THE UK BEFORE THE EUROPEAN COURT OF HUMAN RIGHTS

THE UK BEFORE THE EUROPEAN COURT OF HUMAN RIGHTS

CASE LAW AND COMMENTARY

S. FARRAN

Principal Lecturer at the University of the West
of England, Bristol

BLACKSTONE
PRESS LIMITED

First published in Great Britain 1996 by Blackstone Press Limited,
9-15 Aldine Street, London W12 8AW. Telephone 0181-740 1173

© S. Farran, 1996

ISBN: 1 85431 455 6

British Library Cataloguing in Publication Data
A CIP catalogue record for this book is available from the British Library.

Typeset by Style Photosetting Ltd, Mayfield, East Sussex
Printed by Ashford Colour Press, Gosport, Hampshire

Contents

Preface   vii

Table of Cases   ix

Table of Legislation   xix

Note on References   xxv

Introduction   1

The Convention for the Protection of Human Rights and Fundamental
Freedoms

Chapter 1   19

Article 1 : Securing the rights and freedoms

Chapter 2   27

Article 2 : The right to life

Chapter 3   48

Article 3: Freedom from torture, inhuman and degrading treatment

Chapter 4   80

Article 4: Freedom from slavery and servitude

Chapter 5   83

Article 5: The right to liberty and protection against unlawful detention

Chapter 6   142

Article 6: Fairness in judicial proceedings

Chapter 7   186

Article 7: Protection against retrospective laws

Chapter 8   196

Article 8: Privacy and family life

Chapter 9   244

Article 9: Freedom of thought, conscience and religion

Chapter 10   253

Article 10: Freedom of expression and the protection of democracy

Chapter 11   282

Article 11: Peaceful assembly and public order

Chapter 12   293

Article 12: Marriage

Chapter 13   303

Article 13: Effective remedies

Chapter 14   325

Article 14: The enjoyment of protected rights free from discrimination

Chapter 15   343

Permitted exceptions and restrictions on exceptions:
Articles 15, 16, 17 and 18

Chapter 16   352

The First Protocol

Chapter 17   384

Remedies and Reforms: Article 28 Friendly Settlements and
Just Satisfaction under Article 50

Conclusion   389

Index   393

Preface

The cases in this book have been collected together in order to present a coherent picture of the UK's situation as regards those human rights protected under the European Convention on Human Rights. Both those cases which have been adjudicated by the European Commission of Human Rights and those which have been referred to the European Court of Human Rights are included. Reference is also made to some cases which have been rejected on various grounds, in order to show the extent and the limits of recourse to Strasbourg. While the collection of cases seeks to be comprehensive, it is not exhaustive.

It should be remembered at the outset that these are alleged infringements and do not indicate in all cases that the UK has been found liable. Nevertheless, the nature and range of these cases reflect actual or implied deficiencies in the protection of certain human rights issues in domestic law. The case law also places the UK in the European context of human rights, and although it is not the purpose of this book to draw comparisons with the human rights record of other signatories to the Convention, the collection should provide sufficient material for any reader wishing to do so.

While a great many cases are not referred to Strasbourg, the case law is not insignificant. Not only does it form a coherent part of the jurisprudence of human rights for UK lawyers, but it can also act as a catalyst for change. The UK's frequent appearances before the European Court of Human Rights or the Commission may, in the long run, be seen as a positive influence on the development of English Law in this field, rather than as a negative criticism.

Commentary on the case law includes details about the domestic law relevant to the case, indications of how decisions have led to changes in that law, and highlights areas where the UK has been faced by particular human rights challenges. There is also comment on the approach adopted by the Commission and the Court in interpreting the written text of the Convention, a method of statutory interpretation which has some marked differences from that applied in the UK.

The law as seen from the perspective of cases brought before the Commission and the Court presents an interesting and very unusual view of domestic law. The reader encounters many areas of law which might not otherwise form the subject matter of his or her studies or practical experience. What is more, because applicants may allege violations of a number of different Articles of the Convention, a variety of legal issues come together in a way which might not normally be anticipated or encountered. All of these factors present the possibility of considering the law and its effect in a new light.

The approach adopted in this book is to consider each Article in turn. This necessarily means some fragmenting of the cases, with the result that a complex case raising issues relating to more than one Article may be referred to in more than one chapter. Cases included are drawn from those reported up until December 1995.

Sue Farran
July 1996

Table of Cases

App. No. 3505/68 v UK — 3
App. No. 7379/76 v UK (1977) 8 D & R 211 — 12
App. No. 7879/77 v UK — 234
App. No. 7931/77 v UK — 234
App. No. 7936/77 v UK — 234
App. No. 8245/78 v UK (1981) 24 D & R 98 — 70
App. No. 8416/79 v UK (1980) 19 D & R 244 — 9
App. No. 8566/79 v UK 5 EHRR 265 — 373
App. No. 8575/79 v UK 20 D&R 202 — 3
App. No. 8715/79 v UK 5 EHRR 268 — 149
App. No. 9119/80 v UK 8 EHRR 45 — 50, 373
App. No. 9261/81 v UK (1982) 28 D & R 177 — 354, 364
App. No. 9282/81 5 EHRR 268 — 233
App. No. 9303/81 v UK 9 EHRR 513 — 373
App. No. 9329/81 v UK 5 EHRR 286 — 10, 148
App. No. 9348/81 v UK 5 EHRR 465 — 9, 21
App. No. 9369/81 v UK 5 EHRR 601 — 208
App. No. 9444/81 v UK 6 EHRR 50 — 283
App. No. 9461/81 v UK 5 EHRR 465 at 480 — 372
App. No. 9480/81 v UK 9 EHRR 91 — 9
App. No. 9488/81 v UK 5 EHRR 289 — 233
App. No. 9521/81 v UK 5 EHRR 581 — 218
App. No. 9606/81 v UK 5 EHRR 291 — 51
App. No. 9615/81 v UK 5 EHRR 581 — 260, 353
App. No. 9620/81 v UK 5 EHRR 486 — 9
App. No. 9606/82 v UK 5 EHRR 291 — 51
App. No. 9658/82 v UK 5 EHRR 603 — 327
App. No. 9659 v UK 5 EHRR 581 — 253, 305
App. No. 9702/82 v UK 5 EHRR 293 — 327
App. No. 9730/82 v UK 5 EHRR 581 — 327
App. No. 9773/82 v UK 5 EHRR 296 — 293
App. No. 9793/82 v UK 7 EHRR 135 — 327
App. No. 9803/82 v UK 5 EHRR 465 — 147
App. No. 9810/82 v UK 5 EHRR 581 — 51

App. No. 9813/82 v UK 5 EHRR 513   245, 283
App. No. 9825/82 v UK and Ireland 8 EHRR 45   9, 11, 20
App. No. 9856/82 v UK 10 EHRR 547   9, 54
App. No. 9867/82 v UK 5 EHRR 465   217
App. No. 9884/82 v UK 5 EHRR 298   217
App. No. 9918/82 v UK 5 EHRR 268   293
App. No. 9966/82 v UK 5 EHRR 268   9, 211
App. No. 10039/82 v UK 7 EHRR 409   9
App. No. 10067/82 v UK 5 EHRR 516   51
App. No. 10083/82 v UK 6 EHRR 50, (1983) 33 D & R 270   196, 197, 254
App. No. 10117/82 v UK 7 EHRR 140   3
App. No. 10165/82 v UK 5 EHRR 516   50
App. No. 10184/82 v UK 5 EHRR 516   218
App. No. 10228/82 v UK 7 EHRR 135, (1984) 37 D & R 96   327, 372, 373, 374
App. No. 10229/82 v UK 7 EHRR 135, (1984) 37 D & R 96   327, 372, 373, 374
App. No. 10317/83 v UK 6 EHRR 310   254
App. No. 10331/83 v UK 6 EHRR 467   197, 283
App. No. 10390/83 v UK 8 EHRR 252   353
App. No. 10427/83 v UK 9 EHRR 369   327
App. No. 10496/83 v UK 7 EHRR 135   9
App. No. 10622/83 v UK 8 EHRR 45   210
App. No. 10843/84 v UK 8 EHRR 45   210
App. No. 11486/85 v UK 9 EHRR 350   211, 305
App. No. 11864/85 v UK   3
App. No. 11949/86 v UK 10 EHRR 123   305, 326, 353
App. No. 11970/86 v UK 11 EHRR 46   198
App. No. 12040/86 v UK   147
App. No. 12513/86 v UK 11 EHRR 46   199, 208
App. No. 99732 v UK 5 EHRR 268   146
A v UK App. No. 6840/74, 3 EHRR 131, (1980) 20 D & R 5, (1980)
    23 Yearbook 416, Council of Europe Report 16 July 1980   48, 77, 385, 388
A, B, C and D v UK App. No. 3039/67, (1967) 10 Yearbook 506   362
Abdulaziz, Cabales & Balkandali v UK App. Nos 9214/80, 9473/81, 9474/81,
    5 EHRR 132, 6 EHRR 28, 7 EHRR 471, Series A, Vol. 94, (1982)
    29 D & R 194   218, 305, 310, 331
Abed Hussain v UK App. No. 21928/93, Council of Europe Report
    55/1994/502/584   137
A-G v BBC [1981] AC 303   4
A-G v Guardian Newspapers (No. 2) [1990] 1 AC 109   4
Ahmad v UK App. No. 8160/78 4 EHRR 126   244, 245, 247, 326
Air Canada v UK App. No. 18465/91, 20 EHRR 150, Series A, Vol. 316 178, 369
Alam, Mohamed & Singh, Mohamed Khan Harbhajan v UK App.
    Nos 2991/66 & 2992/66, unreported   141, 198
Allgemeine Gold und Silberscheideanstalt AG v UK App. No. 9118/80,
    7 EHRR 251, 9 EHRR 1, (1983) 32 D & R 159, Series A, Vol. 108 353, 365
Arrondelle v UK App. No. 7889/77 5 EHRR 118, (1980) 19 D & R 186,
    (1980) 23 Yearbook 167, (1982) 26 D & R 5   3, 385
Arrowsmith v UK App. No. 10295/82 & App. No. 7050/75, 6 EHRR 558,
    (1980) 19 D & R 5   245, 246, 261
Artingstoll v UK App. No. 25517/94 19 EHRR CD 92   197, 282

Ashingdane v UK App. No. 8225/78, 4 EHRR 590, Series A, Vol. 93,
    7 EHRR 528, (1982) 27 D & R 5   114, 119, 147, 157
Associated Provincial Picture Houses Ltd v Wednesbury Corp.
    [1948] 1 KB 223   318
Association X v UK App. No. 7154/75 (1979) 14 D & R 33   32

B v UK App. No. 9840/82 Series A, Vol. 121 10 EHRR 87   212, 214
Baggs, Powell & Raynor v UK App. No. 9310/81 9 EHRR 235,
    12 EHRR 355, Series A, Vol. 241, (1987) 52 D & R 29 (Baggs)   3, 223, 305
Banstonian Co. Northern Shipbuilding and Industrial Holding Ltd v UK
    App No. 9265/81 5 EHRR 465   362
Belgian Linguistic Case, The Series A, Vol. 6 1 EHRR 252   326, 372, 379
Benham v UK App. No. 19 380/92 18 EHRR CD 105, Council of Europe
    Report 29 November 1994   139
Boner v UK App. No. 187711/91 19 EHRR 246   183, 184
Bowman, Phyllis v UK (App. No. 24839/94)   280
Boyle v UK App. No. 16580/90, 19 EHRR 179, Series A, Vol. 282-B   215, 388
Boyle and Rice v UK App. Nos 9659/82 and 9658/82 Series A, Vol. 131,
    10 EHRR 425   304, 312
Brady v UK App. No. 8575/79 3 EHRR 297   9, 143, 254
Brannigan and McBride v UK App. Nos 14553-14554/89 17 EHRR 539,
    Series A, Vol. 258-B   109, 318, 344, 346
Brind and Others v UK App. No. 19714/91 18 EHRR CD 76   280
Brogan and Others v UK App. Nos 11209/84, 11234/84, 11266/84,
    11386/85 11 EHRR 117, Series A, Vol. 145-B, (1990) 75 D & R 21
                               102, 110, 111, 344, 348, 349, 350, 386
Brown v UK App. No. 11129/84 8 EHRR 252, (1985) 42 D & R 269   146
Bryan v UK App. No. 19178/91 18 EHRR CD 18   146, 184
Buckley v UK App. No. 20348/92 19 EHRR CD 20,
    Council of Europe Report 11 January 1995   197, 225, 243
Burns, Lorraine v UK App. No. 23413/94 (pending)   47

Campbell v UK App. No. 11240/81 11 EHRR 46   212
Campbell v UK App. No. 13590/88 15 EHRR 137, Series A, Vol. 233-A   234
Campbell & Cosans v UK App. Nos 7511/76, 7743/76, 3 EHRR 531,
    4 EHRR 293, Series A, Vol. 48, (1981) 24 Yearbook 468
                               48, 50, 64, 373, 374, 388
Campbell and Fell v UK App. Nos 7819/77 & 7878/77 5 EHRR 207,
    7 EHRR 165 Series A, Vol. 80   10, 144, 159, 233, 308, 388
Caprino v UK App. No. 6871/75 4 EHRR 97, (1981) 22 D & R 5,
    (1981) 24 Yearbook 468   85
Chahal v UK App. No. 22414/93 20 EHRR CD 19 (pending)   79, 140, 198, 324
Chappell v UK App. No. 10461/83 Series A. Vol. 152   221
Chappell v UK App. No. 3798/68 10 EHRR 510   244, 245, 283
Chater v UK App. No. 11723/85 10 EHRR 503   353
Cheal v UK App. No. 10550/83 8 EHRR 45   283
Church of X v UK App. No. 3798/68 (1969) 12 Yearbook 306   3, 244, 245, 326
Clarke v UK App. No. 15767/89 Resolution DH (94) 57   134
Colman v UK App. No. 16632/90 18 EHRR 119, Series A, Vol. 258-D   254, 385
Corbett v Corbett [1970] 2 WLR 1306   296, 301
Corralyn Roberts v UK App. No. 21178/93 19 EHRR CD 50   198

Cossey v UK App. No. 10843/84 13 EHRR 622, Series A, Vol. 184   199, 210, 297
Costello-Roberts App. No. 5229/71 & 13134/87, 19 EHRR 112, Series A,
    Vol. 247-C
                                                           21, 48, 66, 304
Council of Civil Service Unions and Others v UK App. No. 11603/85
    (1987) 50 D&R 228
                                                                    283, 286
CR & SW v UK App. Nos 20166/92, 20190/92 18 EHRR CD 119   187

Dahanayake v UK App. No. 9435/81 5 EHRR 144   9
Darnell v UK App. No. 15058/89 18 EHRR 205, Series A, Vol. 272   171
De Courcy v UK App. No. 3457/68 (1969) 12 Yearbook 284   3, 147
Derbyshire County Council v Times Newspapers Ltd [1992] 3 WLR 28   4, 5
DS v UK App. No. 22095/93 unreported   181
Dudgeon v UK App. No. 7525/76 3 EHRR 40, 4 EHRR 149, Series A,
    Vol. 45   199, 202, 334, 386, 387, 388
Dugan v UK App. No. 21437/93 18 EHRR CD 174   184
Dyer v UK App. No. 10475/83 7 EHRR 469, (1984) 39 D & R 246   147, 336

E v UK App. No. 20118/92 15 EHRR CD 61   198
East African Asians v UK App. Nos 4403/70 et seq. 3 EHRR 76, (1994)
    78-A D & R 5   48, 69, 328, 331
Engel v Netherlands (No. 1) 1 EHRR 647   159
English Electric Co. and Vickers Ltd v UK App. No. 9263/81 5 EHRR 465   362

Factortame Ltd v Secretary of State for Transport [1991] 1 All ER 70   4
Featherstone, Re (1953) 37 Cr App R 146 (DC)   126
Findlay v UK App. No. 2107/93 unreported   184
Firsoff v UK App. No. 20591/92 15 EHRR CD 111   200, 305
Fox, Campbell and Hartley v UK App. Nos 12244/86, 12245/86, 12383/86,
    13 EHRR 157, Series A, Vol. 182   93, 97, 98, 99, 101

G, H and I v UK App. Nos 18600/91, 18601/91 and 18602/91
    15 EHRR CD 41
                                                                      242
Gaskin v UK App. No. 10454/83, 9 EHRR 235, 12 EHRR 36, Series A,
    Vol. 160, (1986) 45 D & R 91   255, 275
Gay News & Lemon v UK App. No. 8710/79 5 EHRR 123, (1982)
    28 D & R 77 (as X Ltd & Y v UK)   187, 244, 245, 260, 335
Gerrard, Harold v UK (App. No. 21451/93)   248
Gillow v UK App. No. 9063/80 5 EHRR 581, 7 EHRR 292, 11 EHRR 325,
    Series A, Vol. 109   145, 146, 148, 221, 340, 354, 362
Golder v UK App. No. 4451/70 1 EHRR 524, Series A, Vol. 18
                               143, 147, 149, 214, 227, 230, 294, 388
Goodwin v UK App. No. 17488/91 unreported   280
Granger v UK App. No. 11932/80 12 EHRR 451, 469 Series A, Vol. 174
                                                  169, 182, 183, 305
Greenock Ltd v UK (1985) 42 DJR 33   12
Gregory v UK App. No. 22299/93 19 EHRR CD 82   184, 342
Gribler v UK App. No. 12523/86 10 EHRR 546   214

H v UK App. No. 9580/81 Series A, Vol. 120   212, 385
H v UK App. No. 18187/91 16 EHRR CD 44   245
Halford v UK App. No. 20605/92 19 EHRR CD 43   243, 280, 342

Halil, Ahmet & Sabah v UK App. No. 11355/85 8 EHRR 252   51, 218
Hamer v UK Council of Europe Report, para. 71   293, 294
Handyside v UK 1 EHRR 737   13, 33, 253, 255, 345, 353
Harper v UK App. No. 11746/85 9 EHRR 235   80
Herrick v UK App. No. 11185/84 8 EHRR 45   48, 49, 223
Hewitt & Harman v UK App. No. 12175/86 14 EHRR 657
    (1991) 67 D & R 88   241, 283, 306
Hilton v UK App. No. 5613/72 3 EHRR 104 Council of Europe Report
    6 March 1978   72
Hodgson, Woolf Productions v UK App. No. 11553/85 & 11658/85
    10 EHRR 503, (1987) 51 D & R 136   8, 145, 253, 306
Howard v UK App. No. 10825/84 9 EHRR 91   223, 355
Hussain v UK (unreported)   325
Hussain & Singh v UK App. No. 21928/93 & 23389/94, Council of Europe
    55/1994/502/584   140
Hyde v Hyde (1986) 1 P & Divorce 130   297

ISKCON & Others v UK App. No. 20490/92 18 EHRR CD 133,
    (1991) 76-A D & R 90   250, 353

James v U. K. (see Trustees of the late Duke of Westminster's Estate v UK)   338
James v UK App. No. 20447/92 18 EHRR CD 131   147
Johnson v UK 9 EHRR 386   335
Johnson v UK App. No. 10389/83 9 EHRR 350   202
Johnson, Stanley v UK App. No. 22520/93 unreported   140

Kamal v UK App. No. 8378/78 4 EHRR 244   218
Kaplan v UK App. No. 7598/76 4 EHRR 64, (1981) 24 Yearbook 461,
    (1979) 20 D & R 120, (1981) 21 D & R 5, Council of Europe Report
    17 July 1980, (1985) 42 D&R 205   8, 153, 305
Kelly v UK 8 EHRR 45, (1985) 42 D & R 205   27
Kelly v UK App. No. 17579/90 16 EHRR CD 20, (1993) 74 D & R 139
                                                    11, 12, 27, 34, 48
Kennedy Lindsay and Others v UK App. No. 8364/78 (1979) 22 Yearbook
    344, (1979) 15 D & R 247   381
Kilburn v UK App. No. 10991/84 8 EHRR 45   327, 353
Kiss v UK App. No. 6224/73 19 EHRR CD 17   147
Knuller v DPP [1973] AC 435   188

Lamguindaz v UK App. No. 16152/90, 17 EHRR 213, Series A,
    No. 258-C, Resolution DH (93) 55   198, 385
Lant v UK App. No. 11046/84 9 EHRR 235, (1986) 45 D & R 236   199
Laskey, Jaggard & Brown v UK App. Nos 21627/93, 21974/93, 21826/93
    Council of Europe Report 26 October 1995   242, 243, 325
Liberal Party and Others v UK App. No. 8765/79 4 EHRR 106, (1981)
    24 Yearbook 320, (1981) 21 D & R 211   254, 304, 330, 381
Lindsay v UK App. No. 11089/84 9 EHRR 555   326, 336, 354
Lithgow v UK App. No. 9006/80 5 EHRR 491, 8 EHRR 329
    see also Scotts of Greenock Ltd v UK App No. 9599/87 (1987) 51 D & R 34
                                                          147, 305, 360
Lochrie, Steven v UK App. No. 22614/93   184

Lockwood v UK App. No. 18824/91 15 EHRR CD 48   304
Lukka v UK App. No. 12122/86 9 EHRR 513   54, 218, 326
Lyttle v UK App. No. 11650/ 85 9 EHRR 350   92

Magee v UK App. No. 24892/94 19 EHRR CD 91   8
Malone v UK App. No. 8691/79 4 EHRR 330, 7 EHRR 14, 5 EHRR 385,
    Series A, Vol. 82   199, 236, 241, 386, 388
Masefield v UK App. No. 11469/85 9 EHRR 91   223
Maxwell v UK App. No. 18949/91 15 EHRR CD 101, 19 EHRR 97,
    Series A, Vol. 300-C   11, 148, 181, 184
McCallum v UK App. No. 9511/81 13 EHRR 597, Series A, Vol. 183
                                                     234, 255, 305
McCann, Farrell & Savage v UK 21 EHRR 97, Series A, Vol. 324,
    Council of Europe Report   28, 39
McComb v UK App. No. 1061/83 15 EHRR CD 110   236
McCotter v UK App. No. 18632/91 15 EHRR CD 98   198
McCourt v UK App. No. 20433/92 15 EHRR CD 110   199
McEldowney, Sean and Kathleen & Others v UK Resolution DH (94) 31   384
McFeeley v UK App. No. 8317/78 3 EHRR 161 (1980) 23 Yearbook 256,
    (1980) 20 D & R 44, (1984) 38 D & R 11   8, 48, 51, 75, 144, 244, 245, 282
McGinley, Kenneth and Edward Egan v UK App. Nos 21825/93 and 23414/94 185
McLaughlin v UK App. No. 19759/91 18 EHRR CD 84   279, 304, 327
McLuskey v UK App. No. 7931/77 (1987) 51 D & R 5   234
McMichael v UK App. No. 16424/90, 15 EHRR CD 80, 20 EHRR 205,
    Series A, Vol. 308, Council of Europe Report 51/1993/446/525   175, 212, 341
McVeigh, O'Neil & Evans v UK App. Nos 8027/77, 8022/77, 8025/77
    5 EHRR 71, Council of Europe Report 1982   87
Miloslavsky, Nikolae Tolstoy v UK App. No. 18139/91 20 EHRR 442,
    Series A, Vol. 316   147, 264
Mobin Ahmed and Others v UK App. No. 22954/93 20 EHRR CD 72 280, 292, 383
Monnell & Morris v UK App. Nos 9562/81 & 9818/82 7 EHRR 557,
    10 EHRR 205, Series A, Vol. 115   112, 144, 148, 149, 166, 170, 339
Moody, James v UK App. No. 19178/91   184
Munro v UK App. No. 10594/83 10 EHRR 516, (1987) 52 D & R 158
                                                     325, 327, 339
Murray, John v UK App. No. 18731/91 18 EHRR CD 1, 19 EHRR 193
    Council of Europe Report 27 June 1994   96, 173, 184, 200, 305, 325

N v UK App. No. 20100/92 16 EHRR CD 28   134, 198

O v UK App. No. 9276/81 Series A, Vol. 120 Series B, Vol. 107   212, 214
Observer and Guardian v UK App. No. 13585/88 14 EHRR 153, Series A,
    Vol. 216   270, 305, 326
Oldham v UK App. No. 17143/90 Resolution DH (94) 58   134

P, K and G v UK App. No. 13195/87 Resolution DH (94) 59   134
Patel v UK App. No. 8844/80 4 EHRR 256   379
Paton v UK App. No. 8416/78 3 EHRR 408, (1980) 19 D & R 244
    (as X v UK)   10, 27, 28, 30, 211
Paul Matthew Coyne v UK App. No. 25942/94   185
Pinder v UK App. No. 10096/82 7 EHRR 465   147, 335

Powell & Rayner v UK App. No. 9310/81 12 EHRR 288, 355 Series A,
   Vol. 172 (*see also* Baggs, Powell & Rayner v UK)   3, 197, 304, 320
Powell v UK 9 EHRR 241   353, 354
Prem Singh v UK App. No. 23389/94 *see* Hussein & Singh v UK   135
Pullar v UK App. No. 22399/93 unreported   185

R v HM Customs and Excise, ex parte Leonard Haworth (1985) unreported   369
R v Hull Prison Board of Visitors, ex parte St. Germain and Others
   [1979] QB 425   66
R v R [1991] 4 All ER 481   194
R v UK App. No. 10496/83 10 EHRR 74, Series A, Vol. 121   212, 305, 385
R v UK App. No. 18711/91 15 EHRR CD 100   11
Rai, Allmond & 'Negotiate Now' v UK App. No. 25522/94
   19 EHRR CD 93, (1995) 81-A D & R 146   291
Rayner v UK (1986) 47 D & R 5   223
Reed v UK App. No. 7630/76 3 EHRR 136, (1980) 23 Yearbook 111   10, 48, 50
Rees v UK App. No. 9532/81 6 EHRR 603, 7 EHRR 429, 9 EHRR 56,
   (1984) 36 D & R 78, Series A, Vol. 106   199, 208, 295, 299, 300, 301, 302
Republic of Ireland v UK 2 EHRR 25, Series A, Vol. 25,
   (1972) 15 Yearbook 76, (1976) 19 Yearbook 512
                              48, 49, 50, 72, 87, 106, 330, 345, 346, 348
Roe v Wade 410 US 113 (1973)   31
Ryder v UK App. No. 12360/86 11 EHRR 80   353

S v UK App. No. 19085/91 15 EHRR CD 106   198
S & M v UK App No. 21325/93 18 EHRR CD 172   149, 325
Saunders v UK App. No. 19178/91 18 EHRR CD 23   184
Sheffield v UK (Application No. 22985/93)   302, 324
Sibson v UK App. No. 14327/88 17 EHRR 193, Series A, Vol. 258-A   289
Silver & Others v UK App. Nos 5947/72, 6205/73, 7052/75, 7061/75,
   7107/75, 7117/75, 7136/75 3 EHRR 475, Series A, Vol. 61
            229, 233, 303, 305, 306, 309, 310, 313, 314, 315, 386, 387, 388
Smith, Carol and Steve v UK App. No. 22902/93 (unreported) Info. No. 122 325
Soering v UK 11 EHRR 439, Series A, Vol. 161
                        23, 30, 48, 50, 54, 55, 145, 315, 319, 320
Springer v UK App. No. 9083/80 5 EHRR 11   9
Stanford v UK App. No. 16757/90 Series A, Vol. 282   144, 145
Stewart v UK App. No. 10044/82 7 EHRR 409, (1984) 39 D & R 162   31
Stubbings v UK App. No. 22083/93 18 EHRR CD 185, 19 EHRR CD 32
   Council of Europe Report 22 February 1995   147, 180, 184, 342
Sunday Times v UK 2 EHRR 245, Series A, Vol. 30
                        33, 253, 255, 265, 326, 345, 387
Sunday Times (No. 2) App. No. 13166/87 3 EHRR 317, Series A, Vol. 217
                                  186, 189, 275, 326
SW v UK and CR v UK Council of Europe Press Release (20–27 April 1995)   194

Taylor v UK App. No. 20448/92 unreported   140
Taylor, Crampton, Gibson & King v UK App. No. 23412/94
   18 EHRR CD 215, (1994) 79-A D & R 127   37
Temple v UK App. No. 10530/83 8 EHRR 318 (1985) 42 D & R 171   11, 12

Thynne, Wilson & Gunnell v UK App. Nos 1178/85, 11978/86, 12009/86,
13 EHRR 666, Series A, Vol. 190-A   130, 134
Times Newspapers and Neil v UK App. No. 18897/91 15 EHRR CD 49,
(1992) 73 D & R 41   271, 275
Times Newspapers and Others v UK App. No. 10234/83 8 EHRR 54   9
TM v UK App. No. 24835/94   141
Trustees of the Late Duke of Westminster's Estate (James) v UK
App. Vol. 8793/79 (James App. No. 8795/79) 5 EHRR 440, 8 EHRR 123,
Series A, Vol. 98   354
Tyrer v UK 2 EHRR 1 Series A, Vol. 26   48, 50, 61

Uppal and Others v UK (No. 1) App. No. 8244/78 3 EHRR 391,
(1980) 17 D & R 149   217
Uppal & Others v UK (No. 2) App. No. 8224/78 3 EHRR 399,
(1980) 20 D & R 29   143, 385

V v UK App. No. 19804/92 15 EHRR CD 108   145
V, W, X, Y & Z v UK App. No. 22170/93 unreported   242
Vickers plc v UK App. No. 9313/81 5 EHRR 465 *see also*
English Electric Co. and Vickers Ltd v UK   362
Vilvarajah & Others v UK App. Nos 13163/87, 13164/87, 13165/87,
13447/87, 13448/87 14 EHRR 248, Series A, Vol. 215   48, 51, 178, 318
Vosper plc v UK App. No. 9262/81 5 EHRR 465   362

W v UK App. No. 9749/82, 10 EHRR 29, Series A, Vol. 121   212, 305, 385, 386
W, H & A v UK App. No. 21681/93 19 EHRR CD 60   135
W, X, Y & Z v UK App. Nos. 3435/67, 3436/67, 3437/67, 3438/67
(1968) 11 Yearbook 562   80, 81, 198
Ward v UK App. No. 19526/92 16 EHRR CD 25, (1990) 75 D & R 217   134
Watts v UK App. No. 10818/84 9 EHRR 123   11
Weeks v UK App. No. 9787/82 6 EHRR 467, 7 EHRR 409, 436,
10 EHRR 293, (1984) 35 D & R 104, Series A, Vol. 114   124, 131
Welch v UK App. No. 17440/90 16 EHRR CD 42, 20 EHRR 247,
Series A, Vol. 307-A   187, 191
Weston v UK App. No. 8083/77 3 EHRR 402   85
Whiteside v UK App. No. 20357/92 18 EHRR CD 126 (1994) 76-B   221
Wiggins v UK App. No. 7456/76 (1979) 13 D & R 40   340
Wilde, Greenhalgh & Parry v App. Nos 22382/93 19 EHRR CD 86,
(1995) 80 D & R 132   202
Wingrove v UK App. No. 17419/90 19 EHRR CD 54, (1994)
76-A D & R 26   280
Wynne v UK App. No. 15484/89 19 EHRR 333, Series A, Vol. 294-A   135

X v UK App. No. 3485/68 (1969) 12 Yearbook 288   80
X v UK App. No. 3505/68 (1969) 12 Yearbook 298   10
X v UK App. No. 4607/70 (1971) 14 Yearbook 634   148
X v UK App. No. 4623/70 (1972) 15 Yearbook 394   145
X v UK App. No. 6406/73 3 EHRR 302   10
X v UK App. No. 6998/75 4 EHRR 188, Series A, Vol. 46   9, 118, 387
X v UK App. No. 6998/75 5 EHRR 162 Series A, Vol. 55   254

X v UK App. No. 7215/75 3 EHRR 63, Council of Europe Report
  (cited as Wells v UK) 12 October 1978   254
X v UK App. No. 8233/78 3 EHRR 271   145
X v UK App. No. 8600/79 4 EHRR 350   3
X v UK App. No. 9054/80 5 EHRR 260   196, 282
X v UK App. No. 20657/92 15 EHRR CD 113   144
X v UK App. No. 8874/80 4 EHRR 252   380
X v UK DH (83) 2   388
X & the Association of Z v UK App. No. 4515/70 (1971) 14 Yearbook 538   254
X, Cabales & Balkandali v UK (see Abdulaziz et al. v UK)   9, 48
X, Mr and Mrs and their son v UK App. No. 8566/79 5 EHRR 265   373
X & Y v UK App. No. 5269/71 unreported   199
X, Y, Z, V & W v UK App. No. 3325/67 unreported   198, 325
X, Y & Z v UK App. No. 21830/93 unreported   199, 210, 243, 324

Y v UK App. No. 14229/88 17 EHRR 238, Series A, Vol. 247-A   48, 50, 385
Yarrow plc and Three Shareholders v UK App. No. 9266/76 5 EHRR 465   8, 362
Young, James & Webster v UK App. Nos 7601/76, 7806/77,
  5493/72 3 EHRR 30, 4 EHRR 38, Series A, Vol. 44
                                        21, 283, 290, 304, 386, 387, 388

Table of Legislation

Abortion Act 1967   31, 211
Access to Personal Files Act 1987   277
Administration of Justice 1970
   s.31   277
Adoption (Scotland) Act 1978   213
Aircraft and Shipbuilding Industries Act
   1977   305, 360, 362
Armed Forces Act 1966   82
Army Act 1955   82

Birth and Death Registration Act
   1953   297, 298
British Nationality Act 1964   329
British Nationality Act 1981   72, 221
Broadcasting Act 1981   280

Caravan Sites Act 1968   225, 227
Children Act 1989   215, 388
   s.34(3)   217
Children and Young Persons Act 1933
   s.1(1)   69
   s.53(1)   137
Civil Aviation Act 1982   3, 224, 324
   s.76   147, 224, 305, 323
   s.77   224
Commonwealth Immigrants Act 1960
   220
Commonwealth Immigrants Act 1962
   71, 72, 328, 329
Commonwealth Immigrants Act 1968
   71, 72, 220, 328, 329
Contempt of Court Act 1981   306, 387
   s.4(2)   306
   s.10   280

Criminal Appeal Act 1968   112
   s.29   112, 167
   s.29(1)   113, 168
Criminal Justice Act 1948   63
Criminal Justice Act 1967   127, 128
   s.62(2)   125
   s.62(5)   136
   s.62(9)   127
Criminal Justice Act 1972   202
Criminal Justice Act 1982
   s.8(1)   139
Criminal Justice Act 1991   134, 135
   s.34   135
   s.39(5)   136
Criminal Justice and Public Order Act
   1994   202, 227
Criminal Justice (Scotland) Act 1980
   207
Criminal Law Act 1967
   s.3   36
   s.3(1)   32
Criminal Law Act 1977
   s.62   92
Criminal Law Act (Northern Ireland)
   1967
   s.3   33
Criminal Law Amendment Act 1885
   203
Crown Proceedings Act 1947   335
   s.10   147
Customs and Excise Act 1952
   s.44   368
   s.288   368, 369
   s.304   369

Customs and Excise Management Act
    1979   371, 372
  s.139   370
  s.139(1)   180
  s.141(1)   180, 370, 371
  s.152   369
  Sch.3
    para.6   180

Drug Trafficking Offences Act 1986
    191, 192, 193
  s.2(3)   193

Education Act 1944
  s.30   248, 326, 374
Education (No.2) Act 1986   374, 388
Education (No.2) Act 1987   69, 374
Education (Scotland) Act 1962   376
Employment Act 1980   22, 286, 388
Employment Act 1982   11, 388
Employment Protection Act 1975
    288, 289
Employment Protection Act 1978
    288, 290
Employment Protection
    (Consolidation) Act 1978   22,
    286, 288
  s.58(3)   291
  s.138   287
European Convention on Extradition
    1957   25
Extradition Act 1870
  s.11   316
Extradition Act 1970   55

Family Law Reform Act 1969   202

Guardianship of Minors Act 1971   217

Homicide Act 1957   25
Housing Act 1969   338, 354
Housing Act 1974   354
Housing Act 1975   341
Housing Act 1980   354
Housing and Building Control Act
    1984   354
Human Fertility and Embryology Act
    1990   210

Immigration Act 1971   218, 220, 221,
    311, 329, 334

Immigration Act 1971 continued
  s.13   52, 318, 319
Immigration Appeals Act 1969   71,
    328
Incitement to Disaffection Act
    1934   246, 247, 261, 262, 263,
    264
Incitement to Mutiny Act 1797   264
Income and Corporation Taxes Act
    1970   336
Insurance Companies Act 1974   153
  s.29   154, 305
Interception of Communications Act
    1985   199, 388

Land Compensation Act 1973   224,
    322, 323
Law Reform (Parent and Child)
    (Scotland) Act 1986   214
Leasehold Reform Act 1967   338, 354,
    357
Leasehold Reform Act 1979   354
Legal Aid Act 1988   149
Limitation Act 1980   180, 181
Local Authority Services Act 1970
  s.7   276

Matrimonial Causes Act 1973   297
  s.11   296
Mental Health Act 1959   115, 117,
    118, 120, 122, 130
  s.60   77, 114, 118
  s.65   77, 118
  s.66   121
  s.66(3)   122, 123
  s.141   117, 118, 147, 157, 158
Mental Health Act 1983   85, 118, 159
  s.139   147, 159
Mental Health (Amendment) Act 1983
    387

National Health Service Act 1977
  s.3   158
Naval Enlistment Act 1884   82
Noise Abatement Act 1960   324
Northern Ireland (Emergency
    Provisions) Act 1973   105
Northern Ireland (Emergency
    Provisions) Act 1978   75, 96, 98
  s.1   93
  s.6   96

Northern Ireland (Emergency
   Provisions) Act 1987– *continued*
s.14 97, 98, 99, 101, 102, 200
Sch.3
   para.5(2) 104
Northern Ireland (Emergency
   Provisions) Act 1987 175
s.15(1) 173

Obscene Publications Act 1959 256,
   258, 259, 260
s.4 259
Obscene Publications Act 1964 256,
   258, 259
Offences Against the Person Act 1861
   242
  s.42 69
  s.47 69
  s.61-s.62 202
Official Secrets Act 1911 275, 286

Parks Regulation (Amendment) Act
   1926 292
Perjury Act 1911 297
  s.3(1) 208
Police and Criminal Evidence Act
   1984 106
Post Office Act 1969 199
  s.29 306
  s.80 239
Prevention of Terrorism (Temporary
   Provisions) Act 1974 108
Prevention of Terrorism (Temporary
   Provisions) Act 1976 92, 108
  s.12-s.13 92
Prevention of Terrorism (Temporary
   Provisions) Act 1978 96
  s.11(1) 95, 96
Prevention of Terrorism (Temporary
   Provisions) Act 1984 92, 103,
   108, 109, 111, 346
  s.12 102, 104, 106, 108, 109, 111,
   344, 350
  s.12(4) 102
  s.12(6) 106
  s.14 105
Prison Act 1952 232, 233
Prison Rules Act 1964 230
Prisons (Scotland) Act 1952 235
Prisons (Scotland) Act 1989 235

Representation of the People Act
   1949 305, 331, 381
Representation of the People Act
   1969 202

Security Service Act 1989 242
Sexual Offences Act 1956 200, 202,
   335
Sexual Offences Act 1967 200, 201,
   202, 205, 207, 335
Sexual Offences (Scotland) Act 1976
   207
Social Work (Scotland) Act 1968 213
Solicitors Act 1874 3
Special Powers Act (Northern Ireland)
   1922
  reg.10 96

Town and Country Planning Act 1990
   146
Trade Union and Labour Relations Act
   1974 21, 22, 248, 283, 286
Trade Union and Labour Relations
   (Amendment) Act 1976 21, 22,
   286
Trafalgar Square Act 1844 292

European legislation
European Agreement Relating to
   Persons Participating in
   Proceedings of the European
   Commission and Court of Human
   Rights 1969 236
European Convention on Human
   Rights 1-17
  First Protocol 1, 222, 304, 352-83
   art.1 178, 193, 197, 221, 222,
   224, 256, 321, 336, 337, 338,
   340, 341, 345, 352-72
   art.2 21, 48, 64, 246, 276, 327,
   353, 372-81
   art.3 254, 292, 330, 331, 354,
   381-3
   art.4 352, 365
   art.5-art.6 352
  Second Protocol 1
  Third Protocol 1
  Fourth Protocol 2
   art.3(2) 72
  Fifth Protocol 1

European Convention on Human
  Rights – *continued*
Sixth Protocol 2, 30
Seventh Protocol 2
Eighth Protocol 1, 6
Ninth Protocol 2, 6, 13
Tenth Protocol 2
Eleventh Protocol 2, 15, 16
art.1 5, 15, 19–26, 28, 67, 270
art.2 9, 20, 27–47, 48, 55, 211, 343,
  345, 376
art.2(1) 27, 28, 29, 31, 43
art.2(2) 27, 28, 33, 35, 36, 43
art.2(2)(a) 33, 34, 35, 43, 46
art.2(2)(b) 33, 35, 36, 43
art.2(2)(c) 33, 34, 35, 43
art.3 1, 10, 20, 23, 24, 30, 42, 47,
  48–79, 115, 140, 276, 304, 310,
  315, 316, 317, 318, 320, 324,
  328, 343, 345, 373, 374, 377,
  386
art.3(3) 106
art.4 1, 20, 30, 80–2, 115, 196
art.4(1) 31, 80, 343, 345
art.4(2) 80
art.4(3) 80
art.4(3)(b) 81
art.5 20, 28, 31, 42, 51, 80, 83–141,
  157, 228, 246, 324, 329, 339,
  345, 346, 348, 349, 386, 389
art.5(1) 79, 83, 84, 85, 86, 87, 88,
  89, 90, 92, 93, 94, 95, 96, 97, 98,
  99, 100, 101, 102, 103, 105, 107,
  112, 114, 116, 117, 118, 120,
  122, 126, 127, 129, 133, 139,
  140, 152
art.5(1)(a) 88, 112, 114, 118, 119,
  121, 126, 127, 128, 129, 131,
  133
art.5(1)(b) 87, 88, 89, 90, 91, 92
art.5(1)(c) 87, 88, 91, 93, 94, 95,
  96, 97, 98, 99, 100, 101, 103,
  104, 105, 112
art.5(1)(d) 88
art.5(1)(e) 88, 115, 116, 117, 118,
  119, 120, 121, 122, 123, 126,
  128, 131, 133
art.5(1)(f) 87, 88, 91
art.5(2) 83, 84, 87, 91, 92, 93, 94,
  95, 96, 98, 101, 102, 106, 118,
  120, 124, 127, 345

European Convention on Human
  Rights – *continued*
art.5(3) 83–4, 87, 102, 104, 105,
  106, 107, 108, 109, 110, 111,
  118, 127, 344, 345, 347, 348,
  349, 350
art.5(4) 84, 85, 86, 87, 92, 93, 102,
  104, 106, 107, 108, 111, 115,
  116, 117, 118, 120, 121, 122,
  123, 124, 126, 127, 129, 130,
  131, 132, 133, 134, 135, 136,
  137, 138, 139, 140, 141, 152,
  153, 305, 345
art.5(4)(e) 123
art.5(5) 84, 87, 92, 93, 95, 96, 98,
  101, 102, 104, 107, 108, 109,
  110, 111, 127, 130, 132, 134,
  139, 140, 347
art.5(6)-(8) 84
art.6 3, 20, 28, 31, 41, 81, 140,
  142–85, 191, 228, 229, 264, 268,
  305, 309, 321, 323, 339, 340,
  342, 389
art.6(1) 28, 119, 142, 144, 145,
  146, 148, 149, 150, 151, 152,
  153, 154, 155, 156, 157, 158,
  161, 162, 163, 165, 166, 168,
  169, 170, 171, 172, 173, 174,
  175, 176, 177, 178, 179, 180,
  181, 182, 184, 185, 212, 213,
  214, 215, 228, 229, 234, 264,
  277, 305, 306, 321, 323, 328,
  335, 339, 342
art.6(2) 142, 166, 173, 174, 175
art.6(3) 23, 142, 145, 169, 173, 328
art.6(3)(a)-(b) 166
art.6(3)(c) 55, 140, 149, 166, 168,
  169, 170, 171, 173, 174, 175,
  182, 184
art.6(3)(d) 144, 148
art.7 20, 163, 186–95, 260, 343,
  345
art.7(1) 186, 188, 189, 191, 192,
  193
art.7(2.1) 186
art.8 4, 9, 20, 28, 31, 48, 66, 67, 79,
  81, 87, 96, 140, 143, 159, 175,
  180, 185, 196–243, 255, 276,
  293, 294, 296, 298, 299, 304,
  306, 307, 308, 309, 310, 312,
  321, 322, 323, 324, 328, 331,

European Convention on Human
    Rights – *continued*
        332, 333, 334, 335, 340, 341,
        342, 354, 362, 363, 364, 376,
        389
    para.2   43, 204
    art.8(1)   87, 196, 205, 209, 216,
        223, 224, 226, 228, 229, 234,
        238, 239, 241, 242, 294
    art.8(2)   87, 88, 196, 201, 203, 204,
        205, 211, 213, 216, 219, 226,
        230, 231, 232, 234, 238, 239,
        240, 334, 364
    art.9   1, 3, 8, 20, 21, 28, 31, 76, 204,
        244–52, 261, 263, 284, 286, 290,
        291, 326, 376, 378
    art.9(1)   244, 247, 249, 251
    art.9(2)   244, 245, 248, 249, 251
    art.9(3)   248
    art.10   8, 20, 21, 28, 189, 199, 204,
        229, 232, 241, 242, 246, 248,
        253–80, 284, 286, 290, 291, 292,
        306, 330, 331, 342, 345, 376,
        378, 382, 385
    art.10(1)   88, 253, 254, 259, 268,
        270, 277
    art.10(2)   88, 190, 204, 247, 253,
        254, 255, 256, 257, 258, 259,
        261, 262, 263, 267, 268, 269,
        270, 272, 273, 274, 277, 279
    art.11   20, 21, 22, 23, 25, 28, 241,
        242, 282–92
    art.11(1)   282, 287
    art.11(2)   282, 283, 285, 287, 288,
        290
    art.12   20, 208, 219, 293–302
    art.13   20, 21, 23, 28, 48, 52, 55, 66,
        79, 81, 152, 153, 178, 185, 222,
        224, 229, 241, 242, 276, 278,
        284, 303–24, 342, 347, 352
    art.14   9, 20, 175, 180, 181, 212,
        219, 246, 248, 254, 279, 300,
        310, 312, 325–42, 352, 360, 380,
        381, 382, 383
    art.15   20, 42, 87, 88, 109, 110, 344,
        345, 346, 347, 348, 349, 350,
        351
    art.15(1)   34–5, 343, 347
    art.15(2)   343
    art.15(3)   109, 110, 343, 348, 350
    art.16   20, 343, 345

European Convention on Human
    Rights – *continued*
    art.17   20, 343, 345, 378
    art.18   20, 116, 117, 344, 345
    art.19   6, 101
    art.20-art.23   6
    art.24   7, 20
    art.25   7, 8–9, 12, 20, 31, 66, 238,
        389
    art.25(1)   8
    art.26   9–12, 50, 137, 256, 313, 389
    art.27(2)   36, 39, 189, 211, 252,
        304, 322, 323, 337, 381
    art.28   16, 384, 386, 388
    art.28(1)(a)   13
    art.28(1)(b)   13, 78
    art.28(2)   7
    art.30   16
    art.32(1)   15
    art.33   25
    art.36   6
    art.40(6)   17
    art.43   16
    art.47   17
    art.50   14, 47, 86, 108, 171, 184,
        194, 214, 257, 275, 384, 385,
        386, 387, 388
    art.54   15, 279, 289, 387, 388
    Preamble   330

German legislation
    Basic Law   31

Gibraltar legislation
    Gibraltar Constitution
        art.2   40

Guernsey legislation
    Housing Control (Guernsey) Law
        1969   341
    Housing Law 1957   341
    Housing Law 1969   222, 340
    Housing Law 1975   222, 340, 364,
        365
        s.5   364

Isle of Man legislation
    Petty Sessions and Summary
        Jurisdiction Act 1927
        s.56(1)   63
    Summary Jurisdiction Act 1960
        s.8   63
        s.10   63

Jersey legislation
  Island Planning (Jersey) Law 1964
    223

Rome Convention 1952
  art.1   324
Treaty of Rome
  art.30   369
Vienna Convention
  art.31   150
  art.32   152

International legislation
Extradition Treaty 1872 (UK/Germany)
  55
Extradition Treaty 1972 (UK/US)   23,
  55
International Covenant on Economic,
  Social and Cultural Rights 1966
  288
International Labour Convention No.87
  1948
  arts.2–5   289
  art.11   289
United Nations Convention against
  Torture and Other Cruel, Inhuman
  and Degrading Treatment or
  Punishment 1984   25
  art.3   58

United Nations Convention relating to
  the Status of Refugees 1951   51,
  319
  art.33   25
  Protocol 1967   51
United Nations Convention on the
  Rights of the Child 1991
  art.28   21
United Nations Covenant on Civil and
  Political Rights 1966   30, 58, 288
  art.4   351
  art.8   81
  art.14(1)   144
United Nations Universal Declaration
  of Human Rights   1, 2
  art.16
    para.1   296
  art.20
    para.2   285

US legislation
American Convention on Human
  Rights 1969   30, 31, 58
Code of Virginia 1950   26
US Constitution
  Eighth Amendment   57

Note on References

Each case coming before the Commission and the Court is given an Application Number which consists of a number and then the last two figures of the year in which the application was first made. Sometimes a case is identified only by the Application Number and the defendant State, e.g. *Application 9348/81* v *UK*; at other times the applicant is referred to as 'X', or in some cases by the first initial of his or her name, e.g. 'A'. Once the case comes before the Court, this initial may be replaced by the full name, or it may not (an example of this mode of citation appears in the case of Caroline Cossey, cited as *C* v *UK* Application No. 10843/84 before the Commission, and cited as *Cossey* v *UK* or *Cossey Case* 16/1989/176/232 before the Court). Yet other cases are referred to from the outset by the full name of the applicant. If there are a number of applicants, all their names might be given, or only the first and then 'and Others'. Cases before the Court are also given a number indicating their place on the roll of cases heard by the Court that year. Thus in a citation such as *Welch* v *UK* 1/1994/448/527, the first number is the case's position on the list of cases referred to the Court in the relevant year, the year being indicated by the second number; the last two numbers indicate the case's place on the list of cases referred to the Court since its creation and on the list of corresponding originating applications to the Commission.

The judgments of the Court, the reports of the Commission and resolutions or decisions of the Committee of Ministers may be published in full or summary form, and can be found in a number of sources. These include:

The Yearbook of the European Convention on Human Rights (Yearbook)
The Publications of the European Court of Human Rights:
Series A: The Judgments of the Court (which may include the Commission's Opinion)
Series B: The Reports of the Commission
Decisions and Reports of the Commission (D & R) (which may be in summarised form)
The edited *European Human Rights Reports* published by Sweet & Maxwell (European Law Centre) (EHRR)

LEXIS in the Europe Library under Cases
The British Yearbook of International Law (BYIL)

The Council of Europe also issues Information Sheets twice a year with
extracts from cases, reports, plenary sessions etc., and the Registrar of the
European Court of Human Rights issues press releases on a regular basis
concerning cases referred to it and judgments made. The European Commission also issues reports, including surveys of its activities and statistics on an
annual basis, and Information Notes on each session of the Commission. Not
all cases are fully reported, and it can happen that a case is declared admissible
by the Commission and then no more is heard of it. This may be because a
friendly settlement has been reached, or because the case had been dropped by
the applicant or simply because the case is one of a number of unreported cases.
The time-scale involved in the procedures may also mean that a case is lost
sight of for several years.

A number of different sources have been used in this book. The relevant
source for each extract cited is indicated in each chapter, while more extensive
referencing can be found in the Table of Cases to assist readers who may not
always have access to a particular source.

ACKNOWLEDGMENTS

Extracts from the *Yearbook of the European Convention on Human Rights* are
reproduced with the permission of the Council of Europe. The author and
publishers also wish to thank Sweet & Maxwell Limited for permission to
reproduce extracts from the *European Human Rights Reports*.

INTRODUCTION

THE CONVENTION FOR THE PROTECTION OF HUMAN RIGHTS AND FUNDAMENTAL FREEDOMS

INTRODUCTION

The Role of the European Convention on Human Rights

Impetus for an agreement directed at protecting the rights of people in Europe came from the reaction to the horrors and atrocities of the Second World War. A number of the Articles reflect the historical context in which the Convention was drafted, for example Article 3 prohibiting torture and inhuman or degrading treatment, Article 4 prohibiting slavery, and Article 9 protecting freedom of religion. Today some of these Articles give rise to very little case law, largely because of social and political changes. The objective of the Convention was to seek to prevent similar infringements of human rights in the future. It was intended as a flexible and adaptable instrument of human rights' protection.

The Convention was drafted in 1949, having been strongly influenced by the United Nations Declaration of Human Rights which had been adopted by the United Nations General Assembly the previous year. The United Kingdom was a signatory to the Convention in 1950 and the Convention came into force in 1953. The Convention is binding in international law on all its signatories.

The original Convention has been added to by way of further protocols. The UK signed the First Protocol (which came into force on 18 May 1954) on 3 November 1952 (subject to reservations); the Second Protocol on 6 May 1963 (came into force on 21 September 1970); the Third Protocol on 6 May 1963 (entry into force 21 September 1970); the Fifth Protocol on 10 February 1966 (entry into force 20 December 1971); and the Eighth Protocol on 19 March 1985 (entry into force 1 January 1990 subject to declarations and territorial declarations). It also signed the Fourth Protocol on 16 September 1963, but has not ratified it. The UK has not signed the Sixth, Seventh or Ninth Protocols. It has signed the Tenth Protocol (on 25 March 1992), but this is not yet in force, and Eleveth Protocol, which is also not yet in force.

The introduction to the Convention is as follows:

The Governments signatory hereto, being Members of the Council of Europe,
Considering the Universal Declaration of Human Rights proclaimed by the General Assembly of the United Nations on 10th December 1948;
Considering that this Declaration aims at securing the universal and effective recognition and observance of the rights therein declared;
Considering that the aim of the Council of Europe is the achievement of greater unity between its members and that one of the methods by which that aim is to be pursued is the maintenance and further realisation of human rights and fundamental freedoms;
Reaffirming their profound belief in those fundamental freedoms which are the foundation of justice and peace in the world and are best maintained on the one hand by an effective political democracy and on the other by a common understanding and observance of the human rights upon which they depend;
Being resolved, as the governments of European countries which are likeminded and have a common heritage of political traditions, ideals, freedom and the rule of law to take the first steps for the collective enforcement of certain of the rights stated in the Universal Declaration,
Have agreed as follows;

after which follows the various Articles setting forth the rights agreed on as being important.

The Right of Individual Petition

Initially the purpose of the Convention was directed at preventing large scale infringements of human rights by States which were parties to it. However, the Convention also provided the possibility for a State to recognise the jurisdiction of the Commission in the case of individual petitioners (Article 25). This right of individual petition became effective on 5 July 1955 after six of the High Contracting Parties made declarations recognising the competence of the Commission to receive such petitions.

The UK recognised the right of individual petition in 1966. This recognition originally was for a period of five years, but has been renewed on a regular basis. However, the possibility of non-renewal remains. The current right of individual petition was renewed in January 1996 and lasts for five years. In 1981, the UK extended the right of individual petition to its overseas territories, with the exclusion of Hong Kong.

It is this right of individual petition that has given rise to the bulk of the cases coming before the Commission, so that today the Convention can be seen as being a bulwark against specific infringements of human rights rather than large scale violations, although individual cases may be representative of violations affecting certain sectors or groups of the population.

This collection of cases and commentary focuses on individiual applications rather than inter-State ones, although these – which are very few in number – are referred to from time to time and are deserving of study in their own right.

The rights protected by the Convention are primarily civil and political rather than social or economic. Moreover, the protection of such rights afforded by the Convention can be divided into substantive rights and procedural rights. As will be seen from the case law, while an applicant may fail in a claim regarding the infringement of a substantive right, the same claim may succeed on procedural grounds.

Certain rights have been held to be clearly outside the scope of the Convention. These include: the right to retrial (*App. No. 3505/68* v *UK*); the right of foreign nationals to enter or to reside in a country other than their own (*Church of X* v *UK* (1969) 12 *Yearbook* 306); the right to be accorded a pardon, or to obtain a reopening of proceedings after the determination of a criminal charge; the right to institute private prosecution for perjury or to instigate extradition proceedings (*De Courcy* v *UK* (1969) 12 *Yearbook* 284); the classification of a prisoner (*App. No. 10117/82* v *UK* 7 EHRR 140, and *App. No. 8575/79* v *UK* 20 D & R 202).

Applications can be admitted from individual persons, non-governmental organisations or groups of individuals provided that the alleged violation concerns them directly. Whether a corporation can bring an application on behalf of its members was considered in the case of *Church of X* v *UK* (above). Here it was held that as a corporation is a legal and not a natural person, it is incapable of exercising or having certain rights under the Convention – in this case under Article 9. A corporation may, however, have certain procedural rights – for example under Article 6. If an application is brought by an organisation on behalf of its members then the identity of these individuals must be disclosed as anonymous petitions are not considered.

Applications can be brought only against a Contracting Party to the Convention or its agents, not against private individuals or bodies whose acts do not entail the responsibility of a Contracting Party. Thus the Commission may not admit applications directed against corporate bodies (*App. No. 11864/85* v *UK* – application against a bank held to be inadmissible). However, the responsibility of a State may be engaged where it is not immediately apparent that the violation is caused by the State. For example, in several cases the UK has been held accountable for alleged violations concerning aircraft noise because the British Aviation Authority – which is responsible for the planning and construction of civil airports – is a State body, and also because air traffic is regulated by legislation passed by the State (Civil Aviation Act 1982) (*Arrondelle* v *UK* 5 EHRR 118, *Baggs* v *UK* 9 EHRR 235, *Powell and Raynor* v *UK* 12 EHRR 135). Whether an organisation over which the State has some indirect control will involve the liability of the State was raised but left unanswered in the case of *X* v *UK* App. No. 8600/79 4 EHRR 350, concerning the Law Society, which, although it is not a servant or agent of the State, was created by Royal Charter and exercises its regulatory powers under legislation delegated under the Solicitors Act 1874. Its activities are also subject to the supervision of the Master of the Rolls, who is a member of the judiciary and of the government of the day.

The Relationship between the Convention and the UK

While in some countries international treaties automatically become part of the domestic law of the signatory State, this is not the case with the UK

Consequently the Convention and its Protocols are not part of domestic law. Moreover, because the UK has no Bill of Rights, fundamental rights such as those found in the Convention are not embodied in any separate form, but are protected – in so far as they are recognised and protected at all – in much the same way as other rights. As can be seen from an examination of the case law involving the UK before both the Commission and the European Court of Human Rights, certain rights included in the Convention are better protected in the UK than others. For example, applications relating to Article 8 (the right to private and family life) appear frequently, often in conjunction with alleged infringements of other rights. The preponderance of such applications is attributable not only to the domestic law applicable in this area, but also to the fact that this Article is broad in scope, and over the years the Court and the Commission have adopted a fairly fluid approach to the interpretation and application of such Articles.

As with other international treaty obligations, the Convention is applicable in the interpretation of statute law, because it is a generally recognised principle of construction that Parliament does not intend to legislate contrary to the UK's international obligations. However, if a statute is unambiguous and does conflict with international obligations the courts can not avoid this. Where either a statute or the common law is ambiguous the courts may consider the Convention, but much will depend on the inclination of the judge. Some judges have indicated a willingness to have regard to the Convention (e.g. Lord Scarman in *A-G* v *BBC* [1981] AC 303, Lord Goff in *A-G* v *Guardian Newspapers (No. 2)* [1990] 1 AC 109); others have been more reluctant. However, the House of Lords has indicated that where the law is either unclear or ambiguous, or concerns an issue not yet ruled on, the courts ought to consider the implications of the Convention (*Derbyshire County Council* v *Times Newspapers Ltd* [1992] 3 WLR 28).

The Convention may also infiltrate UK domestic law more indirectly by influencing European Union law. The European Court of Justice in Luxembourg has suggested that the Convention can be referred to as a source of general principles of EU law and that EU law should be understood as influenced by those principles. As some EU law can have a direct effect on the UK without further legislation, and in some cases override domestic legislation (*Factortame Ltd.* v *Secretary of State for Transport* [1991] 1 All ER 70), decisions and principles relating to human rights may infiltrate UK law without Parliamentary intervention.

Although the Court and the Commission do not necessarily feel bound by their decisions in previous cases, – and therefore the doctrine of precedent might not apply as strongly as in UK law – it is not unusual to find references to 'the consistent case law' of the Commission or the Court. Thus effectively certain precedents are established and used as guidelines for adjudicating later cases.

The relevance of Convention case-law to domestic law
An individual cannot directly complain of the infringement of Articles under the Convention before an English court, but in the light of the House of Lords

ruling in *Derbyshire County Council* v *Times Newspapers Ltd* (above), could argue a case on the basis of the principles and decisions of the European Court of Human Rights, and the reports of the Commission.

More important is the consideration that quite often individual complaints taken to Strasbourg benefit a wider sector than simply the applicant, particularly when the decision leads to a change in the law. The case law of the Court and the Commission can thus be seen as human rights lobby. The body of case law relating to the UK presents an interesting picture of the protection of human rights in this country. Against it can be set the reforms that have followed major decisions, and it might be asked whether but for the Convention and the UK's frequent appearances before the Commission and the Court these reforms would have come about.

The preamble to the Convention indicates that one of the aims is to achieve greater unity between States which are signatories to the Convention, and to maintain fundamental freedoms through a common understanding and observance of human rights. It is by means of the case law that a common understanding begins to emerge, through the development and encouragement of common standards. Although the case law dealt with here concerns the UK, the standards reflected in the reports of the Commission and the judgments of the Court are not particular to the UK. When the Commission or the Court refers to its established case law, this includes cases involving many different signatory States. The principles for which the Commission and Court strive remain the same, it is only the specific facts and the nature of the alleged violations which differ. Consequently the body of jurisprudence is relevant in two ways. First, the cases involving the UK form part of the general body of case law which will be used as a basis for future judgments. Although the rule of precedent does not apply in the same way as in English law, and indeed the Court is not and cannot be bound by its own previous judgments (Rule 51(1), Rules of Court), it does usually follow and apply its own precedents in the interests of legal certainty and the orderly development of the Convention case law. Secondly, this general body of case law and the cases which reflect upon the national law of the UK in particular, provide a contextual background for human rights issues in the UK, whether these are raised by cases coming before the courts or when new legislation is being drafted or debated.

PROCEDURE FOR TAKING A CASE TO STRASBOURG

The importance of the Convention is that not only is it a statement of ideals, but it is also practically enforceable. When it came into force a procedural machinery was established to supervise the implementation of the rights protected by its Articles and Protocols. This means that while Article 1 provides that:

> The High Contracting Parties shall secure to everyone within their jurisdiction the rights and freedoms defined in Section I of this Convention

where Contracting Parties fail to do this, there is an external enforcement process.

The Enforcement Machinery

This machinery, established under Article 19, consists of the Commission of Human Rights, which receives and examines complaints about the infringement of human rights by States, and the European Court of Human Rights, which adjudicates on cases which are referred to it by the Commission. The Committee of Ministers of the Council of Europe – which consists of the Foreign Ministers of the High Contracting Parties – also has a role in adjudicating certain cases, but more importantly in monitoring the compliance of an offending State with the decision of the Court or Commission.

The procedure for applicants

Procedure is by way of petition to the Secretary-General of the Council of Europe, whether the applicant is a State, i.e. a High Contracting Party, or an individual. The Secretary-General forwards the petition to the Commission.

Following Resolution (63)18, adopted on 25 October 1963 by the Committee of Ministers, the Commission may grant legal aid to an applicant. The provisions governing the grant of legal aid are set out in the Addendum to the Commission's Rules of Procedure. In 1994 the budget for legal aid was 480,000 FF and legal aid was granted in 78 cases (*Survey of Activities and Statistics*, European Commission (1994), p. 17).

The Commission

The Commission consists of one member for every member State, elected by the Committee of Ministers of the Council of Europe (Article 21). As of December 1994 there were 28 members elected for a period of six years. There is a procedure for ensuring a change of membership fairly constantly (Article 22). Such members must not be government representatives (Article 23) and are expected to have substantial legal experience and a recognised competence in human rights matters. Members of the Commission are independent and exercise their functions in an individual, rather than a national, capacity. Indeed, a member may not preside in cases in which the High Contracting Party of which they are a national, or in respect of which they were elected, is a party (Rule 10). The Commission draws up its own rules of procedure (Article 36).

The current rules of procedure entered into force on 28 June 1993. When the Commission sits – which is not on a permanent basis, but must be for at least 16 weeks in each year – it sits *in camera*. It may sit in plenary sessions – generally with a quorum of seven members – in chambers – of which there are two, each with a quorum of seven members – or in committees consisting of three members (Article 20). The last two forms of organisation were introduced in 1980 under the Eighth Protocol. The purpose of the committees is to filter out applications. If its members are unanimous then an application can be declared inadmissible by the committee. Under the Ninth Protocol – which entered into force on 1 October 1994, but has not yet been signed by the UK – an individual may initiate proceedings before the European Court of Human Rights directly, irrespective of whether the Commission or the State concerned has referred the case to the Court. However, a committee will filter out cases which it unanimously considers raise no serious questions concerning the interpretation or the application of the Convention, or any other element which could justify examination by the Court.

Although the Commission is assisted by a Secretariat consisting of 49 lawyers, 36 administrative assistants, four translators and various temporary staff, it has a huge backlog of cases. At the end of 1994, 59 per cent of applications were still awaiting a first examination by the Commission (*Survey of Activities and Statistics*: (1994)). Even so, during 1994, the Secretariat had opened 9,968 provisional files and registered 2,944 individual applications under Article 25. The Commission had considered 2,173 applications during the year, with 3,498 still pending before it.

The procedure before the Commission

In carrying out its task to ensure the observance of the engagements undertaken by the High Contracting Parties under the Convention, the Commission:

(a) rules on the admissibility of applications introduced under Articles 24 and 25 in which violations are alleged;

(b) establishes all the facts of those applications which are declared admissible and places itself at the disposal of the parties to secure a friendly settlement;

(c) draws up a report in accordance with Article 28, para. 2, once a friendly settlement is reached;

(d) draws up a report for the Committee of Ministers if a friendly settlement is not reached, and expresses an opinion as to whether or not the facts disclose a violation of any article in the Convention;

(e) refers the case to the European Court of Human Rights, where appropriate, for a decision;

(f) assists the Court in any case brought before it through its delegates who take part in the proceedings;

(g) assists the Committee of Ministers to determine, where appropriate, the amount of compensation payable for damage resulting from a violation of the Convention.

The Commission will rule on the admissibility of an application either immediately the application comes before it, or, if the case raises difficult or serious issues of law and fact, after further examination and consideration. Before the Commission examines the substance of the petition it must be satisfied that the applicant:

(a) has exhausted all domestic remedies;

(b) has presented the petition within six months of the final decision reached through the above remedies;

(c) is not anonymous;

(d) raises a matter which is not substantially the same as one already ruled on by the Court or Commission;

(e) is not using the procedure as an abuse of right or on the grounds of a manifestly ill-founded claim.

These requirements have in themselves raised certain interpretation problems and the case law of the Court and Commission throws some light on what compliance entails.

Deciding on Admissibility

In order for a claim to be declared admissible, the Commission must be persuaded not only that there are questions of law and fact to be answered regarding the infringement of one or more of the substantive rights protected under the Convention and its Protocols, but also that certain procedural requirements have been met. In defending a claim the Government will invariably argue that the latter have not been complied with.

The right of petition must be directed at protecting one of the rights set out in the Convention. Thus the procedure must not be used for the purpose of attracting media attention or propaganda. However, if there is publicity or there are motives of publicity or political propaganda, these factors will not necessarily amount to an abuse of petition where there are nevertheless valid claims falling under the provisions of the Convention. If the applicant is seeking to exploit the proceedings or to capitalise on them for political purposes, and there is no support for claimed infringements of protected rights, then there may be an abuse of petition (*McFeeley* v *UK* 3 EHRR 161, 185).

Article 25

Article 25
1. The Commission may receive petitions addressed to the Secretary-General of the Council of Europe from any person, non-governmental organisation or group of individuals claiming to be the victim of a violation by one of the High Contracting Parties of the rights set forth in this Convention, provided that the High Contracting Party against which the complaint has been lodged has declared that it recognises the competence of the Commission to receive such petitions. Those of the High Contracting Parties who have made such a declaration undertake not to hinder in any way the effective exercise of this right.

Following this article, an individual applicant can complain to the Commission only of alleged violations of his or her own Convention rights. The applicant must be a 'victim'. Thus the National Union of Journalists could not, for example, claim to be a victim even though one of its members was, because the measures complained of were not directed at the Union (*Hodgson, Woolf Productions and the National Union of Journalists and Channel Four Television* v *UK* 10 EHRR 503). Similarly an applicant could not bring a complaint under Articles 9 and 10 concerning the oath required of Queen's Counsel in Northern Ireland when the applicant had not yet been invited to become a Queen's Counsel (*Magee* v *UK* 19 EHRR CD 91).

Where measures are directed at a corporate organisation which have a direct effect on its members, however, then a member may be a victim. For example, a shareholder of a company may be a victim of measures directed against a company, particularly if the applicant is a majority shareholder (*Kaplan* v *UK* 4 EHRR 64, compared with *Yarrow plc and Three Shareholders* v *UK* 5 EHRR 465). An *actio popularis* cannot be brought before the Commission (*App. No.*

9825/82 v *UK and Ireland* 8 EHRR 45), neither can the law be complained of *in abstracto*; the applicant must have been brought within the ambit of the applicable law which has been applied to his or her detriment, even if no specific measures have been taken to implement the law directly against the applicant (*Springer* v *UK* 5 EHRR 11). Some rights are extensive enough to include applicants who are victims indirectly, for example in the case of Article 2, next-of-kin may claim to be victims (*App. No. 8416/79* v *UK* 19 D & R 244, and *App. No. 9348/81* v *UK* 5 EHRR 506). Similarly in the case of complaints under Articles 8 and 14, applicants may validly claim to be victims where, for example, detrimental measures under the Immigration Rules have been applied to members of their family (*X, Cabales and Balkandali* v *UK* Series A, Vol. 94). A parent may, in normal circumstances, bring an application on behalf of his or her child, but this does not apply where legal and parental responsibilities towards the child have been terminated by an adoption order, even if that adoption proceeded without the parent's consent (*App. No. 9966/82* v *UK* 5 EHRR 299). However, a parent may make a claim under Article 8 concerning his or her own family life, even if the children have been made wards of court and the local authority has assumed parental rights (*App. No. 10496/83* v *UK* 7 EHRR 135).

If the original applicant has died, whether the next-of-kin can continue the application will depend on the circumstances of the case and whether the applicant's interest was of such a nature that it could be transferred. For example, where the original complaint concerned the continued compulsory detention of the deceased applicant in a mental hospital, the Commission held that this interest was not transferable in the absence of any questions of general interest being raised (*App. No. 9480/81* v *UK* 9 EHRR 91, compared to *X* v *UK* 4 EHRR 188).

If an applicant has brought about the consequences of the alleged violation through his or her own conduct, it may be argued that the applicant cannot claim to be a victim. Similarly if the situation has changed so that the applicant is no longer a victim, for example where an illegal immigrant is subsequently allowed to remain in the UK and no longer faces the possibility of deportation (*App. No. 9620/81* v *UK* 5 EHRR 486, *Dahanayake* v *UK* 5 EHRR 144, and *App. No. 9856/82* v *UK* 10 EHRR 503 at 547), or where prison condition have improved so that the treatment received is no longer 'inhuman and degrading' (*Brady* v *UK* 3 EHRR 297).

A victim must be someone directly affected, so the Commission has held that the concept cannot be interpreted so broadly as to include every journalist or newspaper in the UK who, or which, might conceivably be affected by a House of Lords ruling restricting publication of certain news (*App. No. 10039/82* v *UK* 7 EHRR 409); and although newspaper publishers and journalists *may* be directly affected by the law on contempt of court and claim to be victims under Article 25, the Commission still has to examine whether they actually *are* victims (*Times Newspapers Ltd* v *UK* 8 EHRR 54).

Article 26

Article 26

The Commission may only deal with the matter after all domestic remedies have been exhausted, according to the generally recognised rules of international law . . .

In order to satisfy this requirement, if there is a remedy which the applicant is in normal circumstances obliged to exhaust before the Commission can deal with the case, then this must be exhausted. Certain remedies may be deemed not to be normal, for example it has been held that an application for an order of *habeas corpus* 'cannot be considered as part of the normal appeal procedure in the United Kingdom judicial system' (*X* v *UK* (1969) 12 *Yearbook* 298). There may also be circumstances when the normal remedy cannot be exhausted, in which case the applicant is absolved from the obligation. For example, in *Reed* v *UK* 3 EHRR 136, a prisoner alleging that assaults in prison amounted to a violation of Article 3 (inhuman and degrading treatment or punishment) could not pursue the normal remedy of a civil action for damages, because he was denied access to a solicitor in order to seek legal advice. Although there was an internal complaints procedure, the Commission found that neither this nor a public prosecution of the offender provided the applicant with a domestic remedy. Moreover, the ruling of the Commission in the *Reed* case indicated that it is of fundamental importance that if there is an existing domestic remedy for an alleged violation of the Convention, this must, in principle, be immediately available to every aggrieved person. However, the Commission has accepted that in certain cases a limited period may elapse while internal complaints procedures are followed. The time taken for this must not, however, encroach upon the immediacy and effectiveness of the domestic remedy.

Exhaustion of domestic remedies does not simply mean submitting a case to the various competent courts, but also that the substance of any complaint made before the Commission subsequently, is raised during the domestic proceedings concerned (*App. No. 9329/81* v *UK* 5 EHRR 286).

According to the *jurisprudence constante* of the Commission, a person is not required to pursue ineffective remedies offering no prospect of success. However, the mere existence of doubts as to the prospect of success 'does not absolve an applicant from exhausting a given remedy since it is for the domestic courts to determine the matter in the first instance' (*X* v *UK* App. No. 6406/73 3 EHRR 302). It is not always clear whether in fact a certain remedy is available in the circumstances of the case. If there is settled legal opinion which indicates that a particular remedy is not available then there is no obligation for the applicant to make use of it. The existence of a remedy must be sufficiently certain before there can be an obligation to exhaust it. Indeed, one of the things that the case may do is to clarify whether or not a remedy is applicable or not (as happened with the writ of *certiorari* in the context of adjudications by Prison Board of Visitors in *Campbell and Fell* v *UK* 7 EHRR 165).

Thus a domestic remedy must not only be that which would normally apply, but must be immediate, adequate and sufficient redress for the alleged grievance(s). If the Commission considers that although there are domestic remedies available these do not constitute effective remedies, these need not be exhausted. For example, in the case of *Paton* v *UK* 3 EHRR 408, the effective remedy would have been an injunction to prevent the abortion of the baby the applicant had fathered. However, the abortion had already taken place, and as equity will not act in vain this remedy was no longer applicable.

It may be the case that there is no domestic remedy which meets the situation. For example, in the case against the UK and Ireland (*App. No. 9825/82 v UK and Ireland* 8 EHRR 45) the Commission found that there was no domestic remedy in respect of the alleged failure to prevent the murder of the applicant's husband. Similarly, if the remedy is deemed to be one which is essentially discretionary it may be considered not to be effective and sufficient. For example, where the possibility exists for applying for compensation for dismissal (*Temple* v *UK* 8 EHRR 318 and *Watts* v *UK* 9 EHRR 123; Employment Act 1982).

Similarly, the opportunity to request an authority to reconsider a decision it has already taken does not generally constitute a sufficient remedy for the purposes of Article 26. For example, failure to re-apply to the Legal Aid Board which has already refused an initial application for legal aid, does not amount to a failure to exhaust domestic remedies (*R* v *UK* 15 EHRR CD 100 and *Maxwell* v *UK* 15 EHRR CD 101).

It should be noted that the burden of proving the existence of available and sufficient domestic remedies lies upon the State invoking the rule (*Kelly* v *UK* 16 EHRR CD 21); consequently many of the initial arguments put forward by the Government will focus on this aspect rather than seeking to refute allegations of violations, because if the Government can establish that some domestic remedy has not been exhausted then the case will be declared inadmissible.

Article 26 goes on to state that an application must be brought to the Commission within six months of the final decision being taken. The date on which the final decision was taken refers to 'the final decision involved in the exhaustion of all domestic remedies according to the generally recognised rules of international law. In English law this excluded orders of *habeas corpus*, which the Commission has held do not form part of the normal appeal procedure in criminal cases. The purpose of the six-month rule as stated in *Kelly* v *UK* (1985) 42 D & R 205 is:

> . . . to promote certainty of the law and to ensure that cases raising issues under the Convention are dealt with within a reasonable time. Furthermore it ought also to protect the authorities and other persons concerned from being under any uncertainty for a prolonged period of time. Finally, it should provide the possibility of securing the facts of the case which otherwise could fade away, making a fair examination of the question at issue next to impossible.

The six-month rule:

> . . . marks out the temporal limits of supervision carried out by the organs of the Convention and signals to both individuals and State authorities the period beyond which such supervision is no longer possible. (*App. No. 9825/82* v *UK and Ireland* 8 EHRR 45 at 49, para. 13)

The relevant date of the introduction of an application is the date of the first letter to the Commission indicating an intention to lodge an application and the nature of the complaint (*Kelly* v *UK*). If, however, there is a substantial delay or interval between this letter and the submission of further information regarding the application, the Commission may examine the particular circumstances of the case in order to decide what date is to be the relevant date from which to calculate the running of the six-month period. The reason why the Commission retains this discretion is that:

> . . . it would be contrary to the spirit and the aim of the six-month rule . . . if, by any initial communication, an applicant would set in motion the proceedings under Article 25 of the Convention and then remain inactive for an unexplained and unlimited period of time. (*Kelly* v *UK*, p. 78)

The Commission generally, therefore, not only rejects applications where the applicant has submitted the application more than six months after the date of the final decision, when there were no special circumstances suspending or interrupting the running of the six-month period, but also rejects applications which have been submitted within the six-month period but where pursuit of the case has been unreasonably delayed.

Where the violation of the Convention is a continuing state of affairs then the six-month rule does not apply until the continuing state of affairs ceases to exist. In determining whether or not there is a continuing state of affairs, a distinction has to be made between a state of affairs which relates to continuing restriction on substantive Convention rights, and a situation where the domestic law is such that until it changes the situation – for everyone – will continue indefinitely. If the latter is the case, then 'the person affected suffers no additional prejudice beyond that which arose immediately and directly from the initial measure' (*Temple* v *UK* 8 EHRR 319).

If there are no domestic remedies which must be exhausted then the relevant date for the running of the six months is the act or decision complained of, which is taken as the relevant 'final decision' (*App. No. 7379/76* v *UK* 8 D & R 211). So the six-month period referred to in Article 26:

> . . . may begin to run either from the date of a 'final decision' taken in the exhaustion of an effective and sufficient domestic remedy, or from the date of the act or decision complained of where such an act or decision finally determines the applicant's position on the domestic level. However in the Commission's opinion Article 26 cannot be interpreted so as to require an applicant to seize the Commission at any time before his position in connection with the matter complained of has been finally determined or settled on the domestic level. Only when there has been a '*final* decision' (*décision interne définitive*) or some equivalent act or measure, does the six month period start to run. (*Sir William Lithgow* v *UK* cited as *Greenock Ltd* v *UK* (1985) 42 DJR 33 at 41 (Report on admissibility).)

Examination of the Case

Once the Commission has decided that the petition is admissible it must ascertain all the facts. Much of this is done through the compilation of written documents. Both parties must assist in furnishing whatever information is required in order to establish all the facts, and both parties have the opportunity to comment on the petition.

Article 28

1.   In the event of the Commission accepting a petition referred to it:

(a)   it shall, with a view to ascertaining the facts, undertake together with the representatives of the parties an examination of the petition and, if need be, an investigation, for the effective conduct of which the States concerned shall furnish all necessary facilities, after an exchange of views with the Commission . . .

ARRIVING AT A SOLUTION

Friendly Settlements

The primary aim of the procedural machinery is to encourage a friendly settlement or resolution. Cases may be withdrawn if a friendly settlement is reached in the interim. Once a full set of facts is established then the Commission makes itself available to the parties in line with the provision in Article 28, para. 1(b):

(b)   it [the Commission] shall . . . place itself at the disposal of the parties concerned with a view to securing a friendly settlement of the matter on the basis of respect for human rights as defined in this Convention.

If a friendly settlement is secured then the Commission reports to the parties, the Committee of Ministers, and the Secretary-General of the Council of Europe, giving a brief statement of the settlement and the facts of the case. Examples of friendly settlements include offers of compensation and the payment of costs, undertakings to change rules or internal guidelines, or the introduction of reforming legislation.

Taking the Case Further

If a friendly settlement cannot be reached the case must proceed. The Commission sends a private report to the Committee of Ministers and to the parties. The report states the facts and expresses the opinion of the Commission as to whether the facts disclose a breach of the Convention or not. This opinion is not legally binding. The Commission may also make any proposals regarding disposal of the matter which it thinks fit. The Commission may decide to refer the matter to the Court of Human Rights, in which case this decision must be made within three months. Alternatively the State against whom the claim is brought, or the State of whom the individual applicant is a national or a State which is an applicant, can refer the matter to the Court. Under the Ninth Protocol, an individual has an absolute right to bring the case to the Court directly, subject only to the filtering procedure via the committee stage mentioned above. However this procedure is not yet available to UK applicants.

Generally the Court will consider only matters which have been raised before the Commission and have been declared to be admissible by the Commission. However, the Court has held that it may:

. . . take cognisance of every question of law arising in the course of the proceedings concerning the facts submitted to its examination by a Contracting State or by the Commission (*Handyside* v *UK* Series A, Vol. 24, para. 41)

and may have regard to articles other than those raised before the Commission. It cannot, however, act as a court of appeal where the Commission has rejected a claim, or part of a claim, as inadmisssible.

The organisation and working of the Court

The purpose of the Court is essentially the same as that of the Commission, namely to ensure the observance of the engagements undertaken by the Contracting States under the Convention. The number of judges of the Court is equal to that of the member States of the Council of Europe. No two judges can be nationals of the same State. The member States of the Council of Europe nominate a list of possible judges and these are then elected by the Consultative Assembly, for nine years. They may be re-elected and, as with the members of the Commission, they sit in their individual capacity and are expected to be impartial and fully independent.

The Court – which is not a permanent court – may sit as a plenary court, which is exceptional, or in chambers, which is more usual. A chamber consists of nine judges including, as *ex officio* members, the President or Vice-President and the judge who is a national of any State Party concerned. The nine judges are chosen by lot, drawn by the President. Under certain conditions, and since October 1993, the Court may sit as a Grand Chamber consisting of 19 judges. Under the Convention it draws up its own rules of procedure – the current rules in use entered into force on 1 February 1994. The Court is assisted by a registry. It elects the Registrar and the Deputy Registrar itself, but other officials are appointed by the Secretary-General of the Council of Europe with the agreement of the President of the Court or the Registrar.

The procedure is generally written, although there are exceptions to this, and affidavits and other documents are filed with the Court's registry in compliance with time limits and procedures established by the President. This is the first stage. Once the case is ready for hearing the President fixes a date for the oral proceedings which are, in principle, public. The Commission may assist the Court by enlightening it on certain points. It does not take part directly but is present as 'defender of the public interest'. Since 1983, the applicant may indicate that he or she wishes to take part in the proceedings. In principle he or she will be represented by an advocate. Where an applicant has received legal aid to present the case before the Commission this will be continued for the proceedings before the Court, or the President may grant legal aid at any time at the applicant's request. If the applicant is subsequently awarded any sum to compensate for costs and expenses, the legal aid advance will be reimbursed from this.

During the proceedings the President may invite other parties to submit written observations to assist in the proper administration of justice, provided any submissions are submitted within a stipulated time limit.

Final judgments of the Court are given by a majority. The enforcement of judgments is the responsibility of the Committee of Ministers.

The Court's jurisdiction extends to all cases concerning the interpretation and application of the Convention, but only in so far as States have declared that they recognise the jurisdiction of the Court.

Where the Court finds that there has been an infringement of one or more of the articles of the Convention, it has the power to order the offending State to make just compensation (Article 50). If changes to domestic law are needed then the government of the respective state will be free to determine what those should be in order to comply with its obligations under the Convention.

The Committee of Ministers

Within the framework of the Convention the Committee of Ministers has two tasks. First, when a case has not been referred to the European Court within three months from the date of the transmission of the Commission's report to the Committee of Ministers (Article 32, para. 1), the Committee of Ministers is required to decide whether or not provisions of the Convention have been violated. Secondly, when the European Court has made a final ruling on a case, it is up to the Committee of Ministers to supervise the execution of the judgment of the Court in accordance with Article 54 of the Convention.

In the first case, if it finds that there has been a violation of the Convention, the Committee decides what measures the offending State must take and sets a time limit for compliance. If this is not met then the Committee must meet again and decide – by a two-thirds majority – what steps should be taken. It also publishes the report of the Commission.

The decision of the Committee of Ministers is binding on any High Contracting Party concerned and imposes an obligation in international law on that party to amend its domestic law if necessary, to compensate the individual victim and to take any other steps required by the Court or the Committee.

Sanctions operate not only via the Committee of Ministers and at the level of foreign relations, but also because the Commission and Court can be seen as an international arena in which the domestic legislation of any State which is a party to the Convention is subject to scrutiny by judges and experts from other countries. Thus the Court and the Commission themselves operate as a watchdog of human rights, and the reports of their decisions create a body of commentary on the extent to which Article 1 is being complied with.

Procedural reforms under the Eleventh Protocol

The Eleventh Protocol is directed at amending the control mechanism of the European Convention and aims to enhance the efficiency of the means of protection, to shorten the procedural measures involved and to maintain the present high quality of human rights protection by establishing a single European Court of Human Rights. The Protocol was adopted on 11 May 1994, but will not enter into force until one year after all the States which are parties to the Convention have ratified it. The UK ratified this Protocol on 9 December 1994. It was hoped that ratification would be completed by the end of 1995, in which case the Protocol and the new judicial machinery would have come into place in 1996/97. This has not happened, and it now seems probable that ratification may not be completed even by the end of 1996.

The need for reform has been occasioned by the increasing number of applications brought before the Commission and Court, and the expansion of the Council of Europe. A resolution to consider changes was adopted in March 1985 at the European Ministerial Conference on Human Rights in Vienna. The Parliamentary Assembly of the Council of Europe adopted a recommendation for reform in October 1992 (Recommendation 1194 (1992)), and a decision to reform the control machinery of the Convention was taken by the Heads of State and Government of the Council of Europe member States in the Vienna Declaration on 9 October 1993.

The Protocol establishes a single permanent court, consisting of a number of judges equal to that of the High Contracting Parties to the Convention. This alters the present position which is that of one judge for each member State of the Council of Europe. Judges will be elected by the Parliamentary Assembly, each Contracting Party nominating a list of three. Terms of office will be for six years, although initially half of those elected will hold office for only three years. Who these are to be will be determined by lot by the Secretary-General of the Council of Europe. Judges may be re-elected, up to the age of 70. As at present, although the new Court may sit in plenary session – for example, to elect its President and Vice-Presidents, to set up chambers and to adopt the rules of the Court – it will generally sit in Committees (of three judges), chambers (of seven judges) and occasionally in a Grand Chamber (of 17 judges). All inter-State applications will be heard by this Grand Chamber.

Applications will initially be considered by a committee which may, by unanimous vote, declare an application inadmissible (new Article 28). The right to submit individual applications will be made automatic, whereas at present there is an optional clause to this effect in the Convention. If no decision is made by the committee, or if further examination of the application is necessary then a chamber will decide on the admissibility and merits of individual applications. Inter-State applications will be considered by a chamber, not a committee. If a case raises serious questions of interpretation of the Convention or any of the Protocols, or the resolution of the case appears to be inconsistent with a judgment previously delivered by the Court, then it may be referred to the Grand Chamber (new Article 30). The Grand Chamber will also consider requests for advisory opinions.

The jurisdiction of the Court remains the same as before, i.e. to hear all matters concerning the interpretation and application of the Convention and protocols. It can receive applications from a High Contracting Party or an individual, from a non-governmental organisation, or from a group of individuals claiming to be the victim of a violation by one of the High Contracting Parties of the rights set out in the Convention and Protocols. The admissibility criteria remain the same as at present.

Under the new procedure it is the Court which will examine the case and seek to secure a friendly settlement of the matter. The hearings will be public and documents deposited with the Registrar will be accessible to the public unless, in exceptional circumstances, the President of the Court decides otherwise. Judgments of the chambers are final, although exceptionally a party to a case may request that the case be referred to the Grand Chamber. The Grand Chamber will therefore act as a court of appeal where there is a serious question on interpretation or application of the Convention or the protocols, or a serious issue of general importance (new Article 43). Any such request must be made within three months of the judgment.

The Committee of Ministers will retain its role of supervising the execution of judgments and, by a majority vote, may ask the Court for its advisory opinion on legal questions relating to the scope and interpretation of the Convention and protocols provided that these do not fall outside the competence conferred on the Court under Article 47. It will, however, lose its role as a decision-making body as regards individual and State applications.

As part of the interim arrangements, the Parliamentary Assembly recommended that the new Court start with a clean sheet, and that any cases pending before either the Commission or the existing Court be finished by these institutions rather than taken on mid-way by the new Court, as currently provided for under Article 40, para. 6 of the Convention (Opinion No. 178 (1994)). The Assembly expressed the opinion that this would mean that the existing Court would continue for 18 months and the Commission for two and a half years after the establishment of the new Court. Given the current length of proceedings these time spans may be optimistic.

Further reading

There are a number of general texts which include information on the background to the Convention and the operational procedures of the Commission and the Court, as well as more specific journal articles.

Drzemczewski, A., 'Growing Impact of the European Human Rights Convention upon National Case Law' (1987) 84 *Law Society Gazette* 561

Drzemczewski, A., 'The Need for a Radical Overhaul' (1993) 143 *New Law Journal* 126

Fawcett, J. E. S., *The Application of the European Convention on Human Rights* (2nd ed., 1987, Clarendon)

Feldman, D., *Civil Liberties and Human Rights* (1993, Clarendon)

Fenwick, H., *Civil Liberties* (1994, Cavendish)

Gearty, C. A., 'The European Court of Human Rights and the Protection of Civil Liberties: An Overview' (1993) 52 *Cambridge Law Journal* 89

Lester, A., 'Fundamental Rights: the United Kingdom Isolated?' [1984] *Public Law* 46

Marston, G., 'The United Kingdom's Part in the Preparation of the European Convention of Human Rights 1950' (1993) 42 *International and Comparative Law Quarterly* 796

Morris, P., 'Individual Application to the European Commission of Human Rights' (1985) 135 *New Law Journal* 1017

Mowbray, A., 'Procedural Developments and the European Convention on Human Rights' [1991] *Public Law* 353

Mowbray, A., 'Reform of the Control System of the European Convention on Human Rights' [1993] *Public Law* 419

Mowbray, A., 'A New European Court of Human Rights' [1994] *Public Law* 540

Muchlinski, P., 'Status of the Individual under the European Convention on Human Rights and Contemporary International Law' (1985) 34 *International and Comparative Law Quarterly* 376

Robertson, A. H. and Merrills, J. G., *Human Rights in Europe* (3rd ed., 1993, Manchester)

Schermers, H., 'Factual Merger of the European Court and Commission of Human Rights' (1986) 11 *European Law Review* 350

Schermers, H., 'The European Court of Human Rights after the Merger' (1993) 18 *European Law Review* 493

Stone, R., *Civil Liberties* (1994, Blackstone Press)

Warbrick, C., 'Rights, the European Convention on Human Rights and English Law' (1994) 19 *European Law Review* 34

CHAPTER 1
ARTICLE ONE

Article 1
The High Contracting Parties shall secure to everyone within their jurisdiction the rights and freedoms defined in Section I of this Convention

1.1 THE SCOPE OF THE ARTICLE

This article sets a limit, primarily territorial, on the reach of the Convention. This was clearly stated in *Soering* v *UK* Series A, Vol. 161 in which the Court held:

> . . . the engagement undertaken by a Contracting State is confined to 'securing' . . . the listed rights and freedoms to persons within its own 'jurisdiction'. Further the Convention does not govern the actions of States not Parties to it, nor does it purport to be a means of requiring the Contracting States to impose Convention standards on other States . . .
> In interpreting the Convention regard must be had to its special character as a treaty for the collective enforcement of human rights and fundamental freedoms. Thus, the object and purpose of the Convention as an instrument for the protection of individual human beings require that its provisions be interpreted and applied so as to make its safeguards practical and effective. In addition, any interpretation of the rights and freedoms guaranteed has to be consistent with 'the general spirit of the Convention, an instrument designed to maintain and promote the ideals and values of a democratic society'. (paras 86 and 87)

In the *Soering* case, Article 1 could not be interpreted so as to establish a general principle that a Contracting State could not surrender an individual under its extradition obligations unless the Contracting State was satisfied that the country of destination met the conditions and standards implied by the articles of the Convention. Nevertheless, the Court held that the responsibility of the State could be engaged for breaches of Convention rights beyond its jurisdiction, even though there would be no question of adjudicating on the receiving, non-Contracting State for human rights violations under the Convention.

In the case of *Republic of Ireland* v *UK* 2 EHRR 25, the question was raised whether Article 1 could be the subject of a separate breach since the rights and freedoms secured are those mentioned in Section I of the Convention, i.e. Articles 2 to 18. Previously the Court had held that where there was a breach of one of the articles in Section I, a violation of article 1 followed automatically but added nothing to the breach. Article 1 could not be violated *in abstracto*. However, this case presented the Court with the opportunity to reconsider this matter. The Irish Government argued that the UK was in breach of an inter-State obligation arising from Article 1, separately from its obligations towards individuals. The Court held:

> . . . such a breach results from the mere existence of a law which introduces, directs or authorises measures incompatible with the rights and freedoms safeguarded. (Series A, Vol. 25, para. 240)

However, a breach can be found only if the law which is challenged is sufficiently clear so as to make the breach immediately apparent, otherwise there must be a breach which is referable to the interpretation and application of the offending law *in concreto*. Although the Court found two practices of breaches of Article 3, which automatically infringed Article 1 as well, it found, in the circumstances of the case, no breach *in abstracto* evident in the legislation in force at the relevant time in Northern Ireland.

This issue could not have arisen in the case of an individual applicant, as under Article 25 an applicant, must establish that he or she is a victim of a violation. Under Article 24, however, which refers to inter-State applications, a Contracting State is able to refer any alleged breach of the provisions of the Convention by another Contracting State to the Commission.

At inter-State level an independent breach of Article 1 might be established, whereas in the case of individual applications a breach of Article 1 can arise only in connection with a breach of one of the other articles in Section I of the Convention.

In interpreting the words 'within their jurisdiction' the Commission has stated that:

> . . . the High Contracting Parties are bound to secure the said rights and freedoms to all persons under their actual authority and responsibility, not only when the authority is exercised within their own territory but also when it is exercised abroad . . .
> the authorised agents of the State, including diplomatic or consular agents and armed forces, not only remain under its jurisdiction when abroad but bring any other persons or property 'within the jurisdiction' of that State, to the extent that they exercise authority over such persons or property. In so far as, by their acts or omissions the responsibility of the State is engaged. (*App. No. 9825/82* v *UK and Ireland* 8 EHRR 45 at 49, para. 25)

Thus a complaint brought against both the UK and the Republic of Ireland concerning the situation in Northern Ireland, did not engage the responsibility of the latter because it could not be said that the applicant came within the jurisdiction of the Republic of Ireland. Northern Ireland or parts of it could not be considered as national territory of the Republic of Ireland because the constitutional claims to such territory were not recognised by the international community and, secondly, it could not be said that the authorised agents of the Republic were exercising any authority over the applicant. Similarly, where the direct victim of a violation was in Southern Ireland (Ballybay, County Monaghan) at the relevant time, he was not within the jurisdiction of the UK and therefore his wife could not claim to be an indirect victim as a result of his murder (*App. No. 9348/81* v *UK* 5 EHRR 465).

In comparison, a complaint which concerned an agreement between British Rail and the trade unions was held to involve the UK because although the proximate cause of the dispute was this agreement, the underlying complaint concerned the domestic law which, the applicants alleged made lawful violations of rights and freedoms under the Convention (*Young, James and Webster* v *UK* 4 EHRR 38). Similarly in the case of *Costello-Roberts* 19 EHRR 112, the question arose as to whether the responsibility of the State would be engaged on account of the administration of corporal punishment in an independent (non-State) school. It was held that the responsibility of the State was so engaged because, first, Contracting States have an obligation under Article 1 to secure to children within their jurisdiction the guarantees of the Convention; secondly, the State obliges parents to educate their children or to have them educated and therefore has the task of supervising educational standards; and, thirdly, the combination of State and private schools is tolerated and encouraged by the State, and the right to education secured by the State under the First Protocol, Article 2 and reinforced under Article 28 of the United Nations Convention on the Rights of the Child – which was ratified by the UK in December 1991 – means that both the education and the disciplinary systems of a school engage the liability of the State.

1.2   THE CASES

Young, James and Webster v *UK*
Series A, Vol. 44

The facts
The applicants were all former employees of British Rail. After commencing their employment a closed shop agreement was concluded between three trade unions and British Rail whereby membership of one of the unions was a condition of employment. All three applicants refused to join a trade union and in due course each was dismissed in 1976. They were unable to claim unfair dismissal, because under the Trade Union and Labour Relations Act (TULRA) 1974, as modified by the Trade Union and Labour Relations (Amendment) Act 1976, the basic rule was that the dismissal of an employee for refusal to join a specified union in a closed shop situation was to be regarded as fair for the purposes of the law on unfair dismissal. The applicants brought complaints under Articles 9, 10, 11, and 13. Before these could be considered the Commission had to decide if the responsibility of the UK was engaged.

The Commission's opinion
The Government had conceded that if there was found to be a violation of any of the articles of the Convention, or a relevant interference with any of the

applicants' rights under the Convention which could be properly regarded as a direct consequence of the TULRA 1974 and the 1976 amending Act, then the UK would be responsible by virtue of the enactment of the legislation.

The Commission expressed the opinion that:

> . . . Under Article 1 of the Convention each Contracting State 'shall secure to everyone within [its] jurisdiction the rights and freedoms defined in . . . [the] Convention'; hence, if a violation of one of those rights and freedoms is the result of non-observance of that obligation in the enactment of domestic legislation, the responsibility of the State for that violation is engaged. Although the proximate cause of the events giving rise to this case was the 1975 agreement between British Rail and the railway unions, it was the domestic law in force at the relevant time that made lawful the treatment of which the applicants complained. The responsibility of the respondent State for any resultant breach of the Convention is thus engaged on this basis. . . . (para. 49)

The judgment of the Court

Before the Court the Government argued that if a breach of the UK's obligations under Article 11 were disclosed then the responsibility of the UK was engaged exclusively by reason of the enactment of the Acts of 1974 and 1976 and was not engaged on the ground either that British Rail was an organ of the State, or that the Government of the UK was to be regarded as the employer of British Rail or the applicants. The Court accepted the report of the Commission in this respect. The Court also reached the same conclusion as the Commission, namely that there had been a violation of Article 11, and thus the responsibility of the UK was engaged.

Comment

Subsequent to the dismissal of the applicants the law was changed. First, the Employment Protection (Consolidation) Act 1978 was repealed, although its provisions concerning unfair dismissal were substantially re-enacted. The only ground for claiming that the dismissal was unfair in a closed shop situation at that stage was on the grounds of genuine religious objection. The Employment Act 1980 amended the 1978 Act, and although it remained the case that dismissal of an employee who refused to join a union in a closed shop situation was not to be regarded as unfair, three exceptions were introduced whereby such dismissal was unfair if:

> (a) the employee objects on grounds of conscience or other deeply-held personal conviction to being a member of any or a particular union; or
>
> (b) the employee belonged, before the closed shop agreement or arrangement came into effect, to the class of employees covered thereby and has not been a member of a union in accordance therewith; or
>
> (c) in the case of a closed shop agreement or arrangement taking effect after 15 August 1980, either it has not been approved by the vote in a ballot of not less than 80% of the employees affected or, although it is so approved, the employee has not since the balloting been a member of a union in accordance therewith. (para. 26)

Further, a code of practice which came into effect in December 1980 recommended that closed shop agreements should protect basic individual rights and be applied flexibly and tolerantly with due regard to the interests of individuals, unions and employers.

The law had therefore changed while this case was being heard. However, even if it had arisen after these reforms, the European Court might still have found that the restrictions which compulsory trade union membership imposed on freedom of association, as guaranteed by Article 11, were not 'necessary in a democratic society'.

Soering v UK
Series A, Vol. 161

The facts

The applicant, a West German, was charged with murdering his girlfriend's parents in Bedford County, Virginia, USA. The applicant and his girlfriend were students at the University of Virginia but left the United States in October 1985, seven months after the homicides. They were arrested in England in April 1986 in connection with a cheque fraud, and in 1986 the applicant made a sworn affidavit admitting to the murders. The Government of the United States, under the terms of an Extradition Treaty of 1972 between the USA and the UK, applied for the applicant and his girlfriend to be extradicted. The UK sought for an assurance that, if convicted, the applicant would not receive the death penalty. The UK was informed that its representations on this matter would be made known to the judge. In 1987, the applicant's girlfriend was extradited to the United States and, after pleading guilty as an accessory to the murder, was sentenced to 90 years' imprisonment. In 1988, the Secretary of State signed a warrant ordering the applicant's surrender to the United States' authorities. The applicant's actual removal was delayed due to interim measures taken by the Commission and the European Court.

In his application to the Commission, the applicant stated that, notwithstanding the assurances given to the UK, there was a serious likelihood that he would be sentenced to death if extradited to the USA. He claimed violations of Article 3, Article 6, para. 3, and Article 13.

The Commission's opinion

The Commission expressed the opinion that there had been a breach of Article 13 but not of the other two articles.

In considering the applicability of Article 1, and the possibility that extradition might give rise to an issue under Article 3, the Commission expressed the opinion that:

> . . . if a Convention State deports or extradites a person within its jurisdiction to another country where he is subjected to treatment in violation of the Convention the deporting or extraditing State is not responsible as such for the violation which is only opposable to the receiving State where the actual treatment (for example, treatment prohibited by Article 3) takes place. The deportation or extradition, however, can under certain circumstances involve the responsibility of the deporting or extraditing Convention State. If, for example, a Convention State deports or extradites a person to a country where it is certain or where there is a serious risk that the person will be

subjected to torture or inhuman treatment the deportation or extradition would, in itself, under such circumstances constitute inhuman treatment for which the deporting or extraditing State would be directly responsible under Article 3 of the Convention. The basis of State responsibility in such cases lies in the exposure of a person by way of deportation or extradition to inhuman or degrading treatment in another country.

. . . For these reasons the Commission considers that if conditions are such that there exists a serious risk of treatment in breach of Article 3 of the Convention, the deportation or extradition of an individual to face such conditions incurs the responsibility under Article 1 of the Convention of the Contracting State which so decides. . . .

. . . The task of the Commission is thus to assess the existence of a serious danger for the person deported or extradited, or whose deportation or extradition is imminent. (paras 96, 98, and 99)

Before the responsibility of the Contracting State could be engaged the Commission had to assess the existence of a serious danger for the person deported or extradited. It therefore had to consider whether the possibility of the death penalty and the 'death row phenomenon' alleged by the applicant amounted to a breach of Article 3:

. . . its task under Article 3 is to assess the existence of an objective danger that the person extradited would be subjected to treatment contrary to this provision. Moreover, it recalls that the State's obligation under Article 1 of the Convention is to secure the rights and freedoms defined in Section I to every person within its jurisdiction, regardless of his or her nationality or status. It follows, from both provisions read together, that the assessment of the risk that a person might be subject to inhuman treatment contrary to Article 3 depends on an objective assessment of conditions in the country concerned and is independent of the nationality of the applicant or the possibility of extraditing him to his own country. (para. 149)

After a detailed consideration of all the evidence (see Articles 2 and 3), the Commission expressed the opinion that the treatment that the applicant was likely to endure did not attain the degree of seriousness envisaged by Article 3 of the Convention on the grounds that:

. . . In the first place the Commission observes that . . . the delays in the appeal system . . . are, in the main, attributable to the inmates' voluntary action in pursuing State and Federal appeals. It is significant that the automatic appeal procedure to the Virginia Supreme Court only lasts six to eight months. Further, there is no indication that the machinery of justice to which the applicant would be subjected is an arbitrary or unreasonable one. On the contrary the Commission observes that the death penalty scheme in Virginia contains numerous safeguards against arbitrariness and that the appeal system has, as its fundamental purpose, the avoidance of the arbitrary imposition of the death penalty and protection of the prisoner's right to life.

. . . Finally, the Commission notes that the important mitigating factors in the present case, namely, the age and mental condition of the applicant, are matters which can be fully taken into consideration by both the judge and jury at the sentencing phase and in any subsequent State and Federal appeals.
. . .

The Commission concludes, by six votes to five that the extradition of the applicant to the United States of America in the circumstances of the present case would not constitute treatment contrary to Article 3 of the Convention. (paras 152–154)

The judgment of the Court

The Court accepted that extradition agreements have the beneficial purpose of preventing fugitive offenders from evading justice, and that this should not be ignored in determining the scope and application of the Convention and of Article 3 in particular. The Court also accepted that:

> . . . the United Kingdom has no power over the practices and arrangements of the Virginia authorities which are the subject of the applicant's complaints. It is also true that in other international instruments cited by the United Kingdom Government – for example the 1951 United Nations Convention relating to the Status of Refugees (Article 33), the 1957 European Convention on Extradition (Article 11) and the 1984 United Nations Convention against Torture and Other Cruel, Inhuman and Degrading Treatment or Punishment (Article 3) – the problems of removing a person to another jurisdiction where unwanted consequences may follow are addressed expressly and specifically.
>
> These considerations cannot, however, absolve the Contracting Parties from responsibility under Article 3 for all and any foreseeable consequences of extradition suffered outside their jurisdiction. (para. 86)

The Court considered all the circumstances of the case and agreed with the Commission that:

> . . . the machinery of justice to which the applicant would be subject in the United States is in itself arbitary nor unreasonable, but, rather, respects the rule of law and affords not inconsiderable procedural safeguards to the defendant in a capital trial. Facilities are available on death row for the assistance of inmates, notably through provision of psychological and psychiatric services.
>
> However, in the Court's view, having regard to the very long period of time spent on death row in such extreme conditions, with the ever-present and mounting anguish of awaiting execution of the death penalty, and to the personal circumstances of the applicant, especially his age and mental state at the time of the offence, the applicant's extradition to the United States would expose him to a real risk of treatment going beyond the threshold set by Article 3. A further consideration of relevance is that in the particular instance the legitimate purpose of extradition could be achieved by another means which would not involve suffering of such exceptional intensity or duration.
>
> Accordingly, the Secretary of State's decision to extradite the applicant to the United States would, if implemented, give rise to a breach of Article 3. (para. 111)

It therefore held that the Secretary of State's decision to extradite the applicant to the United States would, if implemented, give rise to a breach of Article 3, and that therefore the responsibility of the UK under Article 1 was engaged.

Comment

Although the applicant was a German national and there was an Extradition Treaty between the UK and Germany, the case could not be tried in Germany – despite representations to that effect – because although the German courts had jurisdiction to try the applicant, the evidence submitted by the German court was insufficient to constitute a *prima facie* case, consisting, as it did, only of the applicant's admissions. The offence was not triable in the UK – where the penalty for murder is life imprisonment and not death (Homicide Act 1957) – because the English courts do not exercise criminal jurisdiction in respect of acts of foreigners abroad.

Extradition treaties impose international obligations on the contracting States. Proceedings for extradition are brought before a magistrate by the Secretary of State. The magistrate must be satisfied that there is sufficient evidence to put the accused on trial. A writ of *habeas corpus* may be used to challenge the committal proceedings and to ensure that the magistrate has jurisdiction. The Secretary of State may also exercise his discretion not to sign the extradition warrant. The procedure of judicial review is available to challenge both the exercise of the Secretary of State's discretion and his decision to sign the warrant, on the basis of illegality, irrationality or procedural impropriety. Failure to consider whether or not there was a breach of the European Convention on Human Rights is not a ground for judicial review. In the applicant's case leave to apply for judicial review was rejected.

The law governing the definition and sentence for murder in Virginia is governed by the Code of Virginia 1950. Capital murder, which includes 'the wilful, deliberate and premeditated killing of more than one person as a part of the same act or transaction' is punishable as a Class 1 felony for which the sentence is death or imprisonment for life. The death sentence can be passed only if the prosecution prove beyond a reasonable doubt the existence of one of two aggravating circumstances, i.e. future dangerousness and/or vileness. Proof of multiple wounds sustained by a victim, particularly neck wounds inflicted in a savage, methodical manner – as was the case here – has been held to satisfy the test of 'vileness'. The death penalty was resumed in 1977 after a moratorium imposed by the US Supreme Court. At the date of this case seven people had been executed by electrocution. The death penalty has been considered judicially and held to be constitutional. Provisions for mandatory review are considered to prevent its imposition being arbitrary or capricious.

CHAPTER 2
ARTICLE TWO

Article 2

1. Everyone's right to life shall be protected by law. No one shall be deprived of his life intentionally save in the execution of a sentence of a court following his conviction of a crime for which this penalty is provided by law.

2. Deprivation of life shall not be regarded as inflicted in contravention of this Article when it results from the use of force which is no more than absolutely necessary:

(a) in defence of any person from unlawful violence;

(b) in order to effect a lawful arrest or to prevent the escape of a person lawfully detained;

(c) in action lawfully taken for the purpose of quelling a riot or insurrection.

2.1 THE SCOPE OF THE ARTICLE

In order to engage the responsibility of the State, any complaint brought under this article will usually involve agents of the State such as the armed forces (*Kelly* v *UK* 16 EHRR CD 20; *McCann, Farrell and Savage* v *UK* Series A, Vol. 324), the police (*Kelly* v *UK* 8 EHRR 45), or prison officers, who have in some way been involved in the death of a person, usually a close relative of the applicant. The application may be brought on behalf of the deceased whom it is alleged has been a victim of the violation, or by a near relative who may also qualify as a victim either in his or her own right or because he or she was closely affected by the events on which the violation claimed is based (e.g., in *Paton* v *UK* (1980) 19 D & R 244, it was accepted that a 'a potential father is so closely affected by the termination of his wife's pregnancy that he may claim to be a victim').

The question of what is meant by a 'right to life' was raised in a case brought against the UK and Ireland (*App. No. 9825/82* v *UK and Ireland* 8 EHRR 49). The applicant complained of violations of the Convention under this article on behalf of herself in respect of the murder of her husband. She acknowledged that the murder itself did not ground a claim because no Government could guarantee the life of any citizen absolutely. However, she claimed that Article 2 required the Government to provide:

> . . . a proper level of general security in each locality where persons are under attack or living under the threat or fear of terrorism or paramilitary influence. (8 EHRR 45 at 50, para. 1)

Article 2, para. 1 indicates that everyone's right to life 'shall be protected by law'. The applicant argued that in interpreting this, and in order to secure the rights and freedoms defined in the Convention, the UK should:

> . . . protect the right to life not only by criminal prosecution of offenders but also by such preventative control, through deployment of its armed forces, as appears necessary to protect persons who are considered to be exposed to the threat of terrorist attacks. (para. 17)

The Commission has stated that Article 2 may give rise to positive obligations on the part of the State (*App. No. 9348/81* v *UK* 5 EHRR 465 at 504), but expressed the opinion that this cannot include a positive obligation to exclude any possible violence, or to protect a person from possible violence indefinitely.

In this case, involving the situation in Northern Ireland, the Commission did not find that it was the task of the Commission to consider in detail the appropriateness and efficiency of the measures taken by the UK to combat terrorism in Northern Ireland, although it noted that in fact the UK had taken a number of positive measures concerning the use and deployment of armed and security forces, some of whom had lost their own lives in combating terrorism (p. 505, para. 16).

In a more recent case the Commission and the Court were called on to consider measures taken to combat terrorism outside Northern Ireland (*McCann, Farrell and Savage* v *UK* Series A, Vol. 324). From this case it is clear that any deprivation of life which a Contracting State seeks to justify under any of the exceptions set out in para. 2 of Article 2, will be subject to careful scrutiny. The use of force must be not more than 'absolutely necessary' for the achievement of one of the purposes set out in sub-paras (a)–(c).

The question of who falls under Article 2 was considered in the *Paton* case ((1980) 19 D & R 244). In interpreting 'everyone' and 'life' the Commission considered the ordinary meaning of the provision in the context of this particular article and the Convention as a whole, and found the following:

> . . . the term 'everyone' . . . . is not defined in the Convention. It appears in Article 1 and in Section I, apart from Article 2(1), in Articles 5, 6, 8 to 11 and 13. In nearly all these instances the use of the word is such that it can apply only postnatally. None indicates clearly that it has any possible prenatal application, although such application in a rare case – e.g. under Article 6(1) – cannot be entirely excluded. (para. 7)

The Commission went on to consider the exclusions set out in the Article which limit 'everyone's right to life'. It found that all these limitations could apply only to persons already born, thus both the general usage of the term and the context of Article 2 tend towards the interpretation that 'everyone' does not include the unborn.

As to whether 'life' includes only the life of a person already born or also the unborn life of a foetus – which was the question in issue in the *Paton* case – the Commission noted that this term was also not defined in the Convention. The Commission:

> . . . observes that the term 'life' may be subject to different interpretations in different legal instruments, depending on the context in which it is used in the instrument concerned. (para. 16)

The alternatives open to the Commission were to interpret Article 2:

(a)   as not covering the foetus at all;
(b)   as recognising a 'right to life' of the foetus with certain implied limitations; or
(c)   as recognising an absolute 'right to life' of the foetus.

The Commission considered and rejected the third possibility on the grounds that:

> . . . The 'life' of the foetus is intimately connected with, and it cannot be regarded in isolation of, the life of the pregnant woman. If Article 2 were held to cover the foetus and its protection under this Article were, in the absence of any express limitation, seen as absolute, an abortion would have to be considered as prohibited even where the continuance of the pregnancy would involve a serious risk to the life of the pregnant woman. This would mean that the 'unborn life' of the foetus would be regarded as being of a higher value than the life of the pregnant woman. The 'right to life' of a a person already born would thus be considered as subject not only to the express limitations mentioned in paragraph 8 above but also to a further, implied limitation.
>
> . . . The Commission finds that such an interpretation would be contrary to the object and purpose of the Convention. It notes that, already at the time of the signature of the Convention (4 November 1950), all High Contracting Parties, with one possible exception, permitted abortion when necessary to save the life of the mother and that, in the meanwhile, the national law on termination of pregnancy has shown a tendency towards further liberalisation. (paras 19 and 20)

As regards the second option, in the case before it the Commission was only being asked to consider the 'right to life' of the foetus in the initial stage of pregnancy, as an abortion was carried out at ten weeks. The Commission considered that Article 2, para. 1 is subject to an implied limitation justifying the termination of a pregnancy in its early stages in order to protect the life and health of the woman. The Commission considered that:

> . . . it is not called upon to decide whether Article 2 does not cover the foetus at all or whether it recognises a 'right to life' of the foetus with implied limitations. (para. 23)

The question therefore remains unanswered.

Article 2 provides an exception from contravention in the case of the death penalty. There is a paradox here, in that while Article 3 prohibits inhuman and degrading treatment, Article 2 permits capital punishment.

Although most European States no longer have the death penalty, this issue has been raised in connection with Article 3, in the case of *Soering* v *UK* Series A, No. 161. In this case the Court held that Article 3 must be 'construed in harmony with the provisions of Article 2'. Article 3 cannot be interpreted to include a general prohibition on the death penalty because this would nullify the clear wording of Article 2. However, as indicated in the report of the Commission in the *Soering* case, 'extradition of a person to a country where he risks the death penalty cannot, in itself, raise an issue either under Article 2 or Article 3 of the Convention'. Article 3 may be raised, however, in respect of the manner or circumstances in which such a penalty is implemented (see Chapter 3).

In a separate, although concurring, judgment in the *Soering* case, Judge de Meyer expressed the opinion that to extradite someone to a State where he or she would be exposed to the death penalty not only amounted to inhuman and degrading treatment (Article 3), but also to a violation of the right to life and would be a breach of the extraditing State's obligations under Article 2.

It has been suggested that the fact that most Contracting States have abolished capital punishment could be used to reinterpret the provisions of Article 2 and to abrogate the exception. However, the Sixth Protocol – which came into force in 1985 – provides a normal method of amendment to the text by allowing Contracting States to accept the obligation to abolish capital punishment by signing and ratifying this Protocol. The UK has not yet done so, and so the possibility of reintroducing capital punishment remains open to it. It should also be noted that Article 2 itself contains no safeguards concerning the death penalty as far as age or mental capacity of a condemned accused. However, youth or psychiatric impairment might be taken into account in bringing a possible death sentence within the scope of Article 3, and these factors are included in other instruments which reflect the mores of a large number of States, such as the 1966 International Covenant on Civil and Political Rights (Article 2) and the 1969 American Convention on Human Rights (Article 4).

2.2 THE CASES

Paton v *UK*
(1980) 19 D & R 244 (cited as *X* v *UK*)

The facts
The applicant was the husband of Joan Paton. The marriage was not a happy one and had broken down to the extent that husband and wife were living separately. The applicant was told by his wife that she was pregnant and intended to have an abortion. The applicant applied for a High Court injunction to prevent the abortion. The President of the Court rejected the application for an injunction on the grounds that:

> . . . an injunction could be granted only to restrain the infringement of a legal right;
> that in English law the foetus has no legal rights until it is born and has a separate

existence from its mother, and that the father of a foetus, whether or not he is married to the mother has no legal right to prevent the mother from having an abortion, if the provisions of the 1967 [Abortion] Act have been complied with. (para. 7)

The abortion was carried out and the applicant applied to the Commission contending that the UK law violated Articles 2 and/or 5, 6, 8, and 9 of the Convention.

The Commission's opinion

The Commission accepted the applicant, as a potential father, as a victim within the meaning of Article 25, and that he had exhausted all possible domestic remedies because, as the abortion had taken place, no further remedies by way of injunction would be relevant.

The problems of interpreting the meaning and scope of Article 2, in order to decide whether the unborn foetus was included within the provisions of the Convention, have been indicated above. In the end the Commission found:

> . . . that the authorisation, by the United Kingdom authorities, of the abortion complained of is compatible with Article 2(1), first sentence because, if one assumes that this provision applies at the initial stage of the pregnancy, the abortion is covered by an implied limitation, protecting the life and health of the woman at that stage, of the 'right to life' of the foetus. (para. 23)

The applicant's complaint was therefore found to be inadmissible as being manifestly ill-founded.

Comment

Several previous applications had been made to the Commission concerning the abortion law of High Contracting Parties, either under Article 2, as here, or under Article 8. In two of these the Commission had declared the applications inadmissible on the grounds that the applicants were not victims of the abortion laws complained of. In one application admitted under Article 8, no breach had been found and the question of whether the unborn child was covered by Article 2 had been left open.

The interpretive technique used in this case illustrates the range of sources that the Commission may call on. It considered both the English and French wording of Article 2 and referred to a decision of the Austrian Constitutional Court – which found that Article 2 did not cover unborn life – the American Convention on Human Rights 1969 – which does extend the right to life to the unborn from the moment of conception (Article 4(1)) – the German Federal Constitutional Court's interpretation of the right to life in the Basic Law of Germany – which includes unborn human beings – and a decision of the American Supreme Court (*Roe* v *Wade* 410 US 113 (1973)) – which appeared to favour a viability test.

Stewart v *UK*
(1984) 39 D & R 169

The facts

The applicant was the mother of a child who had been killed by a plastic baton round (plastic 'bullet') fired by a British soldier in Northern Ireland, in 1976.

Domestic proceedings against the Ministry of Defence had been taken by the applicant, as the administratrix of the deceased, based on assault, battery and trespass to the person. These had not been successful either at first instance or on appeal. The appeal judge had found that the incident occurred during a riot in which the deceased was participating and that the firing was reasonable for the prevention of crime under s. 3(1) of the Criminal Law Act 1967.

The applicant complained that the death of her son resulted from the use of force which was in contravention of Article 2.

The Commission's opinion

First, the Commission indicated that it was not called upon to consider or comment on the wider issue of the use of plastic baton rounds as a means of riot control, but only to examine the specific circumstances of the incident with a view to establishing whether the degree of force used was in conformity with Article 2. In doing this the Commission noted that although the applicant disputed the findings of fact of the trial judge:

> . . . the national judge, unlike the Commission, has had the benefit of listening to the witnesses at first hand and assessing the credibility and probative value of their testimony after careful consideration. Accordingly, in the absence of any new evidence having been brought before the Commission and of any indications that the trial judge incorrectly evaluated the evidence before him, the Commission must base its examination of the Convention isues before it on the facts as established by national courts. (para. 8)

In interpreting Article 2 the Commission acknowledged that this article:

> . . . constitutes one of the most important rights of the Convention, from which no derogation is permissible, even in times of public emergency. (para. 11)

> . . . There are four situations in which the deprivation of the right to life will not amount to a violation of the Article. These are 'exhaustive and must be narrowly interpreted'. (para. 13)

The Commission had to consider whether Article 2 encompassed only intentional killing, or whether it included unintentional killing:

> . . . In paragraph 2 no express mention is made of whether the provision covers only intentional or unintentional or both types of deprivation of life. This question has been raised, in the present case, by the respondent Government who submit that Art. 2 extends only to intentional acts and has no application to negligent or accidental acts. (para. 13)

In an earlier case (*Association X v UK* 14 D & R 33) the Commission had adopted a broad approach in which it stated that the right enjoined the State 'not only to refrain from taking life "intentionally" but, further, to take appropriate steps to safeguard life'.

> . . . The Commission considers that the above interpretation, which views the sphere of protection afforded by Art. 2 as going beyond the intentional deprivation of life, flows from the wording and structure of Art. 2. In particular, the exceptions enumerated in paragraph 2 indicate that this provision is not concerned exclusively with intentional killing. Any other interpretation would hardly be consistent with the

object and purpose of the Convention or with a strict interpretation of the general obligation to protect the right to life. In the Commission's opinion the text of Art. 2, read as a whole, indicates that paragraph 2 does not primarily define situations where it is permitted intentionally to kill an individual, but defines the situation where it is permissible to 'use force' which may result, as the unintended outcome of the use of force, in the deprivation of life. The use of the force – which has resulted in a deprivation of life – must be shown to have been 'absolutely necessary' for one of the purposes in subparagraphs (a), (b) or (c) and, therefore, justified in spite of the risks it entailed for human lives. (para. 15)

'Absolutely necessary', which had been interpreted in both the *Handyside* v *UK* case (1 EHRR 737) and *The Sunday Times* v *UK* case (2 EHRR 245), meant conforming to a pressing social need in which the interference with a Convention right was proportionate to the legitimate aim pursued.

The Commission therefore considered that:

... Art. 2(2) permits the use of force for the purposes enumerated in subparagraphs (a), (b) and (c) subject to the requirement that the force used is strictly proportionate to the achievement of the permitted purpose. In assessing whether the use of force is strictly proportionate, regard must be had to the nature of the aim pursued, the dangers to life and limb inherent in the situation and the degree of the risk that the force employed might result in loss of life. The Commission's examination must have due regard to all the relevant circumstances surrounding the deprivation of life. (para. 19)

First the Commission had to examine whether the aim pursued in using the force was permissible, and whether the action was 'lawfully taken for the purpose of quelling a riot'.

While accepting that the term 'riot' may be subject to a number of different interpretations the Commission did not consider it necessary to attempt an exhaustive definition.

... In the present case, the Commission considers that an assembly of 150 persons throwing missiles at a patrol of soldiers to the point that they risked serious injury must be considered, by any standard, to constitute a riot. There can be no doubt also, in view of the decisions of the Northern Ireland courts, that the action of the soldiers was lawful under Northern Irish law (s. 3 of the Criminal Law Act (Northern Ireland) 1967). The aim pursued, therefore, falls within subparagraph (c). (para. 25)

In assessing the question of proportionality the Commission had to bear in mind the situation confronting the soldiers, the degree of force used, the risk of deprivation of life as a result, and also the situation of continuous public disturbance in Northern Ireland which had led to much loss of life. Against this background the Commission noted that:

... the use of the plastic baton round in Northern Ireland has given rise to much controversy and that it is a dangerous weapon which can occasion serious injuries and death, particularly if it strikes the head. However, information provided by the parties concerning casualties, compared with the number of baton rounds discharged, shows that the weapon is less dangerous than alleged.

... It recalls that the group of soldiers were confronted with a hostile and violent crowd of 150 persons who were attacking them with stones and other missiles, and, further, that the soldier's aim was disturbed at the moment of discharge when he was struck by several missiles.

. . . The Commission is of the opinion, taking due account of all the surrounding circumstances, referred to above, that the death of Brian Stewart resulted from the use of force which was no more than 'absolutely necessary' 'in action lawfully taken for the purpose of quelling a riot . . .' within the meaning of Art. 2(2)(c). In view of this finding the Commission does not consider it necessary to examine the respondent Government's alternative plea that the force was no more than 'absolutely necessary' 'in defence of any person from unlawful violence' under subparagraph (a). (paras 28–30)

Comment

The use of the 'baton round' had been introduced in Northern Ireland in 1970. Initially rubber bullets were used, but between 1973 and 1975 these were gradually replaced by plastic bullets. Tests indicated that the use of this weapon could cause death and serious injury, particularly at short range. Guidelines were issued to soldiers concerning the use of baton rounds. Prior to the death of the applicant's son another child had been killed, and between 1976 and 1982 a further nine people were killed, including four children. On 13 May 1982 the use of such baton rounds was condemned by a majority vote in the European Parliament.

Kelly v *UK*
(1993) 74 D & R 139

The facts

The applicant's son was shot by soldiers in Belfast when he sought to evade a roadblock set up to stop the car in which he was joyriding with four other youths. The applicant brought an action against the Ministry of Defence for assault, battery and negligence, alleging that his son's death was the result of excessive and unreasonable force. The trial judge found that the use of force was justified on the grounds that the soldiers had formed a genuine belief that the occupants of the car were escaping terrorists. In deciding that the belief was reasonable in the circumstances the court considered:

. . . In the present case the mischief which the soldiers intended to prevent by firing at the driver of the car was the escape of a number of terrorists, as I have found they reasonably thought the occupants of the car to be. Ex hypothesi the driver at least out of those occupants was regarded by the soldiers as a person who was so intent on escaping capture that he was prepared to break through a checkpoint by knocking vehicles out of his path, reckless of injury to any persons who might be in the way. A person so determined to escape capture, and probably his associates, would be likely to be active and committed terrorists, who would very probably continue to commit terrorist crimes if allowed to go free. The checkpoint was the only place at which it was likely to be possible to stop them, and if they escaped it they would retain their liberty to engage in attacks upon the community of the nature perpetrated by terrorists organisations. The harm to which the occupants of the car were exposed when the soldiers aimed at the driver was predictable and grave and the risk of its occurrence was high. But in my opinion the kind of harm to be averted (as the soldiers reasonably thought) by preventing their escape was even graver – the freedom conferred on active and dangerous terrorists to resume their activities of dealing in death and destruction and, in Lord Diplock's words,

> encouraging the continuance of the armed insurrection and all the misery and destruction of life and property that terrorist activity in Northern Ireland has entailed. [Attorney General for Northern Ireland's Reference 1976 N.I. 169]

> In my judgment the justification for opening fire upon the car has been shown to be sufficient, and I accordingly hold that the defendant has dischared the burden of proving that the act of the soldiers in firing at it was the use of such force as was reasonable in the circumstances in the prevention of crime . . . (p. 143).

The applicant appealed to the Court of Appeal alleging, *inter alia*, that the judge had erred in holding that the act of the soldiers in firing was the use of reasonable force or for the purpose of the prevention of crime. The Court of Appeal in Northern Ireland dismissed the applicant's appeal on 10 October 1989, finding that the judge had correctly applied the law as to the justified use of force.

Leave to appeal to the House of Lords was refused. The applicant complained before the Commission that the death of his son was a deprivation of life contrary to Article 2, and that the use of force was not justified under Article 2, para. 2(a), (b) and (c).

The applicant submitted that the killing of his son could not be regarded as 'absolutely necessary' for one of the purposes specified in Article 2, para. 2.

The Government submitted that the use of force pursued the objective of effecting a lawful arrest and was not disproportionate to that aim.

The Commission's opinion

At the outset the Commission indicated that any justification for the deprivation of life would be narrowly interpreted.

> . . . The use of force which has resulted in a deprivation of life must have been shown to have been 'absolutely necessary' for one of the purposes set out in the second paragraph. The Commission has held that the test of necessity includes an assessment of whether the interference was proportionate to the legitimate aim pursued and that the qualification of the word 'necessary' by the adverb 'absolutely' indicates that a stricter and more compelling test of necessity must be applied than in context of other provisions of the Convention.

More specifically, the Commission considered that:

> . . . Article 2(2) permits the use of force for the purposes enumerated in sub-paragraphs (a), (b) and (c) subject to the requirement that the force used is strictly proportionate to the achievement of the permitted purpose. In assessing whether the use of force is strictly proportionate, regard must be had to the nature of the aim pursued, the dangers to life and limb inherent in the situation and the degree of the risk that the force employed might result in loss of life. The Commission's examination must have due regard to all the relevant circumstances surrounding the deprivation of life. (p. 145)

The Commission took into account the judgment of the High Court judge and his finding that the intention of the soldiers in shooting at the car covered both the prevention of crime and the effecting of a lawful arrest and was therefore justified under s. 3 of the Criminal Law Act 1967.

Having examined the procural aspects of the High Court hearing as well as the judgment, the Commission expressed the opinion that:

> ... the shooting in this case was for the purpose of apprehending the occupants of the stolen car, who were reasonably believed to be terrorists, in order to prevent them carrying out terrorist activities. Accordingly, the action of the soldiers in this case was taken for the purpose of effecting a lawful arrest within the meaning of Article 2(2)(b) of the Convention. It is unnecessary in view of this finding to examine the judge's application and interpretation of the concept 'prevention of crime,' being a justification for the use of force under domestic law which does not appear in Article 2.

> The Commission has therefore examined whether the force used in pursuit of the above aim was 'absolutely necessary,' in particular whether it was strictly proportionate, having regard to the situation confronting the soldiers, the degree of force employed in response and the risk that the use of force could result in the deprivation of life.

> In this regard, the applicant has submitted that the use of force was disproportionate and excessive, given the possibility that a car which goes through a checkpoint could be driven by joyriders or by drunken, inadvertent or frightened motorists. The Commission recalls, however, that the High Court judge expressly addressed this issue and found that the soldiers reasonably believed the occupants to be terrorists. This finding is supported by the suspicion already existing with regard to the car, which was known to have been stolen and had been seen in questionable circumstances in the vicinity of the house and car of a member of the security forces. It was reinforced by the determined and even desperate efforts made by the driver of the car to escape the checkpoint, which was not found to be indicative of joyriders or drunken motorists.

> ... The Commission notes that the High Court judge commented that there was a high probability that shots fired at the driver would kill him or inflict serious injury. The situation facing the soldiers, however, had developed with little or no warning and involved conduct by the driver putting them and others at considerable risk of injury. Their conduct must also be assessed against the background of the events in Northern Ireland, which is facing a situation in which terrorist killings have become a feature of life. In this context the Commission recalls the judge's comments that, although the risk of harm to the occupants of the car was high, the kind of harm to be averted (as the soldiers reasonably thought) by preventing their escape was even greater, namely the freedom of terrorists to resume their dealing in death and destruction.

> The Commission concludes therefore, having regard to all the surrounding circumstances, that the use of force in the present case was justified in terms of Article 2(2) of the Convention. It follows that the application must be rejected as being manifestly ill-founded within the meaning of Article 27(2) of the Convention. (pp. 146–7)

Comment

While the Commission and the European Court of Human Rights try to develop common standards for the protection of human rights, exceptional circumstances pertaining in specific member States may have to be taken into account in assessing whether certain violations are justified. The situation in

Northern Ireland is a case in point. A number of cases involving the UK raise issues concerning the treatment of individuals in Northern Ireland or in connection with the political situation in Northern Ireland. The Commission and the Court are not unsympathetic to the difficulties of the situation and, as indicated in this case, will try to assess the facts against the particular background of the events, while at the same time seeking to achieve a balance between what is justified in unusual circumstances and the protection of human rights for all individuals regardless of their political beliefs.

Taylor, Crampton, Gibson, King v *UK*
(1994) 79-A D & R 127

The facts
The case concerned the infliction of grievous bodily harm and murder, by a nurse, Beverley Allitt, during a period of ten weeks when she worked as a nurse in the children's ward of Grantham Hospital. Nurse Allitt was subsequently convicted of the murder of four children – including Liam Taylor – the attempted murder of three children – including Paul Crampton and Bradley Gibson – and of causing grievous bodily harm to six children – including Christopher King.

The parents of the children pressed for a public inquiry so that all the causes of the tragedy could be examined and so that witnesses could be compelled to give evidence. An internal inquiry under the chairmanship of Sir Cecil Clothier was held, and its report was published in 1994. This report made a number of criticisms, but commented only indirectly on the parents' allegations that the hospital had been underfunded and improperly staffed.

The applicants complained that they had been victims of a violation of Article 2. They submitted that:

> . . . the State, in relation to its positive obligation to protect the right to life where an unlawful killing or life-threatening attack takes place in an environment for which it is responsible, must show that it has sought out the perpetrator and brought him/her to justice; that appropriate mechanisms exist for compensating the victims and that appropriate mechanisms exist to enable the State to determine whatever lessons needs to be learnt to prevent or deter the repetition of such unlawful killings. This, they argue, requires in the circumstances of this case the provision of an independent, public inquiry.
>
> The applicants submit that the inquiry in this case was neither public nor had the power to compel witnesses or obtain discovery of documents and the terms of reference made no mention of the district health authority or the RHA and their management. Members of the panel were not independent of the RHA. The parents were unable to attend or be represented by a lawyer of their choosing and there was no examination or cross-examination of witnesses by counsel. The inquiry was accordingly ineffective and fatally flawed. The responsibility of the district health authority and the RHA for the events which happened was not examined, e.g. the inadequate system of incident reporting; staff shortages and weak leadership. It also ignored the role played by the organisation of the National Health Service generally, i.e. Grantham Hospital to qualify as a District General Hospital had to run a particular level of service and the exigencies of this meant that if Ward Four had been

closed (as it should have been because it was understaffed to a critical level in the applicants' submission) the hospital would have lost two consultants and its status.

The applicant parents complain both on behalf of their children and on their own behalf. They allege that they continue to be affected by the systematic shortcomings which risk other tragic events occurring in the future. (p. 134)

The Commission's opinion

The Commission accepted that Article 2 may contain a procedural element. The protection of rights under the Convention must be effective. Any deprivation of life must receive public and independent scrutiny, the minimum threshold of which will depend on the circumstances.

In this case the Commission noted that:

. . . the attacks on the children, including the applicant children, were prosecuted as criminal acts and that the nurse, Beverly Allitt, was convicted on counts of murder, attempted murder and grievous bodily harm, for which she received sentences of life imprisonment. The facts of the case were subject in the context of those criminal proceedings to investigation and public examination and cross-examination of the people involved (save Allitt herself who chose not to give evidence).

The applicants allege however that the responsibility for events goes beyond the individual criminal responsibility of Allitt herself and that the case raises questions of responsibility for the appointment of an individual like Allitt, the procedural inadequacies for dealing with untoward incidents and emergencies, and the failure to respond promptly and effectively to the series of sudden collapses of children in one ward. This requires, they submit, a public and independent inquiry at which they would be provided with legal aid to be able to have witnesses cross-examined by counsel. The Allitt Inquiry however sat in private, its terms of reference were agreed with the RHA, whose responsibility was at stake, and it had no powers of compulsion.

The Commission notes that the Inquiry which was held into the Allitt affair was presided over by Sir Cecil Clothier, an ex-Ombudsman, and it is satisfied that the Inquiry was effectively independent of the parties involved in the case. Further, while the Inquiry did not have powers to compel discovery or witnesses, it does not appear that the Inquiry was refused access to any document or that any witness refused to attend. The applicants have not referred to any item of evidence or testimony that was omitted from the investigation. Moreover, the terms of reference of the Inquiry covered aspects of operational responsibility of both the hospital and the RHA. While the Inquiry did not conduct itself in public, its findings and recommendations were made public. The Report identified a number of shortcomings which could have contributed to the ease with which and the length of time over which Allitt had conducted her attacks, and it made recommendations to avoid the same mistakes being repeated in future. To the extent that the applicants allege any other aspects of negligence on the part of the health authorities which contributed to the failure to protect the children in their care from injury, it would be possible for the applicants to institute proceedings alleging negligence and/or breech of statutory duty, in which it would be possible to seek discovery of documents and to have witnesses examined and cross-examined.

The Commission acknowledges that neither the criminal proceedings nor the Inquiry addressed the wider issues relating to the organisation and funding of the National Health Service as a whole or the pressures which might have led to a ward being run subject to the shortcomings apparent on Ward Four. The procedural element contained in Article 2 of the Convention however imposes the minimum requirement that where a State or its agents potentially bear responsibility for loss of life the events in question should be subject to an effective investigation or scrutiny which enables the facts to become known to the public, and in particular to the relatives of any victims. The Commission finds no indication that the facts of this case have not been sufficiently investigated and disclosed, or that there has been any failure to provide a mechanism whereby those with criminal or civil responsibility may be held answerable. The wider questions raised by the case are within the public domain and any doubts which may consequently arise as to policies adopted in the field of public health are, in the Commission's opinion, matters for public and political debate which fall outside the scope of Article 2 and the other provisions of the Convention.

The Commission concludes that the present application does not disclose any failure by the State to comply with the positive obligations, including any procedural requirements, imposed by Article 2 of the Convention. It follows that it must be rejected as being manifestly ill-founded within the meaning of Article 27(2) of the Convention.

Held: full Commission unanimously, Article 2, application inadmissible. (pp. 136–7)

McCann and Others v *The United Kingdom*
Council of Europe Report (17/1994/464/545)

The facts
The applicants were the representatives of three Provisional IRA members who had been shot dead in Gibraltar by members of the SAS on 6 March 1988. The events leading to their deaths concerned security reports of a planned terrorist attack by the Provisional IRA (PIRA) on Gibraltar. It was suspected that the PIRA would use a car bomb to carry out the attack in the vicinity of the changing of the guard by the Royal Anglian Regiment on 8 March 1988. The three deceased were known to be members of the PIRA and had been previously convicted for terrorist related offences. A surveillance operation was carried out by the Gibraltar Police and military personnel, including members of the SAS. The three deceased entered Gibraltar on 6 March 1988, and Savage was seen to park a car in the area where it was suspected that the attack would take place. This car was latter described as suspect by a bomb disposal adviser, i.e. it might contain a bomb. The three were not intercepted at the border but watched and followed once they were in Gibraltar. During the course of the surveillance it was decided to arrest the suspects on suspicion of conspiracy to murder. The military took control at this point, and approached the suspects. As the soldiers approached McCann and Farrell, these two made sudden movements and the soldiers opened fire. Savage was shot very shortly afterwards in a similar situation.

At the inquest held by the coroners court in Gibraltar, the jury returned a verdict of lawful killing on 30 September 1988. An action against the Ministry of Defence in the High Court of Justice in Northern Ireland had been commenced on 1 March 1990, but the Secretary of State for Foreign Affairs had issued certificates excluding proceedings against the Crown. Application for judicial review of the validity of these certificates was refused. The applicants applied to the Commission alleging a breach of Article 2. In 1993 the Commission of Human Rights declared the application admissible.

Report of the Commission

The Commission expressed the opinion that:

> . . . the situations where deprivation of life may be justified are exhaustive and must
> be narrowly interpreted.
>   The use of force which has resulted in a deprivation of life must be shown to have
> been 'absolutely necessary' for one of purposes set out in the second paragraph. (paras
> 181 and 182)

Although in the context of other Convention articles this meant that the
interference must have been proportionate to the legitimate aim pursued, in the
context of Article 2 the adverb 'absolutely' indicated that a stricter and more
compelling test of necessity had to be applied.

The Commission accepted that the inquest had conducted a detailed
fact-finding examination of the case, but the Commission noted that the
verdict of the jury related solely to whether the killing was lawful or not. The
jury were not asked directly to consider the question involving State responsibility which was now before the Commission, nor was the Commission bound
by the domestic decision but had to examine the case as a whole to decide
whether the circumstances indicated a justification compatible with the
provisions of the Convention.

The first sentence of Article 2 imposes a positive duty not only to refrain
from taking life 'intentionally', but also to take steps to safeguard life. The
Commission therefore agreed with the applicants that:

> . . . this requires that the domestic law of a State regulates, in a manner compatible
> with the rule of law, the permissible use of lethal force by its agents. (para. 187)

The applicable law was set out in Article 2 of the Gibraltar Constitution, and
the Commission found no indication that this law failed to offer the requisite
general protection against the arbitrary use of lethal force by State authorities.
The Commission also expressed the view, however, that:

> . . . it is essential both for the relatives and for public confidence in the administration
> of justice and in the State's adherence to the principles of the rule of law that a killing
> by the State is subject to some form of open and objective oversight. (para. 192)

In considering the procedural safeguards applicable in this case, the Commission noted that the inquest had been extremely thorough and subjected the
actions of the agents of the State to extensive, independent and highly public
scrutiny, thereby providing sufficient procedural safeguards.

In considering whether the deprivation of life was justified under the second
paragraph of Article 2, the Commission had to consider if the use of force was
more than was 'absolutely necessary'. In this respect the Commission noted
that:

> . . . First, a policy of shooting to kill terrorist suspects in preference to the
> inconvenience of resorting to the procedures of criminal justice would be in flagrant
> violation of the rights guaranteed under the Convention. A terrorist who is suspected
> of having committed or of intending to commit an act of violence continues to enjoy
> the protection of the right to life guaranteed by Article 2 of the Convention and the

right to a fair trial in the determination of any criminal charges brought against him or her as guaranteed under Article 6 of the Convention.

. . . Second, the Commission recognises that the United Kingdom owed a responsibility not only to the three terrorist suspects in this case but was also under a positive obligation with respect to safeguarding the lives of the people in Gibraltar. The existence of any risk and the extent of such risk to other persons must therefore be given particular significance when assessing the necessity for the use of lethal force in this case, and whether the action taken was strictly proportionate to that risk. (paras 206 and 207)

The Commission rejected the applicants' theory that there was a conspiracy to kill the suspected terrorists from the outset. The Commission was satisfied that there was an arrest policy, and that the suspects were shot by the soldiers in the belief that they were about to detonate a bomb. The Commission did not disagree with the evidence presented at the inquest in this respect.

The Commission was concerned that the soldiers shot to kill. The Commission expressed the opinion that although from the soldiers' perspective the shooting of the three suspects could be considered as absolutely necessary for the legitimate aim of the defence of others from unlawful violence:

. . . the United Kingdom bears a wider responsibility for the way in which the operation was planned and executed. This case may be distinguished from the *Kelly* case . . . where the situation at the roadblock developed without any warning. In the present case, the authorities had been aware of the threat posed by the ASU and had been planning for months their response.

. . . In these circumstances, the use of lethal force would be rendered disproportionate if the authorities failed, whether deliberately or through lack of proper care, to take steps which would have avoided the deprivation of life of the suspects without putting the lives of others at risk. (paras 234–235)

The applicants criticised the conduct of the operation, claiming that erroneous assessments and assumptions had been made and relied on to provide a basis for the actions taken. However, the Commission was satisfied that these assessments existed as possibilities which could not be discounted in the circumstances.

. . . Having regard therefore to the possibility that the suspects had brought in a car bomb on 6 March, which if detonated would have occasioned the loss of many lives and the possibility that the suspects could have been able to detonate it when confronted by the soldiers, the Commission finds that the planning and execution of the operation by the authorities does not disclose any deliberate design or lack of proper care which might render the use of lethal force against McCann, Farrell and Savage disproportionate to the aim of defending other persons from unlawful violence. Consequently, the Commission is satisfied that the deprivation of life resulted from the use of force that was no more than 'absolutely necessary' for that purpose.

. . . The Commission concludes, by 11 votes to 6, that there has been no violation of Article 2 of the Convention. (paras 250 and 251)

A number of dissenting opinions were given. Messrs Trechsel and Ermacora expressed the opinion that there was not sufficient regard for the lives of the suspected terrorists; in particular the alternative of shooting to wound rather than to kill was not sufficiently considered. Mrs Liddy, and Messrs Reffi and Nowicki expressed the opinion that in the circumstances the UK had not sufficiently considered other possibilities – for example, that the suspects did not have the means to detonate a bomb, that there was in fact no bomb, that a detonator would not be easy to conceal about the person, that shooting the suspects might activate any such detonator, that the suspected car had not been a bomb but was a blocking car being used to reserve a parking space, that the suspects were on a reconnaissance mission – and therefore that:

> . . . the planning and execution of the operation disclosed a failure properly to balance the possible risks represented by the suspects on 6 March against their right to life. The three suspects could have been arrested without the use of lethal force and insufficient care was taken to ensure that that was the course adopted. The use of lethal force against the three suspects was disproportionate to the aim of defending other persons from unlawful violence. The deprivation of life was consequently not the result of the use of force which was no more than 'absolutely necessary' for that purpose. (para. 17)

Mr Loucaides expressed the opinion that the deprivation of life was not shown to be necessary, because it did not fall within one of the exceptions. The fact that the soldiers may have been mistaken in their assessment of the facts did not exonerate the UK.

> . . . The Convention provides that 'the High Contracting Parties shall secure to everyone within their jurisdiction the rights and freedoms' defined in the Convention. The terms of the Convention do not appear to allow mistakes or errors as a justification or defence for failing to secure the rights in question. The test of whether there is a violation of such right is objective. A violation is sufficiently established if it is proved that the State concerned has actually caused the interference with a right or failed to secure the right in circumstances that do not satisfy strictly the conditions of any permissible justification. In this sense, State liability under the Convention for breach of its provisions is strict.
>
> The fact that the mistake can exculpate the agents of the State labouring under it from personal criminal responsibility under the domestic law cannot be sufficient to exculpate also the State from responsibility under the Convention. Indeed to accept otherwise would lead to absurd results in respect of State responsibility for interferences with the rights set out in the Convention (e.g. Article 5) and in particular as regards the application of permissible limitations and restrictions on such rights. . . .

The judgment of the Court
The Court adopted an approach to the interpretation of Article 2, that:

> . . . the object and purpose of the Convention as an instrument for the protection of individual human beings requires that its provisions be interpreted and applied so as to make its safeguards practical and effective . . .
>
> . . . It must also be borne in mind that, as a provision which not only safeguards the right to life but sets out the circumstances when the deprivation of life may be justified, Article 2 ranks as one of the most fundamental provisions in the Convention – indeed one which, in peacetime, admits of no derogation under Article 15. Together with Article 3 of the Convention, it also enshrines one of the basic values of the democratic societies making up the Council of Europe. As such, its provisions must be strictly construed.

... The Court considers that the exceptions delineated in paragraph 2 indicate that this provision extends to, but is not concerned exclusively with, intentional killing. As the Commission has pointed out, the text of Article 2, read as a whole, demonstrates that paragraph 2 does not primarily define instances where it is permitted intentionally to kill an individual, but describes the situations where it is permitted to 'use force' which may result, as an unintended outcome, in the deprivation of life. The use of force, however, must be no more than 'absolutely necessary' for the achievement of one of the purposes set out in sub-paragraphs (a), (b) or (c) (see application no. 10444/82, *Stewart v the United Kingdom*, 10 July 1984, Decisions and Reports, volume 39, pp. 169–171).

... In this respect the use of the term 'absolutely necessary' in Article 2 § 2 indicates that a stricter and more compelling test of necessity must be employed from that normally applicable when determining whether State action is 'necessary in a democratic society' under paragraph 2 of Articles 8 to 11 of the Convention. In particular, the force used must be strictly proportionate to the achievement of the aims set out in sub-paragraphs 2(a), (b) and (c) of Article 2.

... In keeping with the importance of this provision in a democratic society, the Court must, in making its assessment, subject deprivations of life to the most careful scrutiny, particularly where deliberate lethal force is used, taking into consideration not only the actions of the agents of the State who actually administer the force but also all the surrounding circumstances including such matters as the planning and control of the actions under examination. (paras 146–150)

On the facts of the case before it, the main question for the Court concerned the proportionality of the State's response to the perceived threat of a terrorist attack.

Like the Commission, the Court held that the prohibition on arbitrary killing included the need for adequate and effective procedures to review the use of lethal force. The Court was, however, satisfied that the inquest carried out a thorough, impartial and careful examination of the circumstances surrounding the killings. There was, therefore, no breach of Article 2, para. 1 on this ground.

In applying Article 2 to the facts of this case the Court noted that the establishment and verification of facts is primarily a matter for the Commission, although the Court is not bound by the Commission's findings of fact and remains free to make its own appreciation of fact. In the present case, the facts were not in dispute; the conclusions to be drawn from them were. The Court accepted the Commission's establishment of the facts. As regards the appreciation of these, the Court observed that:

... the jury had the benefit of listening to the witnesses at first hand, observing their demeanour and assessing the probative value of their testimony.

Nevertheless, it must be borne in mind that the jury's finding was limited to a decision of lawful killing and, as is normally the case, did not provide reasons for the conclusion that it reached. In addition, the focus of concern of the Inquest proceedings and the standard applied by the jury was whether the killings by the soldiers were reasonably justified in the circumstances as opposed to whether they were 'absolutely necessary' under Article 2 § 2 in the sense developed above (see paragraphs 120 and 148–49 above).

... Against this background, the Court must make its own assessment whether the facts as established by the Commission disclose a violation of Article 2 of the Convention. (paras 170 and 171)

In assessing all the issues in the light of all the material placed before it by the applicants and the UK Government and, where necessary, material obtained by its own motion, the Court, similarly to the Commission, observed that:

> ... it would need to have convincing evidence before if could conclude that there was a premeditated plan (to kill the suspects). (parenthesis added) (para. 179)

The Court rejected as unsubstantiated the applicants' allegations that there was a plot to kill the suspects.

As regards the conduct and planning of the operation, the applicants had alleged that the killings resulted from incompetence and negligence in the planning and conduct of the anti-terrorist operation, and a failure to maintain a proper balance between the need to meet the threat posed and the right to life of the suspects. The Government had argued that the measures taken were absolutely necessary in the light of intelligence assessments, to defend persons from unlawful violence.

The Court noted that:

> ... In carrying out its examination under Article 2 of the Convention, the Court must bear in mind that the information that the United Kingdom authorities received that there would be a terrorist attack in Gibraltar presented them with a fundamental dilemma. On the one hand, they were required to have regard to their duty to protect the lives of the people in Gibraltar including their own military personnel and, on the other, to have minimum resort to the use of lethal force against those suspected of posing this threat in the light of the obligations flowing from both domestic and international law.
>
> ... Several other factors must also be taken into consideration.
>
> In the first place, the authorities were confronted by an active service unit of the IRA composed of persons who had been convicted of bombing offences and a known explosives expert. The IRA, judged by its actions in the past, had demonstrated a disregard for human life, including that of its own members.
>
> Secondly, the authorities had had prior warning of the impending terrorist action and thus had ample opportunity to plan their reaction and, in coordination with the local Gibraltar authorities, to take measures to foil the attack and arrest the suspects. Inevitably, however, the security authorities could not have been in possession of the full facts and were obliged to formulate their policies on the basis of incomplete hypotheses.
>
> ... Against this background, in determining whether the force used was compatible with Article 2, the Court must carefully scrutinise, as noted above, not only whether the force used by the soldiers was strictly proportionate to the aim of protecting persons against unlawful violence but also whether the anti-terrorist operation was planned and controlled by the authorities so as to minimise, to the greatest extent possible, recourse to lethal force. The Court will consider each of these points in turn. (paras 192–194)

The Court carefully examined the circumstances surrounding each of the killings. Having done so the Court considered that:

> ... the use of force by agents of the State in pursuit of one of the aims delineated in paragraph 2 of Article 2 of the Convention may be justified under this provision where it is based on an honest belief which is perceived, for good reasons, to be valid at the time but which subsequently turns out to be mistaken. To hold otherwise would be to

impose an unrealistic burden on the State and its law enforcement personnel in the execution of their duty, perhaps to the detriment of their lives and those of others.

It follows that, having regard to the dilemma confronting the authorities in the circumstances of the case, the actions of the soldiers do not, in themselves, give rise to a violation of this provision.

. . . The question arises, however, whether the anti-terrorist operation as a whole was controlled and organised in a manner which respected the requirements of Article 2 and whether the information and instructions given to the soldiers which, in effect, rendered inevitable the use of lethal force, took adequately into consideration the right to life of the three suspects. (paras 200 and 201)

The Court accepted that there was an intention to arrest the suspects at an appropriate stage. The Government had argued that arrests had not been made at the time of the killings because of the risk of having insufficient evidence with which to charge the suspects. In this respect the Court observed that:

. . . the danger to the population of Gibraltar – which is at the heart of the Government's submissions in this case – in not preventing their entry must be considered to outweigh the possible consequences of having insufficient evidence to warrant their detention and trial. In its view, either the authorities knew that there was no bomb in the car – which the Court has already discounted . . . – or there was a serious miscalculation by those responsible for controlling the operation. As a result, the scene was set in which the fatal shooting, give the intelligence assessments which had been made, was a foreseeable possibility if not a likelihood.

The decision not to stop the three terrorists from entering Gibraltar is thus a relevant factor to take into account under this head. (para. 205)

As regards the assessments and intelligence that the attack would be carried out by means of a car bomb, the Court considered that a number of key assessments were made, which ultimately turned out to be erroneous, although they were all possible hypotheses. However, the Court held that:

. . . insufficient allowances appear to have made for other assumptions. For example, since the bombing was not expected until 8 March when the changing of the guard ceremony was to take place, there was equally the possibility that the three terrorists were on a reconnaissance mission. While this was a factor which was briefly considered, it does not appear to have been regarded as a serious possibility. . . .

In addition, at the briefings or after the suspects had been spotted, it might have been thought unlikely that they would have been prepared to explode the bomb, thereby killing many civilians, as Mr McCann and Ms Farrell strolled towards the border area since this would have increased the risk of detection and capture . . . It might also have been thought improbable that at that point they would have set up the transmitter in anticipation to enable them to detonate the supposed bomb immediately if confronted. . . .

Moreover, even if allowances are made for the technological skills of the IRA, the description of the detonation device as a 'button job' without the qualifications subsequently described by the experts at the Inquest, of which the competent authorities must have been aware, over-simplifies the true nature of these devices. (para 208)

The problem with these hypotheses was that they were conveyed to the soldiers as certainties. This made the use of lethal force almost unavoidable. Moreover, the Court held that:

. . . the failure to make provision for a margin of error must also be considered in combination with the training of the soldiers to continue shooting once they opened fire until the suspect was dead. As noted by the Coroner in his summing up to the jury at the Inquest, all four soldiers shot to kill the suspects . . . Against this background, the authorities were bound by their obligation to respect the right to life of the suspects to exercise the greatest of care in evaluating the information at their disposal before transmitting it to soldiers whose use of firearms automatically involved shooting to kill.

. . . Although detailed investigation at the Inquest into the training received by the soldiers was prevented by the public interest certificates which had been issued . . . it is not clear whether they had been trained or instructed to assess whether the use of firearms to wound their targets may have been warranted by the specific circumstances that confronted them at the moment of arrest.

Their reflex action in this vital respect lacks the degree of caution in the use of firearms to be expected from law enforcement personnel in a democratic society, even when dealing with dangerous terrorist suspects, and stands in marked contrast to the standard of care reflected in the instructions in the use of firearms by the police which had been drawn to their attention and which emphasised the legal responsibilities of the individual officer in the light of conditions prevailing at the moment of engagement. . . .

This failure by the authorities also suggests a lack of appropriate care in the control and organisation of the arrest operation.

. . . In sum, having regard to the decision not to prevent the suspects from travelling into Gibraltar, to the failure of the authorities to make sufficient allowances for the possibility that their intelligence assessments might, in some respects at least, be erroneous and to the automatic recourse to lethal force when the soldiers opened fire, the Court is not persuaded that the killing of the three terrorists constituted the use of force which was no more than absolutely necessary in defence of persons from unlawful violence within the meaning of Article 2 § 2(a) of the Convention. (paras 211–213)

The Court concluded by finding that the UK had breached Article 2 of the Convention.

Comment
Clearly this is a very serious finding, although the fact that the Court departed from the opinion of the Commission should not be regarded as that surprising given the number of dissenting opinions expressed in the Commission's report. Moreover, it should be noted that the violation by the UK was established only by a majority of one, the vote being 10 votes to 9.

Dissenting opinions were given by Judges Ryssdal, Bernhardt, Vilhjalmsson, Golcuklu, Palm, Pekkanen, Freeland, Baka and Jambrek. In their dissenting opinion they expressed the view that insufficient weight had been given to the inquest finding. They also expressed the view that the Court should avoid the benefit of hindsight; the situation had to be assessed as it appeared at the time. Relevant in this context was the fact that while the authorities had to act within the law, it was known that the suspects intended to ignore both the law and the right to life of both soldiers and innocent civilians. The judges accepted that the UK had to respect the rights of both suspects and others under Article 2, but held that in the circumstances it was inevitable that there was a grave danger that their right to life and that of others might be in conflict. The assessments made by the security forces in the circumstances were reasonable, for example that the car was a car bomb, that the suspects intended to detonate such a bomb by remote control, and that their movements indicated an intention to carry this out.

It might be noted that the Court was not prepared to award any damages to the applicants under Article 50 as just satisfaction. Indeed the Court held that:

> ... as the three terrorist suspects who were killed had been intending to plant a bomb in Gibraltar, the Court does not consider it appropriate to make an award under this head. (para. 219)

However, the Government did pay the legal costs of the applicants.

Cases pending under this Article

Lorraine Burns v *UK* (Application No. 23413/94), concerning the alleged failure of the authorities to provide the applicant's father with information and advice on the risks of exposure to nuclear tests in the Pacific; information which would have allowed earlier diagnosis and treatment of the illness from which the applicant is now suffering, declared admissible (Articles 2 and 3).

CHAPTER 3

ARTICLE THREE

Article 3
No one shall be subjected to torture or to inhuman or degrading treatment or punishment.

3.1 THE SCOPE OF THE ARTICLE

The application of this article of the Convention is relatively broad. Cases involving the UK in which the provisions of the article have been pleaded include: the infliction of corporal punishment (*Y* v *UK*, *Tyrer* v *UK*, *Costello-Roberts* v *UK*), detention in seclusion (*A* v *UK*, *Mc Feeley* v *UK*), assault (*Reed* v *UK*), disruption of normal family life (*X*, *Cabales and Balkandali* v *UK*), the application and operation of immigration controls (*East African Asians* v *UK*), refusal to grant political asylum (*Vilvarajah and Others* v *UK*), extradition to face a possible death penalty (*Soering* v *UK*) and, most notably, the treatment of terrorist suspects (*The Republic of Ireland* v *UK*).

Article 3 may be pleaded in isolation, but also, and more often, in conjunction with other articles, particularly Article 8 (*Herrick* v *UK*, *X*, *Cabales and Balkandali* v *UK*, *Y* v *UK*), Article 2 (*Soering* v *UK*, *Kelly* v *UK*) and the First Protocol, Article 2 (*Campbell and Cosans* v *UK*), or in conjunction with one of the procedural articles such as Article 13 (lack of effective domestic remedies).

Through the case law the meaning of Article 3 has been given some clarification, and the following guidelines emerge.

3.1.1 Torture

In the case of *Ireland* v *UK* (1976) 19 *Yearbook* 512, referring to the reasoning adopted in the *Greek* case (12 *Yearbook* 501), the Commission found that 'all torture must be inhuman and degrading treatment' (19 *Yearbook* at 748).

'Torture' described inhuman treatment which often had a purpose, such as obtaining information or confessions, or the infliction of punishment, and was generally an aggravated form of inhuman treatment. The Commission has recognised that torture may include non-physical torture, for example the infliction of mental suffering by creating a state of anguish and stress.

Not all abuse suffered by detainees will amount to torture. The Commission recognised in both the earlier *Greek* case and the *Ireland* v *UK* case that certain rough treatment may be experienced by detainees, and even taken for granted, although this will naturally vary between different societies. It should also be noted that techniques which by themselves may simply be degrading or inhuman, when applied in combination may amount to torture. This was the conclusion of the Commission in the *Ireland* v *UK* case, in connection with the five interrogation techniques used on IRA suspects. In its report the Commission expressed the opinion that:

> . . . the systematic application of the techniques for the purpose of inducing a person to give information shows a clear resemblence to those methods of systematic torture which have been known over the ages. Although the five techniques – also called 'disorientation' or 'sensory deprivation' techniques – might not necessarily cause any severe after-effects the Commission sees in them a modern system of torture falling into the same category as those systems which have been applied in previous times as a means of obtaining information and confessions. ((1976) 19 *Yearbook* at 794)

On the facts of the case the Court held that the five techniques did not amount to torture:

> . . . Although the five techniques, as applied in combination, undoubtedly amounted to inhuman and degrading treatment, although their object was to extract confessions, the naming of others and/or information and although they were used systematically, they did not occasion suffering of the particular intensity and cruelty inplied by the word torture as so understood. (Series A, Vol. 25, para. 167)

It would seem, therefore, that establishing torture may be fairly difficult and that an applicant is much more likely to succeed in a claim for inhuman or degrading treatment.

3.1.2   Inhuman or Degrading Treatment

Inhuman treatment covers:

> . . . at least such treatment as deliberately causes severe suffering, mental or physical, which in the particular situation is unjustifiable . . .

while

> . . . treatment of an individual may be said to be degrading if it grossly humiliates him before others or drives him to act against his own will or conscience. (*Ireland* v *UK* (1976) 19 *Yearbook* at 748)

If the treatment includes elements of a normal, official procedure designed to humiliate (*Y* v *UK* 17 EHRR 238) it may be regarded as degrading. However, if the treatment or punishment is moderate or reasonable it may not amount to an infringement of Article 3; for example, in *Herrick* v *UK* 8 EHRR 45 (planning control restrictions) and *App. No. 10165/82* v *UK* 5 EHRR 516 (supervision of visiting arrangements for prisoners). There has therefore to be some degree of severity or immoderate use of force, and the humiliation and debasement must be more than the usual element of humiliation involved in any punishment (*Tyrer* v *UK* 2 EHRR 1).

As stated in *Ireland* v *UK*:

> . . . ill-treatment must attain a minimum level of severity if it is to fall within the scope of Article 3. The assessment of this minimum is, in the nature of things, relative; it depends on all the circumstances of the case, such as the duration of the treatment, its physical or mental effects and, in some cases, the sex, age and state of health of the victim, etc. (Series A, Vol. 25, para. 162)

The Commission has held that:

> . . . a particular treatment or punishment will not be 'degrading' unless the person concerned has undergone, either in the eyes of others or in his own eyes, humiliation or debasement attaining a minimum level of severity. (*App. No. 9119/80* v *UK* 8 EHRR 45 at 48)

Thus threatened punishment – as in the above case – may not amount to degrading or inhuman treatment. Mere apprehension of punishment will not always be sufficient (*Campbell and Cosans* v *UK* 4 EHRR 293).

Whether treatment or punishment is inhuman may also depend on evidence of aggravating circumstances, such as delay between sentence and punishment, a formalised procedure, the involvement of strangers in the infliction of the punishment or supervision of the treatment. This was considered in some detail in the case of *Soering* v *UK* Series A, Vol. 16.

3.1.3   Treatment or Punishment

The conduct complained of will normally have to be some form of institutionalised violence, which is therefore expressly or implicitly approved of by those in authority acting as representatives of the UK. For example, in the case of *A* v *UK* 3 EHRR 131, detention in a secure single room in a mental institution was provided for under the hospital guidelines, while in *Y* v *UK* 17 EHRR 238, corporal punishment was part of the disciplinary rules.

However, infringements of Article 3 may still be claimed even if the treatment or conduct is not institutionalised (*Reed* v *UK* 3 EHRR 136), provided that the applicant has complied with requirements under Article 26 (exhaustion of domestic remedies) and brought the complaint within the time limit.

Particularly important when considering the application of Article 3, is the fact that the case law of the Commission and the Court indicates that it can be pleaded when there is a fear or apprehension of such treatment or punishment. This aspect is particularly relevant in those cases concerning claims for political asylum brought against the UK, or claims that a threatened deportation will amount to a breach of the article. In this context it has been held that although the Convention does not guarantee a right to asylum or freedom from deportation as such, the deportation of an individual could, in certain exceptional circumstances, raise an issue under Article 3. However, it must be established that deportation proceedings have been instigated and that there is a real risk of persecution in the country to which the applicant is being deported. Distress, inconvenience or frustration caused by immigration procedures and the threat of deportation is not sufficient to amount to severe ill-treatment or degrading treatment (*App. No. 9810/82* v *UK* 5 EHRR 581, *App. No. 9606/81* v *UK* 5 EHRR 291, *App. No. 10067/82* v *UK* 5 EHRR 516).

Where an applicant has in some way contributed to or aggravated the alleged infringement, a claim may fail. For example, in *Halil, Ahmet and Sabah* v *UK* 8 EHRR 252 at 305, the applicants' entry as illegal immigrants and consequent deportation did not evoke great sympathy from the Commission. Similarly, in *McFeeley* v *UK* (1984) 38 D & R 11, the Commission noted:

> . . . the fact that the protest campaign was designed and coordinated by the prisoners to create the maximum publicity and enlist public sympathy and support for their political aims. That such a strategy involved a self-inflicted debasement and humiliation to an almost sub-human degree must be taken into account. (para. 45)

3.2 THE CASES

The type of infringements claimed under Article 3 against the UK can be grouped under a number of sub-headings.

3.2.1 Deportation/extradition

The right to political asylum, or to be granted the right of residence, is not contained in the Convention or its Protocols, and the Court and the Commission have recognised that Contracting States have the right to control the entry, residence and expulsion of aliens. However, where an asylum seeker is expelled, an issue under Article 5 may arise if there are substantial grounds for believing that this person faces a real risk of torture or inhuman or degrading treatment or punishment.

Similar considerations may apply in the case of extradition proceedings, where, although the UK may have obligations under international treaties, these have to be weighed against the UK's obligations under the Convention.

Whether the risk is real in the case of each applicant depends on the weight of evidence available at the time of expulsion.

Vilvarajah and Others v *UK*
Series A, Vol. 215

The facts
This case involved claims by Tamils from Sri Lanka, who had claimed political asylum under the United Nations Convention of 1951 Relating to the Status of Refugees (as amended by the Protocol of 1967). Under the Convention an applicant for political asylum must show 'a well-founded fear of prosecution'. Although the applicants had suffered various brutalities at the hands of the Sri Lankan and IPKF personnel, including the search and destruction of property,

detention, torture and assault, their requests for asylum, which were referred to the Refugee Section of the Immigration and Nationality Department of the Home Office and the Secretary of State, were rejected. Ultimately they were deported to Sri Lanka where they were subject to further ill-treatment, including arrest, detention and denunciation by informers concerning their political affiliations. Proceedings for judicial review of the Secretary of State's decision in order to have it quashed were brought, but were unsuccessful before the House of Lords. Following successful appeals to the Adjudicator under s. 13 of the Immigration Act 1971, the applicants were subsequently allowed to return to the UK in 1989, and granted exceptional leave to remain for 12 months while further applications for asylum were considered.

The applicants lodged their claim with the Commission in 1987, prior to their removal to Sri Lanka in 1988, alleging violations of Articles 3 and 13.

The Commission's opinion

The Commission confirmed the consistent case law that:

> . . . Contracting States have an obligation under Article 3 of the Convention not to send people to countries where there are substantial grounds for believing that they would be in danger of being subjected to treatment proscribed by Article 3. (para. 137)

However, in some respects the facts of this case were distinguishable from others in that:

> . . . The risks that the applicants ran of such treatment followed from the general situation and were risks shared by all non-combatants resulting from security operations in the north and east of Sri Lanka and there and elsewhere the risk shared by all of being subjected to security checks and interrogation. (para. 138)

The question which had to be answered was whether the UK had rightly assessed the possible risks faced by the asylum seekers on their return to Sri Lanka. The information coming out of the country was unclear. Although there was no serious dispute as to the facts, it was the interpretation of these which was important.

The Commission noted that:

> . . . in February 1988 there was the appearance of an improvement in the situation in the north and east of Sri Lanka. There the Sinhala dominated security forces were no longer in charge, the IPKF having taken over from them. Though there was still occasional fighting between units of the IPKF and groups of Tamil militants who rejected the Accord, the major fighting at Jaffna had ended. The voluntary repatriation of Tamil refugees under a UNHCR programme, constituted on the basis of a memorandum of understanding with the Government of Sri Lanka signed on 31 August 1987, began at the end of December 1987. Between April and August 1988 over 5,000 Tamils had returned under the UNHCR arrangements to the Jaffna district. Others had returned independently. It would therefore appear that, in the view of UNHCR at least, the position had improved to the extent that the return of a large number of refugees was justifiable. The improvement was relative and though many Tamils were going about their ordinary affairs in Sri Lanka, they, and young Tamils in particular, were at risk of interrogation, arrest and detention, which in some

instances were accompanied by treatment proscribed by Article 3, and indeed three of the applicants allege that they were detained and ill-treated after their return. The general situation in Sri Lanka was however at that time such that the decision of the U.K. to send the applicants back to Sri Lanka cannot be said to have been unreasonable or arbitrary. Undoubtedly the applicants, like all other Tamils in Sri Lanka, were exposed to the possibility of ill-treatment by the IPKF or the Sri Lanka police. Nevertheless, it cannot be said that the risk to each member of the Tamil community, or indeed to each young male member, was such as to constitute in the removal of the applicants to Sri Lanka a violation of Article 3 of the Convention. The general instability in Sri Lanka created risks for all non-combatants in certain areas and the Commission does not find that the applicants can be said to have faced greater personal risks on their return in February 1988. (para. 143)

The Commission therefore concluded that there had been no violation of Article 3, although the President had to make a casting vote in this case. There were seven dissenting opinions which expressed the view that there had been a violation of Article 3.

The judgment of the Court
The Court confirmed that:

> ... Contracting States have the right, as a matter of well-established international law and subject to their treaty obligations including Article 3, to control the entry, residence and expulsion of aliens. (para. 102)

However, it accepted that:

> ... expulsion by a Contracting State of an asylum seeker may give rise to an issue under Article 3, and hence engage the responsibility of that State under the Convention, where substantial grounds have been shown for believing that the person concerned faced a real risk of being subjected to torture or inhuman or degrading treatment or punishment in the country to which he was returned. (para. 103)

With reference to the case before it the Court indicated that the relevant time for assessing the risk was at the time of expulsion, although the Court could take into account information which came to light subsequently. In order to satisfy the requirements of Article 3, the applicant would have to show that there were substantial grounds for believing the existence of a risk of Article 3 treatment. The Court held:

> ... the existence of the risk must be assessed primarily with reference to those facts which were known or ought to have been known to the State at the time of the expulsion ...
> The Court's examination of the existence of the risk of ill-treatment must necessarily be a rigorous one in view of the absolute character of this provision and the fact that it enshrines one of the fundamental values of the democratic societies making up the Council of Europe. (paras 107 and 108)

In considering whether the removal of the applicants exposed them to a real risk of inhuman treatment the Court held that:

> ... The evidence before the Court concerning the background of the applicants, as well as the general situation, does not establish that their personal position was any

worse than the generality of other members of the Tamil community or other young male Tamils who were returning to their country. Since the situation was still unsettled there was the possibility that they might be detained and ill-treated as appears to have occurred previously in the cases of some of the applicants . . . A mere possibility of ill-treatment, however, in such circumstances, is not in itself sufficient to give rise to a breach of Article 3.

. . . It is claimed that the second, third and fourth applicants were in fact subjected to ill-treatment following their return. Be that as it may, however, there were no special distinguishing features in their cases that could or ought to have enabled the Secretary of State to foresee that they would be treated in this way.

. . . In addition, the removal to Sri Lanka of the fourth and fifth applicants without identity cards is open to criticism on the basis that it was likely to make travelling more difficult for them because of the existence of numerous army checkpoints. It cannot be said however that this fact alone exposed them to a real risk of treatment going beyond the threshold set by Article 3.

. . . The Court also attaches importance to the knowledge and experience that the UK authorities had in dealing with large numbers of asylum seekers from Sri Lanka, many of whom were granted leave to stay, and to the fact that personal circumstances of each applicant had been carefully considered by the Secretary of State in the light of a substantial body of material concerning the current situation in Sri Lanka and the position of the Tamil community within it.

. . . In the light of these considerations the Court finds that substantial grounds have not been established for believing that the applicants would be exposed to a real risk of being subjected to inhuman or degrading treatment within the meaning of Article 3 on their return to Sri Lanka in February 1988.

. . . Accordingly, there has been no breach of Article 3. (paras 111–116)

Comment

The situation in Sri Lanka had changed slightly when this case was brought. An Accord had been signed between Sri Lanka and India on 29 July 1987, and the Indian Army had entered Tamil areas in order to protect the community there. However, the Accord was rejected by Tamil extremists and fighting had broken out between them and the IPKF – the Indian Peace Keeping Forces. Incidents of arbitrary detention, torture, destruction, indiscriminate shelling and atrocities were reported. In 1988 – when the applicants were returned to Sri Lanka – civil disturbances were still occurring. The United Nations High Commissioner for Refugees (UNHCR) had organised a voluntary repatriation for Tamil refugees since December 1987. Many of these had gone to India, but some had returned to Sri Lanka. At the same time, however, Amnesty International, the British Refugee Council and the UNHCR had urged the UK Government not to send Tamils back to Sri Lanka because of the instability at that time and because of reported human rights violations by the Sri Lankan security forces and the IPKF. It was these conflicting views which made the interpretation and assessment of the facts difficult.

Other decisions involving political asylum seekers include *Lukka* v *UK* 9 EHRR 513 and *App. No. 9856/82* v *UK* 10 EHRR 547. The emphasis that emerges from these decisions is not only that there must be substantial grounds of the risk of inhuman or degrading treatment or torture, but that in the case of the applicant this must be a real risk. This aspect arose in the following case.

Soering v UK
Series A, Vol. 161

The facts

The main facts of the case have been mentioned in Chapter 1. Briefly, the applicant had been indicted for the murder in 1985 of his girlfriends' parents in the State of Virginia, USA. At the time of the indictment he and his girlfriend were in England, where they were arrested on unconnected charges relating to cheque fraud. The USA sought the extradition of the accused and his girlfriend under extradition arrangements between the two countries (Extradition Treaty 1972). Because the accused was a German national, the Federal Republic of Germany also sought his extradition to face trial on these charges in Germany under the Extradition Treaty 1872 between the Federal Republic of Germany and the United Kingdom. However, there was insufficient evidence for a prima facie case before the German court, plus the possible difficulty in obtaining the attendance of witnesses from America. The crime with which he was accused carried a possible death sentence in Virginia. No such sentence would apply either in the UK or in Germany for a similar crime.

Under the Extradition Act 1970, a magistrate, at the request of the Secretary of State for Home Affairs, issued a warrant for the applicant's arrest. He was arrested in December 1986. In 1987 the United States, through its diplomatic channels, requested his extradition; committal proceedings took place in London and the applicant was committed to await the Secretary of State's order for his return to the United States. Application for judicial review was refused because the Secretary of State had not yet made the order. The applicant petitioned the Secretary of State to exercise his discretion not to issue the order for his extradition. This was rejected and the order was issued in 1988. Pending the outcome of proceedings before the Commission and the Court the applicant was detained in a prison hospital in the UK.

In 1988 the applicant applied to the Commission on the grounds that there was a serious likelihood that he would be sentenced to death if extradited to the United States of America, and that in the circumstances he would be subjected to inhuman and degrading treatment and punishment contrary to Article 3 of the Convention. He also alleged violations of Article 6, para. 3(c) and Article 13.

The Commission's opinion

The breach complained of referred not to the punishment that the applicant faced – see Article 2 and the exceptions thereunder but to the 'death row phenomenon', particularly the exceptional delay in carrying out the death penalty in Virginia and the protracted period of detention in prison awaiting execution pending the exhaustion of collateral State and Federal appeals.

The Commission accepted that while the death penalty cannot raise an issue under Article 3, protracted delay in carrying it out might do so:

> ... The notion of inhuman treatment covers at least such treatment as deliberately causes severe suffering, mental or physical. (para. 104)

However, the issue before the Commission in this case was anticipatory in nature, i.e. would a breach occur if the respondent government decided to implement the extradition order.

First the Commission had to examine:

> ... whether there is a serious risk of the applicant being sentenced to death and thus exposed to 'death row.' It must assess whether the risk that the applicant will be sentenced to death is a real one before examining the severity of the treatment to which he could be exposed. (para. 110)

The Government had argued that assurances had been given by the competent USA authorities that the UK's request that the death sentence should not be carried out would be brought before the judge. Also that the applicant faced no real risk of the death penalty because he could plead insanity – which was a complete defence under Virginian law – and rely on mitigating factors such as his age, absence of previous criminal record, high scholastic achievements and mental state. The applicant contested these, on the grounds that he was not insane at the time of the offence, that the law of Virginia did not recognise diminished responsibility and that his age would not necessarily be taken into account. He further questioned the efficacy of the assurances given.

The Commission observed that:

> ... irrespective of whether the sentencing judge can have regard to the representation made to him on behalf of the respondent Government, he is not obliged under Virginia law to accept it. Moreover, as an independent judge, under a legal duty to consider 'any and all' relevant facts in order to assure that the penalty is 'appropriate and just,' it cannot be assumed that he will have regard to the diplomatic considerations relating to the two countries which have been alluded to by the Government. Further it has not been shown that such a representation to the judge could have an impact on the carrying out of the penalty if imposed.
>
> ... Against the above background the Commission finds that, notwithstanding the assurance and the existence of mitigating factors, the risk that the applicant will be sentenced to death is a serious one. (paras 119 and 120)

In considering whether the 'death row phenomenon' attained a sufficient degree of seriousness for Article 3, the Commission accepted that:

> ... on the evidence available to it, that the average time spent on death row in Virginia is between six and eight years, although it notes that the statistics are based only on the seven executions which have taken place since the death penalty was re-introduced in Virginia in 1977. The Commission cannot lose sight of the reality that death row inmates contribute significantly to the 'death row phenomenon' through the exercise of their State and Federal rights of appeal. It is significant, in this regard, that the direct automatic appeal to the Supreme Court of Virginia takes six to eight months and that the remaining delays are brought about by the exercise of these rights of appeal.
>
> ... The Commission has previously recognised the essential dilemma of the 'death row phenomenon' in the *Kirkwood* case. A prolonged appeal system generates acute anxiety over long periods owing to the uncertain, but possibly favourable, outcome of successive appeals. On the other hand, an acceleration of the system would result in earlier executions in cases where appeals were unsuccessful. . . .

... As in the *Kirkwood* case, the Commission must take into account in assessing the seriousness of the delays the momentous significance of these appeals for the inmate whose life depends upon the outcome. The inmate on 'death row' is not the victim of an unjust system which permits those who have been sentenced to death to languish in prison until the State decides to implement the sentence. On the contrary, a significant part of the delay which forms the basis of the present complaint derives from a complex of procedures which are designed to protect human life and to protect against the arbitrary imposition of the death penalty. As the Commission remarked in the *Kirkwood* case:

> In these circumstances the tradition of the rule of law which underlies the principles of the Convention requires painstaking thoroughness in the examination of any case the effects of which will be so irremediably decisive for the appellants in question ...

... Finally, as in the *Kirkwood* case, the Commission attaches great importance to the fact that it would be open to the applicant to raise before United States and Virginia courts the complaint that the 'death row phenomenon' constitutes cruel and unusual punishment contrary to the Eighth Amendment of the United States Constitution.

... Against the above background, the Commission does not consider that the length of time spent on death row due to the appeal system attains the degree of severity envisaged by Article 3 of the Convention. (paras 126–130).

The Commission was further satisfied that the applicant's age and mental condition would be taken into account by the judge and jury under Virginia law and that therefore no question of inhuman treatment arose in this respect.

As far as the conditions of the prisoners on death row were concerned, while the Commission accepted that the day-to-day conditions must be tense and stressful, this was largely due to the nature of the detention centre, the sentences faced by the prisoners and the need for high security. As far as the death sentence itself was concerned, the question of execution by electrocution had been examined previously by the Virginia Supreme Court and found not to amount to 'cruel and unusual punishment' contrary to the Eighth Amendment of the United States Constitution. The Commission attached substantial weight to this and did not consider that either the conditions of detention or the execution procedures attained a level of severity contrary to Article 3.

The Commission attached significance to the fact that there existed complex and detailed measures relating to the appeals system and to ensure compliance with the United States Constitution. In particular the Commission observed that:

> ... although the delays in the appeal system appear to be longer in the present case, they are, in the main, attributable to the inmates' voluntary action in pursuing State and Federal appeals. It is significant that the automatic appeal procedure to the Virginia Supreme Court only lasts six to eight months. Further, there is no indication that the machinery of justice to which the applicant would be subjected is an arbitrary or unreasonable one. On the contrary the Commission observes that the death penalty scheme in Virginia contains numerous safeguards against arbitrariness and that the appeal system has, as its fundamental purpose, the avoidance of the arbitrary imposition of the death penalty and protection of the prisoner's right to life.
> ... Finally, the Commission notes that the important mitigating factors in the present case, namely, the age and mental condition of the applicant, are matters

which can be fully taken into consideration by both the judge and jury at the sentencing phase and in any subsequent State and Federal appeals.

. . .

The Commission concludes, by six votes to five that the extradition of the applicant to the United States of America in the circumstances of the present case would not constitute treatment contrary to Article 3 of the Convention. (paras 152–154)

The judgment of the Court

In finding Article 3 applicable the Court first held that:

. . . Article 3 makes no provision for exceptions and no derogation from it is permissible under Article 15 in time of war or other national emergency. This absolute prohibition on torture and on inhuman or degrading treatment or punishment under the terms of the Convention shows that Article 3 enshrines one of the fundamental values of the democratic societies making up the Council of Europe. It is also to be found in similar terms in other international instruments such as the 1966 International Covenant on Civil and Political Rights and the 1969 American Convention on Human Rights and is generally recognised as an internationally accepted standard.

The question remains whether the extradition of a fugitive to another State where he would be subjected or be likely to be subjected to torture or to inhuman or degrading treatment or punishment would itself engage the responsibility of a Contracting State under Article 3. That the abhorrence of torture has such implications is recognised in Article 3 of the United Nations Convention Against Torture and Other Cruel, Inhuman or Degrading Treatment or Punishment, which provides that 'no State Party shall . . . extradite a person where there are substantial grounds for believing that he would be in danger of being subjected to torture.' The fact that a specialised treaty should spell out in detail a specific obligation attaching to the prohibition of torture does not mean that an essentially similar obligation is not already inherent in the general terms of Article 3 of the European Convention. It would hardly be compatible with the underlying vaues of the Convention, that 'common heritage of political traditions, ideals, freedom and the rule of law' to which the Preamble refers, were a Contracting State knowingly to surrender a fugitive to another State where there were substantial grounds for believing that he would be in danger of being subjected to torture, however heinous the crime allegedly committed. Extradition in such circumstances, while not explicitly referred to in the brief and general wording of Article 3, would plainly be contrary to the spirit and intendment of the Article, and in the Court's view this inherent obligation not to extradite also extends to cases in which the fugitive would be faced in the receiving State by a real risk of exposure to inhuman or degrading treatment or punishment proscribed by that Article.

. . . What amounts to 'inhuman or degrading treatment or punishment' depends on all the circumstances of the case. Furthermore, inherent in the whole of the Convention is a search for a fair balance between the demands of the general interest of the community and the requirements of the protection of the individual's fundamental rights. As movement about the world becomes easier and crime takes on a larger international dimension, it is increasingly in the interest of all nations that suspected offenders who flee abroad should be brought to justice. Conversely, the establishment of safe havens for fugitives would not only result in danger for the State obliged to harbour the protected person but also tend to undermine the foundations of extradition. These considerations must also be included among the factors to be taken into account in the interpretation and application of the notions of inhuman and degrading treatment or punishment in extradition cases.

... It is not normally for the Convention institutions to pronounce on the existence or otherwise of potential violations of the Convention. However, where an applicant claims that a decision to extradite him would, if implemented, be contrary to Article 3 by reason of its foreseeable consequences in the requesting country, a departure from this principle is necessary, in view of the serious and irreparable nature of the alleged suffering risked, in order to ensure the effectiveness of the safeguard provided by that Article.

... In sum, the decision by a Contracting State to extradite a fugitive may give rise to an issue under Article 3, and hence engage the responsibility of that State under the Convention, where substantial grounds have been shown for believing that the person concerned, if extradited, faces a real risk of being subjected to torture or to inhuman or degrading treatment or punishment in the requesting country. The establishment of such responsibility inevitably involves an assessment of conditions in the requesting country against the standards of Article 3 of the Convention. Nonetheless, there is no question of adjudicating on or establishing the responsibility of the receiving country, whether under general international law, under the Convention or otherwise. In so far as any liability under the Convention is or may be incurred, it is liability incurred by the extraditing Contracting State by reason of its having taken action which has as a direct consequence the exposure of an individual to proscribed ill-treatment.

...

B. *Application of Article 3 in the particular circumstances of the present case*
... The extradition procedure against the applicant in the United Kingdom has been completed, the Secretary of State having signed a warrant ordering his surrender to the United States' authorities, this decision, albeit as yet not implemented, directly affects him. It therefore has to be determined on the above principles whether the foreseeable consequences of Mr Soering's return to the United States are such as to attract the application of Article 3. This inquiry must concentrate firstly on whether Mr Soering runs a real risk of being sentenced to death in Virginia, since the source of the alleged inhuman and degrading treatment or punishment, namely the 'death row phenomenon,' lies in the imposition of the death penalty. Only in the event of an affirmative answer to this question need the court examine whether exposure to the 'death row phenomenon' in the circumstances of the applicant's case would involve treatment or punishment incompatible with Article 3. (paras 88–92)

In considering whether the applicant faced a real risk of the death penalty the Court held:

... Whatever the position under Virginia law and practice, and notwithstanding the diplomatic context of the extradition relations between the United Kingdom and the United States, objectively it cannot be said that the undertaking to inform the judge at the sentencing stage of the wishes of the United Kingdom eliminates the risk of the death penalty being imposed. In the independent exercise of his discretion the Commonwealth's Attorney has himself decided to seek and to persist in seeking the death penalty because the evidence, in his determination, supports such action. If the national authority with responsibility for prosecuting the offence takes such a firm stance, it is hardly open to the Court to hold that there are no substantial grounds for believing that the applicant faces a real risk of being sentenced to death and hence experiencing the 'death row phenomenon'. (para. 98)

The Court then considered whether exposure to this 'death row phenomenon' would mean that extradition would amount to a breach of Article 3. It considered all the evidence and concluded:

... For any prisoner condemned to death, some element of delay between imposition and execution of the sentence and the experience of severe stress in conditions necessary for strict incarceration are inevitable. The democratic character of the Virginia legal system in general and the positive features of Virginia trial, sentencing and appeal procedures in particular are beyond doubt. The Court agrees with the Commission that the machinery of justice to which the applicant would be subject in the United States is in itself either arbitrary nor unreasonable, but, rather, respects the rule of law and affords not inconsiderable procedural safeguards to the defendant in a capital trial. Facilities are available on death row for the assistance of inmates, notably through provision of psychological and psychiatric services.

However, in the Court's view, having regard to the very long period of time spent on death row in such extreme conditions, with the ever-present and mounting anguish of awaiting execution of the death penalty, and to the personal circumstances of the applicant, especially his age and mental state at the time of the offence, the applicant's extradition to the United States would expose him to a real risk of treatment going beyond the threshold set by Article 3. A further consideration of relevance is that in the particular instance the legitimate purpose of extradition could be achieved by another means which would not involve suffering of such exceptional intensity or duration.

Accordingly, the Secretary of State's decision to extradite the applicant to the United States would, if implemented, give rise to a breach of Article 3. (para. 111)

Comment

There is provision in the extradition treaty between the UK and the USA which provides:

> If the offence for which extradition is requested is punishable by death under the relevant law of the requesting Party, but the relevant law of the requested Party does not provide for the death penalty in a similar case, extradition may be refused unless the requesting Party gives assurances satisfactory to the requested Party that the death penalty will not be carried out.

> ... In the case of a fugitive requested by the United States who faces a charge carrying the death penalty, it is the Secretary of State's practice, pursuant to Article IV of the United Kingdom—United States Extradition Treaty, to accept an assurance from the prosecuting authorities of the relevant State that a representation will be made to the judge at the time of sentencing that it is the wish of the United Kingdom that the death penalty should be neither imposed nor carried out ... (*Soering*, para. 37)

Such an assurance had been sought in this case. However, while the treaty is binding between States, the assurance sought had been made by the Commonwealth's Attorney for Bedford County, Virginia, and his undertaking fell short of the assurances indicated in the treaty. Indeed, all he had certified was that if the applicant was convicted of capital murder as charged, the representations of the UK would be made to the judge at the time of sentencing. Given the division of jurisdiction between the Federal Courts and the State Supreme Court, it was accepted that this undertaking was probably the best that could be obtained in the circumstances.

Details on the law of the State of Virginia concerning procedures for sentencing and the appeals system procedures for those sentenced to death are given in the judgment of the court.

3.2.2 Corporal Punishment

Tyrer v *UK*
Series A, Vol. 26

The facts

The applicant was sentenced to three strokes of the birch by a juvenile court in the Isle of Man when he was 15. He had been convicted of assault occasioning actual bodily harm to a fellow school pupil. The birching was carried out at a police station in the presence of his father and a doctor. He complained to the Commission that the UK, being responsible for the Isle of Man's international relations, was in breach of Article 3. He subsequently tried to withdraw the case but the Commission decided that it raised issues of such importance that pursuant to its own rules of procedure it could not accede to his request because the case raised questions of a general character.

The Commission's opinion

The Commission expressed the opinion that:

> . . . judicial corporal punishment, being degrading, constituted a breach of Article 3 and that, consequently, its infliction on the applicant was a violation of that provision. (para. 28, Court Judgment)

The judgment of the Court

The Court did not consider that the facts of the case amounted to torture. The notions relevant to this case were 'inhuman punishment' and 'degrading punishment'. It held that the level of punishment in this case was not so severe as to be inhuman. Therefore the question was, was it degrading?

The Court noted:

> . . . first of all that a person may be humiliated by the mere fact of being criminally convicted. However, what is relevant for the purposes of Article 3 is that he should be humiliated not simply by his conviction but by the execution of the punishment which is imposed on him. In fact, in most if not all cases this may be one of the effects of judicial punishment, involving as it does unwilling subjection to the demands of the penal system. . . . It would be absurd to hold that judicial punishment generally, by reason of its usual and perhaps almost inevitable element of humiliation, is 'degrading' within the meaning of Article 3. Some further criterion must be read into the text. Indeed, Article 3, by expressly prohibiting 'inhuman' and 'degrading' punishment, implies that there is a distinction between such punishment and punishment in general.
>
> In the Court's view, in order for a punishment to be 'degrading' and in breach of Article 3, the humiliation or debasement involved must attain a particular level and must in any event be other than that usual element of humiliation referred to in the preceding subparagraph. The assessment is, in the nature of things, relative; it depends on all the circumstances of the case and, in particular, on the nature and context of the punishment itself and the manner and method of its execution. (para. 30)

In considering the circumstances and context of the case, the Court was not persuaded that such punishment did not outrage public opinion:

. . . even assuming that local public opinion can have an incidence on the interpretation of the concept of 'degrading punishment' appearing in Article 3, the Court does not regard it as established that judicial corporal punishment is not considered degrading by those members of the Manx population who favour its retention: it might well be that one of the reasons why they view the penalty as an effective deterrent is precisely the element of degradation which it involves. As regards their belief that judicial corporal punishment deters criminals, it must be pointed out that a punishment does not lose its degrading character just because it is believed to be, or actually is, an effective deterrent or aid to crime control. Above all, as the Court must emphasise, it is never permissible to have recourse to punishments which are contrary to Article 3, whatever their deterrent effect may be. (para. 31)

The Attorney-General for the Isle of Man pointed out that the punishment was carried out in private and without publicity, in the presence of a doctor and a parent or guardian. The Court accepted that there were certain safeguards, such as the right of appeal against sentence, a prior medical examination, the regulation of the dimensions of the birch and the number of strokes and the presence of police officers. Nevertheless the Court held that other circumstances may still make the punishment degrading:

. . . The very nature of judicial corporal punishment is that it involves one human being inflicting physical violence on another human being. Furthermore, it is institutionalised violence, that is in the present case violence permitted by the law, ordered by the judicial authorities of the State and carried out by the police authorities of the State. Thus, although the applicant did not suffer any severe or long-lasting physical effects, his punishment – whereby he was treated as an object in the power of the authorities – constituted an assault on precisely that which it is one of the main purposes of Article 3 to protect, namely a person's dignity and physical integrity. Neither can it be excluded that the punishment may have had adverse psychological effects.

The institutionalised character of this violence is further compounded by the whole aura of official procedure attending the punishment and by the fact that those inflicting it were total strangers to the offender.

Admittedly, the relevant legislation provides that in any event birching shall not take place later than six months after the passing of sentence. However, this does not alter the fact that there had been an interval of several weeks since the applicant's conviction by the juvenile court and a considerable delay in the police station where the punishment was carried out. Accordingly, in addition to the physical pain he experienced, Mr Tyrer was subjected to the mental anguish of anticipating the violence he was to have inflicted on him.

. . . In the present case, the Court does not consider it relevant that the sentence of judicial corporal punishment was imposed on the applicant for an offence of violence. Neither does it consider it relevant that, for Mr Tyrer, birching was an alternative to a period of detention: the fact that one penalty may be preferable to, or have less adverse effects or be less serious than, another penalty does not of itself mean that the first penalty is not 'degrading' within the meaning of Article 3.

. . . Accordingly, viewing these circumstances as a whole, the Court finds that the applicant was subjected to a punishment in which the element of humiliation attained the level inherent in the notion of 'degrading punishment' as explained at paragraph 30 above. The indignity of having the punishment administered over the bare posterior aggravated to some extent the degrading character of the applicant's punishment but it was not the only or determining factor.

The Court therefore concludes that the judicial corporal punishment inflicted on the applicant amounted to degrading punishment within the meaning of Article 3 of the Convention. (paras 33–35)

Comment

Since 1950 the UK has not regarded international treaties which apply to the UK as extending to the Isle of Man. In 1953 the Convention was extended to the Isle of Man.

Judicial punishment on the mainland of the UK was abolished under the Criminal Justice Act 1948, and in Northern Ireland in 1968. The Court of Tynwald – the legislative body on the Isle of Man – had considered its abolition in 1963 and 1965, but decided to retain it, reaffirming this view in 1977.

The applicable law in the Isle of Man was stated to be as follows:

> . . . Section 56(1) of the Petty Sessions and Summary Jurisdiction Act 1927 (as amended by s. 8 of the Summary Jurisdiction Act 1960) provided that the penalty for assault and provoking language or behaviour tending to a breach of the peace was a fine not exceeding £30 or up to six months' imprisonment, and, in the case of a male child (i.e. aged 10–13) or male young person (i.e. aged 14–16), to be whipped in addition to or instead of either of these.
>
> Section 10 of the Act of 1960 provided that the instrument used was to be a cane in the case of a child and otherwise a birch rod; that the court must specify the number of strokes which was not to exceed six strokes for a child and 12 for a young person; that the punishment was to be inflicted privately as soon as practicable after sentence and never more than six months after the passing of sentence; that it was to be carried out by a constable in the presence of an officer of higher rank and the parent or guardian if he desired to be present.
>
> A directive of the Lieutenant-Governor prescribed the dimensions of the instrument. For a child, it was to be a light cane not exceeding four feet in length and not more than half an inch in diameter. In the case of a person between 14 and 20, the birch rod was not to exceed nine ounces in weight; the overall length was to be 40 inches; the handle length was to be 15 inches; the circumference of the spray at the centre was to be six inches; of the handle at the top of the binding, three and a half inches; and of the handle six inches from the end, three and a quarter inches. The magistrates were required to consider a medical report before imposing sentence. The doctor who was required to be present could stop the birching at any time. The directive was amended following the Commission's Report to the effect that the punishment was to be administered over the person's ordinary cloth trousers. (para. 25)

When this judgment was given, the UK Government informed the Lieutenant Governor of the Isle of Man that judicial corporal punishment was in breach of the Convention. The First Deemster of the Isle of Man – the chief judicial officer – drew the attention of all persons entitled to pass such sentences to the judgment.

In a lengthy dissenting judgment, Judge Sir Gerald Fitzmaurice questioned the absolute character given to Article 3 and the consequent need to put a gloss on this by the use of concepts such as degrees of severity, what constitutes torture or degrading treatment and what justifies it. As far as the level of humiliation involved in this case was concerned, Judge Fitzmaurice disagreed that in the circumstances this amounted to degrading treatment. He expressed the opinion that in this case what the majority of the Court was doing was to hold that the punishment itself was degrading, not the circumstances in which it was inflicted. Such reasoning would leave open the possibility of finding all punishment degrading – which it was often intended to be. The Judge indicated that he could not agree with the view that all corporal punishment was degrading – particularly for juvenile offenders compared to adult offenders – although it might be undesirable.

Campbell and Cosans v UK
Series A, Vol. 48

The facts

Mrs Campbell's son attended a school in Scotland where corporal punishment was permitted. He had in fact never be subjected to such punishment, but Mrs Campbell requested a guarantee from the Strathclyde Regional Council – which was responsible for the school – that her son would not be subject to such punishment. The Council refused to give any such guarantee.

Mrs Cosan's son, Jeffrey, attended a different school in Scotland, and had been told that he would receive corporal punishment for taking a short cut home through the cemetery adjoining the school. He refused to accept the punishment and was suspended. The school offered to lift the suspension several months later provided that Mr and Mrs Cosans accepted the disciplinary regime at the school. They refused to do so and Jeffrey never returned to school.

The main claims of the applicants fall under Article 2 of the First Protocol relating to education, but the applicants also complained of a violation of Article 3.

The Commission's opinion

The Commission did not consider that the facts of the cases amounted to either torture or inhuman treatment or punishment. The only question left to be considered, therefore, was whether either of the children had been subjected to degrading treatment or punishment.

In considering the circumstances of the case the Commission could distinguish between this case and that of *Tyrer*.

> ... In contrast to Mr Tyrer, the present applicants' children have on no occasion been subjected to corporal punishment. It is true that it was decided that Jeffrey Cosans should be so punished for having tried to take a short cut home from school. However, this decision was never carried out although it was maintained in force for about four months. Consequently, what has to be ascertained in these cases is whether the mere threatened or potential use of corporal punishment can be considered to attain the level of severity that can be classified as 'degrading' within the meaning of Article 3.
>
> ... As previously stated, the Commission does not exclude that young and sensitive children may suffer adverse effects by the use of violence around them and by the fact that they are themselves under the threat in principle or corporal punishment if they misbehave. The Commission does not consider, however, that such effects alone are sufficient to amount to degrading treatment or punishment as understood by Article 3 of the Convention. Moreover, on the facts of the cases it cannot be established that

the applicants' children have suffered any adverse psychological or other effects which could be imputed to the use of corporal punishment in their schools.

. . . The Commission points out, furthermore, that the test referred to above for measuring the severity of a punishment in the light of Article 3 cannot, in principle, be made in cases like the present ones where there has been no concrete act of physical chastisement. It makes no difference in this respect that there was a decision to punish Jeffrey Cosans: since the decision was never executed, the test for measuring the severity equally cannot be made.

. . . Without prejudging the question whether corporal punishment as a disciplinary measure at school may *per se* be considered as a degrading punishment within the meaning of Article 3, the preceding considerations lead the Commission to conclude that the mere fact that the applicants' children attended an educational system which provides for the use of physical chastisement does not constitute degrading treatment as understood by this provision. (paras 121–124)

The Commission expressed the opinion, therefore, that there was no violation of Article 3. Mr Klecker, however, expressed a strong dissenting opinion (at paras 3–8).

The judgment of the Court
In deciding whether treatment is inhuman or degrading the Court held that it is not necessary that such treatment is actually inflicted provided that:

. . . it is sufficiently real and immediate, a mere threat of conduct prohibited by Article 3 may itself be in conflict with that provision. Thus, to threaten an individual with torture might in some circumstances constitute at least 'inhuman treatment'.

. . . Although the system of corporal punishment can cause a certain degree of apprehension in those who may be subject to it, the Court nevertheless shares the Commission's view that the situation in which the applicants' sons found themselves did not amount to 'torture' or 'inhuman treatment', within the meaning of Article 3: there is no evidence that they underwent suffering of the level inherent in these notions as they were interpreted and applied in *Ireland* v *United Kingdom* (1978) 2 EHRR 25, paras 167 and 174.

. . . In the present case, no 'punishment' has actually been inflicted. Nevertheless, it follows from that judgment that 'treatment' itself will not be 'degrading' unless the person concerned has undergone – either in the eyes of others or in his own eyes – humiliation or debasement attaining a minimum level of severity. That level has to be assessed with regard to the circumstances of the case.

. . . As to whether the applicants' sons were humiliated or debased in their own eyes, the Court observes first that a threat directed to an exceptionally insensitive person may have no significant effect on him but nevertheless be incontrovertibly degrading; and conversely, as exceptionally sensitive person might be deeply affected by a threat that could be described as degrading only by a distortion of the ordinary and usual meaning of the word. In any event, in the case of these two children, the Court, like the Commission, notes that it has not been shown by means of medical certificates or otherwise that they suffered any adverse psychological or other effects . . .

Jeffrey Cosans may well have experienced feelings of apprehension or disquiet when he came close to an infliction of the tawse . . . but such feelings are not sufficient to amount to degrading treatment, within the meaning of Article 3.

The same applies, *a fortiori*, to Gordon Campbell since he was never directly threatened with corporal punishment. . . . It is true that counsel for his mother alleged at the hearings that group tension and a sense of alienation in the pupil are induced by the very existence of this practice but, even if this be so, these effects fall into a different category from humiliation or debasement.

. . . To sum up, no violation of Article 3 is established. This conclusion renders it unnecessary for the Court to consider whether the applicants are entitled, under Article 25 of the Convention, to claim that their children were victims of such a violation, an issue that was examined by the Commission and was the subject of submissions by the Government. (paras 26–28 and 30–31)

Comment

The applicable law in Scotland was stated in the report of the Commission as follows:

. . . The use of corporal punishment in Scottish schools is controlled by the civil and criminal law. The general principle is that a person is liable to criminal or civil proceedings for assault with the exception of teachers who may apply corporal punishment in moderation to ensure discipline in the schools. Excessive, arbitrary or cruel punishment would be illegal.

. . . Corporal punishment, when exercised in the schools attended by the present applicants' children, takes the form of striking the palm of a pupil's hand with a leather strap called a 'tawse'. For incidents of misconduct committed in the classroom, punishment is administered by the teacher, there and then, in the presence of the class. For incidents of misconduct outside the classroom and for serious misconduct, punishment is administered by the headmaster or deputy headmaster, in his room. (paras 19 and 20)

Nevertheless, at the time of the case there does appear to have been some movement towards reform. A booklet entitled *Elimination of Corporal Punishment in Schools: Statement of Principles and Code of Practice* had been issued in 1968 by a consultative body, advocating a gradual move towards the eradication of such punishment as a measure of discipline in schools. The code of practice contained in the booklet was not binding.

Costello-Roberts v *UK*
Series A, Vol. 247-C

The facts

The case concerned the corporal punishment of a seven-year-old pupil by the headmaster of a private boarding school. The punishment consisted of three strokes with a rubber-soled gym shoe on the buttocks, through the boy's shorts, and was given to the boy because he had acquired five demerit marks. The punishment was administered three days after the fifth demerit mark had been awarded. Mrs Costello-Roberts learnt of the 'slippering' from her son. She expressed her concern and disgust to the school and informed the headmaster that she did not want her son to be corporally punished. The headmaster suggested that she remove her son from the school as she did not want him to be educated within the school's framework for discipline and punishment. The child was removed at the end of that term.

Mrs Costello-Roberts and her son, Jeremy, lodged an application with the Commission in January 1986 submitting that his corporal punishment constituted a breach of Article 3. They also complained of violations of Articles 8 and 13.

The Commission's opinion

The two questions which faced the Commission were: Could the responsibility of the State be engaged in the case of a private school? Had the punishment been inhuman or degrading?

In answering the first point the Commission held that the UK had obligations under the Convention to ensure a legal system which provides adequate protection for children's physical and emotional integrity.

> ... The Commission considers that Contracting States do have an obligation under Article 1 of the Convention to secure that children within their jurisdiction are not subjected to torture, inhuman or degrading treatment or punishment, contrary to Article 3 of the Convention. This duty is recognised in English law which provides certain criminal and civil law safeguards against assault or unreasonable punishment. Moreover, children subjected to, or at risk or being subjected to ill-treatment by their parents, including excessive corporal punishment, may be removed from their parents' custody and placed in local authority care. The Commission also notes that the State obliges parents to educate their children, or have them educated in schools, and that the State has the function of supervising educational standards and the suitability of teaching staff even in independent schools. Furthermore, the effect of compulsory education is that parents are normally obliged to put their children in charge of teachers. If parents choose a private school, the teachers assume the parental role in matters of discipline under the national law while the children are in their care, by virtue of the 'in loco parentis' doctrine. In these circumstances the Commission considers that the United Kingdom has a duty under the Convention to secure that all pupils, including pupils at private schools, are not exposed to treatment contrary to Article 3 of the Convention. The Commission considers that the United Kingdom's liability also extends to Article 8 of the Convention in order to protect the right to respect for private life of pupils in private schools to the extent that corporal punishment in such schools may involve an unjustified interference with children's physical and emotional integrity. (para. 37)

In deciding whether the treatment received by Jeremy was inhuman or degrading the Commission, referring to the case of *Tyrer*, noted that:

> ... for corporal punishment to be degrading, within the meaning of Article 3 of the Convention, the humiliation and debasement involved must attain a particular level of severity over and above the usual element of humiliation involved in any kind of punishment. The assessment of such matters is necessarily relative: it depends upon all the circumstances of the case and, in particular, on the nature and context of the punishment itself and the manner and method of its execution ... (para. 41)

In considering the circumstances of this particular case the Commission found that:

> ... the punishment inflicted on the applicant, although probably pedagogically undesirable given his age and sensitivity, could not be said to have reached the level of severe ill-treatment proscribed by Article 3 of the Convention. Three smacks on the buttocks, through shorts, with a soft-soled shoe, apparently causing no visible injury, cannot be compared to the thrashing suffered by Anthony Tyrer when he was birched as a form of judicial corporal punishment. Nor can the applicant's situation be compared to that of a teenage girl being punished by a man in the presence of another man, by having her hand caned so hard that it caused bruising. ... The Commission

considers, therefore, that the mild punishment of the present applicant did not constitute degrading treatment within the meaning of Article 3 of the Convention. (para. 42)

There was therefore no violation of Article 3.

There were, however, dissenting opinions concerning this article from Mrs Thune and Mr Geus, who considered that if a 'wide assessment of all the factual circumstances' were made, and the situation assessed as a whole as it appeared to the pupil concerned, then there was a violation of Article 3. There was also a dissenting opinion from Mr Loucaides.

The judgment of the Court
The Court reasoned as follows:

(a) The State had an obligation to secure to children their right to education; a school's disciplinary system fell within the ambit of the right to education.

(b) The fundamental right of everyone to education was a right guaranteed equally to pupils in State and independent schools.

(c) The State could not absolve itself from responsibility by delegating its obligations to private bodies or individuals.

Therefore 'in the particular domain of school discipline, State responsibility could be engaged'.

In order for the punishment to be 'degrading':

. . . the humiliation or debasement involved must attain a particular level of severity, and must in any event be other than that usual element of humiliation inherent in any punishment. (para. 30)

The applicant had maintained that:

. . . although the actual physical force to which he had been subjected had been moderate, there had, nevertheless, been an assault on his dignity and physical integrity. He relied, in particular, on the dissenting opinions of three members of the Commission. The degrading character had, he claimed, been aggravated by his age at the time, the fact that he had been at the school for only about five weeks, the humiliating site of the punishment, the impersonal and automatic way in which it had been administered as a result of 'totting up' demerit marks for minor offences, and the three-day wait between the 'sentence' and its implementation. (para. 29)

The Court accepted that in considering all the circumstances of the case the Court might take into account:

. . . factors such as the nature and context of the punishment, the manner and method of its execution, its duration, its physical and mental effects and, in some instances, the sex, age and state of health of the victim. (para. 30)

The Court distinguished this case from that of *Tyrer*, however.

. . . Beyond the consequences to be expected from measures taken on a purely disciplinary plane, the applicant has adduced no evidence of any severe or long-lasting effects as a result of the treatment complained of. A punishment which does not occasion such effects may fall within the ambit of Article 3, provided that in the particular circumstances of the case, it may be said to have reached the minimum threshold of severity required. While the Court has certain misgivings about the automatic nature of the punishment and the three-day wait before its imposition, it considers that minimum level of severity not to have been attained in this case.

Accordingly, no violation of Article 3 has been established. (para. 32)

Comment

In English law there are various criminal offences of assault: common assault (Offences Against the Person Act 1861, s. 42); assault occasioning actual bodily harm (s. 47 of the 1861 Act); assault or ill-treatment of a child (Children and Young Persons Act 1933, s. 1(1)). It is also possible to bring a civil action for trespass to the person. In this case the police decided not to prosecute due to lack of evidence. Prior to 1987 it was a defence in the case of civil and criminal actions if the person against whom the claim was made was a teacher administering reasonable and moderate physical punishment with a proper instrument in a decent manner. As from 15 August 1987, i.e. after the events giving rise to this case, the Education (No. 2) Act 1987 removed this defence in civil proceedings for teachers in most State and State-assisted schools.

The Court indicated that even a punishment that did not occasion severe or long-lasting effects *might* fall within the ambit of Article 3, provided that the minimum threshold of severity had been met. This left the door open for cases where it might be difficult to establish or quantify long-lasting effects, but did little to clarify where the threshold lay. Misgivings were expressed about the automatic nature of the corporal punishment and the wait of three days that the boy had to endure before the punishment was carried out, but neither of these factors changed the outcome.

A further case involving corporal punishment was *Y v UK* (App. No. 14229/88, Series A, No. 247-A), in which a 15-year-old school boy had been caned by the headmaster of the independent school he attended, as a punishment for alleged bullying. In this case, however, a friendly settlement had been reached whereby the Government of the UK had agreed to pay the applicant £8,000 plus costs. The applicant withdrew the case from the Court, and as there were no public policy reasons against striking the case out, the case was struck off the list.

3.2.3 Inhuman and Degrading Treatment of Immigrants

East African Asians v UK
(1994) 78-A D & R 5

The facts

The applicants were citizens of the UK and colonies, and husbands of Commonwealth citizens already resident in the UK They had been refused admission into the UK to join their wives, although the legislation in force would have permitted wives to come into the UK to join their husbands.

The question before the Commission was whether the discriminatory effect of the legislation applicable at the time could be regarded as degrading treatment under Article 3, on the grounds that:

... to single out a group of persons for differential treatment on the basis of race may constitute a special form of affront to human dignity and might therefore be capable of constituting degrading treatment. (p. 62)

The Commission's opinion

At the outset the Commission had to clarify the grounds on which this application was admissible, as the Convention does not guarantee the right to enter and reside in a particular country. (See, for example, *App. No. 8245/78* v *UK* 24 D & R 98.) Therefore the use of immigration controls are not in themselves infringements of the Convention. However, where these operate in a discriminatory manner then such discrimination may amount to degrading treatment:

... discrimination based on race could, in certain circumstances, of itself amount to degrading treatment within the meaning of Article 3 of the Convention. The Commission recalls in this connection that, as generally recognised, a special importance should be attached to discrimination based on race, that publicly to single out a group of persons for differential treatment on the basis of race might, in certain circumstances, constitute a special form of affront to human dignity. (para. 207)

The refusal of a right not falling under the Convention could therefore be brought under the Convention only if the circumstances of that refusal violated another right already included in the Convention. In this context the Commission referred to the case law concerning the right of asylum and the right of an alien not to be expelled:

... Although neither of these rights is guaranteed by the Convention, the Commission has nevertheless found that the contracting parties agreed to restrict the free exercise of their powers under general international law, including the power to control the entry and exit of aliens, to the extent and within the limits of the obligations which they assumed under this treaty. In certain exceptional circumstances, the deportation of a person may thus be contrary to the Convention and, in particular, constitute 'inhuman treatment' within the meaning of Article 3 thereof.
... The Commission finds that the above considerations concerning the position of aliens apply, *mutatis mutandis*, to the present applications brought by citizens. It concludes that although the right to enter one's country is not protected by the Convention, the refusal of this right may in certain special circumstances, nevertheless, violate quite independently another right already covered by this treaty. It follows that, in the present cases, the Commission is not being called upon to consider the rights of entry or residence as such, but that it is being invited to examine the different question whether the decisions complained of amount to 'degrading treatment' in the sense of Article 3. (pp. 54–5)

In order to apply the provisions of Article 3 to the circumstances of the case the Commission undertook a careful examination of the meaning of the term 'degrading treatment':

... As a general definition of the term 'degrading treatment', the applicants submit that the treatment of a person is degrading 'if it lowers him in rank, position, reputation or character, whether in his own eyes or in the eyes of other people'.
The Commission finds this broad interpretation of the ordinary meaning useful when defining the term 'degrading treatment' in Article 3 of the Convention. In view

of the particular context in which the term is used in Article 3, the Commission considers, however, that the above interpretation must be narrowed.

Article 3 states that no one shall be subjected to 'torture or to inhuman or degrading treatment or punishment'. The term 'degrading treatment' in this context indicates that the general purpose of the provision is to prevent interferences with the dignity of man of a particularly serious nature. It follows that an action, which lowers a person in rank, position, reputation or character, can only be regarded as 'degrading treatment' in the sense of Article 3, where it reaches a certain level of severity.

. . . The Government suggests a further limitations they submit that the term 'degrading treatment' must be interpreted as referring to physical acts only.

. . . The Commission considers that such interpretation of 'degrading treatment' would be too restrictive. Even in the case of torture and inhuman treatment such a physical element is not essential. (p. 55)

The Commission considered that discrimination based on race, could, in certain circumstances amount to degrading treatment. It was not necessary for the Commission to consider whether all racial discrimination in immigration control was degrading, only:

. . . whether the legislation applied in the applicants' cases, i.e. the Commonwealth Immigrants Act 1962 as amended by the Commonwealth Immigrants Act 1968 and the Immigration Appeals Act 1969, discriminated on the ground of race or colour and, if that be the case, whether its application in the following special circumstances of the present cases constituted 'degrading treatment' in the sense of Article 3 of the Convention . . . (p. 57)

The Commission therefore expressed the opinion that:

. . . the legislation applied in the present cases discriminated against the applicants on the grounds of their colour or race. It has also confirmed the view, which it expressed at the admissibility stage, that discrimination based on race could, in certain circumstances, of itself amount to degrading treatment within the meaning of Article 3 of the Convention.

The Commission recalls in this connection that, as generally recognised, a special importance should be attached to discrimination based on race; that publicity to single out a group of persons for differential treatment on the basis of race might, in certain circumstances, constitute a special form of affront to human dignity; and that differential treatment of a group of persons on the basis of race might therefore be capable of constituting degrading treatment when differential treatment on some other ground would raise no such question.

. . . The Commission considers that the racial discrimination, to which the applicants have been publicly subjected by the application of the above immigration legislation, constitutes an interference with their human dignity which, in the special circumstances described above, amounted to 'degrading treatment' in the sense of Article 3 of the Convention.

. . . It therefore *concludes*, by six votes against three votes, that Article 3 has been violated in the present cases. (p. 62)

However, the Commission expressed the opinion that the situation concerning the applications brought by British protected persons was different because:

— according to English law, British protected persons, although not aliens, are not British subjects;

— they became and remained subject to immigration control under the Commonwealth Immigrants 1962 Act;

— their position as regards entry to the United Kingdom was not changed by the Commonwealth Immigrants 1968 Act;

— the immigration legislation concerned did not distinguish between different groups of British protected persons on any ground of race or colour.

. . . The Commission considers that, in view of the above circumstances, the legislation complained of cannot in the present cases of British protected persons be regarded as discriminatory and even less as constituting degrading treatment in the sense of Article 3 of the Convention.

. . . The Commission therefore *concludes* unanimously that Article 3 has not been violated in these cases. (pp. 63–4)

Comment

The situation in which East African Asians found themselves was considerably aggravated by the policies of Africanisation which were implemented in the 1960s in Tanzania, Uganda and Kenya following independence. As indicated in the report of the Commission:

. . . most of the Asians concerned were deprived of their livelihood and rendered destitute; their trading licences and trading areas were restricted and their continued residence in East Africa became illegal; being refused entry by the only State of which they were citizens – the United Kimgdom – they had no other country to which they could make out a claim for admission. (p. 61)

During the course of the proceedings the applicants were eventually given permission to stay permanently in the UK.

The category of British Overseas Citizens was created by the British Nationality Act 1981, which clarified the legal status of certain classes of immigrants. Such Citizens did not have the right of abode in the UK. Entry into the UK for these citizens was by way of limited quotas for which vouchers were issued according to certain selection criteria. The *East African Asians* case was decided against the background of the Commonwealth Immigrants Act 1968.

The only right of entry protected by the Convention is under the Fourth Protocol, Article 3(2), which has not been ratified by the UK and therefore would not apply.

3.2.4   Prisoners and Detainees

An important inter-State case concerning this aspect of Article 3 was *Republic of Ireland* v *UK* Series A, No. 25. There have, however, also been individual applications concerned with the treatment of prisoners and detaineees.

Hilton v *UK*
Report of the Commission, Council of Europe

The facts
The applicant was convicted in 1971 of malicious wounding and was sentenced to four years' imprisonment. His complaint concerned his treatment during his detention in prison in Leeds and Liverpool. He alleged a number of incidents

of ill-treatment, harassment and victimisation, which were further aggravated by racial prejudice shown towards him by prison staff and hostility from other prisoners following an unjustified rumour that he had been convicted of a sexual offence. His complaints included:

- reduction in prison wages due to change of prison work following a hand injury,
- refusal by the authorities to afford him protection from other prisoners by removing him from association with other prisoners,
- refusal of his applications for transfer to another prison following an alleged assault by a prison officer,
- lack of exercise,
- failure to provide a personal escort for his protection,
- abusive and threatening language used against him, and
- abuse of disciplinary measures by prison staff, including strip searches and cell searches.

The evidence placed before the Commission indicated that:

> . . . By the end of the applicant's detention in Liverpool prison he was in a depressed state. He came to feel that he was like an animal, to such an extent that he would roll in his own excrement on the floor of his cell. It is recorded that early in January he was found one day at 4.00 in the morning 'to have made a small cut on his wrist with glass broken from his mirror' and had rubbed 'his own excreta on to his body, his face, his hair, and into the wound' (report of the Liverpool Prison Governor to the Regional Office). (para. 59)

The Government contested a number of the applicant's allegations. He was examined in prison to ascertain the state of his mental health, but there was no evidence that he was suffering from any form of mental disorder; indeed, the applicant resented any suggestion that he was not mentally healthy. For the greater part of his sentence he spent the time removed from association with other prisoners in accordance with rule 43(1) of the Prison Rules, either at his own request or for disciplinary reasons. The Government submitted that:

> . . . there was no evidence of any ill-treatment of the applicant and therefore no evidence of a possible breach of Article 3 of the Convention. In their opinion the applicant's allegations can only be considered to be a 'total misrepresentation' or gross exaggeration of what actually happened. (para. 62)

The degraded state which the applicant reached by the end of his imprisonment was, according to the Government, of his own doing.
    The applicant contended that:

> . . . The alleged assaults and abuse from prison staff . . . constituted mental and physical torture. Furthermore, he submitted that his detention removed from association with other prisoners under rule 43 of the Prison Rules was not for his own protection but was 'undue, unjust and unjustified punishment', inordinately long, consisting of 23 hours a day solitary confinement, involving loss of privileges and causing him severe mental strain and degradation.
> . . . Finally, he contended that the cumulative effect of solitary confinement, alleged ill-treatment deliberately inflicted, the refusal by all concerned to investigate, or cause

to be investigated, the complaints of brutality he was making against prison officers, the incessant complaints that were made against him and subsequent disciplinary proceedings which allegedly ignored the rules of natural justice and the continuous loss of privileges, resulted in his total degradation and constituted a breach of Article 3 of the Convention. (paras 72 and 73)

The Commission had to decide whether the treatment of the applicant, either in particular instances or in general, amounted to inhuman or degrading treatment or punishment.

The Commission's opinion
The guidelines to be followed by the Commission were those established in previous case law, notably in the *Greek* case (1969) *Yearbook* 186, that:

... Treatment or punishment of an individual may be said to be degrading if it grossly humiliates him before others or drives him to act against his will or conscience. (para. 79)

However, the criteria for individual applicants might be different from those concerning inter-State cases, where the degrading treatment has usually arisen in emergency situations and involves treatment akin to torture or torture. It would not be necessary, therefore, to find that all the treatment complained of was 'atrocious' or 'gross', provided that it attained a minimum level of severity.

The Commission expressed the opinion that on the evidence, it could not be established that specific incidents of ill-treatment were in breach of Article 3.

In considering whether the general treatment he received, either by act or omission, amounted to a breach of the article, the Commission examined whether the applicant could be said to have been treated generally in a degrading manner. The Commission expressed the opinion that:

... There is no evidence that the applicant was deliberately treated in a degrading manner. But such factors as the conditions of over-crowding and understaffing disclosed by this application and the rigorous, impersonal application of disciplinary measures, on occasions to the point of absurdity (for example, the applicant's punishment for putting his hands in his pockets) all had their depressing and discouraging effect upon the applicant.

... Equally, the applicant's own personality was a contributing factor. Even though he was not deemed certifiably mentally ill, he was a stressful personality unable to accept the realities of imprisonment. He overreacted and was over-sensitive to all disagreements associated with his imprisonment. The applicant was particularly sensitive about references to the colour of his skin, but the Government informed the Commission that no account is taken of a prisoner's race, thus perhaps ignoring very real problems which may arise in certain circumstances. It is evident, nevertheless, that the applicant constituted a provocation for the staff and presented them with a particularly difficult situation: whether to ignore him, humour him, oblige him to conform or try to help him.

... The Commission has considered whether the authorities' failure to cope with such an odd personality amounted to a breach of Article 3 of the Convention.

... In this respect the Commission has noted the various positive efforts, albeit unsuccessful, which the prison authorities made to help the applicant: his transfer to Liverpool prison and, at the end of his sentence, to Hull prison; the more or less continued observation made by the prison medical staff of the applicant's mental health to see whether he should be transferred to a special mental hospital such as Broadmoor; the accession to the applicant's request to be removed from association with other prisoners in order to re-establish his confidence in the staff; the restoration of lost remission for sociable behaviour, again in an effort to re-establish this confidence; and the visits by the prison chaplain, other religious functionaries and welfare officers.

. . . In the opinion of the prison authorities the applicant could not have been put in a special mental hospital and he was not suitable for one special prison existing at that time for persons who would normally be removed from association with other prisoners under rule 43 of the Prison Rules because of hostility they would face for their previous convictions, usually for sexual offences. The applicant was unsuitable for such a prison as he had no such record and would not have integrated with such prisoners as he was an abrasive character. Moreover, there were, and still are, regrettable limitations on normal prisons, because of understaffing and overcrowding, which make it difficult to give special attention to an individual prisoner's problems.

. . . The Commission concludes therefore that the general treatment of the applicant, although extremely unsatisfactory in all the circumstances of the case, did not amount to degrading treatment contrary to Article 3 of the Convention. (paras 97–102)

Three members of the Commission expressed a dissenting opinion, that the general treatment of the applicant 'in its cumulative effect' constituted degrading treatment.

McFeeley v *UK*
(1984) 38 D & R 11

The facts
The applicants were prisoners in the Maze Prison in Northern Ireland. All of them had been convicted of offences under the Northern Ireland (Emergency Provisions) Act 1978. Between June 1972 and March 1976, prisoners involved in paramilitary organisations had been given the status of 'special category' prisoners and were treated differently from ordinary prisoners. This classification was phased out from March 1976 following recommendations of the Gardiner Committee Report of the previous year. At the same time as the phasing out, new rules were introduced regarding the earning of remission (Treatment of Offenders (Northern Ireland) Order 1976, SI 1976 No. 226).

In order to express protest at the failure of the Government to recognise them as political prisoners, the applicants refused to comply with certain prison regulations, including the requirement to wear prison uniform. Various disciplinary steps were taken against the prisoners, which gave rise to a number of complaints against the UK.

Their complaints concerning Article 3, which followed as a result of disciplinary proceedings taken against them, were:

(i)   they complain, jointly and severally, that the combination of disciplinary awards and conditions of detention in the H-blocks constitutes an inhuman and degrading system of treatment;

(ii)   they also complain, jointly and severally that, taken *separately*, the system of continuous and cumulative sanctions, the imposition of 'isolation' punishment and collective punishments constitutes inhuman and degrading punishment;

(iii)   they further complain that the combination of disciplinary punishments and their conditions of detention amounts to an administrative practice of inhuman and degrading treatment in breach of Article 3;

(iv)   The applicants Hunter and Nugent complain separately of certain features of the prison regime. Thus both state that the imposition of a restricted diet (No. 1 diet) amounts to inhuman and degrading punishment. The applicant Hunter complains that an award of 'isolation' punishment on 19 April 1978 was a disproportionate sanction for the offence involved and thus amounted to inhuman punishment. (para. 32)

The Commission had to consider to what extent, if at all, the inhuman and degrading treatment was a consequence of the applicants' own acts; for example, their refusal to leave their cells to use the dining room, toilets or washroom or to take exercise. Also to consider whether the reaction of the prison authorities to the prisoners' refusal to wear prison clothing had been excessive.

The Commission's opinion

The Commission, referring to the decision of the Court in the *Tyrer* case, held that the assessment of whether a punishment is inhuman or degrading:

... is relative, depending on all the circumstances of the case, and in particular, the nature and context of the punishment itself and the manner and method of its execution. (para. 41)

As regards the applicants' claim to special status as political prisoners, the Commission observed:

... that the applicants are seeking to achieve a status of political prisoner which they are not entitled to under national law or under the Convention. Furthermore, although this point has not been argued by the parties in their observations, the Commission does not consider that such an entitlement in the present context can be derived from existing norms of international law. In this regard the Commission recalls its opinion that the applicants' convictions are not protected by the Convention or Article 9 in particular, and that their complaint under this provision has been rejected as incompatible *ratione materiae*. It follows from this that their protest cannot derive any legitimacy or justification from the Convention and cannot be attributed to any positive action on behalf of the respondent Government. Thus the Commission is of the view that the undoubtedly harsh conditions of detention, which developed from the applicants' decision not to wear prison uniform or use the toilet and washing facilities provided and other self-imposed deprivations associated with their protest, cannot engage the responsibility of the respondent Government. (para. 43)

The Commission found no obligation in the Convention which would compel the UK Government to concede to the prisoners' demands, adding that:

it does not consider there to be anything inherently degrading or objectionable about the requirement to wear a prison uniform or to work. (para. 43)

... On the other hand, the Commission considers that in such a situation, the State is not absolved from its obligation under the Convention and Article 3 in particular, because prisoners are engaged in what is regarded as an unlawful challenge to the authority of the prison administration. Although short of an obligation to accept the applicants' demands in the sense described above, the Convention requires that the prison authorities, with due regard to the ordinary and reasonable requirements of imprisonment, exercise their custodial authority to safeguard the health and well-being of all prisoners including those engaged in protest in so far as that may be possible in the circumstances. Such a requirement makes it necessary for the prison authorities to keep under constant review their reaction to recalcitrant prisoners engaged in a developing and protracted protest. (para. 46)

As regards the loss of remission for a disciplinary offence the Commission did not consider this to constitute inhuman or degrading treatment.

As regards loss of privileges, including segregation from other prisoners, referring to previous applications the Commission maintained that:

. . . complete sensory isolation, coupled with total social isolation, can destroy the personality and constitutes a form of inhuman treatment which cannot be justified by the requirements of security or any other reason. On the other hand a distinction has been drawn between this and removal from association with other prisoners for security, disciplinary or protective reasons. The Commission would not normally consider that this form of segregation from the prison community amounts to inhuman treatment or punishment. In making an assessment in a given case, regard must be had to the surrounding circumstances including the particular conditions, the stringency of the measure, its duration, the objective pursued and its effects on the person concerned.

. . . The Commission must observe, however, in the present case, that the form of segregation the applicants are subject to does not amount to solitary confinement or to total social isolation as such. It is more correctly characterised as a form of removal from association with other prisoners. Each of the applicants shares a cell with another prisoner. Moreover, it is still open to the applicants, as is confirmed by the submissions of both parties, to leave their cells for certain purposes, e.g. to take one hour's exercise every day in the open air, to receive visits from lawyers, to attend religious services or to visit the medical or welfare officer, to visit the toilet facilities, to take a shower twice weekly, to visit the library and to collect meals from the dining room.

. . . During this period (of segregation) they were confined to their cells, although they were still entitled one hour's exercise in the open air every day. Their mattresses and bedding were removed during the day-time but returned at night. The Commission notes that this punishment was served in their own cells in the company of a cell mate and not in the punishment block, and that its duration was limited to three out of every 14 days. Moreover, as a regular punishment for the applicants' protest it ended on 6 October 1978. The Commission does not doubt the cumulative harshness of this punishment over a long period but again it must observe that, given the actual conditions in which the punishment was served and its length, the Commission is of the opinion that it did not attain a sufficient level of severity to raise an issue under Article 3.

3.2.5 Others

A v *UK*
(1980) 20 D & R 5

The facts
The applicant was detained as a mental patient in Broadmoor Hospital under orders made in accordance with ss. 60 and 65 of the Mental Health Act 1959.

Following an arson incident in May 1974, he was placed in a secure single room in the hospital's intensive care unit.

The conditions of such detention gave rise to his application to the Commission alleging a breach of Article 3. The applicant complained in particular of the length of time he was subject to solitary confinement, and that he had been deprived of adequate furnishings and clothing.

The Commission's opinion

Following its consideration of the case the Commission placed itself at the disposal of the parties to secure a friendly settlement. (Under Article 28, para. 1(b), the Commission 'shall place itself at the disposal of the parties concerned with a view to securing a friendly settlement of the matter on the basis of respect for human rights as defined by this Convention'.)

Although not admitting liability, the Government offered the applicant an *ex gratia* payment of £500 and published new guidelines on the use of seclusion at Broadmoor. These included the following:

1. New working guidelines concerning the seclusion of patients at Broadmoor Special Hospital have now been introduced and are in operation.

2. These are to apply whenever a patient is compulsorily confined to a secure room between the hours of 7 a.m. and normal bedtime. Rooms used for seclusion are to have at least 4.7 square metres floor space and to have natural lighting.

3. The nurse in charge of a ward may take the initial decision to seclude a patient whose behaviour is, or seems likely to become, so disturbed that it is desirable to isolate him for his own safety or for the safety of others. The unit (or duty) nursing officer and the responsible medical officer, or his deputy, are to be advised at once of the decision and the reason for it.

4. A programme of care for any patient secluded for more than three hours is to be drawn up by the nurse in charge in consultation with the responsible medical officer. This programme is to be reviewed daily.

5. Where for safety or security reasons normal clothing and/or furniture is withdrawn, patients are to be provided with pyjamas or other special clothing (including suitable footwear unless this is specifically banned to prevent harm to himself or others), mattresses and bedding. Disposable bedpans and urinals and toilet paper are also to be provided. Writing materials, reading matter and other items are to be provided on request at the discretion of the nurse in charge.

6. Unless the patient's condition precludes it, he is to be allowed out of his room for toilet purposes and to take exercise (for at least 30 minutes each morning and afternoon (or evening) and to receive visitors.

7. Patients in seclusion are to be observed at irregular intervals not exceeding 15 minutes.

8. A special record book is to be maintained on every ward in which full reports of all occasions on which a patient is secluded will be made. This report, which will be cross-referenced with the daily ward report and patient's clinical records, will record, *inter alia,* the time the seclusion started and ended, the reason for it, details of clothing, bedding etc. supplied and observations and reviews made.

9. If the patient is secluded for more than 24 hours, the Hospital Management Team should be informed and if the seclusion lasts for a continuous period of seven days, the Hospital Management Team should make a full report to the hospital managers. Reports should therafter be made to the hospital managers weekly for as long as seclusion continues.

While not conceding that the new guidelines would necessarily prevent a recurrence of the same type of incident, the applicant accepted the friendly settlement.

Comment

Although the matter was resolved by a friendly settlement, the case had raised an admissible issue regarding Article 3. Moreover, it would seem that the new guidelines published in response to the case did not, and were not intended to, introduce radical changes or improvements:

> ... The main effect of the guidelines is to clarify previously unwritten practices rather than to introduce changes. (Minister for Health, Sir George Young, 16 January 1980)

Cases pending under this article

Karamjit Chahal, Darshan Kaur Chahal, Kiranpreet Kaur Chahal and Bikaramjit Singh Chahal v *UK* (Application No. 22414/93). This case was declared admissible by the Commission in September 1994. The main applicant, Mr Chahal, faced deportation to India following a recommendation by the Home Secretary on the grounds of national security. As a Sikh militant supporting the movement for an independent Sikh homeland in India, he claimed political asylum on the ground that he would face torture and persecution if deported. In its report of 27 June, the Commission expressed the opinion that there had been a violation of Articles 3 and 8, 5, para. 1(1) and 13. This case has been referred to the Court by the Commission.

Further reading

Andrews, J., 'Detention of the Mentally Ill in the UK' (1985) 10 *European Law Review* 373

Bonner, D., 'The Beginning of the End for Corporal Punishment' (1979) 42 *Modern Law Review* 580

Drzemczewski, A., 'Human Rights. Recent Developments' (1978) 12 *The Law Teacher* 49

Gandi, S., 'Spare the Rod: Corporal Punishment in Schools and the ECHR' (1984) 33 *International and Comparative Law Quarterly* 488

MacEwan, N., 'Corporal Punishment' (1982) 27 *Journal of Law and Society* 294

Phillips, B., 'The Case for Corporal Punishment in the United Kingdom. Beaten into Submission in Europe?' 43 *International and Comparative Law Quarterly* 153

Spjut, R. J., 'Torture under the European Convention on Human Rights' (1979) 73 *American Journal of International Law* 267

Watson, R., 'Britain Strapped' (1982) *Forum* 7

Zellick, G., 'Corporal Punishment on the Isle of Man' (1978) 27 *International and Comparative Law Quarterly* 665

CHAPTER 4
ARTICLE FOUR

Article 4
1.   *No one shall be held in slavery or servitude.*
2.   *No one shall be required to perform forced or compulsory labour.*
3.   *For the purpose of this Article the term 'forced or compulsory labour' shall not include:*
     (a)   any work required to be done in the ordinary course of detention imposed according to the provisions of Article 5 of this Convention or during conditional release from such detention;
     (b)   any service of a military character or, in case of conscientious objectors in countries where they are recognised, service exacted instead of compulsory military service;
     (c)   any service exacted in case of an emergency or calamity threatening the life or well-being of the community;
     (d)   any work or service which forms part of normal civic obligations.

4.1   SCOPE OF THE ARTICLE

Applications concerning Article 4 are rare. Cases where the application has been dismissed as manifestly ill-founded include *Harper* v *UK* App. No. 11746/85 9 EHRR 235, concerning a change in the compulsory retirement age, and *X* v *UK* App. No. 3485/68 (1969) 12 *Yearbook* 288, concerning compulsory labour in prison. However, the extent and application of the article were considered in the case of *W, X, Y and Z* v *UK* (1968) 11 *Yearbook* 562). Here it was made clear that the exceptions applied only to forced or compulsory labour under Article 4, para 2. Thus there is an absolute prohibition on slavery or servitude. The complaints which have arisen, however, have all been brought under the exceptions.

4.2   THE CASES

W, X, Y and Z v UK
(1968) 11 *Yearbook* 562

The facts
The applicants were all young men who had joined the army or navy at the age of 15 or 16, with the consent of their parents. The period of their contracts was for nine years, which was calculated from the date at which they reached the age of 18, and they could not leave the services before this time except in exceptional circumstances. The complaints included alleged violations of Articles 6, 8, and 13, as well as Article 4.

The claim under Article 4 was for discharge, and therefore relief, from 'oppressive compulsory service tantamount to the status of servitude'.

The Government argued that any service of a military character was excluded from Article 4 by reason of para. 3(b), and that therefore neither the term 'forced or compulsory labour' nor the term 'slavery or servitude' could apply to the situation of the applicants. It was further submitted that the term 'servitude' connoted a condition comparable to slavery:

> . . . that is to say, it implies a deprivation of freedom and personal rights which quite patently does not exist in the case of persons serving in the armed forces of the Crown . . . (p. 576)

and that:

> . . . an essential feature of servitude is that it has been forced upon a person against his will, in circumstances where he has no genuine freedom of choice. In the United Kingdom, no one is required to enter upon military service and a person who does so chooses this course freely . . . (p. 576)

The applicants, on the other hand, interpreted the article differently, arguing that while the term 'forced or compulsory labour' might not apply to military service by reason of the exclusion of para. 3(b), this exclusion did not extend to include 'servitude or slavery', against which – it was argued – the drafters of the Convention intended an absolute prohibition.

The Commission's opinion
In seeking to clarify the interpretation of Article 4, the Commission referred to the background to the provision. The form of drafting applied in Article 4 was taken from Convention No. 29 of the International Labour Office, concerning Forced or Compulsory Labour, 1930, and drafted on the basis of earlier proposals for Article 8 of the United Nations Covenant on Civil and Political Rights. In the light of this interpretation exercise the Commission found that military service included both compulsory military service and voluntary enlistment. Therefore the exception under para. 3(b) would apply to a complaint of 'forced or compulsory labour'. However, the Commission found that 'servitude' and 'forced or compulsory labour' were distinguishable and to be treated differently, and:

... that although they must in fact often overlap, they cannot be treated as equivalent, and that the clause excluding military service expressly from the scope of the term 'forced or compulsory labour' does not forcibly exclude such service in all circumstances from an examination in the light of the prohibition directed at 'slavery or servitude'. (p. 596)

The Commission therefore proceeded to an examination of the situation. It decided that:

... generally the duty of a soldier who enlists after having attained the age of majority, to observe the terms of his engagement and the ensuing restriction of his freedom and personal rights does not amount to an impairment of rights which could come under the terms 'slavery or servitude'. (p. 596)

Although the applicants had entered the armed forces below the age of majority, it was conceded that both the age of majority and the minimum age of recruitment varied from country to country. In considering the particular situation of the applicants the Commission found that:

the young age at which the applicants entered into the services cannot in itself attribute the character of 'servitude' to the normal condition of a soldier; ...
[C]onsequently the terms of service if not amounting to a state of servitude for adult servicemen, can neither have that character for boys who enter the services with their parents' consent. (p. 598)

The Commission therefore found that there was no violation of Article 4.

Comment

The relevant legislation under which the applicants had enlisted was the Armed Forces Act 1966, which had replaced the Naval Enlistment Act 1884 and the Army Act 1955. Parental consent was required by law for anyone under the age of $17\frac{1}{2}$.

The case indicates the way in which the Commission sets about interpreting the various articles, referring to the legislative history behind an article and by comparing the terminology of similar provisions in other human right documents. The Commission may also refer to debates surrounding the drafting of an article and to any notes.

CHAPTER 5

ARTICLE FIVE

Article 5

1.   Everyone has the right to liberty and security of person. No one shall be deprived of his liberty save in the following cases and in accordance with a procedure prescribed by law:

(a)   the lawful detention of a person after conviction by a competent court;

(b)   the lawful arrest or detention of a person for non-compliance with the lawful order of a court or in order to secure the fulfilment of any obligation prescribed by law;

(c)   the lawful arrest or detention of a person effected for the purpose of bringing him before the competent legal authority on a reasonable suspicion of having committed an offence or when it is reasonably considered necessary to prevent his committing an offence or fleeing after having done so;

(d)   the detention of a minor by lawful order for the purpose of educational supervision or his lawful detention for the purpose of bringing him before the competent legal authority;

(e)   the lawful detention of persons for the prevention of the spreading of infectious diseases, of persons of unsound mind, alcoholics or drug addicts or vagrants;

(f)   the lawful arrest or detention of a person to prevent his effecting an unauthorised entry into the country or of a person against whom action is being taken with a view to deportation or extradition.

2.   Everyone who is arrested shall be informed promptly, in a language which he understands, of the reasons for his arrest and of any charge against him.

3.   Everyone arrested or detained in accordance with the provisions of paragraph 1(c) of this Article shall be brought promptly before a judge or

other officer authorized by law to exercise judicial power and shall be entitled to trial within a reasonable time or to release pending trial. Release may be conditioned by guarantee to appear for trial.

4.   Everyone who is deprived of his liberty by arrest or detention shall be entitled to take proceedings by which the lawfulness of his detention shall be decided speedily by a court and his release ordered if the detention is not lawful.

5.   Everyone who has been the victim of arrest or detention in contravention of the provisions of this Article shall have an enforceable right to compensation.

5.1 SCOPE OF THE ARTICLE

Article 5 contains a number of procedural safeguards which may be argued separately or in combination.

5.1.1 The Right to Liberty and Lawfulness of Detention

The first sentence of Article 5, para. 1 refers to 'liberty and security of person'. Whether these are two different rights was raised in the case of the *East African Asians* v *UK* 3 EHRR 76. The Commission expressed the opinion that 'liberty and security of person' had to be read as a whole and that, consequently, 'security' should be understood in the context of 'liberty' (para. 220). The two are therefore closely connected. However, the Commission held that the term 'security' was not otiose:

> . . . In the Commission's view, the protection of 'security' is in this context concerned with *arbitrary* interference, by a public authority, with an individual's personal 'liberty'. Or, in other words, any decision taken within the sphere of Article 5 must, in order to safeguard the individual's right to 'security of person', conform to the procedural as well as the substantive requirements laid down by an already existing law.
>
> This interpretation is confirmed both by the text of Article 5 and by the preparatory work of the Convention, which show that the protection against arbitrary arrest and detention was one of the principal considerations of the drafters of this treaty. ((1994) 78-A D & R, p. 5)

Under para. 1, deprivation of liberty is authorised in six separate categories of cases. Circumstances which do not fall under one of these categories are not therefore justified. Paragraphs 2–5 apply whether the deprivation of liberty falls under one of the categories enumerated in Article 5, para. 1 or not.

While it has been held that Article 5, para. 1 provides an exhaustive list of circumstances in which detention and deprivation of liberty may be justified, these categories are not mutually exclusive; and although it is essential that at any given time at least one of the sub-paragraphs should apply, it is possible that the detention of a person may be justified under more than one sub-paragraph, or that the justification may change with a change in circumstances (see, for example, *McVeigh, O'Neil and Evans* v *UK* 5 EHRR 71).

Any deprivation of liberty must follow conviction by a competent court. Thus, where a solicitor was arrested pursuant to a bench warrant for contempt of court, this was held to be 'in accordance with procedure prescribed by law' within the meaning of Article 5, para. 1, even though the Court of Appeal subsequently found that the behaviour complained of did not amount to contempt (*Weston* v *UK* 3 EHRR 402).

In this respect there must be a sufficient causal connection, rather than simply that the detention follows the conviction in point of time (*Monnell and Morris* v *UK* 10 EHRR 205). Differences in approach to sentencing procedures, and whether the sentence begins to run from the date of conviction or not until avenues of appeal have been exhausted, have been held to be differences of form rather than substance. Both may comply with Article 5, para. 1, which is silent as to the permissible forms of legal machinery whereby a person may be lawfully detained after conviction. It is legitimate that sentencing procedures may vary from one State to another and still comply with the Convention.

One consideration which has been raised under the first part of this article is the detention of mental patients. The purpose of the protection under Article 5, para. 1 is to shield a person from arbitrary detention, therefore the detention of someone believed to be of unsound mind can be effected only on the basis of objective medical expertise, and the mental disorder must be one warranting detention. However, the Commission has recognised that a wide discretion must be afforded to the national authority to order emergency confinements in circumstances where a person may present a danger to himself or herself or to others. The Commission has therefore found that the provisions of the Mental Health Act 1983 are not in breach of Article 5, affording as they do limited remedies by way of an application for *habeas corpus* and a civil action for false imprisonment under s. 139 (*James* v *UK* 18 EHRR CD 131).

Detention may also be justified if it is done with a view to deportation (Article 5, para. 1(f): see, for example, *Zamir* v *UK* 5 EHRR 242). In this respect, although the Convention does not require any judicial review of the deportation proceedings, the legality of the detention itself falls under Article 5, para. 4. Where a remedy is available which may satisfy the provisions of Article 5, para. 4, an applicant must endeavour to make use of it. The Commission cannot find a violation on the basis of a hypothetical situation (*Caprino* v *UK* 4 EHRR 97).

Whenever a person is detained he or she must, according to Article 5, para. 2, be informed of the reasons for this. The Commission has held that this applies not only to the reasons for the initial arrest – in which case it will usually be the police who must supply reasons – but also to all cases of justifiable detention, including the recall of a mental patient, or the revocation of a life licence. The purpose of this part of the article is adequately to inform any detained person of the reasons for his or her arrest so that the lawfulness thereof can be challenged, if necessary, under Article 5, para. 4. Although there is no duty to keep the detainee constantly informed of the reasons for the detention, if these reasons change or new facts arise concerning the detention then the detainee ought to be informed of these.

Review of the lawfulness of detention may be claimed under Article 5, para. 4 even if the detention is lawful under Article 5, para. 1 (*Caprino* v *UK* 4 EHRR 97). The purpose of judicial control of the lawfulness of the detention is to safeguard the liberty of the individual and to prevent arbitrary measures of detention. Therefore any procedure considered under Article 5, para. 4 must cover the substantive grounds of detention, although there need not be unlimited powers of review. The extent of the review procedures will vary according to the kind of deprivation of liberty in question. Article 5, para. 4 envisages only remedies available during the period of detention, not those which may be available after release, e.g. an action for damages for false imprisonment. According to the Court in the case of *Brogan* v *UK*:

> . . . The notion of 'lawfulness' under paragraph 4 has the same meaning as in paragraph 1; and whether an 'arrest' or 'detention' can be regarded as 'lawful' has to be determined in the light not only of domestic law, but also of the text of the Convention, the general principles embodied therein and the aim of the restrictions permitted by Article 5 § (1). (Series A, Vol. 145-B, para. 65)

In interpreting what is meant by 'a court' for the purposes of Article 5, para. 4, it is clear that this need not necessarily be a judicial body provided that it has the necessary independence and offers sufficient procedural safeguards appropriate to the category of deprivation of liberty being dealt with. Therefore the cases have indicated that while Mental Health Review Tribunals may fulfil this function (*X* v *UK* 4 EHRR 188), Parole Boards do not (*Weeks* v *UK* 7 EHRR 409); and it was doubtful whether, in the case of *Ireland* v *UK*, the Commissioner or Detention Appeal Tribunal set up under the Detention of Terrorists Order 1972, could be regarded as 'courts' within the meaning of the provision. As the Commission indicated in the *Weeks* case (referring to the case of *X* v *UK*):

> . . . The term 'court' serves to denote 'bodies which exhibit not only common fundamental features, of which the most important is independence of the executive and of the parties to the case . . . , but also the guarantees' – 'appropriate to the kind of deprivation of liberty in question' – 'of a judicial procedure', the forms of which may vary from one domain to another. . . .
> In addition, the existence of the 'court' remedy must be sufficiently certain, failing which it will lack the accessibility and effectiveness which are required by Article 5 § (4). (Series A, Vol. 114, paras 92–93)

If a breach of one of the provisions of Article 5 is established then the victim of such a violation may be able to claim a right to compensation. As Article 5 is not considered to be part of the domestic law of the UK, no claim for compensation for a breach thereof will succeed before the domestic courts unless the breach is at the same time a breach of UK law. It is likely, therefore, in the case of the UK that if a violation of Article 5 is established an order for compensation – for example under Article 50 – may be made.

5.2 THE CASES

5.2.1 Pre-trial Detention

The deprivation of liberty in the context of arrest and detention for the prevention of offences against public order or State security does not fall into one of the authorised categories. Consequently a number of cases concerning the arrest and detention of suspected terrorists or members of proscribed organisations have been brought against the UK in the context of the situation in Northern Ireland. This issue was considered extensively in the case of *Republic of Ireland* v *UK* (Decision on admissibility (1972) 15 *Yearbook* 76, Report of the Commission (1976) 19 *Yearbook* 512, Decision of the Court 18 January 1978, Series A, Vol. 25, 2 EHRR 25). Article 5 is not an entrenched right, however, and is subject to the 'right to derogation' under Article 15. This was the case in this inter-State case.

McVeigh, O'Neill and Evans v *UK*
Council of Europe Report

The facts
The applicants were arrested by the police in 1977 when they arrived in Liverpool from Ireland. They were detained under the Prevention of Terrorism (Supplemental Temporary Provisions) Order 1976. They were searched, questioned and photographed, and had their fingerprints taken, but were not charged. They were detained for a total of about 45 hours. They complained before the Commission of breaches of Articles 5 and 8.

The Commission's opinion
The points before the Commission were:

— 1. Whether the arrest and detention of the applicants was compatible with Article 5(1) of the Convention, and in particular whether it was justified under any of sub-paras (b), (c) or (f) of that provision;
— 2. Whether the applicants were informed of the reasons for their arrest as required by Article 5(2);
— 3. Whether there was any breach of Article 5(3) in so far as it guarantees a right to persons detained under Article 5(1)(c) to be brought promptly before a judge or other judicial officer;
— 4. Whether the applicants were deprived of their right, under Article 5(4), to take proceedings whereby the lawfulness of their detention could be determined;
— 5. Whether there was any breach of Article 5(5) in so far as it guarantees an enforceable right to compensation;
— 6. Whether the searching, questioning, fingerprinting and photographing of the applicants and the retention of relevant records involved an interference with their right to respect for private life guaranteed by Article 8(1) of the Convention and, if so, whether such interference was justified under Article 8(2);
— 7. Whether the fact that Mr McVeigh and Mr Evans were prevented from joining their wives was an interference with their right to respect for private

a   n   d

family life under Article 8(1) and, if so, whether such interference was justified under Article 8(2);
— 8. Whether the fact that Mr McVeigh and Mr Evans were prevented from communicating with their wives was:
— a. an interference with their right to respect for private and family life under Article 8(1) and, if so, whether such interference was justified under Article 8(2); or

— b.   an interference with their freedom of expression under Article 10(1) and, if so, whether such interference was justified under Article 10(2). (para. 152)

First, the Commission noted that its function was not to examine the domestic legislation *in abstracto*, but to confine itself to the present application. Secondly, the Commission noted that:

> . . . the measures at issue here were taken under legislation which was enacted, and has been applied, for the purpose of combating a campaign of terrorism. This legislation admittedly involves temporary and abnormal restrictions within the field of Convention rights. There is no question but that the right to personal liberty as normally applied within the United Kingdom has been to some extent circumscribed by the legislation, and by the powers of arrest and detention applied to the present applicants in particular. The terrorist campaign in Great Britain, which has led to the introduction and continuance of the legislation, has arisen out of, and is in reality merely an extension of, the emergency situation in Northern Ireland. Various derogations from the Convention have been made by the respondent Government under Article 15 of the Convention in respect of that situation. . . . Nonetheless, the Government have not sought to invoke Article 15 in respect of the situation in Great Britain. In respect of the present applications they have based their case solely on the contention that the measures taken did not breach the applicants' rights under the substantive provisions of the Convention. (para. 155)

Nevertheless the Commission had to bear the context of the case in mind:

> . . . It is well established in the case-law of the Court that the Convention must be interpreted and applied in the light of present-day conditions. . . . The existence of organised terrorism is a feature of modern life whose emergence since the Convention was drafted cannot be ignored any more than the changes in social conditions and moral opinion which have taken place in the same period. . . . It faces democratic Governments with a problem of serious organised crime with which they must cope in order to preserve the fundamental rights of their citizens. The measures they take must comply with the Convention, and the Convention organs must always be alert to the danger in this sphere adverted to by the Court, of 'undermining or even destroying democracy on the ground of defending it'. However, as both the Commission and Court observed . . . some compromise between the requirements for defending democratic society and individual rights is inherent in the system of the Convention . . . Particularly in assessing such matters as the 'necessity' for a given measure in a 'democratic society' (*cf.* para. (2) of Art. 8 etc.), specific requirements of the situation facing the society in question must be taken into account. (para. 157)

As the applicants had not been charged with any offences, the Commission decided to approach the case on the basis that they were innocent.

Considering first the provisions of Article 5, para. 1, the Commission noted that in order for an arrest and detention to be justified it must fall within one of the categories set out in Article 5, para. 1(a) to (f). These had to be narrowly interpreted, and were exhaustive although not mutually exclusive. In considering which of these sub-paragraphs might have applied to the circumstances, the Government had argued that para. 1(b) applied because the arrest and detention were to secure the fulfilment of certain obligations prescribed by law, namely to submit to further examination.

The Commission noted that:

... Although the 'obligation' must thus be 'specific and concrete', Article 5(1)(b) does not require that it should arise from a court order. The case of non-compliance with such an order is covered specifically in the first leg of this provision. However, detention is authorised only to 'secure the fulfilment' of the obligation. It follows that, at the very least, there must be an unfulfilled obligation incumbent on the person concerned and the arrest and detention must be for the purpose of securing its fulfilment and not, for instance, punitive in character. As soon as the relevant obligation has been fulfilled, the basis for detention under this leg of Article 5(1)(b) ceases to exist.

... This branch of Article 5(1)(b) is primarily intended, in the Commission's opinion, to cover the case where the law permits detention as a coercive measure to induce a person to perform a specific obligation which he has wilfully or negligently failed to perform hitherto.

... Nonetheless, the wording of Article 5(1)(b) does not expressly require that there should have been such deliberate or negligent failure on the part of the detainee. It requires only that the <u>purpose</u> of the detention should be to secure the fulfilment of the obligation. This does not expressly exclude the possibility of detention in the absence of a prior breach of legal duty. However, in the Commission's opinion, the mere combination of an unfulfilled obligation (even if 'specific and concrete'), coupled with the relevant purpose, is not enough for the purposes of Article 5(1)(b). To hold that it was would open up a clear possibility of arbitrary detention, thus ignoring the object and purpose of Article 5(1) and the importance of the right to liberty in a democratic society. (paras 172–174)

In examining the obligation involved in the relevant legislation, the Commission noted that the provisions of the 1976 Order created an overall obligation to submit to examination:

... The concept of 'examination' is not expressly defined in the legislation. However, it clearly includes questioning and searching of the examinee for the purpose of determining the matters set out in Article 5(1)(a) to (c) of the order. If the person examined is detained, it may also include measures such as fingerprinting and photography. In practice, it also includes checking of police records and other external investigations. In essence it is thus a process of investigation or a form of security check limited in scope, *inter alia*, by the purposes set out in Article 5(1) of the order. (para. 179)

However, arrest and detention were not an inherent feature of this 'examination'. Indeed, most people who were so examined were not detained. Nevertheless, the Commission accepted that arrest and detention may enable a more prolonged examination:

... The Commission finds that the purpose of the detention 'pending . . . examination' of the present applicants was essentially to secure their compliance with the overall obligation to submit to examination. It was not based on any specific failure on their part to fulfil the legal obligations incumbent on them in connection with their initial examination. The basis of the arrest was not, for instance, any refusal or failure to answer questions or produce evidence of their identity. The examining officer may have suspected that they had not answered his initial questions correctly, but he was not in a position to say with any certainty that this was the case. The purpose of their arrest was not therefore to compel them to rectify any specific prior breach of legal duty. It was to compel them to submit to the further examination which the examining officer considered necessary. (para. 181)

The Commission had to consider whether the obligation was sufficiently 'concrete and specific' to fall within the scope of Article 5, para. 1(b). In considering this, the Commission noted that the obligation to submit to examination is distinct from the obligation to submit to detention. Detention is not an inherent feature of examination. The Commission further noted that:

... The obligation to submit to examination does not amount to a general obligation to submit to questioning or interrogation on any occasion, or for any purpose. (para. 186)

Despite this, the Commission expressed the opinion that:

... In all the circumstances, the Commission consider that the obligation imposed on the present applicants to submit to examination was a specific and concrete obligation and that the United Kingdom authorities were therefore in principle entitled under Article 5(1)(b) to resort to detention to secure its fulfilment. In reaching this conclusion the Commission has particularly taken into account the fact that the obligation in question arises only in limited circumstances, namely in the context of passage over a clear geographical or political boundary. Furthermore, the purpose of the examination is limited and directed towards an end of evident public importance in the context of a serious and continuing threat from organised terrorism. (para. 188)

However:

... the mere existence of an unfulfilled obligation (albeit 'specific and concrete') is not of itself enough to justify arrest or detention under Article 5(1)(b). There must be specific circumstances which warrant the use of detention as a means of securing the fulfilment of the obligation. The Commission must therefore still consider whether such circumstances were present in this case.

The Commission has already observed that the applicants' detention was not based on any prior voluntary failure to fulfil obligations incumbent on them such as a refusal to cooperate in the initial examination. It reiterates that, in the absence of such circumstances, detention cannot normally be justified under Article 5(1)(b). In general only a person's refusal or neglect to comply with an obligation can justify his detention in order to secure its fulfilment. However, as the Commission has indicated above, the possibility that there may be other circumstances justifying detention under this provision is not excluded by the wording of Article 5(1)(b) and in its view there may be other limited circumstances of a pressing nature which could justify such detention.

... In considering whether such circumstances exist, account must be taken, in the Commission's opinion, of the nature of the obligation. It is necessary to consider whether its fulfilment is a matter of immediate necessity and whether the circumstances are such that no other means of securing fulfilment is reasonably practicable. A balance must be drawn between the importance in a democratic society of securing the immediate fulfilment of the obligation in question, and the importance of the right to liberty. The duration of the period of detention is also a relevant factor in drawing such a balance. (paras 189–191)

Taking into account that the scope of the security checks was essentially directed at combatting terrorism, and that for the greater part they were administered without resorting to detention, the Commission expressed the opinion that the detention was not improper or arbitrary:

> ... In the exceptional context of the case, it concludes that there were thus sufficient circumstances to warrant their arrest and detention for some 45 hours for the purpose of securing fulfilment of the obligation incumbent on them to submit to examination.
> ... It is not in dispute that the arrest and detention were in accordance with domestic law and the Commission finds nothing to suggest that it was both 'in accordance with a procedure prescribed by law' and 'lawful' as these concepts in Article 5(1) have been interpreted by the Court. It concludes that their arrest and detention were justified under Article 5(1)(b) in order to secure the fulfilment of an obligation prescribed by law. (paras 195–196)

In considering whether the arrest and detention were also justified under Article 5, para. 1(c), the Commission considered that the circumstances did not establish that there was any sufficiently precise suspicion or belief to satisfy the requirements of this sub-paragraph. Nor was there enough evidence of any sufficiently firm intention to bring the applicants before a 'competent legal authority'. Similarly, there was insufficient evidence to justify the detention under Article 5, para. 1(f), because there was no sufficiently firm intention to use the powers against the applicants with a view to deporting them. It had not been shown that the arrest and detention were to prevent the applicants from making an unauthorised entry.

Because the detention was justified under sub-paragraph (b), no violation of Article 5, para. 1 was established.

The applicants also complained under Article 5, para. 2, that they had not been given sufficient reasons for their arrests. There was no dispute as to the promptness of the reasons given, simply their sufficiency. The Commission noted that:

> ... There is no dispute in the present case that the applicants were sufficiently informed of the legal basis for their detention. The sole question is whether they should have been informed of the grounds for suspicion against them. The Commission has already observed in its decision on admissibility that such information does not appear relevant to the lawfulness of their detention in domestic law, since the existence of 'suspicion' is not a prerequisite for a lawful arrest under the 1976 order. Equally the existence of 'suspicion' is not a substantive requirement of Article 5(1)(b) of the Convention. Only Article 5(1)(c) requires it and, in the Commission's opinion, the applicants detention was not covered by that provision.
> ... In the present case the applicants were informed of the nature of the obligation incumbent on them. In the written notifications served on them they were expressly required to submit to 'further examination'. Furthermore, as a matter of substance, the Commission considers that the information given them was quite sufficient in the circumstances to make it clear that this consisted of a form of security check to establish whether they were involved in terrorism.
> ... The applicants were, in the Commission's opinion, thus sufficiently informed of the legal basis for the detention in domestic law and of the substantive reasons for their detention under Article 5(1)(b) of the Convention. They were given the essential facts relevant to the lawfulness of their detention under both domestic law and the Convention. That is sufficient for the purposes of Article 5(2). (paras 209–211)

There had not, therefore, been a breach of Article 5, para. 2.

As regards the lawfulness of their detention, and a possible breach of Article 5, para. 4, the Commission noted that the remedy of *habeas corpus* was available to the applicants. The Commission could find no reason to suppose that this remedy would have been insufficient in the present case, because the courts could have examined whether the applicants had been lawfully required to submit to examination. There had, therefore, been no breach of Article 5, para. 4. No right to compensation under Article 5, para. 5 arose because the applicants had not been the victims of any violation of other provisions of the article.

Mr Trechsel gave a dissenting opinion based on the view that Article 5, para. 1(b) should not be extensively interpreted to justify arrest and detention in other circumstances of a pressing nature not included in the sub-paragraphs. He did not believe that the obligation to submit to questioning and searching warranted detention of more than a few hours:

> . . . It appears thus that the deprivation of liberty imposed upon them in fact amounted to what is sometimes referred to as a 'fishing expedition': measures of coercion which are normally admissible only on condition that there exists reasonable suspicion against the person concerned are applied not in order to ascertain whether such suspicion is well-founded, but in order to find out whether there are any grounds for suspicion at all.
>
> However, this is a procedure which the Convention clearly wanted to outlaw, as the reference to 'reasonable suspicion'/'raisons plausibles de soupçonner' indicates. The condition thus set ought not to be frustrated by what I consider to be an excessively broad construction of Article 5(1)(b).
>
> I therefore conclude that, in the present case, there has been a violation of Article 5(1) of the Convention (p. 71).

Comment
The 1976 legislation was initially enacted for 12 months, and then renewed periodically. Under s. 12 of the Act, a constable could arrest without warrant a person he reasonably suspected of being guilty of an offence under the Act. Such an arrested person could be held for 48 hours and then for an extended period of up to five days if so authorised by the Secretary of State. Under s. 13 of the Act, the Secretary of State was empowered to make provision for the examination, arrest and detention of persons arriving at or leaving Great Britain or Northern Ireland. These powers of arrest and detention were operated in conjunction with other means of control at the ports.

At the relevant time there was no statutory provision governing the rights of a detained person to contact his or her family, friends or solicitor. Provision for this was made in the Judges' Rules and Administrative Directions to the Police, none of which had the force of law.

The legal situation changed following the events giving rise to this case. Under s. 62 of the Criminal Law Act 1977 – which came into force in 1978 – an arrested person had the right to have one person, named by him, informed of his arrest and where he was being detained.

A similar case, involving the arrest and detention of the applicant under the Prevention of Terrorism (Temporary Provisions) Act 1984, arose in *Lyttle* v *UK*

9 EHRR 350. This case was distinguishable from the *McVeigh* case, inasmuch as the applicant was not detained coming into Great Britain but as he was preparing to leave it. Even so, the Commission expressed the opinion that the legislation provided for the possibility of security checks both on entering and leaving the mainland.

Fox, Campbell and Hartley v *UK*
Series A, Vol. 182

The facts

The applicants were detained in Northern Ireland for periods ranging between 30 and 44 hours under s. 1 of the Northern Ireland (Emergency Provisions) Act 1978. They were not charged with any offences, neither were they brought before a judge or given any opportunity to apply for release or bail. Both Fox and Campbell initiated proceedings for *habeas corpus* but were released before the judge heard the applications.

Before the Commission, all three applicants claimed that their arrest and detention were not justified under Article 5, para. 1, and that there had been breaches of Article 5, paras 2, 4 and 5.

The Commission's opinion

The Commission, in considering the claim under Article 5, para. 1, held that the facts did not disclose that the arrests had been based on reasonable suspicion, although the Commission did not agree with the applicants that the arrests had not been with the purpose of bringing them before a competent legal authority.

The Commission also found that the applicants had not been sufficiently informed of the reasons for their arrests, in breach of Article 5, para. 2.

As regards Article 5, para. 4, the Commission expressed the opinion that the safeguards contained in this part of the article were not applicable where, as in the applicants' case, they had been released before a determination of the lawfulness of their detention could take place. However, one member of the Commission dissented on this point, expressing the view that this part of the article should be equally applicable whether the detention was for a short or long period. As neither the available remedy of *habeas corpus* nor a claim for damages for false imprisonment could examine whether the detention was based on reasonable suspicion, Article 5, para. 4 was not complied with.

The judgment of the Court

While the applicants did not contest that their arrest was lawful, they claimed that they had not be arrested on reasonable suspicion of having committed an offence. They alleged that the reason for their arrest was not to bring them before a competent authority but to gather information.

The Court held that:

> ... Article 5, para 1(c) speaks of a 'reasonable suspicion' rather than a genuine and *bona fide* suspicion. The Court's task, however, is not to review the impugned legislation *in abstracto* but to examine its application in these particular cases.

. . . The 'reasonableness' of the suspicion on which an arrest must be based forms an essential part of the safeguard against arbitrary arrest and detention which is laid down in Article 5, para. 1(c). The Court agrees with the Commission and the Government that having a 'reasonable suspicion' presupposes the existence of facts or information which would satisfy an objective observer that the person concerned may have committed the offence. What may be regarded as 'reasonable' will however depend upon all the circumstances.

In this respect, terrorist crime falls into a special category. Because of the attendant risk of loss of life and human suffering, the police are obliged to act with utmost urgency in following up all information, including information from secret sources. Further, the police may frequently have to arrest a suspected terrorist on the basis of information which is reliable but which cannot, without putting in jeopardy the source of the information, be revealed to the suspect or produced in court to support a change.

As the Government pointed out, in view of the difficulties inherent in the investigation and prosecution of terrorist-type offences in Northern Ireland, the 'reasonableness' of the suspicion justifying such arrests cannot always be judged according to the same standards as are applied in dealing with conventional crime. Nevertheless, the exigencies of dealing with terrorist crime cannot justify stretching the notion of 'reasonableness' to the point where the essence of the safeguard secured by Article 5, para 1(c) is impaired . . . (paras 31–32)

In considering whether the suspicions of the Government were reasonable the Court indicated that:

. . . Certainly Article 5(1)(c) of the Convention should not be applied in such a manner as to put disproportionate difficulties in the way of the police authorities of the Contracting States in taking effective measures to counter organised terrorism. It follows that the Contracting States cannot be asked to establish the reasonableness of the suspicion grounding the arrest of a suspected terrorist by disclosing the confidential sources of supporting information or even facts which would be susceptible of indicating such sources or their identity.

Nevertheless the Court must be enabled to ascertain whether the essence of the safeguard afforded by Article 5(1)(c) has been secured. Consequently the respondent Government has to furnish at least some facts or information capable of satisfying the Court that the arrested person was reasonably suspected of having committed the alleged offence. This is all the more necessary where, as in the present case, the domestic law does not require reasonable suspicion, but sets a lower threshold by merely requiring honest suspicion.

. . . The Court accepts that the arrest and detention of each of the present applicants was based on a *bona fide* suspicion that he or she was a terrorist, and that each of them, including Mr Hartley, was questioned during his or her detention about specific terrorist acts of which he or she was suspected. (paras 34–35).

However, the fact that two of the applicants had previous convictions for acts of terrorism was not sufficient to justify their arrest seven years later. As the Government had not provided any further material to indicate what the genuine suspicion was based on, the Court held that its explanations had not met the minimum standard set by Article 5, para. 1(c) for judging the reasonableness of a suspicion for the arrest of an individual. There had therefore been a violation of Article 5, para. 1.

As regards Article 5, para. 2, the Court held that:

. . . Paragraph (2) of Article 5 contains the elementary safeguard that any person arrested should know why he is being deprived of his liberty. This provision is an integral part of the scheme of protection afforded by Article 5: by virtue of paragraph (2) any person arrested must be told, in simple, non technical language that he can understand, the essential legal and factual grounds for his arrest, so as to be able, if he sees fit, to apply to a court to challenge its lawfulness in accordance with paragraph (4). Whilst this information must be conveyed 'promptly' (in French: '*dans le plus court délai*'), it need not be related in its entirety by the arresting officer at the very moment of the arrest. Whether the content and promptness of the information conveyed were sufficient is to be assessed in each case according to its special features.

. . . On being taken into custody, Mr Fox, Ms Campbell and Mr Hartley were simply told by the arresting officer that they were being arrested under section 11(1) of the 1978 Act on suspicion of being terrorists. This bare indication of the legal basis for the arrest, taken on its own, is insufficient for the purposes of Article 5(2), as the Government conceded.

However, following their arrest all of the applicants were interrogated by the police about their suspected involvement in specific criminal acts and their suspected membership of proscribed organisations. There is no ground to suppose that these interrogations were not such as to enable the applicants to understand why they had been arrested. The reasons why they were suspected of being terrorists were thereby brought to their attention during their interrogation.

. . . Mr Fox and Ms Campbell were arrested at 3.40 p.m. on 5 February 1986 at Woodbourne RUC station and then separately questioned the same day between 8.15 p.m. and 10.00 p.m. at Castlereagh Police Office. Mr Hartley, for his part, was arrested at his home at 7.55 a.m. on 18 August 1986 and taken to Antrim Police Station where he was questioned between 11.05 a.m. and 12.15 p.m. In the context of the present case these intervals of a few hours cannot be regarded as falling outside the constraints of time imposed by the notion of promptness in Article 5(2).

. . . In conclusion there was therefore no breach of Article 5(2) in relation to any of the applicants. (paras 40–43)

In considering whether the applicants had been able to challenge the lawfulness of their detention, the Court noted that two of the three applicants had in fact instituted *habeas corpus* proceedings, and as they were released before these could be heard, the Court could not decide *in abstracto* whether the scope of the remedies available was sufficient or not.

Because there had been a breach of Article 5, para. 1 which could not give rise to an enforceable claim in Northern Ireland, either before or after the finding by the Court, there had been a violation of Article 5, para. 5.

Three judges expressed a dissenting opinion that there had been no violation of Article 5, para. 1(c), because the arrests had been made based on a *bona fide* suspicion. They expressed the view that:

. . . In cases such as these it is not possible to draw a sharp distinction between genuine suspicion and reasonable suspicion. Having regard to all the circumstances and to the facts and information before the Court, including in the case of Mr Fox and Ms Campbell the fact that they had previously been involved in and convicted of terrorist activities, we are satisfied that there were reasonable grounds for suspicion justifying the arrest and detention of the appliants in accordance with Article 5, para. 1(c). We also see no reason to doubt that the applicants were detained and questioned with a view to criminal proceedings if sufficient and usable evidence had been obtained. It is true that they were released without any charges being brought against them, but this in no way invalidates the measures taken since it is the purpose of such investigation to find out whether suspicion is confirmed and supported by any additional evidence. For these reasons we conclude that there was no breach of Article 5, para. 1(c).

Comment

The 1978 Act allowed for the arrest without warrant of any person suspected of being a terrorist. The Act made provision for detention up to 72 hours. The legislation was subject to periodic renewal by Parliament, and the powers under the 1978 Act were renewable every six months until they were repealed in 1987. The origins of the power of arrest without warrant appear to have come from the 1922 Special Powers Act (Northern Ireland), Regulation 10. The fact that such arrest could be used for interrogation does not appear in the Act but was inferred; the original power was for the preservation of peace and maintenance of order. In a report published in 1984, Sir George Baker indicated that although the UK could issue a notice of derogation concerning Article 5, this was undesirable if the UK could take action to avoid relying on such derogation. He recommended that new wording should be introduced which required reasonable suspicion for arresting without a warrant. This recommendation was given effect in 1987 when s. 11(1) of the 1978 Act was replaced by s. 6 of the Northern Ireland (Emergency Provisions) Act. This was subsequent to the facts of this case.

Murray v *UK*
Council of Europe Report of the Commission. Series A, Vol. 300-A,
Judgment of the Court

The facts

The first applicant, Mrs Murray, was arrested in her home and detained under the Northern Ireland (Emergency Provisions) Act 1978, on suspicion of being involved in the collection of money for purchasing arms for the IRA. She was subsequently released without charge. During the period she was detained – approximately two hours – she refused to answer questions. She subsequently brought an action against the Ministry of Defence for false imprisonment and other torts. Her claim was unsuccessful both before the court of first instance and before the Court of Appeal. She was given leave to appeal to the House of Lords, but was again unsuccessful.

Before the Commission she complained that her arrest and detention for questioning had violated Article 5, paras 1 and 2, for which she had no enforceable right to compensation as guaranteed by Article 5, para. 5. The other applicants, who were members of the same family living in the house, alleged violations of Article 5, paras 1, 2 and 5 as a result of being required to assemble for half an hour in one room of the house. Mrs Murray also complained that the taking and keeping of a photograph of her and personal details about her, had been in breach of her rights under Article 8. Along with the other applicants she complained that the entry into and search by the Army of their home were contrary to Article 8.

The Commission's opinion

There was no dispute that the arrest and detention were 'lawful'. The applicant complained, however, that her arrest and detention under s. 14 of the Northern Ireland (Emergency Provisions) Act 1978, were in breach of Article 5, para. 1, particularly subpara. (c).

> ... The applicant's first contention was that she was not arrested for the purpose of bringing her before a competent legal authority, but merely for the purpose of interrogating her. Her second contention concerned the absence of any standard of reasonable suspicion in the legislation which authorised her detention. Whilst the arresting officer may have subjectively and honestly suspected the first applicant of having committed an offence, that suspicion has not been shown to have been objective or reasonable, given that section 14 of the 1978 Act did not require the arresting officer to hold a reasonable degree of suspicion. The absence of the requirement of reasonableness was, in her submission, given the Court's judgment in the *Fox, Campbell and Hartley* case in breach of Article 5(1) of the Convention. The Government contended, *inter alia*, that, although the legislation did not require reasonable suspicion on arrest, in the present case the arresting officer had held reasonable suspicion that the applicant had committed the criminal offence of fund raising for the IRA, connected with her brothers' criminal conviction in the United States of America. They submitted that there existed specific and strong grounds, founded on information received from a reliable source, for the army's suspicions against her. However, the sensitivity of the material underlying the suspicion was such that the Government were unable to disclose it publicly. (para. 60)

Referring to the Court's judgment in the case of *Fox, Campbell and Hartley* above, the Commission noted that:

> ... the test for lawful arrest, under comparable provisions of the 1978 Act concerning police powers of arrest, was a subjective one of honest suspicion on the part of the arresting officer, whereas Article 5(1)(c) of the Convention requires an objective test of reasonable suspicion. This presupposes the existence of facts or information which would satisfy an objective observer that the person concerned may have committed an offence. What may be regarded as reasonable will however depend on the circumstances of a particular case. Whilst terrorist crime presents special problems and the competent authority may arrest someone on the basis of reliable sources which must remain confidential for their protection and future efficacy, nevertheless the exigencies of dealing with terrorist crime cannot justify stretching the notion of 'reasonableness' to the point where the essence of the Article 5(1)(c) safeguard is impaired. Although the Contracting State cannot be asked to reveal its confidential sources of information, the Commission and the Court cannot be satisfied that the requirements of Article (5)(1) have been fulfilled unless the Contracting State has furnished at least some specific facts of information capable of showing the Convention organs that there was reasonable suspicion against the person concerned. (para. 61)

The Commission could find no significant distinction between this present case and that of *Fox, Campbell and Hartley*. The Government had provided no objective evidence to support the suspicion that the applicant was involved in the offence of collecting money to purchase arms for the IRA.

> ... Moreover, the Commission emphasises that the legislation itself, section 14 of the 1978 Act, did not require the arresting army officer to hold a reasonable suspicion,

and that it has since been amended to include the reasonableness standard. In these circumstances, the Commission is of the opinion that the elements provided by the Government are insufficient to support the conclusion that there was 'reasonable suspicion' against the present applicant in accordance with the minimum standard set by Article 5 para. 1(c) of the Convention. In the light of this opinion the Commission does not consider it necessary to go into the first applicant's other complaint under Article 5(1)(c) of the Convention concerning the purpose of her arrest. (para. 63)

There had, therefore, been a violation of Article 5, para. 1.

As regards the issues raised under Article 5, para. 2 and the question whether the applicant had been informed sufficiently promptly of the reasons for her arrest, the Commission noted that she had been informed by the arresting army officer that she was being arrested under s. 14. However, the Commission noted that:

> . . . the Court held in its *Fox, Campbell and Hartley* judgment that a mere reference to a comparable section of the 1978 Act on arrest was insufficient information for the purposes of Article 5(2) of the Convention, but that during interrogation there was no reason to suppose that the applicants in that case were unable to deduce from the questions put to them why they had been arrested. On the same basis, the Commission finds that a mere reference to section 14 of the 1978 Act on arrest was insufficient in the present case.
>
> . . . The question remains whether the first applicant was able to understand from her inverview why she had been arrested. On this point the arresting officer has indicated in the domestic proceedings that the first applicant had been asked questions about money and America. On the basis of this very vague indication, it is impossible, however, to draw any conclusions as to whether the requirements of Article 5(2) were satisfied. (paras 67 and 68)
>
> . . . In the Commission's opinion, the information provided shows that questions were asked which were related to the suspicions against the applicant. However, it has not been shown that these questions were sufficiently precise to constitute information about the reasons for the applicant's arrest as required by Article 5(2) of the Convention. (para. 70)

As the Commission had found that there were breaches of both Articles 5, para. 1 and Article 5, para. 2, and that these violations could not give rise to a right to compensation before the Northern Irish courts, Article 5, para. 5 had also been violated.

Dissenting opinions were given by Mr Schermers and by Sir Basil Hall. The latter dissented on the grounds that the question for the Commission was not whether the arresting officer – an army corporal – had reasonable suspicions on which to base the arrest, but whether the military authorities had such suspicions. He also expressed the opinion that the applicant had been sufficiently informed of the grounds for her arrest.

The judgment of the Court

The Court differed in its conclusions from the Commission. The Commission had suggested that an objective standard was required regarding the grounds of suspicion on which to base an arrest. The Court held that:

> . . . Mrs Murray was arrested and detained by virtue of section 14 of the 1978 Act. This provision, as construed by the domestic courts, empowered the Army to arrest

and detain persons suspected of the commission of an offence provided, *inter alia*, that the suspicion of the arresting officer was honestly and genuinely held. It is relevant but not decisive that the domestic legislation at the time merely imposed this essentially subjective standard: the Court's task is to determine whether the objective standard of 'reasonable suspicion' laid down in Article 5 § 1 was met in the circumstances of the application of the legislation in the particular case. (para. 50)

In considering what was reasonable the Court took into account the special nature of terrorist crime, the threat it poses to democratic society and the exigencies of dealing with it, in interpreting and applying the relevant provisions of the Convention.

The Court noted that Article 5, para. 1(c) does not presuppose that:

. . . '. . . [investigating authorities] should have obtained sufficient evidence to bring charges, either at the point of arrest or while [the arrested person is] in custody. Such evidence may have been unobtainable or, in view of the nature of the suspected offences, impossible to produce in court without endangering the lives of others'. The object of questioning during detention under sub-paragraph (c) of Article 5(1) is to further the criminal investigation by way of confirming or dispelling the concrete suspicion grounding the arrest. Thus, facts which raise a suspicion need not be of the same level as those necessary to justify a conviction or even the bringing of a charge, which comes at the next stage of the process of criminal investigation.
    . . . The length of the deprivation of liberty at risk may also be material to the level of suspicion required. . . . (paras 55 and 56)

In Mrs Murray's case the length of detention was limited by statute to a maximum of four hours.

The Court recognised that:

. . . the use of confidential information is essential in combating terrorist violence and the threat that organised terrorism poses to the lives of citizens and to democratic society as a whole. This does not mean, however, that the investigating authorities have *carte blanche* under Article 5 to arrest suspects for questioning, free from effective control by the domestic courts or by the Convention supervisory institutions, whenever they choose to assert that terrorism is involved.
    . . . As to the present case, the terrorist campaign in Northern Ireland, the carnage it has caused over the years and the active engagement of the Provisional IRA in that campaign are established beyond doubt. The Court also accepts that the power of arrest granted to the Army by section 14 of the 1978 Act represented a bona fide attempt by a democratically elected parliament to deal with terrorist crime under the rule of law. That finding is not altered by the fact that the terms of the applicable legislation were amended in 1987 as a result of the Baker Report so as to include a requirement that the arrest should be based on reasonable, rather than merely honest, suspicion.
    The Court is accordingly prepared to attach some credence to the respondent Government's declaration concerning the existence of reliable but confidential information grounding the suspicion against Mrs Murray. (paras 58–59)

In considering the point made by the Commission that the Government had not furnished sufficient evidence to establish that Mrs Murray was reasonably suspected of having committed an offence, the Court noted that in this case – unlike the situation in the case of *Fox, Campbell and Hartley* – the national courts had conducted a full review of the facts. Because of this, it could not be excluded that:

> . . . all or some of the evidence adduced before the national courts in relation to the genuineness of the suspicion on the basis of which Mrs Murray was arrested may also be material to the issue whether the suspicion was 'reasonable' for the purposes of Article 5 § 1(c) of the Convention. At the very least the honesty and bona fides of a suspicion constitute one indispensable element of its reasonableness.
>
> In the action brought by Mrs Murray against the Ministry of Defence for false imprisonment and other torts, the High Court judge, after having heard the witnesses and assessed their credibility, found that she had genuinely been suspected of having been involved in the collection of funds for the purchase of arms in the United States for the Provisional IRA. The judge believed the evidence of the arresting officer, Corporal D, who was described as a 'transparently honest witness', as to what she had been told at her briefing before the arrest. Likewise as found by the judge, although the interview at the Army centre was later in time than the arrest, the line of questioning pursued by the interviewer also tends to support the conclusion that Mrs Murray herself was suspected of the commission of a specific criminal offence.
>
> . . . Some weeks before her arrest two of Mrs Murray's brothers had been convicted in the United States of offences connected with purchase of arms for the Provisional IRA. As she disclosed in her evidence to the High Court, she had visited the United States and had contacts with her brothers there. The offences of which her brothers were convicted were onces that implied collaboration with 'trustworthy' persons residing in Northern Ireland.
>
> . . . Having regard to the level of factual justification required at the stage of suspicion and to the special exigencies of inivestigating terrorist crime, the Court finds, in the light of all the above considerations, that there did exist sufficient facts or information which would provide a plausible and objective basis for a suspicion that Mrs Murray may have committed the offence of involvement in the collection of funds for the Provisional IRA. On the particular facts of the present case, therefore, the Court is satisfied that, notwithstanding the lower standard of suspicion under domestic law, Mrs Murray can be said to have been arrested and detained on 'reasonable suspicion' of the commission of a criminal offence, within the meaning of sub-paragraph (c) of Article 5 § 1. (paras 61–63)

The applicant complained that her arrest had not been for the purpose of bringing her before a 'competent legal authority'. The Commission had not felt the need to consider this point as it had already found that the arrest was not based on reasonable suspicion. The Court, however, had to do so.

> . . . The Court's task is to determine whether the conditions laid down by paragraph (c) of Article 5(1), including the pursuit of the prescribed legitimate purpose, have been fulfilled in the circumstances of the particular case. However, in this context it is not normally within the province of the Court to substitute its own finding of fact for that of the domestic courts, which are better placed to assess the evidence adduced before them. In the present case no cogent elements have been produced by the first applicant in the proceedings before the Convention institutions which could lead the Court to depart from the findings of fact made by the Northern Ireland courts.
>
> . . . Mrs Murray was neither charged nor brought before a court but was released after an interview lasting a little longer than one hour. This does not necessarily mean, however, that the purpose of her arrest and detention was not in accordance with Article 5 § 1(c) since 'the existence of such a purpose must be considered

independently of its achievement'. As the domestic courts pointed out, in view of her persistent refusal to answer any questions at the Army centre it is not surprising that the authorities were not able to make any headway in pursuing the suspicions against her. It can be assumed that, had these suspicions been confirmed, charges would have been laid and she would have been brought before the competent legal authority. (paras 66 and 67)

The Court was satisfied that the arrest and detention had been effected for purposes within the scope of Article 5, para. 1(c). There had therefore been no violation of Article 5, para. 1.

In considering whether Mrs Murray had been informed sufficiently promptly of the reasons for her arrest, the Court noted that:

> ... The first applicant maintained that at no time during her arrest or detention had she been given any or sufficient information as to the grounds of her arrest. Although she had realised that the Army was interested in her brothers' activities, she had not, she claimed, understood from the interview at the Army centre that she herself was suspected of involvement in fund-raising for the Provisional IRA. The only direct information she was given was the formal formula of arrest pronounced by Corporal D. (para. 73)

Unlike the Commission, the Court held that:

> ... it must have been apparent to Mrs Murray that she was being questioned about her possible involvement in the collection of funds for the purchase of arms for the Provisional IRA by her brothers in the United States. Admittedly, 'there was never any probing examination of her collecting money'—to use the words of the trial judge—but, as the national courts noted, this was because of Mrs Murray's declining to answer any questions at all beyond giving her name. The Court therefore finds that the reasons for her arrest were sufficiently brought to her attention during her interview.
> ... Mrs Murray was arrested at her home at 7.00 a.m. and interviewed at the Army centre between 8.20 a.m and 9.35 a.m. on the same day. In the context of the present case this interval cannot be regarded as falling outside the constraints of time imposed by the notion of promptness in Article 5(2). (paras 77 and 78)

There had, consequently, been no breach of Article 5, para. 2, and as a result no violation of Article 5, para. 5.

Three judges expressed a joint dissenting opinion. They were not convinced of the reasonableness of the suspicion that Mrs Murray had committed the relevant offence, and were not persuaded that this case differed substantially from that of *Fox, Campbell and Hartley*. Further, they were not prepared to allow the review undertaken by the national courts to displace or influence the task of the European Court – in compliance with its duties under Article 19 of the Convention – to ensure the observance of the articles of the Convention.

Comment

As indicated in the report of the Commission, since the circumstances giving rise to the case, s. 14 of the 1978 Act had been amended to include a reasonableness standard. This amendment, which was introduced in June 1987, had occurred as a result of recommendations made in the Baker Report, which had been commissioned by the Government to review the operation of the 1978 Act and to consider whether the right balance was struck between the liberties of the individual and the powers needed by the security forces to combat terrorism.

Brogan and Others v *UK*
Series A, Vol. 145-B

The facts
The applicants were arrested and detained under s. 12 of the Prevention of Terrorism (Temporary Provisions) Act 1984. Brogan was detained for five days and 11 hours, Coyle for six days and $16\frac{1}{2}$ hours, McFadden for four days and six hours, and Tracey for four days and 11 hours.

> . . . All of the applicants were informed by the arresting officer that they were being arrested under section 12 of the 1984 Act and that there were reasonable grounds for suspecting them to have been involved in the commission, preparation or instigation of acts of terrorism connected with the affairs of Northern Ireland. They were cautioned that they need not say anything, but that anything they did say might be used in evidence.
> . . . On the day following his arrest, each applicant was informed by police officers that the Secretary of State for Northern Ireland had agreed to extend his detention by a further five days under section 12(4) of the 1984 Act. None of the applicants was brought before a judge or other officer authorised by law to exercise judicial power, nor were any of them charged after their release. (paras 23 and 24)

The applicants complained before the Commission that there had been breaches of Article 5, paras 1, 2, 3, 4 and 5. The claim concerning Article 5, para. 2 was subsequently withdrawn.

Although the UK could have derogated from the provisions of Article 5, it had in fact withdrawn its notice of derogation on 22 August 1984, prior to the facts of the case occurring.

The Commission's opinion
While the violations alleged had to be considered without any reference to derogation, the Commission recognised that it must not lose sight of the general context of the concrete case before it.

> . . .It is against the background of a continuing terrorist threat in Northern Ireland and the particular problems confronting the security forces in bringing these responsible for terrorist acts to justice that the issues in the present case must be examined. In such a situation the Convention organs must remain vigilant that a proper balance is struck between the protection of individual rights and the need to defend democratic society against the threats posed by organised terrorism. In the Commission's opinion it is inherent in the whole of the Convention that a fair balance has to be struck between the general interest of the community and the interests of the individual. (para. 80)

As no charges had been brought against the applicants the Commission also indicated that it would proceed on the basis that they were innocent of any involvement with terrorism.

In considering the claim under Article 5, para. 1, the Commission noted that:

. . . Article 5(1)(c) contains important safeguards against arbitrary deprivation of liberty. In particular,
— the arrest and detention must be 'in accordance with a procedure prescribed by law' and 'lawful'
— there must exist a reasonable suspicion of having committed an offence
— the arrest and detention must be effected for the purpose of bringing the suspect before the competent legal authority. (para. 85)

The Commission noted that the 1984 Act required:

. . . a reasonable suspicion that a person is or has been concerned in the commission, preparation or instigation of acts of terrorism. Although this suspicion does not necessarily have to relate to a specific criminal offence but may be of a more general character, the Commission considers that it is sufficient to satisfy the requirements of Article 5(1)(c). On this point, the Commission recalls that, in the case of *Ireland* v *United Kingdom*, the European Court of Human Rights observed that the criteria of 'commission or attempted commission of any act of terrorism,' on which to ground an arrest, 'were well in keeping with the idea of an offence' under Article 5 § 1(c). (para. 89)

As to whether there was a sufficient intention to bring the applicants before a competent authority, the Commission noted that:

. . . the reasonable suspicion referred to in Article 5 § 1(c) does not mean that the suspected person's guilt can at that stage be established and proven. In earlier cases, the Commission has pointed out that it could not be a condition for arrest and detention pending trial that the commission of the offence with which the applicant is charged has been established. It is the purpose of the investigation to find the evidence required, and detention is a measure which facilitates the proper conduct of the investigation.
. . . It follows that, after a person has been arrested, it will normally depend on the result of further investigation and questioning whether he will eventually be charged and brought to trial before a court.
. . . It is true that, unless the arrested person is released promptly, he will have to be brought before a judge or other officer authorised to exercise judicial power, whose task it is to decide whether continued detention is justified. However, when the suspicion is not confirmed during the interrogation which often takes place immediately after the arrest, the arrested person will normally be released, and in such cases he will not be brought before a court for the purpose of considering the detention issue.
. . . Consequently, insofar as Article 5 § 1(c) requires that the arrest of detention shall be for the purpose of bringing the arrested or detained person before the competent legal authority, the purpose is mostly a conditional one. Its realisation will depend on whether the existing suspicion is subsequently confirmed during the interrogation of the arrested or detained person or by the investigation in general.
. . . As stated above, the Commission accepts that the applicants were arrested on reasonable suspicion of involvement in specific terrorist acts. If these suspicions had been confirmed during their interrogation after their arrest or by other evidence, the Commission has no doubt that they would have been charged with criminal offences and brought before a court. It follows that the applicants were arrested for the purpose of bringing them before the competent legal authority within the meaning of Article 5 § 1(c) of the Convention.
. . . The Commission concludes, by an unanimous vote, that there has been no breach of Article 5 § 1 of the Convention. (paras 93–98)

As regards the alleged violations of Article 5, para. 3, the Commission noted that established case law suggested that a period of four days had been held to satisfy the requirement of promptness required by this part of Article 5. The Commission therefore assessed the periods in the present case against this background. The Commission was aware, however, that:

> ... it must strike a fair balance between the interests of the individual and the general interest of the community. In so doing, the Commission takes into account that the struggle against terrorism may require a particular measure of sacrifice by each citizen in order to protect the community as a whole against such crimes. Moreover, the Commission also bears in mind the context in which the applicants were arrested and the reality of problems presented by the arrest and detention of suspected terrorists which have been alluded to by the government and which may not be present in ordinary criminal cases.
>
> ... Taking all these elements into account, the Commission has reached the conclusion that the periods of five days 11 hours (Brogan) and six days 16½ hours (Coyle) do not satisfy the requirement of promptness, whereas the period of four days 6 hours (McFadden) and four days 11 hours (Tracey) are compatible with that requirement.
>
> ... The Commission concludes, by ten votes to two that there has been a breach of Article 5(3) of the Convention in the cases of the applicants Brogan and Coyle and, by eight votes to four that there has been no breach of Article 5 § 3 in the cases of the applicants McFadden and Tracey. (paras 106–108)

With respect to Article 5, para. 4, the Commission noted that:

> ... Article 5 § 4 requires that judicial control covers not only the formal legality of the detention in domestic law but also the substantive justification for the detention under Article 5.
>
> ... In the present case it is clear that it was open to the applicants to seek the remedy of habeas corpus or to institute proceedings for false imprisonment. Neither of these remedies is precluded by the effect of paragraph 5 § 2 of Schedule 3 of the 1984 Act. Moreover, it is clear that the courts in Northern Ireland can examine procedural and substantive questions relating to the lawfulness of arrest and detention, in particular, the 'reasonableness' of the suspicion of involvement in terrorist acts.
>
> ... It is true that a court could not, under Northern Ireland law, examine whether the applicants' arrest and detention fully complied with Article 5 § 1 (c) and Article 5 § 3 of the Convention. However, the Commission considers it sufficient for the purposes of Article 5 § 4 of the Convention that judicial control can encompass the procedural and substantive basis of detention. In the Commission's opinion such control should be wide enough to bear on those conditions which according to the Convention are essential for the lawful detention of a person. It is clear that the scope of judicial review available under Northern Ireland law, in respect of arrest and detention under section 12, satisfies this standard.
>
> ... The Commission concludes, by 10 votes to 2, that there has been no breach of Article 5 § 4 of the Convention. (paras 111–114)

In the case of Brogan and Coyle, the Commission held that as it had found a breach of Article 5, para. 3, they were entitled to compensation under Article 5, para. 5, because they did not have an enforceable right to compensation under national law – the Convention not being part of domestic law. As there had been no violation of any other part of Article 5 in the case of McFadden and Tracey, they had no right to compensation under Article 5, para. 5.

Four members of the Commission expressed a dissenting opinion on Article 5, para. 3, in as much as they were of the view that no distinction ought to be made between the circumstances of the four applicants, and that in all four cases there had been insufficient promptness in meeting the requirements of this part of the article.

Sir Basil Hall expressed a partly dissenting opinion on this point, holding that there had not been a violation of Article 5, para. 3 in the case of Brogan and Coyle.

The judgment of the Court

While there was no dispute over the lawfulness of the applicants' arrest and detention, in as much as these were in accordance with a procedure prescribed by law, the applicants claimed that they had not been arrested on suspicion that they had committed an offence, nor was the purpose of their arrest to bring them before a competent legal authority.

The Court considered the provisions and aim of the 1984 Act:

> ... Section 14 of the 1984 Act defines terrorism as 'the use of violence for political ends', which includes 'the use of violence for the purpose of putting the public or any section of the public in fear.' The same definition of acts of terrorism—as contained in the Detention of Terrorists (Northern Ireland) Order 1972 and the Northern Ireland (Emergency Provisions) Act 1973—has already been found by the Court to be 'well in keeping with the idea of an offence'.
>
> In addition, all of the applicants were questioned within a few hours of their arrest about their suspected involvement in specific offences and their suspected membership of proscribed organisations.
>
> Accordingly, the arrest and subsequent detention of the applicants were based on a reasonable suspicion of commission of an offence within the meaning of Article 5 § 1(c). (para. 51)

Further, the Court considered that:

> ... The fact that the applicants were neither charged nor brought before a court does not necessarily mean that the purpose of their detention was not in accordance with Article 5 § 1(c). As the government and the Commission have stated, the existence of such a purpose must be considered independently of its achievement and sub-paragraph (c) of Article 5 § 1 does not presuppose that the police should have obtained sufficient evidence to bring charges, either at the point of arrest or while the applicants were in custody.
>
> Such evidence may have been unobtainable or, in view of the nature of the suspected offences, impossible to produce in court without endangering the lives of others. There is no reason to believe that the police investigation in this case was not in good faith or that the detention of the applicants was not intended to further that investigation by way of confirming or dispelling the concrete suspicions which, as the Court has found, grounded their arrest. Had it been possible, the police would, it can be assumed, have laid charges and the applicants would have been brought before the competent legal authority.
>
> Their arrest and detention must therefore be taken to have been effected for the purpose specified in paragraph (1)(c).
>
> ... In conclusion, there has been no violation of Article 5 § 1. (paras 53 and 54)

The question whether there had been a violation of Article 5, para. 3 related to whether the applicants had been brought promptly before a judge or other officer. The Court noted that under the ordinary law in Northern Ireland, an arrested person must be brought before a magistrates' court within 48 hours, while under the Police and Criminal Evidence Act 1984, in the rest of the UK the maximum period of permitted detention was four days, with judicial approval being required at the 36-hour stage.

The Court held that:

. . . The fact that a detained person is not charged or brought before a court does not in itself amount to a violation of the first part of Article 5 § 3. No violation of Article 5(3) can arise if the arrested person is released 'promptly' before any judicial control of his detention would have been feasible. If the arrested person is not released promptly, he is entitled to a prompt appearance before a judge or judicial officer.

The assessment of 'promptness' has to be made in light of the object and purpose of Article 5. The Court has regard to the importance of this Article in the Convention System: it enshrines a fundamental human right, namely the protection of the individual against arbitrary interferences by the State with his right to liberty. Judicial control of interferences by the executive with the individual's right to liberty is an essential feature of the guarantee embodied in Article 5(3), which is intended to minimise the risk of arbitrariness. Judicial control is implied by the rule of law, 'one of the fundamental principles of a democratic society. . . , which is expressly referred to in the Preamble to the Convention' and 'from which the whole Convention draws its inspiration'.

. . . The obligation expressed in English by the word 'promptly' and in French by the word '*aussitôt*' is clearly distinguishable from the less strict requirement in the second part of paragraph 3 ('reasonable time' '*délai raisonnable*') and even from that in paragraph 4 of Article 5 ('speedily'/'*à bref délai*'). The term 'promptly' also occurs in the English text of paragraph 2, where the French text uses the words '*dans le plus court délai*'. As indicated in the *Ireland v United Kingdom* judgment, 'promptly' in paragraph 3 may be understood as having a broader significance than '*aussitôt*', which literally means immediately. Thus confronted with versions of a law-making treaty which are equally authentic but not exactly the same, the Court must interpret them in a way that reconciles them as far as possible and is most appropriate in order to realise the aim and achieve the object of the treaty.

The use in the French text of the word '*aussitôt*' with its constraining connotation of immediacy, confirms that the degree of flexibility attaching to the notion of 'promptness' is limited even if the attendant circumstances can never be ignored for the purposes of the assessment under paragraph 3. Whereas promptness is to be assessed in each case according to its special features, the significance to be attached to those features can never be taken to the point of impairing the very essence of the right guaranteed by Article 5 § 3, that is the point of effectively negativing the State's obligation to ensure a prompt release or a prompt appearance before a judicial authority.

. . . The instant case is exclusively concerned with the arrest and detention, by virtue of powers granted under special legislation, of persons suspected of involvement in terrorism in Northern Ireland. The requirements under the ordinary law in Northern Ireland as to bringing an accused before a court were expressly made inapplicable to such arrest and detention by section 12(6) of the 1984 Act. There is no call to determine in the present judgment whether in an ordinary criminal case any given period, such as four days, in police or administrative custody would as a general rule be capable of being compatible with the first part of Article 3 § 3. (paras. 58–60)

None of the applicants were brought before a judge or a judicial officer, and therefore the Court had to consider whether there were special features which could be relied on which were sufficient to give a different meaning to the term 'prompt'. The Court recognised that:

> . . . The investigation of terrorist offences undoubtedly present the authorities with special problems, partial reference to which has already been made under Article 5 § 1. The Court takes full judicial notice of the factors adverted to by the government in this connection. It is also true that in Northern Ireland the referral of police requests for extended detention to the Secretary of State and the individual scrutiny of each police request by a Minister do provide a form of executive control. In addition, the need for the continuation of the special powers has been constantly monitored by Parliament and their operation regularly reviewed by independent personalities. The Court accepts that, subject to the existence of adequate safeguards, the context of terrorism in Northern Ireland has the effect of prolonging the period during which the authorities may, without violating Article 5 § 3, keep a person suspected of serious terrorist offences in custody before bringing him before a judge or other judicial officer.
>
> The difficulties, alluded to by the government, of judicial control over decisions to arrest and detain suspected terrorists may affect the manner of implementation of Article 5 § 3, for example in calling for appropriate procedural precautions in view of the nature of the suspected offences. However, they cannot justify, under Article 5 § 3, dispensing altogether with 'prompt' judicial control. (para. 61)

However, the Court held that:

> . . . the scope for flexibility in interpreting and applying the notion of 'promptness' is very limited. In the Court's view, even the shortest of the four periods of detention namely the four days and six hours spent in police custody by Mr McFadden, falls outside the strict contraints as to time permitted by the first part of Article 5 § 3. To attach such importance to the special features of this case as to justify so lengthy a period of detention without appearance before a judge or other judicial officer would be an unacceptably wide interpretation of the plain meaning of the word 'promptly'. An interpretation to this effect would import into Article 5 § 3 a serious weakening of a procedural guarantee to the detriment of the individual and would entail consequences impairing the very essence of the individual and would entail consequences impairing the very essence of the right protected by this provision. The Court thus has to conclude that none of the applicants was either brought 'promptly' before a judicial authority or released 'promptly' following his arrest. The undoubted fact that the arrest and detention of the applicants were inspired by the legitimate aim of protecting the community as a whole from terrorism is not on its own sufficient to ensure compliance with the specific requirements of Article 5 § 3.
>
> There has thus been a breach of Article 5 § 3 in respect of all four applicants. (para. 62)

As far as Article 5, para. 4 was concerned, the Court was satisfied that the remedy of *habeas corpus*, and a possible action for false imprisonment, met the requirements of this part of the article. As there had been a violation of Article 5, para. 3, however, there was a right to compensation under Article 5, para. 5:

> . . . In the instant case, the applicants were arrested and detained lawfully under domestic law but in breach of paragraph (3) of Article 5. This violation could not give rise, either before or after the findings made by the European Court in the present judgment, to an enforceable claim for compensation by the victims before the domestic courts, this was not disputed by the government.

Accordingly, there has also been a breach of paragraph 5 in this case in respect of all four applicants. This finding is without prejudice to the Court's competence under Article 50 in the matter of awarding compensation by way of just satisfaction. (para. 67)

Dissenting opinions were given by eight judges and partially dissenting opinions by two of the judges. The dissenting opinions were based primarily on the interpretation of 'promptly' in Article 5, para. 3, and whether the circumstances of the case should allow greater flexibility than that adopted by the Court.

Comment

The 1984 Act replaced and re-enacted provisions previously found in the 1974 and 1976 Acts. The 1984 Act proscribed two organisation in Northern Ireland, the IRA and the INLA. All the Acts had been subject to periodic reviews commissioned by the Government and presented by Parliament. The conclusion of these was that:

> . . . in view of the problems inherent in the prevention and investigation of terrorism, the continued use of the special powers of arrest and detention was indispensable. The suggestion that decisions extending detention should be taken by the courts was rejected, notably because the information forming the basis of those decisions was highly sensitive and could not be disclosed to the persons in detention or their legal advisers. For various reasons, the decision fell properly within the sphere of the executive. (para. 29, Judgment of the Court)

The 1984 Act was due to expire in 1989, and to be replaced with permanent legislation. Section 12 of the Act, under which the applicants were arrested and detained, provided that:

> (1) . . . [A] constable may arrest without warrant a person who he has reasonable grounds for suspecting to be:
> . . .
> (b) a person who is or has been concerned in the commission, preparation or instigation of acts of terrorism to which this Part of this Act applies;
> . . .
> (3) The acts of terrorism to which this Part of this Act applies are:
> (a) acts of terrorism connected with the affairs of Northern Ireland;
> . . .
> (4) A person arrested under this section shall not be detained in right of the arrest for more than 48 hours after his arrest; but the Secretary of State may, in any particular case, extend the period of 48 hours by a period or periods specified by him.
> (5) Any such further period or periods shall not exceed five days in all.
> (6) The following provisions (requirement to bring accused person before the court after his arrest) shall not apply to a person detained in right of the arrest
> . . .
> (d) Article 131 of the Magistrates' Courts (Northern Ireland) Order 1981;
> . . .
> (8) The provisions of this section are without prejudice to any power of arrest exercisable apart from this section.

Under common law there was no power to arrest and detain a person simply for the purpose of making inquiries. There had to be reasonable suspicion that the person had committed an arrestable offence. Under the 1984 Act reasonable suspicion was required by the arresting officer.

Brannigan and McBride v *UK*
Series A, Vol. 258-B

The facts
The applicants had been arrested and detained in Northern Ireland under s. 12 of the Prevention of Terrorism (Temporary Provisions) Act 1984. Brannigan was detained for a period of six days, 14 hours and 30 minutes, during which he was interrogated and denied access to books, newspapers, radio, television and writing materials. Access to a solicitor was initially delayed for 48 hours and then granted. McBride was detained for four days, six hours and 25 minutes. He was subject to the same regime as Brannigan.

Both applicants complained before the Commission of breaches of Article 5, para. 3, that they were not brought promptly before a judge, and also breaches of Article 5, para. 5.

The Commission's opinion
The applicants relied on the decision in the *Brogan* case (above), in which the Court had held that detention for periods of over four days without charge and without being brought before a judge constituted a breach of Article 5, paras 3, and 5. The Commission considered that the applicants in the present case were in an identical position to the applicants in the *Brogan* case, there was therefore a breach of Article 5. However, since the *Brogan* case, a notice of derogation had been issued by the UK. The Commission had to consider, therefore, whether the potential breaches of Article 5 had been met by the UK's derogation under Article 15.

The Government submitted that the derogation was of very limited scope in so far as it affected Article 5, para. 3, and affected only the requirement of promptness (the Commission having previously held that up to four days' detention without being brought before a judicial authority satisfied the requirement of promptness).

The Commission referred to the text of the derogation and noted that:

> . . . the derogation purports to authorise the further detention of suspected terrorists for questioning without charge. Article 5(3) is, however, concerned with bringing persons reasonably suspected of having committed a criminal offence promptly before a judicial authority for the purpose of examining the question of deprivation of liberty or for the purpose of deciding on the merits of any charge brought against them. In respect of persons arrested under the legal provision applied in the case of *Brogan and Others*, the United Kingdom are not willing to comply with this obligation and the derogation must therefore be interpreted as derogating from the requirements of Article 5(3). The Commission finds that the derogation complies with the requirements of Article 15(3) of the Convention. The fact that it was not made until 1988, rather than at the first appearance of the relevant legislation in 1974, does not, in the Commission's view, affect its validity. Until that time the United Kingdom

authorities considered that the executive powers of extended detention under the Prevention of Terrorism legislation were compatible with Article 5(3) of the Convention. It was legitimate for the United Kingdom to reconsider their position on derogation when informed by the Convention organs that this was not actually the case. The fact that the derogation is expressed as an interim measure while the Government continues its examination of the possibilities for judicial authorisation of extended detention is consistent with the nature and spirit of Article 15, and in particular paragraph 3 . . . (para. 56)

The Commission noted that the applicants did not dispute that in certain circumstances it might be necessary to detain suspected terrorists for up to seven days to combat terrorism. The main issue, however, was that the powers of extending detention rested with the executive and not with the judiciary. The Commission therefore had to examine whether these measures were necessary to respond to the exigencies of the public emergency existing at the time.

In this matter the Commission was prepared to give the State a wide margin of appreciation as to what might be the most prudent or expedient policy to combat terrorism:

. . . In the light of these circumstances, the Commission considers that the United Kingdom have not overstepped their margin of appreciation in vesting in the executive rather than the judiciary the power to extend the detention of persons suspected of being involved in terrorist offences for up to seven days. (para. 62)

Since the requirements of Article 15 (derogation) had been met, Article 5, para. 3 had not been violated and consequently no right to compensation arose under Article 5, para. 5.

Mr Frowein expressed a dissenting opinion on the grounds that derogation from Article 5, para. 3 could not be established as being strictly required, and that judicial control under this part of the article was an essential protection for personal liberty.

Sir Basil Hall, concurring with the majority but expressing a separate opinion, expressed the view – as he had done in the *Brogan* case – that in the case of Northern Ireland the notion of 'promptness' needed to be interpreted more flexibly.

Three of the Commission dissented on the grounds that derogation was not strictly required by the exigencies of the situation, and that therefore there had been violations of Article 5, paras 3 and 5.

The judgment of the Court
The Court, referring to its judgment in the case of *Brogan and Others*, in which it had held that the shortest period in that case had been found to be in breach of Article 5, para. 3, held that as both periods of detention were longer in this case, there had been a breach of Article 5, para. 3, and that Article 5, para. 5 had not been complied with.

The Court, like the Commission, then had to consider whether the derogation from Article 5 was valid. This point had been left open in the *Brogan* case. The Court noted that the real point at issue was the power given to the executive, rather than to the judiciary, to extend detention. However, the Court indicated that:

... the introduction of a 'judge or other officer authorised by law to exercise judicial power' into the process of extension of periods of detention would not of itself necessarily bring about a situation of compliance with Article 5(3). That provision—like Article 5(4)—must be understood to require the necessity of following a procedure that has a judicial character although that procedure need not necessarily be identical in each of the cases where the intervention of a judge is required. (para. 58)

In the circumstances the Court held that the Government had not exceeded its margin of appreciation in deciding against judicial control.

The Court was satisfied that there were sufficient safeguards against arbitrary behaviour and 'incommunicado detention':

... In the first place, the remedy of *habeas corpus* is available to test the lawfulness of the original arrest and detention. There is no dispute that this remedy was open to the applicants had they or their legal advisers chosen to avail themselves of it and that it provides an important measure of protection against arbitrary detention (see the above-mentioned *Brogan and Others* judgment, Series A no. 145-B, pp. 34–35, §§ 63–65). The Court recalls, in this context, that the applicants withdrew their complaint of a breach of Article 5 § 4 of the Convention (see paragraph 33 above).
... In the second place, detainees have an absolute and legally enforceable right to consult a solicitor after forty-eight hours from the time of arrest. Both of the applicants were, in fact, free to consult a solicitor after this period . . .
Moreover, within this period the exercise of this right can only be delayed where there exists reasonable grounds for doing so. It is clear from judgments of the High Court in Northern Ireland that the decision to delay access to a solicitor is susceptible to judicial review and that in such proceedings the burden of establishing reasonable grounds from doing so rests on the authorities. In these cases judicial review has been shown to be a speedy and effective manner of ensuring that access to a solicitor is not arbitrarily withheld . . .
It is also not disputed that detainees are entitled to inform a relative or friend about their detention and to have access to a doctor.
... In addition to the above basic safeguards the operation of the legislation in question has been kept under regular independent review and, until 1989, it was subject to regular renewal. (paras 63–65)

The Court concluded that:

... the derogation lodged by the United Kingdom satisfies the requirements of Article 15 and that therefore the applicants cannot validly complain of a violation of Article 5, para. 3. It follows that there was no obligation under Article 5, para. 5 to provide the applicants with an enforceable right to compensation. (para. 74)

Four judges expressed dissenting opinions based on the grounds that derogation was not justified in the circumstances.

Comment

Under the ordinary criminal law in force in Northern Ireland at the time, a person arrested without a warrant had to be brought before a magistrates' court within 48 hours. This provision was expressly excluded by s. 12 of the 1984 Act. Similarly, whereas under the ordinary law there was no power to arrest and detain a person simply to make inquiries, under the 1984 Act it was legitimate to arrest and question a person even if no specific crime was suspected.

5.2.2   The Detention of Convicted Persons

Monnell and Morris v *UK*
Series A, Vol. 115

The facts
The applicants had been charged with and convicted of criminal offences. Although advised against appeal they had applied for leave to do so and had subsequently been unsuccessful. Under the Criminal Appeal Act 1968, a period spent in custody pending determination of an appeal may count as part of the term of any sentence. However, the Court of Appeal may also direct that such time should not count towards the serving of a sentence. In the applicants' cases loss of time orders were made. Such an order was valid under s. 29 of the Criminal Appeal Act 1968, and in conformity with a Practice Direction issued by the Lord Chief Justice in 1970, and one issued in 1980. The purpose of such loss of time orders is to deter unmeritorious appeals and to facilitate prompt attention to those which are meritorious. Both applicants claimed that these loss of time orders resulted in a deprivation of liberty contrary to Article 5.

The Commission's opinion
The Government contended that the increase in the period of the applicants' detention which resulted from the loss of time orders was part of their lawful detention following conviction by a competent court authorised under Article 5, para. 1.

The Commission accepted that the detention of a person convicted at first instance is to be regarded as falling under Article 5, para. 1 even in cases where, in the case where an appeal is lodged, such person may be considered to be detained on remand. The question was whether the period of detention effectively imposed as a result of the loss of time orders was lawful after conviction by a competent court. The Commission, having examined the purpose of such loss of time orders – which was to deter unmeritorious appeal applicants – concluded that:

> . . . the period of time ordered not to count towards the applicants' sentences imposed by the trial judge cannot be regarded as forming part of their detention after their conviction at first instance, since the express terms of the loss of time orders was to exclude these periods of detention from being so regarded. In these circumstances, and bearing in mind the purpose for which the loss of time orders were made, which was unconnected with the original sentences imposed on the applicants or with the offences for which they were convicted, the Commission finds that the periods of detention which were ordered not to count towards the service of their sentences cannot be regarded as detention under Art. 5(1)(a) of the Convention.
>
> . . . The Commission has considered whether these periods of detention are justified under any of the other paragraphs of Art. 5(1) of the Convention, but does not find any of them applicable. In particular, the Commission observes that Art. 5(1)(c) was only applicable to the applicants' detention prior to the dates on which they were convicted and sentenced by the Crown Court.
>
> . . . The Commission concludes, by ten votes to one, that there has been a breach of Art. 5(1) of the Convention in regard to both applicants. (paras 122–124)

The judgment of the Court

The principal issue was whether the periods in detention were undergone after conviction by a competent court. While it was clear that both applicants had been convicted initially by a competent court, the issue focused on the subsequent loss of time ordered by the Court of Appeal and whether this could be regarded as detention after conviction, or, as argued by the applicants, whether it was a further period of imprisonment imposed not for an offence but for seeking leave to appeal.

The Court did not accept the Government's argument that the loss of time order was not a fresh sentence but simply a means of giving directions as to the mode of execution of the original sentence.

> . . . In the Court's view, a direction for loss of time cannot be qualified simply as a decision laying down the manner of execution of the original detention order by the trial court, since it effectively imposes a period of imprisonment in addition to that which would result from the sentence. The effect of a loss-of-time direction, as the Form AA warns intending applicants for leave to appeal, is a later date of release. This was recognised by the Court of Appeal itself in Mr Monnell's case when it expressed its decision as being that his time in prison should be extended.
>
> . . . As the Commission and its Delegate observed, the relevant additional period of deprivation of liberty was imposed by the Court of Appeal on Mr Monnell and Mr Morris for reasons unconnected either with the facts of the offence or with the character and criminal record of the offender, that is to say, with the elements on which the conviction and sentence at first instance were based: it was ordered, in line with the deterrent policy enunciated in the Practice Directions of 1970 and 1980, for having persisted with an unmeritorious application for leave to appeal. Thus, in Mr Morris' case, the Court of Appeal spoke in its judgment in terms of his having to pay the penalty for having renewed a hopeless application.
>
> Under the express terms of section 29(1) of the Criminal Appeal Act 1968, the direction that the Court of Appeal may make is that a specified period in custody is not to be reckoned as part of any sentence of imprisonment being served by the appellant. (paras 43 and 44)

However, this did not mean that such orders necessarily led to violations of Article 5.

> . . . Whilst the loss of time ordered by the Court of Appeal is not treated under domestic law as part of the applicants' sentences as such, it does form part of the period of detention which results from the overall sentencing procedure that follows conviction. As a matter of English law, a sentence of imprisonment passed by a Crown Court is to be served subject to any order which the Court of Appeal may, in the event of an unsuccessful application for leave to appeal, make as to loss of time. Section 29(1) of the 1968 Act is couched in rather wide and flexible terms. However, the power of the Court of Appeal to order loss of time, as it is actually exercised, is a component of the machinery existing under English law to ensure that criminal appeals are considered within a reasonable time and, in particular, to reduce the time spent in custody by those with meritorious grounds waiting for their appeal to be heard; this is made patently clear in the 1965 report of the Interdepartmental Committee on the Court of Criminal Appeal and in the two Practice Directions issued by the Lord Chief Justice. In sum, it is a power exercised to discourage abuse of the court's own procedures. As such, it is an inherent part of the criminal appeal

process following conviction of an offender and pursues a legitimate aim under sub-paragraph (a) of Article 5(1). (para. 46)

The Court concluded that:

. . . there was a sufficient and legitimate connection, for the purposes of the deprivation of liberty permitted under sub-paragraph (a) of Article 5(1), between the conviction of each applicant and the additional period of imprisonment undergone as a result of the loss-of-time order made by the Court of Appeal. The time spent in custody by each applicant under this head is accordingly to be regarded as detention of a person after conviction by a competent court, within the meaning of sub-paragraph (a) of Article 5(1).

. . .

. . . More generally, the Court is satisfied in the circumstances of the present case as to the lawfulness and procedural propriety of the contested periods of loss of liberty. To begin with, it has not been disputed that the relevant rules and procedures under English law were properly observed by the English courts in relation to the making of the loss-of-time orders. Further, contrary to the submissions of the applicants, the Court finds that these orders depriving the applicants of their liberty issued from and were executed by an appropriate authority and were not arbitrary.

The contested deprivation of liberty must therefore be found to have been both lawful and effected in accordance with a procedure prescribed by law, as those expressions in Article 5(1) have been interpreted in the Court's case law.

. . . There has accordingly been no breach of Article 5(1) in the present case in respect of either applicant. (paras 48, 50 and 51)

Dissenting opinions were given by Judges Pettiti and Spielman, who considered the situation in UK law from a comparative perspective, noting in particular that the vast majority of the member States of the Council of Europe do not have a loss of time system, and that in most of these the right of appeal is automatic. In considering whether the use of loss of time orders was compatible with the Convention, the judges considered that certain elementary guarantees were required, including fixed criteria and objective reasons for the making of such orders.

5.2.3   The Detention of Mental Patients

Ashingdane v *UK*
Series A, Vol. 93

The facts
The applicant was convicted of dangerous driving and unlawful possession of firearms. The court which tried him made a hospital order under s. 60 of the Mental Health Act 1959. The effect of this order was to restrict his discharge, and to make this dependent on a decision by the Home Secretary. On several occasions the applicant's case was considered by the Mental Health Review Tribunal, which considered that he was not ready to be discharged or transferred. In 1978 the Home Secretary, on the recommendation of specialist reports, agreed to the applicant's transfer to a local psychiatric hospital. However, industrial action at the local hospital meant that he could not be transferred there. No suitable alternative accommodation could be found and

so the applicant remained at Broadmoor. The applicant commenced legal proceedings against the local authority and the unions. Before the Commission he complained of violations of Articles 3, 4, and 5. Under Article 5 he complained that his detention was not covered by Article 5, para. 1(e) since he was not of unsound mind.

The question before the Commission was whether his detention during this period was lawful in view of the applicant's claim that the authorities were in breach of their duty to provide him with alternative accommodation in another form of institution. This raised the question not only whether detention should be lawful, but also whether measures taken – such as decisions on transfer or the location of detention – should also be lawful.

The Commission's opinion
First, the Commission noted that:

> . . . the provisions of the Mental Health Act 1959, relevant to the applicant's case, fall within the ambit of Article 5, para. 1(e) and that there is no dispute between the parties that the applicant's compulsory detention was in accordance with a procedure prescribed by law. Medical opinion has throughout considered the applicant's compulsory confinement necessary due to the persistence of mental disorder, diagnosed by various doctors as paranoid schizophrenia. On this basis, the Commission is able to conclude that the applicant's mental ill-health has been established, and that he was compulsorily and justifiably detained, in accordance with domestic law, as a person of unsound mind. (para. 73)

In considering whether Article 5, para. 1(e) encompassed both the actual detention and the treatment of the detained patient, the Commission expressed the opinion that the provisions covered the question of actual detention only, not treatment; the latter might, however, fall under other articles such as Article 3.

Although the Commission noted that the applicant should have been transferred from Broadmoor to Oakwood hospital as of 1 March 1979 – and was not due to industrial action – the Commission considered that the applicant's treatment in either place was not fundamentally different. The detention remained lawful, and his treatment was not neglected.

As far as the applicant's claim under Article 5, para. 4 was concerned, the Commission expressed the view that:

> . . . patients compulsorily detained for indefinite periods are entitled to a periodic review of the lawfulness of their detention, . . . The facts of the present case, in the context of the applicant's status as a restricted patient, do not detract from this conclusion. However, as the Government have pointed out, the present applicant's claim can be distinguished from that of X (Series A No. 46) (parentheses added) who was concerned only with the question of deprivation of liberty, namely the lawfulness of renewed detention on recall to hospital. The present applicant's claim involves questions of suitable treatment and hospital accommodation.
> . . . The Commission has above excluded this latter element from the scope of Article 5, para. 1(e) of the Convention (paras 75–77). The scheme of Article 5 is such that Article 5, para. 4 entitles the detainee to have the lawfulness of his detention tested by a court in the light of those exclusive categories of deprivation of liberty

envisaged by Article 5, para. 1. As the applicant's claim does not concern deprivation of liberty, as such, and does not fall under Article 5, para. 1, it follows that it is not a claim requiring judicial determination under Article 5, para. 4 of the Convention. (paras 84 and 85)

The judgment of the Court

It was accepted by the applicant that his detention was in accordance with a procedure established by law; however, he claimed that at no time had his mental disorder been of such a nature or degree that his compulsory confinement was warranted.

Referring to its previous case law, the Court stated that there were three minimum conditions which have to be satisfied in order for there to be lawful detention of a person of unsound mind within the meaning of Article 5, para. 1(e). These are that:

> . . . except in emergency cases, a true mental disorder must be established before a competent authority on the basis of objective medical expertise; the mental disorder must be of a kind or degree warranting compulsory confinement; and the validity of continued confinement depends upon the persistence of such a disorder. The Court's task in verifying the fulfilment of these conditions is limited to reviewing under the Convention the decisions taken by the national authorities. (para. 37)

In the present case the Court considered that the applicant's detention was justified:

> . . . The medical reports submitted in evidence, including those made by independent doctors at the request of the applicant, gave as the reasons for his initial and continued detention that he was diagnosed as suffering from paranoid schizophrenia, that his condition needed to be controlled by medication and supervision, that he was unwilling or unable to co-operate voluntarily in such treatment, and that if he were released into the community he might be dangerous. . . . (para. 38)

The Court affirmed that Article 5, para. 1(e) is not simply concerned with restrictions on liberty of movement, but with deprivation of liberty, in which the Court must consider all the relevant circumstances. Whether the applicant was at Broadmoor or at Oakwood, he was still detained and his liberty was restricted. The question was the extent to which lawful detention could be construed to include reference not only to actual deprivation of liberty of mental health patients, but also to matters relating to execution of the detention, such as the place, environment and conditions of detention. In considering this the Court held that:

> . . . Certainly, the 'lawfulness' of any detention is required in respect of both the ordering and the execution of the measure depriving the individual of his liberty. Such 'lawfulness' presupposes conformity with domestic law in the first place and also, as confirmed by Article 18, conformity with the purposes of the restrictions permitted by Article 5(1). More generally, it follows from the very aim of Article 5(1) that no detention that is arbitrary can ever be regarded as 'lawful'. The Court would further accept that there must be some relationship between the ground of permitted deprivation of liberty relied on and the place and conditions of detention. In principle, the 'detention' of a person as a mental health patient will only be 'lawful' for the purposes of sub-paragraph (e) of paragraph 1 if effected in a hospital, clinic or other

appropriate institution authorised for that purpose. However, subject to the fore-going, Article 5(1)(e) is not in principle concerned with suitable teatment or conditions. (para. 44)

The Court noted that:

... at all times the purpose of Mr Ashingdane's detention related to his mental illness. This was so even though the immediate cause of the delay in his tansfer from the special security hospital to his local hospital was industrial rather than therapeutic, a circumstance which the Commission described as 'deplorable'. It is clear, however, that the delay was not in conscious disregard of Mr Ashingdane's mental welfare. Efforts were made to find a solution as soon as possible. The evidence before the Court suggests that any course other than that adopted by the responsible authorities would probably have been impracticable. In any event, the Court is satisfied that the applicant's continued detention was not arbitrary or effected for an ulterior purpose, contrary to Article 5(1)(e) read in conjunction with Article 18.

... This conclusion does not alter the unfortunate fact that the applicant suffered, in human terms, an injustice in having to endure the stricter regime at Broadmoor for nineteen months longer than his mental state required. The Government themselves have expressed sympathy at his plight and their great regret at the events giving rise to the application. The problem of transfer from the 'special' hospitals in England and Wales, which lay at the root of the present case, was undoubtedly a serious one for those affected. However, the injustice suffered by Mr Ashingdane is not a mischief against which Article 5(1)(e) of the Convention protects. (paras 48 and 49)

The Court could not, therefore, find any violation of Article 5, para. 1.

As far as the applicant's complaints under Article 5, para. 4 were concerned, the Court pointed out that:

... Article 5(4) does not guarantee a right to judicial control of the legality of all aspects or details of the detention. The scheme of Article 5, when read as a whole as it must be, implies that in relation to one and the same deprivation of liberty the notion of 'lawfulness' should have the same significance in paragraphs 1(e) and 4. Thus, the domestic remedy available under paragraph 4 should enable review of the conditions which, according to paragraph 1(e), are essential for the 'lawful detention' of a person on the ground of unsoundness of mind.

However, the claims that the applicant was prevented by operation of section 141 of the 1959 Act from pursuing before the national courts do not fall within the scope of the judicial determination of 'lawfulness' which Article 5(4) guarantees. As noted above, in his domestic litigation the applicant did not challenge the legal basis for his detention as a person of unsound mind under the 1959 Act or seek his release from the reality of detention: he was claiming an entitlement to accommodation and treatment in the more 'appropriate' conditions of a different category of psychiatric hospital, a matter not covered by paragraph 1(e) of Article 5.

Accordingly, the dismissal of his actions against the responsible authorities did not give rise to a breach of Article 5(4). (para. 52)

Judge Pettiti expressed a dissenting opinion. He considered that the Court had not sufficiently considered whether the continued detention was arbitrary or effected for an ulterior purpose. In the light of the evidence that the specialist report had indicated that the applicant should be treated in an ordinary psychiatric hospital, and that the difficulties in transferring him to a suitable place were due to industrial action, the judge expressed the view that the

Government had not done all that was required of it. The continued detention of the applicant at Broadmoor was therefore unlawful.

Comment

At the time of the facts giving rise to this case the law relating to the compulsory confinement of mentally disordered persons was to be found in the Mental Health Act 1959. The Act was largely repealed and replaced by the Mental Health Act 1983. Section 60 of the 1959 Act empowered criminal courts to direct that certain persons could be dealt with by way of medical treatment rather than punishment. Under s. 65, the power to make such orders as hospital orders could be enlarged by directing that the hospital order be subject to special restrictions in respect of discharge, either without a time limit or during a specified period. Periodic review of a restricted patient's case was made by the Mental Health Review Tribunal. Since 1983, these tribunals have the power to direct the absolute or conditional discharge of restricted patients. The 1983 Act also removed the immunity from claim which existed under s. 141 of the 1959 Act, in respect of civil actions in tort brought by mental patients in connection with their detention.

X v UK
Series A, Vol. 46 Judgment of the Court
4 EHRR 188 Opinion of the Commission

The facts

The application was commenced by X and subsequently continued by his next-of-kin. X had been convicted of an offence in 1968 and sent to a secure mental hospital. He was conditionally discharged in 1971, but recalled to the mental hospital in 1974. Following an application to the Mental Health Review Tribunal and favourable medical reports, he was again conditionally discharged in 1976. During his period of recall in 1974 he had applied unsuccessfully for a writ of *habeas corpus*. His application to the Commission was a complaint under Article 5, paras 1 and 4 concerning the period of detention in 1974, on the grounds that his recall was unjustified, that he was not given sufficient reasons for his re-detention and that he had no effective way of challenging the lawfulness of the authorities' action.

The Commission's opinion

The first question the Commission had to resolve was whether the applicant's detention fell under Article 5, para. 1(a) – lawful detention after criminal conviction – or Article 5, para. 1(e) – lawful detention of a person of unsound mind.

The Commission observed that:

> . . . the two provisions are fundamentally different: Article 5(1)(a) justifies the detention of a person whenever the mere formal condition of a conviction is fulfilled, whereas Article 5(1)(e) requires the observance of material criteria, such as the existence of the specific condition of mental ill-health, in order to justify detention Nevertheless, at first sight, it could be said that both provisions applied to the

applicant's situation in view of his formal criminal conviction in 1968 and his undisputed mental ill-health at that time.

. . . However, in the Commission's opinion, only Article 5(1)(e) applies whenever the case of an accused person of unsound mind is disposed of by committal to a mental hospital for treatment, rather than punishment.

. . . 'Conviction' within the meaning of Article 5(1)(a) refers narrowly to the conviction and sentence of a person found guilty of a criminal offence, with the attendant notions of social blame and punishment. Moreover, in principle, detention in accordance with Article 5(1)(a) follows a procedure which respects the guarantee of a fair hearing provided for in Article 6(1) of the Convention.

. . . On the other hand, Article 5(1)(e) of the Convention provides for the detention of a person by virtue of the specific state of his mental health, irrespective of criminal conduct, as a person of unsound mind, by definition, cannot be held fully responsible for his acts. Periodic control of this justification for detention is necessary in view of the changeable nature of mental ill-health. The mere fact that such a person had an equitable criminal procedure prior to his detention should not deprive him of such further guarantees. (4 EHRR 188, paras 79–82)

The Commission expressed the opinion that the justification for the detention of the applicant fell under Article 5, para. 1(e), although it noted that the same guarantees of Article 5 applied whether a person was detained under this sub-paragraph or under Article 5, para. 1(a).

Whether his detention was justified under this sub-paragraph depended on whether it complied with the three conditions previously established by the Court (see *Ashingdane*, above). There was a dispute between the applicant and the Government concerning his mental health. The Commission indicated that it had limited scope for review in these circumstances. It could review the decisions of the competent authorities only to consider whether there was a prima facie case:

. . . To avoid arbitrary detention, it must be shown that there is objective medical evidence of the detainee's mental disorder, warranting compulsory confinement, and continued confinement may only be justified if the disorder persists. (4 EHRR 188, para. 92)

In the applicant's case the Commission noted the following facts:

. . . The applicant was first committed to Broadmoor Hospital because of his mental ill-health, established after he had violently attacked a workmate. Periodic medical opinion justified his continued detention and subsequent discharge on a conditional basis only, medical supervision being required. As an out-patient the applicant was thought by medical opinion to be coping, although it was conceded that a rapid deterioration in the applicant's condition was still a possibility. For example, in a medical report annexed to an affidavit for the *habeas corpus* proceedings, one of the consultant psychiatrists treating the applicant as an out-patient was particularly anxious about the applicant's volatile mental health and potentially violent behaviour, He expressed no surprise that the applicant was recalled at the mere hint of a crisis. Such a hint was notified by the applicant's wife who renounced previous progress reports she had made to the probation officer supervising the applicant's well-being. Her allegations concerning the applicant's disturbing behaviour, although not verified, alarmed the responsible medical officer at Broadmoor Hospital. In view of his knowledge of the applicant's medical background, he was concerned that a difficult family situation was arising in which the applicant might have broken down and reverted to violent behaviour.

 . . . In the Commission's opinion the arrest and detention of a patient on the indications of a member of the patient's family may run a serious risk of being an unjustified deprivation of liberty and ought only to be effected in exceptional circumstances. In view of the fact, however, that the present case concerned the *recall* of a mental health patient, who was on conditional release only, and whose medical history indicated a certain danger of violent behaviour, a *prima facie* justification existed for the applicant's speedy recall and further medical examination at the first sign of any possible emergency.

 . . . Furthermore on recall and examination, the applicant's responsible medical officer was of the opinion that he should be further detained for treatment. This medical opinion was maintained until December 1975 when, on the advice of the Mental Health Review Tribunal, to whom the applicant had referred his case, and the Broadmoor medical staff, the Home Secretary agreed in principle to the applicant's being allowed limited periods of leave of absence under close supervision. However, treatment was still considered by the medical staff to be necessary throughout. The Commission finds no reason to doubt the competence of the medical staff concerned.

 . . . Thus the Commission considers that the Government have submitted sufficient indications that the applicant's re-arrest and further detention in order to verify the exact state of his mental health was justified.

 . . . The Commission is of the opinion therefore that the applicant's detention in Broadmoor Hospital, particularly as regards his recall, constituted 'the lawful detention of [a person] of unsound mind' within the meaning of Article 5(1)(e) of the Convention. (4 EHRR 188, paras 94–98)

The applicant also complained that at the time of his recall he was not adequately informed of the reasons for his recall. The Commission, while accepting that Article 5, para. 2 applied to the circumstances, noted that there may be particular difficulties in complying with it in the case of certain mental patients. Nevertheless, mental patients are not excluded from the provisions of this sub-paragraph. On the evidence it was not clear whether the applicant's rights had been observed in this respect, but it was clear that insufficient reasons had been given to persons acting on his behalf, i.e. his solicitors, and there had therefore been a violation of Article 5, para. 2.

As regards Article 5, para. 4, the Government had contended that this provision did not require periodic judicial determination of the state of a person's mental health. While it was agreed that the initial detention under the Mental Health Act 1959 was lawful, the dispute related to the recall in 1974. The question for the Commission, therefore, was whether Article 5, para. 4 required the possibility of further periodic judicial review of the lawfulness of detention of persons of unsound mind. The Commission expressed the opinion that such review was required in the case of mentally ill persons. Further, that the scope of review should include the material grounds for detention.

 . . . The Convention guarantees to everyone the right to personal freedom. Article 5(1) sets out an exhaustive list of exceptional cases of permissible arrest or detention. Deprivation of liberty for any other reasons would be incompatible with the Convention. Article 5(4) provides for a special judicial control of the legality of detention which, to be of any effect, cannot, in the case of persons of unsound mind, be limited to the mere formal legality under domestic law. (4 EHRR 188, para. 131)

The remedy of *habeas corpus*, which was available to the applicant and had in fact been unsuccessfully applied for, extended only to a review of whether the original detention had been *intra vires*; the Commission found that it did not satisfy the requirements of Article 5, para. 4.

Further, although review by the Mental Health Tribunal was available, and indeed used by the applicant, such a review took place six months after the event complained of and therefore did not satisfy the requirement of speed provided for in Article 5, para. 4. Moreover, the Commission noted that the Tribunal could not order release but could give only an advisory opinion to the Home Secretary. There had, therefore, been a violation of Article 5, para. 4.

The judgment of the Court
The Court held that the detention of the applicant fell under both Article 5, para. 1(a) and Article 5, para. 1(e):

> ... In the Court's view, there was, in the full sense of the term, a 'conviction' that is to say, finding of guilt 'by a competent court' and, following and dependent upon that conviction, a 'lawful detention' ordered by the same court. Sub-paragraph (a) therefore applies. However, the court did not deal with X by way of punishment but, being satisfied that he was suffering from a mental disorder warranting his confinement in a mental hospital for treatment committed him to Broadmoor. Consequently, sub-paragraph (e), in so far as it relates to the detention of 'persons of unsound mind', also applies. It accordingly follows that, initially at least, the applicant's deprivation of liberty fell within the ambit of both sub-paragraphs.
>
> Having regard to the reasons for X's recall to hospital in 1974 and subsequent detention there until 1976, sub-paragraph (e) likewise covers the second stage of his deprivation of liberty. The particular circumstances of this case, and notably the fact that X was conditionally released and enjoyed a lengthy period of liberty before being redetained, may give rise to some doubts as to the continued applicability of sub-paragraph (a). The Court does not judge it necessary to decide the point, however, since it must in any event verify whether the requirements of sub-paragraph (e) were fulfilled and no problem arises in the present case as regards compliance with the requirements of sub-paragraph (a). (para. 39)

In considering whether the recall of the applicant complied with sub-paragraph (e), the Court noted that s. 66 of the Mental Health Act 1959 was framed in very wide terms, although it was apparent that the Home Secretary's discretionary power was not unlimited. The Court also noted that in emergency cases, such as might arise where a mental patient was recalled, some departure from the express or implied principles of the Convention might be justified:

> ... Clearly, where a provision of domestic law is designed, amongst other things, to authorise emergency confinement of persons capable of presenting a danger to others, it would be impracticable to require thorough medical examination prior to any arrest or detention. A wide discretion must in the nature of things be enjoyed by the national authority empowered to order such emergency confinements. ...

Having regard to the foregoing considerations, the conditions under the 1959 Act governing the recall to hospital of restricted patients do not appear to be incompatible with the meaning under the Convention of the expression 'the lawful detention . . . of persons of unsound mind'. What remains to be determined is whether the manner in which section 66(3) was in fact applied in relation to X gave rise to a breach of Article 5(1)(e). (para. 40)

There may, moreover, be circumstances in which the protection of the public interest prevails over the individual's right to liberty to the extent of justifying an emergency confinement in the absence of the usual protection afforded by Article 5.

The Court was satisfied that:

. . . On the facts of the present case, there was sufficient reason for the Home Secretary to have considered that the applicant's continued liberty constituted a danger to the public, and in particular to his wife.

. . . While these considerations were enough to justify X's recall as an emergency measure and for a short duration, his further detention in hospital until February 1976 must, for its part, satisfy the minimum conditions described above (at para. 40). These conditions were satisfied in the case of X: having examined X after his readmission to Broadmoor, the responsible medical officer was of the opinion that he should be further detained for treatment. This opinion was maintained until December 1975 when an improvement in his condition was noted; up till then the medical reports indicated that he continued in a psychotic state. . . . Like the Commission the Court has no reason to doubt the objectivity and reliability of this medical judgment.

. . . In conclusion, there was no breach of Article 5(1). (paras 45–47)

As far as the alleged breach of Article 5, para. 4 was concerned, the Court held that:

. . . By virtue of Article 5(4) a person of unsound mind compulsorily confined in a psychiatric institution for an indefinite or lengthy period is in principle entitled, at any rate where there is no automatic periodic review of a judicial character, to take proceedings at reasonable intervals before a court to put in issue the 'lawfulness' . . . of his detention, whether that detention was ordered by a civil or criminal court or by some other authority.

. . . It is not within the province of the Court to enquire into what would be the best or most appropriate system of judicial review in this sphere, for the Contracting States are free to choose different methods of performing their obligations. Thus, in Article 5(4) the word 'court' is not necessarily to be understood as signifying a court of law of the classic kind, intergrated within the standard judicial machinery of the country. This term, as employed in several Articles of the Convention (including Art. 5(4)), serves to denote—

bodies which exhibit not only common fundamental features, of which the most important is independence of the executive and of the parties to the case, but also the guarantees ('appropriate to the kind of deprivation of liberty in question') of [a] judicial procedure,

the forms of which may vary from one domain to another.

. . . To sum up, during the period of his detention subsequent to his readmission to Broadmoor Hospital in April 1974 X should have been enabled to take proceedings attended by such 'guarantees'. At that stage, the proceedings that had been held in 1968 before the Sheffield Assizes were no longer sufficient to satisfy the requirements of Article 5(4). (paras 52–54)

In considering whether the availability of *habeas corpus* proceedings satisfied the requirements of Article 5, para. 4, the Court observed that:

... In habeas corpus proceedings, in examining an administrative decision to detain, the court's task is to enquire whether the detention is in compliance with the requirements stated in the relevant legislation and with the applicable principles of the common law. According to these principles, such a decision (even though technically legal on its face) may be upset, *inter alia*, if the detaining authority misused its powers by acting in bad faith or capriciously or for a wrongful purpose, or if the decision is supported by no sufficient evidence or is one which no reasonable person could have reached in the circumstances. Subject to the foregoing, the court will not be able to review the grounds or merits of a decision taken by an administrative authority to the extent that under the legislation in question these are exclusively a matter for determination by that authority. . . . As X's case well exemplifies, when the terms of a statute afford the executive a discretion, whether wide or narrow, the review exercisable by the courts in habeas corpus proceedings will bear solely upon the conformity of the exercise of that discretion with the empowering statute.

In the present case, once it was established that X was a patient who had been conditionally discharged whilst still subject to a restriction order, the statutory requirements for recall by warrant under section 66(3) of the 1959 Act were satisfied. . . . This being so, it was then effectively up to X to show, within the limits permitted by English law, some reason why the apparently legal detention was unlawful. The evidence adduced by X did not disclose any such reason and the Divisional Court had no option but to dismiss the application.

. . . Although X had access to a court which ruled that his detention was 'lawful' in terms of English law, this cannot of itself be decisive as to whether there was a sufficient review of 'lawfulness' for the purposes of Article 5(4) In Article 5(1)(e) as interpreted by the Court, the Convention itself makes the 'lawfulness' of the kind of deprivation of liberty undergone by X subject to certain requirements over and above conformity with domestic law. Article 5 must be read as a whole and there is no reason to suppose that in relation to one and the same deprivation of liberty the significance of 'lawfulness' differs from Article 5(4)(e) to Article 5(4).

. . . Notwithstanding the limited nature of the review possible in relation to decisions taken under section 66(3) of the 1959 Act, the remedy of the habeas corpus can on occasions constitute an effective check against arbitrariness in this sphere. It may be regarded as adequate, for the purposes of Article 5(4), for emergency measures for the detention of persons on the ground of unsoundness of mind. Such measures, provided they are of short duration, are capable of being 'lawful' under Article 5(e) even though not attended by the usual guarantees such as thorough medical examination. . . . The authority empowered to order emergency detention of this kind must in the nature of things enjoy a wide discretion, and this inevitably means that the role of the courts will be reduced.

On the other hand, in the Court's opinion, a judicial review as limited as that available in the habeas corpus procedure in the present case is not sufficient for a continuing confinement such as the one undergone by X. Article 5(4), the Government are quite correct to affirm, does not embody a right to judicial control of such scope as to empower the court, on all aspects of the case, to substitute its own discretion for that of the decision-making authority. The review should, however, be wide enough to bear on those conditions which, according to the Convention, are essential for the 'lawful' detention of a person on the ground of unsoundness of mind, especially as the reasons capable of initially justifying such a detention may cease to exist. . . . This means that in the instant case Article 5(4) required an appropriate procedure allowing a court to examine whether the patient's disorder still persisted and whether the Home Secretary was entitled to think that a continuation of the compulsory confinement was necessary in the interests of public safety.

. . . The habeas corpus proceedings brought by X in 1974 did not therefore secure him the enjoyment of the right guaranteed by Article 5(4), this would also have been the case had he made any fresh application at a later date. (paras 56–59)

The Court accepted the need to take a comprehensive view of all the possible remedies available, not just one. The Government had submitted that these included a recommendation from the responsible medical officer for the patient's discharge, the intervention of a Member of Parliament, a direct request from the patient to the Home Secretary for release, or referral of the case to a Mental Health Review Tribunal.

The Court dismissed the first three on the grounds that they involved no independent review procedure. As regards the fourth, the Court considered that such a tribunal could be regarded as a court within the meaning of Article 5. However, such tribunals lacked sufficient competence to decide on the lawfulness of the detention, or to order release if the detention was unlawful. There was therefore a breach of Article 5, para. 4.

As far as the alleged violation of Article 5, para. 2 was concerned, the Court did not feel it was necessary to resolve the conflicting arguments on this point as clearly the need to inform the applicant of the reasons for his recall were implicit in the provisions of Article 5, para. 4.

Comment

In response to criticisms of the European Commission concerning Article 5, para. 2, the UK Government had in fact introduced changes in the procedures for informing recalled patients of the reasons for their re-detention in 1980. The procedure operated in two stages whereby the person taking the patient into custody informed the patient in simple terms that he or she was being recalled on the authority of the Home Secretary, and that a further explanation would be given. Detailed reasons would then be given within 72 hours of the recall. Such reasons also had to be given to a responsible member of the patient's family, or to his or her legal adviser, and to the officer who supervised the patient during his or her release.

5.2.4   Life Sentences

Weeks v UK
Series A, Vol. 114

The facts

In 1966, at the age of 17, the applicant had been convicted of armed robbery and sentenced to an indeterminate life sentence. There was insufficient evidence to justify his committal to a mental institution, but there was evidence that he had mental problems. In 1969 he suffered a mental breakdown and was treated in a psychiatric hospital. He was released on licence in 1976. While out on licence he committed a number of minor offences, and in 1977 his licence was revoked by the Home Secretary, under s. 62(2) of the Criminal Justice Act 1967. The Parole Board considered his case on several occasions and recommended his release to the Home Secretary. This was eventually effected in 1982.

The applicant's complaint related to his re-detention in 1977, after he had been at liberty for 15 months. He contended that the minor offences which he committed were not sufficient to justify his re-detention, and that he was unable to have the lawfulness of this recall determined by a court.

The Commission's opinion

The Commission paid particular attention to the facts of the original criminal offence. The sum that the applicant had stolen was 35 pence. The gun he had used was a starting pistol. At his trial the judge had sentenced him to an indeterminate life sentence so that the Home Secretary could monitor his progress and authorise his release when it would be safe to do so. Alternatively, the Home Secretary could order his transfer to a mental hospital if his mental health deteriorated.

> . . . In the Commission's view it is clear that the applicant's case fails to be distinguished from that of a person who has received a life sentence because of the gravity of the offence he has committed. The essential difference lies in the fact that it was not the intention of the sentencing judge that the applicant should necessarily serve a long term of imprisonment, rather that he should only remain in prison as long as he was a danger to the public. For this reason he was not given a determinate sentence, since by the end of a fixed term he might still remain a danger to the public. With the stress on the length of imprisonment was dependent on the improvement made by the applicant as assessed by the Home Secretary.
>
> . . . In these circumstances the Commission considers that the present case is analogous to cases concerning habitual or recidivist offenders who are placed by order of a court at the Government's disposal and released when the authorities consider that they no longer pose a danger to society. It is against the background of the principles developed in such cases that the Commission must examine the present application. . . . (paras 69 and 70)

While the Convention allows a measure on indeterminacy in sentencing, and the sentencing of criminal offenders falls outside the scope of the Convention, in cases such as this, where the prisoner is meant to be detained only as long as he poses a threat to public safety, there must be a sufficient connection between the original conviction and the decision to re-detain. The Commission had to examine whether there was a sufficient connection. In this regard the Commission noted that:

> . . . It is clear from the incidents which had occured in prison prior to his release in 1977 that the applicant had a violent disposition which erupted from time to time, particularly when he drank heavily. After his conviction for minor offences he was specifically warned by the Home Office in a letter dated April 1977 that his licence could be revoked by the Home Secretary if his behaviour continued to give cause for concern. The decision by the Home Secretary to revoke his licence and recall him was

finally prompted by his unstable and disturbed behaviour in late June 1977 when he fired an air pistol and, while in a violent and agitated mood, attempted to hang himself in police custody. (para 78)

There had not, therefore, been a breach of Article 5, para. 1.

As regards the alleged violation of Article 5, para. 4, although the applicant was detained under Article 5, para. 1(a) rather than under subpara. (e), the particular facts of his case rendered it inconsistent with the purpose of Article 5 to regard his application as immune from subsequent review of lawfulness, which would be the requirement in the case of detention under Article 5, para. 1(e). The Commission expressed the opinion that:

> . . . the applicant, in the instant case, should have been able to avail himself of an appropriate procedure allowing a court to examine whether his behavioural problems still persisted and whether the Home Secretary was entitled to think that continued detention was necessary in the interests of public safety. (para. 89)

The Government had submitted that the applicant could have instituted proceedings for judicial review or applied for a writ of *habeas corpus*. However, the Commission noted that the domestic law of the UK clearly indicated that a writ of *habeas corpus* was not available in the case of a person serving a sentence passed by a competent court (*Re Featherstone* (1953) 37 Cr App R 146 (DC). The possibility of initiating *habeas corpus* could not, therefore, be said to satisfy Article 5, para. 4 in the circumstances.

As far as judicial review was concerned, the Commission considered that this remedy remained very uncertain and did not meet the requirements of accessibility and effectiveness. Also the Commission considered that:

> . . . the scope of judicial review is not wide enough to be brought to bear on the factors which govern the lawfulness of the applicant's detention, namely, whether his behavioural problems continue to exist and the reasonableness of the Home Secretary's decision that the applicant remains a danger to public safety.
>
> The Commission finds, therefore, that judicial review does not enable the applicant to determine the lawfulness of his re-detention. (para. 100)

As far as the Parole Board was concerned, the applicant had pointed out that legal advice was not available to an applicant to bring a case before the Board, neither was he allowed to be present or to have a representative. He could not be informed of the evidence put before the Board, and could not question or call any witnesses. Moreover, the Parole Board did not have the power to order release; its role was advisory. The Commission considered that:

> . . . the Parole Board lacks the necessary procedural guarantees, in respect of such a serious deprivation of liberty, to be considered a 'court' for the purposes of this provision. It is unnecessary, in the present case, to decide whether the Parole Board can also be considered to be independent of the parties. The Commission finds, therefore, that the Parole Board does not satisfy the requirements of Art. 5(4).
>
> . . . It follows from the above that the applicant was unable to have the lawfulness of his re-detention determined by a court or to have a periodic review of the lawfulness of his continued detention at reasonable intervals throughout his imprisonment.
>
> . . . The Commission concludes, by seven votes to four, that there has been a breach of Art. 5(4). (paras 104–106)

A dissenting opinion was expressed by Mr Danelius, joined by three other members of the Commission. He expressed the opinion that as the applicant had been sentenced by a competent court initially, the fact that the trial judge and the Court of Appeal judge referred to the possibility of his release after some time did not alter the legal effect of the original sentence, given by a competent court. Further rights to review the lawfulness of this were not, therefore, necessary.

The judgment of the Court

In its submissions the Government had drawn a distinction:

> ... between liberty, properly understood, and a life prisoner being permitted to live on licence outside prison. In the latter case, the Government explained, the prisoner was still serving his sentence, albeit outside prison as a result of a privilege granted to him by the Home Secretary, but his right to liberty had not been restored to him. In sum, it was one and the same deprivation of liberty in June 1977 as in December 1966, based on his original conviction and sentence, and no new issue arose under Article 5. (para. 39)

The Court did not accept this line of reasoning. It held that:

> ... All persons, whether at liberty or in detention, are entitled to the protection of Article 5, that is to say, not to be deprived, or to continue to be deprived, of their liberty save in accordance with the conditions specified in paragraph 1 and, when arrested or detained, to receive the benefit of the various safeguards provided by paragraphs 2 to 5 so far as applicable.
>
> Whether Mr Weeks regained his 'liberty', for the purposes of Article 5 of the Convention, when released on licence in March 1976 is a question of fact, depending upon the actual circumstances of the régime to which he was subject. He was lawfully 'at large', to use the terms of section 62(9) of the 1967 Act when outside prison on licence. Admittedly, for persons sentenced to life imprisonment, any release under the 1967 Act is granted as an act of clemency and is always conditional. The freedom enjoyed by a life prisoner, such as Mr Weeks, released on licence is thus more circumscribed in law and more precarious than the freedom enjoyed by the ordinary citizen. Nevertheless, the restrictions to which Mr Weeks' freedom outside prison was subject under the law are not sufficient to prevent its being qualified as a state of 'liberty' for the purposes of Article 5. Hence, when recalling Mr Weeks to prison in 1977, the Home Secretary was ordering his removal from an actual state of liberty, albeit one enjoyed in law as a privilege and not as of right, to a state of custody. (para. 40)

The Court had to consider whether the fresh deprivation of liberty following the decision to revoke his licence, complied with Article 5, para. 1(a). There was no dispute that the re-detention was lawful under English law, but the Court held that:

> ... The 'lawfulness' required by the Convention presupposes not only conformity with domestic law but also, as confirmed by Article 18, conformity with the purposes of the deprivation of liberty permitted by sub-paragraph (a) of Article 5(1). Furthermore, the word 'after' in sub-paragraph (a) does not simply mean that the detention must follow the 'conviction' in point of time: in addition, the 'detention' must result from, 'follow and depend upon' or occur 'by virtue of' the 'conviction'.

In short, there must be sufficient causal connection between the conviction and the deprivation of liberty at issue. (para. 42)

Although the objectives to be pursued by the Home Secretary in exercising his powers under the Criminal Justice Act 1967 were not spelt out, the purpose of the life sentence in Mr Weeks's case was clear from the court's judgment. This purpose placed the sentence in a special category.

... The intention was to make the applicant, who was qualified both by the trial judge and by the Court of Appeal as a 'dangerous young man', subject to a continuing security measure in the interests of public safety. The sentencing judges recognised that it was not possible for them to forecast how long his instability and personality disorders would endure. According to the very words of Thesiger J, Salmon LJ, they accordingly had recourse to an 'indeterminate sentence': this would enable the appropriate authority, namely the Home Secretary, to monitor his progress and release him back into the community when he was no longer judged to represent a danger to society or to himself, and thus hopefully sooner than would have been possible if he had been sentenced to a long term of imprisonment. In the absence of sufficient medical evidence justifying an order sending him to a mental institution, the only means available under the British sentencing machinery to achieve this purpose was a life sentence. In substance, Mr Weeks was being put at the disposal of the State because he needed continued supervision in custody for an unforeseeable length of time and, as a corollary, periodic reassessment in order to ascertain the most appropriate manner of dealing with him.

The grounds expressly relied on by the sentencing courts for ordering this form of deprivation of liberty against Mr Weeks are by their very nature susceptible of change with the passage of time, whereas the measure will remain in force for the whole of his life. In this, his sentence differs from a life sentence imposed on a person because of the gravity of the offence. (para. 46)

In considering whether the re-detention of Mr Weeks was lawful, the Court noted that:

... the formal legal connection between Mr Weeks' conviction in 1966 and his recall to prison some ten years later is not on its own sufficient to justify the contested detention under Article 5(1)(a). The causal link required by sub-paragraph (a) might eventually be broken if a position were reached in which a decision not to release or to re-detain was based on grounds that were inconsistent with the objectives of the sentencing court. 'In those circumstances, a detention that was lawful at the outset would be transformed into a deprivation of liberty that was arbitrary and, hence, incompatible with Article 5'.

... In the submission of the applicant, the objectives of the courts in 1966 and 1967 as regards the length of his loss of liberty were satisfied on his release in March 1976; the requisite link was broken at that stage, so that his full rights under Article 5 were restored to him and his re-detention fifteen months later was no longer justified under Article 5(1)(e).

The Court does not accept this contention. As a matter of English law, it was inherent in Mr Weeks life sentence that, whether he was inside or outside prison, his liberty was at the discretion of the executive for the rest of his life (subject to the controls subsequently introduced by the 1967 Act, notably the Parole Board). This the sentencing judges must be taken to have known and intended. It is not for the Court, within the context of Article 5, to review the appropriateness of the original sentence, a matter which moreover has not been disputed by the applicant in the present proceedings. (paras 49–50)

In examining the sufficiency of the causal connection, the Court was prepared to allow the national authorities a certain discretion as they were better placed than the Court to assess the evidence. Having considered this the Court was satisfied that there was a sufficient connection between the conviction in 1966 and the re-call in 1977 to satisfy Article 5, para. 1(a).

As far as Article 5, para. 4 was concerned, the Court had to determine:

. . . what new issues of lawfulness, if any, were capable of arising in relation to Mr Weeks' recall to prison and continued detention subsequent to sentence and whether the proceedings available complied with paragraph 4 of Article 5.

. . . Mr Weeks did not dispute that in so far as he may have wished to challenge the lawfulness of his recall or detention in terms of English law he at all moments had available to him a remedy before the ordinary courts in the form of an application for judicial review.

However, for the purposes of Article 5(4), the 'lawfulness' of an 'arrest or detention' has to be determined in the light not only of domestic law but also of the text of the Covention, the general principles embodied therein and the aim of the restriction permitted by Article 5(1).

. . . The Court has already held in the context of paragraph (1)(a) of Article 5 that the stated purpose of social protection and rehabilitation for which the 'indetermi-nate' sentence was passed on Mr Weeks, taken together with the particular circumstances of the offence for which he was convicted, places the sentence in a special category: unlike the case of a person sentenced to life imprisonment because of the gravity of the offence committed, the grounds relied on by the sentencing judges for deciding that the length of the deprivation of Mr Weeks' liberty should be subject to the discretion of the executive for the rest of his life are by their nature susceptible of change with the passage of time. The Court inferred from this that if the decisions not to release or to re-detain were based on grounds inconsistent with the objectives of the sentencing court, Mr Weeks' detention would no longer be 'lawful' for the purposes of sub-paragraph (a) of paragraph (1) of Article 5.

It follows that, by virtue of paragraph (4) of Article 5, Mr Weeks was entitled to apply to a 'court' having jurisdictiion to decide 'speedily' whether or not his deprivation of liberty had become 'unlawful' in this sense; this entitlement should have been exercisable by him at the moment of any return to custody after being at liberty and also at reasonable intervals during the course of his imprisonment.

. . . Article 5(4) does not guarantee a right to judicial control of such scope as to empower the 'court', on all aspects of the case, including questions of expediency, to substitute its own discretion for that of the decision-making authority. The review should, however, be wide enough to bear on those conditions which, according to the Convention, are essential for the lawful detention of a person subject to the special kind of deprivation of liberty ordered against Mr Weeks. (paras 56–59)

In considering whether the Parole Board satisfied the requirements of Article 5, para. 4, the Court, having considered its independence and impartiality and its powers and procedures, concluded that:

. . . neither in relation to consideration of Mr Weeks' recall to prison in 1977 nor in relation to periodic examination of his detention with a view to release on licence can the Parole Board be regarded as satisfying the requirements of Article 5(4). (para. 68)

The Court agreed with the Commission that the remedy of judicial review could of itself neither provide the proceedings required by Article 5, para. 4, nor remedy the inadequacies of the Parole Board. There had therefore been a violation of Article 5, para. 4.

Thynne, Wilson and Gunnell v *UK*
Series A, Vol. 190-A

The facts
The applicants had all been sentenced to discretionary life imprisonment for crimes: Thynne for rape and buggery; Wilson for buggery and indecent assault; and Gunnell for rape. There was evidence in Thynne's case of severe psychopathic disorder; he was therefore sentenced to both an indeterminate life sentence and a hospital order. During his imprisonment he absconded from open prison and committed further offences. In 1983 the prison psychiatrist who examined him considered that there was no further need for psychiatric treatment. His release was not recommended, although in 1985 it was accepted that the punitive element of his sentence had been satisfied. He remained in custody pending further review.

In the case of Wilson, who was sentenced in 1972, his release into a controlled protective environment with psychiatric supervision was recommended in 1981. In 1982 he was released on licence, subject to certain conditions. The following year he was recalled and his licence revoked because his conduct had given cause for concern and he had failed to cooperate with his supervising officer. He remained in custody pending review.

In the case of Gunnell, who was convicted in 1965, there was evidence of mental disorder; however, the sentencing judge decided not to make a hospital order under the Mental Health Act 1959, but to impose an indeterminate life sentence because of the gravity of Gunnell's crimes and the need for punishment in such a case. In 1982 the applicant was released on licence, but following two incidents – from which no charges followed – he was recalled in 1983 and his licence revoked. The Secretary of State did not accept the Parole Board's recommendations for his release in 1983 and he was subsequently detained until he was again released on licence in 1988. In 1990 he was convicted of attempted rape, indecent assault and robbery. He was sentenced to life imprisonment and his life licence revoked.

The applicants complained before the Commission of breaches of Article 5, para. 4 and Article 5, para. 5 (Wilson).

The Commission's opinion
The applicants had submitted that there ought to have been a periodic review by a court of the continued lawfulness of their detention. They argued that as they had been given discretionary life sentences – as opposed to determinate sentences – because they were considered to be mentally unstable and thus a danger to the public, their sentences fell into the same category as that of the *Weeks* case, and therefore required judicial safeguards.

The Commission, referring to the constant case law, noted that:

... where an accused receives a sentence of imprisonment, based solely on the gravity of the offence he has committed and the need for retribution and deterrence, the supervision of the lawfulness of such detention under Article 5(4) is incorporated at the outset in the criminal trial and possible appeals against conviction and sentence.

... In such cases detention is justified under Article 5(1)(a) as the detention of a person after conviction by a competent court. Unlike detention of persons of unsound mind, under Article 5(1)(e), the detention is ordered as a retributive punishment for the immutable fact that the person concerned has been found guilty of an offence ...

... However it is clear that there may be cases if imprisonment where Article 5(4) requires continued supervision of the lawfulness of detention at reasonable intervals throughout imprisonment and a court determination of the lawfulness of recall where a prisoner has been released on parole ... (paras 76–78)

However, the Commission considered that:

... unlike the *Weeks* case, the offences committed by all three applicants were grave. However, it is clear that the sentences in these cases do not fall into the normal category of life sentences whose purpose is solely punitive.

... Each of the applicants was given a discretionary life sentence because the domestic courts considered that, in addition to the need for punishment, they were a danger to the public and that there was a need for supervision by the Home Secretary in order to determine when it would be safe to release them. (paras 79 and 80)

Nevertheless, the Commission recognised that there was a difference between a discretionary and a mandatory life sentence.

... Unlike mandatory life sentences, a discretionary life sentence in the United Kingdom is handed down not only because the offence is a grave one, but because, in addition to the need for punishment, the accused is considered mentally unstable and a danger to the public. In such cases it is for the Home Secretary to assess the risks involved in granting parole. While it is true that all life sentences often involve both punitive and security elements, the discretionary life sentence belongs to a separate category because the sentencing court recognises the mental stability or dangerousness of the accused may be susceptible to change over the passage of time.

... The Commission further observes that the domestic courts have openly stated that a discretionary life sentence is composed of a punitive element, i.e. a specific number of years to be served by the prisoner to satisfy the needs of retribution and deterrence (the 'tariff' period) and a security element based on the need to protect the public. Furthermore, since 1983 it is the practice of the trial judge in such cases to communicate the length of the 'tariff' to the Home Secretary at his request to enable the prisoner's case to be reviewed with a view to parole.

... In addition, had it not been for the presence of mental instability and dangerousness, the applicants would have received a determinate sentence under the law of the United Kingdom leading to an earlier release date.

... Against the above background the Commission considers that once the notional 'tariff' period has been served by the applicants the justification for continued detention depends on whether they remain a danger to the public. The measures ordered against them from this point of view are thus comparable to those in the *Weeks* case ... As in the *Weeks* case the lawfulness of the applicants' continued detention under Article 5(1)(a) of the Covention will depend on whether they remain a danger to the public: see *Weeks*, at para. 58.

... It follows that the applicants are entitled under Article 5(4) to apply to a court to have the lawfulness of their detention reviewed at the moment of any return to custody following release or at reasonable intervals during the course of their imprisonment: see *Weeks*. (paras 81–85)

The Commission considered whether the review of the lawfulness of continued detention should apply only after the expiry of the tariff or punitive period of the sentence, but concluded that as the duration of this was uncertain – because it was communicated by the trial judge to the Home Secretary in confidence – this was not really practical. Therefore the guarantee of Article 5, para. 4 had to be considered as applying throughout the imprisonment.

In this respect the Commission noted that:

> . . . the Government do not contest the Court's finding in the *Weeks* case that the requirements of Article 5(4) were not met by either the Parole Board or the availability of judicial review before the High Court. The Court found that the procedure before the Parole Board could not be considered to be judicial in character since the prisoner has no entitlement to full disclosure of the adverse material which the Board has in its possession. It also found that the scope of judicial review was not wide enough to bear on the conditions essential for the 'lawfulness' of re-detention in the sense of Article 5(4) of the Convention. (paras 60 to 69).
>
> . . . The Commission therefore finds that the second and third applicants (Messrs Wilson and Gunnell) were not able to have the lawfulness of their detention determined by a court at the moment of their re-detention and at reasonable intervals throughout their imprisonment.
>
> . . . The Commission also finds that Mr Thynne was not able to have the lawfulness of his detention reviewed by a court at reasonable intervals.
>
> . . . *Conclusion*
> The Commission concludes:
> — by 10 votes to 2 that there has been a violation of Article 5(4) in the case of Mr Wilson;
> — by 10 votes to 2 that there has been a violation of Article 5(4) in the case of Mr Gunnell;
> — by 10 votes to 2 that there has been a violation of Article 5(4) in the case of Mr Thynne. (paras 88–91)

As regards Mr Wilson's claim under Article 5, para. 5, as the Commission had found a violation of Article 5, para. 4, and as it did not accept the restrictive interpretation placed on this paragraph by the Government that:

> . . . the aim of Article 5(5) is limited to ensuring that the victim of an 'unlawful' arrest or detention should have an enforceable right to compensation. (para. 94)

it expressed the opinion that Mr Wilson had an enforceable claim under Article 5, para. 5.

Mr Martinez, in a dissenting opinion, expressed the view that because of the gravity of the offences committed, this case was distinguishable from the *Weeks* case, and that the sentences were in the nature of being prison sentences of an indeterminate length, therefore not requiring compliance with Article 5, para. 4, because the original sentencing procedure was lawful.

The judgment of the Court
In considering the application of Article 5, para. 4 to the facts of the present case, the Court noted that:

. . . the concept of lawfulness under Article 5(4) requires that the detention be in conformity not only with domestic law but also with the text of the Convention, the general principles embodied therein and the aim of the restrictions permitted by Article 5(1).

. . . In cases concerning detention of persons of unsound mind under Article 5(1)(e) where the reasons initially warranting detention may cease to exist the Court has held that 'it would be contrary to the object and purpose of Article 5 . . . to interpret paragraph 4 . . . as making this category of confinement immune from subsequent review of lawfulness merely provided that the intitial decision issued from a court . . . .' This interpretation of Article 5(4) has also, in certain circumstances, been applied to detention 'after conviction by a competent court' under Article 5(1)(a). What is of importance in this context is the nature and purpose of the detention in question, viewed in the light of the objectives of the sentencing court, and not the category to which it belongs under Article 5(1). (paras 68 and 69)

The Court noted that:

. . . Each of the applicants was thus sentenced to life imprisonment because, in addition to the need for punishment, he was considered by the courts to be suffering from a mental or personality disorder and to be dangerous and in need of treatment. Life imprisonment was judged to be the most appropriate sentence in the circumstances since it enabled the Secretary of State to assess their progress and to act accordingly. Thus the courts' sentencing objectives were in that respect similar to those in *Weeks*, but also took into account the much greater gravity of the offences committed.

. . . As regards the nature and purpose of the discretionary life sentence under English law, the Government's main submission was that it is impossible to disentangle the punitive and security components of such sentences. The Court is not persuaded by this argument: the discretionary life sentence has clearly developed in English law as a measure to deal with mentally unstable and dangerous offenders; numerous judicial statements have recognised the protective purpose of this form of life sentence. Although the dividing line may be difficult to draw in particular cases, it seems clear that the principles underlying such sentences, unlike mandatory life sentences, have developed in the sense that they are composed of a punitive element and subsequently of a security element designed to confer on the Secretary of State the responsibility for determining when the public interest permits the prisoner's release. This view is confirmed by the judicial description of the 'tariff' as denoting the period of detention considered necessary to meet the requirements of retribution and deterrence.

. . . It is clear from the judgments of the sentencing courts that in their view the three applicants, unlike Mr Weeks, had committed offences of the utmost gravity meriting lengthy terms of imprisonment. Nevertheless, the Court is satisfied that in each case the punitive period of the discretionary life sentence has expired.

In the case of Mr Thynne, it was accepted that by the end of 1984 risk was the sole remaining consideration in his continued detention.

In addition to the life sentence imposed on him for the offence of buggery, Mr Wilson was sentenced in 1972 to seven years imprisonment for each of the nine other counts to be served concurrently. In the circumstances of his case, it would seem reasonable to draw the conclusion that the punitive period of his life sentence had expired when he was released in 1982 and that thereafter his re-detention pursuant to that sentence depended solely on the risk factor.

In Mr Gunnell's case, too, it may be taken that, notwithstanding the gravity of his offences on which the courts laid particular emphasis, the applicant had served the punitive period of his sentence by March 1982, the date fixed for his provisional release. (paras 72, 73 and 75)

The Court held that factors such as mental instability and dangerousness are susceptible to changes over time, and that new issues of lawfulness may arise concerning the continued detention of such persons. In this case it was clear that the punitive element of sentence in each of the applicant's cases had expired. They were, therefore, entitled to subsequent judicial control as guaranteed by Article 5, para. 4. In considering whether the available remedies satisfied this requirement the Court noted that:

> ... Article 5(4) does not guarantee a right to judicial control of such scope as to empower the 'court' on all aspects of the case, including questions of expediency, to substitute its own discretion for that of the decision-making authority; the review should, nevertheless, be wide enough to bear on those conditions which, according to the Convention, are essential for the lawful detention of a person subject to the special type of deprivation of liberty ordered against these three applicants.
> ... The Court sees no reason to depart from its finding in the *Weeks* judgment that neither the Parole Board not judicial review proceedings—no other remedy of a judicial character being available to the three applicants—satisfy the requirements of Article 5(4). Indeed, this was not disputed by the Government. (paras 79 and 80)

There had therefore been a violation of Article 5, para. 4. In the case of Mr Wilson, the Court agreed with the Commission that there had been a violation of Article 5, para. 5.

Judge Thor Vilhjalmsson expressed a dissenting opinion based on the view that the original sentencing procedure had incorporated the requirements of Article 5, para. 4. He expressed the view that neither the *Weeks* case, nor the case of *X* v *UK* provided sufficient precedents for the Court's ruling in this case.

Comment

This case had far-reaching implications, not only for other similar cases pending before the Commission (see, for example, *Ward* v *UK* 16 EHRR CD 25), but also for the operation of UK law. Following the decision certain changes were introduced both in the determination of the tariff period and in the procedures before the Parole Board, which was itself reconstituted (see Criminal Justice Act 1991).

The Committee of Ministers declared in September 1994 that it was satisfied with the measures taken by the UK in the Criminal Justice Act 1991, and in a number of cases negotiated awards have been made to applicants establishing violations of Article 5, para. 4 occurring before the Act: see, for example, *P, K and G* v *UK* App. No. 13195/87 Resolution DH (94) 59 – in which a sum of £5,150 was awarded; *Clarke* v *UK* App. No. 15767/89 – payment of £500 in respect of non-pecuniary damage (Resolution DH (94) 57); *Oldham* v *UK* App. No. 17143/90 – payment of £500 for non-pecuniary damage and £100 in respect of costs (Resolution DH (94) 58).

It should be noted that entitlement to take proceedings to have the lawfulness of detention examined by a court applies only once the tariff period of the sentence has expired (*N* v *UK* 15 EHRR CD 47). The changes implemented following the decsion in *Thynne, Wilson and Gunnell* did not extend to mandatory life sentences. Indeed, s. 34 of the 1991 Act specifically excluded from review a discretionary life prisoner who was also serving a mandatory life sentence. This was considered in the case of *Wynne* v *UK* App. No. 15484/89, declared admissible 15 October 1992, Report of the Commission 4 May 1993, Decision of the Court 18 July 1994, Series A, No. 294-A, 19 EHRR 333. In this case, the Court, following its own case law, considered that mandatory sentences were imposed because of the gravity of the offence. Whereas a discretionary life sentence could be said to have a protective purpose, a mandatory life sentence was viewed as essentially punitive in nature. It should also be noted that the new measures introduced under the Criminal Justice Act 1991, do not extend to Northern Ireland – see *W, H and A* v *UK* 19 EHRR CD 60 – nor do they extend to persons being detained 'at Her Majesty's Pleasure', an issue which was considered in the following two cases.

Prem Singh v *UK*
Council of Europe Report 55/1994/502/584

The facts
In this case the applicant was 15 when he was convicted of murder in 1973. In 1990 he had been released on licence, but this licence was revoked in 1991 following charges of dishonesty, fraud and threatening behaviour.

The Parole Board, which considered various representations by the applicant, did not permit him to see certain police and probation officers' reports, on the basis of which a decision not to recommend his release was made. This failure to disclose the relevant documents had led to the quashing of the Parole Board's decision in April 1993. The Parole Board then reconsidered the case, but did not hold an oral hearing. Again it decided not to recommend his release.

In 1994, recommendation for the applicant's release was eventually made, but the Secretary of State decided not to accept this recommendation.

The applicant complained to the Commission under Article 5, para. 4, that he was unable to obtain a review by a court of the lawfulness of his continued detention.

The Commission's opinion
The Commission recalled that the Court had distinguished between the different forms of life imprisonment in its earlier case law:

> . . . Mandatory life imprisonment is imposed because of the inherent gravity of the offence (i.e. in cases of murder) and applied automatically regardless of considerations pertaining to the dangerousness of the offender. No right to review of subsequent release on licence arises in such cases. The discretionary life sentence however has a special indeterminate character and has been developed as a measure to deal with mentally ill and unstable offenders. The discretionary sentence serves a preventative rather than a punitive purpose and because of the presence of factors (e.g. dangerousness, instability) which are susceptible of change with the passage of time, new issues of lawfulness of continued detention may arise which require the possibility of recourse to a body satisfying the requirements of Article 5 para. 4 . . .
> (para. 61)

Although the sentence of detention at Her Majesty's pleasure were imposed automatically on juveniles in the case of murder, this differed from the mandatory sentence for adults convicted for murder, in that the former was indeterminate, while the latter was fixed at the term of life. The Commission considered that:

> . . . a distinction must be drawn between a sentence which is fixed by the judiciary at a maximum of life leaving a discretion to the executive as to whether the individual is released earlier and a sentence which has no fixed term and the limits of which are to be defined by the executive. (para. 62)

The Commission considered that the special regime which applied to young offenders was geared to the special considerations which apply in such cases, where the offenders are potentially dangerous but have formative years ahead of them and may change with maturation.

The Commission recalled that in this case:

> . . . the applicant was sentenced at the age of 15 and spent the following 17 years in prison – over half of his life and a significant part of his adolescence and young adulthood. The element of his sentence attributed to the purpose of retribution expired in or about 1990 and consideration of risk and dangerousness would appear to be the determining factor in his continuing detention. His release and subsequent recall to prison were determined primarily with regard to considerations of risk. Since, therefore, issues may arise with the passage of time relating to the justification for the applicant's continued detention, the Commission finds that he is entitled under Article 5 para. 4 to have the lawfulness of that detention decided by a court. (para. 65)

In considering whether the procedures available to the applicant before the Parole Board met the requirements of Article 5, para. 4, the Commission noted that the procedures applicable to the Board's examination of the applicant's case had varied with the circumstances. The Commission therefore considered the various occasions:

> . . . On 19 December 1991, immediately following the applicant's recall, the Board had the power to direct his release pursuant to section 62(5) of the Criminal Justice Act 1967. However, the documents before it were not disclosed to the applicant. When the Board examined the case on 30 July 1992 following the applicant's acquittal, it did not have the power to direct release and there was also no disclosure of documents. The Commission finds that on each of these occasions the Board did not satisfy the requirements of Article 5 para. 4, given the procedural shortcoming in failing to make available the material before the Board either taken alone or combined with the lack of power to direct release.
>
> . . . Following the decision of the Divisional Court . . . the Parole Board's decision of 19 December 1991 was quashed and in the procedure which culminated in its decision of 18 June 1993, it had power to direct release pursuant to section 39(5) of the Criminal Justice Act 1991 which had come into force. The applicant also had sight for the first time of the relevant material before the Board for the purpose of making written representations concerning the allegations against him. (paras 73 and 74)

The Commission noted that:

> . . . when the applicant was recalled to prison, it was against a background of allegations of misconduct and deception. The applicant considered that he had

explanations for the alleged shortcomings in his behaviour and, *inter alia*, submitted statements from his girlfriend and landlady which contradicted the factual basis for the assessment of his conduct as disclosing unreliability and deceptiveness. It appears to the Commission that in the circumstances of this case the opportunity for the Board to hear the relevant witnesses, and for the applicant to be able to cross-examine the witnesses against him, would have been necessary for a proper and fair resolution of the issues arising as to the applicant's bona fides.

. . . Further, the Commission recalls that the Board in its review of 18 June 1993 was reconsidering its original decision to revoke the applicant's licence. The Commission has held in the context of Article 26 of the Convention that the opportunity of requesting an authority to reconsider a decision taken by it does not generally constitute an effective remedy for the purposes of exhaustion of domestic remedies (see e.g. No. 11932/86, Dec. 9.5.88, DR 56 p. 199). While it appears that the composition of the Board may have differed on both occasions, the Commission considers that a prisoner would have legitimate grounds to fear that the principal issue in the case – whether his continued presence in the community constituted a risk – was prejudged. It is not apparent from the material before the Commission that the Board recommends recall on the basis that this is a provisional view based on prima facie evidence and subject to fresh consideration in light of a prisoner's representations. The Commission notes that the reasons given to the applicant for his recall were framed in unconditional findings and assessments as to his conduct and the resulting risk. Pursuant to the relevant statutory provisions, a review of the decision to recall was only undertaken on the applicant's request, such reviews not being required automatically . . .

. . . While it would not necessarily raise an issue of structural independence where, for example, the same judicial instance (differently constituted) reconsidered the merits of a case, the Commission considers that the function and powers of the Parole Board as it currently operates in relation to the detainees at Her Majesty's pleasure vary significantly. The Commission has found above that the Board fails to have the characteristics of a 'court-like body' when it exercises a merely advisory function. Similarly, the procedure by which it recommended recall had, in the Commission's view, an executive or administrative character.

. . . The Commission is therefore of the opinion that the review conducted by the Parole Board on 18 June 1993 lacked the necessary judicial guarantees and did not afford the applicant an effective opportunity of influencing the outcome of the proceedings . . . (paras 76–79)

There was consequently a violation of Article 5, para. 4. The case was referred to the European Court of Human Rights.

Abed Hussain v *UK*
Council of Europe Report

The facts
At the age of 16 the applicant had been convicted of the murder of his baby brother, and sentenced to be detained at Her Majesty's Pleasure under s. 53(1) of the Children and Young Persons Act 1933. On four occasions his release had been considered by the Parole Board. On the first two occasions the applicant had no opportunity to see the reports of the Board, or to appear before it. On the third occasion the decision – in this case not to transfer him to an open

prison – was communicated to him three months after it had been made. On the fourth occasion the Board decided to transfer the applicant to an open prison.

The applicant complained to the Commission that throughout this period he had been unable to obtain review by a court of the lawfulness of his continued detention, and that there had been a violation of Article 5, para. 4.

The Commission's opinion

The Commission had to decide whether detention at Her Majesty's Pleasure should be assimilated to discretionary life sentences for adults – as argued by the applicant – for which the European Court had held that judicial rather than executive control was required; or whether it was equivalent to a term of mandatory life imprisonment – as argued by the Government – for which there was no entitlement to periodic judicial review, the requirements of Article 5, para. 4 being satisfied by the original trial and appeal.

The Commission noted that:

> . . . sentences of detention at Her Majesty's pleasure are imposed automatically in the cases of murder by juveniles (under eighteen years). To that extent, the detention has a similarity with the mandatory sentence imposed in respect of murder by adults. The adult sentence however is fixed at the term of life: detention at Her Majesty's pleasure is on its face indeterminate. Though impliedly a sentence of detention may authorise detention for life, the Commission considers that a distinction must be drawn between a sentence which is fixed by the judiciary at a maximum of life leaving a discretion to the executive as to whether the individual is released earlier and a sentence which has no fixed term and the limits of which are to be defined by the executive.
>
> . . . The Commission has had regard to the origins of the term 'detention at Her Majesty's pleasure' which applied in 1800 to the detention of insane offenders and in which context it had a clearly preventative purpose. Juveniles under eighteen have been excluded from the regime of mandatory life imprisonment and also from the notion of 'custody for life' which applies to offenders between 18 and 21. The application of the term of detention at Her Majesty's pleasure to juveniles would appear to the Commission to reflect an intention of imposing a distinct regime of detention geared to the special considerations which apply in dealing with very young offenders who are potentially dangerous but who still have formative years ahead of them and may change with maturation. (paras 51 and 52)

In this case the applicant had already spent 16 years in prison. As issues might arise relating to the justification for his continued detention once the period for retribution had been served, the Commission expressed the opinion that he was entitled to have the lawfulness of his detention decided by a court.

The Commission had to consider whether the Parole Board, which considered applications for release on licence, met the requirements of Article 5, para. 4. Referring to its earlier case law the Commission recalled that:

> . . . the Court in the *Weeks* and *Thynne, Wilson and Gunnell* cases . . . found that neither the Parole Board (pre-1992) nor the possibility of judicial review satisfied the requirements of Article 5 para. 4 of the Convention in respect of prisoners serving terms of discretionary life imprisonment. The Court held in the *Weeks* case . . . that the Parole Board which could only recommend release lacked the necessary power of

decision. Further, in view of the failure to provide prisoners with full disclosure of the adverse material before the Board the procedures did not allow the proper participation of the person adversely affected by the contested decision and could not be regarded as judicial in character. It did not find it necessary to rule on whether an oral hearing would be required.

. . . The Commission has found above that when considering whether to recommend the release of a person detained at Her Majesty's pleasure the Parole Board is dealing with issues relating to the lawfulness of a deprivation of liberty of an individual. In this context, the 'court' required by Article 5 para. 4 should have the power to order release and it is essential that the procedures followed should afford proper guarantees that enable an individual to participate effectively in the proceedings before it . . . Where questions arise involving, for example, the assessment of character or personal attitudes, it may be essential for the proper and fair examination of the issues that the detained person be given the opportunity to participate in an oral hearing and, if there are disputed issues of fact, the possibility to have witnesses examined and cross-examined and their credibility established in person . . . (paras 57 and 58)

Although certain changes had been introduced in 1992 which made the Parole Board more effective, these did not apply to non-discretionary life sentences, and so in respect of cases such as the applicant's the Parole Board had no decision-making power.

The Commission concluded, therefore, that there had been a violation of Article 5, para. 4.

The case was referred to the European Court of Human Rights.

Comment
Detention 'at Her Majesty's Pleasure' originated in an Act of 1800, and was particularly directed at defendants who had been acquitted of a charge of murder, treason or felony on the grounds of insanity. In 1908 this form of sentence was introduced for offenders aged 10 to 16, and in 1933 was extended to those under 18. Where the offence of murder is committed by persons between the ages of 18 and 21 the sentence is custody for life (s. 8(1) of the Criminal Justice Act 1982).

5.2.5   The Lawfulness of Other Forms of Detention

Benham v *UK*
Council of Europe Report

The facts
The applicant, who was unemployed, was detained by magistrates following his failure to pay the community charge tax. The magistrates order his committal because they found that his failure to pay was due to 'his culpable neglect'. The applicant was not legally represented before the magistrates' court. Twelve days after his detention he was granted bail; a subsequent appeal to the Divisional Court was allowed and the magistrates court order was set aside. Legal aid and representation was available to the applicant for the appeal.

The applicant complained of breaches of Article 5, para. 1, based on his detention for failure to pay; Article 5, para. 5, on the grounds that he had not been able to bring an action for damages in respect of the detention; and Article 6, para. 3(c), concerning the refusal of legal aid.

The Commission's opinion

The Government conceded that the magistrates had erred in law, but considered that they:

> ... did not act in excess of their jurisdiction, and their decision was therefore not unlawful either in domestic law or under Article 5(1) of the Convention. . . . [C]onsequently, in the absence of a violation of Article 5, Article 5(5) of the Convention does not apply. (p. 106)

The Government also argued that the proceedings neither involved criminal actions nor did they determine any civil right or obligation and therefore could not be held to fall under Article 6. Thus the question of legal aid entitlement did not arise.

The Commission recalled that no claim arose under Article 5, para. 5 unless a breach of one of the other paragraphs of Article 5 had been established. First, therefore, it had to consider whether there had been a breach of any of these, in particular Article 5, para. 1.

Comment

The magistrates had arrived at their finding of culpable neglect to pay the community charge on the basis that Mr Benham had left his employment shortly before he became liable to pay the tax and had no paid employment since. Whether suitable employment was in fact available was not reported. However, the magistrates believed that he had the potential to earn money. The process of appeal was by way of judicial review, during which it was held that the finding of culpable neglect could not be sustained on the evidence and the committal to prison was wrong.

Cases pending under this article

Chahal v *UK* (Application No. 22414/93.) This case, which concerned a claim for political asylum by a Sikh activist facing deportation from Britain, raised issues under Articles 3, 5, and 8. The issue relating to Article 5 concerned the prolonged detention undergone by the applicant while facing deportation. The Commission declared the application admissible in September 1994 (10 EHRR CD 193), and in June 1995 the Commission expressed the opinion that there would be a violation of Articles 3 and 8 if the applicant were deported, and that there had been a violation of Article 5, para. 1. The case has now been referred to the European Court.

Taylor v *UK* (Application No. 20448/92), concerning alleged violations of Article 5, para. 4 and the lawfulness of the applicant's detention on the basis of a discretionary life sentence, has been declared admissible by the Commission.

Hussain and Singh v *UK* (Application Nos 21928/93 and 23389/94) have been referred to the European Court and were heard on 27 September 1995.

Stanley Johnson v *UK* (Application No. 22520/93). This application, which concerned the continued detention of the applicant in a psychiatric institution, was declared admissible on 18 May 1995 (Information Note No. 126). The Commission is now seeking to effect a friendly settlement.

TM v *UK* (Application No. 21848/93), concerning the time taken to review the detention of the applicant by the Parole Board (Article 5, para. 4), has been declared admissible.

Raymond Baxter v *UK* (Application No. 24835/94), concerning the alleged absence of any court review of detention 'at Her Majesty's Pleasure' in breach of Article 5, para. 4, declared admissible.

CHAPTER 6
ARTICLE SIX

Article 6

1. In the determination of his civil rights and obligations or of any criminal charge against him, everyone is entitled to a fair and public hearing within a reasonable time by an independent and impartial tribunal established by law. Judgment shall be pronounced publicly but the press and public may be excluded from all or part of the trial in the interests of morals, public order or national security in a democratic society, where the interests of juveniles or the protection of the private life of the parties so require, or to the extent strictly necessary in the opinion of the court in special circumstances where publicity would prejudice the interests of justice.

2. Everyone charged with a criminal offence shall be presumed innocent until proved guilty according to law.

3. Everyone charged with a criminal offence has the following minimum rights:

   (a) to be informed promptly, in a language which he understands and in detail, of the nature and cause of the accusation against him;

   (b) to have adequate time and facilities for the preparation of his defence;

   (c) to defend himself in person or through legal assistance of his own choosing or, if he has not sufficient means to pay for legal assistance, to be given it free when the interests of justice so require;

   (d) to examine or have examined witnesses against him and to obtain the attendance and examination of witnesses on his behalf under the same conditions as witnesses against him;

   (e) to have the free assistance of an interpreter if he cannot understand or speak the language used in court.

6.1   THE SCOPE OF THE ARTICLE

6.1.1   Civil Rights

It has been suggested that 'civil rights' applies only to those rights which are justiciable as such in the courts of the country concerned, i.e. proceedings before courts of law, and that therefore any right relating to administrative proceedings is not a right covered by Article 6. Moreover, any civil claim must be one that is capable of being submitted to a court (*Golder* v *UK* 1 EHRR 524). Article 6 does not in itself guarantee any particular content for civil rights and obligations in the substantive law of the Contracting States (*James* v *UK* 8 EHRR 123). However, the Commission and Court have constantly held that the term 'civil rights and obligations' cannot be construed as a mere reference to the domestic law of the Contracting Party but must be interpreted independently. Whether a right or obligation is of a civil nature does not depend on the particular procedure prescribed by domestic law for its determination, but solely on an analysis of the claim itself. It has therefore been argued that 'civil' should be widely interpreted and that the use of the term is primarily to distinguish 'civil' rights from criminal charges.

However, the Commission has held that where a right is determined by public law, through acts of public administration, Article 6 may not apply – for example, the determination of the category into which a prisoner falls is an administrative decision (*Brady* v *UK* 3 EHRR 297. In particular, this reasoning has been applied to cases involving immigrants and the decision to grant or refuse them entry, and the proceedings by which such decisions are reached, and in cases of deportation (*Uppal and Other* v *UK (No. 2)* 3 EHRR 391). Nevertheless, the determination of rights which are not deemed to fall under this article may adversely affect other rights which do – for example, a deportation decision may impinge on a right to family life, which is recognised as a civil right. Thus in the case of *Mohamed Alam and Mohamed Khan, Harbhajan Singh* v *UK* App. Nos 2991/66 and 2992/66, the Commission expressed the opinion that if the applicants had a right under Article 8, then they would have a 'civil right' and as such would have a right to the protections guaranteed by Article 6.

In some circumstances it may be unclear whether or not there is a right which falls under Article 6. In the case of *McFeeley* v *UK* 3 EHRR 161, the Commission had to consider whether Article 6 applied to the disciplinary adjudications of the prison governor. The Court has indicated that while States may maintain a distinction between a disciplinary charge and a criminal charge, the Court can examine whether any such charge counts as a criminal charge for the purposes of Article 6. In doing so the Court will consider:

[1]   whether the provisions defining the offence charged belong, according to the legal system of the respondent State, to criminal law, disciplinary law or both concurrently;
[2]   the very nature of the offence;
[3]   the degree of severity of the penalty that the person concerned risks incurring.
(3 EHRR 161, para. 93)

In the case of *McFeeley*, although the accumulated effect of the disciplinary measures taken against the applicant was harsh, the Commission considered that the measures were nevertheless disciplinary and not criminal.

The wording of Article 6 was taken over from the early drafts of Article 14, para. 1 of the United Nations Covenant on Civil and Political Rights. Initially the term 'civil' was not included in the drafts, but was inserted later following discussions of the United Nations Commission for Human Rights. From these discussions it appears that it was generally agreed that 'a right to determination by a court of a question concerning military service and taxes would be excluded from the field of application of the provision'. Similarly, it has been held that disputes between civil servants and the State do not involve the 'determination of civil rights and obligations', neither does Article 6 give an automatic right to a medical examination – for example, in personal injury cases (*Campbell and Fell V UK* 5 EHRR 207).

6.1.2   Fair Hearing

The concept of a fair hearing involves a number of issues. For example, is the hearing public or private; is the defendant given a chance to present his or her case; is the judge fair and impartial in his instructions to the jury, etc. In this context a number of principles emerge from the case law, for example:

> . . . that in principle, all evidence must be adduced in the presence of the accused at a public hearing with a view to adversarial argument, but this does not mean that a statement from a witness must always be made in court and in public if it is to be admitted in evidence. The defendant must be given an adequate and proper opportunity to challenge and question the witnesses against him. (*X v UK* 15 EHRR CD 113)

However, a decision by a court – as in the above case – to screen witnesses from the applicant did not interfere with the applicant's rights under either Article 6, para. 1 or Article 6, para. 3(d).

Generally a fair hearing will require the presence of the applicant or a representative; indeed the Commission has held that:

> . . . in certain classes or in certain sets of circumstances a 'fair' hearing is scarcely conceivable without the presence in person of the party concerned. However, the extent to which such presence is actually required will depend upon the nature of the hearing in question, and in particular upon the scope of the powers enjoyed by the court before which the hearing is held, and the significance of this hearing in the context of the proceedings as a whole. (*Monnell and Morris v UK* Series A, No. 115, para. 130)

In a criminal trial Article 6 read as a whole guarantees an accused person the right to participate effectively:

> . . . This includes not only the right to be present but also to hear and follow proceedings. Such rights are implicit in the very notion of an adversarial procedure . . . (*Stanford v UK* Series A, Vol. 282)

However, it is for the accused or his or her lawyer to bring to the court's attention any difficulties in hearing or following the proceedings. The

Contracting States are required to intervene only if a failure by counsel or the accused's representative is manifest, or is sufficiently brought to the attention of the Court. For example, in the *Stanford* case, poor court acoustics could have given rise to an issue under Article 6 had the accused's hearing problems been brought to the attention of the trial judge.

The right to a fair trial may extend beyond the immediate jurisdiction of the member State. In the case of *Soering* v *UK* 11 EHRR 439, the Court, agreeing with the Commission, held that:

> an issue might exceptionally be raised under Article 6 by an extradition decision in circumstances where the fugitive has suffered or risks suffering a flagrant denial of a fair trial in the requesting country. (Series A, Vol. 161, para. 113)

In order for the hearing to be fair, the applicant must be capable of understanding what is going on and of comprehending the course of the proceedings and of conducting a defence (*V* v *UK* 15 EHRR CD 108). The concept of a fair hearing of a 'civil right' does not include the right to report on all matters stated in open court (*Hodgson, Woolf Productions* 10 EHRR 503).

A violent press campaign may render a decision unfair, but the applicant must show that, first, the campaign is violent and, secondly, that it led to the deprivation of a fair trial or violated the presumption of innocence. The implementation of security arrangements at a trial cannot in itself be considered to be unfair, and although the Commission has indicated that handcuffing an accused could be undesirable if it gave the jury any impression which went against a presumption of innocence, this was not necessarily to be assumed (*Welch* v *UK* 16 EHRR CD 42).

In the context of criminal trials Article 6, para. 3 applies. The Commission has indicated that the meaning of 'determination of any criminal charge' within Article 6, para. 1 includes:

> . . . not only the determination of the guilt or innocence of the accused, but also in principle the determination of his sentence; and the expression 'everyone charged with a criminal offence' in Art. 6(3) includes persons who, although already convicted, have not been sentenced. (*X* v *UK* (1972) 15 *Yearbook* pp. 394–6)

In criminal matters, the requirement that an accused person should have a public hearing 'within a reasonable time' is 'designed to avoid that a person charged should remain too long in a state of uncertainty about his fate' (*X* v *UK* 3 EHRR 271, para. 62). The period of time which must be taken into account in order to determine whether or not it is reasonable runs from the day on which the person is charged, i.e. the moment at which a person is substantially affected as a result of the suspicion against him or her. The end of the period is when the person so charged ceases to be affected as a result of these suspicions – in the case of criminal charges this moment will usually be when the accused is found guilty or acquitted, or where the proceedings are discontinued. However, an accused cannot rely on Article 6, para. 1 to claim a right of access to the courts in order that a pending charge against him or her should be heard. Nor can the accused use Article 6 to prevent the prosecution from dropping the charge or deciding to discontinue proceedings (*X* v *UK* 3 EHRR 271).

In considering whether a period of time is not reasonable the Commission will take into account all the relevant factors, including the complexity of the case, whether other charges were pending, whether the matter is at first instance or on appeal, whether there have been valid reasons for adjournment, etc. Thus in the above case of *X* v *UK*, a period of four years and eight months was held not to exceed the limits of what could be considered reasonable in the circumstances.

6.1.3   Independent and Impartial Tribunal

The Commission has interpreted the independence of any tribunal to mean that it is independent from the executive and from the parties. In this respect, in order for the proceedings to be fair, not only must justice be done but it must be seen to be done. However, this does not necessarily mean that the composition of the court on appeal or a re-hearing must be different. This approach is influenced by the practice in a number of member States' legal systems of referring a case back to the court of first instance where the court of appeal allows an appeal on a question of law. In such circumstances the Commission has held that:

> ... It is clear [therefore] that the mere fact that a court has previously been seised with the same case does not render it incapable of satisfying the requirements of impartiality imposed by Art. 6(1) of the Convention. In such circumstances the judges of fact and law retain the same function in respect of the proceedings. They remain subject to the requirements of impartiality, which imply *inter alia*, that they must not have been involved previously in the proceedings in question in a different capacity, such as a prosecutor or advocate. (*Gillow* v *UK* Series A, Vol. 109, para. 179)

The tribunal must be independent and impartial. This involves an examination of the facts. Thus in the case where an inspector refused an appeal against an enforcement notice to comply with planning controls, the Commission had to consider whether the inspector who determined the appeal was 'an independent and impartial tribunal established by law'. The Commission was satisfied that he came within the concept of a 'tribunal' and was established 'by law' (the Town and Country Planning Act 1990); but because he served the Secretary of State, the Commission held that he was not sufficiently independent to comply with the provisions of Article 6. However, this could be remedied by the possibility of further appeal to the High Court (*John Bryan* v *UK* 18 EHRR CD 18).

Where the impartiality of the tribunal or court is in question, it is not sufficient merely to establish that there was no actual likelihood of bias on the part of the judge. An objective approach must be followed in order to establish whether the judge 'offered guarantees sufficient to exclude any legitimate doubt [of bias]' (*Brown* v *UK* 8 EHRR 252).

Even where the same court tries a number of different actions involving the applicant, provided there is no evidence of bias or unfairness, the provisions of Article 6 will not necessarily be violated (*App. No. 99732* v *UK* 5 EHRR 268, in which a number of motoring charges against the applicant were heard by the same bench of magistrates in separate trials).

6.1.4   Access to Court

A fair hearing relates to the procedures observed during the judicial process. Clearly there is some overlap between this aspect of Article 6 and that of access to court. However, the question of whether the hearing is fair may not arise if there are, at the outset, problems in gaining access to the judicial process. Cases in which access to court has been considered include *Kiss* v *UK* 19 EHRR CD 17, in which a prisoner was refused permission by the Home Secretary to take legal proceedings against a prison officer for alleged assault, and *Stubbings* v *UK* 19 EHRR CD 32, which concerned the operation of limitation bars.

The fact that an action is unlikely to succeed if brought to court, is not the same as depriving an applicant of the right of access to court.

The right of access to court is not absolute but may be subject to limitations (*Golder* v *UK* Series A, Vol. 18; *Ashingdane* v *UK* Series A, Vol. 93) – for example, in the case of minors, vexatious litigants, persons of unsound mind and persons declared bankrupt. Access to court may also be limited or denied on the facts of a particular case, for example, where the Official Receiver believes that the costs will outweigh the sum claimed and therefore be detrimental to existing creditors (*App. No. 12040/86* v *UK*, or where the domestic court requires an appellant to find security for the costs of an appeal (*Nikolai Tolstoy Miloslavsky* v *UK* Series A, Vol. 316), or by statute (see, for example, *Ashingdane* v *UK* Series A, Vol. 93 (Mental Health Act 1959, s. 141) and *James* v *UK* 18 EHRR CD 131 (Mental Health Act 1983, s. 139)). Under the Crown Proceedings Act, the Crown is immune from civil liability where a certificate issued under s. 10 certifies that an injury incurred by a member of the Armed Forces was incurred in the course of employment and entitles the holder to enhanced pension rights (*App. No. 9803/82* v *UK* 5 EHRR 465; *Pinder* v *UK* 7 EHRR 464; *Dyer* v *UK* 7 EHRR 469). Similarly, under s. 76 of the Civil Aviation Act 1982, no action lies in respect of trespass or nuisance caused by the flight of an aircraft at a reasonable height.

Limited access may arise where an individual is denied access but collective access is permitted – for example, through a representative of stockholders. Such limitations, provided they are directed at a legitimate aim, will not infringe Article 6 (*Lithgow* v *UK* 8 EHRR 329). However, the Commission has indicated that any limitations imposed must not restrict or reduce the access left to the individual in such a way and to such an extent that the very essence of the right is impaired. There must, therefore, be a reasonable relationship of proportionality between the means employed and the legitimate aim sought to be achieved.

Article 6 does not guarantee any rights to a retrial, and therefore proceedings concerning applications for retrial fall outside the scope of the article (*De Courcy* v *UK* (1969) 12 *Yearbook* 284). Article 6 cannot:

> ... be interpreted so as to require the existence of a further jurisdiction to review or expand on the jurisdiction provided by an inferior court, where that first court is capable of determining all questions of fact and law. (*App. No. 11949/86* v *UK* 10 EHRR 123)

Neither does the article guarantee an appeal in criminal proceedings or compel Contracting States to set up courts of appeal or cassation. It has been held that:

> . . . It is not the Court's function to indicate the measures to be taken by national authorities to ensure that their appeals system satisfies the requirements of Article 6. Its task is solely to determine whether the system chosen by them leads to results which are consistent with Article 6. (*Maxwell* v *UK* Series A, Vol. 300-C, para. 40)

Under the legal system applicable in England and Wales – not Scotland (see *Granger* v *UK* 12 EHRR 451) – where leave to appeal has to be applied for and there is no automatic right to appeal, a number of cases have raised issues concerning the appeals procedure.

Where appeal courts are set up, the guarantees under Article 6 continue to apply to the appeal proceedings as these form part of the whole proceedings which determine the criminal charge at issue.

In examining the fairness of appeal proceedings in the context of the proceedings as a whole, the Commission has held:

> . . . it should consider first the powers of the Court of Appeal and the scope of the hearing for leave to appeal, including the question whether it is a review of a lower court's decision, or whether it is a full rehearing. In addition, the Commission considers it necessary, in the light of the answer to this first question, to examine how the applicants' actual interests were presented and protected in the proceedings in question. (*Monnell and Morris* v *UK* Series A, Vol. 115, para. 131)

6.1.5   Equality of Arms

This principle, of procedural equality of the accused with the prosecution, has been held consistently to be an inherent element of the notion of a fair hearing. Essentially this means that both parties to an action must have access to evidence used in the trial, including the right to challenge and cross-examine evidence used.

Certain evidence may not necessarily be available to an applicant; for example, the Commission has held that Article 6, para. 1 cannot be interpreted to give the parties to proceedings a general right to the tape recording of the proceedings (*Gillow* v *UK* 7 EHRR 292).

Similarly, it is not the Commission's task to examine whether a domestic court has evaluated the evidence correctly, only to consider whether the evidence for and against the accused has been presented in such a manner that the accused has had a fair trial (*App. No. 9329/81* v *UK* 5 EHRR 268). Also the Commission has constantly held that Article 6, para. 3(d) does not give an accused person the right to call witnesses without restriction (*X* v *UK* (1971) 14 *Yearbook* 634 at 658).

An issue which has created some problems in this context is the hearsay rule, whereby evidence of previous statements made by persons who do not give oral testimony at the trial is excluded. There are some exceptions – for example, in criminal cases confessions may be used against the person who made them provided they were made voluntarily, as may statements which can be seen as part of the event itself. Moreover, evidence which goes to the issue of the state of mind of the maker of the statement will be regarded as original evidence rather than hearsay, provided it is not intended to prove the truth of what the maker of the statement said. The Commission has found that the hearsay rule is legitimate and not in principle contrary to Article 6 in as much as its purpose in the jury trial system is to ensure that the best evidence is before the jury, who can evaluate the credibility and demeanour of the witness. It also avoids undue weight being given to evidence which cannot be tested by cross-examination.

6.1.6   Legal Aid

Equality of arms may also raise issues concerning access to legal aid. In this respect there is a distinction between civil and criminal proceedings.

Article 6 does not expressly guarantee legal aid in civil proceedings. While this may be implicit in protecting access to court, the Commission has constantly held that the means by which effective access to court in civil cases is ensured falls within a State's margin of appreciation. Thus limitations on legal aid for certain civil actions will not violate Article 6, para. 1 – for example, under the schedule of proceedings provided for in the Legal Aid Act 1988, legal aid is not available for defamation proceedings (see *S and M* v *UK* 18 EHRR CD 172). The question for the Commission or the Court will always be to examine whether, despite the absence or availability of legal aid, access to court was effectively denied to the litigant, either as plaintiff or defendant.

In the case of criminal proceedings, Article 6, para. 3(c) guarantees the right to free legal assistance subject to two conditions: (i) that the individual concerned does not have sufficient means to pay for legal assistance, and (ii) that the 'interests of justice' require that legal aid be granted. In interpreting this last provision the Court has stated that:

> ... The interests of justice cannot ... be taken to require an automatic grant of legal aid whenever a convicted person, with no objective likelihood of success, wishes to appeal after having received a fair trial at first instance in accordance with Art. 6. (*Monnell and Morris* v *UK* Series A, Vol. 115, para. 67)

Thus in determining 'when the interests of justice so require', the Court or Commission will look at the nature of the proceedings involved, the powers of the court, the capacity of the unrepresented accused – or appellant if the case has gone on appeal – to present legal argument, and the importance of the issue at stake in view of the severity of the sentence.

The right to legal assistance does not extend to guaranteeing the accused the right to choose his or her official lawyer, or to be consulted by the court on the question of such a lawyer's selection (*App. No. 8715/79* v *UK* 5 EHRR 268).

6.2   THE CASES

Golder v *UK*
Series A, Vol. 18

The facts
The applicant, a prisoner, complained that he had been denied permission to consult a solicitor with a view to bringing defamation proceedings against a

prison officer. The officer had accused him of being involved in a prison disturbance, a charge which the applicant denied, but which led to various sanctions being imposed on him under the rules relating to prison discipline. He was eventually cleared of any involvement with the disturbances.

The Commission's opinion

The case raised important questions concerning the right of access to the courts under Article 6. Until this point this question had not been expressly decided, although it had also been raised in *Knechtl v UK* App. No. 4115/69. The Commission had to consider if such a right was guaranteed, whether there were any limitations applicable.

The Commission considered unanimously that there was a violation of Article 6, para. 1.

The judgment of the Court

The Court considered that there were two distinct issues to be decided:

(i) Is article 6(1) limited to guaranteeing in substance the right to a fair trial in legal proceedings which are already pending, or does it in addition secure a right to access to the courts for every person wishing to commence an action in order to have his right to have his civil rights and obligations determined?

(ii) In the latter eventuality, are there any implied limitations on the right of access or on the exercise of that right which are applicable in the present case? (para. 25)

The question whether Golder would have continued in his action once he had received a solicitor's opinion did not have to be considered. The relevant facts were that:

. . . Golder had made it most clear that he intended 'taking civil action for libel'; it was for this purpose that he wished to contact a solicitor, which was a normal preliminary step in itself and in Golder's case probably essential on account of his imprisonment. By forbidding Golder to make such contact, the Home Secretary actually impeded the launching of the contemplated action. Without formally denying Golder his right to institute proceedings before a court, the Home Secretary did in fact prevent him from commencing an action at that time, 1970. Hindrance in fact can contravene the Convention just like a legal impediment. (para. 26)

The Court had to consider whether this hinderance violated any right under the Convention, particularly Article 6. There was no dispute that the action Golder intended to take was a 'civil right' within the meaning of the article. The Court therefore had to interpret the scope and application of Article 6:

. . . In the way in which it is presented in the 'general rule' in Article 31 of the Vienna Convention, the process of interpretation of a treaty is a unity, a single combined operation; this rule, closely integrated, places on the same footing the various elements enumerated in the four paragraphs of the Article.

. . . The terms of Article 6(1) of the European Convention, taken in their context, provide reason to think that this right is included among the guarantees set forth.

. . . The clearest indications are to be found in the French text, first sentence. In the field of *contestations civiles* (civil claims) everyone has a right to proceedings instituted by or against him being conducted in a certain way—'*équitablement*' (fairly), '*publiquement*' (publicly), '*dans un délai raisonnable*' (within a reasonable time), etc.—but also and primarily '*à ce que sa cause soit entendue*' (that his case be heard) not by any authority whatever but '*par un tribunal*' (by a court or tribunal) within the meaning of Article 6(1). The Government have emphasised rightly that in French '*cause*' may mean '*procès qui se plaide*'. This, however, is not the sole ordinary sense of this noun; it serves also to indicate by extension '*l'ensemble des intérêts à soutenir, à faire prévaloir*'. Similarly, the '*contestation*' (claim) generally exists prior to the legal proceedings and is a concept independent of them. As regards the phrase '*tribunal indépendant et impartial, établi par la loi*' (independent and impartial tribunal established by law), it conjures up the idea of organisation rather than that of functioning, of institutions rather than that of procedure.

The English text, for its part, speaks of an 'independent and impartial tribunal established by law'. Moreover, the phrase 'in the determination of his civil rights and obligations', on which the Government have relied in support of their contention, does not necessarily refer only to judicial proceedings already pending: as the Commission have observed, it may be taken as synonymous with 'wherever his civil rights and obligations are being determined'. It too would then imply the right to have the determination of disputes relating to civil rights and obligations made by a court or 'tribunal'.

. . .

While the right to a fair, public and expeditious judicial procedure can assuredly apply only to proceedings in being, it does not, however, necessarily follow that a right to the very institution of such proceedings is thereby excluded; the Delegates of the Commission rightly underlined this at paragraph 21 of their memorial. Besides, in criminal matters, the 'reasonable time' may start to run from a date prior to the seisin of the trial court, of the 'tribunal' competent for the 'determination . . . of (the) criminal charge'. It is conceivable also that in civil matters the reasonable time may begin to run, in certain circumstances, even before the issue of the writ commencing proceedings before the court to which the plaintiff submits the dispute. (paras 28–32)

Further, the Court considered that belief in the 'rule of law' underlying the Convention ought to be given practical effect. In the context of civil matters such a rule was hardly conceivable without the possibility of having access to the courts:

. . . The principle whereby a civil claim must be capable of being submitted to a judge ranks as one of the universally 'recognised' fundamental principles of law; the same is true of the principle of international law which forbids the denial of justice. Article 6(1) must read in the light of these principles.

Were Article 6(1) to be understood as concerning exclusively the conduct of an action which had already been initiated before a court, a Contracting State could, without acting in breach of that text, do away with its courts, or take away their jurisdiction to determine certain classes of civil actions and entrust it to organs dependent on the Government. Such assumptions, indissociable from a danger of arbitrary power, would have serious consequences which are repugnant to the aforementioned principles and which the Court cannot overlook.

It would be inconceivable, in the opinion of the Court, that Article 6(1) should describe in detail the procedural guarantees afforded to parties in a pending lawsuit and should not first protect that which alone makes it in fact possible to benefit from such guarantees, that is, access to a court. The fair, public and expeditious characteristics of judicial proceedings are of no value at all if there are no judicial proceedings.

. . . Taking all the preceding considerations together, it follows that the right of access constitutes an element which is inheret in the right stated by Article 6(1). This is not an extensive interpretation forcing new obligations on the Contracting States: it is based on the very terms of the first sentence of Article 6(1) read in its context and having regard to the object and purpose of the Convention, a lawmaking treaty, and to general principles of law.

The Court thus reaches the conclusion, without needing to resort to 'supplementary means of interpretation' as envisaged at Article 32 of the Vienna Convention, that Article 6(1) secures to everyone the right to have any claim relating to his civil rights and obligations brought before a court or tribunal. In this way the Article embodies the 'right to a court', of which the right of access, that is the right to institute proceedings before courts in civil matters, constitutes one aspect only. To this are added the guarantees laid down by Article 6(1) as regards both the organisation and composition of the court, and the conduct of the proceedings. In sum, the whole makes up the right to a fair hearing. The Court has no need to ascertain in the present case whether and to what extent Article 6(1) further requires a decision on the very substance of the dispute (English 'determination', French '*décidera*'). (paras 35 and 36)

Next the Court had to consider whether there was any justified limitation on the exercise or enjoyment of this right. The Court held that the right of access to a court was not absolute – for example, most of the national laws of the member States limited access to the court in the case of minors or persons of unsound mind. It was not the function of the Court to prescribe admissible limitations in the case of convicted prisoners. Nevertheless, the Court held that it was not for the Home Secretary to decide on the action contemplated by Golder, but the task of an independent and impartial tribunal. The refusal of permission to allow Golder to consult a solicitor consequently amounted to a failure to respect Golder's right of access to a court and violated Article 6, para. 1.

Comment

Under the Prison Rules 1964, a prisoner was not permitted to communicate with any person in connection with any legal or other business without the permission of the Home Secretary. Therefore any prisoner wishing to obtain legal advice in connection with prison treatment had to obtain permission from the Secretary of State before communicating with his solicitor.

In interpreting Article 6, para. 1 reference was made to the relationship between this article and others in the Convention, particularly Article 5, para. 4 and Article 13. The Government had argued that as the last two articles provided an express right of access to the courts, it was unnecessary to find a similar right under Article 6, para. 1, particularly as there was no express provision. The Commission's response to this was that:

. . . Articles 5(4) and 13, as opposed to Article 6(1), are 'accessory' to other provisions. Those Articles, they say, do not state a specific right but are designed to afford procedural guarantees, 'based on recourse', the former for the 'right to liberty', as stated in Article 5(1), the second for the whole of the 'rights and freedoms as set forth in this Convention'. Article 6(1), they continue, is intended to protect 'in itself' . . . (para. 33)

The Court was of the view that:

> . . . the interpretation which the Government have contested does not lead to confounding Article 6(1) with Articles 5(4) and 13, nor making these latter provisions superfluous. Article 13 speaks of an effective remedy before a 'national authority' (*'instance nationale'*) which may not be a 'tribunal' or 'court' within the meaning of Articles 6(1) and 5(4). Furthermore, the effective remedy deals with the violation of a right guaranteed by the Convention, while Articles 6(1) and 5(4) cover claims relating in the first case to the existence or scope of civil rights and in the second to the lawfulness of arrest or detention. What is more, the three provisions do not operate in the same field. The concept of 'civil rights and obligations' is not co-extensive with that of 'rights and freedoms as set forth in this Convention', even if there may be some overlapping. As to the 'right to liberty', its 'civil' character is at any rate open to argument. Besides, the requirements of Article 5(4) in certain respects appear stricter than those of Article 6(1), particularly as regards the element of 'time'. (para. 33)

The approach of the Court illustrates the interpretative approach adopted to deal with a new issue. The articles are considered both in isolation and in the context of the Convention as a whole. Moreover, the Convention is considered both as a free-standing document – often with its terms having autonomous meanings attributed to them – and in the light of its historical background and the wider framework of other international treaties concerning human rights. In this case, broader, philosophical and jurisprudential concepts were also referred to, particularly the idea of the 'rule of law'.

The ruling in the *Golder* case was applied in the case of *Hilton* v *UK* 3 EHRR 104, the facts of which arose prior to the *Golder* decision but in the light of which the Commission expressed the opinion that a refusal of the Home Secretary to allow the applicant to institute civil proceedings amounted to a denial of access to the courts, and was consequently in breach of Article 6, para. 1.

The *Golder* decision was also influential in the case of *Kiss* v *UK* 19 EHRR CD 17, in which the applicant, a prisoner, was denied permission to pursue an action against a prison officer for alleged assault and was punished with 80 days' loss of remission for making false and malicious allegations. The Government accepted that in the light of the *Golder* case, he had been hindered in his access to the courts.

Kaplan v *UK*
Council of Europe Report

The facts
Following certain business transactions, the applicant was declared by the Secretary of State for Trade – exercising powers conferred on him by the Insurance Companies Act 1974 – not to be a fit and proper person to control his company. On the basis of that finding trading restrictions were imposed on his company Indemnity Guarantee Assurance Ltd (IGA). Neither the applicant nor the company was given a hearing. The applicant submitted that:

> . . . the finding of unfitness against him and the decision to impose restrictions on the company's business were decisive of 'civil rights and obligations' of himself and the

company. Secondly, he submits that the allegations made against him amounted, in substance, to a criminal charge. Article 6(1) was thus applicable and entitled him and the company to a hearing before an independent and impartial tribunal, which they did not receive. (para. 122)

The Commission's opinion
The Commission expressed the opinion – and this was not in dispute – that neither the Secretary of State for Trade, nor the officials who heard the representations of the applicant and the company, were a 'tribunal' for the purposes of Article 6; nor was there any public hearing. The main question however, was whether Article 6 applied at all. The Commission emphasised that:

> ... it is not itself concerned with the merits of the Secretary of State's decisions and in particular with the question whether he was right or wrong to make the finding of unfitness against the applicant. The case is concerned with the procedures which were followed or were available. Furthermore the Commission does not consider it relevant whether or not the Secretary of State or his officials were treating the matters complained of as affecting the applicant's civil rights and obligations. The questions at issue under Article 6 must, in the Commission's view, be resolved in the light of an objective examination of the relevant facts and domestic law, and not by reference to any attitude or views the domestic authorities may have held on those questions. The relevant facts and law have been rehearsed in detail by the parties and are largely undisputed. ... (para. 125)

In considering, first, whether any civil rights were in issue, the Commission had to examine whether the direct effect of the administrative acts complained of was to 'create, modify or annul legal rights or obligations of a "civil" character' (para. 132). The Commission had to consider the content and effects of such rights, the object and purpose of the Convention and the national legal systems of other Contracting States.

First, the Commission considered whether the applicant's and the company's 'right' to conduct an insurance business was affected. The Commission noted that:

> ... There is no doubt that until the Secretary of State issued the notice of requirements, IGA was entitled by law to carry on insurance business within the limits imposed by its existing authorisations and the general law. In particular, it was entitled to do so by entering into certain forms of insurance contract. Unless and until the Secretary of State removed that entitlement by exercising the appropriate powers under the Act, no-one could lawfully prevent IGA from thus conducting its business. In the Commission's opinion, IGA thus had a 'right', within the ordinary meaning of the word, to conduct insurance business. It had initially been conferred by the Secretary of State when he authorised the company and he was entitled, under certain conditions, to interfere with it, or even effectively to remove it as he did here. However, these factors do not, in the Commission's opinion, alter its character as a 'right' for the purposes of Article 6(1) at least.
>
> ... The direct legal effect of the Secretary of State's action was that the existing 'right' of IGA to conduct insurance business was restricted in the manner set out in the notice under section 29 of the 1974 Act. Effectively IGA was prohibited from entering into new business. Its 'right' to conduct insurance business was thus affected. (paras 136 and 137)

The Commission expressed the opinion that the right to carry on a commercial activity in the private sector – albeit subject to administrative authorisation and supervision in the public interest – was a civil right, for the purposes of Article 6. However, any effects on the applicant's personal position were merely incidental consequences.

The applicant did not contend that the action taken by the Secretary of State was unlawful, but that the decision should have been taken in the first place by a tribunal satisfying Article 6. The Commission therefore had to consider two issues:

> . . . The first is whether Article 6(1) applies directly to all procedures whereby decisions affecting 'civil rights' are taken. In other words does it confer a right to have such decisions taken in the first place by a tribunal satisfying Article 6(1) and not by an administrative authority at all? If not, the second question arises, namely whether, once such a decision has been taken by an administrative authority exercising a discretionary power, the right of access to court guaranteed by Article 6(1) implies that there must be access to a tribunal with full jurisdiction to re-examine the whole matter and to substitute its own discretion for that of the administrative authority. (para. 145)

In this regard the Commission noted that:

> . . . it is a feature of the administrative law of all the Contracting States that in numerous different fields public authorities are empowered by law to take various forms of action impinging on the private rights of citizens. . . .
>
> . . . Article 6(1) may be applicable in cases concerning the exercise of such public powers. Nevertheless, Article 6 does not, in the Commission's opinion, prohibit the conferment on public authorities of powers to take action affecting the private rights of citizens. It does not go so far as to provide that all acts, decisions or measures which affect private rights must themselves be taken by a tribunal. Such a conclusion, apart from being in conflict with the common position in the Contracting States both today and when the Convention was drafted, would also not be warranted, in the Commission's opinion, by a proper interpretation of Article 6(1).
>
> . . . It is plain from the text of Article 6(1) that it does not directly protect the individual's 'civil rights' as such against acts or decisions which modify, annul or otherwise interfere with them. In many circumstances the private rights of an individual are liable to be affected not only by the lawful acts of public authorities but also by those of other individuals or entities exercising countervailing private rights of their own, and indeed by circumstances of a purely factual nature such as the effluxion of time. The mere fact that an individual's private rights are adversely affected by the acts of another party, whether a public authority or not, does not therefore involve a violation of Article 6(1).
>
> . . . The Commission has thus to some extent recognised in its previous case-law that Article 6(1) is not necessarily applicable to all stages of an administrative process affecting 'civil rights'. Its minority in the *Ringeisen* case, which considered Article 6(1) applicable to the appeal proceedings in question there, made clear that it did not consider it directly applicable to the process whereby administrative decisions affecting civil rights are themselves taken. The Commission has held that where Article 6(1) applies to an administrative process, it may be sufficient that a court procedure is available at some stage after the initial administration decision. (paras 150–153)

The Commission expressed the opinion that the essential role of Article 6, para. 1 was:

. . . to lay down guarantees concerning the mode in which claims or disputes concerning legal rights and obligations (of a 'civil' character) are to be resolved. A distinction must be drawn between the acts of a body which is engaged in the resolution of such a claim or dispute and the acts of an administrative or other body purporting merely to exercise or apply a legal power vested in it and not to resolve a legal claim or dispute. Article 6(1) would not, in the Commission's opinion, apply to the acts of the latter even if they do affect 'civil rights'. It could not be considered as being engaged in a process of 'determination' of civil rights and obligations. Its function would not be to decide ('*décidera*') on a claim, dispute or '*contestation*'. Its acts may, on the other hand, give rise to a claim, dispute or '*contestation*' and Article 6 may come into play in that way.

. . . As to the present case, the Commission notes that the Secretary of State was not engaged in the resolution of a dispute between parties concerning civil rights. He proposed to take action affecting (as the Commission has found) the company's private rights. He considered the objections put forward and then acted. He took action in the exercise of his legal powers which affected 'civil rights' but was not engaged in the 'determination' of a dispute or '*contestation*' concerning civil rights and obligations. In the Commission's opinion, the procedures leading to the finding of unfitness against the applicant and the imposition of restrictions on IGA did not therefore themselves have to comply with Article 6(1). The fact that the relevant decisions were not taken by a tribunal after a fair and public hearing does not therefore involve a breach of this provision. (paras 154 and 155)

In considering whether there was an infringement of the company's or the applicant's access to court, the Commission noted that the applicant had not been denied access to court – for example, to challenge the decision of the Secretary of State by way of judicial review – although the scope of judicial review might be limited:

. . . An interpretation of Article 6(1) under which it was held to provide a right to a full appeal on the merits of every administrative decision affecting private rights would therefore lead to a result which was inconsistent with the existing, and long-standing, legal position in most of the Contracting States. (para. 161)

While it was important that the principle of the rule of law was observed, and that the jurisdiction of the courts was not removed altogether, the Commission observed that:

. . . it is plain that not every grievance or dispute, even arising from an act which has affected 'civil rights', gives rise to a right of access to court. In the Commission's opinion there must be a legal element. A person may be aggrieved by action affecting his private rights whether taken by a public authority or a private individual. However, if he accepts that the opposing party was fully entitled to act as he did, by virtue for instance of powers or rights conferred by statute or by contract, then he would have no claim to bring before a court under the applicable domestic law.

. . . In deciding whether a right of access to court arises, the nature of the claim or dispute under the relevant domestic law is thus of critical importance. This is not to say that the right can only arise where there is a formal right of action in domestic law. To hold that the Convention right was thus restricted would be to open up precisely the possibility referred to by the Court that a State could, without breaching Article 6(1), remove the jurisdiction of its courts in this field. The question whether there is a *'contestation'* or civil claim or dispute must therefore be examined as one of substance. Where an individual objects to action affecting his private rights, the test must be whether he is in substance claiming that the adverse party has acted in a way he was not entitled to act under the applicable domestic law. (paras 163 and 164)

As there was no dispute in this case concerning the facts or the lawfulness of the measures taken, the Commission concluded that the applicant had not been a victim of any breach of Article 6, para. 1 as regards the determination of any civil right.

Further, the Commission expressed the opinion that he had not been the victim of any breach of this article in so far as it guaranteed a right to a hearing before a tribunal in the determination of a 'criminal charge'. Indeed the applicant had not be subject to any penalties which could properly be considered to make the proceedings fall into the category of penal proceedings.

Ashingdane v *UK*
Series A, Vol. 93

The facts
This case, which has been considered under Article 5, concerned the applicant's committal to a mental hospital following conviction for various criminal offences, and his continued detention.

Under s. 141 of the 1959 Mental Health Act, the applicant claimed that he was barred from bringing any action against the Department of Health and Social Security and the local Health Authority, concerning his continued detention.

The Commission's opinion
The Commission noted that:

> . . . the applicant sought to bring a claim in domestic courts for breach of a statutory duty to provide appropriate hospital care for his mental state of health. The claim arose out of the inability, and hence refusal, of the Secretary of State and Health Authority to transfer the applicant from a secure mental hospital to a normal one, because of industrial action by nursing staff. . . . (para. 90)

The Commission expressed the opinion that while one of the principles of Article 6 is to guarantee an individual the right of access to court, national courts have the right to decide disputes concerning the exercise of this right. The Commission expressed the opinion that the applicant was not denied access to court. The question was whether the operation of s. 141 unduly restricted his right of access. In this regard the Commission expressed the opinion that:

> . . . section 141 of the 1959 Act does extinguish certain of the possible civil claims of mental health patients and of other persons concerned with the functioning of that Act. The Commission agrees with the parties that it is immaterial whether the measure is of a substantive or procedural character. It suffices to say that section 141

acted as an unwaivable bar, which effectively restricted the applicant's claim in tort. (para. 93)

The judgment of the Court

The Court noted that the applicant had access to the High Court and the Court of Appeal, but was told in each that his actions were barred by operation of law. However, the Court held that:

> . . . This of itself does not necessarily exhaust the requirements of Article 6(1). It must be still be established that the degree of access afforded under the national legislation was sufficient to secure the individual's 'right to a court', having regard to the rule of law in a democratic society.
>
> Certainly, the right of access to the courts is not absolute but may be subject to limitations; these are permitted by implication since the right of access, 'by its very nature calls for regulation by the State, regulation which may vary in time and place according to the needs and resources of the community and of individuals'. In laying down such regulation, the Contracting States enjoy a certain margin of appreciation. Whilst the final decision as to observance of the Convention's requirements rests with the Court, it is no part of the Court's function to substitute for the assessment of the national authorities any other assessment of what might be the best policy in this field.
>
> Nonetheless, the limitations applied must not restrict or reduce the access left to the individual in such a way or to such an extent that the very essence of the right is impaired. Furthermore, a limitation will not be compatible with Article 6(1) if it does not pursue a legitimate aim and if there is not a reasonable relationship of proportionality between the means employed and the aim sought to be achieved.
>
> . . . Section 141 of the 1959 Act placed a hindrance on Mr Ashingdane's recourse to the national courts. According to the concurring evidence before the Court, the mischief that section 141 sought to avoid was the risk of those responsible for the care of mental patients being unfairly harassed by litigation.
>
> Whilst that objective is in itself legitimate in relation to hospital staff as individuals, the protection from suit enjoyed by the Department of Health and Social Security and by the local Health Authority in the actions brought by Mr Ashingdane calls for closer scrutiny. (paras 57 and 58)

The Court accepted that s. 141 of the 1959 Act hindered the applicant's access to the courts. The Court also accepted that this had a legitimate objective – namely to protect those responsible for the care of mental patients from unfair harassment – but the immunity from suit enjoyed by the Department of Health and Social Security and the local Health Authority needed to be scrutinised.

The claims which the applicant wished to make related to the authorities' failure to provide him with alternative hospital accommodation – a claim founded on s. 3 of the National Health Service Act 1977. The Court found that s. 141 only partially precluded the authorities from being sued, and that it would have still been open to the applicant to bring an action based on negligence or bad faith, subject to obtaining leave from the High Court.

The Court held that:

> . . . In view of all these circumstances, the restriction imposed in the present case by operation of section 141 of the 1959 Act, in limiting any liability of the responsible authorities arising from section 3 of the 1977 Act to acts done negligently or in bad

faith, did not impair the very essence of Mr Ashingdane's 'right to a court' or transgress the principle of proportionality.

This conclusion is not invalidated by the fact that the protection from suit hitherto afforded to the responsible authorities was removed by the 1983 Act, so that there would today be no similar bar on proceedings such as those Mr Ashingdane wished to bring.

... Accordingly, even assuming it to be applicable to the facts of the present case, Article 6(1) has not been violated. (paras 59 and 60)

Comment

Restriction on liability from suit was abolished under the Mental Health Act 1983, s. 139, which removed the protection from the Secretary of State for Social Services and the Health Authorities. In the case of other defendants, where previously an applicant had to satisfy a judge that there was 'substantial ground' for the allegation of bad faith or negligence, the only requirement was to obtain leave of the court.

Campbell and Fell v *UK*
Series A, Vol. 80

The facts

The applicants were prisoners, convicted of offences believed to be connected with terrorist activities of the IRA. While in Albany prison they were involved in a prison disturbance which led to disciplinary proceedings being taken against them by the Prison Board of Visitors, resulting in loss of remission and loss of certain privileges. Both applicants sought permission from the Home Secretary to consult a lawyer with a view to taking legal action against prison officers for injuries sustained during the disturbances. Eventually both were able to obtain legal advice and instituted actions against individual prison officers.

Before the Commission each applicant:

(a)   alleged that he had been convicted by the Board of Visitors of disciplinary charges amounting in substance to 'criminal' charges, without having been afforded a hearing complying with the requirements of Article 6 of the Convention;

(b)   contended that the delay in allowing him to obtain legal advice following the incident of 16 September 1976 involved breaches of his right of access to court, guaranteed by Article 6, and of his right to respect for correspondence, guaranteed by Article 8;

(c)   maintained that the refusal to allow independent medical examination involved a further infringement of his rights under Article 6;

(d)   made a number of other complaints, notably concerning his treatment during and after the aforementioned incident. (para. 53)

The Commission's opinion

First, the Commission had to consider whether Article 6 was applicable to proceedings of the Board of Prison Visitors on the basis that the charges were criminal rather than disciplinary. In order to do this the Commission adopted the criteria used by the Court in the context of military service (*Engel* v *Netherlands (No. 1)* 1 EHRR 647), which were:

[1]   whether the provisions defining the offence charged belong, according to the legal system of the respondent State, to criminal law, disciplinary law or both concurrently;

[2]   the very nature of the offence;

[3]   the degree of severity of the penalty which the person concerned risks incurring. (para. 119)

However, the Commission noted that these criteria had to be applied in the prison sphere with due regard to the circumstances of the prisoner.

Examining the various charges which had been made against the applicants, the Commission noted that:

... the offences of 'mutiny or incitement to mutiny' and 'gross personal violence to an officer' are covered by disciplinary law, namely paragraphs (1) and (2) of Rule 47 of the Prison Rules. It is also not disputed that the acts charged were concurrently offences under the general criminal law.

... In the case of a prisoner, in the Commission's opinion, if the legal rule allegedly contravened is one which governs order within a prison, the State is in principle entitled to deal with the matter under disciplinary law. The offences charged in the present case were both plainly offences against internal prison order. Accordingly, from that point of view the offences were such that, in, principle they could have been dealt with under disciplinary law, subject to the penalty at risk being of a disciplinary rather than a criminal nature.

... Of the various penalties which were, or could have been, imposed here, only the loss of remission is such as could, in itself, bring the matter within the criminal sphere, in the Commission's opinion. The other possible penalties, such as loss of privileges and cellular confinement, are in its view typical disciplinary penalties affecting the prisoner's status within the prison and nothing else. An award of loss of remission, on the other hand, may have a serious impact on liberty by prolonging the period which the prisoner has to spend in prison. In the present case the period of remission at risk was also very long. (paras 121–123)

The Commission did not consider that loss of remission could be considered as a further sentence of imprisonment, because it did not alter the original basis for detention. The Commission noted that many of the Contracting States had systems in which parole, remission or conditional release operated.

... In the Commission's opinion a refusal to grant release under such a system before the end of a sentence, plainly does not involve any 'deprivation of liberty' over and above that imposed by the sentencing court. In the present case there was a 'forfeiture' of remission but the decision was essentially no different in its effects from the case of a refusal to grant release. The fixing of a provisional release date at the beginning of the applicant's sentence did not reduce the sentence to a lesser one than had been passed by the court and subsequent decisions which resulted in the applicant's detention being prolonged beyond the provisional release date cannot be said to have increased the sentence. (para. 127)

An award of loss of remission was therefore in the nature of a disciplinary penalty.

However, the Commission held that the present case differed from previously considered cases due to the severity of the penalties:

... In the first place both the offences charged were 'especially grave offences' and the period of loss of remission which the Board of Visitors could award was accordingly not subject to any limit under the Prison Rules. Within the confines of the overall period of one-third of the original ten-year sentence (3 years and 4 months subject to previous losses), any period of loss of remission could thus be awarded . . . Furthermore, the possibility of a very substantial period of loss of remission being awarded was not merely a theoretical one. The very serious nature of the allegations against the applicant made this a real possibility *ab initio*, and this possibility in fact materialised in the award of 570 days which was made.

. . . Even though there is a possibility of having lost remission restored, such an award is plainly likely to have a very serious impact on the prisoner. In the Commission's view, it went beyond what could properly be considered as a purely 'disciplinary' penalty and fell within the criminal sphere.

. . . The Commission considers that the charges against the applicant were therefore 'criminal' charges for the purposes of Article 6 of the Convention and its provisions were accordingly applicable to the proceedings before the Board of Visitors. In view of this conclusion it is unnecessary to consider the question of the applicability of Article 6 from the point of view of 'civil rights and obligations'.

. . . The Commission concludes that the proceedings against Mr Campbell before the Board of Visitors involved the determination of 'criminal charges' and that Article 6 of the Convention was applicable to those proceedings accordingly. (paras 129–132)

The Commission then considered the claims relating to a 'fair hearing'. Mr Campbell had not attended the hearings concerning him, but the Commission was not convinced that he could not have done so, had he wished to. His reasons for not doing so included an allegation that he did not believe that he would receive a 'fair hearing'. The Commission therefore considered the independence and impartiality of the Board of Visitors when exercising its disciplinary functions:

. . . In accordance with the case-law of the Commission and Court Article 6(1) requires that the tribunal should be 'independent' both from the Executive and from the parties. The Commission recognises that in exercising its disciplinary functions a Board of Visitors is under a legal obligation to act independently of the parties and with impartiality between them. However, independence of the Executive requires more than that, in the Commission's view. To be truly 'independent' the 'tribunal' must be independent of the Executive in its functions and as an institution. Such independence forms an additional practical guarantee that the tribunal will act fairly and objectively and ensures that justice is seen to be done. Despite the legal obligation incumbent on them to act judicially, the Commission does not consider that a Board of Visitors satisfies the additional requirement of possessing the necessary institutional independence of the prison administration. Its members are appointed for limited periods by the Home Secretary, the Minister in charge of the prison administration, and its other functions are such as to bring it into day-to-day contact with the officials of the prison in such a way as to identify it with the administration of the prison. The Commission does not therefore consider tha this requirement of Article 6(1) was met in this case.

. . . Furthermore, it appears that the proceedings before the Board of Visitors also did not satisfy several of the other requirements of Article 6 concerning the procedure to be followed. Thus the proceedings did not take place in public and judgment was not pronounced publicly. Furthermore, the applicant was not afforded the opportunity to obtain legal advice and assistance before the hearing of his case, or legal representation at the hearing.

... The Commission concludes by 9 votes with 3 abstentions that the proceedings before the Board of Visitors in Mr Campbell's case involved a breach of his rights under Article 6 of the Convention. (paras 137–139)

The applicants had not been able to seek legal advice concerning the legal actions they wished to institute against prison officers for assault until they had complied with the 'prior ventilation rule', whereby any complaint had to be investigated internally. The consequence of this was that there had been a delay of four to five months in seeking legal advice. In considering whether this violated Article 6 – particularly the right of access to a court – the Commission, while acknowledging that this right was not absolute, expressed the opinion that:

... the imposition of a substantial period of delay on a person's access to court may of itself breach Article 6(1), regardless of whether it is shown actually to affect the prospects of any action which might be instituted. (para. 149)

The Commission considered that:

... the ordinary and reasonable requirements of imprisonment can justify a system of internal inquiry into prisoners' complaints, so that these can be promptly investigated and necessary corrective action taken within the prison. It may therefore be justifiable to require prisoners to give certain details of their complaints to the prison authorities before allowing them facilities to obtain legal advice and institute proceedings. A system requiring the disclosure of such information need not, in the Commission's view, involve any substantial delay in affording access to court or prejudice the fairness of any subsequent proceedings. There is certainly no evidence that the present applicants have had to disclose information in a way which could prejudice prospects of a fair hearing. . . . (para. 150)

However, this did not mean that any internal investigation should be given unlimited priority, thereby delaying access to a court for a considerable time.

... The Commission therefore considers that the delay imposed on the applicants' access to legal advice pending the internal investigation involved an unjustified interference with their right of access to court under Article 6(1). (para. 151)

Father Fell had further complained that initially he was not permitted to consult with his lawyer out of hearing of a prison officer. The Commission expressed the opinion that:

... there may be specific circumstances in which some interference in the contact between a lawyer and other persons may be justified. However, in its view a general prohibition on privileged contact between prisioners and their lawyers prior to the commencement of litigation, which is not dependent on specific security consider-ations, impinges too broadly on the right of access to court and cannot be considered compatible with Article 6(1). In this connection the Commission observes that privileged contact prior to the commencement of litigation may be just as important as privileged contact after proceedings have been instituted. Although much of a lawyer's interview with his client at this stage might be concerned with eliciting the factual basis of his complaint, other matters such as tactics in pursuing the claim, which the client may legitimately wish to keep secret, may also have to be discussed. The Commission does not therefore consider that the restriction at issue in the present case was compatible with Article 6(1).

. . . The Commission concludes by a unanimous vote that the refusal to allow Father Fell to consult in private with his lawyer was in breach of Article 6(1) of the Convention. (paras 159 and 160)

The judgment of the Court

Similarly to the Commission, the Court had first to determine whether Article 6 was applicable, or whether the charges against the applicants were disciplinary rather than criminal. While holding that the meaning of 'criminal' was autonomous under Article 6, the Court noted that:

> (a) The Convention is not opposed to the Contracting States creating or maintaining a distinction between criminal law and disciplinary law and drawing the dividing line, but it does not follow that the classification thus made is decisive for the purposes of the Convention.
> (b) If the Contracting States were able at their discretion, by classifying an offence as disciplinary instead of criminal, to exclude the operation of the fundamental clauses of Articles 6 and 7, the application of these provisions would be subordinated to their sovereign will. A latitude extending thus far might lead to results incompatible with the object and purpose of the Convention. (para. 68)

The reasoning adopted in previous cases concerning military disciplinary offences could not be blindly applied in the context of the present case. The Court indicated that:

> . . . It is well aware that in the prison context there are practical reasons and reasons of policy for establishing a special disciplinary regime, for example security considerations and the interests of public order, the need to deal with misconduct by inmates as expeditiously as possible, the availability of tailor-made sanctions which may not be at the disposal of the ordinary courts and the desire of the prison authorities to retain ultimate responsibility for discipline within their establishments.
> However, the guarantee of a fair hearing, which is the aim of Article 6, is one of the fundamental principles of any democratic society, within the meaning of the Convention. . . . (para. 69)

Nevertheless, the principles of previous cases could be applied to the custodial context to assist in determining whether the proceedings against the applicants were criminal or disciplinary. In applying these:

> . . . The first matter to be ascertained is whether or not the text defining the offences in issue belongs, according to the domestic legal system, to criminal law, disciplinary law or both concurrently.
> It is clear that, in English law, the offences with which Mr Campbell was charged belong to disciplinary law: Rule 47 states that conduct of this kind on the part of a prisoner shall be 'an offence against discipline' and the Rules go on to provide how it shall be dealt with under the special prison disciplinary regime. . . . (para. 70)

However, the Court noted that:

> . . . the indications so afforded by the national law have only a relative value; the very nature of the offence is a factor of greater import.
> In this respect, it has to be borne in mind that misconduct by a prisoner may take different forms; certain acts are clearly no more than a question of internal discipline, whereas others cannot be seen in the same light. Firstly, some matters may be more serious than others; in fact, the Rules grade offences, classifying those committed by

Mr Campbell as 'especially grave'. Secondly, the illegality of some acts may not turn on the fact that they were committed in prison: certain conduct which constitutes an offence under the Rules may also amount to an offence under the criminal law. Thus, doing gross personal violence to a prison officer may correspond to the crime of 'assault occasioning actual bodily harm' and, although mutiny and incitement to mutiny are not as such offences under the general criminal law, the underlying facts may find a criminal charge of conspiracy. It also has to be remembered that, theoretically at least, there is nothing to prevent conduct of this kind being the subject of both criminal and disciplinary proceedings.

The Court considers that these factors, whilst not of themselves sufficient to lead to the conclusion that the offences with which the applicant was charged have to be regarded as 'criminal' for Convention purposes, do give them a certain colouring which does not entirely coincide with that of a purely disciplinary matter. (para. 71)

A further criterion to be applied was the nature and degree of severity of the penalty. The Court found that:

> . . . the forfeiture of remission which Mr Campbell risked incurring and the forfeiture actually awarded involved such serious consequences as regards the length of his detention that these penalties have to be regarded, for Convention purposes, as 'criminal'. By causing detention to continue for substantially longer than would otherwise have been the case, the sanction came close to, even if it did not technically constitute, deprivation of liberty and the object and purpose of the Convention require that the imposition of a measure of such gravity should be accompanied by the guarantees of Article 6. This conclusion is not altered by the fact that a considerable number of days of remission were subsequently restored to the applicant. . . .
>
> . . . Taking into account, therefore, both the 'especially grave' character of the offences with which Mr Campbell was charged and the nature and severity of the penalty that he risked incurring—and did in fact incur—the Court finds that Article 6 is applicable to the Board of Visitors' adjudication in his case. . . . (paras 72 and 73)

Having found that Article 6 was applicable, the Court proceeded to examine Mr Campbell's claim that he had not had a 'fair hearing'. The Court was satisfied that the Board of Visitors was a 'tribunal established by law'. The Court had to considered next, if the Board was sufficiently independent.

> . . . In determining whether a body can be considered to be 'independent'—notably of the executive and of the parties to the case—the Court has had regard to the manner of appointment of its members and the duration of their term of office, the existence of guarantees against outside pressures and the question whether the body presents an appearance of independence.
>
> The factors which were relied on in the present case as indicative of the Board's lack of 'independence' will be considered in turn.
>
> . . . Members of Boards are appointed by the Home Secretary, who is himself responsible for the administration of prisons in England and Wales.
>
> The Court does not consider that this establishes that the members are not independent of the executive: to hold otherwise would mean that judges appointed by or on the advice of a Minister having responsibilities in the field of the administration of the courts were also not 'independent'. Moreover, although it is true that the Home Office may issue Boards with guidelines as to the performance of their functions, they are not subject to its instructions in their adjudicatory role.
>
> . . . Members of Boards hold office for a term of three years or such less period as the Home Secretary may appoint.

The term of office is admittedly relatively short but the Court notes that there is a very understandable reason: the members are unpaid and it might well prove difficult to find individuals willing and suitable to undertake the onerous and important tasks involved if the period were longer.

The Court notes that the Rules contain neither any regulation governing the removal of members of a Board nor any guarantee for their irremovability.

Although it appears that the Home Secretary could require the resignation of a member, this would be done only in the most exceptional circumstances and the existence of this possibility cannot be regarded as threatening in any respect the independence of the members of a Board in the performance of their judicial function.

It is true that the irremovability of judges by the executive during their term of office must in general be considered as a corollary of their independence and thus included in the guarantees of Article 6(1). However, the absence of a formal recognition of this irremovability in the law does not in itself imply lack of independence provided that it is recognised in fact and that the other necessary guarantees are present.

... There remains the question of the Board's independence having regard to the fact that it has both adjudicatory and supervisory roles.

In that latter role, a Board is, as the Government pointed out, intended to exercise an independent oversight of the administration of the prison. In the nature of things, supervision must involve a Board in frequent contacts with the prison officials and just as much with the inmates themselves; yet this in no way alters the fact that its function, even when discharging its administrative duties, is to 'hold the ring' between the parties concerned, independently of both of them. The impression which prisoners may have that Boards are closely associated with the executive and the prison administration is a factor of greater weight, particularly bearing in mind the importance in the context of Article 6 of the maxim 'justice must not only be done: it must also be seen to be done'. However, the existence of such sentiments on the part of inmates, which is probably unavoidable in a custodial setting, is not sufficient to establish a lack of 'independence'. This requirement of Article 6 would be satisfied if prisoners were reasonably entitled, on account of the frequent contacts between a Board and the authorities, to think that the former was dependent on the latter; however, the Court does not consider that the mere fact of these contacts, which exist also with the prisoners themselves, could justify such an impression.

... In the light of the foregoing, the Court sees no reason to conclude that the Board in question was not 'independent', within the meaning of Article 6. (paras 78–82)

There was no evidence to suggest that the Board was not also impartial.

The Court noted that the hearing before the Board was not a public hearing:

... It is true that ordinary criminal proceedings—which may well concern dangerous individuals or necessitate the production of a prisoner before the court—nearly always take place in public, notwithstanding the attendant security problems, the possible propagation of malicious allegations and the wishes of the accused. However, the Court cannot disregard the factors cited by the Government, notably the considerations of public order and the security problems that would be involved if prison disciplinary proceedings were conducted in public. Such a course would undoubtedly occasion difficulties of greater magnitude than those that arise in ordinary criminal proceedings. A Board's adjudications are, as befits the character of disciplinary proceedings of this kind, habitually held within the prison precincts and the difficulties over admitting the public to those precincts are obvious. If they were held outside, similar problems would arise as regards the prisoner's transportation to and attendance at the hearing. To require that disciplinary proceedings concerning convicted prisoners should be held in public would impose a disproportionate burden on the authorities of the State.

... The Court therefore accepts that there were sufficient reasons of public order and security justifying the exclusion of the press and public from the proceedings against Mr Campbell. There was accordingly no violation of Article 6(1) in this respect. (paras 87 and 88)

Nevertheless, there was no justifiable reason why the decision of the Board should not have been made public, and to this extent there was a violation of Article 6, para. 1.

Although the Court did not find any violation of Article 6, paras 2, or 3(a), it did consider that there had been a breach of Article 6, para. 3(b) and (c), in as much as Mr Campbell had not received legal assistance to prepare his defence or to represent him at the hearing.

The Court also held that both applicants had experienced delay in gaining access to legal advice to pursue claims concerning personal injuries, and that this delay constituted a denial of access to the courts.

The Court also agreed with the Commission's view that the absence of privileged contact between lawyer and client – in the case of Father Fell – amounted to a violation of Article 6, para. 1.

Four judges disagreed with the majority view concerning the criminal nature of the proceedings, preferring the view that these proceedings were essentially disciplinary, despite the seriousness of the sanction of loss of remission.

Comment

A number of changes took place prior to the case coming to the Court. First, The Court of Appeal in *R v Hull Prison Board of Visitors, ex parte St. Germain and Others* [1979] QB 425, held that the writ of *certiorari* might be used to control disciplinary proceedings before the Boards of Visitors.

Secondly, from 6 August 1975, the rules concerning the need for prisoners to petition the Home Secretary for permission to seek advice from a lawyer in order to institute civil proceedings were changed. Under Instruction 45/1975, prisoners were given the right to correspond with a solicitor for the purpose of obtaining legal advice. However, facilities for obtaining legal advice – by correspondence or visit – still required that the complaint be raised through internal channels first.

Thirdly, changes were made concerning visits by legal advisers, whereby such interviews could be held out of hearing but within sight of prison officers, or in some circumstances privately.

Fourthly, from 1 December 1981, the prior ventilation rule was replaced by a simultaneous ventilation rule under new Orders (Order 5B34j).

Monnell and Morris v UK
Series A, Vol. 115

The facts

This case concerned loss of remission of sentence by the applicants, following their unsuccessful applications for leave to appeal. Their Article 6 claim related to the hearings of their applications for leave to appeal by the Court of Appeal.

The Commission's opinion

The Commission observed that:

> ... although Art. 6 does not guarantee an appeal in criminal proceedings, where the opportunity to lodge an appeal in regard to the determination of a criminal charge is provided under domestic law, the guarantees of Art. 6 continue to apply to the appeal proceedings, since those proceedings form part of the whole proceedings which determine the criminal charge at issue . . . (para. 127)

The main issue in the applicants' case was whether they should have been present in order for the hearing to be a 'fair hearing'. The Commission recognised that:

> ... 'in certain classes or in certain sets of circumstances a "fair" hearing is scarcely conceivable without the presence in person of the party concerned'. However, the extent to which such presence is actually required will depend upon the nature of the hearing in question, and in particular upon the scope of the powers enjoyed by the court before which the hearing is held, and the significance of this hearing in the context of the proceedings as a whole. . . . (para. 130)

Further:

> ... in order to examine the fairness of the appeal proceedings in the context of the proceedings as a whole, it should consider first the powers of the Court of Appeal and the scope of the hearing for leave to appeal, including the question whether it is a review of a lower court's decision, or whether it is a full rehearing. In addition, the Commission considers it necessary, in the light of the answer to this first question, to examine how the applicants' actual interests were presented and protected in the proceedings in question. (para. 131)

In the case of the applicants, the proceedings for application for leave to appeal did not involve a full rehearing but an examination of the grounds for appeal:

> ... the nature of the hearing is therefore to determine whether or not a prospective appellant has shown grounds which would justify hearing an appeal, and not to determine the outcome of any such appeal, where leave is granted. (para. 135)

Nevertheless, because the Court of Appeal had the power to order 'loss of time' in the case where leave to appeal was refused, under s. 29 of the Criminal Appeal Act 1968, the Commission had to consider:

> ... the actual protection which was afforded to the applicants at the hearings of their applications for leave to appeal, and whether this protection allowed the applicants a fair hearing in the determination of their criminal charges, viewed as a whole. (para. 140)

In examining the principle of 'equality of arms' the Commission noted that:

> ... both applicants had requested leave to be present at the hearing of their application for leave to appeal and at any subsequent hearings if their applications were granted, although in both cases these requests were refused. The applicants were not otherwise represented by a barrister or by a solicitor before the court. Similarly, however, the prosecution was not represented in relation to the applicants' leave to appeal applications, and thus, as between the prosecution and the defendants, equality of arms was formally respected. (para. 141)

However, the Commission had to consider whether there were special circumstances which made it necessary for the applicants to be present, particularly the risk faced by the applicants concerning loss of time if their application for leave to appeal was unsuccessful. In this respect the Commission noted that:

> ... although there was no power for the Court of Appeal to increase the sentences which had been imposed on conviction if an appeal was actually heard, where leave to appeal was refused as in the present cases, the Court of Appeal was empowered to make loss of time orders, which resulted in the applicants' period of imprisonment being increased. (para. 144)

In such circumstances the Commission expressed the opinion that Article 6 requires that the accused person must normally be present and be able to be heard, unless there is some justification for an exception. The Commission could find no such justification in the circumstances and expressed the opinion that there had been a violation of Article 6, paras 1 and 3(c).

The judgment of the Court
There was no dispute that Article 6 was applicable to the present case, nor was it disputed that neither applicant was present or heard in oral argument in the leave-to-appeal proceedings. The Court held that:

> ... The manner in which paragraph 1, as well as paragraph 3(c), of Article 6 is to be applied in relation to appellate or cassation courts depends upon the special features of the proceedings involved. Account must be taken of the entirety of the proceedings conducted in the domestic legal order and of the rôle of the appellate or cassation court therein. As the Commission put it in its report, in order to determine whether the requirements of fairness in Article 6 were met in the present case, it is necessary to consider matters such as the nature of the leave-to-appeal procedure and its significance in the context of the criminal proceedings as a whole, the scope of the powers of the Court of Appeal, and the manner in which the two applicants' interests were actually presented and protected before the Court of Appeal. (para. 56)

The Court noted that:

> ... Although not expressly provided for in the text of section 29(1) of the Criminal Appeal Act 1968, the basis on which loss of time was ordered against Mr Monnell and Mr Morris was, in line with the stated policy and practice of the Court of Appeal, the unmeritorious character of their own applications for leave to appeal. The nature of the issue to be decided for the ordering of loss of time was not such that their physical attendance was essential to assist the Court of Appeal in its determination.
>
> In the opinion of the Court, Article 6 required that Mr Monnell and Mr Morris be provided, in some appropriate way, with a fair procedure enabling them adequately and effectively to present their case against the possible exercise to their detriment of the power under section 29(1) of the 1968 Act. . . . (para. 61)

The Court reviewed the procedure followed in the applicants' case.

First, the principle of equality of arms was satisfied, in as much as neither the applicants nor the prosecution were represented before either the single judge or the full Court of Appeal which considered the application for leave to appeal. Secondly, both applicants received legal aid for legal advice on appeal. Counsel advised them that there was no reasonable prospect of success. Despite this, applications for leave to appeal were lodged and renewed on official forms, thereby giving the applicants the opportunity to submit written grounds of appeal. Thirdly, both applicants were advised of the need to seek legal advice and the risks of an unsuccessful application.

The Court held that in the circumstances:

> . . . the interests of justice and fairness could . . . be met by the applicants being able to present relevant considerations through making written submissions.
>
> . . .
>
> . . . Having regard to the special features of the context in which the power to order loss of time was exercised and to the circumstances of the case, the Court finds that neither Mr Monnell nor Mr Morris was denied a fair procedure as guaranteed by paragraphs 1 and 3(c) of Article 6. There has accordingly been no breach of either of these provisions of the Convention. (paras 68 and 70)

Judge Gersing expressed a dissenting opinion, on the ground that Article 6 was not applicable to the present case because the leave-to-appeal proceedings could not be said to determine the criminal charge against the applicants.

Granger v *UK*
Series A, Vol. 174

The facts
The applicant was charged with perjury concerning evidence which he had given in a criminal trial. He was found guilty and sentenced to five years' imprisonment. He applied for legal aid to fund his appeal. Application for legal aid was refused by the Supreme Court Legal Aid Committee of the Law Society of Scotland since it was not satisfied that the applicant had substantial grounds for appeal. He continued his appeal, partially assisted by a solicitor who provided free legal assistance, but who did not have the right of audience to appear before the appeal court. The applicant presented his own appeal, which failed.

The applicant claimed before the Commission that his rights under Article 6, paras 1 and 3(c) had been violated as a result of the refusal to grant him legal aid.

The Commission's opinion
It was not in dispute that Article 6, para. 3(c) was applicable to the proceedings before the High Court:

> . . . Art. 6(3) contains an enumeration of specific rights of the defence. They exemplify the notion of fair trial in respect of typical procedural situations which arise in criminal cases, but their intrinsic aim is always to ensure, or contribute to ensuring, the fairness of the criminal proceedings as a whole. The guarantees enshrined in Art. 6(3) must accordingly be interpreted in the light of the function which they have in the overall context of the proceedings . . .
>
> . . . The right to free legal assistance guaranteed by Art. 6(3)(c) is subject to two conditions; that the individual concerned does not have sufficient means to pay for legal assistance and that 'the interests of justice' require it. It is not in dispute that the

first condition was satisfied in the present case. The only issue is whether 'the interests of justice' required that the applicant be granted legal aid before the High Court. (paras 46 and 47)

However, the Commission distinguished between this case and that of *Monnell and Morris*, because in this case the proceedings took the form of a full oral hearing before the High Court at which the prosecution was well represented.

The Commission therefore had to consider the 'interests of justice' in the light of the particular circumstances, including the importance of what was at stake for the applicant. In this respect the Commission noted that the case involving the applicant's perjury had been regarded as being of sufficient gravity for the Solicitor General (Scotland) to appear for the Crown both at the trial and on appeal. Moreover, prior to the appeal reference had been made to the Lord Advocate concerning two points of law arising out of the judge's directions to the jury during the applicant's trial, and the trial judge had indicated that the case was one of exceptional difficulty and complexity.

The Commission therefore found that:

> ... the appeal could not be said to be frivolous or without substance but that it raised legal issues, which the applicant could not be expected to comprehend or to present to the court. The situation which in fact developed in the course of the two hearings in his appeal was that the applicant, who stood alone, had in apparent opposition to him the Solicitor General and counsel, supported by a representative of the Crown Office. He read two speeches which were unintelligible to him, as in all probability was the long speech of the prosecution in reply. The technical discussion which followed would also have been beyond his comprehension. Consequently, the Commission finds that the interests of justice required that the applicant be granted free legal aid for representation at his appeal. (para. 52)

There had therefore been a violation of Article 6, para. 3(c). No separate issues arose under Article 6, para. 1.

The judgment of the Court

The Court considered the two aspects of Article 6 together:

> ... In this connection, the Court recalls that the manner in which paragraph (1), as well as paragraph (3)(c), of Article 6 is to be applied in relation to appellate or cassation courts depends upon the special features of the proceedings involved; account must be taken of the entirety of the proceedings conducted in the domestic legal order and of the rôle of the appellate or cassation court therein.
>
> ... The question whether the interests of justice required a grant of legal aid must be determined in the light of the case as a whole. In that respect not only the situation obtaining at the time the decision on the application for legal aid was handed down but also that obtaining at the time the appeal was heard are material.
>
> ... Mr Granger had been convicted on indictment of perjury and sentenced to five years' imprisonment. There can thus be no question as to the importance of what was at stake in the appeal.
>
> Before the High Court of Justiciary, the Solicitor General, on account of his familiarity with the case, appeared for the Crown and addressed the judges at length. On the other hand, the applicant, as was not contested, was not in a position fully to comprehend the pre-prepared speeches he read out or the opposing arguments submitted to the court. It is also clear that, had the occasion arisen, he would not have

been able to make an effective reply to those arguments or to questions from the bench.

The foregoing factors are of particular weight in the present case in view of the complexity of one of the issues involved. Whilst the High Court of Justiciary apparently had little trouble in disposing of four of Mr Granger's grounds of appeal, the same did not apply to the remaining one. After hearing argument, it decided that this ground – which turned on what the Solicitor General himself described at the European Court's hearing as the 'difficult' distinction between 'precognitions' and other statements – deserved more detailed consideration. It adjourned its hearing and called for a transcript of the evidence given at the applicant's trial, so as to be able to examine the matter more thoroughly. It thus became clear that this ground of appeal raised an issue of complexity and importance.

In this situation some means should have been available to the competent authorities, including the High Court of Justiciary in the exercise of its overall responsibility for ensuring the fair conduct of the appeal proceedings, to have the refusal of legal aid reconsidered. According to the scheme in operation at the relevant time, however, the Legal Aid Committee's decision of 11 July 1985 was stated to be final. The Government, it is true, maintained that as a matter of practice the decision could have been reviewed after the High Court had called for a transcript of the evidence and adjourned its hearing of the appeal. In fact no such review took place. It would appear to the Court that in all the circumstances of the case it would have been in the interests of justice for free legal assistance to be given to the applicant at least at that stage for the ensuing proceedings. . . . (paras 44 and 46–47)

The Court concluded that there had been a violation of para. 3(c) taken together with para. 1. The Court made an award under Article 50 for Mr Granger's legal expenses.

Comment

Because this case took place in Scotland there was no need for the applicant to apply for leave to appeal, this being granted automatically under Scots law.

Darnell v UK
Series A, Vol. 272

The facts

The applicant was dismissed from his post as a consultant microbiologist with Trent Regional Health Authority in 1984, following disciplinary proceedings. He appealed to the Secretary of State who confirmed termination of his employment in 1986. In an application for judicial review to the High Court the applicant successfully challenged the fairness of the procedure leading to his dismissal. The decision was declared invalid and the Secretary of State was asked to reconsider the matter, which he did, but in 1988 confirmed the original dismissal. A further application for judicial review was rejected. Concurrent proceedings before the industrial tribunal had been stayed pending the outcome of the appeal to the Secretary of State and the judicial review applications. These were then recommenced, and in 1990 the industrial tribunal held that the dismissal had not been unfair. The appeal to the Employment Appeal Tribunal was dismissed in 1993.

In the interim, following the exhaustion of judicial review proceedings, the applicant brought the case to the Commission at the end of 1988.

The Commission's opinion

The main grounds of the complaint under Article 6, para. 1 concerned the length of proceedings relating to the termination of employment by the Regional Health Authority: in fact a delay of nine years until the final decision by the Employment Appeal Tribunal. The Government had actually conceded that this delay was unreasonable and had made a public apology.

The Commission indicated the general principles applicable to 'reasonableness' in the length of proceedings:

> . . . According to the case law of the European Court of Human Rights, the reasonableness of the length of proceedings must be assessed in the light of the particular circumstances of the case and having regard to the criteria laid down in the Court's case law, in particular the complexity of the case and the conduct of the applicant and of the relevant authorities.
>
> . . . The Commission notes that the case was of no particular complexity and that in any case, by the time the paragraph 190 appeal was lodged on 23 May 1984, the compilation of the documentary evidence and the hearing of witnesses had already concluded. (paras 54 and 55)

Although the applicant was partially to blame for some of the delays, the Commission considered that:

> . . . the authorities have not acted as diligently and expeditiously as was required in this case. In taking this view, the Commission has had regard to the importance of what was at stake for the applicant. The proceedings were decisive for the applicant's continued employment with the RHA, even though he continued to receive his salary until the conclusion of the proceedings. Although his right to practise his profession remained unaffected, his dismissal effectively made it difficult, if not impossible, for him to work as a consultant microbiologist. Yet it took the Secetary of State nearly two years to reconsider the case and take a decision – confirming the applicant's dismissal – following the Divisional Court's finding that the procedure leading to the termination of the applicant's employment in February 1986 had been unfair. At the same time, these delays caused the proceedings in the Industrial Tribunal to be unduly long as they were stayed for over four years, pending the results of the applicant's appeal to the Secretary of State and the Judicial review proceedings.
>
> . . . In the light of these circumstances, the Commission considers that the length of the proceedings complained of was excessive and failed to satisfy the 'reasonable time' requirement.
>
> . . . The Commission concludes unanimously that in this case there has been a violation of Article 6(1) of the Convention. (paras 57–59)

The matter was referred to the Court.

The judgment of the Court

The Court held that whatever the exact period was – and there was some dispute about this – the lapse of time between the initial application to the industrial tribunal and the judgment of the Employment Appeal Tribunal could not in the circumstances be regarded as 'reasonable'.

The Court held that, despite the apology of the UK, Mr Darnell should receive some compensation for the damage caused to his professional career by the time lost from the practice of medicine and awarded him £5,000 plus legal costs and expenses.

John Murray v UK
Council of Europe Report

The facts

The complaint brought by the applicant concerned criminal proceedings against him following his arrest in January 1990 in a house in which a Provisional IRA informer had been held captive. Following his arrest he asked to consult his solicitor, but access to a solicitor was delayed under s. 15(1) of the Northern Ireland (Emergency Provisions) Act 1987. When the applicant did at last see his solicitor he was advised to remain silent and did so. He was subsequently charged and tried for several offences. He was found guilty of aiding and abetting the false imprisonment of a person. Appeal against his conviction was dismissed.

Before the Commission the applicant complained that he had been deprived of the right to remain silent, and that the adverse inferences drawn as a result of his silence meant that he incriminated himself, contrary to the generally recognised rule in international law that an accused person cannot be required to incriminate himself (Article 6, para. 1). Also that the operation of the procedure meant that the burden of proof was placed on the accused contrary to the principle of the presumption of innocence (Article 6, para. 2). He also complained that he had been denied legal assistance (Article 6, para. 3).

The Government submitted that there were safeguards provided in the proceedings:

> ... before any interference is drawn, the prosecution must have established a prima facie case against the accused; the judge has a discretion whether to draw an interference and is limited to drawing only such inferences as may be proper. The Order, in the Government's submission, merely allows the trier of fact to draw such inferences as common sense dictates. In the present case, there was a formidable case against the applicant which called for evidence from the applicant if there was an innocent explanation for his conduct. Furthermore, the burden of proof remained throughout on the prosecution. (para. 49)

The Commission's opinion

The relevant provisions of Article 6 were paras 1, 2 and 3(c).

As regards the right to silence, the Commission noted that this right is not expressly guaranteed in the provisions of Article 6. However, the right to silence might apply when read with the right against self-incrimination, which is an inherent part of the protection of the Article.

> ... The essential issue under Article 6(1) remains, in the Commission's view, whether an applicant received a fair trial. Whether a particular applicant has been subject to compulsion to incriminate himself in such a way as to render the criminal proceedings unfair or as to deprive him of the presumption of innocence will depend on an assessment of the circumstances of the case as a whole. (para. 56)

The Commission noted that in this case no penalty was imposed on the applicant for exercising his right to silence. However, strong inferences were drawn from his failure to answer certain questions. Nevertheless, the Commission noted that other evidence besides such inferences was presented to the court. Also the Commission noted that:

. . . a judge is not required to draw inferences and may only draw such inferences, and such a degree of inferences, as may be proper. In the context of Northern Ireland where judges sit without a jury, a judge gives a reasoned judgment as to the basis on which he decides to draw adverse inferences and the weight which he gives them. Whether he has properly exercised his discretion may then be examined by the Court of Appeal in Northern Ireland.

. . . In the present case, the Commission recalls that, in accordance with the requirements of the Order, the applicant was warned in effect that there was a prima facie case against him, i.e. a basis on which he could be convicted, and that, if he did not answer it, inferences might then be drawn. The Commission notes that there was evidence against the applicant in the testimony of L as to the applicant's involvement and in the statements of the police who had found the applicant at the top of the stairs in the house and in the mangled tape in the bathroom nearby. Both the trial judge and the Court of Appeal considered that this constituted a formidable case against the applicant in relation to the charge of aiding and abetting the false imprisonment of L. The applicant however did not give evidence in court to counter the prosecution case. The Commission finds that the adverse inferences drawn against him as a result were a formal expression of the inevitable doubt that no innocent explanation for conduct may exist where an accused, against whom considerable suspicion already lies, fails to offer any innocent explanation. (paras 59 and 60)

The Commission was satisfied that there were sufficient safeguards, and that:

. . . the provisions of the 1988 Order constitute a formalised system which aims at allowing common sense implications to play an open role in the assessment of evidence. The Commission finds no indication on the facts of this case that it deprived the applicant of the right to silence or that the consequences which flowed from his exercise of that right were unfair.

. . . Consequently, the Commission finds that the applicant was not deprived of a fair trial contrary to the requirements of Article 6(1) of the Convention nor that his right to presumption of innocence was violated contrary to Article 6(2) of the Convention. (paras 64 and 65)

There was therefore no violation of Article 6, paras 1 or 2.

As regards access to a solicitor, the Commission recalled that:

. . . the Convention does not expressly guarantee the right of an accused to communicate freely with his defence counsel for the preparation of his defence or otherwise, or for the defence counsel to be present during pre-trial examinations. Article 6(3)(c), which reflects a specific aspect of the general concept of a fair trial set out in (1) of the same Article, confers the right on an accused to defend himself through legal assistance. The Commission recalls that the Convention is intended to guarantee rights which are not theoretical or illusory but rights that are practical and effective; this is of particular relevance to the rights of the defence given the prominent place held in a democratic society by the right to a fair trial. Restrictions on an accused's access to his lawyer and the refusal to allow the lawyer to attend during examinations of his client may influence the material position of the defence at the trial and therefore also the outcome of the proceedings. The Court and the Commission have accordingly considered that guarantees of Article 6 normally extend to an accused the right to assistance and support by a lawyer throughout the proceedings.

. . . In the absence, however, of an express provision it cannot be excluded that the right of access to and support by a lawyer during proceedings may be susceptible to restrictions. Regard must be had to the circumstances of the case, including the nature, duration and effect of any restriction, to determine whether, in the context of the proceedings as a whole, an accused has been deprived of a fair hearing. (paras 69 and 70)

In the circumstances:

. . . The fact that, according to the 1988 Order, adverse inferences could be drawn from the applicant's failure to answer questions by the police or to account for certain facts already at the pre-trial stage is an element which made it particularly important for the applicant to be assisted by his solicitor at an early stage.

. . . The Commission is therefore of the opinion that in the present case the applicant's rights of defence were adversely affected by the restrictions on his access to a solicitor and that these restrictions were not in conformity with his right to a fair hearing under Article 6(1) and his right to legal assistance under Article 6(3)(c) of the Convention. (paras 72 and 73)

A number of separate opinions were given. Mr Schermers, while agreeing that there had been a violation of Article 6 concerning the absence of a solicitor, expressed the opinion that full access to a solicitor is not required. Mr Busuttil and Mr Loucaides expressed the opinions that there had also been violations of Article 6, paras 1 and 2, the latter emphasising that the presumption of innocence safeguarded under the article entailed the right to remain silent.

Comment
The Northern Ireland (Emergency Provisions) Act 1987, empowered the police to delay access to a solicitor for 48 hours if they considered that such access would interfere with police operations against terrorism. The procedure of cautioning an accused about the adverse inferences which might be drawn from his or her silence was provided for under the Criminal Evidence (Northern Ireland) Order 1988.

Under Article 4 of the 1988 Order, a court or jury may draw such inferences from the refusal of an accused to give evidence in his or her own defence as appear proper, or, on the basis of such inferences, treat the refusal as amounting to corroboration of any evidence given against the accused.

McMichael v *UK*
Series A, Vol. 308

The facts
This case, which also raised issues under Articles 8 and 14, concerned care proceedings in Scotland.

Mrs McMichael, who at the time was not married to Mr McMichael, gave birth to a son in 1987. As the mother was mentally ill, the baby was taken into care at the request of the Strathclyde Regional Council. From December 1987 a children's hearing made a number of decisions affecting the child, taking into account material in documents which – in line with the applicable procedural rules – were not disclosed to the child's mother or natural father. Two appeals were made against the children's hearings, one of which was abandoned and one upheld in the Sheriff Court. In both appeals documents lodged with the court were not disclosed to the mother.

The substance of the complaint under Article 6, para. 1 was that the applicants had not received a fair hearing before the children's hearing and had not had access to confidential reports and other documents submitted to the hearing. The Commission declared admissible the complaint by the mother, but a similar complaint by the father was dismissed because:

(a)   initially he had not been on the child's birth certificate and so had no *locus standi* to participate in the proceedings;

(b)   even when his name was added to the birth certificate, he did not acquire parental rights thereby as the child's natural father, and had consequently not been a party to the care proceedings.

The Commission's opinion

In considering the father's claim under Article 6, para. 1, the Commission expressed the opinion that this was inadmissible.

As far as the mother of the child was concerned, the Commission was satisfied that there was a 'genuine' and 'serious' dispute over her rights relating to 'family life' concerning the placing of the child in care, and the termination of access.

In considering the various proceedings which had taken place involving the child, the Commission expressed the opinion that:

> ... the children's hearing is not a tribunal or court within the meaning of Article 6(1) of the Convention. It is not intended to be by the relevant legislation and its members fail to offer the necessary guarantees of independence. Consequently the proceedings before the children's hearing did not comply with Article 6 of the Convention. (para. 114)

whereas the Sheriff Court was a tribunal within the meaning of Article 6. However, the Commission noted that:

> ... Article 6(1) does not require that the procedure which determines civil rights and obligations is conducted at each of its stages before tribunals meeting the requirements of Article 6(1). A procedure not complying with Article 6(1) may thus precede the determination of civil rights by a tribunal which has full jurisdictional control over the prior procedure and itself provides the requisite guarantees of Article 6(1). (para. 116)

Although the mother could appeal against the decisions of the children's hearing to the Sheriff Court, the Commission noted that the applicant had restricted access to certain relevant information:

> ... While however the reports and documents before the children's hearing are lodged by the Reporter before the Sheriff Court, these remain undisclosed to a parent such as the second applicant even though they are of relevance to the determination of the issues.
>
> ... The Commission finds that this reveals a basic inequality *vis-à-vis* the other parties and places the parent at a substantial disadvantage both in respect of his or her lodging of the appeal and in the subsequent presentation of the appeal. In these circumstances, the Commission considers that the second applicant's right to a fair hearing was impaired.
>
> ...

. . . The Commission concludes unanimously that there has been a violation of Article 6(1) of the Convention in respect of the second applicant. (paras 119–121)

Two members of the Commission expressed a partially dissenting opinion as regards the first applicant. They expressed the view that Article 6, para. 1 ought to have applied to the father as well, as there was no dispute that he was in fact the father of the child. He had no standing before the children's hearing because he had not acquired a parental rights order; but there was no guarantee that any such application would have been successful. It was wrong, therefore, to make his claim under Article 6 dependent on such an order.

The judgment of the Court

The Court agreed with the Commission that the father, the first applicant, could not claim that the care proceedings determined any of his 'civil rights' under Scots law.

The Court did not feel it necessary to resolve the dispute as to whether or not the children's hearing could be regarded as a tribunal. It held that Article 6, para. 1 was applicable to care proceedings before the children's hearing and the Sheriff Court. The Court was appreciative of the sensitivity of care proceedings, accepting that:

. . . in this sensitive domain of family law there may be good reasons for opting for an adjudicatory body that does not have the composition or procedures of a court of law of the classic kind. . . . Nevertheless, the right to a fair – adversarial – trial means the opportunity to have knowledge of and comment on the observations filed or evidence adduced by the other party. (para. 80)

The fact that certain documents were not disclosed to the applicant affected her ability to influence the outcome of the children's hearing and her ability to assess the chances of making an appeal to the Sheriff Court.

In considering the role of the Sheriff Court, the Court held that:

. . . in relation to disputes (*contestations*) between a parent and a local authority over children taken into care, the Sheriff Court satisfies the conditions of Article 6(1) as far as its composition and jurisdiction are concerned. However, the requirement of an adversarial trial was not fulfilled before the Sheriff Court, any more than it had been on the relevant occasions before the children's hearing.

. . .

. . . This being so, Mrs McMichael did not receive a 'fair hearing', within the meaning of Article 6(1), at either of the two stages in the care proceedings concerning her son A. There has accordingly been a breach in Article 6(1) in her respect. (paras 83 and 84)

Comment

The UK Government had already conceded before the Commission the absence of a fair trial before the children's hearing and before the Sheriff Court. A friendly settlement could have been reached before the case came before the Court. As it was the Court ordered the Government to pay financial compensation fof £8,000 for distress, sorrow and injury to health, on the basis that some of the trauma, anxiety and feeling of injustice experienced by the applicant could be attributed to her inability to see the confidential documents in question.

Air Canada v UK
Council of Europe Report

The facts

The applicants' commercial aircraft was seized by officers of the Commissioners of Customs and Excise when it was discovered that it was carrying prohibited drugs. It was subsequently returned to the company on condition that the company paid £50,000. A complaint was brought under Article 6, para. 1 and Article 1 of the First Protocol – relating to the peaceful enjoyment of possessions.

The Commission's opinion

The applicants complained that they had been subjected to a criminal penalty, namely the seizure of their aircraft and the subsequent fine; alternatively, that this seizure amounted to a determination of the company's civil rights and obligations without court proceedings in breach of Article 6, para. 1.

The applicants claimed that the fine amounted to a penalty which was intended to punish and that it was criminal in nature. The Commission, however, took the view that measures such as confiscation orders do not amount to criminal charges within the meaning and scope of Article 6. The Commission noted that:

> . . . In the present case, the applicant company was the object of proceedings which led to the condemnation of its aircraft as forfeited. Those proceedings established precisely that no element of fault needed to attach to the applicant company for the aircraft to be liable to forfeiture. The condition of payment of £50,000 for return of the aircraft must be seen as a measure limiting the harm caused to the applicant company, and not as a separate 'measure' or 'penalty' for specific behaviour which has given rise to a 'charge'.
>
> . . . The Commission thus finds that the proceedings involved in the present case did not imply the 'determination of any criminal charge'. (paras 50 and 51)

As regards the applicant's civil rights, the Commission, following established case law, accepted that Article 6 was applicable to any action founded on pecuniary subject matter, and that therefore the proceedings in this case determined the applicant's civil rights. The applicants claimed that:

> . . . the customs officer who seized the aircraft was neither independent, impartial nor a tribunal. It considers that the statutory rights of appeal to a court were inappropriate and that the remedy of judicial review was not adequate to remedy the injustice in the light of the width of discretion given to the Customs by the statute and the discretionary nature of judicial review itself. (para. 54)

The Government relied on the case of *Vilvarajah and Others v UK* Series A, Vol. 125, to support the contention that judicial review satisfied the requirements of Article 6. The Commission noted, however, that case concerned judicial review in the context of Article 13. The Commission recalled that:

> . . . it is the function of Article 6 of the Convention to secure procedural rights in connection with the determination of civil rights and obligations. It does not in itself guarantee any particular content for these rights and obligations. The issues before

the High Court and the Court of Appeal were undoubtedly severely circumscribed by the questions before those courts and, indeed, by the strict wording of the statute. Such matters, however, relate to the content of the rights and obligations. The applicant company has not pointed to any matters which could amount to a possible violation of Article 6 of the Convention in conection with the condemnation proceedings. (para. 56)

Further, as the applicant company had not in fact made an application for judicial review of the decision to return the seized aircraft or the payment of £50,000, the Commission was unable to ascertain whether the scope of such review in this case would have complied with Article 6.

Mr Trechsel and Mrs Liddy expressed a dissenting opinion based on the view that the seizure of the aircraft and the levy of the fine was to exert pressure on Air Canada and to operate as a strong warning to improve cargo security. The sum paid was therefore in the nature of a penalty, and Air Canada was therefore faced with a criminal charge. Article 6 should apply. Mr Marxer also agreed with this approach.

The judgment of the Court

The Court agreed with the Commission that the matters complained of did not involve the determination of a criminal charge. As far as the civil rights infringed were concerned, the Court noted that:

. . . the applicant's complaint related to both the seizure of the aircraft and the payment of £50,000.

. . . As regards the seizure, the relevant provisions of United Kingdom law required the Commissioners to take proceedings for forfeiture once the seizure of the aircraft had been challenged. Such proceedings were in fact brought and, with the agreement of the parties, were limited to the determination of specified questions of law. In such circumstances, the requirement of access to court inherent in Article 6(1) was satisfied.

. . . Furthermore, it was also open to Air Canada to bring judicial review proceedings contesting the decision of the Commissioners to require payment as a condition for the return of the aircraft. As noted above, had such proceedings been brought, Air Canada could have sought to contest the factual grounds on which the exercise of discretion by the Commissioners was based. However, for whatever reason, such proceedings were not in fact instituted. Against this background, the Court does not consider it appropriate to examine in the abstract whether the scope of judicial review, as applied by the English courts, would be capable of satisfying Article 6(1) of the Convention.

. . .

. . . Accordingly, there has been no violation of Article 6(1) of the Convention. (paras 60–63)

Judge Walsh expressed a dissenting opinion on the grounds that the term 'criminal' bore an autonomous meaning in the Convention and one of the criteria to be taken into account should be the severity of the penalty. As the penalty imposed was in accordance with the law, judicial review proceedings would not have helped the applicants. In effect the applicants were penalised for criminal acts of persons unknown to them and for whom they were not responsible. Judge Pekkanen agreed with this line of reasoning concerning judicial review.

Judge Martens and Judge Russo similarly expressed the opinion that the confiscation was within the ambit of criminal law, aiming as it did to penalise the applicants and to deter a repetition of the offence by putting pressure on Air Canada to tighten its security.

Comment

The Commissioners derived their power to seize the aircraft from the provisions of the Customs and Excise Management Act 1979, ss. 139(1), 141(1) and Schedule 3, para. 6. The Commissioners had threatened Air Canada with forfeiture of the plane. Their power to do this had been challenged in 1988 by Air Canada before the High Court, which had found in favour of Air Canada. The Commissioners' appeal to the Court of Appeal against this decision had been upheld in 1990 and leave to appeal to the House of Lords by Air Canada had been refused.

Stubbings J.L. and J.P. v UK
Council of Europe Report

The facts

This case, involving three applicants, concerned the operation of time limits on civil claims. All three applicants had been subject to violent sexual and physical abuse as children, which had led to severe psychological problems. The connection between the former and the latter was not appreciated until the applicants became adults. The first applicant's case became a test case for the other two. She brought a civil action for damages in trespass against her abusers in 1987, but this was struck out as being time-barred by the Limitation Act 1980. The matter was taken to appeal, the Appeal Court applying a different interpretation of the law and holding that the action was not time-barred. This judgment was reversed, however, by the House of Lords. Subsequently both the second and third applicants were advised that there was no point in continuing their civil actions because these too would be found to be time-barred in the light of the House of Lords ruling.

The applicants therefore complained to the Commission, which found their application admissible, on the grounds that:

> . . . they are denied access to a court as a result of the limitation period applied in respect of their claims arising out of incidents of abuse which they suffered during their childhood (para 46).

Points of issue concerned violations of Article 6(1) alone or with Article 14 and Article 8.

The Commission's opinion

The Commission accepted that the applicants had been denied access to court as a result of the limitation periods imposed in respect of their claims. There was no dispute that these claims related to the determination of rights of a civil character.

The applicants complained that the nature of the injury was such that an inflexible time limit operated in an arbitrary and disproportionate way. The

Commission recalled, however, that the right of access to the court under Article 6, para. 1 was not absolute and that States may regulate this within their margin of appreciation, provided such limitation does not restrict or reduce access to such an extent that the very right is impaired, and provided that the limitation pursues a legitimate aim and there is proportionality between the means employed and the aim. In this respect the Commission found that:

> ... it must generally be accepted in the interests of good administration of justice that there are time limits within which prospective proceedings must be introduced. It agrees with the Government that time limits imposed on the introduction of claims pursue the legitimate aim of preventing stale claims and the possible injustice to defendants faced with evidential difficulties in contesting allegations relating to distant events and of promoting legal certainty. (para. 53)

Although the applicants' claim under Article 6 failed, the Commission did consider that there had been a violation of Article 6, para. 1 taken in conjunction with Article 14, because of the discriminatory effect of the operation of limitation periods between intentional and unintentional injury. The case was referred to the Court.

Comment
The applicants's civil action was based in the tort of trespass. Under the Limitation Act 1980, actions for negligence, nuisance or breach of duty impose a time limit of three years from the date on which the plaintiff had knowledge that he or she had grounds to bring a claim. The applicant in this case had this knowledge in September 1984, and sought to bring the claim in August 1987. The High Court Master ruled that the action was time-barred on the grounds that 'the date of knowledge was more than three years prior to the date on which proceedings were instituted'. On appeal the Appeal Court held that this date was not at the age of 19, when her mental problems began, but the date at which she became aware of the possible link between the abuse and the psychological problems. The House of Lords, however, held that as her action lay in tort, under the 1980 Act there was an inflexible limit of six years from the date of majority, for claiming for any tort committed against the applicant in her minority.

See similarly *D.S.* v *UK* App. No. 22095/93, in which the Commission expressed the opinion on 22 February 1995 that there had been a breach of Article 6, para. 1 read with Article 4. The case has also been referred to the Court.

Maxwell v UK
Series A, Vol. 300-C

The facts
The applicant had been found guilty of assault in May 1990, and sentenced to five years' imprisonment. He had legal aid for the preparation of his defence and for his representation by counsel at the trial. He was, however, refused legal aid for an appeal and could find no lawyer to represent him. Counsel who had represented him at his trial advised against appeal, as did subsequent lawyers.

The applicant therefore represented himself in March 1991, but his appeal was dismissed. The court – in this case the High Court of Justiciary, as the case was heard in Scotland – was satisfied that the grounds of appeal had no substance and that there had been no miscarriage of justice.

The applicant complained to the Commission of a violation of Article 6 on the grounds that refusal of legal aid for his appeal was a violation of the article, and that as very serious matters were at stake in his appeal, the interests of justice required that he receive legal representation.

The Commission's opinion

The Commission concluded that there had been a violation of Article 6, para. 3(c).

In considering the scope of the words 'in the interests of justice', the Commission indicated that each case must be examined on its facts:

> ... while the likelihood of success and the availability of legal assistance at other stages of the proceedings are significant factors to be taken into account, they are not the sole criteria. Other factors ... include the importance of what is at stake for the applicant, e.g. the severity of the sentence; the personal ability of the applicant and the nature of the proceedings, e.g. the complexity or importance of the issues or procedures involved. (para. 45)

The Commission distinguished this case from the *Granger* case (above) on the question of complexity, but was satisfied regarding the question of importance of what was at stake. Although there were factors in the Scottish appeal procedure which were beneficial, the Commission held that:

> ... The effectiveness of the contribution, by an unaided applicant, to appeal hearings at which the prosecution is represented by counsel, and consequently the fairness of those proceedings, must be seriously in doubt. Consequently, having regard in the present case to the nature of the proceedings and the length of sentence at stake, the Commission finds that the interests of justice required the provision of legal assistance. (para. 47)

Dissenting opinions were expressed by two members of the Commission who considered that there had been no violation of Article 6, para. 3(c), either alone or as an element in the right to a fair hearing under Article 6, para. 1.

The judgment of the Court

The Court accepted that there were differences between the *Granger* case and this one, and that the introduction of new practices following the *Granger* case which were more favourable to an unrepresented appellant were undoubtedly a positive development. Nevertheless, it was clear that although the legal issues in this case may not have been particularly complex, without the services of a legal practitioner Mr Maxwell was unable competently to address the court on these legal issues and thus to defend himself effectively. The Court particularly took note of the appeal court's wide powers, and of the fact that its decision was final and of the length of the sentence imposed. The Court therefore considered that the interests of justice required that the applicant be granted legal aid for representation at the hearing of his appeal, and that failure to do this amounted to a violation of Article 6, para. 3(c).

Comment

In Scotland, there is an automatic right of appeal available for a person convicted of a criminal charge. No leave of appeal is required as in England and Wales. The High Court of Justiciary, in its appellate role, has wide powers to dispose of appeals. The procedure is not limited to specific grounds; any alleged miscarriage of justice may be challenged. Legal aid is administered by the Scottish Legal Aid Board. It is not granted automatically for appeals, but where it has been granted for a trial on indictment it may be extended to pay for consideration and advice by a solicitor on the question of appeal and to obtain an opinion on the prospect of an appeal from the counsel who acted at the trial. Further legal aid must be reapplied for and will be granted only if the grounds for appeal appear to be substantial and there is evidence that a solicitor is willing to act for the appellant. There is no formal review procedure, although the application may be reconsidered by an external reporter.

Reforms in this procedure were introduced in 1990 following the *Granger* decision. These were:

> ... In any appeal where legal aid has been refused and the court considers that prima facie an appellant may have substantial grounds for taking the appeal and it is in the interests of justice that the appellant should have legal representation in arguing his grounds, the court shall forthwith adjourn the hearing and make a recommendation that the decision to refuse legal aid should be reviewed. (*Practice Note*: Lord Justice General to all Appeal Court Chairmen and Clerks, 4 December 1990)

If a recommendation is made then legal aid is automatically granted.

Despite the improvements which have come about since *Granger*, in the case of *Boner* v *UK*, declared admissible 9 December 1991, Report of the Commission 4 May 1993, Decision of the Court 28 October 1994, Series A, Vol. 300-B 19 EHRR 246, the Court indicated that:

> ... The legal issue in this case may not have been particularly complex. Nevertheless, to attack in appeal proceedings a judge's exercise of discretion in the course of a trial requires a certain legal skill and experience. That Mr Boner was able to understand the grounds for his appeal and that counsel was not prepared to represent him does not alter the fact that without the services of a legal practitioner he was unable competently to address the court on this legal issue and thus to defend himself effectively.
>
> Moreover, the Appeal Court, as stated, had wide powers to dispose of his appeal and its decision was final. Of even greater relevance, however, the applicant had been sentenced to eight years' imprisonment. For Mr Boner therefore the issue at stake was an extremely important one.
>
> ...
>
> The situation in a case such as the present, involving a heavy penalty, where an appellant is left to present his own defence unassisted before the highest instance of appeal, is not in conformity with the requirements of Article 6.
>
> ... Given the nature of the proceedings, the wide powers of the High Court, the limited capacity of an unrepresented appellant to present a legal argument and, above all, the importance of the issue at stake in view of the severity of the sentence, the Court considers that the interests of justice required that the applicant be granted legal aid for representation at the hearing of his appeal.

In conclusion, there has been a violation of paragraph 3(c) of Article 6. (paras 41 and 43–44)

In both the *Maxwell* and the *Boner* cases the Scottish Legal Aid Board had rejected applications for legal aid for the appeal stage because it considered that there were no substantial grounds for an appeal. In neither case did the applicants have any legal knowledge themselves.

The judgments of the Court in the *Boner* and *Maxwell* cases were delivered together. Mr Boner was awarded FF 7,500.28 (less the FF 16,275.79 already paid by way of legal aid) under Article 50, for costs and expenses. In the case of Mr Maxwell, the Court was unable to speculate as to the outcome of the appeal had legal aid been granted, and therefore rejected his claim for an award under Article 50.

Cases and Reports pending under this article

Dugan v *UK* (Application No. 21437/93), 18 EHRR CD 174. This case was declared admissible by the Commission in May 1994. The complaint concerned the length of time proceedings had taken from initial arrest in May 1981 to sentence in September 1993, a period of 12 years and three months.

Gregory v *UK* (Application No. 22299/93). The applicant was tried for and convicted of robbery. Indications of racial bias among the jury emerged during the jury discussions. The applicant's complaint of a breach of Article 6 concerning the right to an independent and impartial tribunal, was declared admissible by the Commission in April 1993. In its report of 18 October 1995, the Commission expressed the opinion that there had been no violation of Article 6. The case has now been referred to the Court.

John Murray v *UK*. This case was referred by the Commission to the Court, which held its hearing on 20 June 1995 (Press Release of the Registrar of the Court 19–20 June 1995).

Stubbings v *UK* (Application No. 22083/93), concerning the operation of limitation periods barring access to the court, has been referred to the Court.

John Bryan v *UK* (Application No. 19178/91), concerning whether the High Court's scope to review a decision by an inspector appointed by the Secretary of State for the Environment was sufficient to comply with Article 6, para. 1, was referred to the Court, which held its hearing on 23 May 1995. In a judgment delivered on 22 November 1995, the Court held that there was no violation of Article 6, para. 1 (Press Release 22 November–18 December 1995).

Ernest Saunders v *UK* (Application No. 19178/91), concerning complaints relating to a fair trial when statements made to the DTI were subsequently used in criminal proceedings, has now been referred to the Court after the Commission found there had been a violation of Article 6, para. 1 (18 EHRR CD23).

James Moody v *UK* (Application No. 22613/93) and *Steven Lochrie* v *UK* (Application No. 22614/93), concerning the refusal to award defence costs following acquittal, were both declared admissible by chambers of the Commission.

Findlay v *UK* (Application No. 22107/93). This case concerned the conduct of the applicant's court-martial hearing and the procedures for reviewing this.

His complaints concerning Article 6 were that the review procedures were largely administrative in nature and conducted in private. He challenged the independence and the impartiality of the procedure, particularly the powers and conduct of the Convening Officer and the Judge Advocate, on the grounds that there are close connections between the army authorities and the members of the court-martial and the reviewing authorities. In its report of 5 September 1995, the Commission expressed the opinion that there had been a violation of Article 6, para. 1. The case has now been referred to the Court.

Pullar v *UK* (Application No. 22399/93), Report of the Commission 11 January 1995, Council of Europe Press Release 3–23 March 1995, which concerned the applicant's trial by jury in Scotland. One of the jurors had been employed by one of the principal prosecution witnesses and was acquainted with the other principal prosecution witness. This fact did not come to the attention of the applicant or his legal advisers until after the trial, by which time he had been convicted and sentenced. The matter had been brought to the attention of the Sheriff's clerk by both the prosecution witnesses involved, but the clerk had not informed the Sheriff. Appeal to the High Court had been unsuccessful. The Commission expressed the opinion that there had been a violation of Article 6, para. 1. The case has now been referred to the European Court.

Kenneth McGinley and Edward Egan v *UK* (Application Nos 21825/93 and 23414/94), concerning refusal to disclose medical and other records to the applicants who claimed to be victims of radiation during nuclear tests while in the armed forces in the 1950s, declared admissible. (Articles 6, para. 1, 8 and 13.)

Paul Matthew Coyne v *UK* (Application No. 25942/94), concerning the independence and impartiality of a court-martial, declared admissible.

CHAPTER 7

ARTICLE SEVEN

Article 7

1. No one shall be held guilty of any criminal offence on account of any act or omission which did not constitute a criminal offence under national or international law at the time when it was committed. Nor shall a heavier penalty be imposed than the one that was applicable at the time the criminal offence was committed.

2.1 This Article shall not prejudice the trial and punishment of any person for any act or omission which, at the time when it was committed, was criminal according to the general principles of law recognised by civilised nations.

7.1 THE SCOPE OF THE ARTICLE

A number of the other articles in the Convention use the words 'prescribed by law', or 'in accordance with the law'. In the context of the UK this means both statute and common or other customary law. These criteria were considered in the case of *Sunday Times* v *UK*, in which it was stated:

> . . . Firstly, the law must be adequately accessible: the citizen must be able to have an indication that is adequate in the circumstances of the legal rule applicable in a given case. Secondly, a norm cannot be regarded as a 'law' unless it is formulated with sufficient precision to enable a citizen to regulate his conduct: he must be able – if need be with appropriate advice – to foresee, to a degree that is reasonable in the circumstances, the consequences which a given action may entail. Those consequences need not be foreseeable with absolute certainty: experience shows this to be unattainable. Again, whilst certainty is highly desirable, it may bring in its train excessive rigidity and the law must be able to keep pace with changing circumstances. Accordingly, many laws are inevitably couched in terms which, to a greater or lesser extent, are vague and whose interpretation and application are questions of practice. (Series A, Vol. 30, para. 49)

In the case of criminal law it is particularly important that the law is clear. Article 7 makes specific provision which is applicable to the legal basis of any criminal sanction and sets out criteria which are more elaborate than those found in other articles regarding lawfulness, and in particular the possible retrospective effect of the law.

One of the problems that arises in the context of English law is the role of common law rather than statute law. Although the judges are there to apply the law and not to make it, in order to keep the law up to date with changing circumstances it does occasionally happen that a court decision which alters the law precedes Parliamentary action. Where the criminal offence or penalty is established by statute then the question is usually one concerning the date at which the statute came into force (*Welch* v *UK* 16 EHRR CD 42). However, where the law is judge-made, the situation is not so clear. Where an offence is a common law offence the courts may have the function of clarifying or developing vague legal provisions. In doing this the courts must be careful not to extend the application of the law in order to encompass the facts of the cases before them. The rule-making function of the courts must remain within reasonable limits (*Gay News Ltd* v *UK* 5 EHRR 123). The dividing line as to what is reasonable and what is not is not always clear. In the *Gay News* case the Commission stated that:

> . . . it is excluded . . . that any acts not previously punishable should be held by the courts to entail criminal liability, or that existing offences should be extended to cover facts which previously clearly did not constitute a criminal offence. This implies that constituent elements of an offence such as e.g. the particular form of culpability required for its completion may not be essentially changed, at least not to the detriment of the accused, by the case law of the courts. On the other hand it is not objectionable that the existing elements of the offence are clarified and adapted to new circumstances which can reasonably be brought under the original concept of the offence. (vol. 28 D & R 77, para. 9)

In the cases of *CR and SW* v *UK* 18 EHRR CD 119, at the date the applicants committed the alleged offences (1989) the existing law revealed no offence because of the marital immunity from rape. A Criminal Law Revision Committee Report of 1984 had expressed the view that there should be no change in the basic principle of marital immunity; and although the Law Commission's Working Paper on 'Rape within Marriage' (1990) had proposed that the existing principle of marital immunity should be abolished, this had not been undertaken by Parliament at the time of the trials of CR and SW. The only change in the law had been made by the Judicial Committee of the House of Lords. This change related not so much to the constituent elements of the offence, but more fundamentally extended the offence into circumstances in which it formerly had had no application.

7.2 THE CASES

Gay News Ltd and Lemon v UK
Vol 28 D & R 77 (ref. *X Ltd and Y* v *UK*)

The facts
A private prosecution was brought against the applicants who were respectively the publisher and editor of a magazine *Gay News*. The charge was one of

blasphemous libel on the grounds that the applicants had 'unlawfully and wickedly published or caused to be published a blasphemous libel concerning the Christian religion, namely an obscene poem and illustration vilifying Christ in His life and in His crucifixion'.

The trial judge directed the jury that in order to satisfy the requisite elements of this common law offence it was necessary to establish only that the publication complained of vilified Christ in His life and crucifixion. It was not necessary to establish an intention beyond the intention to publish. The applicants were convicted. The House of Lords itself granted leave to appeal, and although the appeal was dismissed, two of the Law Lords concluded that an intent to blaspheme was a necessary element of the offence and that the law in this respect was unclear. The majority of the House of Lords, however, held that such intent was not necessary, although only one held that the law in this regard had always been clear.

Under Article 7, the applicants complained that their conviction was based on legal principles which had not existed, or at least had not been defined with sufficient clarity, at the time of the commission of the offence.

The Commission's opinion
In considering whether Article 7 had been violated, the Commission had to consider whether the courts had remained within reasonable limits in interpreting and applying the common law.

The Commission expressed the opinion that:

... While this branch of the law presents certain particularities for the very reason that it is by definition law developed by the courts, it is nevertheless subject to the rule that the law-making function of the courts must remain within reasonable limits. In particular in the area of the criminal law it is excluded, by virtue of Article 7(1) of the Convention, that any acts not previously punishable should be held by the courts to entail criminal liability, or that existing offences should be extended to cover facts which previously clearly did not constitute a criminal offence. This implies that constituent elements of an offence such as e.g. the particular form of culpability required for its completion may not be essentially changed, at least not to the detriment of the accused, by the case law of the courts. On the other hand it is not objectionable that the existing elements of the offence are clarified and adapted to new circumstances which can reasonably be brought under the original concept of the offence.

... The Commission notes that the Law Commission has criticised the state of the law of blasphemous libel in particular with regard to its lacking clarity, but it nevertheless considers that the courts in the present case in fact did not go beyond the limits of a reasonable interpretation of the existing law. The House of Lords in particular was aware of the limits of its law-making functions in the area of the criminal law which had been circumscribed in the practice statement of 1966 and put into operation in the case of *Knuller* v *DPP* [1973] AC 435. The courts of all degrees confirmed the continued existence of the offence of blasphemous libel. There was only one point which was not clear, namely the particular requirements as to the *mens rea* of a person who commits this offence. The question was answered in the same way by each of the courts. Despite the admission by the Court of Appeal and the majority of the House of Lords that a point of principle was involved in the determination of this question which required clarification, it is equally clear that the application of a test of strict liability and the exclusion of evidence as to the publisher's and editor's intention to blaspheme did not amount to the creation of new law in the sense that earlier case law clearly denying such strict liability and admitting evidence as to the blasphemous intentions was overruled. By stating that the *mens rea* in this offence did only relate to the intention to publish, the courts therefore did not overstep the limits of what can still be regarded as an acceptable clarification of the law. The Commission further considers that the law was also accessible to the applicants and that its interpretation in this way was reasonably foreseeable for them with the assistance of appropriate legal advice. In conclusion therefore the Commission finds that there is no appearance of a violation of Article 7(1) of the Convention in this case, and the applicant's complaint in this respect must accordingly be rejected as being manifestly ill-founded within the meaning of Article 27(2) of the Convention. . . . (paras 9 and 10)

Times Newspapers Ltd and Neil v *UK*
15 EHRR CD 49

The facts
This application was one of three concerning the publication of extracts from *Spycatcher*, the memoirs of Peter Wright, a former member of the British Security Service MI5. The application primarily concerned an alleged violation of Article 10. The issue concerning Article 7 revolved around the application and interpretation of the law on criminal contempt. The relevant facts in this context were those as stated in *Sunday Times* v *UK (No. 2)* Series A, Vol. 217, paras 27–28:

> . . . On 12 July 1987, the *Sunday Times*, which had purchased the British newspaper serialisation rights from Mr Wright's Australian publishers and had obtained a copy of the manuscript from Viking Penguin Incorporated in the United States, printed in its later editions, in order to avoid the risk of proceedings for an injunction, the first instalment of extracts from *Spycatcher*. It explained that this was timed to coincide with publication of the book in the United States, which was due to take place on 14 July. On 13 July the Attorney-General also commenced proceedings against the applicants for contempt of court on the ground that the publication frustrated the purpose of the original injunctions in July 1986.
>
> On 14 July 1987, Viking Penguin Incorporated published *Spycatcher* in the United States of America; some copies had, in fact, been put on sale on the previous day. It was an immediate bestseller. The British Government, which had been advised that proceedings to restrain publication in the United States would not succeed, took no legal action to that end either in that country or in Canada, where the book also became a bestseller.

The original injunctions referred to were injunctions granted to the Attorney-General by the Chancery Division of the High Court to restrain the *Observer* and the *Guardian* newspapers from publishing reports about some of the allegations of misconduct on the part of MI5 contained in the book. Proceedings to prevent publication of the book in Australia had been started in 1985 by the UK.

While the injunctions against the *Observer* and the *Guardian* were still in force, a summary of the allegations was published, first in the *Independent* and then in the *London Evening Standard* and the *London Daily News*. The Attorney-General applied for and was granted leave to move against the publishers and editors of these newspapers for contempt of court. The question at issue was whether newspapers not covered by the injunctions were in contempt of court because they knew that such injunctions existed.

On 2 June 1987, the Vice-Chancellor held that publication of the memoirs did not constitute criminal contempt by newspapers other than those covered by the original injunctions. This ruling was made prior to the *Sunday Times* publishing its extracts, although at the time of that publication the Attorney-General's appeal against the Vice-Chancellor's preliminary ruling was pending. However, Mr Neil, the editor of the *Sunday Times*, received legal advice prior to publication that neither he nor his newspaper would liable for criminal contempt if they published information covered by the existing injunctions.

Shortly after the *Sunday Times* publication, the Vice-Chancellor's ruling was reversed by the Court of Appeal on the grounds that:

> . . . the purpose of the original injunctions was to preserve the confidentiality of the *Spycatcher* material, . . . publication of that material would destroy that confidentiality . . . and therefore interfere with the administration of justice. (Series A, No. 217, para. 30)

An injunction against further publication of extracts by the *Sunday Times* was obtained by the Attorney-General on 16 July 1987. The applicants were tried for contempt in April 1989 and, along with the *News on Sunday* and the *Independent*, found guilty on the ground that:

> . . . The *Sunday Times* had knowingly perpetrated contempt of court in publishing the *Spycatcher* extracts on 12 July 1987. (p. 52)

They were fined £50,000 plus costs.

On appeal the Court of Appeal upheld the judgment but concluded that no fines should be imposed because:

> . . . first, the Vice-Chancellor had given his preliminary ruling that the other newspapers were not in contempt of court, even though the applicants knew that his ruling was subject to an appeal; secondly, the applicants had received legal advice that they would not be in contempt if they published the *Spycatcher* extracts and, thirdly, the publication of the whole book in the United States of America was imminent, thus largely destroying any confidentiality in Mr Wright's material. (p. 53)

In their application to the Commission, the applicants alleged that at the time of their publication, in the light of the preliminary ruling, they were not guilty of an offence, and to find them so was contrary to Article 7.

The Commission's opinion

In considering the application of the law under Article 7, the Commission found that:

> . . . the offence of criminal contempt for which the applicants were found guilty was prescribed by law within the meaning of Article 10(2) of the Convention. (p. 58)

Therefore, the Commission considered that:

... the constituent elements of the common law offence of contempt were sufficiently clear as of 12 July 1987. The fact that the established legal principles involved were applied to novel circumstances does not render the offence retroactive in any way. (p. 58)

Welch v *UK*
Series A, Vol. 307

The facts

The applicant had been charged with drug offences and found guilty on five counts, and sentenced to imprisonment. After the applicant's arrest, but before trial, a new provision had come into force under the Drug Trafficking Offences Act 1986, which made provision for a confiscation order – in this case for £66,914, subsequently reduced on appeal by £7,000.

The applicant complained that:

> ... the confiscation order imposed on him constituted a retrospective criminal penalty. He points to the draconian nature of the order which is calculated on the basis of assumptions that any money received or paid by the defendant in the preceding six years is derived from drug trafficking. The purpose of the order is wider than the removal of profits since it covers all proceeds which have passed through the defendant's hands irrelevant of whether he received any benefit or enrichment. Expenditure by the defendant is not deducted in the calculation but is in fact capable of being added to the total figure. The effect of the order therefore is not, in his submission, to restore the status quo since it will place a defendant in a worse position. Further, there is the imposition of a period of imprisonment in default of payment (up to a maximum of 10 years) which is required to run consecutively to the prison term imposed in respect of the offence. Consequently, the confiscation order is essentially punitive in nature and effect since it arises out of criminal proceedings in which guilt is determined and is contingent upon a subsisting and valid criminal conviction. (para. 40)

The Commission's opinion

The Commission noted that there was no dispute concerning the retrospective effect of the legislation. The question before the Commission was:

> ... whether the confiscation order constituted a penalty imposed in respect of a criminal offence within the meaning of Article 7(1) of the Convention. (para. 42)

The case raised a new problem in as much as the case law of the Commission revealed no established definition of the term 'penalty' within the context of this article, compared to definitions relating to proceedings under Article 6.

In seeking to interpret the term, the Commission considered that:

> ... regard must be had to the essential nature and object of a measure both as stated in domestic law and as revealed in practice. (para. 46)

In this case the Commission considered the background to the Drug Trafficking Offences Act 1986:

> ... the stated purpose of the Act [indicates] that the measure of confiscation was intended to be reparative and preventive—to remove the proceeds of crime from the

offender so that 'crime does not pay' and also to ensure the money could not continue to be used in drug trafficking.

. . . The procedure as enacted provides in practice that at the end of criminal proceedings in which a person in convicted of drug trafficking offences the court will proceed to determine whether the person has benefited from drug trafficking and if so assess the amount to be subject to a confiscation order. The 1986 Act provides for drastic assumptions in making that assessment, in particular that all money passing through the defendant's hands in the past six years will be assumed to be the benefit of drug trafficking. These assumptions however may be shown by the defendant to be incorrect. (paras 47 and 48)

However, the Commission considered that the severity of the measure alone was not decisive of its character.

In considering all the facts, and the intended operation of the law, the Commission concluded that the confiscation order was not punitive and did not constitute a penalty within the meaning of Article 7.

Five members of the Commission expressed a dissenting opinion on the grounds that:

. . . Where a sanction or measure is not strictly speaking a penalty, it may nonetheless have a similar purpose or effect which may bring it within the ambit of Article 7 of the Convention.

As noted by the majority, the 1986 Act provides for drastic assumptions in assessing the amount to be subject to a confiscation order, in particular that all money passing through the defendant's hands in the past six years will be assumed to be the benefit of drug trafficking. The draconian nature of the provisions has been commented upon by the domestic courts, which have taken steps to mitigate the provisions by, for example, insisting on the criminal standard of proof applying to the prosecution as regards whether a person has benefitted from drug trafficking. Nonetheless, once the initial step of establishing that a defendant has benefitted has been accomplished by the prosecution, the burden of proof effectively switches to the defendant to prove that particular assets were in fact not derived from drug trafficking and therefore should not be included in the calculation of the proceeds to be confiscated.

We find in the applicant's argument that the true nature and object of the confiscation is punitive since in practice it goes beyond reparation and prevention in the scope of the proceeds which it can attach, i.e. it is not limited to the actual enrichment or profit. Further, expenditure by the defendant is in fact capable of being added to the total figure assessed. While the severity of the order, combined as it is with sentence, of imprisonment in default, is not decisive in itself, it is nonetheless a significant factor in assessing whether the measure is punitive in its essential effect. . . .

We are aware that the United Kingdom system could be regarded as giving a high standard of procedural protection to suspects as a result of linking confiscation to criminal proceedings with a correspondingly higher burden of proof on the prosecution. However, that link to the criminal conviction combined with the stringency of the measure, particularly the sentence of two years' imprisonment in default, leads us to the view that such confiscation is a measure which in practice is essentially punitive in its nature and effect.

Consequently, we consider that the confiscation order imposed on the applicant was a penalty within the meaning of Article 7(1) of the Convention. We would emphasise, however, that this conclusion is not a criticism of confiscation itself as a means of combating the problems of drug trafficking: merely that the imposition of such a penalty cannot, under the terms of the Article, be imposed retrospectively.

Mr Schermers also expressed a dissenting opinion but on rather different grounds:

> In my opinion, the confiscation of property acquired by crime, even without express prior legislation, is not contrary to Article 7 of the Convention, nor to Article 1 of the First Protocol. In this respect, I can support much of the opinion of the majority. In principle, therefore, I do not consider the 1986 Act as such contrary to the Convention. The importance of effectively fighting crime justifies its drastic assumptions. These drastic assumptions, however, illustrate that, apart from its purpose to 'take back' what was obtained illegally, the Act also includes a punitive element. Without the assumption of an underlying crime, only illegally-obtained profit could be confiscated and only to the extent to which the authorities could prove the unjust enrichment. In my view, the confiscation of property in excess of the amount which the authorities can prove to be obtained from crime is of a punitive character. That part of the confiscation, therefore, may not be retroactively imposed. The facts as presented to the Commission suggest that property in excess of that amount has been confiscated which leads me to the conclusion that there has been a violation of Article 7 of the Convention.

The judgment of the Court
The Court held that as there was no dispute concerning the retroactive imposition of the confiscation order – because the order had been made following a conviction for offences committed before the Act came into force – the only question to be determined was whether the order constituted a penalty under Article 7, para. 1.

In determining what was a penalty the Court held that the concept bore an autonomous meaning under the Convention. The Court did not have to accept the definition of domestic law, but could examine the measure.

> . . . The starting point in any assessment of the existence of a penalty is whether the measure in question is imposed following conviction for a 'criminal offence'. Other factors that may be taken into account as relevant in this connection are the nature and purpose of the measure in question; its characterisation under national law; the procedures involved in the making and implementation of the measure; and its severity. (para. 28)

Like the Commission, the Court took into account the background of the Act:

> . . . which was introduced to overcome the inadequacy of the existing powers of forfeiture and to confer on the courts the power to confiscate proceeds after they had been converted into other forms of assets. The preventive purpose of confiscating property that might be available for use in future drug trafficking operations as well as the purpose of ensuring that crime does not pay are evident from the ministerial statements that were made to Parliament at the time of the introduction of the legislation. However, it cannot be excluded that legislation which confers such broad powers of confiscation on the courts also pursues the aim of punishing the offender. Indeed, the aims of prevention and reparation are consistent with a punitive purpose and may be seen as constituent elements of the very notion of punishment. (para. 30)

On the facts of the case the following elements pointed to a penalty:

> . . . the sweeping statutory assumption in section 2(3) of the 1986 Act that all property assing through the offender's hands over a six-year period is the fruit of drug

trafficking unless he can prove otherwise . . . ; the fact that the order is directed to the proceeds and is not limited to actual enrichment or profit . . . ; the discretion of the trial judge to take into consideration the degree of culpability of the accused . . . ; and the possibility of imprisonment in default of payment. (para. 33)

There was, therefore, a combination of punitive elements which became evident once the realities of the situation were examined, and therefore a breach of Article 7. The UK was ordered to pay the applicant's costs under Article 50 to the sum of £13,852.60 less legal aid paid to the applicant.

Comment
The Court did not question the courts' powers to order confiscation in the general fight against drug trafficking, only the retrospective application of the legislation.

The domestic courts had already commented on the draconian effect of the legislation and had sought to mitigate this by holding that the prosecution had to prove beyond reasonable doubt that a defendant had in fact benefitted from his or her crime. However, the Commission and the Court could not, and indeed did not have to, rely on the *dicta* of the domestic courts as to whether the measure was punitive or not, as these were conflicting.

SW v *UK* and *CR* v *UK*
Council of Europe Press Release (20–27 April 1995)

The facts
In the case of CR, following matrimonial difficulties the wife left the matrimonial home in 1989 and went to live with her parents. She had consulted a lawyer and informed her husband in writing that she intended to petition for divorce. The applicant had also indicated in a telephone conversation that he intended to divorce. Shortly after, while his wife's parents were away, he forced his way into their house and attempted to have sexual intercourse with his wife. He was charged with attempted rape and assault.

The circumstances of SW similarly concerned an unsuccessful marriage. Prior to the events which gave rise to criminal charges, the couple had been sleeping separately but in the same house. On the night in question the wife had informed the applicant that she intended to leave him. He threw her out of the house, but following police intervention she re-entered. Later that same evening the applicant forcibly and violently had sexual intercourse with his wife and assaulted her.

Both of these cases concerned the issue of marital rape, the alleged rapes having taken place prior to the changes in the law brought about by the decision in *R* v *R* [1991] 4 All ER 481. This decision, in which the Court of Appeal had declared anachronistic and offensive the fiction that a husband cannot be guilty of raping his wife, had taken place between the date of the rapes and trial. The applicants complained that they had been charged and convicted in respect of acts which at the relevant time did not constitute a criminal offence and that their convictions were, therefore, a violation of Article 7.

The Commission's opinion
The Commission commented on the development of the law by the case law in this area, and expressed the opinion that the implied agreement to seek a divorce in the case of CR and the withdrawal from cohabitation by the wife, would indicate that in today's society the applicant might foresee that his conduct would be regarded as unlawful. Similarly, although in the case of SW the couple were still living together, anticipation of the abolition of marital immunity from a charge of rape ought to have been foreseen by the applicant. The Commission therefore concluded that there had been no violation of Article 7. The matter was referred to the Court.

The view of the majority, and even the opinions of the minority, indicated that the law on marital rape in the UK was unsatisfactory. Whereas the majority were prepared to accept that anticipated reform was almost inevitable and that therefore the applicants could not genuinely have believed that their conduct was not criminal, the minority opinions were more reserved. The dissenting opinion of Mr Loucaides and Nowicki was:

> . . . the law as regards one of the existing elements of the offence of rape, that is consent, has been fundamentally changed [by the decision in R v R] to the applicant's detriment. It was neither a clarification of the existing elements of the offence in question, nor an adaptation of such elements to new circumstances which could reasonably be brought under the original concept of the offence . . . A change through the case-law of the courts could not have been reasonably foreseeable to the applicant even with the assistance of legal advice.

The judgment of the Court
The Court gave the judgment on 22 November 1995, holding that there had been no violation of Article 7 (Press Release, 22 November–18 December 1995).

Comment
The Commission did not appear to place great importance on the difference in the facts of the two applicants' cases. Whereas the existing exceptions to marital immunity from rape might reasonably have been anticipated to extend to the case of CR, this could not easily be argued to be the situation in the case of SW, where there was still co-habitation and less evidence of agreement to separate.

Further reading
Beddard, R., 'Retrospective Crime' (1995) 145 New Law Journal 663

CHAPTER 8

ARTICLE EIGHT

Article 8
1.   *Everyone has the right to respect for his private and family life, his home and his correspondence.*
2.   *There shall be no interference by a public authority with the exercise of this right except such as is in accordance with the law and is necessary in a democratic society in the interests of national security, public safety or the economic well-being of the country, for the prevention of disorder or crime, for the protection of health or morals, or for the protection of the rights and freedoms of others.*

8.1   THE SCOPE OF THE ARTICLE

The case law of the Commission and of the Court establishes that States not only have to respect the rights guaranteed by this article but also to protect them. This may involve taking positive measures to do so.

8.1.1   Private Life

The right to respect for private life comprises to a certain extent:

. . . the right to establish and to develop relationships with other human beings, especially in the emotional field for the development and fulfilment of one's own personality. (*X* v *UK* 5 EHRR 260 at 263)

. . . To this effect [everyone] must also have the possibility of establishing relationships of various kinds, including sexual, with other persons. (*App. No. 10083/82* v *UK* 6 EHRR 50 at 143)

However, there may be circumstances where this right has to be limited, for example in the case of visiting facilities for prisoners, or the requirement that prisoners wear prison clothes. In such cases any limitation must be reasonable, consistent and justified under Article 8, para. 2.

The Commission has also held that the regulation of professional conduct is not a matter of private life (*App. No. 10331/83* v *UK* 6 EHRR 467, concerning regulation of the legal profession). However, the dividing line between private life and the public sphere may not always be easy to draw. As the Commission has indicated:

> ... there are limits to the personal sphere while a large proportion of the law existing in a given State has some immediate or remote effect on the individual's possibility of developing his personality by doing what he wants to do, not all of these can be considered to constitute an interference with private life in the sense of Art. 8 of the Convention ... the claim to respect for private life is automatically reduced to the extent that the individual himself brings his private life into contact with public life or into close connection with other protected interests. (*App. No. 10331* v *UK* 6 EHRR 143)

Therefore, for example, aiding and abetting suicide, although relevant to the private lives of would-be suicides, did not involve the applicant's rights to privacy (*App. No. 10083/82* v *UK*). Similarly, the criminalisation of homosexual acts between under age persons, even if done in private and with the consent of the participants, might be justified to protect the rights and freedoms of others.

8.1.2   Private Life and Home

The Commission has indicated that the scope of this article cannot be narrowly interpreted so as only to apply to direct measures taken by the State or its representatives against the privacy and/or home of an individual:

> ... It may also cover indirect intrusions which are unavoidable consequences of measures not at all directed against private individuals. (*Powell* v *UK* 9 EHRR 235 at 241)

Consequently, cases raising issues of nuisance, including noise nuisance, have been considered under Article 8 (e.g., *Powell and Baggs* v *UK* App. No. 9310/81). A distinction is made here between the provisions of the First Protocol, Article 1, which is mainly concerned with the arbitrary confiscation of property, and the right of peaceful enjoyment of possessions – although the Commission has recognised that nuisance of a considerable level and frequency may seriously affect the value of real property – and even render it unsaleable – and thus amount to a partial taking of property.

However, the right to private life has its limits. For example, it does not include the right to keep a domestic pet (*Artingstoll* v *UK* 19 EHRR CD 92), nor does it include the right to living accommodation (*Buckley* v *UK* 19 EHRR CD 26).

8.1.3   Family Life

Respect for family life includes the right of any member of the nuclear family – i.e. husband, wife and dependent or minor children – to the consortium of every other member. Included in that consortium is the right of each member to reside in the family's chosen place of residence. The unity of the family is therefore a factor to be considered under Article 8. Consequently, the right to family life may include the right not to have the family unit disrupted, e.g. by refusing entry to one of them (*Alam and Khan* v *UK* App. No. 2991/66, *Singh* v *UK* App. No. 2992/66), or by the deportation of one of them (*Lamguindaz* v *UK*, Judgment of the Court 28 June 1993 resulting in a friendly settlement (DH (93) 55), and recently, *Chahal* v *UK* App. No. 2241/93). However, there are limitations. Deportations may be held not to amount to a breach of Article 8 if there are no legal obstacles to the applicants effectively establishing their family life elsewhere (*X, Y, Z, V, W* v *UK* App. No. 3325/67), or where the disruption caused to the family by deportation is largely of the applicant's own making because he has repeatedly breached immigration controls (*App. No. 11970/86* v *UK* 11 EHRR 46 at 48).

Similarly, the Commission has held that the scope of Article 8:

> . . . presupposes the existence of a family life and the relationship should at least arise from a lawful and genuine marriage, even if family life has not been fully established. (*E* v *UK* 15 EHRR CD 61)

If a couple have married primarily for reasons of immigration, although the marriage may be lawful, as there is no general obligation to respect the choice of residence of a married couple, a State's refusal to grant them residence, where there is no obstacle to them residing elsewhere, will not amount to a violation of the article (*E* v *UK* 15 EHRR 46 and *N* v *UK* 16 EHRR CD 28).

Also, the Commission has held that respect for family life cannot reasonably be given such a wide interpretation as to allow an individual – even a minor – to free himself or herself from the obligations under a long-term service engagement freely entered into but involving a separation from his or her family except for periods of leave (*W, X, Y and Z* v *UK* (1968) 11 *Yearbook* 562).

In certain other circumstances, separating members of a family may amount to a breach of Article 8, for example, by placing children in the care of a local authority and transferring custody to that authority (declared admissible *Corralyn Roberts* v *UK* App. No. 21178/93). In other circumstances the separation of family members may be justified – for example, refusal to transfer an IRA prisoner in prison in England to Northern Ireland in order to be closer to his mother and sister (*S* v *UK* 15 EHRR CD 106). In the context of prisoners the Commission has observed that the concept of 'family life' has to be interpreted more widely than usual, and that:

> . . . Article 8 required the State to assist prisoners as far as possible to create and sustain ties with people outside prison in order to facilitate their social rehabilitation. (*McCotter* v *UK* 15 EHRR CD 98)

Although the essential object of Article 8 is to protect the individual against arbitrary interference by public authorities, there can also be positive obligations inherent in an effective respect for family life. In the case of prisoners in particular, however, a balance has to be struck between the rights of the individual and society in general. According to the case law of the Commission, a prisoner has no right to choose where he will serve his sentence and his separation from his family is an inevitable consequence of his detention. Only in exceptional circumstances would the detention of a prisoner a long way from his home constitute a violation of Article 8.

Similarly, refusal by prison authorities to use the applicant's new name, which he had changed by deed poll while in prison, was held by the Commission to be a question relating to the public administration of prisons and therefore beyond the scope of Article 8 (*Lant* v *UK* 9 EHRR 235).

'Family life' may be understood in a wider context than the nuclear family and include 'close members' of the family, including the applicant's parents. This was raised in *X and Y* v *UK* App. No. 5269/71, where the threatened deportation of a Cypriot from the UK meant that if his wife accompanied him, she would no longer be able to live with her parents. The Commission suggested that there could be such a close link between an applicant and his or her parents that the circumstances might amount to family life. However, taking into account that the applicant was 26 years old, married and living with her husband, working full-time, and that she was not dependent on her parents, nor they on her, on the facts no family life had been established.

The relationship between homosexuals has been held to relate to private rather than family life (*Dudgeon* v *UK* 4 EHRR 149, *App. No. 9369/81* v *UK* 5 EHRR 601 and *App. No. 12513/86* v *UK* 11 EHRR 46 at 49). This has also been the view in transsexual cases (*Rees* v *UK* Series A, Vol. 106, *Cossey* v *UK* Series A, Vol. 184). However, in a recent case the Commission expressed the opinion that the right to family life may apply to transsexuals (*X, Y and Z* v *UK* App. No. 21830/93).

Article 8 cannot be interpreted so as to require a State to provide a particular form of civil proceedings for the relatives of victims of crime, or to provide damages to extended categories of relatives (*McCourt* v *UK* 15 EHRR CD 110).

8.1.4 Correspondence

Correspondence is afforded separate protection under Article 8. Although there is clearly some overlap here with Article 10, the Commission has constantly expressed the opinion that where freedom of expression takes the form of correspondence, then Article 8 is the relevant provision.

8.1.5 Privacy

Intrusions into privacy – and in some cases correspondence – also covers secret surveillance, search and security vetting. Of particular importance in the context of the UK is the existence in England and Wales of laws and practices permitting a system for effecting secret surveillance of communications (Post Office Act 1969, Interception of Communications Act 1985). This has itself been held to amount to an interference with rights under Article 8 (*Malone* v *UK* 7 EHRR 14). However, the Commission has held that the case law concerning secret surveillance cannot be interpreted so broadly as to include every person in the UK who fears or suspects that information may have been compiled about him or her by a security agency. Nevertheless, because of the difficulties faced by an applicant in proving that information has been so compiled and retained, an alleged infringement of Article 8 may be claimed on the basis that such measures permitting secret surveillance exist and that there is a reasonable likelihood that the security service has compiled and retain information concerning private life. The same considerations will apply in the case of police surveillance. Nevertheless, the applicant must establish sufficient evidence that he or she is a person who is likely to be subject to such surveillance. For example, in *Firsoff* v *UK* 15 EHRR CD 111, the applicant, who had been involved in a number of incidents connected with attempts to gain access to the site of Stonehenge for the Summer Solstice, failed to establish a 'reasonable likelihood' that his mail had been interfered with by the police.

An example of grounds for justification for interference can be found in *Murray* v *UK* 19 EHRR 193, which concerned the entry and search of the family home by the Army in connection with suspected IRA offences under s.14 of the Northern Ireland (Emergency Provisions) Act 1978. The interference with the applicants' right to respect for their private and family life was:

(a)   in accordance with the law; and

(b)   necessary in a democratic society because it was directed at the legitimate aim of crime prevention – in this case terrorist crime.

8.2   THE CASES

The cases be can grouped into a number of subject areas, although at times these overlap.

8.2.1   Sexual relationships
X v *UK*
Council of Europe Report (cited as *Wells* v *UK*)

The facts

The applicant was charged with buggery concerning two 18-year-old males. He was found guilty on both counts. He complained to the Commission that the prosecution and imprisonment were an interference with his private life which was not justified, and also that the legal age of consent of 21 for homosexual acts, under the Sexual Offences Acts 1956 and 1967, was an unjustified interference with his private life.

The Commission's opinion

The Commission expressed the view that 'a person's sexual life is an important aspect of his private life'. It accepted that there had been an interference with the private life of the applicant as a result of the prosecution and imprisonment. The question was, therefore, whether such interference was justified.

Firstly, there was no dispute that it was 'prescribed by law'. The stated aims of the laws in question were the protection of health and morals, and the protection of the rights of others. In the light of the evidence presented at the trial, particularly relating to the threat of force and uncertainty as to how consistent the consent given had been, the Commission was satisfied that on the facts of the case the aim of protecting the rights and freedoms of others was justified, and necessary in a democratic society to provide safeguards to those who might be particularly vulnerable because of their age.

In considering whether the legal age of consent constituted an unjustified interference, the Commission expressed the opinion that:

... the legislation which fixes the age of consent, as distinct from its application in a particular case, regulates and affects the private homosexual lives of the applicant and others similarly situated by making it a criminal offence to have homosexual relations with persons under the age of 21. (para. 141)

The Government submitted that while fixing the age of consent might amount to interference with private life, it did not amount to lack of respect for it. The Commission accepted that:

... not all regulation of sexual behaviour could be considered to be an interference with the right to respect for private life. However, in the present case, it is of the opinion that legislation which makes private and consensual homosexual behaviour concerning young men between 18 and 21 a criminal offence amounts to an interference with respect for the applicant's private life which falls to be justified on one of the grounds in paragraph 2 of Article 8. The Commission considers that this statement is given weight by the fact that the age of majority in the United Kingdom for other areas of the law is 18 and that in most other European countries the 'age of consent' for homosexual relations is 18 or below. (para. 144)

The Commission therefore had to examine whether the age limit established in the UK was justified by reasonable and objective arguments. Legislative control of homosexual behaviour was to be found in most European countries, although the age of consent varied. Nevertheless the law must be examined on its own merits and in the context of the society for which it is applicable. The Commission expressed the opinion that:

... the age limit of 21 may be regarded as high in the present era, especially when contrasted with the current position in other member States of the Council of Europe. The Commission is also aware that current trends throughout Europe in relation to private consensual homosexual behaviour tend to emphasise tolerance and understanding as opposed to the use of criminal sanctions. Moreover, as far as the legislative position in the United Kingdom is concerned, the Commission considers that it may be seen as inconsistent to have an age of majority applicable to voting and other legal transactions which is lower than the age of consent for homosexual behaviour.

... However, the Commission cannot disregard the fact that this question was examined by the Wolfenden Committee and that their recommendations were seen fit to be adopted by Parliament and incorporated in the 1967 legislation. Nor can it ignore the fact that the issue has been before Parliament again in a 1977 Private Member's Bill which was not accepted and that it is being currently re-examined by the Criminal Law Revision Committee and the Policy Advisory Committee on Sexual Offences.

... In addition, the Commission takes the view that there is a realistic basis for the respondent Government's opinion that, given the controversial and sensitive nature of the question involved, young men in the 18 to 21 age bracket who are involved in homosexual relationships would be subject to substantial social pressures which could be harmful to their psychological development.

... In this connection, the Commission does not consider that the respondent Government has gone beyond its obligation under the Convention in finding the right balance to be struck.

... Accordingly, the Commission finds that the interference in the applicant's private life involved in fixing the age of consent at 21 is justified as being necessary in a democratic society for the protection of the rights of others. (paras 152–156)

Accordingly no violation was found. Mr Opsahl expressed a separate opinion indicating the problems raised by issues which concern private life but which also affect persons other than the applicant.

Comment

The law governing homosexual conduct in England and Wales was contained in the Sexual Offences Act 1956 as amended by the Sexual Offences Act 1967. The latter Act, introduced by means of a Private Member's Bill to give effect to the recommendations of the Wolfendon Report (1957), allowed homosexual acts committed in private between consenting males who were over the age of 21. The 1956 Act made it unlawful to have heterosexual intercourse with a girl under the age of 16, unless the couple were married. It should be noted that the law relating to sexual offences had been under review since July 1975, and a provisional recommendation that the age of consent should be lowered to 18 had been made by the Policy Advisory Committee on Sexual Offences in 1979. The age of consent was not in line with the age of majority, which had been reduced from 21 to 18 under the Family Law Reform Act 1969, or with the age for voting or serving on a jury, which was similarly 18 under the Representation of the People Act 1969 and the Criminal Justice Act 1972.

The law also makes it an offence where homosexual acts are committed and more than two adult males are present. In the case of *Johnson* v *UK* 9 EHRR 350 at 386, the applicant complained that the very existence of this legislation placed him at risk of interference with his private life. However, since there was no evidence that the applicant himself intended to commit homosexual acts either with a person under 21, or when more than two adult males were present, there was no indication that the legislation constituted an interference with his private life or his home.

Other cases which have concerned the rights of homosexuals to respect for their private life include *Wilde, Greenhalgh and Parry* v *UK* App. No. 22382/93, Report of the Commission January 1995, 19 EHRR CD 86, 80-A D & R 132, in which the complaint of the applicants – who had suffered a number of homophobic attacks – was that the age of consent of 21 for homosexuals, and the consequent criminalisation of homosexual activity for people under that age, created a climate of hostility towards homosexual men. By the time the Commission considered the merits of this case, changes in the law had been introduced by the Criminal Justice and Public Order Act 1994, which reduced the age of consent contained in the Sexual Offences Act 1967, from 21 to 18. The 1994 Act also reduced the age of consent in Scotland. The case was therefore struck out.

The situation concerning consenting adults over the age of 21 was considered in the *Dudgeon* case.

Dudgeon v *UK*
Series A, Vol. 45

The facts

The applicant was resident in Northern Ireland. Under the law applicable to Northern Ireland – although not to the rest of the UK – ss. 61 and 62 of the

Offences Against the Person Act 1861 made buggery (even between consenting adults) a criminal offence. Other laws restricting homosexual conduct were the Criminal Law Amendment Act 1885 concerning the offence of gross indecency between males, and the common law offences of conspiracy to corrupt public morals, conspiracy to outrage public decency and attempting to commit buggery or acts of gross indecency. Although the applicant had neither been charged with nor convicted of any of these offences, he had been questioned by the police. He alleged that the existence of the laws caused him prejudice, fear and distress and interfered with his right to respect for his private life.

The Commission's opinion
The Commission first had to decide whether the applicant was in fact a victim, as he had not been prosecuted under any of the relevant laws. It considered that as he was a male homosexual, he was directly affected by the laws of which he complained, because he was one of a class of persons whose conduct was legally restricted. Whether there had actually been an interference with his private life depended on whether the laws affected homosexual acts in private as well as in public. The applicant complained only about the interference with private consensual acts. As a person's sexual life was recognised as forming part of his private life there was an interference. It was argued by the Government that the laws were applied very rarely to prosecute persons over the age of 21. In considering this the Commission noted:

> . . . it is not in dispute that the laws complained of are on occasions applied so as to prosecute private consensual homosexul acts involving persons under 21 years of age. To the extent that the law makes it a criminal offence for the applicant to commit such acts with a person under that age, the Commission considers that it amounts to an interference with his right to respect for his private life, which falls to be justified under Article 8(2). It imposes a prohibition on the conduct in question which is actually enforced in practice by means of penal sanctions.
> . . . The law also prohibits private consensual homosexual acts involving persons over 21 years of age but, subject to one possible exception, it does not appear to have been enforced by means of criminal proceedings in respect of any such acts since at least 1972. However, it has not fallen into desuetude or lost its legal effectiveness to prohibit such acts. The legal prohibition remains and the possibility of prosecutions by either the public prosecuting authorities or private individuals is open in law. Furthermore it does not appear that there is any clear policy not to prosecute in respect of such acts. Whilst there have been no recent prosecutions, this may well be explained by the evident difficulties in obtaining evidence and the fact that relevant complaints are apparently very rarely made to the police. (paras 92 and 93)

The Commission concluded, therefore, that the legislation complained of did interfere with the applicant's right to respect for his private life.

Whether this right was justified depended on whether the interference was 'in accordance with law', whether it pursued a legitimate aim and whether it was 'necessary in a democratic society'. The Commission was satisfied that the first two criteria had been met. In considering the third, the Commission expressed the view that:

> . . . the interference in the applicant's private life involved in prohibiting male homosexual acts can, in so far as it prevents his having relations with persons under

21 years of age, be justified as necessary in a democratic society for the protection of the rights of others. To the extent that the applicant's conduct is thus restricted, this is compatible with Article 8. (para. 105)

However, the only ground upon which a restriction on private consensual homosexual relations with persons over the age of 21 could be justified would be for the 'protection of morals'. Although the Commission appreciated that in the context of morals the contracting States might have a greater margin of appreciation than in some other cases, nevertheless:

. . . in reviewing the necessity for the restriction in question in the present case, the Commission considers it of considerable importance that it is an interference in *private* life. In its opinion the term 'protection of morals' used in paragraph 2 of Articles 8–11 of the Convention refers primarily to the protection of the moral ethos of society, and the Convention (Articles 8 and 9 in particular) preserves to the individual an area of strictly private morality in which the State may not interfere. That is not to say that interferences in 'private life' may not be 'necessary' for the purpose of protecting the morals of society. However, in this area it is especially necessary to bear in mind that the interference must be justified by 'a pressing social need' in a 'democratic society' and also the Court's reference in the *Handyside* case to 'the demands of that pluralism, tolerance and broadmindedness without which there is no democratic society'.

. . . It is also relevant that the special 'duties and responsibilities' referred to in Article 10(2) and to which the Court also had regard in the *Handyside* case (para. 49), are not referred to in Article 8(2). Indeed Article 8(2) is generally drafted in more restrictive terms than Article 10(2). This appears to reflect the fact that the exercise of the freedoms guaranteed by Article 10, with their public aspect, may call for greater regulation by the State, than does the carrying on of activities within the essentially private sphere covered by Article 8. . . .

. . . As to the particular facts of the case, the Commission again recalls that it is concerned only with the actual effects of the law on the applicant. It must assess whether the interference with the applicant's right to respect for his private life which is has found to exist, notwithstanding the manner in which the laws are applied, is justified as necessary in a democratic society for the protection of morals.

. . . In assessing the requirements of the 'protection of morals' in Northern Ireland, the Commission considers that it must examine the measures in question in the context of Northern Irish society, taking into account the information before it as to the climate of moral opinion in that particular society. The fact that similar measures are not considered necessary in other parts of the United Kingdom, or in other European countries does not mean that they cannot be necessary in Northern Ireland. . . . (paras 108–111)

Despite indications that there was considerable public support for the retention of the current law, it was also evident that there was support for reform. Even if the majority favoured retaining the current law, the Commission indicated that the will of the majority should not be taken as giving them an unqualified right to impose their standards of private sexual morality on the whole of society:

. . . Account must be taken of the effect which allowing the conduct in question is likely to have on the moral standards of society as a whole. However, the available evidence does not suggest that to allow private acts between consenting adults would have any very significant impact on public morality. The rarity of complaints to the police suggests that such conduct in fact gives rise to little or no public offence. The police and public prosecuting authorities evidently do not consider it necessary to enforce the relevant prohibition by taking steps to detect and prosecute offences. Furthermore, whilst it may be true that attitudes towards homosexuality have changed in England since the enactment of the 1967 Act, this appears to be part of a general phenomenon, possibly reflecting increased knowledge on the matter, rather than a direct result of the Act. There is little evidence to suggest that any increase in homosexual conduct has resulted.

. . . The Commission is aware that in the religious and political situation prevailing in Northern Ireland the respondent Government may have had strong reasons for their decision not now to change the law. Nevertheless it must consider whether the reasons given for maintaining the law are relevant and sufficient in the context of Article 8 of the Convention. Whilst the views of local politicians, church leaders and other members of the community may provide a valuable indication of the requirements of 'protection of morals' in the particular community and be entitled to considerable respect, they cannot of themselves be decisive. The Commission must address itself to the question whether it is *necessary* in order to protect the moral standards of the community to interfere with the fundamental right to respect for the private life of persons who, almost by definition, form part of a minority. The criterion to be applied is not whether the prevailing attitude in the community is one of moral disapproval of homosexuality, of tolerance or intolerance, but whether in order to preserve moral standards it is necessary to maintain criminal legislation.

. . . In all the circumstances of the present case, the Commission does not consider it established that there exists any 'pressing social need' related to the protection of morality in Northern Ireland which requires the maintenance in force of the legal prohibition on private consensual male homosexual acts involving persons over 21 years of age. It has not been shown to make any contribution to the moral climate of society which could, within a reasonable relationship of proportionality, justify or counter-balance the inevitable negative effects which it has on the private lives of homosexuals, and the present applicant in particular. It cannot therefore be justified as 'necessary' under Article 8(2). (paras 113–115)

The judgment of the Court

The Court agreed that the existing legislation interfered with the applicant's private life:

. . . the maintenance in force of the impugned legislation constitutes a continuing interference with the applicant's right to respect for his private life (which includes his sexual life) within the meaning of Article 8(1). In the personal circumstances of the applicant, the very existence of this legislation continuously and directly affects his private life: either he respects the law and refrains from engaging (even in private with consenting male partners) in prohibited sexual acts to which he is disposed by reason of his homosexual tendencies, or he commits such acts and thereby becomes liable to criminal prosecution. (para. 41)

In considering whether such interference was justified, the Court recognised that the general aim of the legislation was the protection of morals and moral standards pertaining in Northern Ireland, and also the protection of the rights and freedoms of others:

. . . The Court recognises that one of the purposes of the legislation is to afford safeguards for vulnerable members of society, such as the young, against the consequences of homosexual practices. However, it is somewhat artificial in this context to draw a rigid distinction between 'protection of the rights and freedoms of others' and 'protection of . . . morals'. The latter may imply safeguarding the moral ethos or moral standards of a society as a whole, but may also, as the Government pointed out, cover protection of the moral interests and welfare of a particular section of society, for example schoolchildren. Thus, 'protection of the rights and freedoms of others', when meaning the safeguarding of the moral interests and welfare of certain individuals or classes of individuals who are in need of special protection for reasons such as lack of maturity, mental disability or state of dependence, amounts to one aspect of 'protection of . . . morals'. The Court will therefore take account of the two aims on this basis.

. . .

. . . In practice there is legislation on the matter in all the member States of the Council of Europe, but what distinguishes the law in Northern Ireland from that existing in the great majority of the member-States is that it prohibits generally gross indecency between males and buggery whatever the circumstances. It being accepted that some form of legislation is 'necessary' to protect particular sections of society as well as the moral ethos of society as a whole, the question in the present case is whether the contested provisions of the law of Northern Ireland and their enforcement remain within the bounds of what, in a democratic society, may be regarded as necessary in order to accomplish those aims. (paras 47 and 49)

A measure can be regarded as being 'necessary in a democratic society' only if it responds to a pressing social need. Assessment of that need lies in the first place with the national authorities, who may act within the margin of appreciation allowed to them by the Convention. However, any such measures may be subject to review by the Court. The Court indicated that in this area of interference with a person's private life there must be serious reasons to justify such interference. Moreover, the Court held that:

. . . the notion of 'necessity' is linked to that of a 'democratic society' (two hallmarks of which are tolerance and broadmindedness). (para. 53)

Although the contested measures must be examined in the context of Northern Ireland society and the need for caution and sensitivity to public opinion because of the situation of direct rule, the Court held that it could not overlook changes in attitudes, understanding and tolerance of homosexual behaviour in the other member States of the Council of Europe. The Court held that:

. . . It cannot be maintained in these circumstances that there is a 'pressing social need' to make such acts criminal offences, there being no sufficient justification provided by the risk of harm to vulnerable sections of society requiring protection or by the effects on the public. On the issue of proportionality, the Court considers that such justifications as there are for retaining the law in force unamended are outweighed by the detrimental effects which the very existence of the legislative provisions in question can have on the life of a person of homosexual orientation like the applicant. Although members of the public who regard homosexuality as immoral may be shocked, offended or disturbed by the commission by others of private homosexual acts, this cannot on its own warrant the application of penal sanctions when it is consenting adults alone who are involved.

. . . Accordingly, the reasons given by the Government, although relevant, are not sufficient to justify the maintenance in force of the impugned legislation in so far as it has the general effect of criminalising private homosexual relations between adult males capable of valid consent. In particular, the moral attitudes towards male homosexuality in Northern Ireland and the concern that any relaxation in the law would tend to erode existing moral standards cannot, without more, warrant interfering with the applicant's private life to such an extent. 'Decriminalisation' does not imply approval, and a fear that some sectors of the population might draw misguided conclusions in this respect from reform of the legislation does not afford a good ground for maintaining it in force with all its unjustifiable features. (paras 60 and 61)

The Court concluded, therefore, that there could be no justification for interfering with the applicant's private life so far as it concerned consensual, private, homosexual conduct with persons over the age of 21. Interference with such conduct with persons under that age could be justified in the interests of providing safeguards against exploitation and corruption of those who might be particularly vulnerable due to their youth.

Comment

The law in this area was not only different in Northern Ireland, it was also different in Scotland where the applicable law was contained in the Sexual Offences (Scotland) Act 1976 and the common law. However, in Scotland there was a stated policy by a number of Lord Advocates, that persons who would not be punishable under the 1967 Act, i.e. consenting adults over the age of 21, would not be prosecuted. Before this case was decided by the European Court of Human Rights, the law in Scotland had in fact changed and been brought into line with the 1967 Act through the passing of the Criminal Justice (Scotland) Act 1980. Proposals for reform had been extensively canvassed in Northern Ireland since 1977. Change by means of legislation had been hampered by the constitutional and political situation concerning Northern Ireland. In 1920, all criminal matters fell under the Government of Northern Ireland, and between 1921 and 1972 the Westminster Parliament did not legislate on matters within the competence of the Northern Ireland Parliament. It was only once Westminster rule was resumed in 1972 that Westminster could once more legislate for Northern Ireland in these matters – usually by means of Orders in Council. The Northern Ireland Advisory Commission on Human Rights had reported in 1977 that there was support for bringing the law in line with that pertaining to England and Wales. However, legislation proposed in 1978 was dropped the following year after consultation on a range of views indicated the controversy likely to be aroused by such a proposal.

Although Judge Walsh, in a dissenting opinion, expressed the view that private life related to family life and therefore impliedly marital privacy, the case law does not suggest that this has been the view of the majority of the Commission or Court. The more pertinent question has been whether homosexual relations fall within the ambit of family life *or* private life. It has been consistently held that such relationships fall within private life rather than family life. This has certain consequences; for example, refusal to allow a homosexual to remain in the country under immigration rules has been held not to disclose any violation of Article 8, because it does not interfere with respect for private life (*App. No. 12513* v *UK* 11 EHRR 46). The dividing line is not always very clear; for instance, the threat of deportation of an illegal immigrant has, on occasion, been held to constitute a violation of the right to family life. This approach cannot be applied in the case of a homosexual seeking not to be deported because he has a stable homosexual relationship in the UK (*App. No. 9369/81* 5 EHRR 581 at 601).

Homosexuals are not the only group which has presented special problems for the Commission and Court in interpreting Article 8. Transsexuals have also raised some difficult questions concerning their rights under this provision.

Rees* v *UK
Series A, Vol. 106

The facts

This case, which also raised issues under Article 12, concerned a female to male transsexual. He had undergone sexual reassignment surgery, changed his name and had his driving licence and passport issued in his new name. However, he was unable to change the sex indicated on his birth certificate, and as a result was unable to marry, owing to the fact that in English law marriage is permitted only between a 'man and a woman'. To claim to be a man when his birth certificate stated otherwise would make the applicant liable for perjury under s. 3(1) of the Perjury Act 1911.

Before the Commission the applicant claimed that his right to private life had been violated and that UK law did not confer on him a legal status corresponding to his actual condition.

The Commission's opinion

The Commission accepted the applicant's arguments that:

> . . . sex is one of the essential elements of human personality. If modern medical research into the specific problems of transsexualism and surgery as effected in the present case has made possible a change of sex as far as the normal appearance of a person is concerned Art. 8 must be understood as protecting such an individual against the non-recognition of his/her changed sex as part of his/her personality. This does not mean that the legal recognition of a change of sex must be extended to the period prior to the specific moment of change. However, it must be possible for the individual after the change has been effected, to confirm his/her normal appearance by the necessary documents. (para. 43)

While recognising that there were few occasions when the applicant might have to produce his birth certificate to third parties, the Commission accepted that there were such occasions. The Commission expressed the opinion that:

> . . . The refusal to amend the birth register cannot be justified by any reasons of public interest. The respondent Government have pointed out that the birth register was intended to provide authentic evidence of the events and also to establish the connection of families for the purposes related to succession, legitimacy and the distribution of property. However, none of these purposes will be affected by an entry in the birth register to the effect that at a particular moment a person has changed sex. Nor does such an entry affect the statistical value of birth registers. On the contrary it helps to give a statistical picture corresponding to the actual situation.

. . . The Commission considers that the failure of the United Kingdom to contemplate measures which would make it possible to take account in the applicant's civil status of the changes which have lawfully occurred amounts to a veritable failure to recognise the respect due to his private life within the meaning of Art. 8(1) of the Convention.
. . . The Commission, therefore, unanimously concludes that Art. 8 has been violated. (paras 49–51)

The judgment of the Court
The Court indicated that:

. . . although the essential object of Article 8 is to protect the individual against arbitrary interference by the public authorities, there may in addition be positive obligations inherent in an effective respect for private life, albeit subject to the State's margin of appreciation.
In the present case it is the existence and scope of such 'positive' obligations which have to be determined. The mere refusal to alter the register of births or to issue birth certificates whose contents and nature differ from those of the birth register cannot be considered as interferences. (para. 35)

The notion of what was meant by 'respect' for private life was not clear-cut. There was a diversity of practices in the Contracting States in relation to transsexuals, and some margin of appreciation had to be afforded to States in this area. A fair balance had to be struck between the general interest of the community and the interests of the individual. The Court noted that:

. . . In the United Kingdom no uniform, general decision has been adopted either by the legislature or by the courts as to the civil status of post-operative transsexuals. Moreover, there is no integrated system of civil status registration, but only separate registers for births, marriages, deaths and adoption. These record the relevant events in the manner they occurred without, except in special circumstances, mentioning changes (of name, address, etc.) which in other States are registered.
. . . However, transsexuals, like anyone else in the United Kingdom, are free to change their first names and surnames at will. Similarly, they can be issued with official documents bearing their chosen first names and surnames and indicating, if their sex is mentioned at all, their preferred sex by the relevant prefix (Mr, Mrs, Ms or Miss). This freedom gives them a considerable advantage in comparison with States where all official documents have to conform with the records held by the registry office.
Conversely, the drawback – emphasised by the applicant – is that, as the country's legal system makes no provision for legally valid civil status certificates, such persons have on occasion to establish their identity by means of a birth certificate which is either an authenticated copy of or an extract from the birth register. The nature of the register, which furthermore is public, is that the certificates mention the biological sex which the individuals had at the time of their birth. The production of such a birth certificate is not a strict legal requirement, but may on occasion be required in practice for some purposes.
It is also clear that the United Kingdom does not recognise the applicant as a man for all social purposes. Thus, it would appear that, at the present stage of the development of United Kingdom law, he would be regarded as a woman, *inter alia*, as far as marriage, pension rights and certain employments are concerned. The existence of the unamended birth certificate might also prevent him from entering into certain types of private agreements as a man. (paras 39 and 40)

The Court, however, did not follow the Commission. The Court recognised that to ask the UK to change its system of the registration of births and to determine civil status in the same way as other Contracting States would be unacceptable. The Court acknowledged that:

> . . . the United Kingdom has endeavoured to meet the applicant's demands to the fullest extent that its system allowed. The alleged lack of respect therefore seems to come down to a refusal to establish a type of documentation showing, and constituting proof of, current civil status. The introduction of such a system has not hitherto been considered necessary in the United Kingdom. It would have important administrative consequences and would impose new duties on the rest of the population. The governing authorities in the United Kingdom are fully entitled, in the exercise of their margin of appreciation, to take account of the requirements of the situation pertaining there in determining what measures to adopt. While the requirement of striking a fair balance, as developed in paragraph 37 above, may possibly, in the interests of persons in the applicants situation, call for incidental adjustments to the existing system, it cannot give rise to any direct obligation on the United Kingdom to alter the very basis thereof. (para. 42)

The Court held that there had not been a breach of Article 8 in the case.

The Court did indicate that it was conscious of the problems facing transsexuals and the distress such people suffered, and expressed its willingness to interpret the Convention in the light of present and changing circumstances.

Three judges expressed a dissenting opinion, based on the view that the register of births could be altered by annotation, combined with a right by the applicant to obtain an extract showing only his new sexual identity which would better protect his right to private life.

Comment

This case was followed by that of *Cossey* v *UK* App. No. 10843/84 Report of the Commission 9 May 1989, Judgment of the Court 27 September 1990, Series A, No. 184. Although this case involved a male to female transsexual, the issues were not materially distinguishable from *Rees* and the Court followed the line of reasoning adopted in the *Rees* case.

A slight departure from the previous two cases arose in the case of *X, Y and Z* v *UK* App. No. 21830/93 Report of the Commission 27 June 1995. This case did not involve a claim by the applicant to have his own birth certificate altered, but to be declared the father of the child born to his partner by artificial insemination, on this child's birth certificate. His claim was based on a right to family life rather than private life. As a female to male transsexual he was clearly unable to be the father biologically, but the Human Fertility and Embryology Act 1990 allowed a non-biological father to be registered as the father where he had consented to the treatment. This Act reflects some of the changing circumstances the Court has indicated that it must keep in view. The Commission accepted the applicant's claim, and expressed the opinion that there had been a violation of Article 8. The case has now been referred to the Court.

Other cases in which transsexual issues have been raised are *App. No. 10622/83* 8 EHRR 45 at 89 and *App. No. 10843/84* v *UK (idem)*.

8.2.2   Family Life and the Rights of Parents

Paton v UK
(1980) 19 D & R 244 (cited as *X* v *UK*)

The facts
The facts of this case have been considered under Article 2. The case concerned a claim by the father of an aborted foetus, that he had been denied respect for family life because he had not been consulted about the abortion prior to its occurrence.

The Commission's opinion
While accepting that the father's right to a family life may have been interfered with, first, as regards the fact that he did not give his permission for the abortion, the Commission placed the interests of the applicant's wife above his and recalled that:

> ... the pregnancy of the applicant's wife was terminated in accordance with her wish and in order to avert the risk of injury to her physical or mental health. The Commission therefore finds that this decision, insofar as it interfered in itself with the applicant's right to respect for his family life, was justified under paragraph 2 of Article 8 as being necessary for the protection of the rights of another person. It follows that this complaint is also manifestly ill-founded within the meaning of Article 27(2). (para. 26)

Secondly, in so far as the Abortion Act 1967 – which governed the abortion – denied the father of the foetus a right to be consulted or to make any applications about the proposed abortion, the Commission observed that:

> ... any interpretation of the husband's and potential father's right, under Article 8 of the Convention, to respect for his private and family life, as regards an abortion which his wife intends to have performed on her, must first of all take into account the right of the pregnant woman, being the person primarily concerned in the pregnancy and its continuation or termination, to respect for her private life. ... In the present case the Commission, having regard to the right of the pregnant woman, does not find that the husband's and potential father's rights to respect for his private and family life can be interpreted so widely as to embrace such procedural rights as claimed by the applicant, i.e. a right to be consulted, or a right to make applications, about an abortion which his wife intends to have performed on her. The Commission concludes that this complaint is incompatible *ratione materiae* with the provisions of the Convention within the meaning of Article 27(2). (para. 27)

A number of cases have involved the claims of unmarried fathers to their children – see, for example, *App. No. 11468/85* v *UK* 9 EHRR 350 at 393 – and the Commission has consistently held that the relationship between a parent and child born out of wedlock is covered by the concept of 'family life'. However, there must be a realistic link between the parent and child which establishes family life. If a father's contact with his child was periodically interrupted but he nevertheless showed a continuing interest in the child, this might establish the existence of family life (*App. No. 9966/82* v *UK* 5 EHRR 268 at 299).

The Commission has also held that family life is not a restricted concept. It extends, for example, beyond the natural family relationship to the situation where a child is taken into care by the Social Services (*O* v *UK* Series A, Vol. 120; *H* v *UK* Series A, Vol. 120; *W* v *UK* Series A, Vol. 121; *B* v *UK* Series A, Vol. 121; *R* v *UK* Series A, Vol. 121; *Campbell* v *UK* 11 EHRR 46).

McMichael v UK
Report of the Commission
15 EHRR CD 80
Council of Europe Report 51/1993/446/525

The facts

The applicant was the father of a child born in 1987. At the time of the child's birth the parents were not married, the mother suffered from mental illness, and the applicant was not named on the birth certificate as the father. The child was taken into care shortly after birth. Initially the child's mother had access rights for visits to the child who was placed with foster parents, but the applicant had none, not being recognised at the time as the child's father. A year after the birth the applicant's name was added to the birth certificate, but this did not give him parental rights. However, he was allowed to visit the child for a period of three months, after which access was terminated and the council considered freeing the child for adoption. Three years after the child's birth the parents married, the applicant thereby acquiring parental rights; however, in the same year the council decided to free the child for adoption by the foster parents, the competent court having decided to dispense with the parents' consent.

The applicants complained of breaches of Article 6, para. 1, Article 8 and Article 14 of the Convention, in as much as they had been deprived of the care and custody of their son and of access to him. They alleged that they had not received a fair hearing and had not had access to certain documents.

The Commission's opinion

The Commission noted first, that the case fell within the scope of Article 8 for both applicants:

> . . . While there are no explicit procedural requirements contained in Article 8, the case law of the Commission and Court establish that in this area, where decisions may have a drastic effect on the relations between parent and child and become irreversible, there is particular need for protection against arbitrary interferences. . . .
>
> . . . In the present case there is no doubt as to the importance of what was at stake for the applicants. The children's hearings were taking decisions which determined the future of their relationship with A. The Commission notes the informal nature of the children's hearings which are intended to provide a non-contentious and constructive approach to dealing with questions relating to a child's welfare. Nonetheless it is open to question the effectiveness of a parent's participation in this process if he or she has no sight of reports and documents which are presumably relevant to the proceedings and contain matters at least indirectly relating to the welfare of their child and their own capacities in that respect. The opportunity of appealing to the Sheriff Court either for an alleged failure to give the substance of a

document or on any other ground suffers from the basic defect that the parent has no knowledge of the material's contents to begin with. Further, the Commission notes that even before the Sheriff Court, the parents are not provided with copies of reports or other documents. Without the documents in question, it must also be difficult for a parent to seek independent advice as to their significance or as to the existence of a ground of appeal, advice which takes on added importance where as in this case the parent suffers from emotional or mental problems. (paras 102 and 103)

The Commission expressed the opinion that the interference was clearly in accordance with law, as the measures were taken in accordance with the Social Work (Scotland) Act 1968 and the freeing for adoption order was granted by the Sheriff Court under the Adoption (Scotland) Act 1978. The aims of the measures were legitimate in that they were taken as being in the best interests of A – the child – to protect the child's health and rights.

In considering whether the decisions were necessary, in that they corresponded to a pressing social need, and whether they were also proportionate, the Commission examined the reasons given for the decisions:

> . . . The Commission recalls that the decisions depriving the applicant of the care and custody of A were taken in the light of the facts, established before the Sheriff Court, that the second applicant suffered from a major psychiatric illness and was as a result unable to care adequately for A. The Commission recalls that the decisions of the Children's Hearing regarding the applicants' access to A were made following a three-month period of intensive access during which concern arose as to the effect on A and it appeared that the applicants had made no progress in their ability to care for A. The second applicant also had a recurrence of ill-health during this period and was admitted to hospital. As regards the decision to free A for adoption, the Commission notes the judgment of the Sheriff given as 14 October 1992, where he found that the applicants had failed to demonstrate the capacity for parenting and that, in light of the evidence, it would be wholly contrary to A's welfare for him to be returned to them.
>
> The Commission finds that the above reasons were 'relevant and sufficient' for the decisions in question and were based on a thorough and careful investigation of the case.
>
> The Commission concludes, bearing in mind the margin of appreciation accorded to the domestic authorities, that the interference in the present case was justified under Article 8(2) of the Convention as being 'necessary in a democratic society' for the protection of health and for the protection of the rights of others. (15 EHRR CD 80 at p. 85)

The applicants also complained that they had been unable to see the confidential reports and documents that had been put before the children's hearing at which the future of their child had been decided, and the father further complained that he had no legal rights to custody of A or to participate in the proceedings.

The judgment of the Court

The case was referred to the Court which gave its judgment on 24 February 1995, holding that there had been a violation of Article 8 in respect of both Mr and Mrs McMichael.

In considering the violation of Article 8, the Court considered the operation of the provisions of this article in the light of the alleged breaches under Article 6, para. 1. In this respect the Court pointed out:

... the difference in the nature of the interests protected by Articles 6(1) and 8. Thus, Article 6(1) affords a procedural safeguard, namely the 'right to a court' in the determination of one's 'civil rights and obligations' (see the *Golder* v *the United Kingdom* judgment of 21 February 1975, Series A No. 18, p. 18, para. 36); whereas not only does the procedural requirement inherent in Article 8 cover administrative procedures as well as judicial proceedings, but it is ancillary to the wider purpose of ensuring proper respect for, *inter alia*, family life (see, for example, the *B* v *the United Kingdom* judgment of 8 July 1987, Series A No. 121-B, pp. 72–74 and 75, paras 63–65 and 68). The difference between the purpose pursued by the respective safeguards afforded by Articles 6(1) and 8 may, in the light of the particular circumstances, justify the examination of the same set of facts under both Articles (compare, for example, the above-mentioned *Golder* v *the United Kingdom* judgment, pp. 20–22, paras 41–45, and the *O* v *the United Kingdom* judgment of 8 July 1987, Series A No. 120-A, pp. 28–29, paras 65–67).

As regards the instant case, the facts complained of had repercussions not only on the conduct of judicial proceedings to which the second applicant was a party, but also on 'a fundamental element of [the] family life' of the two applicants (see paragraph 85 above). In the present case the Court judges it appropriate to examine the facts also under Article 8. (para. 91)

The Court found that although the couple acted in concert in their endeavours to recover custody of and have access to their son, and were living together as a family, the care proceedings had not involved Mr McMichael in the way which they could have. The Government had in fact conceded the unfair character of the care proceedings (before the children's hearing and before the Sheriff Court in respect of Mrs McMichael).

The Court noted the concessions made by the UK Government concerning the unfairness of the proceedings and held that:

... in this respect the decision-making process determining the custody and access arrangements in regard to A did not afford the requisite protection of the applicants' interests as safeguarded by Article 8. Having regard to the approach taken in the present judgment in regard to the treatment of the applicants' complaint under Article 8 (see paragraph 90 above), the Court does not deem it appropriate to draw any material distinction between the two applicants as regards the extent of the violation found, despite some differences in their legal circumstances.

... In conclusion, there has been a breach of Article 8 in respect of both applicants. (paras 92 and 93)

Under Article 50, the applicants were awarded £8,000 for non-pecuniary damage.

Three judges gave a dissenting opinion in so far as the first applicant's rights under Article 8 were concerned (Mr McMichael). Because of his different legal status, these judges considered that although there was a joint family life once Mrs McMichael accepted the first applicant's paternity, his lack of legal standing concerning the care proceedings meant that his rights under Article 8 were not breached.

Comment

Under the relevant law – Law Reform (Parent and Child) (Scotland) Act 1986 – the persons who had parental rights over a child were its mother – whether or not she was married to the father of the child, and the father *only* if he were married to the mother either at the time of conception or subsequently. Any other person (including the unmarried father) could apply to the court for an order of parental rights and a court could make such an order if it deemed it to be in the interests of the child.

The Court had no problem in considering the same set of facts in the alleged breach of Article 8 as in that of Article 6, para. 1. It did not have jurisdiction, however, to consider under Article 8 the merits of the care, access and adoption measures since these complaints had been declared inadmissible by the Commission.

It may also be the case that a parent is denied access or contact with a child – which will amount to an interference with rights under Article 8 – but that this is deemed to be justified as being in the best interests of the child. This was the situation in the case of *Gribler* v *UK* 10 EHRR 546.

A claim to family life need not involve only a parent-child relationship, as the case of *Boyle* demonstrates.

Boyle v UK
Series A, Vol. 282-B

The facts
The applicant's sister gave birth to a son in 1980. The applicant formed a close bond with his nephew. In 1989 the child was placed in care under a Place of Safety Order as the result of suspicions that he had been sexually abused by his mother. No charges were brought against her, but a full care order was made out for the child. The applicant made repeated requests for access to his nephew, but apart from one supervised visit was denied access. He was also excluded from the meetings or conferences held by the social services concerning the child. In 1991 the county court made an order freeing the child for adoption. The applicant complained to the Commission in October 1989 that the refusal of the local authority to allow him access infringed his right to respect for family life.

In October 1991 the Children Act 1989 entered into force. Under this Act a non-parental relative could apply for a contact order with a child taken into care. The applicant applied for such an order in December 1991, although his application was refused in February 1992. However, the adoption proceedings were stopped in that year, and in November 1993 the applicant was informed that the local authority was considering reintroducing contact between him and his nephew.

The applicant's claim before the Commission included a complaint that the legal situation prior to the Children Act denied him any possibility of applying to the court for access to the child.

The Commission's opinion
First, the Commission had to consider whether the relationship fell within the scope of 'family life'.

The Commission did not accept the Government's view that the bonds of uncle-nephew were insufficient to constitute 'family life', expressing the opinion that:

. . . cohabitation is . . . not a prerequisite for the maintenance of family ties which are to fall within the scope of the concept of 'family life'. Cohabitation is a factor amongst many others, albeit often an important one, to be taken into account when considering the existence or otherwise of family ties. (para. 43)

The significant factors in this case were that the applicant had frequent contact with the child, spent considerable time with him, lived in close proximity and was referred to in the care proceedings as a 'good father figure'. The Commission was satisfied, therefore, that there was a significant bond between the applicant and his nephew, and that this relationship fell within the scope of the concept 'family life'.

Following the case law relevant to the situation of parents when a child is taken into care, the Commission recalled that:

. . . Where a parent is denied access to a minor child taken into care, there is in general an interference with the parent's right to respect for family life as protected by Article 8(1) of the Convention. This however is not necessarily the case where other close relatives are concerned. Access by relatives to a child is normally at the discretion of the child's parents and, where a care order has been made in respect of the child, this control of access passes to the local authority. A restriction of access which does not deny a recoverable opportunity to maintain the relationship will not of itself show a lack of respect for family life.

. . . The Commission recalls however with regards to the present applicant that apart from one visit in September 1989, all contact with C was prohibited thereby preventing any continuance of the applicant's relationship with him. It finds that this amounts to an interference with the applicant's right to respect for his 'family life' as guaranteed by Article 8(1) of the Convention. (paras 46 and 47)

Although the interference was 'in accordance with the law', the grounds for the termination of access appear to have been that the applicant continued to deny that his sister had sexually abused the child and that in view of this denial the local authority felt that further contact would be detrimental to the child. The Commission did not express an opinion on this reasoning, but recalled that there will have been a failure to respect family life if parents are not involved in the decision-making process where a child is to be placed in care. Although the applicant's relationship would not require the same level of involvement, nevertheless the decision-making process should provide an applicant with the opportunity to make his views known and to have these taken into account. In this case, apart from one discussion in June 1989, there was no consultation with the applicant. The Commission did not express an opinion as to the best forum for such a process, but found that:

. . . the absence of such a forum or mechanism in the present case discloses a fundamental shortcoming since the applicant as a result was not involved in the decision-making procedure to the degree sufficient to provide him with the requisite protection of his interest. Consequently, the interference complained of cannot be regarded as 'necessary' within the meaning of Article 8(2) of the Convention. (para. 58)

Four members of the Commission expressed a dissenting opinion on the grounds that although they accepted that Article 8 has a procedural aspect when children are placed in care – namely the involvement of the parents in the decision-making process – this cannot be extended to more distant relatives to the same degree, and that where these are concerned then the domestic authorities must have a wider discretion.

The judgment of the Court

Because of the change in the law which occurred between the application being admitted by the Commission and the reference of the case to the Court, a friendly settlement had been reached between the Government and the applicant, whereby the Government expressed its regret that the applicant had no statutory right to apply to the court for contact with his nephew prior to the entry into force of s. 34(3) of the Children Act 1989, in November 1991, and offered to make an *ex gratia* payment of £15,000 plus reasonable legal costs to the applicant.

Comment

The Children Act 1989, s. 34(3), enables any person who has the leave of the court to make an application to have the question of contact between the child placed in local authority care and that person determined by a court. Thus grandparents, uncles and aunts, etc. may make such applications. In this case contact between the child and his uncle had been broken in 1989 when the child was nine years old. It was not until late 1993 – when the child was 13 – that there was some indication that such contact might be restored.

In the case of serial relationships the concept of family life becomes more complex. The Commission has stated that Article 8:

> . . . required the United Kingdom authorities to respect not only the 'family life' relationship of the applicant [the ex-husband] with his children, but also the 'family life' of his former wife with the children and her new husband. (*App. No. 9867/82* v *UK* 5 EHRR 465)

Thus where the wife – who had custody of the children – wished to take them with her to South Africa to live with her new husband, the Commission, taking into account the Guardianship of Minors Act 1971 which placed the welfare of the child first and paramount, found that the interference with the applicant's family life was justified.

8.2.3 Family Life and Extradition

The Convention does not guarantee any right to enter and remain in a country of which the applicant is not a national. Therefore Article 8 cannot be relied on to avoid the application of immigration controls or deportation orders. However, occasionally immigration restrictions, or threatened deportation or extradition may involve a right under Article 8 if the implementation of these can truly be said to interfere with family life. Usually a close family connection will have to be established – for example, it is not sufficient simply to claim that a number of brothers and sisters already reside in the UK, unless it can also be shown that there is evidence of sufficiently close links which indicate family life between them (see, for example, *App. No. 9884/82* v *UK* 5 EHRR 298, compared to the situation in the *Uppal* case 3 EHRR 391, in which the family life of three generations was considered). Dependency may be a factor which the Commission will take into account, but this is likely to carry less weight if the applicant is adult and earning. Alternatively the dependency may relate to a child or parent who is dependent on the applicant. If there are other members of the family who also support a parent or child then the applicant's case may be weakened. For example, simply participating in a family business is not sufficient to establish this kind of dependency if there are several members of the family actively engaged in that business.

Even where deportation is recognised as being an interference with family life, it may be found to be justified. For example, in *Halil, Ahmet and Sabah* v *UK* 8 EHRR 252, the deportation of a family of Turkish-Cypriot origin was held to be justified in order to ensure effective immigration controls, this being an element of prevention of disorder under Article 8, para. 2. Similarly, deportation may be justified, even though it interferes with family life, where the husband has blatantly flouted the immigration rules (*App. No. 10184/82* v *UK* 5 EHRR 516) or where the spouse knew at the time of the marriage that his or her immigration status was precarious (*Lukka* v *UK* 9 EHRR 552).

Proof of marriage will not necessarily be sufficient evidence of being a member of a family or of having rights to family life if the links deemed necessary cannot be established. Thus in a case concerning the deportation of a Muslim back to South Yemen, the fact that he had several wives living in the UK did not convince the Commission that deportation would interfere with his right to family life, because it was not clear from the evidence that he had a family life with any of his wives, only that he visited and stayed with his wives and children from time to time (*App. No. 9521/81* v *UK* 5 EHRR 581 at 602).

In so far as the right of spouses to live together might be interfered with by immigration rules, the law as it originally stood entitled a person settled in the UK to be joined by his wife and any children under 18. The law did not afford the same right to wives as to husbands (*Abdulaziz* v *UK* Series A, Vol. 94). However, the Commission has accepted that under the principle of family re-unification it is not unreasonable for a State to establish a domestic verification procedure for claimants (*Kamal* v *UK* 4 EHRR 244).

Abdulaziz, Cabales and Balkandali v *UK*
Series A, Vol. 94

The facts

All the applicants were women; one had been born in the Philippines, one in Malawi and one in Egypt. All three were permanently settled in the UK. In all three cases the husbands of the applicants had not been permitted to remain with them in the UK because under the immigration rules in force at the time – the Immigration Act 1971 – neither the applicants nor their respective parents were born in the UK. Under the Statement of Changes in Immigration Rules which came into force in March 1980 and which applied in the applicants' case, a person who sought to join his wife for permanent settlement in the UK had to show that his wife was a citizen of the UK, who was born in the UK, or one of whose parents was so born. The law was not applied in an identical fashion to wives seeking to join their husbands, in as much as a woman would be given indefinite leave to enter to join her husband settled in the UK provided that he could accommodate and maintain her. Similarly, if a woman entered the country and subsequently married a man lawfully settled in the UK she would be given indefinite leave to remain.

The applicants complained of violations of Articles 8 and 14.

The Commission's opinion

The main thrust of the Commission's opinion focused on the discriminatory nature of the immigration controls in place at the time, and this aspect is therefore considered under Article 14. Clearly the right of the applicants to family life was interfered with as their husbands were not allowed to remain with them. The Government's argument in support of this differential treatment was that this protected the domestic labour market in a time of high and rising unemployment. This was based on the assumption that men were more likely to seek employment than women. The Commission was not convinced by this argument observing that women, including immigrant women, make up a significant proportion of the work force, and in any case, the likely number of husbands excluded as a result of these immigration rules was relatively low and could hardly be said to affect the overall economic situation. Nor was the Commission convinced that the measures were necessary for effective immigration control and the fostering of good race relations. Indeed, reform of the legislation had already shown that such measures were no longer considered necessary.

The Commission therefore concluded that:

> . . . the exclusion of the applicants' husbands from the United Kingdom entailed sexual discrimination in the securement of the applicants' right to respect for family life, the application of the relevant immigration rules being disproportionate to the purported aims of the measure. It is of the opinion, by a unanimous vote, that there has been a violation of Article 14 (on the ground of sexual discrimination), in conjunction with Article 8 in the present applications. (para. 109)

The judgment of the Court

The Court clearly distinguished this case from the situation where a person is seeking not to be deported or to be allowed to enter the country in order to join his or her family. In this case the applicants were the wives, already resident in the UK and in no danger themselves of being deported. Their complaint was that they were being deprived of the society of their spouses. Although Article 8 presupposes the existence of a family, this may extend to include intended family life even if at the time of the claim the family is not yet properly established. The Court further held:

> . . . the expression 'family life', in the case of a married couple, normally comprises cohabitation. The later proposition is reinforced by the existence of Article 12, for it is scarcely conceivable that the right to found a family should not encompass the right to live together. (para. 62)

The applicants contended that they were faced with the dilemma of either moving abroad or of being separated from their respective spouses. While the Court held that:

. . . the duty imposed by Article 8 cannot be considered as extending to a general obligation on the part of a Contracting State to respect the choice by married couples of the country of their matrimonial residence and to accept the non-national spouses for settlement in that country. (para. 68)

Nevertheless, under Article 8 there may be positive obligations inherent in effective 'respect' for family life.

However, the Court held that a Contracting State had a wide margin of appreciation in determining what steps should be taken to ensure compliance with the Convention. In particular the current case involved issues not only of family life but also immigration. The Court held that:

. . . In the present case, the applicants have not shown that there were obstacles to establishing family life in their own or their husband's countries or that there were special reasons why that could not be expected of them. (para. 68)

There was therefore no 'lack of respect' for family life and Article 8, taken alone, had not been violated.

Comment

Originally any persons born in a dominion owing allegiance to the British Crown were British subjects. As the British Empire gave way to the Commonwealth various territories became independent and established their own citizenship laws. Persons who had the citizenship of an independent Commonwealth country had the status under UK law of 'British subject' or 'Commonwealth citizen'. Until 1962, Commonwealth citizens had the right to enter the UK for work and permanent residence without any restriction. In 1960 the Commonwealth Immigrants Act was passed, and a similar Act in 1968, restricting the right of entry of certain classes of Commonwealth citizens, including citizens of the UK and Colonies who did not have close links with Britain.

These Acts were replaced by the Immigration Act 1971, which came into force in 1973. This Act created two new categories of persons: those having the right of abode in the UK (patrials) and those who did not have this right (non-patrials). Only the former were free from immigration controls. The latter could live, work and settle in the UK only if they had permission to do so. Patrials were persons who fell into one of the following classes:

(a) citizens of the United Kingdom and Colonies who had acquired that citizenship by birth, adoption, naturalisation or registration in the British Islands (that is, the United Kingdom, the Channel Islands and the Isle of Man), or were the children or grandchildren of any such persons;

(b) citizens of the United Kingdom and Colonies who had at any time been settled in the British Islands for at least five years;

(c) other Commonwealth citizens who were the children of a person having citizenship of the United Kingdom and Colonies by virtue of birth in the British Islands;

(d) women, being Commonwealth citizens, who were or had been married to a man falling within any of the preceding categories. (para. 14)

The division into patrials and non-patrials meant that not all former citizens of the United Kingdom and Colonies had the right of abode, while a number of persons who were not citizens, for example those with an ancestral link, did have this right, e.g. persons from New Zealand and Australia.

The 1971 Act gave the Home Secretary the authority to lay statements of Rules before Parliament concerning the actual administration of the Act. The Rules in force at the time of this case were the 1980 Rules. Among these were a number of provisions aimed at protecting the domestic labour market because of rising unemployment. The effect of these provisions was to make it harder for immigrants who were likely to be seeking full-time work in order to support a family, to enter and remain in the UK.

Citizenship and immigration law were brought into line under the British Nationality Act 1981, which created three categories: British, British Dependent Territories and British Overseas. Only British citizens were free from immigration controls and Commonwealth citizens having the right of abode under the 1971 Act as at December 1982. In order to acquire British citizenship a person had to be a citizen of the United Kingdom and Colonies with the right of abode under the 1971 Act. Such a person need not be born in the UK or have a parent born in the UK. Citizenship could also be obtained by a process of naturalisation on the basis of residence in the UK. The British Nationality Act 1981 came into force in 1983. Changes to the immigration rules allowing all women who were British citizens to be joined by their husbands and fiancés came into force in January 1983. Under the new rules a husband or fiancé could join his wife in the UK provided that she was a British citizen. Leave for a husband to join his wife who was settled in the UK but not a British citizen, could be granted by the Home Secretary. Such a wife could also become a British citizen by naturalisation. Further changes to the immigration rules were made in 1983.

8.2.4 Respect for the Home

This right may overlap with the Article 1 of the First Protocol, or be pleaded in conjunction with it. Whether it extends to include practical and effective protection from harassment in one's own home was left open in the case of *Whiteside* v *UK* (App. No. 20357/92), which was declared inadmissible due to failure to exhaust all the possible domestic remedies. It does extend to include intrusions into the home (*Chappell* v *UK* Series A, Vol. 152, concerning the use of *Anton Piller* orders), and also nuisance interfering with the use and enjoyment of the home (*Gillow* v *UK* Series A, No. 109).

Gillow* v *UK
Series A, Vol. 109

The facts
This case, which also raised issues under Article 1 of the First Protocol, concerned the refusal of the authorities in Guernsey to allow the applicants to occupy the property they owned on the island. Initially they had residential qualifications owing to employment in Guernsey, but lost these while living abroad. Their application for a licence to occupy the property on their return to the island was rejected, culminating in the conviction of Mr Gillow for unlawful occupation.

The applicants complained that the housing laws in Guernsey constituted an interference with their rights to respect for their home under Article 8.

The Commission's opinion

The Commission expressed the opinion that there had been a breach of both Article 8 and Article 1 of the First Protocol.

The judgment of the Court

When the matter came before the Court it was discovered that the First Protocol was not applicable. The applicants had to rely entirely on Article 8. However, some of the Government's arguments had been removed owing to the fact that it had been clearly established – a point which was disputed before the Commission – that the applicants had no other home.

The Court considered that:

> ... the fact that, on pain of prosecution, they were obliged to obtain a licence to live in their own house on their return to Guernsey in 1979, the refusal of the licences applied for, the institution of criminal proceedings against them for unlawful occupation of the property and, in Mr Gillow's case, his conviction and the imposition of a fine constituted interferences with the exercise of the applicants' right to respect for their home. (para. 47)

In examining whether these interferences were justified, the Court found that the relevant housing legislation – the Housing Law 1975 – was in accordance with the law. The aim of restricting the residential population of the island pursued a legitimate aim, namely to promote the economic well-being of the island. However, this had to be balanced against the applicants' individual right to respect for their home. The Court considered the facts:

> ... The statistics submitted to the Court show that, during the relevant period – 1979 and 1980 – the population of the island had been kept within the levels of recent years, having even marginally declined, and the availability of houses for occupation had not suffered any significant deterioration. Against this background, whilst not overlooking the fact that the average population per square mile of the island was still high in comparison with other countries, the Court considers that insufficient weight was given to the applicants' particular circumstances. They had built Whiteknights as a residence for themselves, and their family. At that time, they possessed residence qualifications and continued to do so until the entry into force of the Housing Law 1969, so that during that period they were entitled to occupy the house without a licence. The property was Mr and Mrs Gillow's place of residence for two years before they left Guernsey in 1960. Thereafter, they had retained ownership of the house and left furniture there. By letting it over a period of eighteen years to persons approved by the Housing Authority, they contributed to the Guernsey housing stock. On their return in 1979, they had no other home in the United Kingdom or elsewhere; Whiteknights was vacant and there were no prospective tenants.
>
> As for the refusals of the temporary licences, the decisions of the Housing Authority were, despite the granting of certain periods of grace, even more striking. Whiteknights needed repairs after eighteen years of rented use, with the result that it could not be occupied in the meantime by anyone other than the applicants.
>
> Finally, as regards the referral of the case to the Law Officers with a view to prosecution, the Government stated that the Housing Authority deferred taking this

course on several occasions. This, however, in the Court's view did not materially alleviate Mr and Mrs Gillow's already precarious situation.

... The Court therefore concludes that the decisions by the Housing Authority to refuse the applicants permanent and temporary licences to occupy Whiteknights, as well as the conviction and fining of Mr Gillow, constituted interferences with the exercise of their right to respect for their home which were disproportionate to the legitimate aim pursued.

There has accordingly been a breach of Article 8 of the Convention as far as the application of the legislation in the particular circumstances of the applicants' case was concerned. (paras 57 and 58)

Other cases in which control of housing has been considered – particularly in the context of planning controls – include: *Herrick* v *UK* 8 EHRR 66, concerning the operation of the 1964 Island Planning (Jersey) Law, which stipulated that permission of the Island Development Committee was required for any development of land in Jersey; *Masefield* v *UK* 9 EHRR 91; and *Howard* v *UK* 9 EHRR 91 at 116.

Baggs, Powell and Raynor v UK
Series A, Vol. 172
(Cases considered separately at the admissibility stage and then joined)

The facts
The facts of these cases are similar. In the *Baggs* case, the applicant complained about noise nuisance amounting to a violation of Article 8. His home and business, as a market gardener and poultry keeper, were located about a quarter of a mile from the western end of the southern runway at Heathrow Airport. Because of the noise nuisance and the consequential devaluation of his property the applicant had applied for planning permission for change of use to commercial property rather than residential, in order to be able to sell the property and move elsewhere. This permission was refused on the ground that the envisaged development would detract from the residential amenities of the neighbourhood.

In the *Powell* case, the property was further from Heathrow. Although it still fell within a Noise and Number Contour, its designation was one under which planning was not refused on the grounds of noise alone. In 1972 a new flight departure route overflew the area, but this route was in use for only about one third of the year in certain weather.

In the *Rayner* case, the property was situated one and a third miles west of Heathrow, in a direct line with the northern runway. It was regularly over-flown 24 hours a day and was in an area regarded as one of high noise annoyance.

The Commission's opinion
The Commission considered that:

... Considerable noise nuisance can undoubtedly affect the physical well-being of a person and thus interfere with his private life. It may also deprive a person of the possibility of enjoying the amenities of his home ... it is not necessary to determine at what level of intensity noise becomes an interference with the rights guaranteed by Art. 8(1). (*Rayner* v *UK* (1986) 47 D & R 5 at 12)

The Commission considered that the facts in the *Baggs* case raised complex questions of law and fact, and declared the complaint admissible as far as Articles 8 and 13 and the First Protocol, Article 1 were concerned. This case was subsequently settled and withdrawn. In considering whether the *Powell* and *Rayner* cases were admissible, however, the Commission found that the interference was justified, on the following basis:

> . . . It is not in question that the construction of Heathrow Airport has a legal basis. Furthermore, it cannot be doubted that the running of an airport and the increasing use of jet aircraft is in the interest of the economic well-being of a country and is also necessary in a democratic society. It is essential for developing external and internal trade by providing speedy means of transportation and it is also an important factor for the development of tourism.
>
> The interference with the applicant's right under Art. 8(1) is also proportionate to the legitimate aim connected with the running of the airport. It is true that where a State is allowed to restrict rights or freedoms guaranteed by the Convention, the principle of proportionality may oblige it to make sure that such restrictions do not create an unreasonable burden for the individual concerned.
>
> . . . The Commission notes in this context that the United Kingdom authorities have . . . taken various measures to control and limit the noise nuisance connected with the running of Heathrow Airport. In the case of *Powell*, the Commission noted that as far as the particular situation of the applicant Powell is concerned, the flight departure route causing disturbance in his area is in operation for only about one third of the year and it was divided into two sections in consequence of the objections raised by the population concerned. Mr Powell's property lies just within the 35 NNI contour which is, according to the uncontested submissions of the respondent Government, an area of low noise annoyance. The Commission cannot, in these circumstances, find that the assumed interference with the applicant Powell's right to respect for private life and for his home is disproportionate to the legitimate aim connected with the running of the airport. . . . (paras 4 and 5 Series A, Vol. 172)

The application was therefore found to be inadmissible as regards Article 8, but admissible with respect to Article 13.

Comment
The statistical growth of the volume and density of traffic handled by Heathrow over the years is clearly set out in the *Baggs* report. A number of measures had been adopted by the Government to deal with the consequential increase in the noise and nuisance factor. These included standards for noise certification, restrictions on night jet movements, noise monitoring, the designation of minimum noise routes, and noise insulation grant schemes for dwellings in the vicinity. The law made provision for liability in the case of material loss or damage to persons or property on land or water caused by an aircraft in flight or an object falling from an aircraft (Civil Aviation Act 1982); and compensation for loss of value of houses and land from airport noise (Land Compensation Act 1973). However, the 1982 Act specifically excluded any action for trespass or nuisance under s. 76 and s. 77.

Respect for the home may also include more widely the right to establish a home and lifestyle of one's choosing.

Buckley v UK
Council of Europe Report

The facts

The applicant was a gypsy who had parked her caravans on land which she had acquired, without the necessary planning permission, from her sister in 1988. Her subsequent planning application was refused and an enforcement notice issued by the District Council for the removal of the caravans. Appeal against the notice was dismissed. The applicant was found guilty of failure to comply with the enforcement notice and fined.

The applicant complained of a violation of Article 8 on the grounds, *inter alia*, that:

> . . . she is prohibited from living in her caravans on her own land where her children can grow up in a stable environment and receive continuous education and that she is also prevented from pursuing the traditional lifestyle of a gypsy.
>
> . . .
>
> . . . She submits that there is an acknowledged shortfall of sites for gypsies in South Cambridgeshire and that local authorities are failing to fulfil their statutory duty to provide sites. (paras 61 and 66)

The applicant further submitted that while the Secretary for State may direct a local authority to make provision for caravan sites, this is a purely discretionary power which has rarely been exercised and which has never been enforced.

Her sister, who owned adjacent land, had been granted personal temporary permission for three caravans, and in 1992 an official site had been opened by the council in the vicinity. Vacancies on this site had been notified to the applicant. The District Council had also granted planning permission for 170 private gypsy caravans. In May 1993, the Department of the Environment informed the local District Council that the area where the applicant lived – South Cambridgeshire – was to be a designated area.

The applicant contended that it was a practical impossibility for her to station her caravans on her sister's site; and that even if there were vacant pitches on the nearby official site, this site had a reputation for being overcrowded and violent, which rendered it an unsafe location for a single woman living alone with her children.

The Government contended, on the other hand, that the applicant was not a victim of any violation as she could either live on the neighbouring land lawfully occupied by her sister, or apply for a place on one of the designated sites. Even if there had been any interference with her rights under Article 8, this was justified under Article 8, para. 2 in the interests of public safety on the road, the economic well-being of the country and the protection of the environment. The designation system – whereby under the Caravan Sites Act 1968 local authorities designate certain sites for gypsies – was a proportionate response to the need to protect public safety on the roads and the rights of others.

The Commission's opinion

The Government contended that the applicant could not bring a claim under Article 8 as she had never lawfully occupied her caravan on the disputed site, and was therefore claiming a right to establish a home rather than a right to respect for an existing home. The Commission expressed the opinion that:

> ... the concept of 'home' within the meaning of Article 8 is not limited to those which are lawfully occupied or which have been lawfully established. 'Home' is an autonomous concept which does not depend on classification under domestic law. Whether or not a particular habitation constitutes a 'home' which attracts the protection of Article 8(1) will depend on the factual circumstances, namely the existence of sufficient and continuous links. (para. 63)

The Commission took into account the fact that the applicant was a gypsy with a particular lifestyle and considered that in the circumstances of the case her complaint fell within the scope of the article.

The question of lawfulness was relevant to considerations under Article 8, para. 2 relating to the interference with her right under Article 8, para. 1. It was not disputed that the interference was lawful or that it was directed at a legitimate aim. The question was whether the measures taken were proportionate and whether they responded to a pressing social need. In cases concerning residence of land without the requisite planning permission the Commission has to:

> ... weigh the general interests of the community in effective planning controls against the applicant's right to respect for her private life, family life and home, rights which are an intrinsic part of her personal security and well-being. In this assessment, the Commission must have regard to whether an excessive burden is placed on the applicant. Relevant to this exercise is consideration of whether there are practical alternatives open to the applicant if she leaves her land. . . . This case presents the special feature that, being a gypsy, the applicant leads a traditional lifestyle which restricts the options open to her. (para. 76)

The Commission did not consider that there was sufficient room on the official sites for the number of gypsies in the area. Moreover, the applicant could not reasonably be expected to move onto a private site as she would have to buy a mobile home on the site in order to do so, and she could not afford this. It was also no longer practical to expect the applicant to move onto her sister's site as other members of the family had done so. The Commission also considered that it was unreasonable to expect the applicant to move onto an official site with a bad reputation when her current site had the advantage of being close to other members of her family. The Commission therefore found that:

> ... the measures taken against the applicant with regard to her continued occupation of her land place her in the position where she is being required either to move off without any specific lawful place where she can go or to apply for a future vacancy on a site which she considers, with reason, to be unsuitable. Both these alternatives offer the prospect of insecurity and the threat of disrupting the stability of her own and her children's existence. Against this, the Commission considers that the factors weighing in favour of the public interest in planning controls are of a slight and general nature. The highway safety aspect does not appear strong in view of the location of an official and unofficial gypsy site along the same road and the fact that two of the gypsy families at the applicant's location have permission to be there. The general amenity of the immediate area would not appear to require special measures of protection in view of the number of authorised gypsy sites already in place, i.e. it is not an area of

untouched countryside or of particular scenic beauty which might weight the balance more heavily towards preservation.

. . . In these circumstances, the burden placed upon the applicant by the enforcement measures is, in the Commission's opinion, excessive and disproportionate. Even having regard to the margin of appreciation accorded to the domestic authorities, the Commission finds that the interests of the applicant in this case outweigh the general interest. It does not consider that this finding is tantamount to rendering gypsies immune from legitimate planning controls. Special considerations arise in the planning sphere regarding the needs of gypsies which are acknowledged in the Government's own policies. Whether the correct balance has been struck between the rights of an individual gypsy or gypsy family and the interests of the general community will depend always on the particular facts of the case.

. . . The Commission finds that in the circumstances of the case the interference cannot be regarded as 'necessary in a democratic society' in pursuit of the aims identified above.

. . . The Commission concludes, by seven votes to five, that there has been a violation of Article 8 of the Convention. (paras 83–86)

The case has now been referred to the Court.

Comment

If the Secretary of State designated an area under the Caravan Sites Act 1968, the result was that it became a criminal offence for gypsies to station their caravans near the highway on any unoccupied land or on any occupied land without the consent of the occupier. Under the Act the Secretary of State could order a local authority to comply with its statutory duty to provide a sufficient number of official sites for gypsies. In this case the Secretary of State found that the concentration of gypsy sites in the area had reached the desirable maximum.

In 1994, the Criminal Justice and Public Order Act abolished the duty of local authorities to provide gypsy sites. New guidelines issued to local authorities by the Department of the Environment in January 1994 are directed at encouraging these authorities, when considering private planning applications by gypsies – which are now the only lawful way in which they can acquire permanent permission to remain on a site – to take into account the nomadic lifestyle of gypsies and to encourage pre-application discussions and meetings. The onus is now, therefore, on gypsies themselves to apply through the standard planning application procedures for permission. This procedure also means that objections to such applications can be made, which may make it very difficult for gypsies to obtain planning permission.

8.2.5 Respect for Correspondence

Interference with this right has been most frequently cited in the case of prisoners.

Golder* v *UK
Series A, Vol. 18

The facts

The applicant was detained in prison on the Isle of Wight. He had been convicted of robbery with violence. While he was in prison there was a demonstration and disturbances involving the prisoners on 24 October 1969. The applicant was accused of having been involved in these and of assaulting a prison officer. He was eventually cleared of all complicity in the events. Shortly after these disturbances he wrote to his MP – who was negotiating for him to be allowed to sit certain examinations – asserting that he had no part in the riots. This letter and a subsequent letter were stopped. A letter to the Chief Constable was also stopped. The grounds for stopping the letters were that the applicant had not raised the matters through the authorised channels. The applicant was also refused permission by the Home Secretary to consult a solicitor.

The applicant's complaint under Article 8 was that no Prison Rule stated specifically that letters complaining of treatment in prison should be stopped, therefore there had been a violation of his rights under this article. Also that the refusal to allow him to consult a solicitor interfered with his rights under Articles 8 and 6.

The Commission's opinion

The Commission declared admissible the applicant's complaint that the refusal to allow him to consult a solicitor was a breach of Article 8, para. 1 read with Article 6, para. 1.

The judgment of the Court

The Home Secretary's refusal to allow Golder to consult a solicitor for the purpose of finding out whether he could commence legal proceedings for defamation against a prison officer who had alleged that he had been involved in the disturbances, effectively interfered with his right to correspond with his solicitor. At this stage, however, there was no actual correspondence which was stopped or censored. The Court held, however, that:

> . . . (i)mpeding someone from even initiating correspondence constitutes the most far-reaching form of 'interference' with the exercise of the 'right to respect for correspondence'; it is inconceivable that should fall outside the scope of Article 8 while mere supervision indisputably falls within it. (para. 43)

The Court therefore held that it could consider whether there had been such an interference. The Court rejected the argument that Article 8 contained an implied limitation in the case of prisoners. The wording of the provision left no room for implied limitations. However, the fact of imprisonment may be relevant in considering justification for interference in as much as the Court accepted that:

> . . . the 'necessity' for interference with the exercise of the right of a convicted prisoner to respect for his correspondence must be appreciated having regard to the ordinary and reasonable requirements of imprisonment. The 'prevention of disorder or crime', for example, may justify wider measures of interference in the case of such a prisoner than in that of a person at liberty. To this extent, but to this extent only, lawful deprivation of liberty within the meaning of Article 5 does not fail to impinge on the application of Article 8. . . . (para. 45)

The Government had argued that the interference was 'necessary' to prevent disorder or crime. The Court could not accept this:

. . . the Court cannot discern how these considerations, as they are understood 'in a democratic society', could oblige the Home Secretary to prevent Golder from corresponding with a solicitor with a view to suing Laird for libel. The Court again lays stress on the fact that Golder was seeking to exculpate himself of a charge made against him by that prison officer acting in the course of his duties and relating to an incident in prison. In these circumstances, Golder could justifiably wish to write to a solicitor. It was not for the Home Secretary himself to appraise – no more than it is for the Court today – the prospects of the action contemplated; it was for a solicitor to advise the applicant on his rights and then for a court to rule on any action that might be brought.

The Home Secretary's decision proves to be all the less 'necessary in a democratic society' in that the applicant's correspondence with a solicitor would have been a preparatory step to the institution of civil legal proceedings and, therefore, to the exercise of a right embodied in another Article of the Convention, that is, Article 6.

The Court thus reaches the conclusion that there has been a violation of Article 8. (para. 45)

Silver and Others v UK
Series A, Vol. 61

The facts

All but one of the applicants were detained in prison and complained of interference with their post by the prison authorities. This interference involved the stopping of letters. Under the Home Secretary's power to pass delegated legislation, a number of restrictions existed to control prisoners' correspondence. Any legal communications relating to proceedings against the Home Secretary arising from prison treatment were subject to the 'prior ventilation rule', whereby all complaints had to go through the internal prison complaints procedure before a prisoner would be given permission to seek legal advice about bringing proceedings. Restrictions were placed on correspondence with MPs and other officials and, although some of these had been removed since December 1975, the prior ventilation rule also applied to such correspondence. The same rule applied in the case of letters to recognised organisations concerned with prisoners' rights, e.g. the Howard League. A prisoner was also only allowed to correspond with close relatives and friends who were known to the prisoner prior to imprisonment and there were restrictions on the subject matter permitted in such letters.

If a prisoner had a complaint about prison treatment then he could petition the Home Secretary, but only one petition at a time was permitted.

In total 62 of the applicants' letters were stopped for various reasons provided for in the Prison Rules. The case before the Commission was whether the censorship of this correspondence amounted to a violation of Article 8. Issues were also raised concerning Article 10, Article 6, para. 1 and Article 13.

The Commission declared the applications admissible on the basis that the interference with the applicants' correspondence was in breach of Article 8, para. 1.

The Commission's opinion

The Government argued that there had been no interference on the grounds that:

... respect for correspondence does not signify total freedom to correspond. .... In the Government's opinion, the ordinary and reasonable requirements of imprisonment permit limitations on prisoners' correspondence. (para. 268)

As in the *Golder* case, the Commission rejected this argument on the ground that there was no implied limitation on the right to respect for correspondence in the case of prisoners due to their particular situation. A prisoner had the same right as a person at liberty. The requirements of imprisonment, might, however, be relevant as justification under Article 8, para. 2, and it was this aspect with which the Commission was primarily concerned.

First, was the interference 'in accordance with the law'? The Commission understood this to be:

... not merely a reference to a State's domestic law but also a reference to the rule of law, or the principle of legality, which is common to democratic societies and the heritage of member States of the Council of Europe. (para. 281)

Therefore the law should be accessible and formulated with sufficient precision. The Prison Rules Act 1964 satisfied this criterion because they were public and made known to prisoners. However, further restrictions under the unpublished administrative guidelines issued by the Home Secretary did not meet this criterion because they were not accessible or foreseeable by a prisoner, who would not be able to regulate his conduct in accordance with them. The Commission had to consider whether the Prison Rules indicated sufficiently that the type of interference complained of was reasonably foreseeable.

In deciding whether the restrictions were 'necessary in a democratic society', the Commission could take into account the context of imprisonment. This required a balance to be struck between the legitimate interests of public order and security and that of the rehabilitation of prisoners. In considering this balance the Commission noted that the restrictions in this case were principally:

— the prohibition on complaints about prison treatment;
— the prohibition on correspondence to persons other than relatives or friends;
— the prohibition on letters dealing with legal matters without the prior leave of the Secretary of State;
— the prohibition on letters containing material intended for publication;
— the prohibition on letters containing material deliberately calculated to hold the prison authorities up to contempt; and
— the prohibition on letters containing representations about trial, conviction or sentence;

and subsidiarily:

— the prohibition on letters attempting to stimulate public agitation or petition;
— the prohibition on letters which circumvent or evade prison regulations; and
— the prohibition on letters containing allegations against prison officers. (para. 296)

The fact that letters concerning prison treatment were subject to the 'prior ventilation rule' was not apparent from the Prison Rules, but was set out in the unpublished Standing Orders. While the Commission accepted that:

... the ordinary and reasonable requirements of imprisonment justify a system of internal inquiry into prisoners' complaints about their treatment or conditions in prison . . . [it did] not consider, however, that the priority of such a system is so justified. (para. 301)

This applied to letters to MPs, to legal representatives, and to other people. The Commission expressed the view that:

... the prohibition on complaints, the rule neither attempting to define 'complaint' nor giving consideration to the security risk of the prisoner or the addressee or the likely effect of the correspondence in question, constitutes an over-broad restriction which cannot be said to be proportionate to the legitimate aims of Government. It has not been shown, therefore, to be a restriction which is 'necessary in a democratic society... for the prevention of disorder' within the meaning of Article 8(2). (para. 323)

As regards the restriction on correspondence with persons other than relatives or friends, the Commission found that although these restrictions could be ascertained from the Prison Rules, these indicated that such correspondence would be restricted only in the interests of 'discipline and good order or the prevention or crime or in the interest of any persons'. However, the Commission found that in the case of the applicants' letters the rule had been interpreted much more extensively, and that this interpretation could not have been foreseen.

Although it was clear from the Prison Rules that the 'prior ventilation rule' must be exhausted in the case of letters dealing with legal matters, the Commission expressed the opinion that such censorship was disproportionate to the aim sought, i.e. the opportunity for the prison authorities to be informed of legal matters involving prisoners and so address complaints internally as quickly as possible. Similar lack of proportionality was to be found in the censorship of all correspondence intended for publication, all correspondence which was contemptuous of the prison authorities, any correspondence which attempted to stimulate public agitation or petition, and any letters containing allegations against prison officers.

The only censorship which the Commission felt generally to be justified under Article 8, para. 2 was the prohibition on letters which circumvented or evaded prison regulations, the prohibition on letters containing threats of violence, and that relating to letters which discussed crime in general or the crime(s) of others.

The judgment of the Court

Before the case came before the Court a number of reforms had been made to the Prison Rules, and the Government did not therefore contest most of the Commission's findings. The Court was asked to take these changes into account, and the hearing before the Court was limited to those issues which were still in dispute. However, at the outset, the Court indicated that it could not take the legal changes into account, because it could not rule on legislation *in abstracto* (although it did express its satisfaction that substantial changes had taken place).

The Court accepted that there were interferences by a public authority with the applicants' correspondence. Whether these were 'in accordance with the law', depended on the interpretation given to the expression 'prescribed by law'. Although Article 8 uses the expression 'in accordance with the law' in the context of correspondence, there is a substantial overlap with the provisions of Article 10 which uses the expression 'prescribed by law'. The Court held that because of this overlap the two expressions must be given the same interpretation. The principles of interpretation had been given in the *Sunday Times* case which concerned Article 10. First, the interference must have some basis in domestic law. The Court accepted that this was the case as regards the Prison Rules and the Prison Act, but not as regards the Orders and Instructions. Similarly, the former complied with the principle of being adequately accessible, while the latter did not. Thirdly, the Court held that:

> . . . a norm cannot be regarded as a 'law' unless it is formulated with sufficient precision to enable the citizen to regulate his conduct: he must be able – if need be with appropriate advice – to foresee, to a degree that is reasonable in the circumstances, the consequences which a given action may entail. (para. 88)

Any law which confers a discretion must indicate the scope of that discretion.

> . . . However, the Court has already recognised the impossibility of attaining absolute certainty in the framing of laws and the risk that the search for certainty may entail excessive rigidity (ibid.). These observations are of particular weight in the 'circumstances' of the present case, involving as it does, in the special context of imprisonment, the screening of approximately 10 million items of correspondence in a year. . . . It would scarcely be possible to formulate a law to cover every eventuality. Indeed, the applicants themselves did not deny that some discretion should be left to the authorities. (para. 88)

As regards the censorship of letters which was still being contested, the Court found that these had been interfered with 'in accordance with the law' and with a legitimate aim, but it had to consider whether the interferences were 'necessary in a democratic society', as it was on this question the Commission had found a violation. The Court reiterated its understanding of this expression as follows:

> (a)   the adjective 'necessary' is not synonymous with 'indispensable', neither has it the flexibility of such expressions as 'admissible', 'ordinary', 'useful', 'reasonable' or 'desirable'.
> (b)   the Contracting States enjoy a certain but not unlimited margin of appreciation in the matter of the imposition of restrictions, but it is for the Court to give the final ruling on whether they are compatible with the Convention.
> (c)   the phrase 'necessary in a democratic society' means that, to be compatible with the Convention, the interference must, *inter alia*, correspond to a 'pressing social need' and be 'proportionate to the legitimate aim pursued'.
> (d)   those paragraphs of an Article of the Convention which provide for an exception to a right guaranteed are to be narrowly interpreted.
> . . . The Court has also held that, in assessing whether an interference with the exercise of the right of a convicted prisoner to respect for his correspondence was 'necessary' for one of the aims set out in Article 8(2), regard has to be paid to the ordinary and reasonable requirements of imprisonment. Indeed, the Court recognises that some measure of control over prisoners' correspondence is called for and is not of itself incompatible with the Convention. (paras 97–98)

In applying these principles to the correspondence which had been stopped, the Court came to the same conclusion as the Commission, i.e. that the stopping of 57 of the letters was not found to be necessary while the remainder were legitimately stopped.

Comment

The Home Secretary is responsible for the control of prisons by virtue of the power vested in him under the Prison Act 1952. He may make rules concerning the management of prisons by means of statutory instruments (Prison Rules). The Rules governing prisoners' correspondence were rules 33 and 34 of the Prison Rules 1964. Under these a prisoner could communicate with someone outside only with the Home Secretary's leave, and the prison governor or his deputy had authority to examine correspondence and stop it if it was found to be objectionable. Confidential management guidelines were issued to prison governors by the Home Secretary in the form of Standing Orders and Circular Instructions.

Some changes had been made to the relevant rules during the course of this case. Since January 1973, a prisoner who was party to legal proceedings could have confidential correspondence with his legal adviser; and since April 1976, a prisoner could seek legal advice about potential civil proceedings. However, before this could be done a prisoner had to apply to the prison governor explaining why he or she was seeking legal advice to initiate such proceedings. If the intended proceedings were against the Home Office in connection with treatment in prison, then the 'prior ventilation rule' had to be complied with.

From 1 December 1981, the directives concerning prisoners' correspondence were substantially revised, so that a prisoner could communicate with any person or organisation, subject to certain limited exceptions. Details of the law can be found in the Decision of the Court, paras 25–50. The most important of these revisions was that the 'prior ventilation rule' was replaced with a 'simultaneous ventilation rule'. Changes were also made, as from 1 December 1981, concerning the complaints procedure, so that prisoners no longer had to wait until one petition had been dealt with before submitting another. Complaints could also be addressed to the Parliamentary Commissioner for Administration (the Ombudsman), either via a Member of Parliament or (since August 1979) directly.

A number of cases were adjourned pending the outcome of the *Silver* case, including *App. No. 9282/81* 5 EHRR 268, *App. No. 9488/81* v *UK* 5 EHRR 289. See also *Campbell and Fell* v *UK* (Series A, No. 80), in which the Court saw no reason to depart from its judgment in the *Silver* case and agreed with the Commission that there had been violations of Article 8 at the time that the case arose. However, it recognised that certain changes had been made to the relevant Standing Rules governing certain of the issues raised in the case, namely, that new Orders (Nos 5B23–5B30) stated that subject to certain exceptions, a prisoner could correspond with any person or organisation provided that regulations relating to the contents of letters were observed as well as the new 'simultaneous ventilation' rule.

A number of cases raised similar issues to those in *Campbell and Fell* and were admitted on the same considerations, e.g. *App. No. 7879/77* v *UK, App. No. 7931/77* v *UK, McLuskey* v *UK* (1987) 51 D & R 5 and *App. No. 7936/77* v *UK*.

In the case of *McCallum* v *UK* Series A, No. 183, concerning restrictions imposed on prisoners' correspondence in Scotland, the reasoning in *Silver* was applied, even though the applicable law was slightly different (see *Campbell* v *UK*).

Campbell v UK
Series A, Vol. 233-A

The facts

The applicant was serving a term of life imprisonment for murder in Scotland. Correspondence with his solicitor and the Commission had been regularly screened and opened by the prison authorities following the Prison Rules and Standing Orders which provided for the opening and reading of such correspondence in order to ensure the prevention of disorder or crime. This interference had taken place despite requests from the applicant's solicitor that such correspondence should be allowed to pass without interference. The applicant complained that this amounted to a breach of Article 8.

The Commission's opinion

This case was distinguishable from that of *Silver* in as much as that case concerned the stopping of letters, while this case concerned the opening of them. The case law of the Commission and the Court indicated that the supervision of prisoners' correspondence could in general be justified under Article 8, para. 2 even though it was a violation under Article 8, para. 1, for the prevention of disorder and crime.

In this case the opening was 'in accordance with law' as the Standing Orders were public and made known to the prisoners and public. The Commission was also satisfied that the measures pursued a legitimate aim. However, the Commission recognised the importance of protecting the confidentiality between a lawyer and his client, and the principle of effective access to court, in the context of both Article 6, para. 1 and Article 8.

Whether the opening of the applicant's general correspondence with his solicitor amounted to an unjustified interference depended on whether it was necessary. The Commission recalled that the case law established that the mere screening of correspondence was a measure falling under Article 8, para. 2. However, as regards the opening of letters to and from a solicitor the Commission noted that a right to respect such correspondence overlapped with Article 6, para. 1, and that in order to be justified there must be a pressing social need. In the circumstances the Commission took into account the professional status of solicitors, the system of sanctioning and controlling them, and the confidential nature of such correspondence. It concluded that while there may occasionally be circumstances justifying the opening of such correspondence, in general this could not be said to be the case, therefore there had been a violation of Article 8 in respect of the general correspondence with the applicant's solicitor.

As regards interference with the applicant's correspondence with the Commission, the Commission noted that many of the complaints it receives are submitted by prisoners concerning their treatment or conditions in prison. It is therefore important that communications of this sort are free from unnecessary constraints.

The judgment of the Court

The Court found that there had been an interference with the applicant's correspondence. This had been carried out 'in accordance with the law' and in pursuit of a legitimate aim. The Court then held that although some measure of control over prisoners' correspondence might be compatible with the Convention:

> . . . It is clearly in the general interest that any person who wishes to consult a lawyer should be free to do so under conditions which favour full and uninhibited discussion. (para. 46)

The Court further held that:

> . . . The right to respect for correspondence is of special importance in a prison context where it may be more difficult for a legal adviser to visit his client in person because, as in the present case, of the distant location of the prison. Finally, the objective of confidential communication with a lawyer could not be achieved if this means of communication were the subject of automatic control. (para. 50)

While the margin of appreciation afforded to Contracting States permits the possibility of examining correspondence where there is reasonable cause, such cause was not established in this case. There was, therefore, no pressing social need for the opening and reading of the applicant's correspondence with his solicitor. Similarly, the Court held that the opening of letters from the Commission was not 'necessary in a democratic society' and that there had been a breach of Article 8.

Two partly dissenting opinions were given. Judge Morenilla dissented on the grounds that regard should have been had to the particular situation pertaining in Scottish prisons at the time and to the character of the applicant himself, in determining whether the interference was justified on the grounds of preventing disorder and crime. Also a distinction should be drawn between 'incoming' and 'outgoing' mail, interference with the former being justified in the circumstances. Judge Sir John Freeland also thought that the different categories of correspondence should be distinguished, interference with general correspondence with a solicitor – which could cover a wide range of topics – being justified.

Comment

At the relevant time the prison system in Scotland was governed by the Prisons (Scotland) Act 1952. These provisions were re-enacted in the Prisons (Scotland) Act 1989. Under these Acts the Secretary of State for Scotland has the power to make Prison Rules, including rules concerning communications between prisoners and the outside. All correspondence to or from a prisoner may be read by the governor of the prison or his deputy. These rules were supplemented by a Standing Order which was available to prisoners and the public.

In between Mr Campbell lodging his application and its being heard, new procedures concerning correspondence between a prisoner and his legal adviser had been introduced following the friendly settlement achieved in the case of *McComb* v *UK* 15 EHRR CD 110. Under these new procedures such correspondence could not be stopped provided that the governor had no reason to believe that it contained other, non-permitted material and provided that the solicitor sent such mail in a sealed envelope bearing the words 'Legal proceedings' and his signature, and placed this within another envelope addressed to the prison governor.

The applicant's right to correspond with the Commission was protected under the European Agreement Relating to Persons Participating in Proceedings of the European Commission and Court of Human Rights of 6 May 1969 (the European Agreement), the relevant provisions of which read as follows:

> 1.   The Contracting Parties shall respect the right of the persons referred to in paragraph 1 of Article 1 of [the] Agreement to correspond freely with the Commission and the Court.
>
> 2.   As regards persons under detention, the exercise of this right shall in particular imply that:
>
>   (a)   if their correspondence is examined by the competent authorities, its despatch and delivery shall nevertheless take place without undue delay and without alteration;
>
>   (b)   such persons shall not be subject to disciplinary measures in any form on account of any communication sent through the proper channels to the Commission or the Court;
>
>   (c)   such persons shall have the right to correspond, and consult out of hearing of other persons, with a lawyer qualified to appear before the courts of the country where they are detained in regard to an application to the Commission, or any proceedings resulting therefrom.
>
> 3.   In application of the preceding paragraphs, there shall be no interference by a public authority except such as is in accordance with the law and is necessary in a democratic society in the interests of national security, for the direction of prosecution of a criminal offence or for the protection of health.

This Agreement is distinct from the Convention and binding on the Contracting Parties, including the UK, as from 1971.

8.2.6   Privacy and Surveillance

Malone v *UK*
Series A, Vol. 82 & 4 EHRR 330

The facts
The applicant, an antique dealer, was arrested and charged with offences relating to the handling of stolen goods. He was eventually acquitted of these charges. He alleged that since about 1971 he had been under police surveillance, which included having his telephone tapped and his telephone calls metered. Also that his correspondence had been intercepted and

tampered with. Following his trial the applicant instituted proceedings against the Metropolitan Police Commissioner complaining about the interception, monitoring or recording of conversations on his telephone. He sought declarations from the court:

—(1)   that interception, monitoring or recording of conversations on his telephone lines without his consent, or disclosing the contents thereof, was unlawful even if done pursuant to a warrant of the Home Secretary;

—(2)   that he had a right of property, privacy and confidentiality in respect of conversations on his telephone lines and that interception, monitoring, recording and disclosure of conversations were in breach thereof;

—(3)   alternatively that he had no remedy under English law for the interception, monitoring, recording or disclosure of conversations;

—(4)   that the interception and monitoring of his telephone lines violated Article 8 of the Convention;

—(5)   alternatively that he had no effective remedy before a national authority for the violation of Article 8 by reason of the interception and monitoring of his telephone conversations. (4 EHRR 330 at 337)

During the course of the case the law relating to telephone tapping was considered at length. However, the Vice-Chancellor, Sir Robert Megarry, concluded his judgment by dismissing the applicant's claim on the grounds that, first:

. . . he had no jurisdiction to make a declaration to the effect that telephone tapping infringed Article 8 of the Convention. The Convention was a treaty which did not have the force of law in England. The power to make declarations was confined to matters that were justiciable in the court. The Convention as a treaty was not so justiciable.

In considering the legality of telephone tapping, the Vice-Chancellor observed that the case concerned only tapping effected from wires which were not on the subscriber's premises. No issue concerning radio apparatus or trespass on premises arose. He held that there was no property right in the words contained in a telephone conversation. There was no general right of privacy in English law nor any particular right to hold a telephone conversation in the privacy of one's home without molestation. Any such right could only be created by the legislature. Nor was there any right of confidentiality in a telephone conversation, whether arising under contract or otherwise. Even if there was, there could (subject to certain requirements) be just cause or excuse for tapping a telephone for the purpose of detecting crime, and the duty could thus be limited, and would be so limited on the facts of this case. Although there was no specific power in law to tap telephones, it was not unlawful since there was nothing (such as a trespass) to make it so. The Convention conferred no direct rights in English law. The court was not faced with the interpretation of legislation whose meaning was in doubt. The Vice-Chancellor commented particularly on the absence of any legal safeguards, as opposed to administrative safeguards unenforceable in law. . . . (4 EHRR 330 at 337–338)

The applicant complained to the Commission that the UK law relevant to telephone tapping and the interception of mail violated Article 8.

The Commission's opinion
The Commission found that:

... the applicant is 'directly affected' by the law and practice in England and Wales under which the secret surveillance of postal and telephone communications on behalf of the police is permitted and takes place. His communications have at all relevant times been liable to such surveillance without his being able to obtain knowledge of it. Accordingly, as has not been disputed, he is entitled to claim, for the purposes of Article 25 of the Convention, to be a 'victim' of the relevant law and practice irrespective of whether or to what extent he is able to show that it has actually been applied to him. In these circumstances the Commission does not find it necessary to consider to what extent, if at all, the applicant's communications have been intercepted, apart from the single admitted instance. It will confine itself to examining the admitted interception and the relevant law and practice to ascertain whether it is compatible with the Convention.

... The Commission finds that the admitted interception of the applicant's telephone conversation was an interference by a public authority with his right to respect for his private life and correspondence guaranteed by Article 8(1). In addition, the existence of the laws and practices which permit and establish a system for effecting secret surveillance of postal and telephone communications in itself amounts to an interference with these rights under Article 8(1) apart from any measures of surveillance actually undertaken. The existence of such interferences is not disputed and as the Commission indicated in the admissibility decision, the principal questions to be considered thus arise under Article 8(2). (paras 114 and 115)

In deciding whether the interference was justified under Article 8, para. 2, the Commission had to examine whether the measures taken were in accordance with the law, and therefore sufficiently accessible and foreseeable. The Commission considered that in the field of secret surveillance it was particularly important that:

... the law should specify clearly the circumstances in which measures interfering with the protected rights may lawfully take place since the opportunity for the courts to determine obscure or disputed questions of law is obviously limited. Accordingly if the individual is to have an adequate indication of what the legal rules applicable in this area are, it is necessary that they should be reasonably clear and unambiguous. Furthermore the law should define the circumstances in which an interference may take place with reasonable precision. . . . (para. 122 Series A, Vol. 82)

While the law did not have to be statute law, it should not be merely a statement of administrative practice. Therefore:

... for an 'interference' to be 'in accordance with the law' it should be carried out under a system of domestic law which, when looked at in all its relevant features, can be seen, with reasonable certainty, to permit interference only in circumstances which are limited or defined with reasonable precision and in principle compatible with the purposes mentioned in Article 8(2). It is not sufficient merely that an interference should be lawful in the sense that it is not unlawful, or that it should be carried out under a publicly announced administrative practice without binding effect on the authorities.

... In the present case the parties are agreed, and the Commission itself is satisfied, that the interception of postal and telephone communications carried out under a warrant issued on behalf of the police in accordance with the official practice for purposes of detection of crime is lawful. . . . (paras 124 and 125 Series A, Vol. 82)

The question was whether the law delimited the circumstances with sufficient precision and certainty. While the Commission was satisfied that a warrant was required to intercept communications, it was not satisfied about the legal regulation of the conditions and procedures for the issue of such warrants. The Commission found that:

> ... Section 80 of the [Post Office Act] 1969 ... does not regulate either the purpose for which warrants may be issued or their content or duration in the manner contended by the Government. In any event it fails to do so with any reasonable degree of clarity in the Commission's view.
>
> ... The position therefore appears to be as follows. Firstly it appears reasonably certain that a postal or telephone communication passing through the relevant public service could not lawfully be intercepted for police purposes save in obedience to a valid warrant under the hand of a Secretary of State. Secondly it does not appear that the purposes for which such warrants may be issued are subject to any, save possibly the very broadest, legal restriction. In any event it cannot be stated with any reasonable degree of certainty that such restrictions exist. Thirdly the scope, form, content and duration of such warrants similarly does not appear to be defined by law, or at any event it cannot be stated with reasonable certainty that they are so defined. Fourthly other matters such as the procedures whereby such warrants are applied for, the persons or authorities who may apply for them, and the handling of information obtained are regulated by administrative practice, not by rules of law.
>
> ... Accordingly in the Commission's opinion it cannot be said, at least with any reasonable certainty, that domestic law lays down even the principal conditions or procedures for the issue of warrants authorising postal and telephone interceptions on behalf of the police. In the Commission's opinion such interceptions are not therefore carried out 'in accordance with the law' for the purposes of Article 8(2).
>
> ...
> ... The Commission concludes by 11 votes with 1 abstention that there has been a breach of the applicant's rights under Article 8 of the Convention by reason of the admitted interception of his telephone conversation and the law and practice governing the interception of postal and telephone communications on behalf of the police. (paras 142–145 Series A, Vol. 82)

The judgment of the Court
In considering whether the interference was justified under Article 8, para. 2, the Court held:

> ... the phrase 'in accordance with the law' does not merely refer back to domestic law but also relates to the quality of the law, requiring it to be compatible with the rule of law, which is expressly mentioned in the preamble to the Convention. The phrase thus implies – and this follows from the object and purpose of Article 8 – that there must be a measure of legal protection in domestic law against arbitrary interferences by public authorities with the rights safeguarded by paragraph 1. Especially where a power of the executive is exercised in secret, the risks of arbitrariness are evident. Undoubtedly, as the Government rightly suggested, the requirements of the Convention, notably in regard to foreseeability, cannot be exactly the same in the special context of interception of communications for the purposes of police investigations as they are where the object of the relevant law is to place restrictions on the conduct of individuals. In particular, the requirement of foreseeability cannot mean that an individual should be enabled to foresee when the authorities are likely to intercept his communications so that he can adapt his conduct accordingly.

Nevertheless, the law must be sufficiently clear in its terms to give citizens an adequate indication as to the circumstances in which and the conditions on which public authorities are empowered to resort to this secret and potentially dangerous interference with the right to respect for private life and correspondence. (para. 67 Series A, Vol. 82)

The Court observed that:

. . . at the very least, in its present state the law in England and Wales governing interception of communications for police purposes is somewhat obscure and open to differing interpretations. The Court would be usurping the function of the national courts were it to attempt to make an authoritative statement on such issues of domestic law. The Court is, however, required under the Convention to determine whether, for the purposes of Article 8(2), the relevant law lays down with reasonable clarity the essential elements of the authorities' powers in this domain.

Detailed procedures concerning interception of communications on behalf of the police in England and Wales do exist. What is more, published statistics show the efficacy of those procedures in keeping the number of warrants granted relatively low, especially when compared with the rising number of indictable crimes committed and telephones installed. The public have been made aware of the applicable arrangements and principles through publication of the Birkett report and the White Paper and through statements by responsible Ministers in Parliament.

Nonetheless, on the evidence before the Court, it cannot be said with any reasonable certainty what elements of the powers to intercept are incorporated in legal rules and what elements remain within the discretion of the executive. In view of the attendant obscurity and uncertainty as to the state of the law in this essential respect, the Court cannot but reach a similar conclusion to that of the Commission. In the opinion of the Court, the law of England and Wales does not indicate with reasonable clarity the scope and manner of exercise of the relevant discretion conferred on the public authorities. To that extent, the minimum degree of legal protection to which citizens are entitled under the rule of law in a democratic society is lacking. (para. 79 Series A, Vol. 82)

The Court found that there had been a breach of Article 8. The Court also held that the metering of the applicant's telephone was a violation of this article, there being no legal rules concerning the scope and manner of the exercise of the discretion enjoyed by public authorities to carry out such metering.

Judge Pettiti gave a concurring but separate opinion emphasising the contemporary dangers of uncontrolled surveillance and interference in private lives via modern technology.

Comment

Suspicion that his telephone had been tapped arose as a result of certain evidence and procedures taken in connection with the applicant's civil trial. The Government would neither confirm nor deny that the telephone had been tapped, and admitted only that one telephone conversation had been intercepted pursuant to a warrant by the Secretary of State.

The law relating to telephone tapping had been considered in the Birkett Report (Cmnd. 283 1957), a Government White Paper 'The Interception of Communications in Great Britain' (Cmnd. 7873 1980) and the Report of Lord Diplock, 'The interception of Communications in Great Britain' (Cmnd. 8191 1981).

Hewitt and Harman v UK
(1991) 47 D & R 88

The facts
Both applicants were involved with the National Council for Civil Liberties
(NCCL); the first applicant was General Secretary between September 1983
and May 1984, and the second was employed as a legal officer from 1978 until
1982. A former intelligence officer of the Security Service (MI5) (Ms Cathy
Massiter) revealed in 1985 that both applicants had been placed by the Security
Service in the category of communist sympathisers due to their prominent
participation in the activities of the NCCL, an organisation which was,
according to Ms Massiter, classified as a communist-controlled subversive
organisation. Both applicants complained that they were the subject of secret
surveillance by the Security Service, that information concerning their activities was compiled and retained by the Security Service, and that the activities
of the Security Service constituted an unjustified interference with their right to
respect for private life. They also brought complaints under Articles 10, 11, and
13.

The Commission's opinion
The Commission had to consider:

> Whether the surveillance of the activities of the applicants by the Security Service and
> the consequent compilation and retention of information concerning their private
> lives constituted a violation of their right to respect for private life contrary to Article
> 8 of the Convention. (para. 23)

In formulating an opinion the Commission, referring in particular to *Malone*
(above), recalled that:

> . . . the storing of information concerning a person's private life in a secret police
> register amounts to an interference with the right to respect for private life as
> guaranteed by Article 8, para 1 of the Convention. . . . It follows that secret surveillance
> activities for the purpose of gathering and storing on file information concerning a
> person's private life also constitutes an interference with this right. (para. 27)

In determining whether in this case the evidence pointed to such an
interference, the Commission recalled that:

> . . . 'an individual may, under certain conditions, claim to be a victim of a violation
> occasioned by the mere existence of secret measures – without having to allege that
> such measures were in fact applied to him'. (para. 29)
>
> . . .
> . . . In the present case the applicants have submitted a detailed affidavit by a former
> intelligence officer of MI5 which indicates that they were the subjects of secret
> surveillance by the Security Service because of their association with the National
> Council for Civil Liberties (NCCL) and that the information gathered about them
> comprises *inter alia* information concerning their private life and is kept in records
> maintained by the Security Service.
> . . . The Commission notes that the applicants do not allege that they were
> subjected to telephone or mail intercepts. Nevertheless Ms Massiter's evidence states

that they had been subject to 'indirect interception,' i.e. the recording of information about them which appeared in the telephone or mail intercepts of others.

... The interception and recording of such information, even though the applicants were not directly subject to interception, amounts in itself to an interference with the applicants' right to respect for private life and correspondence....

... Against the above background the Commission finds that the existence of practices permitting secret surveillance has been established and that there is a reasonable likelihood that the applicants were the subjects of secret surveillance and that the Security Service has compiled and retained information concerning their private lives. It follows that there has been an interference *inter alia* with the applicants' right to respect for their private life under Article 8, para. 1 of the Convention. (paras 33–36)

The next question which had to be considered was whether this interference was justified. First, was it in accordance with law? In seeking to answer this the Commission recalled that:

... the phrase 'in accordance with the law' includes requirements over and above compliance with the domestic law. The 'law' in question must be adequately accessible in the sense that the citizen must be able to have an indication that is adequate in the circumstances of the legal rules applicable to a given case. In addition 'a norm cannot be regarded as law unless it is formulated with sufficient precision to enable the citizen to regulate his conduct. He must be able – if need be with appropriate advice – to foresee, to a degree that is reasonable in the circumstances, the consequences which a given action may entail'. (para. 38)

The Commission therefore found that there had been a violation of Articles 8 and 13, and that it was unnecessary in the circumstances to consider the claims under Articles 10 and 11.

Comment

This case, although it comes after *Malone*, avoids some of the issues raised in that case in as much as there was no direct interception of communications. However, it pre-dates the Security Service Act 1989 which was passed by the UK to place the Security Service on a statutory basis. The unsatisfactory nature of the law prior to the passing of this Act is evident from the Commission's Opinion. However, the case of *G, H and I v UK* 15 EHRR CD 41, raised questions concerning the effectiveness of the new Act, and particularly the onus placed on applicants to establish that they are likely to have been the victims of surveillance – in this case positive vetting for civil service posts.

Cases pending under this article

There are several cases pending under Article 8, some of which raise interesting and novel issues.

V, W, X, Y and Z v UK (Application No. 22170/93) and *Laskey, Jaggard and Brown v UK* (Application Nos 21627/93 and 21974/93). Both these cases concern sado-masochistic sexual acts conducted in private for sexual gratification.

In these cases the applicants were charged with a series of offences under the Offences Against the Person Act 1861, including assault and wounding in connection with sado-masochistic acts between consenting adults in private.

On appeal to the House of Lords on a point of law, their lordships had held that consent was no defence to a prosecution for sado-masochistic acts which inflict actual bodily harm. The applicants complained that the convictions and penalties imposed violated their right to respect for their private life under Article 8 and that there was no justification for interference with such an intimate aspect of their private lives.

The Commission declared the applications admissible on 18 January 1995. In its report of 26 October 1995, the Commission – in the case of *Laskey, Jaggard and Brown* – concluded that there had been no violation of Article 8. The case has now been referred to the Court.

X, Y and Z v *UK* (Application No. 21830/93), concerning the refusal to recognise a female to male transsexual as the father of a child born to his cohabitee through artificial insemination by a donor, has now been referred to the Court.

Buckley v *UK* (Application No. 20348/92), concerning the rights of gypsies to obtain planning permission to occupy sites other than official ones, has been referred to the Court.

Roberts v *UK* (Application No. 21178/93), concerning the right of a mother to have access to her children, has been declared admissible by the Commission (19 EHRR CD 50).

Halford v *UK* (Application No. 20605/92), concerning the interception of the applicant's private telephone conversations by the police, the applicant herself being a senior police officer, has been declared admissible by the Commission.

Harold Gerrard v *UK* (Application No. 21451/93), concerning the alleged opening of a prisoner's correspondence with his lawyer and with the Commission, has been declared admissible.

Further reading
Andrews, J., 'Telephone Tapping in the UK' (1985) 10 *European Law Review* 68
Andrews, J., 'Access to Children in Care' (1988) 13 *European Law Review* 140
Deech, R., 'Unmarried Fathers and Human Rights' (1995) 4 *Journal of Child Law* 3
Douglas, G., Hebenton, B. and Thomas, T., 'The Right to Found a Family' (1992) 142 *New Law Journal* 488
Kodwo Bentil, J., 'Individual Rights and Telephone Tapping by the Police' (1980) 124 *Solicitors Journal* 472
Millns, S., 'Transexuality and the European Convention on Human Rights' [1992] *Public Law* 559
Morton, J., 'The Transsexual and the Law' (1985) 135 *New Law Journal* 1017
Mowbray, A., 'Anton Piller Orders versus Human Rights' (1989) 133 *Solicitors Journal* 1022
Pogany, I., 'Telephone Tapping and the European Convention on Human Rights' (1984) 134 *New Law Journal* 290
Reid, K., 'Child care cases and the European Convention on Human Rights' (1993) 2 *Journal of Child Law* 66

CHAPTER 9

ARTICLE NINE

Article 9

1. Everyone has the right to freedom of thought, conscience and religion; this right includes freedom to change his religion or belief and freedom, either alone or in community with others and in public or in private, to manifest his religion or belief, in worship, teaching, practice and observance.

2. Freedom to manifest one's religion or beliefs shall be subject only to such limitations as are prescribed by law and are necessary in a democratic society in the interests of public safety, for the protection of public order, health or morals, or for the protection of the rights and freedoms of others.

9.1 THE SCOPE OF THE ARTICLE

In deciding what constitutes a religion for the purpose of Article 9, the Commission has traditionally adopted a broad and somewhat vague approach. In cases involving the UK it has been raised in cases concerning Druidism (*Chappell*), pacifism (*Arrowsmith*), veganism (*H v UK*), recognised religions such as the Muslim faith (*Ahmad*), and religions practised by certain cults (*Church of X*). However, it is not so extensive so as to include the right to seek 'special category status' as a political prisoner (*McFeeley*); or to permit the publication of a blasphemous poem suggesting that Christ was a practising, promiscuous homosexual (*Gay News Ltd and Lemon*).

The rights conferred under Article 9 may be possessed and exercised by:

> . . . A church body, or an association with religious and philosophical objects (*Chappell* v *UK* 10 EHRR 510, para. 1);

or by an individual. However, it may be difficult for a corporation to establish that its rights have in fact been infringed compared to the rights of individual members, or indeed an unincorporated association. This was raised and considered in the case of the *Church of X* in which:

... the applicant corporation complains that its own rights to freedom of thought, conscience and religion have been infringed by the policy adopted by the United Kingdom Government . . . whereas the Commission considers, however, that a corporation being a legal and not a natural person, is incapable of having or exercising the rights mentioned in Article 9. ((1969) 12 *Yearbook* 306 at 314)

Article 9 indicates that a belief may be manifested in 'worship, teaching, practice and observance'. The interpretation of this was considered in the case of *Arrowsmith* v *UK* 6 EHRR 558, in which the issue was whether the distribution of leaflets by a pacifist could be regarded as an exercise of the right to freedom of thought, conscience and religion, and the manifestation of a belief. The Commission, while recognising pacifism as a philosophy and therefore as a belief falling within the scope of Article 9, expressed the opinion that the term 'practice' does not 'cover each act which is motivated or influenced by a religion or a belief'. The action or conduct must actually express the belief concerned; consequently a belief in pacificism did not extend to the right to manifest that belief by refusing to pay taxes, some of which might be used to finance armaments. Similarly, the freedom to manifest religion or belief 'in practice' cannot be interpreted to include the right for applicants to wear their own clothes in prison, or to be relieved from the requirement to do prison work (*McFeeley* v *UK* 3 EHRR 161).

The second paragraph of Article 9 provides for a number of exceptions, and so the provision cannot be regarded as conferring an absolute right but one which may justifiably be curtailed – for example, in the interests of maintaining good order in prison in accordance with the Prison Rules (*H* v *UK* 16 EHRR CD 44); in the interests of public safety, health and the rights and freedoms of others (*App. No. 9813/82* v *UK* 5 EHRR 513); for the preservation of ancient monuments (*Chappell* v *UK* 10 EHRR 510); for the protection of public order and the protection of the rights and freedoms of others (*Chappell*); to prevent blasphemy (*Gay News and Lemon* v *UK* 5 EHRR 123).

Even if the restriction is not one which falls under Article 9, para. 2, it is possible that the freedom to practice a particular religion may be influenced by the situation of the person claiming that freedom. This was considered in the case of *Ahmad* v *UK* 4 EHRR 126, in which the contractual obligations of the applicant and the requirements of the education system as a whole limited the right, but did not amount to a violation of Article 9.

It may also be possible to circumvent Article 9 by adopting measures which do not directly infringe the right to freedom of religion. In the case of *Church of X* v *UK* (above) the Government sought to restrict the practice of the Church following the publication of an adverse report on its activities which described the Church as 'a pseudo-philosophical cult the practice of which was potentially harmful to its adherents'. The Government could not prohibit the practice of the Church altogether, but could restrain its educational activities. To this end the College of the Church of X was no longer accepted as an educational establishment for the purposes of Home Office policy concerning the admission of foreign nationals, who consequently would not be regarded as students or granted work permits to teach at the college; neither would foreign delegates intending to attend a conference organised by the Church be admitted into the country.

It should also be noted that Article 9 may be argued in conjunction with Article 10 relating to freedom of expression, which itself contains a number of exceptions, or with Article 2 of the First Protocol.

9.2   THE CASES

Few cases are raised under Article 9 nowadays, its provisions being much more relevant in the light of events which took place during the Second World War – particularly the persecution of Jews.

Arrowsmith v *UK*
3 EHRR 218

The facts
The applicant was a convinced pacifist. She campaigned in support of her views and was active in an organisation advocating the withdrawal of troops from Northern Ireland. In September 1973 she was involved, with others, in the distributing of leaflets pertaining to this campaign, at an Army centre in Wiltshire. The police asked the group to stop distributing the leaflets. The applicant refused. She was arrested for conduct likely to cause a breach of the peace, and subsequently was charged with and tried for offences under the Incitement to Disaffection Act 1934. Her conviction was confirmed by the Court of Appeal, which stated that the leaflets were 'the clearest incitement to mutiny and desertion'.

The applicant complained of violations of Articles 5, 9, 10, and Article 14, read with Article 9 and/or Article 10.

The question before the Commission concerning Article 9 was:

> Whether or not the distribution of the leaflets concerned in this case can be regarded as an exercise of the applicant's right to freedom of thought, conscience and religion as being the manifestation of a belief and if so, whether the applicant's prosecution and conviction under the Incitement to Disaffection Act 1934 for having distributed the leaflets in question was necessary in a democratic society in the interests of public safety, for the protection of public order and the rights of others. (para. 60)

The Commission's opinion
It was accepted that the applicant was a pacifist. The Commission also accepted the Government's definition of pacifism as:

> ... The commitment, in both theory and practice, to the philosophy of securing one's political or other objectives without resort to the threat or use of force against another human being under any circumstances, even in response to the threat of or use of force. (para. 68)

The Commission was satisfied that pacifism as a philosophy fell within the ambit of the right to freedom of thought and conscience. The question therefore was whether the distribution of the leaflets was protected under Article 9 as being the 'manifestation of her pacifist belief'. The applicant's submission was that the distribution of the leaflets was the way in which she practised her belief.

The Commission did not consider that the term 'practice' could cover each act which is motivated or influenced by a religion or belief:

> . . . when the actions of individuals do not actually express the belief concerned they cannot be considered to be as such protected by Article 9(1), even when they are motivated or influenced by it. (para. 71)

The Commission noted that the leaflets were not addressed to the public at large, but specifically at British soldiers who might shortly be posted to Northern Ireland. The contents of the leaflets did not reflect a philosophy but opposition to British policy in Northern Ireland. Consequently, the Commission expressed the opinion that:

> . . . the applicant, by distributing the leaflets, did not manifest her belief in the sense of Article 9(1). It follows that her conviction and sentence for the distribution of these leaflets did not in any way interfere with the exercise of her rights under this provision.
>
> . . . The Commission is therefore unanimously of the opinion that Article 9(1) of the Convention has not been violated. (paras 75 and 76)

Although the Commission was unanimous, two separate opinions were given. Mr Opsahl, in his separate opinion, agreed with the Commission that a distinction could be drawn between manifestation and motivation. Only the latter should fall under Article 9, para. 1, but the line was a hard one to draw. Mr Klecker suggested that in fact a distinction could not be drawn between manifestation and motivation if it was accepted that practical action is an important part of the philosophy of pacifism. He considered that the distribution of the leaflet was an integral part of the applicant's belief. He considered that the Commission's interpretation of Article 9 was too narrow.

Comment

Although there are a number of laws in the UK which protect the armed forces and the police from attempts to subvert their allegiance or persuade them into breaches of duty, these are rarely used. The Incitement to Disaffection Act 1934, under which the applicant was charged, had been used very little since its introduction, and between 1956 and 1974 there were only four prosecutions. The Act had also been under consideration by the Law Reform Commission, although the Commission had not recommended its abolition, believing its existence to be compatible with the exception provided for under Article 10, para. 2 relating to national security. The fact that the applicant was prosecuted under the Act may have been referable to the situation in Northern Ireland at the time.

Ahmad v UK
4 EHRR 126

The facts

The applicant was a devout Muslim. He was also a school teacher. He was employed at a number of schools under the control of the London Education Authority (LEA). As a devout Muslim he was expected to offer prayers every

Friday, at a Mosque if distance permitted, otherwise by himself. During his teaching employment some of the schools he worked at allowed him time off to attend religious services, others did not. Usually if he did take time off, he did not return in time for the lesson immediately after lunch and his colleagues had to cover for him.

During his employment he requested the LEA to allow him to go to the Mosque for Friday prayer and asked that the necessary arrangements be made in the school time-table. The request was refused, and it was suggested that he give up full-time employment and apply for a part-time appointment which would enable him to attend the Mosque. The LEA refused to grant him leave of absence for any part of the Friday afternoon sessions. The applicant then decided to resign his job rather than accept part-time work.

In July 1975 the applicant applied to an industrial tribunal claiming to have been the victim of unfair dismissal under the Trade Union and Labour Relations Act 1974. The tribunal dismissed his application on the grounds that he was bound by his contract to be in school on Friday afternoons and to work full-time. Petition for review of this decision and an appeal to the Employment Appeal Tribunal were unsuccessful, as was appeal to the Court of Appeal.

The applicant claimed that the interpretation of s. 30 of the Education Act 1944 by the tribunals and by the Court of Appeal was in contravention of his rights under Article 9, because this interpretation meant that a practising Muslim could never accept employment as a full-time teacher.

The Commission's opinion
Although the Convention does not guarantee any right to employment as such, or the right to hold a position in public service, the Commission noted that:

> . . . the dismissal of a State official may in certain circumstances raise an issue under specific Convention provisions, such as Article 9 or Article 10. The Commission considers that this jurisprudence applies also in case of alleged forced resignation, or variation of employment, like that of the present applicant. It here notes that, in the United Kingdom, the legislation prohibiting unfair dismissal may also be invoked by employees who claim that they have been unfairly forced to resign. The Commission has consequently examined the applicant's complaint that he was forced to resign from full-time employment, under the specific provisions of Article 9 and of Article 14 in conjunction with Article 9 of the Convention.

> . . . With regard to the applicant's claim, that the school authorities should have arranged their time-table so that he could attend Friday prayers, the Commission further observes that the object of Article 9 is essentially that of protecting the individual against unjustified interference by the State, but that there may also be positive obligations inherent in an effective 'respect' for the individual's freedom of religion. (paras 2 and 3)

Article 9 includes the right of everyone to manifest his or her religion 'either alone or in community with others'. The issues raised in this case refer to the latter form of worship. In interpreting these provisions the Commission:

> . . . examined the ordinary meaning of the guarantee of the freedom of religion in paragraph (1) in the context both of Article 9 and of the Convention as a whole, taking into account the object and purpose of the Convention. It notes that the right to manifest one's religion 'in community with others' has always been regarded as an

essential part of the freedom of religion and finds that the two alternatives 'either alone or in community with others' in Article 9(1) cannot be considered as mutually exclusive, or as leaving a choice to the authorities, but only as recognising that religion may be practised in either form. It observes at the same time that the freedom of religion is not absolute but under the Convention subject to the limitations of Article 9(2). The Commission concludes that the applicant may under Article 9(1) claim the right to manifest his religion 'in community with others'. (para. 5)

Whether it was necessary for the applicant to manifest his religion in this way was a further issue. There was the problem of the inherent conflict with his contractual obligations as a full-time teacher.

. . . In the case of a person at liberty, the question of the 'necessity' of a religious manifestation, as regards its time and place, will not normally arise under Article 9. Nevertheless, even a person at liberty may, in the exercise of his freedom to manifest his religion, have to take into account his particular professional or contractual position. The parties' submissions in the present case concerning the 'necessity' of the applicant's attendance at the mosque are connected with their discussion of his special contractual obligations as a teacher.
. . .
. . . The Commission does not consider that the applicant has convincingly shown that, following his transfer in 1974 to a school 'nearer to mosques', he was required by Islam to disregard his continuing contractual obligations *vis-à-vis* the ILEA, entered into six years earlier in 1968 and accepted throughout the years, and to attend the mosque during school time.
. . .
. . . It finds that, in the present case, the ILEA was during the relevant period (1974/75) in principle entitled to rely on its contract with the applicant. However, the question arises whether, under Article 9 of the Convention, the ILEA had to give due consideration to his religious position.
. . . The Commission here notes that the applicant did not, when he was first interviewed for his teaching position, nor during the first six years of his employment with the ILEA, disclose the fact that he might require time off during normal school hours for attending prayers at the mosque. . . . (paras 7, 9, 13 and 14)

Comment
In the course of its report the Commission noted that in considering the parties' submissions it:

. . . had regard not only to the particular circumstances of the applicant's case but also to its background, as described in the pleadings. It notes that, during the relevant period, the United Kingdom society was with its increasing Muslim community in a period of transition. New and complex problems arose, *inter alia*, in the field of education, both as regards teachers and students. The parties agree that the applicant's case is not an isolated one and that it raises questions of general importance.
. . .
. . . The Commission accepts that the school authorities, in their treatment of the applicant's case on the basis of his contract with the ILEA, had to have regard not only to his religious position, but also to the requirements of the education system as a whole; it notes that the complex education system of the United Kingdom was during the relevant time faced with the task of gradual adaptation to new developments in its

society. The Commission is not called upon to substitute for the assessment by the national authorities of what might be the best policy in this field but only to examine whether the school authorities, in relying on the applicant's contract, arbitrarily disregarded his freedom of religion. (paras 17 and 19)

The problems posed by a multi-cultural, heterogeneous population are reflected in a number of cases involving the UK. These include issues relating to immigration, arranged marriages, definitions of blasphemy, philosophical convictions relating to education, etc. Interpretations and applications of the Convention have to keep abreast of social changes, but it may be many years before an apparent conflict of interests, such as was evident here, comes before the Commission. In the meantime self-help measures are likely to be adopted. In this case two emerged: absenteeism on the part of the applicant for a short while on Friday afternoons, which was, by and large, tolerated by his colleagues; and accommodation measures taken by some employers in the Midlands, as mentioned by the religious leader Dr Pasha, who provided evidence for the applicant.

ISKCON and Others v *UK*
(1991) 76-A D & R 90

The facts
ISKCON acquired a property in 1973 to establish a residential theological college for the teaching and promotion of the religion of Krishna Consciousness, a traditionalist branch of the Hindu Faith. Besides being used as a training college for Hindu priests, the premises were used as a place of pilgrimage and as a centre for devotional services which were open to the public. Festivals were also held on holy days in the Hindu calendar. The original agreement with the local authority was that no more than 1,000 persons would be allowed to visit the property in any one day, except for six festival days in the year when more than this number would be permitted.

Complaints were made about the excessive number of people coming to such festivals and also at other times, causing congestion in the small village in which the property was located and nuisance. ISKCON was served with an enforcement notice alleging material change of use amounting to a breach of planning control.

ISKCON alleged a violation of Article 9. Although the applicants accepted that the enforcement notice was lawful and served a legitimate purpose, they argued that the interference was not necessary in a democratic society and that the attitude of the authorities was not proportionate. They also alleged that the authorities had not given sufficient weight to the importance of the property as a place of worship and inspiration for Hindus.

The Commission's opinion
The applicants asked the Commission to adopt a narrow margin of appreciation under Article 9, in the light of an increasingly ethnically diverse Europe, and to construe the article according to international standards and developments, with particular reference to the United Nations Declaration on the

elimination of all forms of intolerance and discrimination based on religion or belief.

The Commission noted that:

> . . . ISKCON do not allege that the mere existence of planning legislation violated their rights under the Convention. Indeed, the Convention organs have found on several occasions that Contracting States enjoy a wide discretion in regulating planning matters (cf. Eur. Court H.R., *Sporrong and Lonnröth* judgment of 23 September 1982, Series A no. 52, p. 26 para. 69, and, in the context of the United Kingdom legislation, *Chater v the United Kingdom*, No. 11723/85, Dec. 7.5.87, D.R. 52 pp. 250, 256). It is against this background that the Commission must assess the compliance with Article 9 para. 2 of any interference with ISKCON's right under Article 9 para. 1 of the Convention.
>
> ISKCON Ltd is a registered charity in the United Kingdom. It is part of the International Society for Krishna Consciousness, which is the worldwide promoter of Vayishnavism, the worship of Krishna. ISKCON's use of Bhaktivedanta Manor began in 1973 when the Manor was acquired, and developed as the Manor became more successful and better known. The Commission is prepared to assume that the issue of the enforcement notices to limit use of the manor to that which was permitted when ISKCON acquired the manor amounts to an interference with ISKCON's freedom of religion, including the freedom to manifest that religion in worship, teaching, practice and observance.
>
> The Commission finds that the limitation on ISKCON's freedom to manifest its religion was prescribed by law in that the domestic town and country planning legislation was applied. It has not been suggested that that legislation was insufficiently clear or otherwise in conflict with the requirement that it be 'prescribed by law'. (pp. 105–106)

ISKCON accepted that the aim of the interference was to protect the rights of others, namely the residents of the nearby village. The Commission also found the aims of protecting public order and health.

As to whether the response of the local authority was proportionate, the Commission expressed the opinion that:

> . . . the decision of the local authority to control the use of the property by recourse to the statutory enforcement powers, rather than by means of contractual provisions, was (not) in the circumstances disproportionate to the legitimate aim. (p. 106)

As far as ISKCON's allegations that their right to religion had not been sufficiently taken into account was concerned, the Commission noted that:

> . . . although the courts were limited in their review of the Secretary of State's decision to confirm the enforcement notices, the Inspector who held an inquiry into the enforcement notices gave detailed consideration to the special circumstances of the case. Although he came to the conclusion that the special circumstances were not sufficient to outweigh the general planning considerations, the Commission finds that sufficient weight was given to the position of ISKCON and the difficulties faced if the use of Bhaktivedanta Manor was limited to that which was permitted in 1973. In particular, the Commission does not consider that Article 9 of the Convention can be used to circumvent existing planning legislation, provided that in the proceedings under that legislation, adequate weight is given to freedom of religion. In contending

that inadequate weight was given to ISKCON's freedom of religion, the applicants rely on statements in letters sent by Ministers and an official of the Department of the Environment to the effect that the decision on ISKCON's appeal against the enforcement notice was based on the relevant land-use planning grounds and that 'the religious aspects of the Society's activities at Bhaktivedanta Manor were not relevant'. The Commission does not interpret these statements as suggesting that the religious importance of the Manor to the members of ISKCON was not fully taken into account and weighed against the general planning considerations, but rather as making clear that the refusal of planning permission was based on proper planning grounds and not on any objections to the religious aspects of the activities of ISKCON. It is in any event clear from the terms of the Inspector's report and the decision letter of the Secretary of State that considerable weight was attached to the religious needs and interests of the members of ISKCON and to the importance of the Manor in relation to the religious activities of the members.

Accordingly, the Commission finds that the interference with ISKCON's right to freedom of religion under Article 9 of the Convention can be regarded as 'necessary in a democratic society'.

It follows that this part of the application is manifestly ill-founded within the meaning of Article 27 para. 2 of the Convention. (pp. 107–108)

Cases pending under this article

There are no cases currently pending under Article 9 involving the UK.

CHAPTER 10

ARTICLE TEN

Article 10

   1.   *Everyone has the right to freedom of expression. This right shall include freedom to hold opinions and to receive and impart information and ideas without interference by public authority and regardless of frontiers. This Article shall not prevent States from requiring the licensing of broadcasting, television or cinema enterprises.*

   2.   *The exercise of these freedoms, since it carries with it duties and responsibilities, may be subject to such formalities, conditions, restrictions or penalties as are prescribed by law and are necessary in a democratic society, in the interests of national security, territorial integrity or public safety, for the prevention of disorder or crime, for the protection of health or morals, for the protection of the reputation or rights of others, for preventing the disclosure of information received in confidence, or for maintaining the authority and impartiality of the judiciary.*

10.1 SCOPE OF THE ARTICLE

The Commission has held that:

> . . . freedom of expression constitutes one of the essential foundations of a democratic society and one of the basic conditions for its progress and each individual's self-fulfilment. (*Hodgson, Woolf Productions and National Union of Journalists and Channel Four Television* v *UK* (1987) 51 D & R 136 at 143)

The meaning of the words 'freedom of expression' is given some explanation in the text, but this is not exclusive. Thus its extent is left open. It could, for example, include the freedom to create works of art (*App. No. 9659* v *UK* 5 EHRR 581); freedom of publication in newspapers and journals (*Sunday Times* 2 EHRR 245) or in book form (*Handyside* 1 EHRR 737); and television programmes (*Hodgson, Woolf Productions and National Union of Journalists and Channel Four Television* 10 EHRR 503).

However, the concept of expression has limits. It has been held not to encompass any notion of the physical expression of feelings (*X* v *UK* 3 EHRR 63); nor to include the right to vote as such, or to stand for election or any other right covered in Article 3 of the First Protocol (*Liberal Party* v *UK* 4 EHRR 106); nor to entitle a prisoner to know the names of the members of the administrative committee dealing with his prisoner category classification (*Brady* v *UK* 3 EHRR 297), and it cannot be interpreted as guaranteeing the right to entertain in a particular public place (*App. No. 10317/83* v *UK* 6 EHRR 310 – legal restrictions on busking in public places did not interfere with applicants' right; they could busk elsewhere).

The right to impart information may extend to advertising of services or opinions (*X* v *UK* 4 EHRR 35, concerning the right of solicitors to advertise; *Colman* v *UK* Series A, Vol. 258-D). However, freedom to 'impart information and ideas' included under this article:

> . . . cannot be taken to include a general and unfettered right for any private citizen or organisation to have access to broadcasting time on radio and television in order to forward its opinion . . . [although] denial of broadcasting time to one or more specific groups or person may, in particular circumstances, raise an issue under Article 10 alone or in conjunction with Article 14. (*X and the Association of Z* v *UK* (1971) 14 *Yearbook* 538)

Article 10 clearly permits a Contracting State to subject radio and television broadcasting to certain regulations, and the practice in the different States will vary considerably. The Commission has accepted that the provisions of Article 10, para. 1 should be interpreted as permitting a State, in granting a licence to broadcasters, to exclude or restrict certain specified categories of advertisements. Therefore, where political broadcasting time was allowed only to political parties which were either represented in Parliament or had a certain number of candidates standing for election to Parliament, this was not considered to be a violation of the article (*X and the Association of Z* v *UK*). Where the imparting of information gives rise to criminal sanctions, interference with the right may be justified (*App. No. 10083/82* v *UK* 6 EHRR 50 at 140 – the State had a legitimate interest in interfering with those aiding and abetting suicide as an act of voluntary euthanasia).

The freedom conferred by Article 10 does not authorise the publication of defamatory material. If views are published without any prior restraint and these views are subsequently found to be libellous then the rights of others to protect their reputation is covered by Article 10, para. 2 (*S and M* v *UK* 18 EHRR CD 172, criticism of McDonald's business practices which attracted libel proceedings manifestly ill-founded).

The right to receive information relates to information which falls within areas of public interest (*Sunday Times* case, compared, for example, with the *Brady* case), and includes access to newspapers and periodicals which are generally available to the public (*X* v *UK* 5 EHRR 162). The right to receive information prohibits a government from restricting a person from receiving information which others might wish or might be willing to impart to him or her. In the *Brady* case it was suggested that the right to such information ought not to be interfered with by a public authority, but where it is the authority which holds the information and does not wish to impart it, it would seem that this is not a violation of Article 10 (*Gaskin* v *UK* 12 EHRR 36). Where the information relates to correspondence, the applicable provision is Article 8 rather than Article 10 (*McCallum* v *UK* 13 EHRR 587).

The right to freedom of expression is not absolute but is subject to a number of exceptions. The parameters of these exceptions have been closely considered in a number of cases involving the UK, notably *Handyside* v *UK* 1 EHRR 737 and *Sunday Times* v *UK* 2 EHRR 245. The Court has indicated consistently that these must be narrowly interpreted:

> . . . It is not sufficient that the interference involved belongs to that class of the exceptions listed in Article 10(2) . . . neither is it sufficient that the interference was imposed because its subject-matter fell within a particular category. (*Sunday Times* v *UK* Series A, No. 30, para. 65)

Therefore, not only does the right to freedom of expression have to be reasonably secured, enjoyed or exercised, but, because the two paragraphs are interdependent:

> . . . Any restriction affecting the exercise of the right to freedom of expression must be reasonably foreseeable or predictable. (*Sunday Times*, Judge Zekia's concurring opinion, pp. 58–9)

Where a restriction is 'prescribed by law', that law must be adequately accessible and formulated with sufficient precision. Any restriction must also be 'necessary in a democratic society'. It was held in the *Handyside* case that 'necessary' in this context:

> . . . is not synonymous with 'indispensable', neither has it the flexibility of such expressions as 'admissible', 'ordinary', 'useful', 'reasonable' or 'desirable'. (Series A, Vol. 24, para. 48)

There must be 'a pressing social need' implied in the notion of 'necessity' in this context. This means that the interference must have a legitimate aim. Even if this can be established – and the Contracting States have a fairly wide margin of appreciation here – the measures taken will have to be shown to be necessary, in that they must be shown to be proportionate to achieving the aim.

10.2   THE CASES

Most of the cases focus on whether an accepted interference is justified by being brought under Article 10, para. 2.

10.2.1   Forms of Censorship

Handyside v *UK*
Series A, Vol 24

The facts
The applicant was a publisher. In 1971 he prepared for publication a book entitled *The Little Red Schoolbook*. The book was intended for schoolchildren

aged 12 and upward, to be used as a reference book on Education, Learning, Teachers, Pupils and the System. This last chapter included a section on sex, which incorporated subsections on topics such as masturbation, menstruation, contraceptives, pornography etc., together with addresses for seeking further information and help. Once printing was completed the applicant sent out review copies and a press release. As a result of police inquiries following complaints made about the book, the applicant's business premises were searched and a number of the copies of the book were seized together with publicity material. The applicant was subsequently summoned under the Obscene Publications Act 1959 as amended by the Obscene Publications Act 1964, for having obscene books in his possession for publication for gain. The applicant was found guilty and fined. A forfeiture order was made for the destruction of the books. This decision was upheld on appeal.

The applicant complained that the action taken against him was in breach of his rights under Article 10 and under Article 1 of the First Protocol (he also claimed violations of a number of other articles, but these were rejected as inadmissible by the Commission).

The Commission's opinion
The Commission expressed the opinion that there had been no violation of Article 10 of the Convention by eight votes to five. The matter was referred to the Court.

The judgment of the Court
First, the Court held that:

> ... The various measures challenged – the applicant's criminal conviction, the seizure and subsequent forfeiture and destruction of the matrix and of hundreds of copies of the *Schoolbook* – were without any doubt, and the Government did not deny it, 'interferences by public authority' in the exercise of his freedom of expression which is guaranteed by paragraph 1 of the text cited above. Such interferences entail a 'violation' of Article 10 if they do not fall within one of the exceptions provided for in paragraph 2, which is accordingly of decisive importance in this case. (para. 43)

Such infringements must, in the first place, be 'prescribed by law'. The Court found that this requirement was met by the 1959 and 1964 Acts, which had, moreover, been correctly applied by the competent authorities.

Next the Court had to investigate whether the interferences were 'necessary in a democratic society ... for the protection of ... morals'. The aim of the Acts was legitimate, namely the protection of morals in a democratic society. The question was whether the measures taken, i.e. the restrictions and penalties complained of, were appropriate to that aim. This raised the issue of how far the Court was to go in interfering with the UK's margin of appreciation in this sphere. In clarifying the nature of its role, the Court pointed out that:

> ... the machinery of protection established by the Convention is subsidiary to the national systems safeguarding human rights. The Convention leaves to each Contracting State, in the first place, the task of securing the rights and freedoms it enshrines. The institutions created by it make their own contribution to this task but they become involved only through contentious proceedings and once all domestic remedies have been exhausted (Art. 26).

These observations apply, notably, to Article 10(2). In particular, it is not possible to find in the domestic law of the various Contracting States a uniform European conception of morals. The view taken by their respective laws of the requirements of morals varies from time to time and from place to place, especially in our era which is characterised by a rapid and far-reaching evolution of opinions on the subject. By reason of their direct and continuous contact with the vital forces of their countries, State authorities are in principle in a better position than the international judge to give an opinion on the exact content of these requirements as well as on the 'necessity' of a 'restriction' or 'penalty' intended to meet them. The Court notes at this juncture that, whilst the adjective 'necessary', within the meaning of Article 10(2), is not synonymous with 'indispensable', neither has it the flexibility of such expressions as 'admissible', 'ordinary', 'useful', 'reasonable' or 'desirable'. Nevertheless, it is for the national authorities to make the initial assessment of the reality of the pressing social need implied by the notion of 'necessity' in this context.

Consequently, Article 10(2) leaves to the Contracting States a margin of appreciation. This margin is given both to the domestic legislator ('prescribed by law') and to the bodies, judicial amongst others, that are called upon to interpret and apply the laws in force.

. . . Nevertheless, Article 10(2) does not give the Contracting States an unlimited power of appreciation. The Court, which, with the Commission, is responsible for ensuring the observance of those States' engagements, is empowered to give the final ruling on whether a 'restriction' or 'penalty' is reconcilable with freedom of expression as protected by Article 10. The domestic margin of appreciation thus goes hand in hand with a European supervision. Such supervision concerns both the aim of the measure challenged and its 'necessity'; it covers not only the basic legislation but also the decision applying it, even one given by an independent court. In this respect, the Court refers to Article 50 of the Convention ('decision or . . . measure taken by a legal authority or any other authority') as well as to its own case-law.

The Court's supervisory functions oblige it to pay the utmost attention to the principles characterising a 'democratic society'. Freedom of expression constitutes one of the essential foundations of such a society, one of the basic conditions for its progress and for the development of every man. Subject to Article 10(2), it is applicable not only to 'information' or 'ideas' that are favourably received or regarded as inoffensive or as a matter of indifference, but also to those that offend, shock or disturb the State or any sector of the population. Such are the demands of that pluralism, tolerance and broadmindedness without which there is no 'democratic society'. This means, amongst other things, that every 'formality', 'condition', 'restriction' or 'penalty' imposed in this sphere must be proportionate to the legitimate aim pursued.

From another standpoint, whoever exercises his freedom of expression undertakes 'duties and responsibilities' the scope of which depends on his situation and the technical means he uses. The Court cannot overlook such a person's 'duties' and 'responsibilities' when it enquires, as in this case; whether 'restrictions' or 'penalties' were conducive to the 'protection of morals' which made them 'necessary' in a 'democratic society'.

. . . It follows from this that it is in no way the Court's task to take the place of the competent national courts but rather to review under Article 10 the decisions they delivered in the exercise of their power of appreciation.

However, the Court's supervision would generally prove illusory if it did no more than examine these decisions in isolation; it must view them in the light of the case as a whole, including the publication in question and the arguments and evidence adduced by the applicant in the domestic legal system and then at the international level. The Court must decide, on the different data available to it, whether the reasons given by the national authorities to justify the actual measures of 'interference' they take are relevant and sufficient under Article 10(2). (paras 48–50)

In this particular case the Court closely examined the judgment of the domestic court. It took particular notice of the attention paid by the court to the fact that the publication was directed at young people, and concluded that:

... the fundamental aim of the judgment of 29 October 1971, applying the 1959/1964 Acts, was the protection of the morals of the young, a legitimate purpose under Article 10(2). Consequently the seizures effected on 31 March and 1 April 1971, pending the outcome of the proceedings that were about to open, also had this aim. (para. 52)

In considering whether the measures taken were necessary, the court noted that many Contracting States had seizure measures similar to those found under the English Acts, and expressed the view that the seizure of large stocks of the book was necessary if young people were to be protected against reading the book.

The fact that the book had been published freely in other countries which were member States of the Council of Europe, did not mean that the decision taken by the English court was not within the margin of appreciation allowed to the UK. As the Court pointed out:

... The Contracting States have each fashioned their approach in the light of the situation obtaining in their respective territories; they have had regard, *inter alia*, to the different views prevailing there about the demands of the protection of morals in a democratic society. The fact that most of them decided to allow the work to be distributed does not mean that the contrary decision of the Inner London Quarter Sessions was a breach of Article 10. Besides, some of the editions published outside the United Kingdom do not include the passages, or at least not all the passages, cited in the judgment of 29 October 1971 as striking examples of a tendency to 'deprave and corrupt'. (para. 57)

The Court did not consider that the measures taken in the circumstances were draconian or unnecessary. Although it might have been open to the State to request the applicant to expurgate the book or restrict its distribution, Article 10 does not oblige the Contracting States to introduce prior censorship. The Court therefore concluded that no breach of the requirements of Article 10 had been established.

Judge Mosler expressed a dissenting opinion. While accepting that the measures taken had a legitimate aim and were prescribed by law, Judge Mosler argued that:

... Since the criteria in Article 10(2) are autonomous concepts, the Court must investigate both whether it was 'necessary' for the domestic authorities to have recourse to the means they employed to achieve the aim and whether they overstepped the national margin of appreciation with a resultant violation of the common standard guaranteed by an autonomous concept.

What is 'necessary' is not the same as what is indispensable. Such a definition would be too narrow and would not correspond to the usage of this word in domestic law. On the other hand, it is beyond question that the measure must be appropriate for achieving the aim. However, a measure cannot be regarded as inappropriate, and hence not 'necessary', just because it proves ineffectual by not achieving its aim. A measure likely to be effectual under normal conditions cannot be deprived of its legal basis after the event by failure to attain the success which it might have had in more favourable circumstances.

The greater part of the first edition of the book circulated without impediment. The measures taken by the competent authorities and confirmed by the Inner London Quarter Sessions prevented merely the distribution of under 10 per cent of the impression. The remainder, that is about 90 per cent, reached the public including probably, to a large extent, the adolescents meant to be protected . . . . The measures in respect of the applicant thus had so little success that they must be taken as ineffectual in relation to the aim pursued. In fact young people were not protected against the influence of the book that had been qualified as likely to 'deprave and corrupt' them by the authorities, acting within their legitimate margin of appreciation.

The ineffectualness of the measures would in no way prevent their being considered appropriate if it had been due to circumstances beyond the influence and control of the authorities. However, that was not the case. Certainly it cannot be presumed that the measures were not taken in good faith and with the genuine intention of preventing the book's circulation. Above all, the carefully reasoned judgment of the Inner London Quarter Sessions excludes such a presumption. Nevertheless, from an objective point of view, the measures actually taken against the book's circulation could never have achieved their aim without being accompanied by other measures against 90 per cent of the impression. Yet nothing in the case file, in particular in the addresses of those appearing before the Court, shows that action of this kind was attempted.

Under Article 10(2), the authorities' action in certain respects and their lack of action in others must be viewed as a whole. The aim, legitimate under Article 10(2) of restricting freedom of expression in order to protect the morals of the young against *The Little Red Schoolbook*, is one and indivisible. The result of the authorities' action as well as of their inaction must be attributed to the British State. It is responsible for the application of measures that were not appropriate with regard to the aim pursued because they covered only one small part of the object of the prosecution without taking the others into account.

Accordingly, the measures chosen by the authorities were, by their very nature, inappropriate.

. . . It must follow that the action complained of was not 'necessary', within the meaning of Article 10(2), with regard to the aim pursued. Such a measure is not covered by the exceptions to which freedom of expression can be subjected, even if the aim is perfectly legitimate and if the qualification of what is moral in a democratic society remained within the framework of the State's margin of appreciation.

The right enshrined in Article 10(1) is so valuable for every democratic society that the criterion of necessity, which, when combined with other criteria, justifies an exception to the principle, must be examined from every aspect suggested by the circumstances.

Comment

Under the Obscene Publications Act 1959 amended by the 1964 Act, a defence is available under s. 4, if 'it is proved that the publication of the article in question is justified as being for the public good on the ground that it is in the interests of science, literature, art or learning, or of other objects of general concern'. Moreover, the authorities appeared often to adopt a non-contentious approach by simply issuing a warning or caution rather than instituting criminal proceedings. However, the non-contentious procedure was available only if the individual concerned admitted that the article was obscene and consented to its destruction. This non-contentious procedure was abandoned in 1973.

The book had first been published in Danish in 1969, and subsequently in translation in other countries including Belgium, France, Greece, Iceland, Italy, Norway and Sweden. The book was not the subject of proceedings in Northern Ireland, the Channel Islands or the Isle of Man. This fact was relied on by the applicant to support his case that the measures taken were not necessary or proportionate. However, the Obscene Publications Act did not apply to Northern Ireland or to Scotland; although proceedings were commenced in Scotland against a bookseller, these were subsequently dropped. This lack of action by other authorities, together with the toleration of the book in other countries, did not persuade the Court that criminal proceedings and seizure were not necessary and therefore justified. Neither did the fact that about 18,000 copies of a print run of 20,000 escaped seizure and found their way on to the market. (It should be noted that a revised edition of the book came out in November 1971 and there were no criminal proceedings in connection with it.)

The scope of the Obscene Publications Act 1959 was again considered in *App. No. 9615/81* v *UK* 5 EHRR 581, in which the Commission expressed the view that a legal person, here a company, could complain of a violation of a right under Article 10. Also that the right could be invoked by the author or editor, and the publisher.

The problem of censorship also arose in the following case.

Gay News Ltd and Lemon v UK
5 EHRR 123

The facts
This case involved the issue of blasphemous libel. The facts of the case have been mentioned in connection with Article 7. Under Article 10, the applicants complained that their conviction and punishment for blasphemous libel involved a violation of the right to freedom of expression.

The Commission's opinion
There was no doubt that the applicants' freedom of expression had been interfered with. The Commission had to decide whether such interference was justified.

The question whether this interference was prescribed by law caused some problems and had to be decided having regard to Article 7, because of the criminal sanction involved. After consideration the Commission expressed the opinion that the interference was prescribed by law.

In considering whether this interference had a legitimate purpose, the Government had invoked three grounds: the prevention of disorder, protection of morals and protection of the rights of others. However, as noted by the Commission, the Government itself had not undertaken a public prosecution, the matter had arisen by way of a private prosecution. Therefore it could not be said that:

> . . . the public interest (prevention of disorder and protection of morals) was so preponderant that it provided the real basis for the interference with the applicants' right to freedom of expression. In the circumstances, the justifying ground for the restriction must therefore primarily be sought in the protection of the rights of the private prosecutor. The Commission considers that the offence of blasphemous libel as it is construed under the applicable common law in fact has the main purpose to protect the right of citizens not to be offended in their religious feelings by publications. This was the thrust of the arguments put before the jury by the trial judge, arguments which were subsequently confirmed by the higher courts in this case. The Commission therefore concludes that the restriction was indeed covered by a legitimate purpose recognised in the Convention, namely the protection of the rights of others. (para. 11)

To decide whether the restrictions imposed to meet this purpose were necessary, the Commission:

> . . . first observes that the existence of an offence of blasphemy does not as such raise any doubts as to its necessity: If it is accepted that the religious feelings of the citizen may deserve protection against indecent attacks on the matters held sacred by him, then it can also be considered as necessary in a democratic society to stipulate that such attacks, if they attain a certain level of severity, shall constitute a criminal offence triable at the request of the offended person. It is in principle left to the legislation of the State concerned how it wishes to define the offence, provided that the principle of proportionality, which is inherent in the exception clause of Article 10(2), is being respected. The Commission considers that the offence of blasphemous libel as laid down in the common law of England in fact satisfies these criteria. In particular it does not seem disproportionate to the aim pursued that the offence is one of strict liability incurred irrespective of the intention to blaspheme and irrespective of the intended audience and of the possible avoidability of the publication by a certain member of the public. The issue of the applicants' journal containing the incriminated poem was on sale to the general public, it happened to get known in some way or other to the private prosecutor who was so deeply offended that she decided to take proceedings against the publication of this poem, and the outcome of these proceedings showed that not only the private prosecutor herself, but also the judicial authorities of all degrees were convinced of its blasphemous nature. The Commission therefore considers that the application of the blasphemy law could be considered as necessary in the circumstances of this case. . . . (para. 12)

The complaint of the applicants was therefore manifestly ill-founded.

A different form of censorship, but nevertheless a restriction on freedom of expression, arose in the following two cases.

Arrowsmith v UK
3 EHRR 218

The facts
The facts of this case have been indicated under Article 9. The applicant, an avowed pacifist, was convicted under the Incitement to Disaffection Act 1934

for distributing leaflets to troops stationed at an army camp. The content of the leaflets was directed at trying to seduce them from their duty or allegiance in relation to serving in Northern Ireland. The applicant claimed that her rights under Article 10 had been interfered with unjustifiably.

The Commission's opinion

There was no doubt that the applicant's rights had been interfered with. This followed from the applicant's arrest, prosecution and punishment. The only question was whether this had been justified under Article 10, para. 2.

First, the Commission had to consider whether the interference was prescribed by law. Clearly there was a relevant statute, but the applicant argued that the Incitement to Disaffection Act 1934 was vaguely worded and therefore uncertain. The words complained of in particular were 'maliciously and advisedly' and 'to seduce'. However, the Commission considered that the statute was not so vague that it was impossible to determine what acts or omissions were subject to criminal liability.

Next the Commission had to consider whether the law pursued one of the permitted aims stated under the exceptions. The Government's argument was that the Act served to protect national security, the prevention of disorder and the protection of the rights of others. The Commission accepted that:

> . . . the desertion of soldiers can even in peace-time, create a threat to 'national security' in that it tends to weaken the army's role as an instrument destined in a democratic society to protect it from internal or external threats . . . The Commission accepts that the maintenance of 'order' within the armed forces requires strict measures to prevent desertion. (para. 85)

Therefore the aims of the Act were consonant with the provisions of Article 10, para. 2.

Were the actual measures taken against the applicant necessary in a democratic society? The Commission noted that not every violation of the Act resulted in similar measures, as the Director of Public Prosecutions had to consent to prosecution.

The applicant had argued that all she was doing was expressing an opinion and that the soldiers had a right to receive such information. The Commission expressed the opinion that the applicant went further than simply expressing a political opinion. The Commission relied on the evidence of the courts involved in the case:

> . . . The applicant was not convicted for statements showing her discontent with British policy in Northern Ireland. She was convicted because in the leaflets distributed she encouraged individual soldiers to disaffection indicating specific means of assistance.
>
> . . . As regards the justification of prosecution in the applicant's case, the Commission observes that both the Director of Public Prosecutions and the courts dealing with the case attached particular importance to the facts that the leaflet was aimed at and distributed to soldiers who might shortly be posted to Northern Ireland and that the applicant herself had behaved in a way which made it clear that she would go on distributing the leaflets unless strict measures were taken to stop her.

. . . In all these circumstances, the Commission considers that the applicant's prosecution, conviction and sentence under the 1934 Act served an aim which was consistent with Article 10(2) of the Convention, namely the protection of national security and the prevention of disorder within the army. (paras 92–94)

Were the measures nevertheless necessary? The Commission stated that:

. . . The notion 'necessary' implies a 'pressing social need' which may include the clear and present danger test and must be assessed in the light of the circumstances of a given case.

. . . As regards the decision to prosecute the applicant, the Commission notes that the Director of Public Prosecutions took into account, when deciding to consent to prosecution, the difficult situation in Northern Ireland and the possible effect of the campaign, which the applicant supported by distributing the leaflets, if this campaign was not stopped.

. . . The Commission accepts that, in view of the applicant's manifest intention to continue her action unless stopped by prohibitive measures, the decision to prosecute her was necessary for the protection of national security and the prevention of disorder in the army. (paras 95–97)

As regards the sentence which the applicant received, the Commission expressed the opinion that:

. . . the sentence which the applicant finally received and served (seven months' imprisonment), although admittedly severe, was not in the circumstances so clearly out of proportion to the legitimate aims pursued that this severity in itself could render unjustifiable such an interference which the Commission otherwise has held justified.

. . . The Commission is therefore of the opinion by 11 votes against one that the restriction imposed on the applicant's right to freedom of expression was justified under Article 10(2) of the Convention. (paras 99 and 100)

A dissenting opinion was expressed by Mr Opsahl, who was of the view that:

. . . The aim of influencing others who are themselves responsible for their actions is an essential and legitimate aspect of the exercise of freedom of expression and opinion, in political and other matters. If others are in fact led to accept such beliefs, opinions or ideas or make use of information which has been imparted to them with a view to influencing them, they do so mainly on their own responsibility. Whether the matter is seen under Article 9 or Article 10 or both, the justification and need for punishing those, who merely try to influence others by an otherwise 'pure' exercise of these rights, must be examined in this perspective.

. . . On the facts of the present case I consider its nature and essence to be that a political offence was seen as a potential threat to public policy, but that the applicant did not in the circumstances actually endanger national security or undermine order in the army, which are the justifications accepted by the Commission, or at most she did so only very indirectly. No link has been shown to the Commission between her own specific acts and actual dangers to these interests. In fact, under the law applied to her by the domestic courts, the prosecution was not required to show any such link, while she on the other hand was not allowed to show that no such dangers actually existed. (paras 6 and 7)

Mr Klecker also dissented, emphasising the importance of protecting freedom of expression, particularly pacifism, in the contemporary context.

Comment

Mr Opsahl referred in his judgment to the historic background of the Act, and pointed to the danger of applying an Act passed in a totally different political context to the present situation. When the Bill which preceded the Act was before Parliament, there was some debate concerning the actual wording. The Incitement to Mutiny Act 1797, which this Act partially replaced, necessitated trial on indictment in every case, with a maximum penalty of life imprisonment. The 1934 Act permitted a summary procedure and a much reduced maximum penalty.

Tolstoy Miloslavsky v *UK*
Series A, Vol. 316

The Facts

The applicant had written a pamphlet alleging that the warden of Winchester College had been involved in various war crimes concerning the handing over of Cossack and Yugoslav prisoners and refugees to the Soviet authorities. Following the distribution of the pamphlet the applicant had been sued for libel and ordered to pay £1,500,000 in damages. In seeking an appeal against the finding the applicant was ordered to provide security for the costs of the plaintiff should the appeal be unsuccessful – a sum of £124,900. This security was not found and therefore the appeal was dismissed.

The application to the Commission alleged breaches of Article 6: first, that the proceedings had been unfair and, secondly, that there had been a violation of the applicant's right to access to court, because of the requirement to meet the security for the costs of the appeal. The applicant also claimed a breach of Article 10, in that the measure taken (the security) was neither prescribed by law nor necessary.

The Commission's opinion

The Commission declared the application admissible as regards the violation of the right of access to court and the right to freedom of expression. In its report the Commission had found that there was no violation of Article 6, para. 1, but that there was a violation of Article 10. Following unsuccessful attempts to arrive at a friendly settlement the matter was referred to the Court.

The judgment of the Court

The issues before the Court concerned the size of the original libel damages awarded against the applicant by the High Court jury (£1.5 million), and the order made by the Court of Appeal that the applicant deposit a security for the plaintiff's costs in the case of an appeal. The applicant claimed that these constituted an interference with his right to freedom of expression. In particular, that the amount of damages was not prescribed by law.

The Court held that the relevant legal rules concerning damages for libel were formulated with sufficient precision; although there was a considerable degree of flexibility of national laws in this area, this was justified. It was not a requirement of precision that the applicant could foresee the quantum of damages likely to be awarded. Even so, the discretion of the jury in this matter was not unfettered but subject to a number of limitations and safeguards.

Further, the award and the injunction satisfied the requirement of a legitimate aim, i.e. the protection of the reputation of others.

However, the Court did not consider that the size of the award was necessary in a democratic society. The Court had to consider only the assessment of the award by the jury, not the finding of libel. The Court held that:

> The jury had been directed not to punish the applicant but only to award an amount that would compensate the non-pecuniary damage to Lord Aldington. The sum awarded was three times the size of the highest libel award previously made in England and no comparable award had been made since. An award of the size in question must be particularly open to question where the substantive national law applicable at the time failed itself to provide a requirement of proportionality.
>
> At the material time the national law allowed great latitude to the jury as the Court of Appeal could not set aside an award simply on the grounds that it was excessive but only if it was so unreasonable that it could not have been made by sensible people but must have been arrived at capriciously, unconscionably or irrationally. (paras 49 and 50).

The Court therefore found that there had been a violation of the applicant's rights under Article 10. However, as regards the injunction which was framed to prevent the applicant from repeating the libellous allegations, the Court found that this measure did not amount to a disproportionate interference with the applicant's rights under Article 10.

10.2.2   Contempt of Court

Sunday Times v *UK*
Series A, Vol. 30

The facts
Since 1968, the *Sunday Times* had published a number of articles concerning issues raised by controversy concerning the drug Thalidomide, manufactured by Distillers Company (Biochemicals) Ltd and marketed between 1958 and 1961. Use of the drug by pregnant women had resulted in a number of babies being born with deformities, and there were allegations of negligence on the part of the manufacturers. Between 1962 and 1966 writs had been issued by parents and lengthy negotiations for compensation payments were taking place. Some settlements had been agreed. No cases had proceeded to trial at the time that the *Sunday Times* published its articles. Nevertheless, in November 1972, the Attorney-General obtained an injunction restraining the *Sunday Times* from publishing an article which dealt with the testing, manufacture and marketing of the drug. The ground for the injunction was that the article's publication would constitute contempt of court. The High Court granted the injunction, and although it was rescinded by the Court of Appeal, it was restored by the House of Lords in August 1973, finally being discharged in 1976. The article that had given rise to the injunction was published in modified form shortly afterwards.

The *Sunday Times* – the editor, publisher and a group of journalists – claimed that this injunction infringed their right to freedom of expression, which was not justified by a pressing social need.

The Commission's opinion

The Commission expressed the opinion that there had been a breach of Article 10 due to the injunction. The case was referred to the Court.

The judgment of the Court

Clearly there had been an interference with the applicants' freedom of expression. The problem arose as to whether or not it had been 'prescribed by law'. The applicable law at the time was the common law of contempt, which had been described by the Phillimore Report (Cmnd. 5794 (1974)).

Under the common law offence there was – as admitted by the Phillimore Report – 'a lack of clear definition of the kind of statement, criticism or comment that will be held to amount to contempt'. It was also not clear whether publication would amount to contempt only if it appeared after the issue of a writ, or when proceedings were 'imminent'. The High Court in its judgment had indicated that there should be no comment on a case until its conclusion, particularly because in this case any such comment might prejudice the free choice and conduct of the party to the litigation by improperly imposing pressure to settle.

The Court of Appeal had rescinded the injunction on the grounds that the proceedings were dormant and that freedom of expression should prevail. While trial by newspaper should not be allowed:

> ... the public interest in a matter of national concern had to be balanced against the interest of the parties in a fair trial or settlement; in the present case, the public interest in discussion outweighed the potential prejudice to a party. The law did not prevent comment when litigation was dormant and not being actively pursued. Moreover, since the law did not prevent comment on litigation which had ended or had not started, there was nothing to prevent comment on the 62 cases settled in 1968 or the 123 cases in which writs had not been issued. Even in September 1972, the proposed article would not have amounted to contempt: it was fair comment on a matter of public interest; it did not prejudice pending litigation because that litigation had been dormant for years and still was; and the pressure the article was intended to bring to bear was legitimate. In addition, it would be discrimination of the worst kind to continue to enjoin *The Sunday Times* alone when Parliament and other newspapers had discussed the matter since November 1972. (para. 25)

The House of Lords restored the injunction largely on the ground that the proceedings were not dormant.

Although this was a common law offence, the Court observed that the term 'prescribed by law' included both written and common law. In interpreting what this meant the Court held:

> ... the following are two of the requirements that flow from the expression 'prescribed by law'. First, the law must be adequately accessible: the citizen must be able to have an indication that is adequate in the circumstances of the legal rules applicable to a given case. Secondly, a norm cannot be regarded as a 'law' unless it is formulated with sufficient precision to enable the citizen to regulate his conduct: he must be able – if need be with appropriate advice – to foresee, to a degree that is reasonable in the circumstances, the consequences which a given action may entail. Those consequences need not be foreseeable with absolute certainty: experience shows this to be

unattainable. Again, whilst certainty is highly desirable, it may bring in its train excessive rigidity and the law must be able to keep pace with changing circumstances. Accordingly, many laws are inevitably couched in terms which, to a greater or lesser extent, are vague and whose interpretation and application are questions of practice. (para. 49)

The Court considered that both the 'pressure principle' and the 'prejudgment principle' were formulated with sufficient precision to enable the applicants to foresee the consequences that publication might entail. The interference was therefore prescribed by law.

The aim of the law of contempt of safeguarding the impartiality and authority of the judiciary was considered to be a legitimate aim. The Court held that:

... The term 'judiciary' ('*pouvoir judiciaire*') comprises the machinery of justice or the judicial branch of government as well as the judges in their official capacity. The phrase 'authority of the judiciary' includes, in particular, the notion that the courts are, and are accepted by the public at large as being, the proper forum for the ascertaintment of legal rights and obligations and the settlement of disputes relative thereto; further, that the public at large have respect for and confidence in the courts' capacity to fulfil that function. (para. 55)

The more difficult question was whether in fact the interference with the applicants' freedom of expression was directed at this aim. In deciding this the Court considered the reasoning of the House of Lords which was:

— by 'prejudging' the issue of negligence, it would have led to disrespect for the processes of the law or interfered with the administration of justice; it was of a kind that would expose Distillers to public and prejudicial discussion of the merits of their case, such exposure being objectionable as it inhibits suitors generally from having recourse to the courts;
— it would subject Distillers to pressure and to the prejudices of prejudgment of the issues in the litigation, and the law of contempt was designed to prevent interference with recourse to the courts;
— prejudgment by the press would have led inevitably in this case to replies by the parties, thereby creating the danger of a 'trial by newspaper' incompatible with the proper administration of justice;
— the courts owe it to the parties to protect them from the prejudices of prejudgment which involves their having to participate in the flurries of pre-trial publicity.

The Court regards all these various reasons as falling within the aim of maintaining the 'authority . . . of the judiciary' as interpreted by the Court in the second sub-paragraph of paragraph 55 above.

Accordingly, the interference with the applicants' freedom of expression had an aim that is legitimate under Article 10(2). (para. 57)

Was this interference necessary in a democratic society? Although a wide margin of appreciation is given to the Contracting States, it is not unlimited, nor is the margin of appreciation identical for all of the grounds stated under Article 10, para. 2. Thus this case was distinguishable from that of *Handyside* ('the protection of morals') where a wider margin of appreciation might be given than here ('authority of the judiciary').

. . . The domestic law and practice of the Contracting States reveal a fairly substantial measure of common ground in this area. This is reflected in a number of provisions of the Convention, including Article 6, which have no equivalent as far as 'morals' are concerned. Accordingly, here a more extensive European supervision corresponds to a less discretionary power of appreciation. (para. 59)

It was argued, before both the Commission and the Court, that the inclusion of the phrase 'authority of the judiciary' had been essential to cover the institution of contempt of court which was peculiar to common law countries. The Court did not entirely accept this:

. . . However, even if this were so, the Court considers that the reason for the insertion of those words would have been to ensure that the general aims of the law of contempt of court should be considered legitimate aims under Article 10(2) but not to make that law the standard by which to assess whether a given measure was 'necessary'. If and to the extent that Article 10(2) was prompted by the notions underlying either the English law of contempt of court or any other similar domestic institution, it cannot have adopted them as they stood: it transposed them into an autonomous context. It is 'necessity' in terms of the Convention which the Court has to assess, its rôle being to review the conformity of national acts with the standards of that instrument.
. . . the main purpose of the Convention is 'to lay down certain international standards to be observed by the Contracting States in their relations with persons under their jurisdiction'. This does not mean that absolute uniformity is required and, indeed, since the Contracting States remain free to choose the measures which they consider appropriate, the Court cannot be oblivious of the substantive or procedural features of their respective domestic laws. (paras 60 and 61)

The final question before the Court was whether the measure used – the injunction – corresponded to a 'pressing social need'. Was it 'proportionate to the legitimate aim pursued' and were the reasons given by the UK 'relevant and sufficient'? In considering this the Court took into account a number of factors. First, would the publication of the article really have increased the pressure on Distillers to settle? The Court thought not. Secondly, did the proposed article amount to 'trial by media'? The Court held that the article was couched in moderate language. It expressed both sides of the argument. It would not, therefore, have had adverse consequences on the 'authority of the judiciary'. Thirdly, the negotiations had been going on for some time. When the injunction was discharged some of these were still in progress, yet at that stage an injunction was no longer necessary. The Court held that there was sufficient public interest in the issues raised by the thalidomide cases to justify discussion. The public had a right to receive such ideas. Article 10 guarantees the freedom of the press to inform the public, and the right of the public to be properly informed. In weighing the competing interests the Court observed that:

. . . In September 1972, the case had, in the words of the applicants, been in a 'legal cocoon' for several years and it was, at the very least, far from certain that the parents' actions would have come on for trial. There had also been no public enquiry . . .
The Government and the minority of the Commission point out that there was no prohibition on discussion of the 'wider issues', such as the principles of the English law of negligence, and indeed it is true that there had been extensive discussion in various circles especially after, but also before, the Divisional Court's initial decision.

. . . However, the Court considers it rather artificial to attempt to divide the 'wider issues' and the negligence issue. The question of where responsibility for a tragedy of this kind actually lies is also a matter of public interest.

It is true that, if *The Sunday Times* article had appeared at the intended time, Distillers might have felt obliged to develop in public, and in advance of any trial, their arguments on the facts of the case . . .; however, those facts did not cease to be a matter of public interest merely because they formed the background to pending litigation. By bringing to light certain facts, the article might have served as a brake on speculative and unenlightened discussion.

. . . Having regard to all the circumstances of the case and on the basis of the approach described in paragraph 65 above, the Court concludes that the interference complained of did not correspond to a social need sufficiently pressing to outweigh the public interest in freedom of expression within the meaning of the Convention. The Court therefore finds the reasons for the restraint imposed on the applicants not to be sufficient under Article 10(2). That restraint proves not to be proportionate to the legitimate aim pursued; it was not necessary in a democratic society for maintaining the authority of the judiciary.

. . . There has accordingly been a violation of Article 10. (paras 66–68)

Dissenting opinions were expressed by nine judges. The main ground of their dissent rested on the interpretation of 'necessity' of the interference, and the margin of appreciation to be allowed to the UK.

Comment

The unsatisfactory nature of the common law of contempt had already attracted attention. The Interdepartmental Committee on the Law of Contempt had published a report on the effect of the law on tribunals of inquiry in 1969 (Cmnd. 4078), and the Phillimore Committee had been set up in 1971, the report being submitted to Parliament in December 1974 after the *Sunday Times* litigation. The report recommended that the law needed to be reformed in order to redress the balance between public interest in the administration of justice and the freedom of the press. It considered that the balance had shifted too far in favour of the former. There was also a need to achieve greater certainty in the law. The test recommended by the report was:

. . . whether the publication complained of creates a risk that the course of justice will be seriously impeded or prejudiced. (para. 36)

The Committee concluded that:

. . . the law of contempt was required as a means of maintaining the rights of the citizen to a fair and unimpeded system of justice and protecting the orderly administration of the law; however, the operation of that law should be confined to circumstances where the offending act was not within the definition of any other criminal offence and where the achievement of that law's objectives required a summary procedure. The law as it stood contained uncertainties impeding and restricting reasonable freedom of speech and should be amended and clarified so as to allow as much freedom of speech as was consistent with the achievement of the above-mentioned objectives. (para. 36)

Judge Zekia, in a concurring but separate opinion, commented on the way in which this particular case had illustrated the unsatisfactory nature of the common law of contempt:

... The diversity of the criteria adopted in this case by Lord Chief Justice Widgery in the Divisional Court and Lord Denning and his colleagues in the Court of Appeal and the criterion evolved by the majority of the House of Lords illustrate the unsatisfactory and unsettled state of the rules or principles of contempt of court dealing with press publications in pending civil matters. This is especially so when such publications are made in good faith without misrepresentation and are not calculated to interfere with or prejudice the course of justice and, furthermore, when factual accuracy is claimed and the subject matter is of public concern.

... In my view the branch of the common law that concerns contempt of court dealing with publications in the press and other media in connection with pending civil proceedings was – at any rate on the material date – uncertain and unsettled – and unascertainable even by a qualified lawyer – to such an extent that it could not be considered as a prescribed law within the purview and object of Articles 1 and 10(1) and (2) of the Convention. The phrase 'prescribed by law' in its context does not simply mean a restriction 'authorised by law' but necessarily means a law that is reasonably comprehensive in describing the conditions for the imposition of restrictions on the rights and freedoms contained in Article 10(1). As we said earlier, the right to freedom of the press would be drastically affected unless pressmen, with a reasonable degree of care and legal advice, can inform and warn themselves of the risks and pitfalls lying ahead owing to the uncertainties of contempt of court. (paras 27 and 28)

Some interesting differences concerning legal systems emerge from this case, notably the lack of contempt of court proceedings in continental systems and their retention in common law systems. In the former, of course, there may be less trial by jury and decisions tend to be both anonymous and collegial, but presumably the integrity of the judiciary is a common aspiration.

Observer and Guardian v UK
Series A, Vol. 126

The facts

Mr Peter Wright, a former employee of the British Government in the British Security Service (MI5), wrote his memoirs and made arrangements for the book *Spycatcher* to be published in Australia. The book contained material relating to the operation of MI5 including allegations of illegal activities. Part of the material had already appeared in another book by a different author and Mr Wright had given a lengthy television interview prior to publication about the work of MI5.

The Attorney-General instituted proceedings in Australia, in September 1985, to restrain publication of the book on the basis that publication would place Mr Wright in breach of his duty of confidentiality under the terms of his former employment. While the proceedings in Australia were pending the *Observer* and the *Guardian* published short articles on some of the contents of the book. The Attorney-General instituted proceedings against the newspapers for breach of confidence. In June 1986 ex parte interim injunctions were granted. The injunctions were upheld by the Court of Appeal on 25 July 1986 and confirmed on 11 July hearing at an *inter partes* appeal to the House of Lords which was refused by the Court of Appeal but granted by the Appellate Committee of the House of Lords on 6 November 1986.

In Australia, the trial of the action took place in November and December 1986 and judgment was delivered in March 1987. The court rejected the Attorney-General's claim. The Attorney-General appealed. On 24 September 1987 the Court of Appeal of New South Wales dismissed the Attorney-General's appeal. The Attorney-General appealed to the High Court of Australia. This court dismissed his appeal in June 1988, refusing in the interim to grant a temporary injunction to restrain publication of the book in Australia. *Spycatcher* was published in Australia on 13 October 1987.

On 17 April 1987, the *Independent* newspaper published a lengthy summary of the allegations contained in the book and two evening papers published reports on this. Similar material appeared in two Australian newspapers two days later, and in early May in an American newspaper.

The Attorney-General, in his capacity as guardian of the public interest in the due administration of justice, brought an action against the *Independent* and the two other papers for contempt of court. On 2 June 1987, the Vice-Chancellor held that the reports in the *Independent* could not amount to contempt of court because they were not in breach of the express terms of the original injunction against the *Observer* and the *Guardian*. The Attorney-General appealed. On 15 July, the Court of Appeal announced that it would reverse the judgment of the Vice-Chancellor. As a result of the Court of Appeal's decision the injunctions were effectively binding on all the British media. Ultimately the proceedings against the *Independent* and the other two newspapers took place in April 1989. The papers were held by the High Court to have been in contempt of court and fined.

In the meantime, the *Observer* and the *Guardian* applied to have the injunction against them lifted given the change in circumstances, particularly the fact that in May 1987 an American publishing company – Viking Penguin Inc. – announced its intention of publishing *Spycatcher* in America. A ruling on this was deferred pending the outcome of the case against the *Independent*. On 22 July 1987 – a few days after the Court of Appeal had reversed his judgment in the *Independent* case – the Vice-Chancellor discharged the injunction against the *Observer* and the *Guardian*. The Attorney-General appealed and pending his appeal the injunctions against the *Observer* and the *Guardian* continued in force. On 24 July 1987, The Court of Appeal ruled that the injunctions should continue, but in varied form so that a summary in very general terms of Mr Wright's allegations would be permissible but not in greater detail. The House of Lords upheld this ruling on 30 July 1987 and the injunctions continued in force until the trial of the action for breach of confidence in November 1987. Judgment in this trial was given on 21 December 1987 by Scott J, who rejected a claim for permanent injunctions. However, temporary injunctions were imposed pending appeal, first to the Court of Appeal – which upheld the ruling by Scott J – and then to the House of Lords. On 13 October 1988, the House of Lords dismissed the appeal by the Attorney-General and affirmed the judgment of Scott J. The injunctions were then lifted.

On 12 July 1987, the *Sunday Times* began the serialisation of *Spycatcher* (see *Times Newspapers and Neil* v *UK* 15 EHRR CD 49). The Attorney-General brought contempt of court proceedings against the *Sunday Times* for this serialisation and applied for an injunction to restrain the *Sunday Times* from publishing further extracts. A temporary injunction was granted by the Vice-Chancellor. Claims for a permanent injunction were dismissed at the same time that the injunction against the *Observer* and the *Guardian* was discharged.

The *Observer* and the *Guardian* alleged before the Commission that the interlocutory injunctions amounted to an unjustified interference with their freedom of expression.

The Commission's opinion

The Commission considered that the injunctions had constituted an interference with the applicants' right to freedom of expression. The Commission was satisfied that the injunctions were 'prescribed by law'; therefore, the main issue was whether the interference pursued a legitimate aim, and whether the measures taken to achieve that aim were 'necessary in a democratic society'.

The Commission was satisfied that the aim was legitimate, namely to protect the position of the Attorney-General as a litigant pending the trial of the confidentiality claims. This fell within the scope of maintaining the authority and impartiality of the judiciary. Indirectly the original injunctions were also intended to protect national security.

In considering whether these measures were necessary, two separate periods had to be considered: the first from the imposition of the original injunction on 11 July 1986 to 30 July 1987, and the second from 30 July 1987 when the House of Lords refused to discharge the injunction.

11 July 1986–30 July 1987
The Commission accepted that:

> ... the imposition of a temporary injunction to protect the interests of the parties until the full trial, which trial is decisive for the question whether or not material may be published, must, under normal circumstances be considered necessary in a democratic society for maintaining the authority of the judiciary within the meaning of Article 10(2) of the Convention. To find otherwise would be to deprive the trial of its purpose. However, the need for a temporary injunction must be established with particular clarity where it is the Government which relies on a private law concept of a breach of confidence to restrict the dissemination of information which is of considerable interest to the public, as in the present case. Whilst a binding rule of confidentiality between private persons is, in principle, compatible with Article 10 of the Convention, since this Article guarantees individual rights *vis-à-vis* the State, a stricter test of necessity must be applied where the Government seeks to restrict press freedom by that same rule. (para. 79)

The Commission observed that the primary concern of the English courts related to protection of confidentiality and that this influenced the criteria which they applied in assessing the material published. They were much more concerned about material which emanated directly from Mr Wright, rather than other material containing similar information from other sources. The Commission considered that the confidentiality rule which was applied was one based on the 'balance of convenience' and did not meet the necessity test laid down in Article 10, para. 2. Further, the Commission observed that the reports printed in the two newspapers were short, fair and objective. The Government had not sought to prevent disclosure of information on which much of the reports were based. It was not convinced, therefore, that there was a pressing social need for the injunctions, because much of the confidentiality which was supposed to have been protected had already been substantially destroyed. Moreover, the injunctions could not effectively preserve further confidentiality because of the inevitable leaks of the confidential information from other sources. The Commission also expressed the view that in imposing the injunctions the court had:

> ... failed to give sufficient weight to the public's right to know about the workings of government and the duty of the press to denounce alleged misconduct by a governmental authority. (para. 84)

There had therefore been a violation of Article 10 in respect of the first period. A dissenting opinion concerning this period was expressed by five members of the Commission on the ground that the injunctions were justified because the Government had an arguable claim for permanent injunctions against the applicants since it was not clear whether their sources of information included Mr Wright or not.

30 July 1987–13 October 1988
Given the extensive publication of the contents of *Spycatcher* by the end of July 1987, together with publication of the book in America and its importation into the UK – which was not prevented by the Government – the Commission could find no pressing social need for the injunctions. The failure to discharge them was therefore a violation of Article 10.

The judgment of the Court
The Court, like the Commission, concentrated on the question of necessity as it related to the two different periods.

11 July 1986–30 July 1987
The Court noted that although the articles published by the two newspapers were fair, it had emerged during the trial that they wished to publish further information deriving either directly or indirectly from Mr Wright. Had the injunction not been imposed then the newspapers would have been free to publish that material immediately, before the trial of the action for breach of confidence, and this would have effectively deprived the Attorney-General of a right to be granted a permanent injunction had he succeeded on the merits of the case. The Court expressed the view that these reasons were relevant to the aims of protecting national security and maintaining the authority of the judiciary. Therefore the Court held that the grant of injunctive relief was justified as being necessary and the reasons for it were sufficient for the purposes of Article 10, para. 2. The Court then had to consider whether the actual restraints were 'proportionate' to the legitimate aims being pursued.

In considering this the Court noted that the injunctions were not 'blanket' injunctions. The newspapers could pursue independent inquiries and could use previously published work. Moreover, under the terms of the original injunction the newspapers could apply to alter or vary the terms of the injunctions at any time, which they did. Although the injunctions were in place for over a year, the news was not urgent, in as much as it concerned events which had occurred several years earlier, and the aspects concerning the trial of the action were complex and needed time for preparation.

The Court concluded that the injunctions for this period were 'necessary in a democratic society' and that there had not, accordingly, been a violation of Article 10.

30 July 1987–13 October 1988

After publication of *Spycatcher* on 14 July 1987 in America, the contents of the book ceased to be a matter of speculation and their confidentiality was destroyed.

> . . . The fact that the further publication of *Spycatcher* material could have been prejudicial to the trial of the Attorney-General's claims for permanent injunctions was certainly in terms of the aim of maintaining the authority of the judiciary, a 'relevant' reason for continuing the restraints in question. The Court finds, however, that in the circumstances it does not constitute a 'sufficient' reason for the purposes of Article 10. (para. 68)

The Court concluded that the interference was no longer 'necessary in a democratic society' after 30 July 1987. There had therefore been a violation of Article 10.

A number of dissenting opinions were expressed. Judge Pettiti, joined by Judge Pinheiro Farinha, expressed the opinion that there had also been a violation of Article 10 for the first period. Judge Walsh also thought that there was a breach of Article 10 as regards the first period. Like Judge Pettiti, Judge Walsh emphasised the importance of freedom of the press:

> . . . It is clear that the matters the applicants had wished to deal with were of great interest to the public and perhaps even of concern. The public interest invoked by the Government appears to be equated with Government policy. That policy may very well justify, in the Government's view, making every effort to stem leakages from the Security Service or indeed in the interests of that service to take no action at all to deal with the allegations or indeed to pursue Mr Wright in any way available. These are policy matters and are not grounds for invoking the restrictions permitted by Article 10(2). (para. 5)

Judge Martens expressed a dissenting opinion as regards the first period, on the ground that the requirement of necessity was not met. Judge Martens was particularly critical of the onus placed on the defendants in applying for a discharge of the injunctions to show that disclosure of the information was in the public interest and that this interest outweighed the interest in preserving confidentiality. The Judge did not consider the standards applied conformed with the principles derived from Article 10.

Both Judge Pekkanen and Judge Morenilla expressed the opinion that the interference complained of during the first period was not justified, the latter indicating dissatisfaction with the way in which the case had been considered under two distinct periods. The Court's view that prior restraint was not excluded as a possibility under Article 10 was criticised by Judge de Meyer. He expressed the view that:

> . . . in a free and democratic society there can be no room, in times of peace, for restrictions of that kind, and particularly not if these are resorted to, as they were in the present case, for 'governmental suppression of embarrassing information' or ideas.

Four other judges agreed with his view.

Comment

Mr Wright had tried, unsuccessfully, to persuade the UK Government to investigate allegations of unlawful activities within MI5, as had a number of the members of the 1974–79 Labour Government. The two newspapers had also been conducting a campaign for an independent investigation into the workings of the Security Service.

It is notable that the case which triggered these injunctions had been brought under the common law breach of confidence rather than under breach of the Official Secrets Act. This was because the case was being brought against the publishers rather than Mr Wright himself, who would have had to agree to be bound by the provision of the Official Secrets Act when he took up employment with the British Government.

The costs involved in this case – which was not legally aided – were £137,825.05 for the domestic proceedings and £74,605.23 for the Strasbourg proceedings. The Court ordered the UK to pay the applicants £100,000 together with any value added tax, under Article 50. The remainder of the claim was dismissed.

Other cases relating to the publication of *Spycatcher* which were also brought before the Commission were *Sunday Times* v *UK (No. 2)* Series A, No. 217 – concerning the imposition of interlocutory injunctions, and *Times Newspapers Ltd and Neil* v *UK* (1992) 73 D & R 41, 15 EHRR CD 49. In the former case the Court agreed with the Commission that there was a violation of Article 10. Legal costs of £100,000 were awarded to the *Sunday Times* under Article 50 (£50,000 for the domestic proceedings and the same for the Strasbourg proceedings). In the latter case, publication of extracts occurred at a time when the Commission considered that the confidentiality of the material was still worth preserving, therefore the finding of contempt was legitimate and proportionate, and there was no violation of Article 10.

10.2.3   The Receipt and Dissemination of Information

Gaskin v *UK*
Series A, Vol. 160

The facts

As a child the applicant had been taken into care following the death of his mother. While in care he claimed that he was badly treated. When he became an adult he attempted to obtain information kept in records on him, held by the local authority. He succeeded in obtaining certain information, as a result of which he brought an action for damages for personal injuries against the local authority. In connection with these, in 1980 he sought an order for discovery of the local authority's case notes and records concerning him while in care. The local authority acknowledged that it held such information, but objections were made to its discovery on the ground that disclosure would be contrary to the public interest. Such records, which the local authority indicated would be as full and frank as possible, were confidential. It was necessary for the proper functioning of the child care service that this confidentiality be preserved. The court agreed with the local authority and refused to grant the application for discovery. The Court of Appeal dismissed the applicant's appeal and leave to appeal to the House of Lords was refused.

Thereafter the applicant sought access to his record in order to assist him in coping with the psychological problems which he believed originated from his treatment as a child.

Subsequently a new procedure was established relating to access to personal files held by the Social Services Department, and the Child Care Records Sub-Committee was set up. In June 1982 this Committee passed a resolution recommending that such records should be made available to ex-clients once certain information of a confidential nature had been excluded. It recommended that the records should be made available to the applicant, a recommendation which was approved by his local Social Services Committee. However, one councillor disagreed and sought and obtained an injunction restraining the local authority from such disclosure. This action was subsequently discontinued. By subsequent resolutions the local authority confirmed its initial resolution. In August 1983 the Department of Health and Social Security issued a Local Authority Circular under s. 7 of the Local Authority Services Act 1970 setting out the principles relating to disclosure of case records, indicating that in general persons who were the subject of such records should have access to them, provided certain safeguards were followed. Following this, the Attorney-General instituted proceedings for judicial review of the local authority's resolution on the grounds that this was contrary to law and outside its legal powers. A temporary injunction was granted against the local authority. Ultimately these proceedings were withdrawn and the file was eventually released to the applicant in May 1986, once the contributors to the file had given their consent. Where the contributor of the information did not consent to its disclosure, no disclosure was made.

Initially the applicant claimed violations of Articles 3, 8 and 13 and of the First Protocol, Article 2. In its decision relating to admissibility the Commission admitted complaints under Articles 8 and 10.

The Commission's opinion

The issue under Article 10 was whether the applicant's right to receive information had been violated as a result of the refusal to give him access to the file of the local authority.

The Government had contended that Article 10 does not confer a right to receive information from the State if the State does not wish to provide it.

Alternatively, there had been no interference with any right under this article as the applicant had briefly had access to his file in 1978. In the further alternative, any interference was justified under Article 10, para. 2 as being 'necessary in a democratic society' either 'for the protection of the reputation or rights of others' or 'for preventing the disclosure of information received in confidence'.

Following the case law of the Court (notably *Leander* v *Sweden* 9 EHRR 933), the Commission expressed the opinion that Article 10 prohibits a Government from restricting a person from receiving information which others may be willing to impart, but does not confer on an individual the right to information which others are unwilling to impart.

The judgment of the Court

The Court agreed with the opinion of the Commission that there had been no violation of Article 10. Judge Walsh, however, expressed a dissenting opinion, in which he was of the view that Article 10 was applicable but that interference with this right had been justified:

> . . . the applicant's right to receive the information sought from the public authority falls within the guarantee contained in Article 10(1) of the Convention. The information sought was relevant to his legal proceedings. The willingness of Liverpool City Council to furnish the information was curbed by the English courts on the grounds that to do so would be to breach the undisputed confidentiality which covered the documents in question. In my view that fell within the qualification permitted by Article 10(2) of the Convention. In fact 19 of the 46 informants agreed to waive confidentiality and the relevant documents were furnished to the applicant. The applicant's freedom to pursue his legal proceedings is not impaired and he is free to exercise his rights guaranteed by Article 6(1) of the Convention. He can furnish first-hand evidence of the alleged personal injuries suffered by him and examine and cross-examine witnesses in accordance with the rules of English procedural law. The fact that the English courts in their discretion might have given the applicant access to the documents sought does not affect the construction of Article 10(2) of the Convention. The matter was decided in accordance with English law on grounds which, in my view, can in the circumstances of the case be justified as being necessary in a democratic society for preventing the disclosure of information received in confidence relating to a very sensitive area of social welfare.
>
> . . . In my opinion it has not been shown that there has been any breach of the Convention. (paras 2 and 3)

Comment

The application for the order of discovery was made under the Administration of Justice Act 1970, s. 31. In granting this, a judge has discretion and may take into account any factors which seem relevant to its grant or its refusal, balancing the competing interests.

On 1 April 1989, the Access to Personal Files (Social Services) Regulations came into force. These were made under the Access to Personal Files Act 1987, and imposed upon a local authority the duty to give access to personal information held on an individual except for certain information relating to health. This Act and the Regulations apply only to information recorded after 1 April 1989. They had no retrospective effect in the case of Mr Gaskin.

Colman v UK
Series A, Vol. 258-D

The facts

The application was brought by a medical practitioner against the advertising restrictions of the General Medical Council. The applicant had sought to advertise his Holistic Counselling and Education Centre in the local newspaper. Realising that this might be contrary to GMC practice he sought guidance and asked the GMC to review its current policy on advertising – at the time contained in guidelines of November 1986. In response he was advised (i) the GMC did not intend to revise its policy, and (ii) if he advertised as proposed he could face disciplinary action. Legal proceedings against the decision of the GMC to the High Court and the Court of Appeal were unsuccessful and appeal to the House of Lords was refused. However, in the interim the Government had proposed the loosening of advertising restraints in a White Paper, and a report by the Monopolies and Mergers Commission concluded that the GMC's rules were not in the public interest. As a result the Director of Fair Trading had been asked to negotiate with the GMC to implement the report's recommendations.

Consequently, in the same month that Dr Colman applied to the Commission, the GMC revised its advertising rules to allow publication in the press of factual information about doctors' services. The applicant complained that the GMC's policy on advertising prior to May 1990 was in breach of Articles 10 and 13.

The Commission's opinion

The Commission expressed the opinion that there had been an interference with the applicant's freedom of expression by a public authority, but that this was lawful because:

> ... [the interference] pursued legitimate aims, namely the protection of the health of patients and the rights of others, namely doctors. (para. 33)

The key question was whether the interference was necessary.

In assessing this the Commission referred to the constant case law of the European Court of Human Rights:

> ... that the Contracting States have a certain margin of appreciation in assessing the existence and extent of the necessity of an interference, but this margin is subject to a European supervision. (para. 36)

In commercial matters the question was whether the measures taken on a national level were justifiable in principle and proportionate. Some limitations on advertising of the liberal professions may be justified to protect the rights of other practitioners. In assessing the matter the Commission had regard to the fact that not all advertising was forbidden, only that in newspapers. Also, at the material time other Contracting Parties had similar restrictions on such advertising. Also that the Government of the UK was taking active steps to review its policy. The Commission could not:

. . . substitute its own valuation for that of the competent medical authorities in the present case where those authorities, on reasonable grounds, had considered the restrictions to be necessary at the material time. (para. 39)

In a dissenting opinion, M.F. Martinez was of the view that the ban on advertising did constitute an interference with the freedom to communicate information under Article 10; and even if this was permitted by law, it was not necessary for the protection of health, or for the protection of the rights of other doctors. Therefore such interference was not permitted by Article 10, para. 2.

By the time the matter was referred to the European Court, the restrictions on advertising had been relaxed and the applicant agreed to a friendly settlement, under the terms of which the Government, while not admitting any breach of the Convention, agreed to pay the applicant the sum of £12,500. The case was therefore struck out (Resolution DH (93) 44 Committee of Ministers in accordance with Article 54).

Comment

Two points give rise to comment. First, the applicant's contentions about the then current practice of the GMC as regards advertising, proved to be supported by the Monopolies and Mergers Commission and the Government White Paper. It is difficult to assess, therefore, what impact this individual case had on the changes that subsequently took place.

Secondly, in considering whether the interference was necessary the Commission clearly had in mind the needs of the single market when it placed the case in the context of commercial matters. This issue was not fully addressed in the *Colman* case because the applicant was arguing the right to advertise on the grounds of public interest – particularly in alternative medical approaches – rather than publicising his own practice.

Two recent cases involved the broadcasting ban on Sinn Fein imposed by two directives issued on 19 October 1988 by the Secretary of State for the Home Department to the BBC (British Broadcasting Corporation) and ITV (Independent Broadcasting Authority).

McLaughlin v UK
18 EHRR CD 84

The facts

A broadcasting ban covered any broadcast consisting of or including words where the speaker represented Sinn Fein, or where the words supported or solicited support for Sinn Fein. The broadcaster did not have to be a member of Sinn Fein. The applicant complained that as a result of these directives he was prevented from having direct access to the broadcast media, despite the fact that he was a democratically elected Councillor wishing to comment on matters relevant to his constituents. He complained that his rights under Article 10 and 14 were violated in as much as the directions applied only to Sinn Fein.

The Commission's opinion

The Commission expressed the opinion that the applicant's rights under Article 10 had been interfered with. The interference was prescribed by law under a 'Licence and Agreement' 1981 with the BBC and the Broadcasting Act 1981 as regards ITV. This law was accessible as the notices had been announced in Parliament and been the subject of widespread comment in the press. They were also foreseeable as the Home Office had subsequently clarified their scope to the broadcasting authorities.

The aim of the restrictions was to protect the interests of national security, and although the applicant argued that it was not clear how the restrictions were intended to do this, the Commission accepted that the aim was legitimate. The issue was whether the restrictions were necessary in a democratic society.

Bearing in mind the margin of appreciation permitted to States, the limited interference with the applicant's rights and the importance of measures against terrorism, the Commission expressed the opinion that the interference was not disproportionate to the aims pursued. There had, therefore, been no violation of Article 10.

A similar opinion was expressed in the case of *Brind and Others* v *UK* 18 EHRR CD 76.

Cases pending under this article

Goodwin v *UK* (Application No. 17488/91) Report of the Commission 1 March 1994, concerning the application of a journalist who refused to comply with a court order issued under s. 10 of the Contempt of Court Act, to reveal the source of certain unsolicited information which he had used in a journal article on a company. The Commission expressed the view that there had been a violation of Article 10 and referred the case to the Court.

Wingrove v *UK* (Application No. 17419/90) (1994) 76-A D & R 26, Report of the Commission 10 January 1995. This case, which concerned the refusal by the British Board of Film Classification to issue a certificate for a film made by the applicant on the grounds that the film – 'Visions of Ecstasy' – was blasphemous, has been referred to the Court.

Halford v *UK* (Application No. 20605/92), concerning the interception of a senior female police officer's telephone calls, has been declared admissible by the Commission.

Mobin Ahmed and Others v *UK* (Application No. 22954/93), concerning restrictions on the political activities of certain local government officers, has been declared admissible by the Commission.

Phyllis Bowman v *UK* (Application No. 24839/94), concerning the prosecution of the applicant for distributing leaflets during elections publicising views on abortion and embryo experimentation, has been declared admissible.

Further reading

Coliver, S., 'Defamation Jurisprudence of the European Court of Human Rights' (1992) *Journal of Media Law and Practice* 250

Coliver, S., 'Freedom of Expression under the European Convention on Human Rights' (1992) 7 *Interrights Bulletin* 2

Duffy, P.J., 'The Sunday Times Case: Freedom of Expression, Contempt of Court and the European Court of Human Rights' (1980) *Human Rights Review* 17

Feingold, C., 'The Little Red Schoolbook and the European Court of Human Rights' (1978) *Revue des Droits de l'Homme* 21

Mann, F., 'Contempt of Court in the House of Lords and the European Court of Human Rights' (1979) 95 *Law Quarterly Review* 348

Pilmo, P., 'Prior Restraint and Article 10 of the European Human Rights Convention' (1994) 6 *Entertainment Law Review* 194

CHAPTER 11

ARTICLE ELEVEN

Article 11

1. *Everyone has the right to freedom of peaceful assembly and to freedom of association with others, including the right to form and to join trade unions for the protection of his interests.*

2. *No restrictions shall be placed on the exercise of these rights other than such as are prescribed by law and are necessary in a democratic society in the interests of national security or public safety, for the prevention of disorder or crime, for the protection of health or morals or for the protection of the rights and freedoms of others. This Article shall not prevent the imposition of lawful restrictions on the exercise of these rights by members of the armed forces, of the police or of the administration of the State.*

11.1 THE SCOPE OF THE ARTICLE

The concept of freedom of association is concerned with the right to form or to be affiliated with a group or organisation pursuing particular aims. It does not, for example, concern the right of prisoners to share the company of other prisoners or to 'associate' with other prisoners in this sense (*McFeeley* v *UK* 3 EHRR 161); nor does it extend to affording a prisoner the right to receive visits from an acquaintance for the purpose of discussing his medical history (*X* v *UK* 5 EHRR 260 – the right of a prisoner to associate with others does not concern the right to enjoy the personal company of others, specifically in this case the Chairman of the Citizens' Commission on Human Rights). It has also been held that this article does not extend to the right of association with animals (*Artingstoll* v *UK* 19 EHRR CD 92).

Institutions of public law cannot be considered as associations within the meaning of Article 11. Thus in a case concerning compulsory membership of the Bar for barristers, the Commission expressed the opinion that this could not be considered to be a restriction on the right to freedom of association, because the Senate and the Inns of Court and the Bar were founded in common law under the auspices of the judiciary to assist in the proper administration of justice (*App. No. 10331/83* v *UK* 6 EHRR 467 at 583).

The type of rights which have been claimed under Article 11 include: the right of Druids to celebrate the summer solstice at Stonehenge (*Chappell* v *UK* 10 EHRR 510); the right to belong to a trade union (*Council of Civil Service Unions and Others* v *UK* 10 EHRR 269); the right to belong to certain associations (*Hewitt and Harman* v *UK* 14 EHRR 657).

Generally one of the exclusions will prevent a restriction being held to be a breach of the article; for example, in *Chappell*, the interference was held by the Commission to be prescribed by law within the meaning of Article 11, para. 2 (considerations of public safety, damage to the monument, risk of harm and disruption to the public and traffic). Similarly, restrictions on chapel attendance for a prisoner held in a segregated unit were held to be justified under Article 11, para. 2 (*App. No. 9813/82* v *UK* 5 EHRR 513).

The majority of cases involving the UK have concerned trade union membership. The right to form and join trade unions is a special aspect of freedom of association which protects individuals, first and foremost, against State action. The State may interfere with this right only in accordance with the provisions of Article 11, para. 2 (*Young, James and Webster* v *UK* 4 EHRR 38). However, trade unions themselves may restrict or control the right to membership, and the State may not interfere with the regulation and administration of trade unions (*Cheall* v *UK* 8 EHRR 45 – expulsion from a trade union was within the private domain of the union, and therefore not the responsibility of the State). The State will be involved only if there is any abuse of a dominant position by trade unions, for example if they act *ultra vires*. Its responsibility cannot be engaged for the acts or omissions of a trade union – for example, where a trade union refuses to support a member's complaints before an industrial tribunal (App. No. 9444/81 6 EHRR 50 at 136).

11.2   THE CASES

Young, James and Webster v UK
Series A, Vol. 44

The facts
The applicants were former employees of British Rail. During the course of their employment British Rail entered into a closed shop agreement with three trade unions, the National Union of Railwaymen (NUR), the Transport Salaried Staffs' Association (TSSA) and the Associated Society of Locomotive Engineers and Firemen (ASLEF). Membership of one of these trade unions was made a condition of employment. Non-membership was permissible only on the grounds of religious belief. None of the three applicants wished to join a union and they were consequently dismissed. They were unable to complain of unfair dismissal because, under the Trade Union and Labour Relations Act

1974, dismissal on the grounds that the employee refused to join a trade union in an employment situation governed by a closed shop agreement, was not unfair provided that there was no genuine religious objection to such membership in general, or no reasonable objection to membership of a particular trade union.

The change in employment conditions was not a breach of the employment contract by British Rail because the original contracts, signed by the applicants when they commenced employment, included a provision that they were subject to terms and conditions which might from time to time be settled by their employers.

Before the Commission the applicants complained of violations of Articles 9, 10, 11, and 13.

The Commission's opinion

The Commission expressed the opinion that there had been a violation of Article 11, but no violation of Article 13. There were no separate issues arising under the other articles.

The judgment of the Court

The question before the Court was whether Article 11 conferred both a positive right to belong to a trade union, and a negative right not to be compelled to join one. The Commission had not determined this issue. The Court did not directly answer this question but suggested that freedom of association implied some freedom of choice. Therefore the Court held that:

> ... it does not follow that the negative aspect of a person's freedom of association falls completely outside the ambit of Article 11 and that each and every compulsion to join a particular trade union is compatible with the intention of that provision. To construe Article 11 as permitting every kind of compulsion in the field of trade union membership would strike at the very substance of the freedom it is designed to guarantee. (para. 52)

The Court was not called on to review the existence of closed shop agreements in general, but to focus on the facts of the case before it. In the circumstances the Court found that:

> ... The situation facing the applicants clearly runs counter to the concept of freedom of association in its negative sense.
>
> Assuming that Article 11 does not guarantee the negative aspect of that freedom on the same footing as the positive aspect, compulsion to join a particular trade union may not always be contrary to the Convention.
>
> However, a threat of dismissal involving loss of livelihood is a most serious form of compulsion and, in the present instance, it was directed against persons engaged by British Rail before the introduction of any obligation to join a particular trade union.
>
> In the Court's opinion, such a form of compulsion, in the circumstances of the case, strikes at the very substance of the freedom guaranteed by Article 11. For this reason alone, there has been an interference with that freedom as regards each of the three applicants.
>
> ... Another facet of this case concerns the restriction of the applicants' choice as regards the trade unions which they could join of their own volition. An individual does not enjoy the right to freedom of association if in reality the freedom of action or

choice which remains available to him is either non-existent or so reduced as to be of no practical value. (paras 55 and 56)

In considering whether the interference was justified under Article 11, para. 2, the Court was prepared to accept that the interference was prescribed by law, but was not prepared to comment on whether the aim of protecting the rights of others extended to upholding the closed shop agreement as this would involve consideration of such agreements in general.

In considering whether the interference was in fact necessary in a democratic society, the Court held:

> . . . The fact that British Rail's closed shop agreement may in a general way have produced certain advantages is . . . not of itself conclusive as to the necessity of the interference complained of.
>
> . . . Pluralism, tolerance and broadmindedness are hallmarks of a 'democratic society.' Although individual interests must on occasion be subordinated to those of a group, democracy does not simply mean that the views of a majority must always prevail: a balance must be achieved which ensures the fair and proper treatment of minorities and avoids any abuse of a dominant position. Accordingly, the mere fact that the applicant's standpoint was adopted by very few of their colleagues is again not conclusive of the issue now before the Court. (para. 63)

In considering whether the measures taken were proportionate to the legitimate aim pursued, the Court noted that the applicants represented a small minority of employees and that their refusal to join a trade union would not have interfered substantially with the aim of the railway unions to protect their members' interests, because of the agreement with British Rail. Therefore, the Court held that:

> . . . the detriment suffered by Mr Young, Mr James and Mr Webster went further than was required to achieve a proper balance between the conflicting interests of those involved and cannot be regarded as proportionate to the aims being pursued. Even making due allowance for a State's 'margin of appreciation,' the Court thus finds that the restrictions complained of were not 'necessary in a democratic society,' as required by Article 11(2).
>
> There has accordingly been a violation of Article 11. (para. 65)

A separate but concurring opinion was given by six judges, who felt that Article 11 should be interpreted so as to confer a negative as well as a positive aspect of freedom of association. In particular, these judges expressed the view that freedom of association required freedom of choice whether to associate or not, without threat of sanction.

A dissenting opinion was expressed by Judge Sorensen. His opinion was based on the interpretation of Article 11 and the background to its drafting. He suggested that the deliberate omission of any provision comparable to, for example, Article 20, para. 2 of the United Nations Universal Declaration, meant that this should be left to the national regulation of the States which were parties to the Convention. Such an interpretation was consistent with the approach of the International Labour Organisation. He expressed the view, therefore, that what the applicants were really seeking was security of employment – a right not protected by the Convention.

The Court also indicated that in this case Article 11 should be read with Articles 9 and 10, particularly as two of the applicants objected to joining a trade union because of their policies and activities. It was therefore important that their right to a personal opinion – protected under Articles 9 and 10 – should be respected and that they should not be compelled to join an association contrary to their convictions.

Comment

Over the years the law in the UK has varied considerably in the protection it affords to employees against employers and trade unions. Prior to the Trade Union and Labour Relations Act 1974, the applicable law was the Industrial Relations Act 1971, which conferred on employees the right not to be unfairly dismissed; in particular, any dismissal based on an employee's refusal to join a trade union was considered to be unfair. The 1974 Act repealed this, although union resistance to restrictions on closed shop agreements had meant that in practice closed shop employment situations had persisted.

The applicants were dismissed in 1976. In the same year the Trade Union and Labour Relations (Amendment) Act was passed which abolished the reasonable grounds exception to union membership, leaving only religious grounds. In 1978, the Employment Protection (Consolidation) Act was passed which re-enacted the existing provisions. This was amended in 1980 by the Employment Act. The 1980 Act retained the rule that dismissal on the grounds of refusal to join a trade union in a closed shop situation was not unfair, but extended the exceptions as from August 1980. The exceptions under the Act now included: objections on the grounds of conscience or personal conviction; non-membership prior to a closed shop agreement coming into force; non-compliance with the requirements of a balloting majority of 80 per cent, or non-membership subsequent to a valid ballot.

Thus while the right to belong to a trade union has become more protected, with compensation for dismissal if an employee loses his job because he is a member of a trade union, the right of an individual not to belong to a trade union has in certain employment situations been eroded.

Council of Civil Service Unions and Others v UK
(1987) 50 D & R 228

The facts

The case concerned the right of employees at the Government Communications Headquarters (GCHQ) to be trade union members. GCHQ, which is responsible for ensuring the security of the UK's military and official communications and is concerned with national security, was established in 1947. From 1947 to 1984 employees were permitted to be trade union members. Many were members of the Council of Civil Service Unions which was formed as a union in 1980.

It was not until 1983 – as a result of court proceedings concerning an employee and offences under the Official Secrets Act 1911 – that the Government publicly acknowledged the nature of GCHQ's work. Between

February 1979 and April 1981 there were seven occasions when industrial action was taken at GCHQ. On 22 December 1983, the Prime Minister as Minister for the Civil Service gave an oral direction – pursuant to her powers under the Civil Service Order 1982 – that the employment conditions of civil servants should be revised so as to exclude trade union membership. In future staff would only be allowed to be members of a staff association approved by the director of GCHQ. Written directions to this effect in the form of ministerial certificates were issued in January 1984 by the Secretary of State for Foreign and Commonwealth Affairs under the provisions of s. 138 of the Employment Protection (Consolidation) Act 1978.

Staff at GCHQ were given the option of transferring elsewhere in the civil service or taking premature retirement if they did not wish to comply with these instructions. All staff were paid a compensation sum of £1,000.

The applicants were all employed at GCHQ. Following the declaration preventing their being members of a trade union they applied for judicial review of the notice and certificates issued by the Ministers. The High Court found for the applicants declaring that the oral direction and the certificates were invalid, not because the Ministers did not have the requisite power to make them but because the Government had not consulted with the trade unions. Failure to consult when there were expectations that this would be done amounted to a breach of natural justice.

The Court of Appeal set aside this declaration on the grounds that the actions taken concerning GCHQ were actions taken on the grounds of national security, and as Ministers were the only persons who could judge what this required the decisions were not susceptible to judicial review. Any expectation of prior consultation might have to give way to the greater demands of national security.

The House of Lords dismissed an appeal by the applicants. Although it was accepted that the applicants may have had a legitimate expectation to be consulted, the nature of the work at GCHQ could not be compromised either by discussion and publicity, or by industrial action.

The applicants complained to the Commission that the UK had removed the right of GCHQ employees to belong to a trade union and that this was not prescribed by law, or necessary in a democratic society.

The Commission's opinion
The Commission found that there had been an interference with the applicants' right under Article 11, para. 1 – indeed this was not disputed. The Commission had then to examine whether the interference fell under the exceptions provided for under Article 11, para. 2. In this respect the Commission observed that:

> . . . the first sentence of Article 11, para 2 provides criteria for justifying an interference with the rights under Article 11, para 1). The second sentence specifically envisages restrictions on the exercise of these rights by various categories of persons employed by the State. (p. 287)

The Commission therefore had to consider the scope and interpretation of these terms. Referring to other instruments which conferred the right to trade union membership – namely the International Covenant on Civil and Political Rights 1966 and the International Covenant on Economic, Social and Cultural Rights 1966 – the Commission could find no real guidance as the former did not restrict the rights of employees in State administration, while the latter did do so.

The Commission had to examine whether the staff employed at GCHQ fell under the terms 'members of . . . the administration of the State'. The Commission noted that:

> . . . the terms are mentioned, in the same sentence in Article 11, para 2), together with members of the armed forces [and] of the police. In the present case, the Commission is confronted with a special institution, namely GCHQ, whose purpose resembles to a large extent that of the armed forces and the police in so far as GCHQ staff directly or indirectly, by ensuring the security of their respondent Government's military and official communications, fulfil vital functions in protecting national security. (p. 288)

The Commission was therefore satisfied that the employees at GCHQ fell into the category 'members of . . . the administration of the State' in Article 11, para. 2.

The Commission next had to consider whether the interference was lawful. This meant that the measures taken must be in accordance with national law. Under Article 4 of the Civil Service Order in Council 1982, the Minister for the Civil Service had the power to regulate the employment conditions of civil servants. Although this was broadly worded and included no specific reference to trade union membership, it had to be interpreted in the context of the 1975 and 1978 Employment Protection Acts. Both these Acts included the provision that a Ministerial certificate might restrict the rights of trade union membership in the context of national security. The Commission was satisfied that the work of GCHQ involved national security and that the legislation gave GCHQ employees adequate indication that such rights might be curtailed.

The applicants had argued that 'restriction', even if justified, should not amount to 'destruction' of a right. However, the Commission expressed the opinion that it could be interpreted as covering a complete prohibition of the right under Article 11. It was not clear whether the restriction in this context had also to be proportional, but even if this were so, the Commission indicated that in the case of national security a wide margin of appreciation was conferred on Contracting States. The Commission considered that given the vulnerability of GCHQ to industrial action and the vital functions of GCHQ, the measures taken, although drastic, were not arbitrary.

The Commission consequently rejected the complaint as manifestly ill-founded.

Comment

Civil servants – including employees at GCHQ – are employed under the powers of the royal prerogative, which, since 1963, have been vested in the Minister for the Civil Service. Under the Civil Service Order 1982 the relevant Minister may make regulations controlling the Service and give instructions relating to matters other than remuneration. Civil servants are protected under the Employment Protection (Consolidation) Act 1978 and the Employment

Protection Act 1975, except where their employment is certified by a Minister of the Crown as being exempted from the provisions of the Acts for the purpose of safeguarding national security.

The alteration in the terms of employment for the staff at GCHQ attracted the concern of the all-party House of Commons Employment Committee, which urged that the Government and the civil service unions should hold discussions to negotiate an agreement which could meet the objectives of both sides.

A separate action concerning the issues was brought by the General Council of the Trades Union Congress (TUC), which complained to the Director General of the International Labour Organisation (ILO) that the UK was in breach of Articles 2 to 5 and 11 of the 1948 International Labour Convention No. 87 on Freedom of Association. The report of the Committee of Experts on the Application of Conventions and Recommendations indicated that the matter raised complex legal issues which might need to be resolved by the International Court of Justice. This separate action did not exclude the right of the applicants to bring their application before the Commission, because although the rights protected by Articles 2 to 5 were similar to those covered by Article 11, the complainants were different.

Sibson* v *UK
Series A, Vol. 258-A

The facts
The applicant was employed as a heavy goods driver. He was a member of a trade union but his employment did not involve a closed shop agreement. As a result of allegations of dishonesty he was dismissed from his union. He joined another one, but fellow employees threatened to strike unless he was moved to another depot (the possibility of doing this was covered by the terms of his contract). The applicant refused to move or to re-join the first union. His employer advised him that if he reported for work at the depot he would be sent home without pay. The applicant resigned. He brought an action for constructive dismissal against his employer. This action was successful before the industrial tribunal and the Employment Appeals Tribunal but was dismissed by the Court of Appeal.

The applicant complained to the Commission that the compulsion on him to re-join his original trade union or to move to another depot was contrary to his rights under Article 11.

The Commission's opinion
The complaint required the Commission to consider the negative freedom of association aspect of Article 11 which had been raised in *Young, James and Webster*, and also whether the responsibility of the State had in fact been engaged as the actions leading to the dismissal were primarily those of the employer and the trade union. The Commission recalled that:

> . . . The Court has held that for the rights under Article 11 to be effective the State must protect the individual against any abuse of a dominant position by trade unions.

The Court has indicated that compulsion to join a particular trade union may not always be contrary to the Convention. Abuse might, in the Commission's opinion, occur, for example, where the consequences of failure to join a trade union resulted in exceptional hardship such as dismissal. (para. 29)

However, in this case the Commission considered that there had been no unfair or constructive dismissal, but that the applicant had resigned. The contract of employment clearly gave the employer the right to move the applicant to another depot.

Further, the Commission was satisfied that the UK provided sufficient legislative safeguards against abuse by trade unions, etc. in the Employment Protection Act 1978, and that on the facts there was no indication that the UK had failed to provide the applicant with protection against his negative freedom of association right. There was therefore no violation of Article 11.

Six members of the Commission dissented on the grounds that the real reason for asking the applicant to move from one depot to another was not operational but in order to avoid strike action. This motivation amounted to an unjustified interference with the applicant's right to not join a particular trade union. It amounted, therefore, to indirect pressure to compel him to join a particular union against his will. As the domestic law of the UK made this type of treatment lawful – according to the Court of Appeal judgment – the UK's responsibility was engaged.

The judgment of the Court
The Court distinguished this case from that of *Young, James and Webster* on the grounds that:

— the applicant did not object to trade union membership on the basis of any specific convictions (therefore Articles 9 and 10 of the Convention were not applicable here);
— the applicant was not threatened in the same way with loss of livelihood because he had the possibility of going to work at the other depot;
— the employment situation was not a closed shop one.

The Court therefore held that the applicant was not subjected to a form of treatment striking at the very substance of the rights guaranteed by Article 11 and there had accordingly been no violation.

Two judges – Judge Morenilla and Judge Russo – gave a dissenting opinion on the grounds that Article 11 ought to be interpreted in an 'evolutive' way. The notion of 'compulsion' to join a union – which had been declared unlawful under the negative aspect of Article 11 discussed in *Young, James and Webster* – should not be narrowly interpreted to mean simply 'treatment'. The alternatives open to Mr Sibson amounted to compulsion which could not be justified under Article 11, para. 2.

Comment
Had a closed shop agreement been in operation the dismissal would not have been unfair under the Employment Protection (Consolidation) Act 1978,

s. 58(3). The case is distinguishable from *Young, James and Webster* in that the applicant was given a choice (other than union membership or dismissal), namely to move to another depot. However, the two industrial courts held that there had been constructive dismissal and therefore loss of livelihood. The Court of Appeal based its reasoning on an implied mobility term in the contract of employment.

Rai, Allmond and 'Negotiate Now' v UK
(1995) 81-A D & R 146

The facts
The applicants were members of an organisation which sought to promote peace in Northern Ireland and to encourage negotiations to this effect without a prior cease-fire. The organisation was called 'Negotiate Now'. In order to promote their views and attract publicity, the applicants requested permission to hold a rally in Trafalgar Square, London, from the Department of National Heritage. They also informed the Metropolitan Police Commissioner of the proposal and he expressed the view that such a rally would not create a danger to public order. The Department of National Heritage refused the applicants permission for such a rally. The Secretary of State confirmed this refusal on the grounds that it was Government policy since 1972 to refuse permission for any public demonstration or meetings concerning Northern Ireland in Trafalgar Square. Leave for judicial review was refused.

The applicants complained that the ban infringed their freedom to manifest their beliefs in public, the right to freedom of expression and their right to freedom of peaceful assembly. The Commission noted that the submissions primarily related to Article 11, although the applicants invoked Articles 9 and 10 as well.

The Commission's opinion
The Commission noted that:

> ... The problems of freedom of thought and belief and freedom of expression cannot in this case be separated from that of freedom of assembly. (p. 151)

Article 11 was the specific article for assemblies and so the application was considered under this head.

The Commission noted that the applicants' intention to hold a peaceful rally was not disputed. Moreover, that the case law of the Commission established that:

> ... the right to freedom of peaceful assembly, which is a fundamental right in a democratic society, is guaranteed to everyone who has the intention of organising a peaceful demonstration. (p. 152)

Refusal to grant the applicants permission was therefore a restriction on this right.

The question was whether the restriction was 'prescribed by law'. The Commission expressed the opinion that although:

... the power to regulate the use of the Square for assemblies is not subject to defined restrictions, . . . the policy of excepting demonstrations relating to Northern Ireland was the subject of a public statement in the House of Commons and that numerous refusals of demonstrations occurred subsequent to this. It is compatible with the requirements of foreseeability that terms which are on their face general and unlimited are explained by executive or administrative statements, since it is the provision of sufficiently precise guidance to individuals to regulate their conduct rather than the source of that guidance which is of relevance. (p. 152)

The Commission was satisfied that the regulation of assemblies in the Square was sufficiently 'prescribed by law'.

Although the Commission accepted that the sensitive and complex situation in Northern Ireland might justify a general policy of banning demonstrations with the aim of preventing disorder and protecting the rights and freedoms of others, the question of whether this was 'necessary in a democratic society' still had to be considered. The Commission recognised that refusal of permission to the applicants affected their freedom to express their views and beliefs. However, the assessment of whether or not the policy of unconditional negotiation, which they advocated, was controversial fell within the Government's margin of appreciation. In view of the fact that the applicants could hold such an assembly in another place, e.g. Hyde Park, the Commission concluded that the restriction was proportionate and justified.

Comment
Control of Trafalgar Square vests in the Secretary of State for National Heritage pursuant to the Trafalgar Square Act 1844. Under the Parks Regulation (Amendment) Act 1926, regulations may be made by the Commissioners or their successors (now the Secretary of State). Under the Trafalgar Square Regulations 1952, permission is required for any assembly, parade, procession or public speech held or made in Trafalgar Square.

Government policy refusing permission for such events had originated in 1972 following the IRA bombing of Aldershot, on the ground that it would not be fitting to allow any organisation supporting terrorist activities to hold such meetings. In order not to have to distinguish between different organisations a blanket ban would be imposed on any demonstration or meeting having anything to do with the situation in Northern Ireland. Since that date a number of different organisations had been refused permission to hold meetings, but some exceptions had been allowed – 1976 Peace People, 1978 Better Life for All Campaign, 1993 Peace 93.

Cases pending under this article
Mobin Ahmed and Others v *UK* (Application No. 22954/93), concerning restrictions on political activities of certain local government officers (also Articles 10 and Article 3 of the First Protocol) has been declared admissible by the Commission.

CHAPTER 12

ARTICLE TWELVE

Article 12
Men and women of marriageable age have the right to marry and to
found a family, according to the national laws governing the exercise of
this right.

12.1   THE SCOPE OF THE ARTICLE

The right to marry has been interpreted as 'a right to form a legal relationship, to acquire a status' (para. 58) and 'The essence of the right to marry, . . . is the formation of a legally binding association between a man and a woman' (*Hamer v UK* Council of Europe Report, para. 71).

Article 12 guarantees a fundamental right, and although this right must be exercised in accordance with national law, the national law is limited in scope in as much as the national law cannot be so restrictive so as to make this fundamental right redundant. The role of the national law is therefore to 'govern the exercise of this right' (*Hamer*). In doing this national laws may establish rules relating to the formalities for a valid marriage, but:

> . . . national law may not otherwise deprive a person or category of persons of full legal capacity of the right to marry. Nor may it substantially interfere with their exercise of the right. (*Hamer*, para. 62)

Any claim based on Article 12 must relate to a genuine marriage or wish to marry and not simply a marriage of convenience – for example, to obtain admission to the UK (*App. No. 9918/82* v *UK* and *App. No. 9773/82* v *UK*). The right to marry and found a family (Article 12 read with Article 8) does not in principle include the right to choose the geographical location of the marriage.

Often this article is pleaded together with rights under Article 8, but the two are not synonymous. Although the right to found a family under Article 8 is an absolute right, a person may have the right to marry even if the circumstances are such that he or she cannot cohabit or consummate the marriage. Consequently, it appears that the Convention itself does not require consummation or cohabitation for the exercise of the right under Article 12. These aspects may, however, be required under the national laws, or be included in the national legal framework concerning capacity to marry. The Commission has held that:

> ... Article 12 of the Convention therefore guarantees a specific and distinctive right of an independent nature as compared with the right to protection of private and family life guaranteed by Article 8 para. 1 of the Convention.
>
> In fact the distinction between Articles 8 and 12 must be seen essentially as a difference between protection under Article 8 of *de facto* family life irrespective of its legal status . . . and the right under Article 12 for two persons of opposite sex to be united in a formal, legally recognised union. (*Cossey* v *UK* Series A, Vol. 184, para. 43, Commission's Opinion)

It is in the context of capacity and status that most case law has arisen.

12.2 THE CASES

Hamer v *UK*
(1981) 24 D & R 5

The facts
The applicant was prevented from marrying because he was in prison and national law did not permit him to marry in prison. The Home Secretary would not allow him temporary release so that he could marry elsewhere.

The Commission's opinion
The Commission had first to establish whether the fundamental right guaranteed under Article 12 was denied to the applicant or interfered with by the UK authorities. In answering this question the Commission referred to the case law of the Court which had held that:

> ... even though a right is not formally denied, 'hindrance in fact can contravene the Convention just like a legal impediment' and 'hindering the effective exercise of a right may amount to a breach of that right, even if the hindrance is of a temporary character'. (*Golder* v *UK* 1 EHRR 524, para. 65)

The Government argued that the applicant was unable to exercise his right under Article 12 as a result of his own actions. The Commission expressed the opinion that the situation was not one of the applicant's choice. He was not like a priest who chooses not to marry:

> ... nor can it be said that his inability to marry was simply an inevitable result of his imprisonment, or of his actions which led to it, for which the Government were not responsible. Personal liberty is not a necessary precondition to the exercise of the right to marry.
>
> ... The refusal of the necessary permission or facilities is, rather, to be seen as an interference with the relevant Convention right by the competent authorities, which may or may not be justifiable under the Convention. (paras 67 and 68)

In examining whether this interference was justifiable, the Commission expressed the opinion that:

... no general consideration of public interest arising from the fact of imprisonment itself can justify such interference in the case of a prisoner ... no particular difficulties are involved in allowing the marriage of prisoners. In addition there is no evidence before the Commission to suggest that, as a general proposition, it is in any way harmful to the public interest to allow the marriage of prisoners. Marriage may, on the contrary, be a stabilising and rehabilitative influence. (para. 72)

The Commission therefore found that the applicant's right to marry had been violated.

During the examination of the case, the UK Government informed the Committee of Ministers that it accepted the Commission's report and that it had changed its practice with regard to the marriage of prisoners. In a resolution of the Committee of Ministers (Resolution DH(81)5, 2 April 1981) the Committee of Ministers declared that it was satisfied with the reforms implemented by the UK.

Comment

Besides the interpretation that this case establishes concerning the scope of Article 12, the Commission's Report also illustrates more general methods of interpretation. The UK Government had asked the Commission to follow an earlier case involving the Federal Republic of Germany, in which it had expressed the opinion that a refusal to allow a prisoner to marry was not in breach of Article 12. The Commission indicated that the two cases were not directly comparable – because of the particularities of German national law – but more importantly the Commission was not rigorously bound by precedent:

... In any event in interpreting Article 12 of the Convention the Commission must now have regard to subsequent case law of the European Court of Human Rights on the scope of permissible limitations to Convention rights, of prisoners in particular. It must also consider the facts now before it in the light of present-day conditions. In this respect it is relevant to note the general tendency in European penal systems in recent years towards reduction of the differences between prison life and life at liberty and the increasing emphasis laid on rehabilitation. (para. 57)

This suggests that where the UK's national legislation is completely out of line with trends elsewhere, interference with a right may be held to be unjustifiable unless there are special circumstances – for example, the situation in Northern Ireland.

Moreover, although only a violation of Article 12 was being raised in this case, the Commission had regard to the overall situation regarding prisoners and their rights under the Convention. In considering whether the exercise of this particular right by prisoners could be justifiably interfered with, the Commission asked whether its exercise involved any general threat to prison security or good order.

Rees v *UK*
Series A, Vol. 106

The facts

The applicant was born in 1942 and had been recorded in the birth register as female. In 1974 he had undergone medical treatment for physical sexual conversion. He changed his names and had been living as a male, but had not been allowed to change the indication of his sex in the birth register. As a result the applicant was unable to marry because under English law a marriage is void if the parties are not respectively male and female (Matrimonial Causes Act 1973, s. 11, as applied in the case of *Corbett* v *Corbett* [1970] 2 WLR 1306).

The applicant complained before the Commission that the non-recognition of his present status amounted to a violation of his rights under Article 8 and Article 12.

The Commission's opinion
The Commission expressed the opinion that there had not been a violation of Article 12, but was divided in its reasons. One opinion was that the applicant was entitled to marry, but not to marry a woman. This was a direct result of the fact that he was not recognised as a man. As this was a matter which fell under Article 8, there was no separate violation of Article 12.

The other opinion was that a violation of Article 8 did not automatically imply a violation of Article 12. Whereas Article 8 guaranteed 'everyone' the same right, Article 12 had to be read subject to the 'national laws governing the exercise of this right'. Although national laws could not arbitrarily restrict this right, they could impose reasonable limitations based on fundamental concepts of marriage and the family. Therefore national law could impose requirements concerning formalities, age, mental capacity, etc. Further, it could be argued that Article 12 includes the 'physical capacity to procreate' (para. 55). Support for this interpretation was to be found in the preparatory documents for Article 16, para. 1 of the United Nations Declaration of Human Rights, from which the French version of this article was taken. These use the words '*âge nubile*', indicating that the essential purpose of the institution of marriage is the foundation of a family. It follows that:

> . . . a Contracting State must be permitted to exclude from marriage persons whose sexual category itself implies a physical incapacity to procreate either absolutely (in the case of a transsexual) or in relation to the sexual category of the other spouse (in the case of individuals of the same sex).
>
> Such situations whose legal recognition might appear to the national legislator as distorting the essential nature of marriage and its social purpose (*finalité sociale*) justify allowing the State to refuse the right to marry. (para. 55). Opinion of Fawcett, Tenekides, Gözübügük, Soyer and Batliner (Commission)).

The judgment of the Court
The greater part of the Court's judgment dealt with the claims relating to Article 8. As regards Article 12, the Court expressed the opinion that:

> . . . the right to marry guaranteed by Article 12 refers to the traditional marriage between persons of opposite biological sex. This appears also from the wording of the Article which makes it clear that Article 12 is mainly concerned to protect marriage as the basis of the family. (para. 49)

Although the Contracting States had a margin of appreciation in so far as domestic legislation controlling marriage was concerned, the limitations introduced by any domestic law should not 'restrict or reduce the right in such a way that the very essence of the right is impaired' (para. 50). However, in this case the Court held that the legal impediment in the UK on marriage of persons who are not of the opposite biological sex, could not be said to impair the very essence of the right under Article 12. There was therefore no violation of Article 12.

Comment

In the UK transsexuals may change their names by deed poll and also have driving licences issued in their new names, as well as passports and national insurance documents. Surgical treatment for physical sexual conversion, together with hormonal treatment, is supported by the National Health Service. Under the Birth and Death Registration Act 1953, the birth of every child is registered by the Registrar of Births and Deaths for the area in which the child is born. The only alterations permitted to this registration are where there has been a clerical error, or where an error of fact or substance was made when the birth was registered. The birth certificate is a certified copy of this entry.

The recognised criteria for determining sex are: chromosomal sex; gonadal sex (ovaries or testes); apparent sex (external genitalia); and psychological sex. The definitive criteria for the determination of sex, rather than gender, in the case of transsexuals were established in the *Corbett* case. Expert evidence supporting Mr Rees's application emphasised the importance of the fourth criterion – psychological sex. Sex at birth is usually determined by only one of these criteria, i.e. apparent sex.

In English law marriage is defined as 'a voluntary union for life of one man and one woman to the exclusion of all others' (*Hyde* v *Hyde* (1986) 1 P & Divorce 130). A marriage is void if the parties are not respectively male and female (Matrimonial Causes Act 1973).

Production of a birth certificate is not required for marriage, but a notice has to be completed in which the person applying for a marriage licence has to make a solemn declaration that he or she believes that there is no impediment or hindrance to the marriage. Deceitful statements could lead to prosecution under the Perjury Act 1911.

Cossey v *UK*
Council of Europe Report 16/1989/176/232

The facts
The applicant was a transsexual who was registered at birth as being of the male sex. As an adult the applicant underwent extensive medical and surgical treatment to change sex from male to female. In 1973 she changed her name by deed poll to a woman's name; in 1974 she had gender reassignment surgery; in 1976 she was given a UK passport as a female. From 1979 to 1986 she was a successful fashion model. She wished to marry an Italian citizen and inquired whether she could validly contract such a marriage. In 1983 the Director and Registrar General informed the applicant that:

. . . a marriage would be void because English law would treat the applicant as male, notwithstanding her anatomical and psychological status as a woman. The applicant's Member of Parliament informed her in a letter of 30 August 1983 that it would require a change in United Kingdom law to allow her to marry. On 18 January 1984, after another enquiry by the applicant, she was informed on behalf of the Registrar General that she could not be granted a birth certificate showing her sex as female, since a birth certificate records details as at the date of birth. (para. 17)

The legal problem related to the applicant's sex, as registered at birth, and current status. As in the *Rees* case, the difficulty under English law concerned the alteration of the birth certificate. Under the Birth and Death Registration Act 1953, the birth of every child has to be registered. The entry and the subsequent certificate are, as stated in the *Rees* case, records of fact. Clerical errors, or errors of fact or substance made at the time of registration may be corrected. Similarly, in the case of the subsequent legitimation or adoption of a child re-registration will occur.

The applicant complained that under UK law she was unable to claim full recognition of her changed status. In particular she complained that she could not marry an Italian citizen who wished to marry her. She therefore invoked Articles 8 and 12. With reference to Article 12, the applicant complained in particular that:

> . . . she is denied the right to marry a man as she is in this respect treated as a man by the United Kingdom authorities. She states that her sexual conversion enables her to consummate marriage with a man and that she wishes to marry an Italian citizen who also wishes to marry her. (para. 40)

The Commission's opinion

The Commission was bound to take into account the decision of the Court in the *Rees* case, which had been given in October 1986, and its own report on that case. However, this was not of great assistance because in that case five members of the Commission had expressed the opinion that there was no separate violation of Article 12, while five other members of the Commission considered that Article 12 was not violated. Nevertheless, the Commission expressed the opinion that:

> . . . marriage and the foundation of a family are particular events in the life of individuals which go beyond the mere realisation of private and family life as they involve two persons who form a legally and socially recognised union which creates both responsibilities and privileges. Article 12 of the Convention therefore guarantees a specific and distinctive right of an independent nature as compared with the right to protection of private and family life guaranteed by Article 8 para. 1 of the Convention. (para. 43)

Even if there was no violation of Article 8, this did not automatically exclude the possibility of a violation of Article 12.

> . . . As far as the present applicant's right to marry is concerned, the Commission first observes that her application contains a factual element which distinguishes it from the *Rees* case and the other transsexual cases so far considered, in that the present applicant has, according to her uncontested statements, a male partner wishing to marry her.
> . . . The Commission agrees, in principle, with the Court, that Article 12 refers to the traditional marriage between persons of opposite biological sex. It cannot,

however, be inferred from Article 12 that the capacity to procreate is a necessary requirement for the right in question. Men or women, who are unable to have children, enjoy the right to marry just as other persons. Therefore, biological sex cannot for the purpose of Article 12 be related to the capacity to procreate.

... It is certified by a medical expert that the applicant is anatomically no longer of male sex. She has been living after the gender reassignment surgery as a woman and is socially accepted as such.

In these circumstances it cannot, in the Commission's opinion, be maintained that for the purposes of Article 12 the applicant still has to be considered as being of male sex. The applicant must therefore have the right to conclude a marriage recognised by the United Kingdom law with the man she has chosen to be her husband.

... The Commission concludes, by ten votes to six, that there has been a violation of Article 12 of the Covention. (paras 44–47)

Six members of the Commission dissented with this finding. Their reasons for doing so were either that they considered that Articles 8 and 12 could not be completely separated, or they were of the view that this case could not be distinguished from the *Rees* case, in as much as:

(T)he Court's reasoning in the *Rees* case ... was of a general character and based on an evaluation of a principle of United Kingdom law rather than on an assessment of any concrete circumstances pertaining to the specific case. (p. 14, Report of the Commission published by the Council of Europe)

Mr Martinez in a single dissenting opinion expressed concern that the Commission should depart from the judgment of the Court in the *Rees* case by distinguishing it. His objections related to the role of the Commission and its relationship to the Court, and the interpretation and application of Article 12.

The judgment of the Court

Having previously given its decision in the *Rees* case, the Court was not persuaded that there was a material difference between the two cases because:

... In the first place, the fact that Mr Rees had no such partner played no part in the Court's decisions, which were based on a general consideration of the principles involved (see the *Rees* judgment, pp. 14–18 and 19, paras 35–46 and 48–51). In any event, as regards Article 8, the existence or otherwise of a willing marriage partner has no relevance in relation to the contents of birth certificates, copies of which may be sought or required for purposes wholly unconnected with marriage. Again, as regards Article 12, whether a person has the right to marry depends not on the existence in the individual case of such a partner or a wish to marry, but on whether or not he or she meets the general criteria laid down by law.

... Reliance was also placed by the applicant on the fact that she is socially accepted as a woman (see paragraphs 10–12 above), but this provides no relevant distinction because the same was true, *mutatis mutandis*, of Mr Rees (see the *Rees* judgment, p. 9, para. 17). Neither is it material that Miss Cossey is a male-to-female transsexual whereas Mr Rees is a female-to-male transsexual: this – the only other factual difference between the two cases – is again a matter that had no bearing on the reasoning in the *Rees* judgment. (paras 32 and 33)

In considering whether there had been a violation of Article 12, the Court noted similar points to those in its judgment of the *Rees* case, namely:

(a) The right to marry guaranteed by Article 12 referred to the traditional marriage between persons of opposite biological sex. This appeared also from the wording of the Article which made it clear that its main concern was to protect marriage as the basis of the family.

(b) Article 12 laid down that the exercise of the right to marry shall be subject to the national laws of the Contracting States. The limitations thereby introduced must not restrict or reduce the right in such a way or to such an extent that the very essence of the right was impaired. However, the legal impediment in the United Kingdom on the marriage of persons who were not of the opposite biological sex could not be said to have an effect of this kind.

. . . Miss Cossey placed considerable reliance, as did the Delegate of the Commission, on the fact that she could not marry at all: as a woman, she could not realistically marry another woman and English law prevented her from marrying a man.

In the latter connection, Miss Cossey accepted that Article 12 referred to marriage between a man and a woman and she did not dispute that she had not acquired all the biological characteristics of a woman. She challenged, however, the adoption in English law of exclusively biological criteria for determining a person's sex for the purposes of marriage (see paragraph 24 above) and the Court's endorsement of that situation in the *Rees* judgment, despite the absence from Article 12 of any indication of the criteria to be applied for this purpose. In her submission, there was no good reason for not allowing her to marry a man.

. . . As to the applicant's inability to marry a woman, this does not stem from any legal impediment and in this respect it cannot be said that the right to marry has been impaired as a consequence of the provisions of domestic law.

As to her inability to marry a man, the criteria adopted by English law are in this respect in conformity with the concept of marriage to which the right guaranteed by Article 12 refers (see paragraph 43(a) above).

. . . Although some Contracting States would now regard as valid a marriage between a person in Miss Cossey's situation and a man, the developments which have occurred to date (see paragraph 40 above) cannot be said to evidence any general abandonment of the traditional concept of marriage. In these circumstances, the Court does not consider that it is open to it to take a new approach to the interpretation of Article 12 on the point at issue. It finds, furthermore, that attachment to the traditional concept of marriage provides sufficient reason for the continued adoption of biological criteria for determining a person's sex for the purposes of marriage, this being a matter encompassed within the power of the Contracting States to regulate by national law the exercise of the right to marry.

. . . In the context of Article 12 the applicant again prayed in aid Article 14 of the Convention. On this point it suffices to refer to the observations in paragraph 41 above.

. . . The Court thus concludes that there is no violation of Article 12.

Comment

In considering whether or not to depart from its previous line of reasoning in *Rees*, the Court commented on its own *modus operandi*:

. . . the Court is not bound by its previous judgments; indeed, this is borne out by Rule 51 para. 1 of the Rules of Court. However, it usually follows and applies its own precedents, such a course being in the interests of legal certainty and the orderly development of the Convention case-law. Nevertheless, this would not prevent the

Court from departing from an earlier decision if it was persuaded that there were cogent reasons for doing so. Such a departure might, for example, be warranted in order to ensure that the interpretation of the Convention reflects societal changes and remains in line with present-day conditions. . . . (para. 35)

It would have been open to the Court to take a new approach, and indeed this was considered in the judgment in para. 46.

In a dissenting opinion Judge Martens expressed the view that he thought that the Court should have departed from its *Rees* judgment, and had cogent reasons for doing so. The Judge was critical of both the UK treatment of transsexuals in the *Corbett* case, and the reasoning and approach of the European Court in the *Rees* case, particularly the emphasis on biological sex as the decisive factor for sexual identity. He expressed the view that this system (the Biological Sex Determinant (BSD) System) violated the rights guaranteed under Article 12:

> . . . In the *Rees* judgment the question whether the BSD-system violates Article 12 was answered in the negative. The Court's arguments for doing so are conspicuously succinct: they only consist of two short paragraphs, of which the first (paragraph 49) is already decisive. There the Court interprets the words 'men and women' in Article 12 as denoting: 'persons of opposite *biological* sex' (emphasis added).
>
> . . . The Court does not elucidate the term '*biological* sex', but the meaning of that term can be deduced from the judgment.
>
> The arguments on which the Court's interpretation is based seem to echo those used by Mr Justice Ormrod in *Corbett* v *Corbett* as the basis for his opinion that 'sex is clearly an essential determinant of the relationship called marriage'. Whilst the Court speaks of '*traditional* marriage', the learned Judge said that marriage '*always* has been recognised as the union of man and woman' and 'is the institution on which the family is built'. Both this conspicuous similarity of arguments and paragraph 50 of the *Rees* judgment – where the Court, referring to United Kingdom law, notes that under that law persons who are not of the 'opposite biological sex' cannot marry – warrant the conclusion that the Court used the term 'biological sex' in the very same sense as did Mr Justice Ormrod, namely as 'the biological sexual constitution of an individual' which is 'fixed at birth'.
>
> . . . It is true that Article 12, by speaking of 'men and women', clearly indicates that marriage is the union of two persons of opposite sex. That does not necessarily mean, however, that 'sex' in this context must be interpreted as 'biological sex'. Nor can it be maintained that 'tradition' implies that 'sex' in this context can only mean 'the biological sexual constitution of an individual which is fixed at birth'. That interpretation has, therefore, to be supported by further arguments, the more so as it is far from self-evident that, when seeking a definition of what is meant by 'sex' in this context, one should choose one which depends on the situation obtaining when the would-be spouses were born, rather than when they want to marry, especially as the sexual condition of an individual is determined by several factors (viz. chromosomal factors: gonadal factors; genital factors; psychological factors) nearly all of which are (more or less) capable of changing.
>
> . . . This is all the more so because Mr Justice Ormrod's arguments are clearly unacceptable. Marriage is far more than a sexual union, and the capacity for sexual intercourse is therefore not '*essential*' for marriage. Persons who are not or are no longer capable of procreating or having sexual intercourse may also want to and do marry. That is because marriage is far more than a union which legitimates sexual

intercourse and aims at procreating: it is a legal institution which creates a fixed legal relationship between both the partners and third parties (including the authorities); it is a societal bond, in that married people (as one learned writer put it) 'represent to the world that theirs is a relationship based on strong human emotions, exclusive commitment to each other and permanence'; it is, moreover, a species of togetherness in which intellectual, spiritual and emotional bonds are at least as essential as the physical one.

Article 12 of the Convention protects the right of all men and women (of marriageable age) to enter into that union and therefore the definition of what is meant by 'men and women' in this context should take into account all these features of marriage. (paras 4.3.1, 4.3.2, 4.5.1 and 4.5.2)

The Court could seek little help on the matter of transsexualism from the drafting of the article, as transsexualism was not then a legal issue. However, more recently some changes have been made by member States – for example, Sweden in 1972, Germany in 1980 and Italy in 1982 – which have introduced the possibility of a change of legal sex for transsexuals and, subject to certain conditions, acknowledged their right to marry a person of their former sex. A German court judgment of 1978 had also held that there was no public interest reason for refusing to change the sex of a post-operative transsexual in the register of births.

Cases pending under this article

Sheffield v *UK* (Application No. 22985/93) raising similar issues to those of *Rees* and *Cassey* have been declared admissible by the Commission.

Further reading

Armstrong, C. and Walton, T., 'Transsexuals and the Law' (1990) 140 *New Law Journal* 1384

Millns, S., 'Transexuality and the European Convention on Human Rights' [1992] *Public Law Journal* 559

Naldi, G., 'No Hope for Transsexuals' (1987) 137 *New Law Journal* 129

CHAPTER 13
ARTICLE THIRTEEN

Article 13
Everyone whose rights and freedoms as set forth in this Convention are violated shall have an effective remedy before a national authority notwithstanding that the violation has been committed by persons acting in an official capacity.

13.1 THE SCOPE OF THE ARTICLE

In a partially dissenting judgment in the case of *Malone* v *UK* 7 EHRR 14, in which the Court had decided that it was not necessary to examine the claim under Article 13, Judges Matscher and Pinheiro Farinha expressed the opinion that 'Article 13 constitutes one of the most obscure clauses in the Convention and . . . its application raises extremely difficult and complicated problems of interpretation'. Indeed, they went on to remark that the Court and the Commission had avoided analysing this provision for over 20 years. Fortunately in the 1980s there were a number of cases in which the Commission did establish some principles for interpreting Article 13. Two of these cases involved the UK: *Silver* v *UK* Series A, Vol. 61 and *Campbell and Fell* v *UK* Series A, No. 80.

In the case of *Silver* v *UK*, the Court stated:

(a) where an individual has an arguable claim to be the victim of a violation of the rights set forth in the Convention, he should have a remedy before a national authority in order both to have his claim decided, and, if appropriate, to obtain redress . . .

(b) the authority referred to in Article 13 may not necessarily be a judicial authority, but, if it is not, its powers and the guarantees which it affords are relevant in determining whether the remedy before it is effective . . .

(c) although no single remedy may itself entirely satisfy the requirements of Article 13, the aggregate of remedies provided for under domestic law may do so . . .

(d) neither Article 13 nor the Convention in general lays down for the Contracting States any given manner for ensuring within their internal law the effective implementation of any of the provisions of the Convention – for example, by incorporating the Convention into domestic law. (para. 113)

Article 13 cannot therefore be interpreted to require a remedy in domestic law in respect of a 'supposed grievance'; there must be an arguable claim. If there is no arguable claim then Article 13 does not require the provision of an effective remedy (*Lockwood* v *UK* 15 CD 48), so not all claims of alleged breaches of the Convention require a remedy in domestic law (see, e.g., *Boyle and Rice* v *UK* 10 EHRR 425, *Powell and Rayner* v *UK* 12 EHRR 355). The case law of the Court has established a link between this concept of 'arguability' and that of 'manifestly ill-founded'. Thus where a claim is held to be 'manifestly ill-founded' under Article 27, para. 2, it is unlikely that there is an arguable claim if the claim under Article 13 relates to the claim declared to be manifestly ill-founded (*McLaughlin* v *UK* 18 EHRR CD 84). However, there may be cases in which the Court does not exclude a claim from the operation of Article 13, even if the Commission has declared the application manifestly ill-founded. The Court, while not being able to review the merits of the Commission's view that a claim is manifestly ill-founded, may consider those complaints which the Commission has declared admissible, including consideration of whether or not they are arguable (*Boyle and Rice* v *UK* 10 EHRR 425). Arguability will therefore be determined in the light of the particular facts of a claim.

Article 13 guarantees a right to the opportunity for an applicant to make a claim that there has been a breach of a Convention right. See, for example, the case of *Gaskin* 9 EHRR 235, where the availability of proceedings for discovery of documents concerning the applicant's childhood provided such an opportunity, so there was no breach of the article.

It should be noted that the provision of an effective remedy cannot be interpreted to mean that a favourable outcome must be assured. In the case of *Costello-Roberts* v *UK* 19 EHRR 112, the Commission expressed the opinion that despite having an arguable claim concerning his rights under Articles 3 and 8, the applicant would have had no prospect of bringing a successful assault claim against his headmaster, and therefore had no effective remedy before a national authority, because his civil action for assault would have been dismissed on the ground that his punishment fell within the bounds of reasonable and modest chastisement. The Court held, however, that it would have been open to the applicant to institute proceedings for civil assault and the domestic courts had the power to grant appropriate relief. It was not for the Court to speculate whether such proceedings would have been favourable or not. There was therefore no breach of Article 13.

Article 13 does not provide a remedy for applicants who allege that national legislation is not in conformity with the Convention. As was pointed out in *Young, James and Webster* 3 EHRR 20, 'such a remedy would amount to some sort of judicial review of legislation' (para. 177). Thus in *Liberal Party and Others* v *UK* 4 EHRR 106, although it was clear that Article 13 applied as much to the articles of the First Protocol as to the rest of the Convention, it could not be used to examine the application of the Representation of the People Act 1949; in *Kaplan* v *UK* 4 EHRR 64, Article 13 could not be relied on to challenge the right of the Secretary of State for Trade to impose trading restrictions on insurance companies under s. 29 of the Insurance Companies Act 1974; and in *Lithgow and Others* v *UK* 8 EHRR 329, it could not be used to challenge the validity of the Aircraft and Shipbuilding Industries Act 1977.

Just as Article 13 cannot be applied to guarantee a remedy by which legislation can be controlled as to its conformity with the Convention, neither could the Commission examine the power of the courts to impose the equitable remedy of an injunction restraining publication in the case of *Observer and Guardian* v *UK* 14 EHRR 153. However, if applicants are victims of 'norms' which are incompatible with the Convention – as opposed to legislation – then Article 13 may require an effective remedy (*Abdulaziz, Cabales and Balkandali* v *UK* Series A, Vol. 94). Nevertheless Article 13 cannot be interpreted so as to dictate to the Contracting States how the Convention should be given effective implementation in domestic law, nor can it be interpreted to ensure that domestic courts apply the same standards or criteria, or enjoy the same scope of examination in each Contracting State.

Because the Convention is not incorporated into UK law the Commission and European Court of Human Rights usually examine the effectiveness of court and appeal procedures, including the availability of judicial review. Where breach of a civil right is alleged then the application should be brought under Article 6, para. 1, rather than under Article 13, as the former provides a more rigorous procedural guarantee, whereas the provisions of Article 13 are more general (see, for example, *App. No. 11468/85* v *UK* 9 EHRR 350 and *App. No. 11949/86* v *UK* 10 EHRR 123 at 149). The requirements of Article 13 are therefore absorbed by Article 6, where the latter is pleaded (*Silver* v *UK* 4 EHRR 347; *W* v *UK* 10 EHRR 29; *R* v *UK* 10 EHRR 74 and *Granger* v *UK* 12 EHRR 451).

Article 13 is also effectively excluded by a claim under Article 5, para. 4 in the case of an effective remedy to protect the right to liberty and security of the person. If a violation of Article 5, para. 4 is not raised by an applicant, then the Court may refuse to examine whether the less strict requirements of Article 13 were complied with, unless the facts or law incline the Court to do so (*Murray* v *UK* 19 EHRR 193).

Most of the applications which succeed under this article are those where there is clearly either a gap in the available remedies, or the action complained of is specifically excluded from such available remedies. Cases illustrating the former situation include *Silver and Others* v *UK* 5 EHRR 347, *App. No. 9659* v *UK* 8 EHRR 274 and *McCallum* v *UK* 13 EHRR 597 (where there was no effective remedy concerning the validity of a Secretary of State's directive stopping prisoners' letters and its compatibility with the Convention). An example of the latter situation is the case of *Baggs* v *UK* 9 EHRR 235, where there was no specific remedy for individuals who might be affected by aircraft noise in the vicinity of airports because s. 76 of the Civil Aviation Act 1982 excluded liability in nuisance with regard to the flight of aircraft in certain circumstances. Similarly, in *Firsoff* v *UK* 15 EHRR CD 111, under the Post

Office Act 1969, s. 29, the Post Office was protected by a statutory immunity from tort in the case of interference with mail; while in *Hodgson, Woolf Productions and National Union of Journalists and Channel Four Television* v *UK* 10 EHRR 503, it was clear that the Contempt of Court Act 1981 granted the applicants no right to oppose or appeal an Order made under s. 4(2), and that therefore they had no effective remedy in respect of a claim under Article 10. It should be noted that the need to establish that there is an effective remedy available, falls on the defendant Government. Thus in the case of *Hewitt and Harman* v *UK* 14 EHRR 657, the Commission found that the applicants did not have an effective remedy in respect of complaints concerning secret surveillance in breach of Article 8, as the Commission had not been informed of the existence of any effective remedy by the UK.

13.2   THE CASES

Silver and Others v *UK*
Series A, Vol. 61

The facts

This case, which has been considered under Article 8, concerned respect for the private correspondence of prisoners and the interference with that correspondence by the prison authorities. Under Article 13, the applicants submitted that in the UK there was no remedy in respect of their claims under Article 6, para. 1, Article 8 and Article 10, as there were no enforceable rights concerning correspondence.

The Commission's opinion

The Government had argued that Article 13 could be invoked only if a violation of another right under the Convention had been established. Alternatively, that effective remedies were available through the courts, the Ombudsman, or the prison authorities.

The Commission established at the outset that:

> . . . the right under Article 13 is an autonomous one, which may be examined by the Convention organs irrespective of whether they have found a breach of an applicant's other Convention rights. (para. 439)

The Commission must examine in fact what remedies are available and whether these are effective. The authority referred to in Article 13 need not always be judicial. The Commission considered that:

> . . . Article 13 requires the high Contracting Parties to provide domestic remedies whereby an individual's claim of a breach of a Convention right or freedom, at least in substance, may be determined, and redressed should the claim be established. (para. 442)

In the present case the Commission considered the application of Article 13 in respect of the claims made under Article 8. In considering the possible remedies claimed by the Government, the Commission found that:

. . . In the context of prisoners' correspondence, the Commission observes that a prisoner's right to respect for correspondence, freedom of expression and access to courts, or equivalents thereof, do not appear to be enforceable before the English courts, the prison rules, i.e. the domestic law, affording a wide discretion to the prison administration to control prisoners' correspondence and there being no domestic jurisprudence to indicate the possibility of bringing an effective action against the prison administration in this respect.

. . . The Commission finds, therefore, that the English courts were unable to provide an effective remedy in respect of the substance of the applicants' claims under Article 8. (paras 445 and 446)

As far as the Ombudsman was concerned, the Commission observed that:

. . . access to the Ombudsman is indirect, requiring the co-operation of a Member of Parliament, to whom prisoners' access may also be prevented. The Ombudsman's jurisdiction is limited to that of maladministration, thus he could not consider the claim of an interference with a prisoner's right to respect for correspondence pursuant to the correct exercise of the wide discretion afforded to the prison administration to control prisoners' correspondence. It appears, also, that the Ombudsman could not directly grant redress for a legitimate complaint of maladministration as he is limited to reporting the results of his inquiries to the persons concerned or, if necessary, to Parliament.

. . . The Commission finds, therefore, that the Parliamentary Commissioner for Administration was unable to provide an effective remedy in respect of the substance of the applicants' claims under Article 8. (paras 447 and 448)

Further, that:

. . . the powers of the board of visitors, in dealing with prisoners' complaints of censorship of correspondence, are limited to an examination of the correct application of the prison rules and Standing Orders. Even if a board were not satisfied that the regulations had been properly applied they could not enforce their decision, but could only advise the prison governor accordingly, or report their conclusions to the Home Secretary.

. . . The Commission finds, therefore, that the board of visitors was unable to provide an effective remedy in respect of the substance of the applicants' claims under Article 8. (paras 449 and 450)

With regard to the possibility of recourse to the Home Secretary providing an effective remedy, the Commission noted that:

. . . it is the Home Secretary himself who has issued the restrictive Standing Orders in respect of prisoners' correspondence, many of which Orders the Commission considers to be incompatible with the Convention, that it is an acknowledged aim of the prison administration to maintain a uniform censorship practice and that the facts of the present case disclose a consistent denial of redress for censorship complaints where the censorship was in accordance with the regulations. The Commission finds in the circumstances of the censorship system in operation at the time of the prisoner-applicants' detention, that a petition to the Home Secretary could not be considered to have provided an effective remedy in respect of the substance of the applicants' claims under Article 8.

. . . The Commission is of the opinion, by a vote of 14 against one that the absence of effective domestic remedies for the applicants' claims under Article 8 constituted a violation of Article 13 of the Convention. (paras 451 and 452)

The judgment of the Court

In the context of Article 13, the Court decided to consider 'the question of safeguards against abuse of the powers to control prisoners' correspondence' (para. 111). The Court held that:

> ... the application of Article 13 in a given case will depend upon the manner in which the Contacting State concerned has chosen to discharge its obligation under Article 1 directly to secure to anyone within its jurisdiction the rights and freedoms set out in section I. (para 113)

In considering the remedies claimed to be available to the applicants, the Court, like the Commission, found that an application to the Board of Visitors and an application to the Parliamentary Commissioner for Administration (the Ombudsman), did not constitute an effective remedy.

As far as the possibility of the Home Secretary providing an effective remedy was concerned, the Court held that:

> ... if there were a complaint to him as to the validity of an Order or Instruction under which a measure of control over correspondence had been carried out, he could not be considered to have a sufficiently independent standpoint to satisfy the requirements of Article 13 as the author of the directives in question, he would in reality be judge in his own cause. The position, however, would be otherwise if the complainant alleged that a measure of control resulted from a misapplication of one of those directives. The Court is satisfied that in such cases a petition to the Home Secretary would in general be effective to secure compliance with the directive, if the complaint was well-founded. The Court notes, however, that even in these cases, at least prior to 1 December 1981, the conditions for the submission of such petitions imposed limitations on the availability of this remedy in some circumstances . . . (para. 116)

Although the English courts had a certain supervisory jurisdiction over the exercise of powers conferred on the Home Secretary and the prison authorities, this was limited to the established grounds of judicial review. In the circumstances the English courts could not have found that the measures interfering with the prisoners' correspondence were taken arbitrarily, in bad faith, for an improper motive or in an *ultra vires* manner.

The Court held that:

> ... in those instances where the norms in question were incompatible with the Convention and where the Court has found a violation of Article 8 to have occurred there was no effective remedy and Article 13 has therefore also been violated. In the remaining cases, there is no reason to assume that the applicants' complaints could not have been duly examined by the Home Secretary and/or the English courts and Article 13 has therefore not been violated . . . (para. 119)

Campbell and Fell v UK
Series A, Vol. 80

The Facts

The applicants were category A prisoners, convicted of offences relating to terrorist activities of the IRA. During their imprisonment they were charged with disciplinary offences relating to a sit-down protest inside the prison. As a result of these offences they were awarded loss of remission and loss of certain privileges. The applicants complained to the Commission that they had been convicted of disciplinary offences amounting to criminal charges without the benefit of a hearing complying with the requirements of Article 6; that delays in obtaining legal advice caused by the prison authorities had breached the right of access to court under Article 6, and that rights to respect for correspondence had also been violated. Further complaints related to the refusal to allow independent medical examination of alleged injuries sustained in prison, and of treatment before and after the protest.

Under Article 13, Father Fell complained that there was no effective remedy for the complaints under Articles 6 and 8.

The Commission's opinion

The Commission expressed the opinion that Father Fell's complaints relating to Article 6 raised no separate issue under Article 13 as regards access to legal advice, refusal to allow independent medical examination and refusal to allow confidential consultation with his lawyer. The Commission did find, however, that there was no effective remedy available to Father Fell concerning his complaints under Article 8 and that this amounted to a breach of Article 13.

The judgment of the Court

The Court agreed with the Commission as far as the complaints under Article 6 were concerned. With respect to the complaints concerning Article 8, the Court, agreeing with the Commission, held that the complaint about refusal of confidential consultation with the applicant's lawyer fell to be considered with the other complaints under Article 6 and need not be examined under Article 8. However, the Court did feel it was necessary to examine the two remaining complaints, namely restrictions placed on personal correspondence and access to legal advice.

Turning to the first, the Court found that:

... It was not alleged that the restrictions at issue were unlawful under domestic law or resulted from a misapplication of the relevant directives. Again, it was not suggested that any remedies were available to the applicant other than the four channels of complaint examined by the Commission, namely an application to the Board of Visitors, an application to the Parliamentary Commissioner for Administration, the institution of proceedings before the English courts and a petition to the Home Secretary.

The Government accepted, in their memorial to the Court, that prior to December 1981 the first three channels of complaint would not have provided Father Fell with an 'effective remedy', within the meaning of Article 13, in respect of the complaints in question. For the reasons given in its abovementioned *Silver and Others* judgment, the Court finds that this must be so.

... At the hearings before the Court, the Government stated that they did not seek to argue that a petition to the Home Secretary would have provided an 'effective remedy' as regards the delay in allowing contact with a lawyer. However, they suggested that the position might have been otherwise as regards the refusal to allow correspondence with Sister Power and Sister Benedict, had Father Fell established that the authorities had incorrectly applied the relevant directives in treating these two nuns as not being 'close personal friends'.

The Court has found that the restrictions on Father Fell's access to legal advice and on his personal correspondence were the result of the application of norms that were incompatible with the Convention. In such circumstances, as the Court held in its abovementioned *Silver and Others* judgment, there could be no 'effective remedy' as required by Article 13. In particular, a petition to the Home Secretary could only have been effective if the complainant alleged that a measure of control over correspondence resulted from a misapplication of one of the relevant directives. And in the present case, Father Fell made no such allegation nor do the circumstances suggest that he would have been in a position to do so.

. . . As regards the applicant's complaints concerning the two restrictions in question, there has accordingly been a violation of Article 13. (paras 126–128)

Abdulaziz, Cabales and Balkandali v *UK*
Series A, Vol. 94

The facts
This case, which has been considered under Article 8 and which also raised issues considered under Article 14, concerned the refusal of the immigration authorities to allow the applicants' husbands to join them in order to reside permanently in the UK.

The Government contended that as the complaints of the applicants related to primary or secondary legislation, Article 13 could not be relied on. Alternatively, that there were effective remedies in the form of adjudicators, Immigration Appeal Tribunals and representations to the Secretary of State through Members of Parliament.

The Commission's opinion
The Commission, while accepting this limitation on the applicability of Article 13, first had to establish the nature of the measures complained of:

. . . The first question to be determined is the legal nature of the Statement of Changes in Immigration Rules in view of the Government's contention that they are delegated, secondary legislation against which no remedy can be required under Article 13.

. . . It seems, however, that these Rules are not delegated legislation, but a hybrid of delegated legislation and administrative guidelines. Even though Parliament may disapprove of their content the Rules drawn up by the Home Secretary nevertheless come into force until the Home Secretary amends them with a new Statement of the Changes in accordance with the wishes of Parliament. The Home Secretary is thus free to issue whatever Rules he sees fit, subject, presumably, to the ultimate sanction of his political career or a vote of no confidence in the Government should he ignore Parliament's dictate. On the other hand the Rules are binding on the independent appellate bodies; the adjudicator and Immigration Appeal Tribunals are obliged to enforce them.

. . . In the Commission's view, however, it is their origin which is decisive – the power of the Secretary of State to implement such immigration rules as he considers necessary, relegates his Statement of Changes in Immigration Rules to the status of administrative regulations. Accordingly they do not have the aforementioned immunity under Article 13 with regard to legislation.

. . . The Commission finds that the applicants are entitled to an effective domestic remedy under Article 13 for their claims relating to Articles 3, 8 and 14 as regards the application of the Statement of Changes in Immigration Rules, HC 394, in their cases. (paras 126–129)

Then the Commission considered the remedies which the Government claimed to be effective.

Dealing first with the adjudicators and Immigration Appeals Tribunals, the Commission expressed the opinion that:

> . . . Under the Immigration Act 1971 the applicants' husbands had rights of appeal against the Secretary of State's refusal to allow them to remain in (first and third applicants) or enter (second applicant) the United Kingdom. The Commission notes, however, that the appellate authorities are bound to apply the current Statement of Changes in Immigration Rules, HC 394 at the material time. The Rules in HC 394, of which the applicants complain, contained no element of discretion in respect of which the appellate authorities could have substituted their evaluation for that of the Home Secretary. The Rules clearly prohibited the entry or stay of the foreign husbands of women who are not United Kingdom citizens born in the United Kingdom or one of whose parents was born there.
>
> . . . The Commission observes that these authorities may, at their discretion, recommend that the Secretary of State change his decision, making an exception to the Rules, but such recommendations, although taken very seriously by the Secretary of State, are not binding upon him.
>
> . . . The rights of appeal concerning deportation procedures are not relevant to the present cases, no such procedures having been instigated against the applicants' husbands. (paras 131–133)

As far as representation to Members of Parliament were concerned, the Commission considered that:

> . . . It is clear that many Members of Parliament show active concern with the problems of their immigrant constituents. They often make representations to the Secretary of State in the hope of persuading him to exercise his descretion outside the relevant Immigration Rules. However it cannot be overlooked that such representations depend upon the willingness of the Member of Parliament to assist, and are not binding upon the Secretary of State. (para. 134)

While the Secretary of State made the ultimate decision as to whether or not an immigrant might be allowed to reside in the UK, the Commission observed that:

> . . . It is he who issued the restrictive Rules of which the applicants complain, he who refused entry or permission to remain, to him that recommendations can be made by appellate authorities or representations by Members of Parliament and he alone who can waive the Rules when all other avenues have been tried, despite that fact the one of his principal concerns must be to implement a uniform immigration policy. Furthermore, the Commission would add that it has found that the Home Secretary's Immigration Rules HC 394, as applied in the present cases, are not compatible with the Convention by virtue of sexual discrimination. (para. 135)

Furthermore,

> . . . the courts would, like the aforementioned appellate authorities, be obliged to uphold the lawful application of the immigration Rules in question. The refusal of immigration authorities to waive the requirements of the Immigration Rules HC 394

would not have been an exercise of discretion which could have been reviewed by the courts. Moreover they would not have been competent to deal with claims of discrimination or interference with the right to respect for family life allegedly caused by the lawful application of those Rules.

. . . The Commission finds that there is no domestic remedy available to the applicants which presents sufficient guarantees of independence and efficacy, and which could have satisfactorily dealt with their claims of discrimination, unjustified interference with their right to respect for family life or degrading treatment. (paras 136 and 137)

The judgment of the Court

The Court held that the discrimination which had been established under Articles 8 and 14 was the result of norms which were incompatible with the Convention. Because the UK had not incorporated the Convention into its domestic law, there could be no effective remedy:

. . . [R]ecourse to the available channels of complaint (the immigration appeals system, representations to the Home Secretary, application for judicial review) could have been effective only if the complainant alleged that the discrimination resulted from a misapplication of the 1980 (Immigration) Rules. Yet here no such allegation was made nor was it suggested that discrimination in any other way contravened domestic law. (para. 93)

The Court concluded that there had been a violation of Article 13.

Comment

The term 'norms' in this context appears to be used to describe administrative practices which do not originate from regulations or published guidelines or legislation. They are manifestations of attitude or a particular approach to certain situations. The incorporation of the Convention into UK law would presumably make the existence of such norms illegal if they were relied on to inform or govern particular approaches.

Boyle and Rice v *UK*
Series A, Vol. 131

The facts

Three of the applicants were prisoners in Scottish prisons, while the fourth applicant was the father of one of them. Their Article 13 complaint concerned interferences with their correspondence while in prison, interference with rights to family life under Article 8, including visiting rights, and discriminatory prison regimes. In particular, they complained about the differential prison regimes that operated when they were transferred to prison in Edinburgh.

The Commission's opinion

The Government submitted that the applicants' claims were not arguable, or alternatively related to legislation and therefore fell outside the ambit of Article 13. It also submitted that effective remedies existed in the form of complaints procedures to the Visiting Committee, the Secretary of State, and the Parliamentary Commissioner for Administration or the courts.

The Commission, following the interpretation of Article 13 given in *Silver*, expressed the opinion that:

> . . . Article 13 plays a key rôle in the Convention system because it requires the provision of national safeguards against the misuse of power and the infringement of Convention rights. It provides the counterpart of the requirement to exhaust domestic remedies in Article 26 and reflects the subsidiary character of the Convention system to the national systems safeguarding human rights.
> . . . However for Article 13 to apply the claim that a provision of the Convention has been breached must be an arguable one. The Commission considers that an arguable claim falls to be determined on the particular facts of each case and should have the following elements:
> —it should concern a right or freedom guaranteed by the Convention;
> —the claim should not be wholly unsubstantiated on the facts;
> —the claim should give rise to a *prima facie* issue under the Convention. (paras 73 and 74)

While accepting that Article 13 could not be used to control the conformity of legislation with the Convention, the Commission had to decide whether the Prison Rules, Standing Orders and administrative circulars could properly be described as legislation. Following similar reasoning to that followed in the case of *Abdulaziz, Cabales and Balkandali,* the Commission expressed the opinion that the Prison Rules, Standing Orders and administrative circulars amounted to 'norms' rather than legislation, and did not have immunity from Article 13. Therefore the Commission had to consider the effectiveness of the remedies available.

In the light of the *Silver* finding, the Commission expressed the opinion that neither the Visiting Committee, nor the Parliamentary Commissioner offered effective remedies, and that the Secretary of State could be considered to be an effective remedy only in limited circumstances. Similarly, the jurisdiction of the Scottish courts was limited to the established grounds of judicial review. Further, the Commission considered that:

> . . . the lack of effectiveness of each remedy, considered in isolation, is not cured by considering the aggregate of remedies as a whole since the imperfections which taint each single remedy still remain.
> . . . The Commission is aware that in certain cirumstances recourse to a series of remedies may result in redress actually being granted. However the assessment of the effectiveness of a remedy or an aggregate of remedies must be measured according to objective criteria such as the nature and scope and procedural guarantees of the remedies in question and not in terms of a potentially successful outcome. (paras 85 and 86)

Applying Article 13 to the facts, the Commission found that there was no arguable claim concerning the complaints of Mr and Mrs Boyle about their correspondence. There was, however, an arguable claim concerning restrictions on prison visits, and as these restrictions emanated from the relevant norms – i.e. the Prison Rules and Standing Orders – and not from the implementation of those norms, there was no effective remedy to the Secretary of State, and therefore there was a breach of Article 13. The Commission also found that there had been a violation of Article 13 concerning the refusal by the authorities to allow Mr Rice to visit his sick father, but no violation in respect of the discriminatory prison regimes experienced by the applicants.

The judgment of the Court

The Court confirmed the general principles established in the *Silver* case:

> ... Notwithstanding the terms of Article 13 read literally, the existence of an actual breach of another provision of the Convention (a 'substantive' provision) is not a prerequisite for the application of the Article. Article 13 guarantees the availability of a remedy at national level to enforce – and hence to allege non-compliance with – the substance of the Convention rights and freedoms in whatever form they may happen to be secured in the domestic legal order.
>
> However, Article 13 cannot reasonably be interpreted so as to require a remedy in domestic law in respect of any supposed grievance under the Convention that an individual may have, no matter how unmeritorious his complaint may be: the grievance must be an arguable one in terms of the Convention. (para. 52)

In considering whether a finding that a complaint was 'manifestly ill-founded' meant that it was not an arguable claim for the purposes of Article 13, the Court held:

> ... rejection of a complaint as 'manifestly ill-founded' amounts to a decision that 'there is not even a *prima facie* case against the respondent State. On the ordinary meaning of the words, it is difficult to conceive how a claim that is 'manifestly ill-founded' can nevertheless be 'arguable', and *vice versa*.
>
> This does not mean, however, that the Court must hold a claim to be excluded from the operation of Article 13 if the Commission has previously declared it manifestly ill-founded under the substantive Article. The Commission's decision declaring an application admissible determines the scope of the case brought before the Court. The Court is precluded from reviewing on their merits under the relevant Article the complaints rejected as manifestly ill-founded, but empowered to entertain those complaints which the Commission had declared admissible and which have been duly referred to it. The Court is thus competent to take cognizance of all questions of fact and of law arising in the context of the complaints before it under Article 13, including the arguability or not of the claims of violation of the substantive provisions. In this connection, the Commission's decision on the admissibility of the underlying claims and the reasoning therein, whilst not being decisive, provide significant pointers as to the arguable character of the claims for the purposes of Article 13.
>
> ... The Court does not think that it should give an abstract definition of the notion of arguability. Rather it must be determined, in the light of the particular facts and the nature of the legal issue or issues raised, whether each individual claim of violation forming the basis of a complaint under Article 13 was arguable and, if so, whether the requirements of Article 13 were met in relation thereto. (paras 54 and 55)

Considering the individual claims, the Court agreed with the Commission that there was no breach in connection with interference with correspondence. As regards the complaints that some mail had been read aloud and that a letter had been stopped, the Court held that in these cases there were remedies available to the applicants.

As far as limitations on visiting rights were concerned, the Court found that arguable claims were raised under this issue – although such interference might be found to be justifiable – but that effective remedies existed. The fact that use of these might not be successful did not detract from their effectiveness. The Court also held that there was no arguable claim concerning the discriminatory prison regimes.

The Court refrained from elaborating on the interpretation of Article 13. It stated:

> ... During the course of the pleadings before the Court, considerable argument was presented as to the requirements of Article 13 in circumstances where the complaint is directed against the content of the applicable national norms – as laid down in primary legislation, subordinate legislation or internal administrative directives – rather than against the implementation of the norms. In particular, the question was raised whether Article 13 imposed a duty on a Contracting State to make available a remedy enabling an individual to challenge the terms of subordinate legislation, and there was dispute as to the nature of the remedy required by Article 13 when the applicable national norms are themselves fully compatible with the substantive provisions of the Convention.
>
> In view of its above findings in relation to the individual complaints made by the applicants, the Court considers it unnecessary to go into these issues of interpretation in the present case. (para. 87)

Judge de Meyer, in a separate opinion, expressed the view that the requirement of 'arguability' was unnecessary.

Comment

This is one of the few cases which primarily raised issues relating to Article 13 rather than other articles. As such it confirmed the independent existence of rights under Article 13. Some of the claims failed because they were not at the outset arguable, while in other instances there were effective remedies available.

After the events giving rise to the complaints of the applicants, but before the Court hearing, a number of changes were introduced concerning prisoners' correspondence, following the judgment in 1983 in the *Silver* case.

Soering v UK
Series A, Vol. 161

The facts

The applicant faced extradition to the United States of America to face murder charges, and possibly the death sentence if found guilty. The main thrust of his complaint fell under Article 3 and is considered under that Article. Under Article 13 the applicant submitted that:

> ... he has no effective remedy in respect of his complaint under Article 3 of the Convention that he is likely to receive the death penalty and be subjected to the 'death row phenomenon'. He claims that the Secretary of State cannot be regarded as sufficiently independent and impartial to constitute an effective remedy. Furthermore, judicial review of the Secretary of State's decision is limited to the question of whether he acted reasonably and not to whether his decision is in conformity with the Convention.

... The repondent Government contends, in the first place, that Article 13 does not apply because the applicant's complaint under Article 3 of the Convention is not 'arguable'. It further submits that this provision has no application in respect of an anticipated violation of the Convention since it would create potential difficulties for the domestic authorities both in terms of deciding whether a breach of the Convention was likely to occur and the nature of the remedy to be granted. Finally the Government accepts that the courts could not review the exercise of discretion by the Secretary of State on the basis that the applicant might be exposed to treatment in breach of Article 3 but maintains that this provision is satisfied by the following remedies, taken on their own or in aggregate, an action for *habeas corpus*, a petition to the Secretary of State and judicial review of his decision. (paras 159 and 160)

The UK Government argued that because the extradition was governed by an international treaty Article 13 had no application, or alternatively that the aggregate of remedies available in domestic law were effective.

The Commission's opinion
The Commission considered that the applicant had an 'arguable' complaint and that this was so even though the complaint under Article 3 was prospective or anticipatory in nature:

... It follows from the nature of the guarantee under Article 13 that the requirement to provide an effective remedy must also extend in this domain to arguable claims made by a person whose extradition or expulsion is imminent and who may be exposed to harm which is irremediable in nature. Any other interpretation would substantially weaken the guarantee of an effective remedy under this provision.

... As to the effectiveness of the remedies available under United Kingdom law in respect of this complaint, the Commission notes, firstly, that the remedy of *habeas corpus* was open to the applicant after the committal proceedings before Bow Street Magistrates' Court on 16 June 1987. However, it is clear that the courts can only examine the question whether the extradition proceedings were properly conducted in accordance with the law of the United Kingdom and cannot examine the applicant's allegations as to the treatment he would be exposed to in the United States. This remedy is not, therefore, an effective remedy for purposes of this provision.

... Further, as regards a petition to the Secretary of State for Home Affairs, the Commission observes from section 11 of the Extradition Act 1870 that it is incumbent on the Secretary of State to take the final decision to order the applicant's extradition following committal by a Magistrate. Moreover, it is the Secretary of State who orders the Magistrate to arrest a person with a view to extradition. In the light of the Secretary of State's rôle in the extradition procedure it cannot be said that he is independent of the parties in the exercise of his discretion under section 11. For this reason the Commission does not consider that the possibility of petitioning the Secretary of State constitutes an effective remedy under this provision.

... As regards judicial review proceedings following the Secretary of State's order, the Commission notes that it is not contested by the Government that the courts limit their examination to the question whether the Secretary of State has acted illegally, irrationally or improperly and do not examine the applicant's fear that he might be exposed to inhuman or degrading treatment and punishment. Accordingly the Commission does not consider that judicial review proceedings constitute an effective remedy as required by this provision.

... Finally, the Commission does not consider that the above remedies considered in aggregate provide an effective remedy. In the Commission's view the lack of effectiveness of each remedy, considered in isolation, is not cured by considering the aggregate of remedies as a whole since the imperfections which taint each single remedy remain.

. . . It follows that the applicant does not have an effective remedy under the law of the United Kingdom in respect of his complaint under Article 3 as required by Article 13 of the Convention.

. . .

. . . The Commission concludes, by seven votes to four, that there has been a violation of Article 13 in the present case. (paras 163–169)

The judgment of the Court

The Court considered the remedies which the UK Government had suggested were effective, namely an application for *habeas corpus* and an application for judicial review:

. . . Both the applicant and the Commission were of the opinion that the scope of judicial review was too narrow to allow the courts to consider the subject matter of the complaint which the applicant has made in the context of Article 3. The applicant further contended that the courts' lack of jurisdiction to issue interim injunctions against the Crown was an additional reason rendering judicial review an ineffective remedy.

. . . Article 13 guarantees the availability of a remedy at national level to enforce the substance of the Convention rights and freedoms in whatever form they may happen to be secured in the domestic legal order. The effect of Article 13 is thus to require the provision of a domestic remedy allowing the competent 'national authority' both to deal with the substance of the relevant Convention complaint and to grant appropriate relief.

. . . In judicial review proceedings the court may rule the exercise of executive discretion unlawful on the ground that it is tainted with illegality, irrationality or procedural impropriety. In an extradition case the test of 'irrationality,' on the basis of the so-called 'Wednesbury principles,' would be that no reasonable Secretary of State could have made an order for surrender in the circumstances. According to the United Kingdom Government, a court would have jurisdiction to quash a challenged decision to send a fugitive to a country where it was established that there was a serious risk of inhuman or degrading treatment, on the ground that in all the circumstances of the case the decision was one that no reasonable Secretary of State could take. Although the Convention is not considered to be part of United Kingdom law, the Court is satisfied that the English courts can review the 'reasonableness' of an extradition decision in the light of the kind of factors relied on by Mr Soering before the Convention institutions in the context of Article 3.

. . . Mr Soering did admittedly make an application for judicial review together with his application for *habeas corpus* and was met with an unfavourable response from Lloyd LJ on the issue of 'irrationality'. However, as Lloyd LJ explained, the claim failed because it was premature, the courts only having jurisdiction once the Minister has actually taken his decision. Furthermore, the arguments adduced by Mr Soering were by no means the same as those relied on when justifying his complaint under Article 3 before the Convention institutions. His counsel before the Divisional Court limited himself to submitting that the assurance by the United States' authorities was so worthless than no reasonable Secretary of State could regard it as satisfactory under the Treaty. This is an argument going to the likelihood of the death penalty being imposed but says nothing about the quality of the treatment awaiting Mr Soering after sentence to death, this being the substance of his allegation of inhuman and degrading treatment.

There was nothing to have stopped Mr Soering bringing an application for judicial review at the appropriate moment and arguing 'Wednesbury unreasonableness' on the basis of much the same material that he adduced before the Convention institutions in relation to the death row phenomenon. Such a claim would have been given 'the most anxious scrutiny' in view of the fundamental nature of the human right at stake. The effectiveness of the remedy, for the purposes of Article 13, does not depend on the certainty of a favourable outcome for Mr Soering, and in any event it is not for this Court to speculate as to what would have been the decision of the English courts.

... The English courts' lack of jurisdiction to grant interim injunctions against the Crown does not, in the Court's opinion, detract from the effectiveness of judicial review in the present connection, since there is no suggestion that in practice a fugitive would ever be surrendered before his application to the Divisional Court and any eventual appeal therefrom had been determined.

... The Court concludes that Mr Soering did have available to him under English law an effective remedy in relation to his complaint under Article 3. This being so, there is no need to inquire into the other two remedies referred to by the United Kingdom Government.

There is accordingly no breach of Article 13. (paras 119–124)

Comment

The '*Wednesbury*' principles were those enumerated in the case of *Associated Provincial Picture Houses Ltd* v *Wednesbury Corporation* [1948] 1 KB 223. These principles establish a reasonableness test for ministerial decisions. In the case of extradition, the application of the principles would be that a decision to extradite would be irrational if no reasonable Secretary of State could have made such an order in the circumstances. If the decision is found to be irrational it can be quashed.

It should be noted that the remedy of *habeas corpus* depends upon showing a breach of the national laws. It is not available for a claim that detention is illegal by reason only of a breach of the Convention (*Brannigan and McBride* v *UK* 17 EHRR 539).

Vilvarajah and Others v UK
Series A, Vol. 215

The facts

This case, which has been considered under Article 3, concerned claims for asylum by the applicants who were all Tamils from Sri Lanka. They had sought judicial review of the refusals by the UK to grant them asylum. They complained that the refusals infringed Article 13, because they had no effective remedy whereby their claim that they faced the risk of inhuman and degrading treatment under Article 3 could be tested. The remedies that had been available to them were: representations by the UK Immigrants' Advisory Service (UKIAS), representations by Members of Parliament, appeal to an independent Adjudicator under s. 13 of the Immigration Act 1971 and judicial review of the Secretary of State's decision to refuse asylum.

The Commission's opinion

The Commission considered that:

... the UKIAS referral system and representation by Members of Parliament cannot be deemed effective remedies for the purposes of Article 13 of the Convention. Although UKIAS or a Member of Parliament may be able to influence the Secretary of State, who otherwise might have refused an asylum application, their intervention on behalf of an asylum seeker has no mandatory effect on that decision.

... As regards the appeal to an independent Adjudicator under section 13 of the Immigration Act 1971, the Commission finds that in many instances it would fully satisfy the requirements of Article 13 of the Convention. The Adjudicator is empowered to examine the full merits of each case, both as regards fact and law, and may hear evidence. The Adjudicator may also substitute his evaluation for that of the Secretary of State and his decisions are largely binding. However this remedy was fatally flawed in the applicants' cases because it could only be from outside the UK. The Commission finds that the protection required by Article 13 of the Convention cannot be ensured if a person has to return to the very country where he fears persecution before he can effectively appeal against the asylum refusal. (paras 152 and 153)

In considering whether the possibility of judicial review met the requirements of Article 13 in this case, the Commission noted that:

... In the present cases the only ground on which the refusal of the Secretary of State to allow the applicants to remain in the UK could be challenged was that the decision was irrational, that is to say, a decision which no reasonable Secretary of State could have made. The Commission is of the opinion that the consideration of the possible perversity of the executive's decision in these cases is too restrictive an examination in view of what may be at stake, namely the possibility of someone being returned to a country where he would allegedly be a target for arbitrary detention, torture, disappearance or the like.

... The Commission notes that judicial review by the English courts has significantly progressed over the last 20 years to check the arbitrariness of administrative decisions. Furthermore, in asylum cases the courts have examined with care the application of the Immigration Rules and the 1951 Refugee Convention. The position however remains that in judicial review proceedings the courts are concerned with the way in which a decision is taken and not with the merits of a decision. They have deliberately refrained from examining the well-foundedness of the asylum seeker's claims or from reviewing any of the material on which the Secretary of State has based his decision. There is nothing in the facts of the applicants' cases which suggests that the Secretary of State's refusal to grant compassionate leave to remain in the UK could have been the subject of a successful application for judicial review. (paras 155 and 156)

The Commission distinguished this case from the *Soering* case on the ground of the difference in complexity, particularly as to the nature of the risk faced, but nevertheless expressed the opinion that:

... the remedies afforded to asylum applicants, for the purposes of Article 13 of the Convention, should be equal to, if not greater than, the judicial safeguards afforded in extradition proceedings. Yet in the present cases it seems that adequate safeguards were not forthcoming in the judicial review proceedings.

. . . The Commission is not persuaded that the four remedies relied on by the Government could, as an aggregate, be said to satisfy Article 13 of the Convention. In matters as vital as asylum questions it is essential to have a fully effective remedy providing the guarantees of a certain independence of the parties, a binding decision-making power and a thorough review of the reasonableness of the asylum seeker's fear of persecution.

. . .

. . . The Commission concludes, by 13 notes to one, that there has been a violation of Article 13 of the Convention, in that the applicants did not have any effective domestic remedies available to them in respect of their claim under Article 3 of the Convention. (paras 159–161)

The judgment of the Court

Referring to its decision in the *Soering* case, the Court did not consider that there were any material differences between that case and this one:

. . . It is not in dispute that the English courts are able in asylum cases to review the Secretary of State's refusal to grant asylum with reference to the same principles of judicial review as considered in the *Soering* case and to quash a decision in similar circumstances and that they have done so in decided cases. Indeed the courts have stressed their special responsibility to subject administrative decisions in this area to the most anxious scrutiny where an applicant's life or liberty may be at risk. Moreover, the practice is that an asylum seeker will not be removed from the UK until proceedings are complete once he has obtained leave to apply for judicial review.

. . . While it is true that there are limitations on the powers of the courts in judicial review proceedings the Court is of the opinion that these powers, exercisable as they are by the highest tribunals in the land, do provide an effective degree of control over the decisions of the administrative authorities in asylum cases and are sufficient to satisfy the requirements of Article 13.

. . . The applicants thus had available to them an effective remedy in relation to their complaint under Article 3. There is accordingly no breach of Article 13. (paras 125–127)

Judge Walsh, joined by Judge Russo, expressed a partly dissenting opinion that the two cases could be distinguished, and that judicial review did not exist to resolve disputed issues such as arose in this case.

Comment

In the *Soering* case the facts were not in dispute between the parties, whereas the evidence concerning the situation in Sri Lanka for returning Tamils was in dispute. In *Soering* it had been accepted that judicial review might be an effective remedy for the decision of the Secretary of State. Grounds for judicial review of the exercise of executive discretion are illegality, irrationality or procedural impropriety.

Powell and Rayner v UK
Series A, Vol. 172

The facts

The applicants complained of excessive noise levels in connection with the operation of Heathrow Airport which affected their properties situated in the vicinity, and alleged violations of Article 6, para. 1, Article 8, Article 13 and the First Protocol, Article 1.

The Commission rejected the claims under the substantive articles but admitted the claim under Article 13 on the grounds that the applicants had no effective remedy at their disposal for their substantive grievance about the noise nuisance created by Heathrow Airport and its effects on the environment of their homes nearby.

The Commission's opinion

Although the complaints under Articles 6 and 8 and Article 1 of the First Protocol had been declared inadmissible, this did not prevent the Commission from considering the complaint under Article 13. The existence of an actual breach of a substantive article of the Convention was not a prerequisite of a claim under Article 13; all that was required was that the applicants had an arguable claim to a violation of one of the Convention rights and that there existed the availability of a remedy at national level to allege non-compliance with such a right. The Commission therefore considered the claims concerning Article 13.

First, the Commission noted that:

> . . . since it declared the applicants' Art. 13 complaint admissible the applicants no longer maintain in their submissions on the merits that they have an arguable claim under Art. 1 of Prot. No. 1 to the Convention which would require an effective domestic remedy. It also notes that in the present case there was no evidence that the value of the applicants' property has been substantially diminished or that their property has been rendered unsaleable by aircraft noise. In the absence of any interference with the applicants' property rights the Commission declared inadmissible as being manifestly ill-founded the applicants' complaints under Art. 1 of Prot. No. 1. In these circumstances, the Commission is of the opinion that the applicants do not have an arguable claim under this provision. Consequently they are not entitled to an effective domestic remedy under Art. 13 of the Convention in respect of their original allegations under Art. 1 of Prot. No. 1. (para. 51)

The applicants' claim under Article 6, para. 1 had been declared inadmissible, and as this involved the question of access to a court to determine their civil rights concerning noise nuisance, the Commission expressed the opinion that no separate issue was raised under Article 13, because Article 6, para. 1 was the relevant provision. Article 13 could not be interpreted to support a claim for a general right to a court in all circumstances.

As far as Mr Powell's claim under Article 8 was concerned, the Commission had found that this was manifestly ill-founded, and therefore presented no arguable claim relevant for Article 13. In the case of Mr Rayner, however, the Commission expressed the opinion that Mr Rayner did have an arguable claim:

> . . . It notes that his home and farm, which obliges him to be outdoors most of his time, is one and one third miles from, and in the direct line of one of Heathrow's Airport's busy runways. This area is considered to be a high noise nuisance zone, being within the 60 NNI contour area. 60 NNI signifies a very much greater noise level than that experienced by residents in the first applicant's 35 NNI contour area, given the

logarithmic element of the Noise and Number Index . . . This nuisance is recognised by the State which, for example, prohibits any further development in this area and the Government concede that only about 1500 people around Heathrow Airport experience a noise exposure equal to or more than that of the second applicant.

Mr Rayner acquired his home before Heathrow Airport was greatly expanded with the resultant major increase in aircraft traffic. Whilst he has no desire to move away from the area he has good reason, in the Commission's opinion, to complain of and seek redress for the deterioration of the noise climate in his home environment.

. . . The Commission declared Mr Rayner's Art. 8 complaint manifestly ill-founded, because, on balance, the clear interference with his private life and home was considered necessary in a democratic society for the economic well-being of the country. It is implicit in the Commission's consistent case law that the term 'manifestly ill-founded' under Art. 27(2) of the Convention extends further than the literal meaning of the word 'manifestly' would suggest at first reading. In certain cases, where the Commission considers at an early stage in the proceedings that a *prima facie* issue arises, it seeks the observations of the parties on admissibility and merits. The Commission may then proceed to a full examination of the facts and issues of a case, but nevertheless finally reject the applicant's substantive claims as manifestly ill-founded notwithstanding their 'arguable' character. In such cases the rejection of a claim under this head of inadmissibility amounts to the following finding: after full information has been provided by both parties, without the need for further formal investigation, it has now become manifest that the claim of a breach of the Convention is unfounded. Mr Rayner's substantive claim under Art. 8 of the Convention was such a case. The careful consideration which had to be given to this claim and the facts which gave rise to it lead the Commission to the conclusion that it is an 'arguable claim' for the purposes of Art. 13 of the Convention.

. . . The next question to be determined is whether the second applicant has an effective remedy under Art. 13 of the Convention to redress his Art. 8 claim. The applicant submits that he has not, whereas, the Government contends that there is an aggregate of satisfactory remedies available for aircraft noise nuisance: a civil action in nuisance against aircraft operators who fail to abide by flight regulations, a claim for compensation under the Land Compensation Act 1973, sound insulation grants and State imposition and enforcement of aircraft noise controls.

. . . The Commission notes that no civil suit lies in nuisance for the noise annoyance caused by aircraft flying in accordance with aviation regulations even though that annoyance may be generally recognised as high. Moreover for those like Mr Rayner who acquired property before a public utility, such as Heathrow Airport, was expanded and used to maximum capacity, no right to compensation under the Land Compensation Act 1973 is available. Sound insulation is not wholly effective for people living within the high noise, 60 NNI contour, like Mr Rayner, and it seems that despite the noise controls imposed by the Government a high level of aircraft noise is still to be expected. In the particular circumstances of this case, the Commission is of the opinon that none of these remedies could provide adequate redress for the claim of Mr Rayner under Art. 8 of the Convention. It finds, therefore, that the second applicant did not have an effective remedy within the meaning of Art. 13 of the Convention. (paras 58–61)

Three members of the Commission found difficulty with the distinction between an arguable claim and one that was manifestly ill-founded, and expressed the opinion that if a claim was manifestly ill-founded it could not be arguable. They therefore dissented with the majority opinion.

The judgment of the Court

The Court could not review the merits of the complaints which had been declared manifestly ill-founded by the Commission. It therefore had no jurisdiction to rule separately on the claims under Articles 6 and 8 independently of their relevance within the context of Article 13.

The Court had to decide whether a claim that had been found to be manifestly ill-founded by the Commission was nevertheless arguable. It considered the relationship between Article 27, para. 2 and Article 13:

> ... Article 13 and Article 27(2) are concerned, within their respective spheres, with the availability of remedies for the enforcement of the same Convention rights and freedoms. The coherence of this dual system of enforcement is at risk of being undermined if Article 13 is interpreted as requiring national law to make available an 'effective remedy' for a grievance classified under Article 27(2) as being so weak as not to warrant examination on its merits at international level. Whatever threshold the Commission has set in its case law for declaring claims 'manifestly ill-founded' under Article 27(2), in principle it should set the same threshold in regard to the parallel notion of 'arguability' under Article 13.
>
> This does not mean, however, that in the present case the Court is bound to hold Article 13 inapplicable solely as a result of the Commission's decisions of 17 October 1985 and 16 July 1986 declaring the applicant's substantive claims under Articles 6(1) and 8 to be manifestly ill-founded. Whilst those decisions as such are unreviewable, the Court is competent to take cognizance of all questions of fact and law arising in the context of the Article 13 complaints duly referred to it, including the 'arguability' or not of each of the substantive claims. In order to determine the latter question, the particular facts and the nature of the legal issues raised must be examined, notably in the light of the Commission's admissibility decisions and the reasoning contained therein. . . . (para. 33)

Even if the Commission has carefully considered a claim before deciding that it is inadmissible, this does not necessarily mean that the claim is arguable.

The Court decided that there was no arguable claim in respect of Article 6, para. 1 relevant to Article 13, because although s. 76 of the Civil Aviation Act 1982 excluded liability for nuisance in certain circumstances, access to the courts was still available to any person who considered that he had a cause of action in nuisance. The applicability of s. 76 was a question for the courts to decide.

As regards Article 8, the Court noted that although s. 76 limited the possibilities of legal redress, the exclusion of liability in nuisance was not absolute, and where the applicants wished to complain of noise caused by aircraft not satisfying either the condition of reasonable height or compliance with air traffic regulations, there was no bar and therefore they must be regarded as having an effective remedy available to them. There was therefore no violation of Article 13.

Comment

This case was originally joined by two other applicants, the Federation of Heathrow Anti-Noise Groups and Mr Baggs. The case brought by Mr Baggs ended in a settlement, while that of the Federation was declared inadmissible.

There were only limited remedies available to persons complaining about noise nuisance. Under the Land Compensation Act 1973, compensation was available for loss of value of property caused by new or altered public works. This did not cover intensification of existing use. Compulsory purchase of property affected by the development of Terminal 4 at Heathrow was provided for under a scheme drawn up by Heathrow Airport Ltd in 1986, but this was limited to property within a certain noise band and to certain circumstances. The applicants' properties fell outside the relevant contour limitation. The British Airport Authority also funded a scheme for sound insulation of dwellings in the immediate vicinity of the airport. The Noise Abatement Act 1960 specifically exempted aircraft noise from its protection, while the Civil Aviation Act 1982 excluded any action in trespass or nuisance for complaints concerning overflight, provided that the aircraft was flying at a reasonable height above the land and that the various statutory requirements had been complied with. Strict liability applied only for material damage or loss caused, for example, by an aircraft or part thereof falling onto land or water. This limitation was in accordance with Article 1 of the Rome Convention of 1952 on Damage Caused by Foreign Aircraft to Third Parties on the Surface, although as at January 1990 the UK had not ratified this Convention. There are international forums for quieter aircraft, the main one being the International Civil Aviation Organisation. Effect is given to their recommended standards in the UK by means of Air Navigation (Noise Certification) Orders. Heathrow Airport also places restrictions on night movements of aircraft and monitors aircraft noise on take-off. Aircraft must also remain on special noise preferential routes.

Cases pending

Sheffield v *UK* (Application No. 22985/93) which raises similar issues to those under *Cassey* and *Rees* (see Articles 8 and 12), declared admissible 20 EHRR CD 66.

Chahal Family v *UK* (Application No. 22414/93) concerning deportation on the grounds of national security – together with complaints under Articles 3, 5 and 8. Violation of Article 13 found by the Commission (20 EHRR CD 19) now referred to the Court.

Further reading

Hampson, F., 'Concept of an "arguable claim" under Article 13 of the European Convention on Human Rights' (1990) 39 *International and Comparative Law Quarterly* 891

CHAPTER 14

ARTICLE FOURTEEN

Article 14
The enjoyment of the rights and freedoms set forth in this Convention shall be secured without discrimination on any ground such as sex, race, colour, language, religion, political or other opinion, national or social origin, association with a national minority, property, birth or other status.

Article 14 cannot be pleaded in isolation but must be raised in connection with a breach of one of the other articles of the Convention.

14.1   SCOPE OF THE ARTICLE

According to the Court's case law, a difference of treatment is discriminatory if it has no reasonable and objective justification, that is, if it does not pursue a legitimate aim or if there is not a reasonable relationship of proportionality between the means employed and the aim sought to be realised.

Examples where breaches have been alleged are: refusal of legal aid for pursuing a defamation action (*Munro* 10 EHRR 516), although there may be reasonable and objective grounds for the State not to provide litigants with legal aid in defamation cases (*S and M v UK* 18 EHRR CD 172); exclusion of a solicitor from interviews of terrorist suspects in Northern Ireland (*John Murray* 18 EHRR CD 1); differential treatment of convicted murderers on the grounds of status (*Hussain v UK* (unreported)); gypsies (*Carol and Steve Smith* v *UK* (unreported)); immigrants (*X, Y, Z, V and W* v *UK*; transsexuals (*X, Y and Z* v *UK*); discriminatory treatment of certain forms of conduct but not others, e.g. sado-masochistic acts between consenting males compared to boxing (*Laskey, Jaggard and Brown* v *UK* Council of Europe).

Although the guarantees laid down in Article 14 have no independent existence, breach of this article can make unlawful what might otherwise be lawful in terms of other rights guaranteed by the Convention (see the *Belgian Linguistics* case 1 EHRR 252). Moreover, even where an applicant does not invoke Article 14, the Commission may consider the article in conjunction with whatever articles have been invoked. This was done in the case of *Ahmad* v *UK* 4 EHRR 126 (considered under Article 9), which concerned domestic proceedings falling under legislation dealing with religious discrimination (Education Act 1944, s. 30).

It should be noted that Article 14 prohibits discrimination only with regard to the enjoyment of those rights and freedoms set forth under the Convention. Where the right claimed is not in fact one covered by the Convention, a claim under Article 14 must fail. So, for example, where there is no Convention right for a foreign national to be admitted to a country other than his own, discriminatory treatment in terms of restrictions or exclusion of foreign nationals cannot constitute discrimination (*Church of X v UK* (1969) 12 *Yearbook* 306).

Nevertheless, discrimination within the meaning of Article 14 is broad enough to cover any form of discrimination, be it political, racial, social, etc.; it need not be limited in meaning (*Hussain*). An example of this breadth can be found in *App. No. 11949/86* v *UK* 10 EHRR 123, which concerned differences in procedure and available remedies against an order for repossession of a flat by the landlord, between the county court and the High Court. The Commission was prepared to examine this complaint under Article 14, although in the circumstances it found that the difference in treatment pursued a legitimate aim and that therefore there was no violation of the article.

Article 14 safeguards individuals or groups of individuals placed in comparable situations. A case may fail if a comparison cannot be made. For example, in *Sunday Times* v *UK* Series A, Vol. 30 the Court rejected a claim that because the Parliamentary treatment of matters which were *sub judice* was different from the practice of the courts, the applicants were discriminated against, because the situation was not comparable.

Similarly, the *Guardian* and the *Observer* could not complain that an injunction which prevented them publishing a story was discriminatory, because the injunction applied equally to all the British media (*Observer and Guardian* v *UK* 14 EHRR 153). The fact that people in the USA and in other European countries could purchase and read freely distributed copies of the material in question – the book *Spycatcher* – could not be claimed to be discrimination based on national origin because persons who were not resident in the UK were beyond the jurisdiction of the court's injunction and not a comparable group, and the Government's liability under the Convention was limited to its jurisdiction. A similar line of reasoning was followed in *Sunday Times* v *UK* (No. 2) 14 EHRR 229.

Therefore, difference in treatment may not amount to a violation of Article 14. For instance, prisoners may be treated differently to those outside prison because the two groups cannot be regarded as analogous for the purposes of Article 14 (*Lockwood* v *UK* 15 EHRR CD 48). The Commission has also held that cohabitees and married couples are not in analogous situations (*Lindsay* v *UK* 9 EHRR 555); nor are the circumstances of an alleged deserter from the army and a civilian suspected of a criminal offence analogous (*App. No. 10427/83* v *UK* 9 EHRR 369); or the situations of an owner of rent controlled property and another individual who possesses a cash sum which is free to be invested as he wishes (*Kilburn* v *UK* 8 EHRR 45); or the tax regime applicable to a self-employed person compared to that of an employer, who falls into a different tax class for contributions (*App. No. 9793/82* v *UK* 7 EHRR 135).

Frequently the discrimination is found to be justified. For example, where a householder faced criminal sanctions for not completing a census this was held to be justified discrimination on the grounds of practical necessity for the administration of the census and therefore it pursued a legitimate aim and was not disproportionate (*App. No. 9702/82* v *UK* 5 EHRR 293). Similarly in immigration cases discrimination in immigration policy may be justified. For example, where a person is admitted to the UK as a UK passport holder with a special voucher for settlement in the UK, there is objective and reasonable justification for the difference in treatment, namely the prerogative of the State to give preferential treatment to its passport holders (*App. No. 9730/82* v *UK* 5 EHRR 581). Differential visiting and correspondence rights for prisoners in open and closed prisons are justified because of the 'different nature of the security considerations confronting each type of prison' (*App. No. 9658/82* v *UK* 5 EHRR 603). While a ban on broadcasting material favourable to Sinn Fein did not apply to other political parties, it was held to be justified because it pursued a legitimate aim and was proportionate to that aim (*McLaughlin* v *UK* 18 EHRR CD 84). In the case of *Kilburn* v *UK* 8 EHRR 45 at 81, the Commission considered that rent control legislation which regulated the powers of landlords of properties below a certain rateable value, pursued a legitimate aim of social policy and was therefore justified. In a case in which the provision of grammar school places was alleged to be discriminatory in conjunction with Article 2 of the First Protocol, this discrimination was held to be justified because, although a State may not discriminate in the provision of educational facilities actually established by the State, the operation of quotas for places in selective schools, although discriminatory, was reasonable and objective because to exceed the number of places available would be an inefficient use of educational facilities and resources (*App. Nos 10228/82 and 10229/82* v *UK* (1984) 37 D & R 96).

14.2 THE CASES

Most of these cases have been dealt with elsewhere because, by the very nature of Article 14, applicants must bring their complaints under other articles of the Convention as well as under Article 14. In this chapter only the Article 14 issues will be dealt with. Usually if the Court or Commission has found that there has been no violation of any other articles of the Convention then no separate issue will arise under Article 14. Similarly, it often happens that although there has been a violation of one of the other articles, the Court or Commission does not find it necessary to consider alleged violations of Article 14 separately. A typical example of this is *Munro* v *UK* 10 EHRR 516, in which the applicant alleged that the delay in granting him access to a solicitor for 48 hours after his detention, under prevention of terrorism legislation, was discriminatory in as much as he understood that this provision did not apply in England and Wales, only in Northern Ireland. The Commission expressed the opinion that there had been a breach of Article 6, para. 1 read with Article 6, para. 3, but found it unnecessary to consider Article 14 separately.

14.2.1 Racial Discrimination

East African Asians v *UK*
(1994) Vol 78-A D & R 5

The facts

The facts of this case have been considered with reference to Articles 3 and 8. The husbands of the applicants had been refused admission into the UK in circumstances in which wives would have been admitted.

The element of discrimination was integral to the Commission's interpretation of 'degrading treatment' under Article 3. The applicants complained that the legislation in force discriminated against them on the grounds of their race and colour.

The Commission's opinion

The question before the Commission was whether:

. . . the legislation applied in the applicants' cases, i.e. the Commonwealth Immigrants Act 1962 as amended by the Commonwealth Immigrants Act 1968 and the Immigration Appeals Act 1969, discriminated on the ground of race or colour and, if that be the case, whether its application in the following special circumstances of the present cases constituted 'degrading treatment' in the sense of Article 3 of the Convention . . . (p. 57)

In considering the background to the legislation the Commission found that:

. . . the 1968 Act had racial motives and that it covered a racial group. When it was introduced into Parliament as a Bill, it was clear that it was directed against the Asian citizens of the United Kingdom and colonies in East Africa and especially those in Kenya. The Commission refers in this connection to statements made in both Houses of Parliament during the debate on the Bill in February 1968.

It notes in particular that a former Secretary of State for the Colonies had proposed legislation to limit the rights of Asians from Kenya to enter the United Kingdom, and that the main purpose of the Government's Bill was apparently to exclude that 'most of the 200,000 Asians in East Africa would continue to be free to come here at will'.

. . . The Government, while claiming that the Act was based on geography, nevertheless admitted that it had racial motives: the Home Secretary stated in the House of Commons on 27 February 1968 'that the origin of this Bill lies . . . in a considered judgment of the best way to achieve the idea of a multi-racial society'; and the Government submitted in the present proceedings that the Act was intended to promote 'racial harmony'.

. . . The Commission concludes that the Commonwealth Immigrants Act 1968, by subjecting to immigration control citizens of the United Kingdom and colonies in East Africa who were of Asian origin, discriminated against this group of people on grounds of their colour or race. (pp. 58–9)

Two other provisions also had a discriminatory effect – the Commonwealth Immigrants Regulation 1969 and the British Nationality Act 1964, both of which gave preference to white people. The replacement of the 1968 Act with the Immigration Act 1971 did not greatly improve the situation as the distinction between patrials and non-patrials also had a discriminatory effect, because those qualifying as patrials with the right of abode would predominantly be white Commonwealth citizens, while Asian citizens of the UK and Colonies in East Africa would not so qualify. This was further aggravated by Rule 27 of the Immigration Rules for Control of Entry, 25 January 1973.

The Commission concluded that:

> ... the legislation applied in the present cases discriminated against the applicants on the grounds of their colour or race. It has also confirmed the view, which it expressed at the admissibility stage, that discrimination based on race could, in certain circumstances, of itself amount to degrading treatment within the meaning of Article 3 of the Convention.
>
> The Commission recalls in this connection that, as generally recognised, a special importance should be attached to discrimination based on race; that publicly to single out a group of persons for differential treatment on the basis of race might, in certain circumstances, constitute a special form of affront to human dignity; and that differential treatment of a group of persons on the basis of race might therefore be capable of constituting degrading treatment when differential treatment on some other ground would raise no such question. (p. 62)

A distinction was made between the 25 applicants who were citizens of the UK and colonies and six applicants who were British protected persons. As regards the latter, the Commission expressed the opinion that:

> — according to English law, British protected persons, although not aliens, are not British subjects;
> — they became and remained subject to immigration control under the 1962 Act;
> — their position as regards entry to the United Kingdom was not changed by the 1968 Act;
> — the immigration legislation concerned did not distinguish between different groups of British protected persons on any ground of race or colour.
> ... The Commission considers that, in view of the above circumstances, the legislation complained of cannot in the present cases of British protected persons be regarded as discriminatory ... (pp. 63–4)

A claim under Article 5 read with Article 14 failed.

Mr Welter, however, expressed a dissenting opinion concerning discrimination.

Comment

In a Resolution of 21 October 1977 (Resolution DH (77)2), the Committee of Ministers noted that certain measures had been adopted by the UK to facilitate the entry of UK passport holders from East Asia into the UK and that all the applicants had been allowed to settle in the UK. The annual quotas had also been increased and, since 1974, the immigration rules permitted husbands to join wives settled in the UK.

14.2.2   Political Discrimination

While this aspect of discrimination was considered extensively in the inter-State case of *Ireland* v *UK* Series A, Vol. 25, it has not arisen a great deal in individual applications.

Liberal Party and Others v *UK*
(1981) 21 D & R 211

The facts

The complaint of the applicants concerned the British electoral system, which, they alleged, adversely affected their rights under Article 10 and the First Protocol, Article 3, read with Article 14. They claimed that the simple majority system by which the UK Parliament was elected was not representative and had a disproportionate adverse impact on the Liberal Party and its members. It further discriminated against the Liberal Party in favour of the Conservative and the Labour parties.

The claim under Article 14 was based on the following interpretation of the article:

(i)   Article 14 of the Convention safeguards individuals placed in similar situations, from any discrimination in the enjoyment of the rights and freedoms set forth in other provisions of the Convention or its Protocols. It is as though Article 14 formed an integral part of each of the provisions laying down rights and freedoms.

(ii)   The Convention is intended to guarantee not rights that are theoretical or illusory but rights that are practical and effective. Thus, Article 14 protects the practical and effective enjoyment of the rights and freedoms guaranteed by the provisions of the Convention and its Protocols. Article 14 is of particular importance in relation to those provisions of the Convention and its Protocols which, while establishing a right or freedom, give States discretionary power with regard to the steps to be taken to ensure the enjoyment of that right or freedom.

(iii)   Furthermore, Article 14 is of special importance in relation to the enjoyment of the right to vote and the right to stand for election to the legislature in view of the central importance of an 'effective political democracy' to the maintaining of human rights and fundamental freedoms, reaffirmed in the Preamble to the Convention. This is also particularly so of the enjoyment of the rights to freedom of expression which constitutes 'one of the essential foundations of a democratic society'.

(iv)   The Convention, including Article 14, must be interpreted in the light of present day conditions. It is submitted that, in the present case, this includes the substantially changed conditions of political life in the United Kingdom since 1974.
. . . (pp. 113–4)

The Commission's opinion

The Commission had to consider:

(a)   whether a difference of treatment has been made in an area covered by the Convention or its Protocols, between persons in similar circumstances.

(b)   if so, whether the difference of treatment has a legitimate aim; and

(c)   if so, whether there is a reasonable relationship between the means employed and the aim sought to be realised. (p. 114)

While most of the cases concerning discrimination have related to differences in treatment between persons in comparable situations, previous case law (particularly the *East African Asians* case) indicated that:

> ... the concept of discrimination includes not only overt differences of treatment but also differences in impact or effect: that is, a difference of treatment in the sense that a measure which is neutral on its face has a disproportionate adverse impact or effect upon a particular category of person. (p. 115)

The applicants were claiming that the electoral system fitted into this pattern.

In considering the claim under Article 14, the Commission first had to consider whether in fact there was a breach, or possible breach, of a right covered by the other articles and Protocols. In this respect the Commission expressed the opinion that Article 3 of the First Protocol, which gives individuals the right to vote in elections, is not the same as a protection of equal voting influence for all voters. Article 3 of the First Protocol does not bind the States to a particular electoral system or to any requirement of equality in the secret ballot. If the electoral system meant that religious or ethnic groups could never be represented then there might be an issue under Article 14, but this had not been raised in the case of the Liberal Party. There was therefore no violation of Article 14 in conjunction with Article 3 of the First Protocol.

There was also no violation of Article 14 in conjunction with Article 10, because this latter article did not protect the right to vote within the concept of freedom of expression. Article 10 was therefore not applicable in this case and so Article 14 could not be raised.

Comment

Elections are governed by the Representation of the People Act 1949. There have been a number of proposals concerning the introduction of proportional representation, but the current system is one of simple majority. The same system is found in a number of other countries and, even in countries which have a fundamental right to equality of voting, such a system has been held to comply with constitutional requirements (the Commission mentioned the US Supreme Court and the Federal Constitutional Court of the Federal Republic of Germany).

14.2.3 Discrimination on the Grounds of Sex

Abdulaziz, Cabales and Balkandali v UK
Series A, Vol. 94

The facts

This case has been considered under Article 8. The applicants were all women who were settled in the UK. Their husbands had been refused permission to join them. The applicants complained that they were victims of a practice of race and sex discrimination authorised by Parliament, because men who were lawfully resident in the UK – whether or not of British nationality, with the territorial birth link – would be entitled to be joined by their foreign wives. In order for a husband to join his wife for settlement, he had to show that she was a citizen of the United Kingdom and Colonies who was born in the UK, or one of whose parents was so born.

The Commission's opinion

In considering the allegations of sex discrimination made by the applicants, the Commission noted that the Government's justification for this difference in treatment was to protect the domestic labour market in a time of rising unemployment. In this context the Commission noted that:

> ... the elimination of all forms of discrimination against women is an accepted general principle in the member States of the Council of Europe, confirmed in domestic legislation, and regional and international treaties. Significantly, heading the citation of prohibited forms of discrimination under Article 14 of the Convention is that of discrimination on grounds of sex.
>
> ... It is generally recognised that classifications based on sex are to be carefully scrutinised, in order to eliminate invidious disadvantages. It is incumbent on the Commission therefore to examine closely the purported justification upon which are practised differences in treatment on grounds of sex in the securement of Convention rights and freedoms. . . . (paras 102 and 103)

The Commission was not convinced by the Government's argument. Other arguments put forward by the Government to justify discriminatory treatment were also rejected.

The Commission concluded that there had been sex discrimination in the securement of the applicants' right to respect for family life.

In considering whether there had also been racial discrimination, the Commission accepted that:

> ... most immigration policies restricting, as they do, free entry, differentiate on the basis of people's nationality, and indirectly their race, ethnic origin and possibly their colour. But that States give preferential treatment to their own citizens or nationals from countries with whom they have the closest links, excluding other foreigners, cannot be considered to be racial discrimination. However the Commission recognises that the State's discretion in immigration matters is not of an unfettered character, for a State may not implement policies of a purely racist nature, such as a policy prohibiting the entry of any person of a particular skin colour. In this connection the Commission affirms its opinion in the *East African Asians* cases that the singling out of a group of persons for differential treatment on the basis of race might, in certain circumstances, constitute a special form of affront to human dignity. (para. 113)

However, in the circumstances the Commission did not find any evidence of racial discrimination.

One of the applicants, who was a UK citizen but had not been born in the UK (neither had her parents), claimed discrimination on the grounds of birth. The Commission expressed the opinion that:

> ... By implementing a difference in the protection of the right to respect for family life, a difference based, like sex discrimination, on the mere accident of birth, with no account being taken in the Rules of the individual's personal circumstances or merits, discrimination is perpetrated on the ground of birth contrary to Article 14, combined with Article 8. (para. 118)

Although the rules had changed by the time of the hearing, the Commission indicated that the rules which had applied were discriminatory on this ground.

Three members of the Commission expressed the dissenting opinion that there had been racial discrimination.

The judgment of the Court

The Court accepted that the Immigration Rules 1980 had the aim of protecting the domestic labour market. This aim was legitimate, but did not necessarily justify differential treatment for female and male immigrants. The Court held that:

> ... the advancement of the equality of the sexes is today a major goal in the member States of the Council of Europe. This means that very weighty reasons would have to be advanced before a difference of treatment on the ground of sex could be regarded as compatible with the Convention. (para. 78)

The Court was not convinced by the Government's arguments regarding employment and the economic activity of men and women:

> ... the Court is not convinced that the difference that may nevertheless exist between the respective impact of men and of women on the domestic labour market is sufficiently important to justify the difference of treatment, complained of by the applicants, as to the possibility for a person settled in the United Kingdom to be joined by, as the case may be, his wife or her husband. (para. 79)

The Court also accepted that the 1980 Rules had the aim of advancing public tranquillity, but it was not persuaded that this was to be achieved by differential treatment.

The Court concluded that the applicants had been the victims of sex discrimination.

As regards racial discrimination, the Court agreed with the majority of the Commission:

> ... The 1980 Rules, which were applicable in general to all 'non-patrials' wanting to enter and settle in the United Kingdom, did not contain regulations differentiating between persons or groups on the ground of their race or ethnic origin. The rules included in paragraph 2 a specific instruction to immigration officers to carry out their duties without regard to the race, colour or religion of the intending entrant, and they were applicable across the board to intending immigrants from all parts of the world, irrespective of their race or origin.
>
> As the Court has already accepted, the main and essential purpose of the 1980 Rules was to curtail 'primary immigration' in order to protect the labour market at a time of high unemployment. This means that their reinforcement of the restrictions on immigration was grounded not on objections regarding the origin of the non-nationals wanting to enter the country but on the need to stem the flow of immigrants at the relevant time.
>
> That the mass immigration against which the rules were directed consisted mainly of would-be immigrants from the New Commonwealth and Pakistan, and that as a result they affected at the material time fewer white people than others, is not a sufficient reason to consider them as racist in character: it is an effect which derives not from the content of the 1980 Rules but from the fact that, among those wishing to immigrate, some ethnic groups outnumbered others.

The Court concludes from the foregoing that the 1980 Rules made no distinction on the ground of race and were therefore not discriminatory on that account. . . . (para. 85)

The Court did not agree with the Commission that there had been discrimination on the grounds of birth against one of the applicants. The Court found that the aim of the discrimination complained of was legitimate, and could be regarded as having an objective and reasonable justification.

Comment

The relevant law was the Immigration Act 1971 (read with the Statement of Changes in Immigration Rules, HC 394), which was directed at controlling primary immigration – immigration of a person likely to become head of the household and take up employment. Wives and children of persons lawfully in the country – secondary immigration – were subject to less control.

14.2.4 Discrimination on the Grounds of Sexual Orientation

If male homosexuals claim to be discriminated against on the grounds of their sexuality, then the comparable group may be female homosexuals (lesbians) – provided that there is such a comparable group. If the comparable group is a certain form of social organisation, such as the family – rather than private life – then homosexuals may not be able to succeed in establishing discrimination or differential treatment because there is no unit of comparison.

Dudgeon v UK
Series A, Vol. 45

The facts

The facts, which have been considered under Article 8, concerned the prohibition of homosexual conduct in private between consenting adults in Northern Ireland. The applicant complained that he was a victim of a breach of Article 14 read with Article 8, because he was subject to greater interference with his private life by the criminal law than was a person who was not a male homosexual.

The Commission's opinion

The Commission first recalled that:

> . . . Article 14 safeguards individuals, or groups of individuals, placed in comparable situations, from all discrimination in the enjoyment of the rights and freedoms set forth in the other normative provisions of the Convention. (para. 119)

However, not every difference of treatment will violate this provision if there is an objective and reasonable justification. The Commission was satisfied that in this case the interference with the applicant's rights under Article 8 was justified under Article 8, para. 2. This justification could be extended to providing objective and reasonable justification for the resulting differences in treatment between male homosexuals and heterosexuals or female homosexuals. There was not, therefore, a violation of Article 14 read with Article 8.

The judgment of the Court

The Court did not feel it necessary to consider the alleged violation of Article 14 separately, because the substance of the complaint had been absorbed by the alleged violation of Article 8. The Court indicated that:

> ... Where a substantive Article of the Convention has been invoked both on its own and together with Article 14 and a separate breach has been found of the substantive Article, it is not generally necessary for the Court also to examine the case under Article 14, though the position is otherwise if a clear inequality of treatment in the enjoyment of the right in question is a fundamental aspect of the case. (para. 67)

Comment

Other cases in which applicants have complained of discriminatory treatment of homosexuals include: *Gay News Ltd and Lemon* v *UK* 5 EHRR 123, in which the Commission expressed the opinion that prosecution of the applicant for publication of a poem and illustration had been based solely on the blasphemous nature of the publication and not on the applicant's sexual orientation; *Johnson* v *UK* 9 EHRR 386, in which the Commission expressed the opinion that difference in treatment between male homosexuals, heterosexuals and female homosexuals under the Sexual Offences Act 1956 as amended by the Sexual Offences Act 1967, had a reasonable and objective justification in the criterion of social protection; *Wilde, Greenhalgh and Parry* v *UK* (1995) 80-A D & R 132, which concerned the law on homosexuals in Scotland.

14.2.5 Discrimination on the Grounds of Status

Pinder v *UK*
7 EHRR 409

The facts

The applicant claimed that while he was serving in the Air Force he suffered as a result of medical negligence. Under the Crown Proceedings Act 1947, he was unable to sue the Ministry of Defence in negligence because of the statutory immunity contained therein. Instead he received an increased pension entitlement. He claimed that this was less than the amount he would have been awarded under a negligence claim. His claim was based on a violation of Article 6, para. 1 and Article 14.

The Commission's opinion

The Commission found that there was breach of Article 6, para. 1 but that this did not prevent the Commission from considering the claim under Article 14, as there clearly arose an issue under the substantive article.

Clearly there was a difference in treatment between civilians who could sue in tort and the applicant who, as a serviceman, was prevented from doing so. However:

> ... the Commission considers that it is legitimate to single out servicemen because of the high risks of injury and death in their profession as well as the special relationship which exists between the ranks and to regard them as incurring greater risks than other professional groups. In these circumstances, the Commission considers that the

State is entitled under the Convention to make special legislative provision in the event of the risks of injury during service actually materialising.

. . . The Commission is also of the opinion that there exists a reasonable relationship of proportionality between the means chosen, that is, the pension scheme replacing the civil action in tort, and the aim of making special provision for injured servicemen. In making this assessment, it has considered . . . the fairness of the no-fault pension scheme which offers many advantages when compared to the traditional action in negligence, frequently characterised as time-consuming, costly and uncertain. The pension scheme, on the other hand, circumvents the inherent difficulties of establishing negligence by providing immediate and certain coverage of the needs of all injured servicemen who fall within the scheme. In accordance with Art. 4(2) of the 1978 Service Pensions Order, for example, a claimant bears no onus to establish that he fulfils the condition of entitlement of a pension and is entitled to the benefit of any reasonable doubt in this respect. (paras 15 and 16)

The Commission therefore concluded that there had been no violation of Article 14.

Comment
A similar finding was made in the case of *Dyer* v *UK* 7 EHRR 469.

Lindsay v *UK*
9 EHRR 513

The facts
The applicants, a married couple, complained of discrimination in the taxation system. The wife was not working but received some income from investments. The husband was earning and received income from his earnings and from some shared investments. Under the applicable legislation – the Income and Corporation Taxes Act 1970 – the wife's investment income was aggregated with her husband's for taxation purposes. On marriage the wife ceased to have a separate tax-free personal allowance. Although a husband received an increased allowance as a 'married man', this was equivalent only to about one and a half times the personal allowance, not double. This meant that married persons were treated differently from unmarried persons. Similarly, husbands of women who had earned income, as opposed to investment income, could claim an additional earned income allowance. This discriminated between different types of income. There was also discrimination between the sexes in this regard as a husband's personal allowance was not dependent on him having an income or on whether, if he had one, it was earned or unearned. The result in this case was that the couple paid considerably more income tax than they would have had they been separate, or had they opted for separate assessment if the wife had been the main earner.

The Commission's opinion
The Commission considered that taxation is primarily an issue falling under Article 1 of the First Protocol, as a right interfering with the enjoyment of property, but is justified under the second paragraph of that article. However,

as taxation fell within the scope of the rights included under the Convention and its Protocols, the prohibition against discrimination in Article 14 was applicable.

The Commission accepted that there was clearly a difference in taxation depending on whether the husband or the wife was the sole earner. The question was whether this distinction of treatment had an objective and reasonable justification.

The Commission considered that:

> ... it is for the national authorities to make the initial assessment, in the field of taxation, of the aims to be pursued and the means by which they are pursued: accordingly, a margin of appreciation is left to them. The Commission is also of the view that the margin of appreciation must be wider in this area than it is in many others. The Commission recalls in this respect that systems of taxation inevitably differentiate between different groups of tax payers and that the implementation of any taxation system creates marginal situations. The applicants have themselves stated that the situation of which they complain affects only 3 per cent of the tax payers. Also, attitudes as to the social and economic goals to be pursued by the State in its revenue policy may vary considerably from place to place and time to time. A government may often have to strike a balance between the need to raise revenue and reflecting other social objectives in its taxation policies. The national authorities are obviously in a better position than the Commission to assess those needs and requirements.
>
> ... In the light of the above considerations, the Commission concludes that the tax provisions which result in extra tax advantages accruing when a wife is the breadwinner of a family can be said to fall within the margin of appreciation accorded to the national authorities. The Commission therefore finds that the difference in treatment in the present case has an objective and reasonable justification in the aim of providing positive discrimination in favour of married women who work. The Commission also finds that the test of proportionality is satisfied in the present case. It follows that this part of the application is manifestly ill-founded within the meaning of Art. 27(2) of the Convention. (p. 559)

In considering the applicants' complaint that UK tax legislation discriminated against married couples as opposed to unmarried cohabiting couples, the Commission expressed the opinion that the comparison was not a valid one:

> ... The applicants in the present case seek to compare themselves, a married couple, with a man and woman who receive the same income, but who live together without being married. The Commission is of the opinion that these are not analogous situations. Though in some fields, the *de facto* relationship of cohabitees is now recognised, there still exist differences between married and unmarried couples, in particular, differences in legal status and legal effects. Marriage continues to be characterised by a corpus of rights and obligations which differentiate it markedly from the situation of a man and woman who cohabit. The Commission accordingly concludes that the situation of the applicants is not comparable to that of an unmarried couple and that part of the application therefore does not enclose any appearance of a violation of Prot. No. 1 Art. 1 read in conjunction with Art. 14 of the Convention. It follows that this part of the application is manifestly ill-founded within the meaning of Art. 27(2) of the Convention. (pp. 559–60)

There was no discrimination on the grounds of religion because all married couples were treated the same regardless of their religious convictions, or whether they had been married in a church or not.

James v UK/Trustees of the late Duke of Westminster's Estate v UK
Series A, Vol. 98

The facts
Under the Leasehold Reform Act 1967 modified by the Housing Act 1969, the applicants, who held a large number of properties in London on trust for the Duke of Westminster, had to sell certain freehold interests to tenants. The case before the Commission involved 80 such transactions. The main complaint of the applicants related to Article 1 of the First Protocol. Under Article 14, the applicants complained that the operation of the leasehold reform legislation was discriminatory on the ground that it applied only to a restricted class of property, i.e. long leasehold houses occupied by leaseholders, and secondly, the lower the value of the property, the more harshly the landlord was treated, because of the way in which the purchase price was calculated. The Government argued that the legislation was not discriminatory as no distinction was based on the criterion of wealth.

The judgment of the Court
In considering the applicability of Article 14, the Court held that:

> . . . The list of prohibited grounds of discrimination as set out in Article 14 is not exhaustive. On the facts, the legislation does entail differences of treatment in regard to different categories of property owners in the enjoyment of the right safeguarded by Article 1 of Protocol No. 1. In the Court's opinion, the grounds on which those differences of treatment are based are relevant in the context of Article 14 of the Convention and, accordingly, Article 14 is applicable to the present case. (para. 74)

In assessing whether there was an objective and reasonable justification for a difference of treatment, the Court observed that:

> . . . it was inevitable that the contested legislation, being designed to remedy a perceived imbalance in the relations between landlords and occupying tenants under the long leasehold system of tenure, should affect landlords coming within that restricted category rather than all or other property owners. . . . the absence of a mechanism for inquiry into the details and individual merits of each proposed enfranchisement was not judged by the Court to have the consequence of rendering the operation of the legislation unacceptable. The Court sees no cause for arriving at a different conclusion in relation to Article 14 of the Convention: having regard to the margin of appreciation, the United Kingdom legislature did not transgress the principle of proportionality. In the Court's opinion, therefore, the contested distinction drawn in the legislation is reasonably and objectively justified.
>
> . . . The introduction of the rateable-value limits and the institution of two levels of compensation reflect Parliament's desire to exclude from the benefits of enfranchisement the small percentage of better-off tenants not considered to be in need of economic protection and to provide more favourable terms of purchase for the vast majority of tenants, most likely to suffer hardship under the existing system.
>
> . . . In view of the legitimate objectives being pursued in the public interest and having regard to the respondent State's margin of appreciation, that policy of different

treatment cannot be considered as unreasonable or as imposing a disproportionate burden on the applicants. The provisions in the legislation entailing progressively disadvantageous treatment for the landlord the lower the value of the property must be deemed to have a reasonable and objective justification and, consequently, are not discriminatory. (paras 76 and 77)

There had therefore been no violation of Article 14.

Monnell and Morris v *UK*
Series A, Vol. 115

The facts
The applicants claimed discrimination on the grounds that they were detained in prison at the time of applying for leave to appeal against their conviction and sentence. They therefore had to seek leave to be present at the hearing of their application for leave to appeal and were subject to the power which the Court of Appeal had over them as detained persons to loss of time, i.e. the time they had already spent in detention pending appeal would not necessarily be taken into account as part of their sentence already served. People who were not detained at the time of applying for leave to appeal did not suffer these disadvantages, therefore the practice was discriminatory.

The Commission's opinion
The justification given by the UK Government for this practice was to discourage unmeritorious applications for leave to appeal.

This justification was found to be insufficient by the Commission, because it created a special obstacle to access to proceedings for leave to appeal which was discriminatory, and therefore a violation of Article 6, para. 1 read with Article 14.

The judgment of the Court
Once convicted persons in custody set in motion the procedure for leave to appeal they risked, and suffered, loss of liberty in addition to the sentence received in the first instance. Persons at liberty did not run the same risk. Although this was discriminatory the Court considered the difference in treatment to have an objective and reasonable justification:

> ... The aim pursued by the Court of Appeal's power to order loss of time, as it is exercised, is to expedite the process of hearing applications and so to reduce the period spent in custody by an applicant with a meritorious appeal. (para. 73)

Similarly, although a person at liberty did not risk the same sanction from pursuing an application for leave to appeal, the Court felt that this difference of treatment, although contrary to Article 14, was justified. There was therefore no breach of Article 14, either as regards Articles 5 or as regards Article 6.

Munro v *UK*
10 EHRR 503 (1987) 52 D & R 158

The facts
The applicant complained of discriminatory practice regarding the award of legal aid to pursue a defamation action. He alleged that because of his poverty

– compared to a more wealthy person – he was consequently denied the chance to defend a particular civil right because he could not afford a lawyer and because the legal aid provisions did not provide free legal aid for defamation proceedings.

The Commission's opinion

While there clearly was discrimination, this discriminatory practice was justified on the grounds of the need to prioritise legal aid and the risks inherently involved in defamation proceedings, and in particular the risk involved in this case. There was therefore no improper aim, or disproportionate or differential treatment.

Gillow v *UK*
Series A, Vol. 109

The facts

The applicants bought a plot of land in Guernsey and built a house on it. The applicants had residence qualifications to live on the island due to the husband's employment. For some time the applicants lived overseas and the property was let. When the applicants indicated their intention to return to live in the house, they were informed that they would require a licence to do so. Accordingly they applied for a licence and in the meanwhile returned to Guernsey to carry out repairs on the house. The application for a licence was refused. They were prosecuted for unlawful occupation. The applicants complained of violations of Articles 6 and 8, Article 1 of the First Protocol and Article 14.

Under Article 14, they alleged that the laws in Guernsey discriminated in favour of people born or with roots in Guernsey, in comparison with other British citizens, as far as residence qualifications were concerned. Moreover, the housing laws created a category of open market houses which discriminated in favour of the wealthy who were able to purchase houses which were over a certain rateable value and which were not subject to control by the Housing Authority.

The Commission's opinion

In considering the discriminatory effect of the Housing Law 1975, the Commission referred back to a decision concerning the Housing Law 1969 (*Wiggins* v *UK* (1979) 13 D & R 40). The Commission had found that this statute had pursued:

> . . . the legitimate aim of securing that accommodation would be available to persons with a recognised connection with Guernsey; the Commission finds no reason to depart from [this] analysis . . . in the present case, relating to the Housing Law 1975, which it therefore finds to pursue an objective and reasonable aim and not to be discriminatory. In as far as the applicants complain that the existence of the open market sector is also discriminatory, this sector is similar to the unregulated housing position in most parts of the Member States of the Council of Europe, where the right to occupy a given property is free from official control and is open to anyone with sufficient means. The Commission does not find that the existence of such an open market sector raises any issue under the Convention in the present case. Finally, with regard to the question whether there was a reasonable relationship of proportionality

between the means employed and the aims sought to be realised by the Housing Act 1975 in the decision to refuse the applicants licence to occupy Whiteknights, the Commission finds that it is not necessary to pursue this question, since it is already established that the refusal of such licences was disproportionate and a violation of both Art. 8 of the Convention and Prot. No. 1 Art. 1. (para. 184)

There had therefore been no breach of Article 14.

The judgment of the Court

The Court held that preferential treatment for persons with strong attachments to the island was legitimate. Moreover, the control system established by the Housing Law 1957 was not disproportionate to the aim pursued. The difference in treatment therefore had an objective and reasonable justification.

As far as discrimination on the grounds of wealth was concerned, the Court was satisfied that:

> . . . the introduction of rateable-value limits reflects the Government's desire to exclude from the control of the Housing Authority the small percentage of expensive houses (10 per cent) likely to be sought after by better-off persons not considered to be in need of protection, while providing necessary protection for persons of more limited means who have strong connections with Guernsey. The applicants themselves have accepted that it was legitimate for a State to try to ensure adequate housing for the poorer section of the community. In view of the legitimate objectives being pursued in the general interest and having regard to the State's margin of appreciation, that policy of different treatment cannot be considered as unreasonable or as imposing a disproportionate burden on owners of more modest houses like the applicants, taking into account the possibilities open to them under the licencing system.
>
> . . . The Court therefore finds that the facts of the case do not disclose a breach of Article 14 of the Convention, taken in conjunction with Article 8. (paras 66 and 67)

Comment

The law applicable at the time that Mr Gillow bought his land was the Housing Law 1957. This freed from control all houses with a rateable value in excess of £50 per annum. The land which Mr Gillow bought had a rateable value of £49 and did not fall into this category of 'open market houses'. It was therefore a controlled property and could be occupied only by persons who either had a licence or who had residence qualifications, e.g., because of employment. Initially the applicants had such qualifications. They moved away from Guernsey in 1960.

In 1970 the Housing Control (Guernsey) Law 1969 came into force. This gave the Housing Authority discretion to grant residence licences to persons without residence qualifications. A licence could be dispensed with only if the applicants had been resident on 31 July 1968. In 1975 this law was replaced by a new Housing Law.

McMichael v UK
Council of Europe Report 51/1993/446/525

The facts

The case concerned a claim by an unmarried father that he had been a victim of discriminatory treatment because of his lack of any legal right, prior to marriage to the mother, to custody of their child, or to participate in care proceedings concerning the child (Article 14 with Article 6, para. 1 and Article 8). The complaint here was concerned with the status of a natural father under Scots law.

The Commission's opinion
The Commission held that this discrimination was not unlawful because:

> . . . the aim of the relevant legislation [to provide a mechanism for identifying 'meritorious' fathers who might be accorded parental rights] is legitimate and the conditions imposed on natural fathers for obtaining legal recognition of their parental role respect the principle of proportionality. (para. 98)

The judgment of the Court
Under Scots law, a child's father automatically acquired the parental rights of tutory, access and custody only if married to the mother of the child. The natural father of a child born out of wedlock might obtain parental rights by means of an application to the court. Mr McMichael was in a less advantageous position than a married father, but he never sought an order for parental rights. The Court accepted the Commission's opinion that the nature of the relationship between natural fathers and their children will vary greatly. It accepted that the aim of the relevant legislation was:

> . . . to provide a mechanism for identifying 'meritorious' fathers who might be accorded parental rights, thereby protecting the interests of the child and the mother. In the Court's view, this aim is legitimate and the conditions imposed on natural fathers for obtaining recognition of their parental role respect the principle of proportionality. The Court therefore agrees with the Commission that there was an objective and reasonable justification for the difference of treatment complained of. (para. 98)

Cases pending under this article
Halford v *UK* (Application No. 20605/92) 19 EHRR CD 43, concerning a claim of discrimination on the grounds of sex in conjunction with Articles 10 and 13 relating to the interception of communications by the applicant's employer to undermine her proceedings against the employer for sex discrimination. Declared admissible by the Commission, March 1995.

Gregory v *UK* (Application No. 22299/93) 19 EHRR CD 82, concerning a claim of racial bias among jury members in reaching a verdict in a criminal trial in which the applicant was found guilty of robbery (Article 14 claimed with Article 6). See Chapter 6.

Stubbings J. L. and J. P. v *UK* (Application No. 22083/93) 18 EHRR CD 183. This case, which was declared admissible in September 1994, concerns claims under Article 6 relating to access to court for victims of sexual abuse who have had their claims barred by the six-year time-limit for certain tort claims. The applicants complain that the rules governing limitation periods discriminate against them in respect to their right of access to court and in respect of their private life.

CHAPTER 15

PERMITTED EXCEPTIONS AND RESTRICTIONS OF EXCEPTIONS: ARTICLES 15, 16, 17 AND 18

Article 15

1.   In time of war or other public emergency threatening the life of the nation, any High Contracting Party may take measures derogating from its obligations under this Convention to the extent strictly required by the exigencies of the situation, provided that such measures are not inconsistent with its other obligations under international law.

2.   No derogation from Article 2, except in respect of deaths resulting from lawful acts of war, or from Articles 3, 4 (paragraph 1) and 7 shall be made under this provision.

3.   Any High Contracting Party availing itself of this right of derogation shall keep the Secretary General of the Council of Europe fully informed of the measures which it has taken and the reasons therefor. It shall also inform the Secretary General of the Council of Europe when such measures have ceased to operate and provisions of the Convention are again being fully executed.

Article 16

Nothing in Articles 10, 11 and 14 shall be regarded as preventing the High Contracting Parties from imposing restrictions on the political activity of aliens.

Article 17

Nothing in this Convention may be interpreted as implying for any State, group or person any right to engage in any activity or perform any act aimed at the destruction of any of the rights and freedoms set forth herein or at their limitation to a greater extent than is provided for in the Convention.

Article 18
The restrictions permitted under this Convention to the said rights and freedoms shall not be applied for any purpose other than those for which they have been prescribed.

15.1   THE SCOPE OF THE ARTICLES

These articles relate to permitted restrictions on the scope of the articles of the Convention. The most frequently cited article in the context of the UK has been Article 15. On a number of occasions the UK Government has informed the Secretary-General of the Council of Europe of derogations under Article 15 relating to the emergency situation in Northern Ireland. Where an application is made for derogation, the Contracting State is under an obligation to keep the Secretary-General informed of the situation and of any developments pertaining thereto. Examples of such communications from the UK can be found in 14 *Yearbook*, p. 32, 16 *Yearbook*, pp. 26–8, 18 *Yearbook*, p. 18 and 21 *Yearbook*, p. 22.

Once a notice that derogation has been withdrawn is sent to the Secretary-General, the examination of a case – even if it relates to Northern Ireland – must proceed on the basis that the articles of the Convention are fully applicable. This was the position in *Brogan and Others* v *UK* 11 EHRR 117 because withdrawal of derogation had been notified on 22 August 1984, shortly before the complaints raised in the case occurred.

Following the judgment of the Court against the UK in the case of *Brogan and Others*, the UK Government again gave notice of derogation under Article 15 because of the difficulties of judicial control over decisions to arrest and detain suspected terrorists in the circumstances prevailing in Northern Ireland. On 23 December 1988, the UK informed the Secretary-General of the Council of Europe that the Government had availed itself of the right of derogation conferred by Article 15, para. 1. This derogation referred in particular to the exercise of powers of arrest and detention under s. 12 of the Prevention of Terrorism (Temporary Provisions) Act 1984, and the possible inconsistency of these with the provisions of Article 5, para. 3 – as established by the *Brogan* case. The extent of this derogation was considered in the case of *Brannigan and McBride* v *UK* 17 EHRR 539.

The Convention organs have limited powers to examine questions arising under Article 15, as the Contracting State is best placed to determine whether or not the 'life of the nation' is threatened by a public emergency. Therefore each State has a wide margin of appreciation, although it does not have unlimited power because the domestic margin of appreciation is subject to European supervision via the Commission and the Court, which are responsible for ensuring that States do not go beyond the extent strictly required by the exigencies of the crisis. There must, therefore, be compliance with the three requirements of Article 15, para. 1, namely:

(a)   that there be a public emergency threatening the life of the nation;
(b)   that the measures taken are strictly required by the exigencies of the situation; and

(c)   that the derogation is consistent with the High Contracting Party's other international law obligations.

It should be noted that even under Article 15, there can be no derogation from Article 2 – except in respect of deaths resulting from lawful acts of war – nor from Article 3, Article 4, para. 1 and Article 7.

Whereas claims involving Article 16 are rarely raised, Article 18 is occasionally raised in connection with other articles, and may be considered *ex officio* by the Court or the Commission if this is felt to be desirable. This was the case in *Handyside* v *UK* 1 EHRR 737, in which, although not specifically asked to do so, the Commission decided to consider whether the seizure and confiscation of the copies of *The Little Red Schoolbook* raised any issues under Articles 17 and 18, as well as the claimed violations of Article 10 and Article 1 of the First Protocol. In the circumstances, having concluded that the restrictions imposed on publication were legitimate and justified under the latter two articles, the Commission found no reason to examine the complaint under Articles 18 or 17 in any further depth. In *Sunday Times* v *UK* 2 EHRR 245, the applicants raised a claimed violation of Article 18 before the Commission, but this was not maintained before the Court. As in this case the Court found that the interference was not justified under Article 10 it is to be regretted that the Article 18 claim was dropped and not discussed.

15.2   THE CASES

Derogation under Article 15 was particularly relevant in the case of *Ireland* v *UK*, Report of the Commission (1976) 19 *Yearbook* 512 Decision of the Court, Series A, Vol. 25, because both the Commission and the Court found that the measures taken by the UK to detain and interrogate suspected terrorists were in breach of Article 5. Three communications by the UK Government had been sent to the Secretary-General of the Council of Europe – 27 June 1957, 25 September 1969, and 25 August 1971 – informing the Secretary-General of measures taken derogating from the UK's obligations under the Convention, in accordance with the provisions of Article 15. The Commission and the Court therefore had to decide whether the measures actually taken were greater and more extensive than those which would strictly be required to meet with the exigencies of the situation.

Following the Commission, the Court held that in the light of the seriousness and extent of the crisis at the time, far-reaching derogations from paras 2–4 of Article 5 were justified, and that the UK did not exceed the 'extent strictly required' of Article 15, para. 1. Consequently, the Court concluded that as the requirements of Article 15 were met, the derogations from Article 5 were not in breach of the Convention.

Judge Fitzmaurice suggested in his separate opinion that the Court had proceeded in the wrong way in its examination, by first considering the individual articles and then examining these in the light of Article 15. He suggested that the better way of proceeding would have been to start with Article 15:

. . . since, if it was properly invoked, and if the acts or conduct complained of are validated under it, it will become unnecessary to consider whether, had this not been the case, they would have involved derogations from – i.e. infractions of – Article 5. Only if it appeared that Article 15 could not operate in favour of the defendant Government, either because there was no real public emergency or because the acts or conduct in issue went beyond what was required in order to deal with it, would it become essential to investigate the acts or courses of conduct themselves, so as to establish whether they did or did not amount to breaches of Article 5.

. . . If of course the defendant Government has not invoked Article 15 at all, and simply takes its stand on a denial that Article 5 has been infringed (e.g. because the arrest or detention involved came within one of the cases permitted by that provision), then clearly an enquiry into the Article 5 position is all that is necessary or possible. But where Article 15 *was* invoked, this either implies a tacit recognition that Article 5 has, or very possibly has, been infringed, or renders that issue irrelevant except upon the assumption that, in all the circumstances of the case, Article 15 would not in any event validate the infraction. This last matter therefore becomes the primary issue and should be gone into first. . . . (paras 39 and 41)

Not only would this approach have procedural advantages, but also substantive ones:

. . . The Court's present method of dealing with the matter is to hold that there has been a breach of the Convention because of derogations from it under a certain Article – but then to hold that, by reason of the provisions of another Article, these derogations are *excusable*. But this is clearly incorrect. Article 15, where applicable to the facts of the case, does not merely excuse acts otherwise inconsistent with Article 5: it *nullifies* them *qua* breaches of the Convention as a whole – or at least justifies them, so that no breach results.

(b)   This being so, it seems to me that the present system puts the emphasis in the wrong place. It involves only coming to the consequences of the respondent Party having pleaded Article 15, after establishing that there has been a breach of Article 5, thus putting that Party in the posture of being, in principle, a Convention-breaker, although it has taken all the steps necessary to invoke and bring into play Article 15 which specifically provides that, in certain circumstances, 'any High Contracting Party may take measures derogating from . . . this Convention'. Moreover, there being in consequence no breach of the Convention as such, there cannot have been any breach of Article 5 either – for Article 15 has acted retrospectively to prevent that. The respondent Party is therefore left in the invidious and false position of having prima facie violated the Convention, and having merely as it were subsequently atoned for that violation by bringing itself under Article 15 – whereas the true situation is that *such a Party should be deemed never to have breached Article 5 at all* as regards any acts for which Article 15 was invoked and found to be applicable. (para. 42)

This suggested approach was not followed, however, in a subsequent case.

Brannigan and McBride v *UK*
Series A, Vol. 258-B

The facts
Both applicants were arrested and detained without charge in 1984 under the Prevention of Terrorism (Temporary Provisions) Act 1984. Brannigan was

detained for six days, 14 hours and 30 minutes, and McBride for four days, six hours and 25 minutes. During their detention they were interrogated and denied access to books, newspapers, radio and television. Neither were they allowed to associate with other prisoners. After an initial delay, access to a solicitor was granted to each of the detainees. The applicants complained of violations of rights under Article 5, paras 3 and 5 and Article 13.

The Commission's opinion

As the facts were very similar to those in a previous case (see *Brogan*) the Commission considered that there was no reason to depart from the Court's judgment in that case, and accordingly found that there had been a breach of Article 5, paras 3 and 5. However, the Commission then had to consider:

> ... whether these potential breaches of Article 5 of the Convention have been met by the United Kingdom's derogation of 23 December 1988 under Article 15 of the Convention. (para. 42)

The Commission noted:

> (1)   In time of war or other public emergency threatening the life of the nation any High Contracting Party may take measures derogating from its obligations under this Convention to the extent strictly required by the exigencies of the situation, provided that such measures are not inconsistent with its other obligations under international law.
>
> ...
>
> (3)   Any High Contracting Party availing itself of this right of derogation shall keep the Secretary General of the Council of Europe fully informed of the measures which it has taken and the reasons therefor. It shall also inform the Secretary General of the Council of Europe when such measures have ceased to operate and the provisions of the Convention are again being fully executed.
>
> ... Article 15(1) of the Convention lays down three requirements:
>
>   (a)   that there be a public emergency threatening the life of the nation;
>   (b)   that the measures taken are strictly required by the exigencies of the situation; and
>   (c)   that the derogation is consistent with the High Contracting Party's other international law obligations. (para. 43)

The Commission appreciated that there were limits imposed on the Convention organs to examine Article 15 issues, because of the wide margin of appreciation left to the Contracting States to assess the existence and scale of an emergency.

Referring to the *Ireland* v *UK* case, where the Court had no difficulty in concluding that a state of emergency existed in Northern Ireland, the Commission examined whether the situation had changed significantly since then. It expressed the opinion that:

> ... Judging by the statistics on deaths, maimings, explosions and bombings presented to the Commission by the Government, it is clear that the situation in Northern Ireland remains very serious. In 1988 when the derogation was made these figures were still high and the Commission can only conclude in the present cases that there was, and continues to be, a state of emergency in Northern Ireland threatening the life of the nation. (para. 49)

The question was, therefore, whether the measures applied were strictly required by the exigencies of the situation.

The applicants had submitted that any derogation should be strictly construed and that in this case their detention in breach of Article 5 had not come within the stipulations of the derogation. The fact that the impugned legislation had existed without derogation since 1974 – hence the *Brogan* decision – was evidence in itself that derogation was not strictly required by the exigencies of the situation but had been claimed in order to avoid further judgments similar to that of the Court in *Brogan*.

The Commission was satisfied that the derogation complied with the requirements of Article 15, para. 3, even though it was not made until 1988, this did not affect its validity. Until the *Brogan* decision it was clear that the UK considered that the executive powers of extended detention were compatible with the Convention. The *Brogan* decision showed that this was not so, and in these circumstances it was reasonable for the UK to reconsider the question of derogation.

The real question was whether the derogation from the provisions of Article 5, para. 3, whereby persons suspected of committing a criminal offence would be brought promptly before a *judicial* authority, was required by the exigencies of the situation. Under the prevention of terrorism legislation it was the executive rather than the judiciary which was vested with the powers of extended detention. The Government justified this on the grounds that it would place the impartiality and physical integrity of the Northern Ireland judiciary in jeopardy, if the rule of law was not seen to be independent of the executive.

The Commission noted:

... the Government's concern that public confidence in the small Northern Ireland judiciary, already performing difficult tasks at great personal risk, might be seriously undermined if they were to be perceived as a mere arm of the executive in granting extensions of detention on the basis of evidence which could not be disclosed to the detainee. It also notes that there are certain safeguards in the executive system of extension decision which are kept under regular independent review. The applicants have alleged that the executive system is open to abuse. However, they do not allege that it was abusively applied in their cases. Not only are the extension decisions kept under independent review, but so is the Prevention of Terrorism legislation itself. An important feature of that legislation is its temporary status, being voted for a period of five years after full parliamentary scrutiny, with intervening annual or biannual renewals. Finally, the Commission notes that the United Kingdom's derogation of 23 December 1988 is limited in scope to enable the detention of suspected persons without being brought before a judicial authority for a maximum of seven days and that it is therefore much more limited than the derogation which in the case of *Ireland v United Kingdom* was found by the European Court of Human Rights to satisfy the conditions of Article 15. Moreover, during the period of detention the detainee is not totally cut off from the outside world; in particular, he is entitled to have a friend or relative told about his detention, and he may have access to a lawyer and a doctor.

... In the light of these circumstances, the Commission considers that the United Kingdom have not overstepped their margin of appreciation in vesting in the executive rather than the judiciary the power to extend the detention of persons suspected of being involved in terrorist offences for up to seven days.

... Given the undisputed need to have a system of extended detention of suspected terrorists for up to seven days, the limited nature of the Government's derogation, the continuous reviews of the system, the safeguards against abuse and the wide margin of appreciation afforded to States by Article 15 of the Convention, the Commission is of the opinion that the United Kingdom's derogation may be deemed to be strictly required by the exigencies of the public emergency which exists in Northern Ireland. Moreover, there is no reason to doubt that the applicants' detention without being brought before a judicial authority fell within the scope of that derogation. (paras 61–63)

Since the requirements of Article 15 were deemed to have been met, Article 5, para. 3 could not be considered to have been violated.

Mr Fowein, in a dissenting opinion, expressed the view that derogation from Article 5, whereby detention for up to seven days was allowed, had not been shown to be strictly required by the exigencies of the situation; and that as judicial control under Article 5, para. 3 was an essential protection of personal liberty, the decision in *Brogan* should not be lightly departed from.

Three other members of the Commission expressed similar dissenting views and were unable to agree with the majority of the Commission that derogation was strictly required.

The judgment of the Court
The Court recalled that the question whether any derogation from the UK's obligations under Article 5 of the Convention might be permissible, had been specifically left open by the Court in the *Brogan* case. It therefore had to consider whether in fact such derogation was permissible.

The applicants, supported by Amnesty International, Liberty, Interights and the Committee on the Administration of Justice, had argued that any margin of appreciation should be very narrowly interpreted when examining derogation from fundamental procedural guarantees.

The Court recalled that:

... it falls to each Contracting State, with its responsibility for 'the life of [its] nations,' to determine whether that life is threatened by a 'public emergency' and, if so, how far it is necessary to go in attempting to overcome the emergency. By reason of their direct and continuous contact with the pressing needs of the moment, the national authorities are in principle in a better position than the international judge to decide both on the presence of such an emergency and on the nature and scope of derogations necessary to avert it. Accordingly, in this matter a wide margin of appreciation should be left to the national authorities.

Nevertheless, Contracting Parties do not enjoy an unlimited power of appreciation. It is for the Court to rule on whether *inter alia* the States have gone beyond the 'extent strictly required by the exigencies' of the crisis. The domestic margin of appreciation is thus accompanied by a European supervision. At the same time, in exercising its supervision the Court must give appropriate weight to such relevant factors as the nature of the rights affected by the derogation, the circumstances leading to, and the duration of, the emergency situation. (para. 43)

The Court did not doubt that there was a public emergency existing in Northern Ireland at the relevant time. Nevertheless, the Court had to scrutinise the derogation against the background of the importance of Article 5, para. 3

and the *Brogan* judgment. The issue in question was not the existence of the power to detain suspected terrorists for up to seven days, but the exercise of this power without judicial intervention.

The Court first observed that:

> ... the power of arrest and extended detention has been considered necessary by the Government since 1974 in dealing with the threat of terrorism. Following the *Brogan and Others* judgment the Government were then faced with the option of either introducing judicial control of the decision to detain under section 12 of the 1984 Act or lodging a derogation from their Convention obligations in this respect. The adoption of the view by the Government that judicial control compatible with Article 5(3) was not feasible because of the special difficulties associated with the investigation and prosecution of terrorist crime rendered derogation inevitable. Accordingly, the power of extended detention without such judicial control and the derogation of 23 December 1988 being clearly linked to the persistence of the emergency situation, there is no indication that the derogation was other than a genuine response. (para. 51)

The applicants had argued that the derogation was premature, but the Court was not persuaded by this:

> ... While it is true that Article 15 does not envisage an interim suspension of Convention guarantees pending consideration of the necessity to derogate, it is clear from the notice of derogation that 'against the background of the terrorist campaign, and the over-riding need to bring terrorists to justice, the Government did not believe that the maximum period of detention should be reduced.' However it remained the Government's wish 'to find a judicial process under which extended detention might be reviewed and, where appropriate, authorised by a judge or other judicial officer.'
>
> The validity of the derogation cannot be called into question for the sole reason that the Government had decided to examine whether in the future a way could be found of ensuring greater conformity with Convention obligations. Indeed, such a process of continued reflection is not only in keeping with Article 15(3) which requires permanent review of the need for emergency measures but is also implicit in the very notion of proportionality. (para. 54)

In considering whether the absence of judicial control of extended detention was justified, the Court took into account the various reports reviewing the operation of the relevant legislation and the difficulties of investigating and prosecuting terrorist crime. The Court noted that:

> ... It is not the Court's role to substitute its view as to what measures were most appropriate or expedient at the relevant time in dealing with an emergency situation for that of the Government which has direct responsibility for establishing the balance between the taking of effective measures to combat terrorism on the one hand, and respecting individual rights on the other. In the context of Northern Ireland, where the judiciary is small and vulnerable to terrorist attacks, public confidence in the independence of the judiciary is understandably a matter to which the Government attaches great importance. (para. 59)

The Court was, moreover, satisfied that effective safeguards existed against abuse of the power of detention, including the remedy of *habeus corpus*, the absolute and legally enforceable right of detainees to consult a solicitor after 48 hours from arrest, susceptibility to judicial review of any interference with such rights, and regular independent review of the operation of the legislation. The Court concluded that:

> . . . Having regard to the nature of the terrorist threat in Northern Ireland, the limited scope of the derogation and the reasons advanced in support of it, as well as the existence of basic safeguards against abuse, the Court takes the view that the Government has not exceeded its margin of appreciation in considering that the derogation was strictly required by the exigencies of the situation. (para. 66)

Dissenting opinions were given by Judge Pettiti, Judge Walsh, Judge de Meyer, and Judge Makarczyk, all of whom disagreed with the majority that the derogation was necessary. Judge Makarczyk suggested that any decision concerning Article 15 went beyond the confines of the immediate case and affected the integrity of the Convention system of protection as a whole. It was particularly important for new member States or aspiring ones to be clear about the importance of the rule of law. The Court should therefore make it very clear that derogation was to be allowed as a strictly temporary measure, with the onus being on the derogating State to show that the derogation did in fact contribute to the aims allowed for under derogation. The Judge was unconvinced that the UK had discharged this burden of proof. Judge de Meyer shared this view. Judge Pettiti expressed the opinion that derogation must not be seen to operate as a *carte blanche*. The need for derogation must be kept constantly under review; the State's margin of appreciation was not so wide as to exclude the scrutiny of the Court. In his opinion the UK's action fell outside the margin of appreciation which the Court was able to recognise.

Comment

One point raised before the Court was whether it was necessary for a public emergency to have been officially proclaimed before notice of derogation could be made. Such a requirement exists under Article 4 of the 1966 United Nations International Covenant on Civil and Political Rights. The UK is a party to this Covenant, although the situation in Northern Ireland arose prior to the UK's ratification.

The Court did not feel called on to define conclusively what might be meant by 'officially proclaimed', but considered in the circumstances that the emergency situation had been sufficiently formally and publicly indicated by means of a formal announcement by the Secretary of State for the Home Department to the House of Commons on 22 December 1988, when the fact of derogation because of the existence of the emergency was announced.

CHAPTER 16

THE FIRST PROTOCOL

The First Protocol consists of six articles. Article 5 provides:

Article 5
As between the High Contracting Parties the provisions of Articles 1, 2, 3 and 4 of this Protocol shall be regarded as additional articles to the Convention and all the provisions of the Convention shall apply accordingly.

The Protocol entered into force on 18 May 1954. The UK signed it on 20 March 1952, although with reservations.

This chapter considers the first three articles of this Protocol. Article 4 concerns the extension of the Protocol to territories falling under the responsibility of any of the High Contracting Parties, and Article 6 simply states the procedure for the entry into force of the Protocol.

As has been indicated in other articles, particularly Articles 13 and 14, these apply equally to the alleged breach of an article under the First Protocol as under the rest of the Convention.

ARTICLE 1 OF THE FIRST PROTOCOL

Article 1
Every natural or legal person is entitled to the peaceful enjoyment of his possessions. No one shall be deprived of his possessions except in the public interest and subject to the conditions provided for by law and by the general principles of international law.

The preceding provisions shall not, however, in any way impair the right of a State to enforce such laws as it deems necessary to control the use of property in accordance with the general interest or to secure the payment of taxes or other contributions or penalties.

16.1 THE SCOPE OF THE ARTICLE

It has been held that:

> This provision is mainly concerned with the arbitrary confiscation of property and does not in principle, guarantee a right to the peaceful enjoyment of possession in a pleasant environment. (*Powell* v *UK* 9 EHRR 241)

A number of cases involving the protection of property rights ensured by Article 1 have concerned the question of compensation. First, it is clear that the article does not extend to the granting of compensation for the cessation of an unlawful use of property (*Chater* v *UK* 10 EHRR 503 at 534); neither can this article be used as a ground for claiming planning permission to extend the permitted use of property (*ISKCON and Others* v *UK* 18 EHRR CD 133). The second paragraph of the article clearly allows a State to make provisions for the control of property use. Therefore refusal of planning permission and enforcement notices to comply with planning regulations will not normally amount to a breach of Article 1, provided the purpose of such control falls within the permitted exceptions. In this respect the Commission will assess the lawfulness of the interference and the extent to which it served the public interest. A fairly wide margin of appreciation is allowed to States in the planning field, but nevertheless a balance must be struck between the general interest of the community and the protection of individual rights. An example of a case in which interference with property was allowed in order to protect the character of green-belt areas or areas of outstanding natural beauty was *Ryder* v *UK* 11 EHRR 80.

Interference with use can extend beyond planning control to include control of use and such factors as rent control (*Kilburn* v *UK* 8 EHRR 45 at 81), and the temporary or permanent confiscation of property in accordance with criminal law enforcement measures (*App. No. 9615/81* v *UK* – confiscation of obscene magazines held to be both lawful and necessary and in the public interest; similarly *Handyside* v *UK* 1 EHRR 737 – seizure of *The Little Red Schoolbook*). However, in the case of *Allgemeine Gold und Silberscheideanstalt AG* v *UK* 7 EHRR 251 at 314, the Commission held that the continued retention of Krugerrands seized by Customs and Excise from smugglers who had obtained them from the applicants unlawfully, amounted to a violation of Article 1 (although the Court held differently).

It is not possible for an applicant to claim a violation of rights protected by Article 1 on the basis of proposed planning developments which have not yet occurred. For example, where there are proposals for a motorway which may affect the applicant's property, he or she cannot claim to be a victim until the motorway is constructed (*App. No. 10390/83* v *UK* 8 EHRR 252). Where an applicant has been deprived of possessions as a result of private negotiations, the responsibility of the State is not involved. Thus, where the applicant was ordered to forfeit her lease because she refused to pay her landlord a service charge, the Commission found that this was a lease regulated by private law contractual arrangements (*App. No. 11949/86* v *UK* 10 EHRR 123 at 149). The deprivation rule is, therefore, intended to refer to acts whereby the State lays hands on, or authorises a third party to lay hands on, a particular piece of property for a purpose which is to serve the public interest.

It should be noted that although taxation is recognised as being in principle an interference with the right guaranteed by Article 1, this interference is justified according to the second paragraph of the article (*Lindsay* v *UK* 9 EHRR 513).

There is some overlap between Article 8 of the Convention and Article 1 of the First Protocol, particularly in the case of compulsory purchase of property. Here the Commission has recognised that the application of the two provisions must be reconciled. This is done by holding that the measure of necessity referred to in the second sentence of Article 1 of the Protocol, closely resembles the interpretation and application of the notion of justification found in Article 8 (*App. No. 9261/81* v *UK* 28 D & R 177 at 185, *Gillow* v *UK* 7 EHRR 292, *Howard* v *UK* 9 EHRR 91). Therefore it must be shown that the authorities struck a fair balance between the rights of an individual owner and those of the community. The availability of compensation will be a significant factor in considering this balance.

In the case of *Powell* v *UK* 9 EHRR 241, it was observed that in the case of nuisance caused by aircraft noise, because this may seriously affect the value of real property or even render it unsaleable, such interference could amount to a partial taking of property.

16.2   THE CASES

Trustees of the late Duke of Westminster's Estate v *UK*
James v *UK*
Series A, Vol. 98

(*Note*: These two case references are to the same case, James being one of the trustees bringing the application.)

The facts
The applicants were trustees of the estate of the 2nd Duke of Westminster. The estate included a number of leasehold properties. Under the Leasehold Reform Act 1967, as amended by the Housing Acts 1969 and 1974, the Leasehold Reform Act 1979, the Housing Act 1980 and the Housing and Building Control Act 1984, tenants of these properties had acquired the right to buy the properties at a price calculated according to a formula provided by statute.

Between April 1979 and November 1983, around 80 long leasehold properties had been acquired from the estate by tenants under the applicable legislation, and more tenants were expected to exercise this right in the future.

The applicants complained that the compulsory transfer of their property under the Leasehold Reform Act 1967, as amended, gave rise to a violation of Article 1 of the First Protocol, on the grounds that the Act:

(i)   interfered with agreements between the applicants and their tenants freely made before it came into effect;

(ii)   frustrated the expectations with which the applicants entered into the agreements, and on which the terms of such agreements were based;

(iii)   compelled the applicants to sell the properties, against their will, to private individuals for the benefit of those individuals;

(iv)   deprived the applicants of their property at a price always below, and often far below, market value;

(v)   enabled tenants to sell the properties in the open market for large profits after claiming enfranchisement;

(vi)   provided no machinery whereby the applicants can challenge either the validity of or the justification for the deprivation, or the principles upon which the compensation is to be calculated, once only it is established that the tenancy is within the ambit of the Act;

(vii)   made arbitrary distinctions between the properties of which they can be deprived, and those of which they cannot. (para. 34)

The Commission's opinion

The Commission declined to consider each and every transaction. The initial question was whether the UK was responsible as a legislator for facilitating these transactions, the transactions themselves being matters for private law. The essential issue therefore was:

. . . whether the respondent State has breached the applicants' rights under the Convention by empowering tenants to acquire their property on the terms and conditions laid down in the legislation; and this issue has to be determined by considering whether the legislation is compatible with the Convention rather than by separate scrutiny of the individual transactions. (para. 35)

The main dispute related to the terms and conditions of the legislation rather than the manner of its execution by a State authority.

The judgment of the Court

The Court considered that the applicants had been deprived of their possessions – this was not in dispute – therefore the second rule of Article 1, found in the second sentence of the first paragraph, relating to the deprivation of property, had been violated. The issue was whether the deprivation was in the 'public interest'. The applicants' first contention was that:

. . . the 'public interest' test in the deprivation rule is satisfied only if the property is taken for a public purpose of benefit to the community generally and that, as a corollary, the transfer of property from one person to another for the latter's private benefit alone can never be 'in the public interest'. In their submission, the contested legislation does not satisfy this condition.

The Commission and the Government, on the other hand, were agreed in thinking that a compulsory transfer of property from one individual to another may in principle be considered to be 'in the public interest' if the taking is effected in pursuance of legitimate social policies. (para. 39)

The Court agreed that:

. . . a deprivation of property effected for no reason other than to confer a private benefit on a private party cannot be 'in the public interest'. Nonetheless, the compulsory transfer of property from one individual to another may, depending upon the circumstances, constitute a legitimate means for promoting the public interest. In this connection, even where the texts in force employ expressions like 'for the public use', no common principle can be identified in the constitutions, legislation and case law of the Contracting States that would warrant understanding the notion of public interest as outlawing compulsory transfer between private parties. The same may be said of certain other democratic countries; thus, the applicants and the Government cited in argument a judgment of the Supreme Court of the United States of America, which concerned State legislation in Hawaii compulsorily transferring title in real property from lessors to lessees in order to reduce the concentration of land ownership.

. . . Neither can it be read into the English expression 'in the public interest' that the transferred property should be put into use for the general public or that the community generally, or even a substantial proportion of it, should directly benefit from the taking. The taking of property in pursuance of a policy calculated to enhance social justice within the community can properly be described as being 'in the public interest'. In particular, the fairness of a system of law governing the contractual or property rights of private parties is a matter of public concern and therefore legislative measures intended to bring about such fairness are capable of being 'in the public interest', even if they involve the compulsory transfer of property from one individual to another.

. . . The expression *'pour cause d'utilité publique'* used in the French text of Article 1 may indeed be read as having the narrow sense argued by the applicants, as is shown by the domestic law of some, but not all, of the Contracting States where the expression or its equivalent is found in the context of expropriation of property. That, however, is not decisive, as many Convention concepts have been recognised in the Court's case law as having an 'autonomous' meaning. Moreover, the words *'utilité publique'* are also capable of bearing a wider meaning, covering expropriation measures taken in implementation of policies calculated to enhance social justice.

The Court, like the Commission, considers that such an interpretation best reconciles the language of the English and French texts, having regard to the object and purpose of Article 1, which is primarily to guard against the arbitrary confiscation of property. (paras 40–42)

The Court therefore held that:

. . . a taking of property effected in pursuance of legitimate social, economic or other policies may be 'in the public interest', even if the community at large has no direct use or enjoyment of the property taken. The leasehold reform legislation is not therefore *ipso facto* an infringement of Article 1 on this ground. Accordingly, it is necessary to inquire whether in other respects the legislation satisfied the 'public interest' test and the remaining requirements laid down in the second sentence of Article 1. (para. 45)

Whether in fact the relevant legislation complied with this 'public interest' test, depended on what was understood as being 'in the public interest'. In this respect the Court recognised the margin of appreciation afforded to contracting States:

. . . Because of their direct knowledge of their society and its needs, the national authorities are in principle better placed than the international judge to appreciate what is 'in the public interest'. Under the system of protection established by the Convention, it is thus for the national authorities to make the initial assessment both of the existence of a problem of public concern warranting measures of deprivation of property and of the remedial action to be taken. Here, as in other fields to which the safeguards of the Convention extend, the national authorities accordingly enjoy a certain margin of appreciation.

Furthermore, the notion of 'public interest' is necessarily extensive. In particular, as the Commission noted, the decision to enact laws expropriating property will commonly involve consideration of political, economic and social issues on which opinions within a democratic society may reasonably differ widely. The Court, finding it natural that the margin of appreciation available to the legislature in implementing social and economic policies should be a wide one, will respect the legislature's judgment as to what is 'in the public interest' unless that judgment be manifestly without reasonable foundation. In other words, although the Court cannot substitute its own assessment for that of the national authorities, it is bound to review the contested measures under Article 1 of Protocol No. 1 and, in so doing, to make an inquiry into the facts with reference to which the national authorities acted. (para. 46)

In considering whether the aim of the legislation was legitimate, the Court held that:

... The aim of the 1967 Act, as spelt out in the 1966 White Paper, was to right the injustice which was felt to be caused to occupying tenants by the operation of the long leasehold system of tenure. The Act was designed to reform the existing law, said to be 'inequitable to the leaseholder', and to give effect to what was described as the occupying tenant's 'moral entitlement' to ownership of the house.

Eliminating what are judged to be social injustices is an example of the functions of a democratic legislature. More especially, modern societies consider housing of the population to be a prime social need, the regulation of which cannot entirely be left to the play of market forces. The margin of appreciation is wide enough to cover legislation aimed at securing greater social justice in the sphere of people's homes, even where such legislation interferes with existing contractual relations between private parties and confers no direct benefit on the State or the community at large. In principle, therefore, the aim pursued by the leasehold reform legislation is a legitimate one. (para. 47)

The means taken to achieve that aim had to be reasonably proportional. In considering this, the Court held that it was not required to impose a test of strict necessity:

... The availability of alternative solutions does not in itself render the leasehold reform legislation unjustified; it constitutes one factor, along with others, relevant for determining whether the means chosen could be regarded as reasonable and suited to achieving the legitimate aim being pursued, having regard to the need to strike a 'fair balance'. Provided the legislature remained within these bounds, it is not for the Court to say whether the legislation represented the best solution for dealing with the problem or whether the legislative discretion should have been exercised in another way.

. . .

The occupying leaseholder was considered by Parliament to have a 'moral entitlement' to ownership of the house, of which inadequate account was taken under the existing law. The concern of the legislature was not simply to regulate more fairly the relationship of landlord and tenant but to right a perceived injustice that went to the very issue of ownership. Allowing a mechanism for the compulsory transfer of the freehold interest in the house and the land to the tenant, with financial compensation to the landlord, cannot in itself be qualified in the circumstances as an inappropriate or disproportionate method for readjusting the law so as to meet that concern. (para. 51)

The Court further held that the application of rateable value limits to determine which houses might be bought by tenants, fell within the State's margin of appreciation.

The applicants had also complained of the compensation terms offered under the legislation. First, the Court observed that:

> . . . under the legal systems of the Contracting States, the taking of property in the public interest without payment of compensation is treated as justifiable only in exceptional circumstances not relevant for present purposes. As far as Article 1 is concerned, the protection of the right of property it affords would be largely illusory and ineffective in the absence of any equivalent principle. Clearly, compensation terms are material to the assessment whether the contested legislation respects a fair balance between the various interests at stake and, notably, whether it does not impose a disproportionate burden on the applicants.
>
> The Court further accepts the Commission's conclusion as to the standard of compensation: the taking of property without payment of an amount reasonably related to its value would normally constitute a disproportionate interference which could not be considered justifiable under Article 1. Article 1 does not, however, guarantee a right to full compensation in all circumstances. Legitimate objectives of 'public interest', such as pursued in measures of economic reform or measures designed to achieve greater social justice, may call for less than reimbursement of the full market value. Furthermore, the Court's power of review is limited to ascertaining whether the choice of compensation terms falls outside the State's wide margin of appreciation in this domain. (para. 54)

Considering the facts of the case, the Court held that:

> . . . The objective pursued by the leasehold reform legislation is to prevent a perceived unjust enrichment accruing to the landlord on the reversion of the property. In the light of that objective, judged by the Court to be legitimate for the purposes of Article 1, it has not been established, having regard to the respondent State's wide margin of appreciation, that the 1967 basis of valuation is not such as to afford a fair balance between the interests of the private parties concerned and thereby between the general interest of society and the landlord's right of property. (para. 56)

The applicants had also raised the question of whether the general principles of international law requiring prompt, adequate and effective compensation for the expropriation of property of foreigners, also applied to nationals. The Commission had consistently held that these principles did not apply to a State taking the property of its own nationals. The Court clearly adhered to this view:

> . . . In the first place, purely as a matter of general international law, the principles in question apply solely to non-nationals. They were specifically developed for the benefit of non-nationals. As such, these principles did not relate to the treatment accorded by States to their own nationals. (para. 60)

In interpreting the wording of the article, the Court took the reference to the general principles of international law to mean that those principles are incorporated into the article, but only as regards those acts:

> . . . to which they are normally applicable, that is to say acts of a State in relation to non-nationals. Moreover, the words of a treaty should be understood to have their ordinary meaning, and to interpret the phrase in question as extending the general

principles of international law beyond their normal sphere of applicability is less consistent with the ordinary meaning of the terms used, notwithstanding their context.

... The inclusion of the reference can be seen to serve at least two purposes. Firstly, it enables non-nationals to resort directly to the machinery of the Convention to enforce their rights on the basis of the relevant principles of international law, whereas otherwise they would have to seek recourse to diplomatic channels or to other available means of dispute settlement to do so. Secondly, the reference ensures that the position of non-nationals is safeguarded, in that it excludes any possible argument that the entry into force of Protocol No. 1 has led to a diminution of their rights. In this connection, it is also noteworthy that Article 1 expressly provides that deprivation of property must be effected 'in the public interest': since such a requirement has always been included amongst the general principles of international law, this express provision would itself have been superfluous if Article 1 had had the effect of rendering those principles applicable to nationals as well as to non-nationals. (paras 61 and 62)

The Court recognised that there were difficulties in interpreting the provisions of this article and referred to the *travaux préparatoires* as a supplementary means of interpretation:

... Examination of the *travaux préparatoires* reveals that the express reference to a right to compensation contained in earlier drafts of Article 1 was excluded, notably in the face of opposition on the part of the United Kingdom and other States. The mention of the general principles of international law was subsequently included and was the subject of several statements to the effect that they protected only foreigners. Thus, when the German Government stated that they could accept the text provided that it was explicitly recognised that those principles involved the obligation to pay compensation in the event of expropriation, the Swedish delegation pointed out that those principles only applied to relations between a State and non-nationals. And it was then agreed, at the request of the German and Belgian delegations, that 'the general principles of international law, in their present connotation, entailed the obligation to pay compensation *to non-nationals* in cases of expropriation' (emphasis added).

Above all, in their Resolution (52)1 of 19 March 1952 approving the text of the Protocol and opening it for signature, the Committee of Ministers expressly stated that, 'as regards Article 1, the general principles of international law in their present connotation entail the obligation to pay compensation *to non-nationals* in cases of expropriation (emphasis added). Having regard to the negotiating history as a whole, the Court considers that this Resolution must be taken as a clear indication that the reference to the general principles of international law was not intended to extend to nationals.

The *travaux préparatoires* accordingly do not support the interpretation for which the applicants contended.

... Finally, it has not been demonstrated that, since the entry into force of Protocol No. 1, State practice has developed to the point where it can be said that the parties to that instrument regard the reference therein to the general principles of international law as being applicable to the treatment accorded by them to their own nationals. The evidence adduced points distinctly in the opposite direction.

... For all these reasons, the Court concludes that the general principles of international law are not applicable to a taking by a State of the property of its own nationals. (paras 64–66)

In conclusion the Court held:

> ... The 80 enfranchisements complained of by the applicants remained within the framework of the legislation, which framework the Court has found to be compatible with the second sentence of Article 1. These enfranchisements did not result in placing an excessive burden on the applicants, over and above the disadvantageous effects generally inherent for landlords in the application of the scheme set up under the leasehold reform legislation. Accordingly, the requisite balance under Article 1 was not destroyed. (para. 69)

Comment

Although the differential rights conferred on nationals and non-nationals under this article appear to conflict with Article 14 (non-discrimination) and Article 1 (securing the rights of the Convention and its Protocols to nationals and non-nationals alike), the Court held that exceptions may be permitted if indicated in a particular text.

Sir William Lithgow v UK
Series A, Vol. 102

The facts

The applicants were shareholders in a shipbuilding company called John G. Kincaid and Company Ltd. They owned slightly over 28 per cent of the shares. Under a programme of nationalisation of the aircraft and shipbuilding industries provided for by the Aircraft and Shipbuilding Act 1977, the company was nationalised and compensation for shares was paid in accordance to a formula provided for by the 1977 Act. The applicants complained that they had been deprived of their shares without fair compensation.

The judgment of the Court

Clearly the applicants had been deprived of their possessions within the meaning of the second sentence of Article 1. The question was whether this deprivation was 'in the public interest' and 'subject to the conditions provided for by law'.

The Court rejected the applicants' arguments based on the unfairness of the compensation paid and the arbitrary manner in which it was calculated as evidence of sufficient grounds for holding that the deprivation was neither in the public interest nor provided for by law. The Court held:

> ... The Court is unable to accept the first of these contentions. The obligation to pay compensation derives from an implicit condition in Article 1 of Protocol No. 1 read as a whole rather than from the 'public interest' requirement itself. The latter requirement relates to the justification and the motives for the actual taking, issues which were not contested by the applicants.
>
> ... As regards the phrase 'subject to the conditions provided for by law', it requires in the first place the existence of and compliance with adequately accessible and sufficiently precise domestic legal provisions. Save as stated in paragraph 153 below, the applicants did not dispute that these requirements had been satisfied. (paras 109 and 110)

Following its reasoning in *James v UK*, the Court held that the principles of international law referred to in the second sentence of Article 1 were not applicable.

The Court had to consider whether the availability and the amount of compensation were material considerations under the second sentence of the first paragraph of the article. The Court, in agreement with the Commission, observed that:

> . . . under the legal systems of the Contracting States, the taking of property in the public interest without payment of compensation is treated as justifiable only in exceptional circumstances not relevant for present purposes. As far as Article 1 is concerned, the protection of the right of property it affords would be largely illusory and ineffective in the absence of any equivalent principle.
>
> In this connection, the Court recalls that not only must a measure depriving a person of his property pursue, on the facts as well as in principle, a legitimate aim 'in the public interest', but there must also be a reasonable relationship of proportionality between the means employed and the aim sought to be realised. This latter requirement was expressed in other terms in the abovementioned *Sporrong and Lönnroth* judgment by the notion of the 'fair balance' that must be struck between the demands of the general interest of the community and the requirements of the protection of the individual's fundamental rights. The requisite balance will not be found if the person concerned has had to bear 'an individual and excessive burden'. Although the Court was speaking in that judgment in the context of the general rule of peaceful enjoyment of property enunciated in the first sentence of the first paragraph, it pointed out that 'the search for this balance is . . . reflected in the structure of Article 1' as a whole.
>
> Clearly, compensation terms are material to the assessment whether a fair balance has been struck between the various interests at stake and, notably, whether or not a disproportionate burden has been imposed on the person who has been deprived of his possessions. (para. 120)

Not only should compensation be paid, but it should also be reasonably related to the value of the property, otherwise there would be a disproportionate interference. The Court recognised, however, that:

> . . . Article 1 does not, however, guarantee a right to full compensation in all circumstances, since legitimate objectives of 'public interest', such as pursued in measures of economic reform or measures designed to achieve greater social justice, may call for less than reimbursement of the full market value.
>
> In this connection, the applicants contended that, as regards the standard of compensation, no distinction could be drawn between nationalisation and other takings of property by the State, such as the compulsory acquisition of land for public purposes.
>
> The Court is unable to agree. Both the nature of the property taken and the circumstances of the taking in these two categories of cases give rise to different considerations which may legitimately be taken into account in determining a fair balance between the public interest and the private interests concerned. The valuation of major industrial enterprises for the purpose of nationalising a whole industry is in itself a far more complex operation than, for instance, the valuation of land compulsorily acquired and normally calls for specific legislation which can be applied across the board to all the undertakings involved. Accordingly, provided always that the aforesaid fair balance is preserved, the standard of compensation required in a nationalisation case may be different from that required in regard to other takings of property. (para. 121)

In determining a compensation scheme the State had to be afforded a reasonable margin of appreciation:

... A decision to enact nationalisation legislation will commonly involve consideration of various issues on which opinions within a democratic society may reasonably differ widely. Because of their direct knowledge of their society and its needs and resources, the national authorities are in principle better placed than the international judge to appreciate what measures are appropriate in this area and consequently the margin of appreciation available to them should be a wide one. It would, in the Court's view, be artificial in this respect to divorce the decision as to the compensation terms from the actual decision to nationalise, since the factors influencing the latter will of necessity also influence the former. Accordingly, the Court's power of review in the present case is limited to ascertaining whether the decisions regarding compensation fell outside the United Kingdom's wide margin of appreciation; it will respect the legislature's judgment in this connection unless that judgment was manifestly without reasonable foundation. (para. 122)

As to whether the compensation paid had met the required standard, the Court had to consider the terms and conditions of the legislation and its effects. To do this the Court considered the calculation of compensation based on share values, the hypothetical Stock Exchange quotation method of valuation which had been used, and the reference period for valuation. It found that none of these was inconsistent or contrary to Article 1.

As far as the effects of the legislation on the facts of the applicants' case were concerned, the Court considered the absence of allowance for developments between 1974 and 1977 in the companies concerned; the absence of allowance for inflation; and the absence of an element representing the special value of a large or controlling shareholding. It concluded that the effects of the system established by the 1977 Act were not incompatible with Article 1.

An interesting comparative dissenting opinion was given by Judge Pettiti, who considered the issue of nationalisation, the problems of compensation raised thereby, and whether UK law had indeed struck the right balance.

Comment
The impact of nationalisation had been considered in the earlier case of *A, B, C and D* v *UK* (1967) 10 *Yearbook* 506, concerning the nationalisation of British steel.

A number of other cases concerning compensation depended on the outcome of this case, including: *Vosper Plc* v *UK* App. No. 9262/81; *English Electric Co. and Vickers Ltd* v *UK* App. No. 9263/81; *Banstonian Co. Northern Shipbuilding and Industrial Holding Ltd* v *UK* App. No. 9265/81; *Yarrow Plc and Three Shareholders* v *UK* App. No. 9266/81; and *Vickers Plc* v *UK* App. No. 9313/81.

Gillow v *UK*
Series A, Vol. 109

The facts
The facts of this case, which have been considered under Article 8 of the Convention, concerned the right of the applicants to own and occupy property in Guernsey. Since July 1948, the right of residence in Guernsey without a licence was limited by statute. Although the applicants initially had residence

qualifications, these were lost as a result of their absence from the island and changes in the law. Their application for the required licence to occupy the property which they had bought was refused. Mr Gillow was ultimately charged with and fined for unlawful occupation. Under Article 1 of the First Protocol, the applicants complained that their peaceful enjoyment of possessions had been interfered with.

The Commission's opinion

Referring to the three rules which had emerged from the *Lithgow* case, the Commission expressed the opinion that although this case was not directly concerned with deprivation, it was still necessary to consider whether a fair balance had been struck between the demands of the general interests of the community and the requirements of the applicants' fundamental rights. It was therefore necessary to examine whether the refusal to grant occupational licences and the initiation of criminal proceedings had observed this balance.

The Commission considered that the control of use rule, which interferes with the general principle of peaceful enjoyment of possessions, must be narrowly construed. Therefore:

> . . . in exercising its supervisory jurisdiction, the Commission is required to consider two questions: first whether the control legislation pursues a legitimate aim 'in the general interest' and secondly whether the operation of the legislation and the control thereby exercised on the applicants' use of the property is proportionate to the legitimate aim pursued. . . . Hence, in the Commission's opinion the control of the use of property, albeit for a legitimate purpose 'in accordance with the general interest' will violate Prot. No. 1 Art. 1 if it is clearly established that there is no reasonable relationship of proportionality between the interference with the individual's rights and the general interest which gives legitimacy to the aim pursued.
>
> . . .
>
> . . . While therefore the Commission's approach under the deprivation rule and the control of use rule is closely parallel, the measure of proportionality clearly differs in the application of the two rules since, when viewed in the light of the general rule contained in the first sentence of Prot. No. 1 Art. 1, a deprivation of property is inherently more serious than the control of its use, where full ownership is retained. The principal criterion for establishing whether a fair balance has now been struck in the control use of personal property is therefore the use for which that property was intended by the individual owner. (paras 146 and 148)

The applicants' property was clearly intended for residential use. The licensing requirement therefore deprived them of this sole, direct, personal use, although they retained the rights of ownership.

In examining the legitimacy of the relevant legislation in the context of Article 8 of the Convention, the Commission had found that it satisfied the criteria for that article. As greater latitude is allowed to Contracting States under Article 1 of the First Protocol than under Article 8 of the Convention, the legislation must also be deemed to satisfy the requirement of foreseeability and certainty necessary for the requirement of law. The aim, equally, was legitimate.

The question remained whether the control used was proportionate. The Commission expressed the opinion that:

. . . The standard required by the second paragraph of Prot. No. 1 Art. 1 differs in this regard from the requirements of the second sentence of the same provision, as also from the test of necessity and proportionality contained in Art. 8(2). Whereas the Commission has recognised a close parallel between the test of necessity in respect of deprivations of property and interferences with the right to respect for one's home under Art. 8 (e.g. *App. No. 9261/81* v *United Kingdom*, 28 D & R 177 at 185), the test applicable in respect of measures for the control of property is less stringent and must depend principally upon the severity of the restrictions imposed. Hence the measures applied to control the property's use must be considered in the light of the way in which the property could still be used and the purpose for which it was originally intended.

. . . Whiteknights was, as the Commission has already noted, a house built as, and primarily, if not solely, usable as, a private dwelling. The applicants had built the house themselves for their own personal use and it was therefore equipped to some extent for their requirements; in addition it was furnished with their furniture. By virtue of the operation of the Housing Law 1975 the applicants were only entitled to occupy the property lawfully if they were granted a licence to do so. Nevertheless, despite their previous connections with Guernsey, their applications for a long-term licence for two years or longer were refused by the Housing Authority. In consequence the applicants were not able to make personal use of the house despite their close personal connection with it, and, when they nevertheless did so, they were subjected to criminal prosecution. In addition, however, the applicants were specifically refused permission to occupy the property on a temporary basis in order to carry out repairs. The repairs in question, necessitated after eighteen years of tenanted occupation, were quite substantial, including, for example, the replacement of windows and extensive redecoration. While such work was being carried out, the property could not realistically be let or otherwise disposed of but the applicants' personal use of the property was forbidden.

. . . In these circumstances, whilst the Commission does not find that the restrictions in question amounted to a deprivation of the applicants' property, their use of it was nevertheless subject to very severe restrictions.

. . . The reasons given to the applicants for the refusal of a licence to enable them to use the property was their lack of essential employment, the desirability of Whiteknights as accommodation for those with residence qualifications and the adverse housing situation in the controlled sector. Although these are factors reflecting the general interest of providing residential accommodation for the population of Guernsey, their adequacy must be assessed by reference to the proportionality of this aim to the severity of the restriction on the applicants' use of their property. In this respect the Commission notes that under section 5 of the Housing Law 1975 the Housing Authority was empowered to take into account 'such other factors as it may from time to time deem necessary or expedient'. However, owing to the lack of publicity concerning the operation and exercise of the Housing Authority's discretionary powers, and in the absence of fuller reasons given to explain the decision, it is unclear to what extent such factors may have been considered.

. . .

. . . Furthermore, the Commission also notes that the second reason given by the Housing Authority on 27 July 1979 for refusing a licence, namely that Whiteknights was likely to be sought after by persons fulfilling the residence qualifications that the applicants lacked, failed to refer to the fact that the applicants had previously enjoyed such qualifications for a considerable period themselves. The Housing Authority's reason suggests that the Housing Authority assumed that, if the applicants were not able to occupy the property themselves, it would be made available for occupation by others. However, such a view failed to take into account that, since Whiteknights belonged to the applicants, it was for them, and not the Housing Authority, to decide whether or not Whiteknights was at any time to be made available for occupation by anybody except the applicants themselves.

... Whilst the Housing Law 1975 gave the Housing Authority the power to control the applicants' use of their property, the exercise of this power was always subject to the overriding requirement of the first general rule of Prot. No. 1 Art. 1, that the applicants' personal right to the peaceful enjoyment of their possessions be respected. In the Commission's view, the Housing Authority's implication that, if the applicants were not permitted to occupy the property themselves they should make it available for occupation by someone else, failed adequately to take account of their right of ownership of Whiteknights. The Commission cannot either escape the view that this aspect of the Housing Authority's decision was also disproportionate, bearing in mind that, in view of its state of repair, Whiteknights was apparently not in a wholly satisfactory state for occupation under a fresh tenancy and required repairs before it could be sold. (paras 154–157 and 160 and 161)

The Commission therefore found that:

... the refusal of a licence to the applicants to occupy the house on a long term basis, or temporarily to carry out repairs, was *prima facie* disproportionate and failed to pay due respect to their rights to enjoy their possession. (para. 162)

The Commission concluded, therefore, that there was a breach of Article 1 of the First Protocol.

The judgment of the Court
When the matter came before the Court, the claim under the First Protocol was held not to be valid because the Protocol did not apply to Guernsey. This was because, as the island was a territory for the international relations of which the UK was responsible, an express declaration was required under Article 4 of the First Protocol to extend the application of the whole Protocol to the island.

Comment
It does seem rather extraordinary that the Government had not raised this issue before. In fact the Agent of the Government informed the Court only on 10 October 1986, i.e. after the completion of the Commission hearing. The Court then had to consider the situation *ex officio*. It appeared that a general statement had been made concerning the position of the Channel Islands in relation to treaties and international agreements in October 1950. However, Article 4 requires express declaration for its application. As no such declaration had been communicated by the UK to the Council of Europe, the Court could only conclude that the Protocol was not applicable in the present case.

Allgemeine Gold und Silberscheideanstalt AG v *UK*
Series A, Vol. 108

The facts
The applicants, a German company (AGOSI), dealt in gold and silver coins. In 1975 they sold Krugerrands to two individuals. A term of the sale was that

ownership of the coins would remain with the applicants until the cheque had been cleared. The cheque was dishonoured. On being notified of this the company declared the contract void. On the same day the individuals who had purported to purchase the coins attempted to smuggle them into the UK. They were stopped at Dover, searched, and the coins were confiscated by Customs and Excise. The smugglers were charged with and convicted of criminal offences in connection with the coins. The company endeavoured to regain possession of the coins and instituted civil proceedings to this effect. They were unsuccessful. They therefore brought an application before the Commission claiming a violation of Article 1 of the First Protocol.

The Commission's opinion

First, the Commission had to consider whether the forfeiture of the property was a 'deprivation of property' in the sense of the first paragraph of Article 1. The Commission expressed the view that such forfeiture amounted to a control of use rather than deprivation and therefore fell under the second paragraph:

> . . . At the relevant time the importation of Krugerrands into the United Kingdom without appropriate licence was illegal. Forfeiture under these conditions must be viewed as the operation of legislation to control the use of property in accordance with the general interest, within the terms of the second paragraph of Prot. No. 1 Art. 1 to reflect the fact that the legislation enacted in the United Kingdom prohibiting the unlicenced importation of Krugerrands was itself not contrary to Prot. No. 1 Art. 1. Just as the introduction of this legislation to ban the importation of the Krugerrands was in conformity with the Convention, so also was the forfeiture procedure, since it is merely a direct consequence of that legitimate legislation.
>
> . . . For these reasons the Commission is of the opinion that, in as far as forfeiture concerns those who are responsible for smuggling, the standards contained in the first paragraph of Prot. No. 1 Art. 1, for a normal deprivation of property, do not apply; hence it is the less stringent standard of the second paragraph of that provision which is applicable in such circumstances. (paras 75 and 76)

The problem here was that if there was no justification for controlling the use of property belonging to an innocent owner, then there would be a breach of the article:

> . . . The question therefore is whether or not English law as applied in the present case gave the applicant company the opportunity to argue and establish that it was an innocent owner, and, if innocent, the right to recover the coins. The Commission comes to the conclusion that the condemnation proceedings applicable in the present case did not give the applicant company any such opportunity. In fact, as the Court of Appeal stated in its decision, the only relevant matter in the proceedings under English law was that the coins had been brought into the country in breach of customs legislation. (para. 80)

and that:

> . . . Prot. No. 1 Art. 1 requires that under domestic law an owner who establishes his innocence can recover his possessions. The respondent Government have not contended that this is a right protected by English law. They merely submit that innocence would be a factor . . . (para. 89)

The Commission concluded that:

. . . English law did not permit the applicant company to establish its claim to be an innocent owner and thereby to recover the coins as of right. It is apparent that the Convention cannot require complete proof of the innocence of an applicant before a violation could be established in this context. It is rather the failure of the State to provide a specific machinery and opportunity to establish the innocence of the owner, and in such a case a right to recover the goods, which must be seen as falling short of the requirements of Prot. No. 1 Art. 1. Otherwise the guarantee of the property right in the first sentence of Prot. No. 1 Art. 1 would be rendered meaningless whenever property was misused against the will of the owner and this misuse resulted in confiscation. In fact the practice of the Member States of the Council of Europe shows that innocent owners are usually protected in just such circumstances.

. . . In the present case the Commission finds that the applicant company had no opportunity to have its request for the restoration of the coins determined in the manner which permitted its claim of innocence to be examined and the appropriateness of its being subjected to a penalty fully considered save by the availability of a discretionary power to restore the coins by act of grace. As a result the forfeiture was ordered without formal reference to the question of the applicant company's involvement in the wrongdoing for which it was the penalty.

. . . The Commission finds the ordering of forfeiture and the refusal to restore the coins in these circumstances, which interfered with the applicant company's enjoyment of its possessions, was disproportionate and failed to take adequate account of its claim to the enjoyment of the fundamental right to property protected by Prot. No. 1 Art. 1. (paras 90–92)

The Commission therefore expressed the opinion that there had been a breach of Article 1.

The judgment of the Court

The forfeiture of the smuggled Krugerrands amounted to an interference with the applicant's property. This was not in dispute. The prohibition on the importation of gold coins was a control of the use of property, although it also involved a deprivation of property. The applicable part of Article 1 was primarily the second paragraph:

. . . The second paragraph of Article 1 recognises the right of a State 'to enforce such laws as it deems necessary to control the use of property . . . in accordance with the public interest'.

Undoubtedly the prohibition on the importation of Krügerrands into the United Kingdom was in itself compatible with the terms of this provision. Nevertheless, as the second paragraph is to be construed in the light of the general principle enunciated in the opening sentence of Article 1, there must, in respect of enforcement of this prohibition, also be a reasonable relationship of proportionality between the means employed and the aim sought to be realised; in other words, the Court must determine whether a fair balance has been struck between the demands of the general interest in this respect and the interest of the individual or individuals concerned. In determining whether a fair balance exists, the Court recognises that the State enjoys a wide margin of appreciation with regard both to choosing the means of enforcement and to ascertaining whether the consequences of enforcement are justified in the general interest for the purpose of achieving the object of the law in question.

. . . As the Commisssion pointed out, under the general principles of law recognised in all Contracting States, smuggled goods may, as a rule, be the object of confiscation. . . . (paras 52 and 53)

In considering whether it agreed with the applicant company and the Commission that the innocence of the owner was a relevant factor, the Court observed that:

. . . although there is a trend in the practice of the Contracting States that the behaviour of the owner of the goods and in particular the use of due care on his part should be taken into account in deciding whether or not to restore smuggled goods – assuming that the goods are not dangerous – different standards are applied and no common practice can be said to exist. For forfeiture to be justified under the terms of the second paragraph of Article 1, it is enough that the explicit requirements of this paragraph are met and that the State has struck a fair balance between the interests of the State and those of the individual. The striking of a fair balance depends on many factors and the behaviour of the owner of the property, including the degree of fault or care which he has displayed, is one element of the entirety of circumstances which should be taken into account.

. . . Accordingly, although the second paragraph of Article 1 contains no explicit procedural requirements, the Court must consider whether the applicable procedures in the present case were such as to enable, amongst other things, reasonable account to be taken of the degree of fault or care of the applicant company or, at least, of the relationship between the company's conduct and the breach of the law which undoubtedly occurred; and also whether the procedures in question afforded the applicant company a reasonable opportunity of putting its case to the responsible authorities. In ascertaining whether these conditions were satisfied, a comprehensive view must be taken of the applicable procedures.

. . . In the present case, the question of forfeiture was dealt with in two distinct stages: the condemnation proceedings before the courts and the subsequent determination by the Commissioners under section 288 of the 1952 Act whether or not to exercise their discretion to restore the Krügerrands to the applicants. It is uncontested that the question of AGOSI's behaviour was irrelevant in the proceedings before the High Court under section 44 of the Act for the condemnation of the Krügerrands as forfeit. The question of the company's behaviour was, however, implicitly raised in its application to the Commissioners on 1 April 1980, that is after the coins had been formally forfeited by the courts, for the restoration of the Krügerrands under section 288. In accordance with the rules of English law, the Commissioners were bound to be guided by relevant considerations. In the present case, the relevant considerations certainly included the alleged innocence and diligence of the owner of the forfeited coins and the relationship between the behaviour of the owner and the breach of the import laws. (paras 54–56)

If the applicants considered that the Customs and Excise Commissions had not taken into account relevant considerations they could have applied for judicial review. The Court, having examined the availability of this remedy, considered that in the circumstances the scope of judicial review under English law was sufficient to satisfy the requirements of the second paragraph of Article 1.

In conclusion the Court found that:

. . . the procedure available to the applicant company against the Commissioners' refusal to restore the Krügerrands cannot be dismissed as an inadequate one for the purposes of the requirements of the second paragraph of Article 1. In particular, it has not been established that the British system failed either to ensure that reasonable account be taken of the behaviour of the applicant company or to afford the applicant company a reasonable opportunity to put its case.

The fact that the applicant, for reasons of its own, chose not to seek judicial review of the Commissioners' decision of May 1980 and hence did not receive full advantage of the safeguards available to owners asserting their innocence and lack of negligence cannot invalidate this conclusion. Accordingly there has been no breach of Article 1 of Protocol No. 1. (para. 62)

Judge Pettiti expressed a dissenting opinion, holding that there had been a violation of the First Protocol.

Comment

The importation of gold coins without a special licence had been made illegal under s. 304 of the Customs and Excise Act 1952 and the Import of Goods (Control) Order 1954 (SI 1954 No. 23). Under s. 288 of the 1952 Act, the Commissioners of Customs and Excise have a discretion to restore any property seized or forfeited. They decided not to exercise their discretion in the applicant company's favour, although they did not give reasons. During the criminal proceedings a question was raised which had to be referred to the European Court of Justice. This was whether the restriction on the importation of coins was a breach of Article 30 of the Treaty of Rome guaranteeing the free movement of goods. The European Court of Justice held that Article 30 did not apply to the Krugerrands, which were to be regarded as capital rather than goods.

Another interesting aspect which emerged from the case was the difference between the common law approach and the civil law approach to judicial review. In a civil law system, where the State or its agents are involved in a case, there will automatically come a moment at which judicial review is applicable. Under English law a separate procedure and action must be commenced. The applicant company had failed to institute judicial review proceedings, although they had pursued civil proceedings. In a subsequent case a challenge by way of judicial review of equivalent discretionary powers under s. 152 of the Customs and Excise Management Act 1979, had been successful (*R* v *HM Customs and Excise, ex parte Leonard Haworth* (1985) unreported). In the *AGOSI* case, failure to apply for judicial review had not been raised by the UK under the heading of failure to exhaust domestic remedies, but, despite this, the existence of the remedy was not only held to be applicable but on the facts persuaded the Court that its availability satisfied the requirements of guaranteeing a balance between the competing interests.

Air Canada v *UK*
Council of Europe Report

The facts

. . . On 26 April 1987 a Tristar aircraft owned and operated by the applicant company and worth over £60 million, landed at Heathrow airport, London, where it discharged cargo including a container which, when opened, was found to contain 331 kilograms of cannabis resin valued at about £800,000. The airway bill number of the container was false, the applicant company's cargo computer did not hold any details of the consignment and no airway bill had been drawn up and despatched for it.

The aircraft was on a regular scheduled flight starting in Singapore and travelling to Toronto landing en route at Bombay and Heathrow. It was carrying both fare-paying passengers and cargo. (Council of Europe Report, para. 7)

On 1 May, Commissioners of Customs and Excise, acting under s. 139 of the Customs and Excise Management Act 1979, seized the aircraft as liable to forfeiture under s. 141(1) of the Act. The aircraft was delivered back to the applicants later the same day subject to the payment of a penalty of £50,000. The applicants pursued civil proceedings; and although they were successful before the High Court, the Court of Appeal overruled this decision. Leave to appeal to the House of Lords was refused. The applicants complained that the seizure of the aircraft was a violation of their right to peaceful enjoyment of possessions under Article 1. The Commission expressed the opinion that there had been no violation of this article.

The judgment of the Court

Although it was clear that there had been an interference with the applicant company's property, the Court had to resolve whether this amounted to deprivation of property or control of use. Although both of these affect the enjoyment of property and were therefore not distinct in as much as they were interconnected, the applicants had considered that the measure amounted to deprivation, while the Commission and the UK had expressed the view that it amounted to control of use – in the circumstances control of the use of an aircraft which had been employed for the import of prohibited drugs. The Court agreed with this latter view. It observed:

> . . . in the first place, that the seizure of the aircraft amounted to a temporary restriction on its use and did not involve a transfer of ownership, and, in the second place, that the decision of the Court of Appeal to condemn the property as forfeited did not have the effect of depriving Air Canada of ownership since the sum required for the release of the aircraft had been paid. . . .
>
> . . . In addition, it is clear from the scheme of the legislation that the release of the aircraft subject to the payment of a sum of money was, in effect, a measure taken in furtherance of a policy of seeking to prevent carriers from bringing, *inter alia*, prohibited drugs into the United Kingdom. As such, it amounted to a control of the use of property. It is therefore the second paragraph of Article 1 which is applicable in the present case . . . (paras 33 and 34)

Such being the case, the Court then had to consider if this control of use was 'in accordance with the general interest'. This meant that the interference must:

> . . . achieve a 'fair balance' between the demands of the general interest of the community and the requirements of the protection of the individual's fundamental rights. (para. 36)

The Commission had considered that judicial review proceedings would have been available to the applicants if they felt that the measures taken were disproportionate or wrong. The Commission expressed the view that the actions taken were proportionate to the aim of controlling the use of aircraft involved in the importation of prohibited drugs.

The Court observed that the seizure and the requirement of payment conformed with the relevant requirements of the 1979 Act, which did not require a finding of fault or negligence on the part of the applicant company.

The Court held that:

> ... While the width of the powers of forfeiture conferred on the Commissioners by section 141(1) of this Act is striking, the seizure of the applicant's aircraft and its release subject to payment were undoubtedly exceptional measures which were resorted to in order to bring about an improvement in the company's security procedures. These measures were taken following the discovery of a container, the shipment of which involved various transport irregularities, holding 331 kilograms of cannabis resin. ... Moreover, this incident was the latest in a long series of alleged security lapses which had been brought to Air Canada's attention involving the illegal importation of drugs into the United Kingdom during the period 1983-1987. ... In particular, Air Canada – along with other operators – had been warned in a letter dated 15 December 1986 from the Commissioners that, where prohibited goods have been carried, they would consider exercising their powers under the 1979 Act including the seizure and forfeiture of aircraft.
>
> ... Against this background there can be no doubt that the measures taken conformed to the general interest in combatting international drug trafficking. (paras 41 and 42)

Further, the Court agreed with the Commission that the availability of judicial review to challenge actions of the Commissioners of Customs and Excise was an effective remedy, and sufficient in its scope to satisfy the requirements of the second paragraph of Article 1.

To conclude, the Court held that:

> ... taking into account the large quantity of cannabis that was found in the container, its street value ... as well as the value of the aircraft that had been seized, the Court does not consider the requirement to pay £50,000 to be disproportionate to the aim pursued, namely the prevention of the importation of prohibited drugs into the United Kingdom.
>
> ... Bearing in mind the above, as well as the State's margin of appreciation in this area, it considers that, in the circumstances of the present case, a fair balance was achieved. There has thus been no violation of Article 1 of Protocol No. 1. (paras 47 and 48)

Four dissenting opinions were made. Judge Walsh disagreed with the majority on the grounds that to interpret Article 1 as allowing the forfeiture of an innocent person's property for the benefit of the 'general interest', was to exceed the scope of the article. The case was distinguishable from the *AGOSI* case, because in that case the goods seized were contraband; the aircraft was not contraband.

Judge Martens, joined by Judge Russo, preferred to view the seizure of the aircraft not as control of use, but as seizure of property to secure the payment of penalties. This raised the question whether the right of the State to seize a person's property without that person being permitted to prove that he or she was not to blame for that property being used to perpetrate an offence, was compatible with Article 1. Judge Martens expressed the view that the answer to this was in the negative.

Judge Pekkanen dissented from the majority on the grounds that the purpose behind the confiscation of the aircraft was to compel the payment of the penalty, and the penalty was imposed as a condition for the release of the aircraft. Given the wide powers of discretion conferred on the Commissioners under the 1979 Act, the Judge questioned whether the operation of the law was sufficiently foreseeable to meet Convention requirements. The Judge was also not convinced that proportionality had been observed by the Commissioners in their decision-making process.

Further reading

Andrews, J., 'Leasehold enfranchisement and the public interest in the UK' (1986) 11 *European Law Review* 366

Andrews, J., 'Compensation for nationalisation in the UK' (1987) 12 *European Law Review* 65

Andrews, J., 'Housing Law in Guernsey' (1987) 12 *European Law Review* 70

Sherlock, A., 'Council of Europe – Property Rights and the European Convention on Human Rights' (1987) 8 *Business Law Review* 113

ARTICLE 2 OF THE FIRST PROTOCOL

Article 2
No person shall be denied the right to education. In the exercise of any functions which it assumes in relation to education and to teaching, the State shall respect the right of parents to ensure such education and teaching in conformity with their own religious and philosophical convictions.

16.3   THE SCOPE OF THE ARTICLE

Although the definitive case on Article 2 was one involving Belgium (*The Belgian Linguistic case* 1 EHRR 252), it has been raised in a number of cases involving the UK and the principles outlined in the Belgian case have been expressed and applied in these.

Article 2 guarantees a fundamental right to education, but it has also been suggested that the second sentence of the article provides an 'adjunct' to this fundamental right and the article should be interpreted as a whole (*App. Nos 10228/82 and 10229/82* v *UK* 7 EHRR 135 at 141).

In interpreting the article as a whole, the Court has held that there is no positive obligation on the State to provide for or subsidise any particular form of education in order to respect the philosophical convictions of parents. Thus refusal of the authorities to provide financial support for the education of the applicants' children at a Rudolf Steiner school – which gave practical effect to certain educational and philosophical convictions – was not a violation of Article 2, because the State did not prevent the parents from sending their children there and, moreover, it showed respect for the school by granting it charitable status (*App. No. 9461/81* v *UK* 5 EHRR 465).

Generally cases will fail if the State is not made aware of the parents' philosophical or religious convictions. This has been raised in several cases where a school has included the infliction of corporal punishment on pupils as part of the general disciplinary procedure. Corporal punishment and its regulation have been viewed as part of the function assumed by the State in relation to education (see, for example, *Mr and Mrs X and their son v UK* 5 EHRR 265). Once a parent has brought his or her views on corporal punishment to the attention of the relevant authority, then, if those views are ignored, a violation may be established (for instance, if a child has been refused education because a parent will not agree to corporal punishment and no alternative school is found for the child: *App. No. 9303/81 v UK* 9 EHRR 513). If the parent's convictions are not brought to the attention of the authorities then they may be deemed not to have attained a necessary level of cogency. Corporal punishment itself, although it may fall under Article 3 of the Convention, has been held to be a reasonable condition to readmission to a school under this article (*App. No. 9119/80 v UK* 8 EHRR 47).

Ensuring respect for parents' philosophical convictions is, moreover, not without some limitations of a practical nature. An example of acceptable practical limitations can be found in a case where the applicants had entered their respective children for grammar schools, but they had been refused places because the education authority claimed that there were no more places available in the schools and that the admissions quotas could not be exceeded without prejudicing the efficient education of the schools concerned (*App. Nos 10228/82 and 10229/82 v UK* 7 EHRR 135).

If a State does provide education then it has a positive obligation in respect of each and every function undertaken to ensure respect for the parents' philosophical convictions. However, these convictions must achieve a certain level of 'cogency, seriousness, cohesion and importance' (*Campbell and Cosans v UK* 4 EHRR 293 and *App. No. 8566/79 v UK* 5 EHRR 265).

Respect for a variety of convictions does not mean that education provided by the State must be religiously and philosophically neutral. Article 2 of the First Protocol does not prevent a State from imparting, either through teaching or education, information or knowledge of a directly or indirectly religious or philosophical kind.

. . . It does not even permit parents to object to the integration of such teaching or education in the school curriculum, for otherwise all institutionalised teaching would run the risk of proving impracticable. In fact, it seems very difficult for many subjects taught at school not to have, to a greater or lesser extent, some philosophical complexion or implications. The same is true of religious affinities if one remembers the existence of religions forming a very broad dogmatic and moral entity which has or may have answers to every question of a philosophical, cosmological or moral nature.

The second sentence of Article 2 implies on the other hand that the State, in fulfilling the functions assumed by it in regard to education and teaching, must take care that information or knowledge included in the curriculum is conveyed in an objective, critical and pluralistic manner. The State is forbidden to pursue an aim of indoctrination that might be considered as not respecting parents' religious and philosophical convictions. . . .

. . . Thus the essence of Protocol No. 1, Art. 2, is the safeguarding of pluralism and tolerance in public education and the prohibition on indoctrination, parents' religious and philosophical convictions having to be respected, albeit not necessarily reflected, in the State school system.

As regards the circumstances of the present cases, the Commission notes that in the applicants' region there is a dual system of selective and comprehensive public education and that other alternatives, such as private school education or education at home of a sufficient standard, are open to them. The Commission considers, however, that the reasons given for refusing the applicants' children places in the selective State schools, i.e. the unavailability of places, the maintenance of efficient education in such schools and the efficient use and distribution of resources between these and other schools in the area, and the fact that the applicants cannot afford private education, cannot be viewed as conflicting with the requirements of Protocol No. 1, Art. 2.

The Commission also observes that there is no evidence in this case that the applicants' children are being indoctrinated in the respective comprehensive schools which they are attending or that the teaching of the children is not conveyed in an objective, critical or pluralistic manner. Moreover there is no allegation that the comprehensive system denies the applicants their major role in the education of their children, in particular the transmission of their values or philosophical convictions. In the light of the above considerations, the Commission concludes that the respondent Government cannot be said to have overstepped the limits of the obligations it has accepted under Protocol No. 1, Art. 2. It follows that this aspect of the case is manifestly ill-founded within the meaning of Art. 27(2) of the Convention. (*App. Nos 10228 and 10229/82* v *UK* (1984) 37 D & R 96 at 99)

When signing the First Protocol the UK Government made a reservation which provided that:

. . . in view of certain provisions of the Education Acts in force in the United Kingdom, the principle affirmed in the second sentence of Article 2 is accepted by the United Kingdom only so far as it is compatible with the provision of efficient instruction and training, and the avoidance of unreasonable public expenditure.

16.4 THE CASES

Campbell and Cosans v *UK*
Series A, Vol. 48

The facts

The facts of this case, which has been considered under Article 3, were that the first applicant's son was at a school in Scotland where corporal punishment was part of the general disciplinary procedure. Although her son had never been subject to such punishment, the applicant had tried unsuccessfully to obtain guarantees that he would not ever receive it. The second applicant's son was at a different school in Scotland. He had broken one of the school rules and been told to report for corporal punishment. Following his refusal to do so he was suspended from the school, and in fact never returned to school again.

The applicants complained that the existence of corporal punishment in Scottish schools interfered with their rights under Article 2, to ensure the education and teaching of their children in accordance with their philosophical convictions.

The Commission's opinion

First the Commission had to decide if it accepted the Government's argument that corporal punishment constituted a disciplinary measure which was not a function assumed by the State in relation to education and teaching and therefore fell outside Article 2.

Rejecting the Government's view, the Commission held that:

> . . . Although the right guaranteed by the second sentence of Article 2 extends primarily to the content of the school curriculum and the manner in which it is conveyed to school children, it also *inter alia* covers, as stated above, the organisation and financing of public education. The Commission points out, moreover, that the term 'education' is generally understood as meaning not only theoretical instruction in a strict sense, but also generally the development and moulding of children's character and mental powers. The fact that the draftsmen of Article 2 found it necessary to refer both to 'education' and to 'teaching', a term the ordinary meaning of which is more restricted, supports this view.
>
> . . . In the opinion of the Commission this interpretation is further borne out by the very structure and object of Article 2 itself. This Article constitutes a whole which is dominated by its first sentence which provides the fundamental right to education, to which the right set out in the second sentence of Article 2 is an adjunct. . . .
>
> . . . In the light of all the preceding considerations, the Commission concludes that measures used for the purpose of punishing and correcting faults as a matter of discipline must clearly be considered as a function assumed in relation to education and teaching, thus obliging the State to respect the religious and philosophical convictions of parents. The Commission finally points out in this context that it is immaterial whether the functions covered by Article 2 of the Protocol are directly or merely indirectly assumed by the Contracting States. It follows that this Article extends also to education provided by local education authorities. (paras 80–82)

Secondly, the Commission had to examine whether the opinions of the applicants on this matter were 'philosophical convictions', the question of religious convictions not being raised here. The Government had argued that 'convictions' could not be extended to cover preferences in the matter of disciplinary punishments.

The Commission accepted that it would be wrong to distort the meaning of the words 'philosophical' and 'religious'; nevertheless, the issues here concerned the fundamental views of two mothers on the use or threatened use of physical violence on their children. In interpreting the term 'philosophical' which had no single determinate and unqualified meaning, the Commission expressed the opinion that:

> . . . the notion of 'philosophical convictions' has instead to be given an independent content in the light of the context of the second sentence of Article 2 of the Protocol and the object and purpose of this provision.
>
> . . . In the opinion of the Commission it is clear in the first place that 'philosophical convictions' cannot be so interpreted as to cover merely the views of those parents who have such a developed system of thought that it would have the scope of a 'religion' or a 'philosophy' in the strict sense of these terms. Such an interpretation

would inevitably imply that the 'respect' clause of Article 2 of the Protocol would only apply to a comparatively limited number of parents with well-defined and articulate philosophical opinions. The Commission considers that such restrictive interpretation is in the first place excluded by the text itself of Article 2 of the Protocol which guarantees a fundamental right to *all* parents. Secondly, the text of Article 2 speaks of respect for religious *and* philosophical convictions.

. . .

. . . The Commission considers that, as a general idea, the concept of 'philosophical convictions' must be understood to mean those ideas based on human knowledge and reasoning concerning the world, life, society etc., which a person adopts and professes according to the dictates of his or her conscience. These ideas can more briefly be characterised as a person's outlook on life including, in particular, a concept of human behaviour in society. In support of this consideration the Commission recalls that the provisions of the Convention and the Protocol 'must be read as a whole'. Consequently, the provisions of Article 2 of the Protocol

> must be read not only in the light of each other but also, in particular, of Articles 8, 9 and 10 of the Convention which proclaim the right of everyone, including parents and children, 'to respect for his private and family life', to 'freedom of thought, conscience and religion', and to 'freedom . . . to receive and impart information and ideas'.

. . . As regards the present two applicants, the Commission is satisfied that their views on the use or threatened use of physical violence as a means of disciplining young children are indeed views of a clear moral order concerning human behaviour in respect of young children at school and in society at large. Furthermore, on the facts as established by the Commission, there is no indication whatever to show that these views are not genuinely held by them.

. . . The Commission thus arrives at the conclusion that the applicants' opinions are philosophical convictions within the meaning of the second sentence of Article 2 of the Protocol which the State is obliged by that provision to respect. (paras 88 and 89, and 92–94)

Satisfied that the applicants' views amounted to philosophical convictions, the Commission then had to consider whether these had been respected. In this context the Commission recognised that the contracting States had broad competence as to how they carried out functions relating to teaching and education, including the measures for discipline and order. Nevertheless, the Commission felt that under Article 2 a State is required:

> . . . to provide schools in its educational system for the children of parents who express clear convictions about the use of corporal punishment in schools and who wish to have their children exempted from such punishment. (para. 98)

The fact that private schools existed in Scotland which did not have corporal punishment did not provide an acceptable and realistic alternative to the parents. Therefore the Commission found that the UK had failed to respect the applicants' convictions.

In considering whether the UK reservation to Article 2 had any effect, the Commission had to consider the state of the law. The relevant legislation was the Education (Scotland) Act 1962, passed some time after the UK made its reservation. However, the 1962 Act simply re-enacted an earlier provision which had been in force when the UK signed the Protocol. The legislation would therefore be covered by the reservation if this was found to be applicable. The UK Government argued that it would be impractical to have a dual system of State schools in which some had corporal punishment and some did not. The Commission was not persuaded:

> ... The Commission notes that nothing has been submitted to it from which it could be concluded that corporal punishment is of such overriding importance with respect to the education system that it would justify an interference with the applicants' philosophical convictions. In particular, the argument that the maintenance of corporal punishment is necessary for the purpose of making education and teaching possible is in fact contradicted by the *Statement of Principles and Code of Practice* issued by the Liaison Committee on Educational Matters in 1968 and by the Government's own statement before the Commission that they are proceeding by means of negotiations with education authorities to achieve consensus on the matter of abolition of corporal punishment. Furthermore, the Government have submitted no details as to how it could possibly cause any increased public expenditure to respect the applicants' philosophical convictions.
>
> ... In the light of the preceding observations the Commission is satisfied that the United Kingdom reservation has no bearing on the interpretation of Article 2 of the Protocol, since the respondent Government have failed to show that it would in any way be incompatible with the provision of 'suitable instruction and training, and the avoidance of unreasonable public expenditure' to respect the convictions of those parents who, like the present applicants, are against corporal punishment. (paras 104 and 105)

There had therefore been a violation of the applicants' rights under Article 2 of the First Protocol.

The Commission did not consider it necessary to decide whether there had been a separate violation of the first sentence of Article 2 in respect of the suspension of Jeffrey Cosans in as much as he had been denied the right to education. Mr Kiernan expressed a dissenting opinion that the suspension in fact was a separate violation and ought to have been considered as such.

A dissenting opinion was expressed by five of the Commission on the issue of whether the applicants' objections to corporal punishment amounted to 'philosophical convictions'. In their view the primary purpose of Article 2 was to prevent indoctrination; the question of the use of different disciplinary measures did not fall within the envisaged scope of the article. It was suggested that only if the disciplinary measure was such as to be a violation of a child's rights under the Convention, could any view on it be said to amount to a 'philosophical conviction'. As in this case the Commission had found that there was no violation of Article 3, the views of the applicants could not be said to amount to 'philosophical convictions'.

The judgment of the Court
The Court agreed with the Commission that the question of discipline could be included within the scope of Article 2:

> ... the education of children is the whole process, whereby, in any society, adults endeavour to transmit their beliefs, culture and other values to the young, whereas

teaching or instruction refers in particular to the transmission of knowledge and to intellectual development. (para. 33)

The Court did not feel that matters of internal administration, including discipline, could be separated. Even if the day-to-day administration of a school was vested in individual teachers, the State was responsible for formulating general policy, including questions of discipline. The responsibility of the State was, therefore, engaged.

Whether the applicants' views amounted to 'philosophical convictions', the Court held that:

> . . . In its ordinary meaning the word 'convictions', taken on its own, is not synonymous with the words 'opinions' and 'ideas', such as are utilised in Article 10 of the Convention, which guarantees freedom of expression; it is more akin to the term 'beliefs' (in the French text: '*convictions*') appearing in Article 9 – which guarantees freedom of thought, conscience and religion – and denotes views that attain a certain leavel of cogency, seriousness, cohesion and importance.
>
> As regards the adjective 'philosophical', it is not capable of exhaustive definition and little assistance as to its precise significance is to be gleaned from the *travaux préparatoires*. The Commission pointed out that the word 'philosophy' bears numerous meanings: it is used to allude to a fully-fledged system of thought or, rather loosely, to views on more or less trivial matters. The Court agrees with the Commission that neither of these two extremes can be adopted for the purposes of interpreting Article 2: the former would too narrowly restrict the scope of a right that is guaranteed to all parents and the latter might result in the inclusion of matters of insufficient weight or substance.
>
> Having regard to the Convention as a whole, including Article 17, the expression 'philosophical convictions' in the present context denotes, in the Court's opinion, such convictions as are worthy of respect in a 'democratic society' and are not incompatible with human dignity; in addition, they must not conflict with the fundamental right of the child to education, the whole of Article 2 being dominated by its first sentence. (para. 36)

Although the Court noted that changes had been proposed in the Scottish system, these did not amount to 'respect' for the applicants' convictions.

In interpreting this, the Court pointed out that the original draft used the words 'have regard to'; these had been replaced by the word 'respect'. The Court understood this word to mean:

> . . . more than 'acknowledge' or 'take into account'; in addition to a primarily negative undertaking, it implies some positive obligation on the part of the State. This being so, the duty to respect parental convictions in this sphere cannot be overridden by the alleged necessity of striking a balance between the conflicting views involved, nor is the Government's policy to move gradually towards the abolition of corporal punishment in itself sufficient to comply with this duty. (para. 37)

The Court agreed with the Commission that the reservation made by the UK was not of assistance here, because it was not convinced that the UK could not have respected the applicants' rights in some way.

Unlike the Commission, the Court found that it was necessary to consider the separate issue of Jeffrey Cosans's suspension. The complaint under the first sentence of Article 2 related to a right of the applicant's son, while the question of philosophical beliefs related to the parent. The two claims were, therefore, distinct. Although Article 2 constitutes a whole, it is dominated by its first sentence, therefore an issue arising under this is not absorbed by the second sentence. Jeffrey Cosans could have returned to school only if his parents had been prepared to act contrary to their convictions. There was therefore a separate violation of the first sentence of Article 2.

A dissenting opinion was expressed by Judge Sir Vincent Evans, who felt that the Court had given too wide an interpretation to the article and had not sufficiently taken account of the reservation made by the UK.

Patel v UK
4 EHRR 256

The facts

The applicant was admitted to Bradford University to read for a degree in Computer Science and Technology. He failed his first-year examinations and the re-sit examinations, and because of his poor attendance throughout the year was asked to withdraw from the course. He pursued legal proceedings against the university, and eventually the Chancery Division of the High Court held that the court had no jurisdiction in the case, this being a matter exclusively for the Bradford University Visitors. This view was confirmed by the Court of Appeal.

Before the Commission the applicant invoked a number of articles, including Article 2 of the First Protocol.

The Commission's opinion

The Commission referred to the principles of the *Belgian Linguistic* case and noted that there was no absolute right to education. The article could be interpreted by a negative formulation whereby the Contracting Parties:

> . . . do not recognise such a right to education as would require them to establish at their own expense, or to subsidise, education of any particular type or at any particular level. . . .
>
> There never was, nor is now, therefore any question of requiring each State to establish . . . a system [of general and official education], but merely of guaranteeing to persons subject to the jurisdiction of the Contracting Parties the right, in principle, to avail themselves of the means of instruction existing at a given time.
>
> The Convention lays down no specific obligations concerning the extent of those means and the manner of their organisation or subsidisation. . . .
>
> The first sentence of Article 2 of the Protocol consequently guarantees, in the first place, the right of access to educational institutions existing at a given time.

This right, however, requires regulation by the State:

> regulation which may vary in time and place according to the needs and resources of the community and of individuals. It goes without saying that such regulation must never injure the substance of the right to education nor conflict with other rights enshrined in the Convention. (*Belgian Linguistics Case (No. 2)* 1 EHRR 252, para. 5, cited in para. 12)

In the light of these principles the Commission considered that:

... where certain, limited, higher education facilities are provided by a State, in principle it is not incompatible with Article 2 of Protocol No. 1 to restrict access thereto to those students who have attained the academic level required to most benefit from the courses offered.

... Applying this conclusion to the facts of the present case, the Commission notes that the applicant did have an opportunity to pursue the computer science course at Bradford University but he failed the first year examination requirements and had a poor attendance record at compulsory classes. He was not therefore considered of a sufficient academic standard for readmittance to the University to repeat the first year of these studies, although the University did not exclude the possibility that he pursue a different subject. The Commission does not consider therefore that the applicant was unreasonably refused access to university education. (paras 13 and 14)

X v UK
4 EHRR 252

The facts

The applicant was detained in prison serving a five-year sentence. He was a New Zealand citizen and was trying to follow a correspondence course from New Zealand in mechanical engineering while in prison. He had also taken an 'O' level course in mathematics and started an 'A' level course, but had been removed from this as the tutor did not think he could cope with it. He complained that he was not given sufficient time off from his prison work to study and that there were difficulties concerning postal facilities available to him. He alleged violations of Article 2 of the First Protocol and violation of Article 14, on the grounds that he had been discriminated against as a New Zealander, while other prisoners who were of British nationality were given more favourable treatment.

The Commission's opinion

The Commission emphasised that Article 2 does not confer an absolute right to all forms of education. It was not unreasonable to restrict access to certain limited higher education facilities on the basis of academic ability and attainment of certain academic levels.

The Commission noted that:

... the applicant is allowed by the prison authorities to follow a mechanical engineering course, by correspondence, in his spare time. The Commission finds that the prison authorities do not deny the applicant his rights under Article 2 of Protocol No. 1 in refusing him time off prison work to study for this course. Moreover, the Commission notes that the applicant was given an opportunity to pursue an 'A' level course in mathematics but that the course tutor did not consider that the applicant was of a sufficient academic level to continue such studies, he was, therefore, required to withdraw from it. The Commission does not consider therefore that the applicant was unreasonably refused access to the 'A' level course. (para. 14)

As far as the correspondence course was concerned, the Commission noted that:

... The Home Secretary has specified the categories of study for which prisoners are allowed time off work: remedial education, Open University courses and other recognised courses of study which a prisoner had already started prior to his imprisonment. On this basis the applicant has been treated differently from prisoners following these categories of study. However, Article 14 does not prohibit every difference in treatment in the enjoyment of Convention rights and freedoms: '. . . the principle of equality of treatment is violated if the distinction has no objective and reasonable justification'.

. . . The Commission finds that the applicant has not put forward any evidence to cast doubt on the objectivity and reasonableness of giving priority to the aforementioned categories of study for which the prison administration allows time off work.

. . . An examination of the applicant's complaints, including an examination *ex officio*, does not disclose any appearance of a violation of the rights and freedoms set forth in the Convention, in particular in Article 14 and Article 2 of Protocol No. 1.

. . . It follows that this part of the application is manifestly ill-founded within the meaning of Article 27(2) of the Convention. (paras 16–19)

ARTICLE 3 OF THE FIRST PROTOCOL

Article 3
The High Contracting Parties undertake to hold free elections at reasonable intervals by secret ballot, under conditions which will ensure the free expression of the opinion of the people in the choice of the legislature.

In western-style democracies it is not surprising that this article is not raised very often. However, it was considered in the case of *Liberal Party and Others* v *UK*, which concerned the simple majority system, and in *Kennedy Lindsay* v *UK* (1979) 22 *Yearbook* 344, which concerned the system of the single transferable vote for European Assembly elections in Northern Ireland.

Liberal Party and Others v UK
(1981) 24 Yearbook 320

The facts
The applicants complained that they were adversely affected by the British electoral system in breach of rights conferred under Article 3 of the First Protocol. The electoral system, which was governed by the Representation of the People Act 1949 as amended, was based on a simple majority system, which tended to favour the two major political parties, Labour and Conservative, with a corresponding disproportionately adverse effect on the Liberal Party and its members. The applicants argued, and this was not disputed, that a system of proportional representation would benefit the Liberal Party. The applicants claimed that:

(i) Article 3 of the Protocol guarantees the right to vote and the right to stand for election to the legislature. States may impose restrictions on the right to vote and the right to stand, provided that they are not arbitrary and do not interfere with the free expression of the people's opinion. It is for the Commission to decide in each particular case whether this particular condition is fulfilled.

(ii) Article 3 does not impose a particular kind of electoral system which would guarantee that the total number of votes cast for each candidate or group of candidates must be proportionately reflected in the composition of the legislative assembly.

(iii) Accordingly, by virtue of the previous decisions of the Commission it is not open to the applicants, in the circumstances of the present case, to complain that the simple majority system violates Article 3 read in isolation from the other provisions of the Convention and its Protocols; nor do the applicants seek to do so. However, it is submitted that the rights guaranteed by Article 3 are not theoretical or illusory but practical and effective. (pp. 115–16)

The purposes of the applicants in bringing the claim were stated as being:

. . . (a) to secure the effective enjoyment by the applicants and other persons within the jurisdiction of the United Kingdom of the right to vote and the right to stand for elections to the House of Commons, guaranteed by Article 3 of the Protocol, and of the right to freedom of expression, guaranteed by Article 10 of the Convention, without discrimination on grounds of political opinion or party affiliation; and (b) to secure that everyone (including the applicants) will have an effective remedy before a national authority within the United Kingdom for claims of violations of Article 3 of the Protocol and of Article 10 of the Convention read together with Article 14 of the Convention of the kind set forth in the present application. (pp. 119–20)

The Commission's opinion

The question whether the Liberal Party itself, as opposed to any individual member, could claim to have rights protected under Article 3, was left open, as there were sufficient individual applicants for the Commission to proceed.

Referring to previous case law the Commission expressed the opinion that:

. . . Article 3 of the First Protocol may not be interpreted as an Article which imposes a particular kind of electoral system which would guarantee that the total number of votes cast for each candidate or group of candidates must be reflected in the composition of the legislative assembly. Both the simple majority system and the proportional representation system are therefore compatible with this Article. (para. 4)

The Commission noted that:

. . . the applicants do not allege a breach of Article 3 of the Protocol as such, but of the Article in conjunction with Article 14 of the Convention which forbids discrimination in the enjoyment of the rights and freedoms set forth therein. In this respect the applicants have, *inter alia*, submitted that most of the cases which have been considered by the Court and the Commission under Article 14 have involved measures which have, on their face, made differences of treatment between persons in comparable circumstances, or concerned measures which differentiated in their impact or effect upon particular groups of persons. As to their present claim the applicants have stated that the simple majority system has an adverse disproportion-ate impact and effect upon the Liberal Party, Liberal electors and Liberal candidates. In this connection they submitted that if at the general election of 3 May 1979 one of the three proportional systems (national list; additional number system; single transferable vote) had been used, the total number of Liberal Members of the present House of Commons would have borne a much more reasonable relationship to the total number of votes cast in favour of the Liberal candidates throughout the United Kingdom.

. . . The Commission understands this complaint in the sense that the applicants feel discriminated against in that the simple majority system does not enable the number of Liberal Party votes to be properly reflected in the composition of the House of Commons. (paras 5 and 6)

However, whatever the disadvantages of the simple majority system or the advantages of any other system, the Commission had to consider the wording and background of the provisions concerned:

. . . Article 3 of the First Protocol gives an individual right to vote in the election provided for by this Article. Article 14 of the Convention read in conjunction with Article 3 of the First Protocol protects every voter against discrimination directed at him as a person for the grounds mentioned in Article 14. This is not the same as a protection of equal voting influence for all voters. The question whether or not equality exists in this respect is due to the electoral system being applied. Article 3 of the First Protocol is careful not to bind the States as to the electoral system and does not add any requirement of 'equality' to the 'secret ballot'.

. . . Article 3 requires that elections are being held under conditions which will ensure the free expression of the opinion of the people in the choice of the legislature. The applicants seem to suggest that the disadvantage existing for the Liberal Party, as for any smaller party, does not really assure the free expression of the opinion of the people. Although the Commission agrees that this disadvantage exists and may be of considerable political impact it cannot find a violation of Article 3 of the First Protocol alone or in conjunction with Article 14 of the Convention on that basis. . . . (paras 8 and 9)

The Commission did not have to consider in this particular case whether the electoral system operated in such a way as to exclude certain religious or ethnic groups entirely – in which case there might have been a violation of this article read with Article 14.

As it was, the Commission concluded that the application was manifestly ill-founded and revealed no violation of Article 3 of the First Protocol read alone or in conjunction with Article 14.

Cases pending under this article
Mobin Ahmed and Others v *UK* (Application No. 22954/93) concerning restrictions on the political activities of certain local government officers. Declared admissible by the Commission (Information Note No. 128, 27 September 1995).

CHAPTER 17

REMEDIES AND REFORMS: ARTICLE 28 FRIENDLY SETTLEMENTS AND JUST SATISFACTION UNDER ARTICLE 50

The primary aim of the Commission, once it has accepted a petition which has been referred to it and ascertained the relevant facts, is to try to secure a friendly settlement between the parties. Article 28 makes provision for this:

Article 28
In the event of the Commission accepting a petition referred to it:
   (a)   it shall, with a view of ascertaining the facts, undertake together with the representatives of the parties an examination of the petition and, if need be, an investigation, for the effective conduct of which the States concerned shall furnish all necessary facilities, after an exchange of view with the Commission;
   (b)   it shall place itself at the disposal of the parties concerned with a view to securing a friendly settlement of the matter on the basis of respect for human rights as defined in this Convention.

It is not unusual, therefore, for the Commission to publish an admissibility decision concerning a particular application and then to hear no more of the case because a friendly settlement has been reached.

Usually when this is done, the Contracting State against which the application has been brought does not admit or acknowledge any violation of the Convention. It can happen, however, that the friendly settlement is reached only after the Commission has found a violation of the Convention. In such a case a friendly settlement will usually prevent the matter proceeding to the Court (as happened, for example, in the case of *Sean and Kathleen McEldowney and Others v UK* DH (94) 31).

Friendly settlements normally take the form of a lump sum payment, as in *Arrondelle* v *UK* 5 EHRR 118, in which the Government paid the applicant £7,500 to compensate for the reduction in value to her home caused by aircraft noise from Gatwick airport, and her unsuccessful attempts to obtain permission for change of use for her home. Similarly in *A* v *UK* 3 EHRR 131, £500 was paid to the applicant concerning detention in Broadmoor mental institution.

Friendly settlements can take forms other than an *ex gratia* lump sum. In *Uppal and Others* v *UK (No. 2)* 3 EHRR 391 at 399, the settlement took the form of a revocation of the deportation order which had initially prompted the application. Similarly in the case of *Lamguindaz* v *UK* DH (93) 55, 17 EHRR 213, in which the deportation order against the applicant was revoked and he was allowed to re-enter the UK and given indefinite leave to remain and apply for naturalisation.

Sometimes a friendly settlement is reached because the law has been changed between the circumstances giving rise to the application and the hearing by the Commission, or between the report of the Commission and the hearing by the Court. This happened in the case of *Colman* v *UK* 18 EHRR 119, in which the General Medical Council had relaxed its restriction on advertising by the medical profession by the time the case was heard by the Commission. Nevertheless, the Commission considered the case on the basis of the alleged violations of Article 10 prior to the changes, although six members of the Commission did express the view that the applicant had ceased to be a victim of any violation since these changes had occurred. Prior to the case reaching the Court, a friendly settlement facilitated by these changes had taken place and so the case was struck off. Once the friendly settlement has been reached, unless there are public policy considerations for refusing to strike the case out of the list it will be struck out, even if there are reservations about doing so, as in the case of *Y* v *UK* 17 EHRR 238 concerning corporal punishment.

Sometimes the friendly settlement may relate only to costs and expenses being paid (*W* v *UK* Series A, No. 121, *R* v *UK* Series A, No. 121, *H* v *UK* Series A, No. 120).

If the Commission fails to secure a friendly settlement and the matter proceeds to a hearing before the Court then, in the case of a violation being established, Article 50 may apply.

Article 50
If the Court finds that a decision or a measure taken by a legal authority or any other authority of a High Contracting Party is completely or partially in conflict with the obligations arising from the present Convention, and if the internal law of the said Party allows only partial reparation to be made for the consequences of this decision or measure, the decision of the Court shall, if necessary, afford just satisfaction to the injured party.

An applicant may raise a claim under Article 50 at the outset, along with claims under other articles; but the Article 50 claim can be decided only once, and if, a violation is established. Generally the Court will defer ruling on this on the grounds that the matter is not yet ready for settlement. It may happen that an Article 28 settlement is reached in the interim, in which case the Article 50 claim is struck out (this happened in *Malone* v *UK* Series A, No. 82).

As with Article 28 settlements, the 'just satisfaction' afforded to the injured party will usually be the payment of a lump sum. However, the Court will afford 'just satisfaction' under Article 50 only 'if necessary'. In a great many cases the finding of a violation will itself be deemed to be 'just satisfaction'. For example, in the case of *Brogan and Others* Series A, No. 145-B, although violations of Articles 3 and 5 had been established, no pecuniary damages were awarded; similarly in *Silver* v *UK* Series A, No. 61, despite the fact that the applicants claimed that the finding of a violation by the Court of itself could not amount to 'just satisfaction'. Any award is therefore discretionary and the Court has regard to what is equitable in all the circumstances of the case.

If a sum is paid under Article 50, this may be for moral damage, which cannot be sufficiently compensated for by the mere finding of a violation (for example, in the case of *Gillow* v *UK* Series A, No. 109, £10,000 was paid). In other cases the grounds are stated to be simply non-pecuniary damage (for example, in the case of *W* v *UK* App. No. 9749/82, Series A, Vol. 136 13 EHRR 453, the UK was ordered to pay the applicant £12,000 for non-pecuniary damage for loss of real opportunities, mental anguish and distress). Generally the sums awarded are considerably less than those claimed (in *W* v *UK* the applicant originally claimed £100,000). The Court can also award a sum for pecuniary loss, for example lost wages, as happened in the case of *Young, James and Webster* v *UK* Series A, No. 44.

There are, however, recognised limits to the Court's powers to afford 'just satisfaction' to the injured party. For example, in the *Gillow* case, the Court could not order that the residence qualifications for Guernsey, formerly enjoyed by the applicants, be restored to them (13 EHRR 593); nor could it make orders concerning the applicant's child in *W* v *UK* Series A, Vol. 121. In *Dudgeon* v *UK* Series A, Vol. 45, the Court was not empowered to direct the UK to make a declaration that it would not discriminate against the applicant in Civil Service employment.

In making an award under Article 50, the Court may allow payment by the offending State to the applicant(s) for costs and expenses:

> . . . Costs and expenses are recoverable under Article 50 provided that they were incurred by the injured party in order to seek, through the domestic legal order, prevention or rectification of a violation, to have the same established by the Commission and later by the Court or to obtain redress therefor. Furthermore, it has to be established that the costs and expenses were actually incurred, were necessarily incurred and were also reasonable as to quantum. (*Dudgeon* v *UK*, para. 20)

Claims for these are scrutinised very carefully, and generally the Court awards considerably less than is claimed. Not only must all costs be supported by sufficient evidence, but they must also be deemed to be reasonable. Therefore, if certain expenses could have been avoided, the Court will say so and reduce the award accordingly. Only those costs necessarily incurred will be considered. Among the costs claimed which are frequently reduced in quantum by the Court, are costs for lawyers. The Court has justified its refusal to allow high legal fees on the grounds that to permit these would encourage high legal charges and thereby put out of reach the effective protection of human rights for many applicants. The Court has held that:

> . . . Applicants should not encounter undue financial difficulties in bringing complaints under the Convention. (*Young, James and Webster* Series A, Vol. 44, para. 15)

The Court has expressed the hope that lawyers in Contracting States would cooperate to this end in the fixing of their fees. This may be rather over-optimistic, although it is true that some lawyers provide their services free or their fees are met by organisations which seek to advance human rights protection.

If the applicants have received legal aid then any costs awarded will be reduced accordingly, to repay the legal aid received.

If one of the applicants dies before the Article 50 application is resolved, the Court will consider all the circumstances in order to decide whether it is equitable that any award should be paid to the survivor or into the deceased's estate. In principle the Court has recognised that a claim for 'just satisfaction' vested in a deceased person may survive for the benefit of his estate (*X* v *UK* 5 EHRR 192). In the case of *Gillow*, because both husband and wife had been affected by the violation, the surviving wife was allowed to receive the sum paid under the article. Where, however, the violation has really affected only the deceased and was personal in nature, then no sum will be paid into the deceased's estate (*Silver* v *UK* Series A, Vol. 61). However, in this respect a distinction needs to be made between legal costs and expenses and any claim for non-pecuniary costs. In the case of *X* v *UK* 4 EHRR 188, which was proceeded with by the original applicant's relatives, costs and expenses were allowed and paid into the deceased's estate, whereas non-pecuniary compensation was not paid – although there was a dissenting opinion that the estate ought to be entitled to non-material damage if this would have been payable to the deceased.

Besides any remedy afforded to an applicant under Article 50, if a violation of the Convention has been established, further steps may need to be taken. Indeed, often the motive behind bringing the application in the first place has been to bring about a change in the law (see, for example, *Dudgeon* v *UK* Series A, Vol. 45). In all cases the judgment of the Court is transmitted to the Committee of Ministers which supervises its execution (Article 54). In doing this, the Committee of Ministers takes into account measures which have been taken by the offending State as a consequence of the judgment. It is by this mechanism that certain reforms of domestic law have been achieved. For example, following the judgment in *X* v *UK* 4 EHRR 188, amendments were inserted into the Mental Health (Amendment) Bill, which was before Parliament at the time. These were subsequently enacted and became part of the Mental Health (Amendment) Act 1983. Similarly, following the judgment of the Court in the case of *Sunday Times* v *UK* 2 EHRR 245, 3 EHRR 317, the British Government drafted the Contempt of Court Bill, which became the Contempt of Court Act 1981.

Other changes which have been prompted by judgments of the Court have been: amendment of the Prison Rules 1964 (following *Golder* v *UK* Series A, Vol. 18); amendment of closed shop regulations by the Employment Act 1980 and the Employment Act 1982 (following *Young, James and Webster* Series A, Vol. 44); changes in the law relating to homosexuals in Northern Ireland under the Homosexual Offences (Northern Ireland) Order 1982 (SI 1982 No. 1536 (NI 19)) (see *Dudgeon* v *UK* Series A, Vol. 45); the abolition of corporal punishment in State schools under the Education (No. 2) Act 1986 (following *Campbell and Cosans* Series A, Vol. 48); changes in the rules relating to prisoners' correspondence (*Silver and Others* Series A, Vol. 61), and the availability of legal aid for prisoners coming before the Board of Prison Visitors (*Campbell and Fell* Series A, Vol. 80); the passing of the Interception of Communications Act 1985 (following *Malone* v *UK* Series A, Vol. 82); and changes in the law determining *locus standi* for requesting access to a child or the right to oppose an adoption order under the Children Act 1989, following the case of *Boyle* v *UK* Series A, No. 282-B.

Sometimes changes in administrative practices are brought about at an earlier stage as part of the negotiations directed at reaching a friendly settlement. For example, in the case of *A* v *UK* 3 EHRR 131, a number of changes to the use of seclusion at Broadmoor Hospital and improvements in facilities were made, as well as the payment of an *ex gratia* sum to the applicant. Where friendly settlements under Article 28 are reached without the Government admitting any liability or altering its stated opposition to the admissibility and merits of the claim, it is more difficult to ascertain to what extent the approaches of the Commission to secure the friendly settlement may have led to changes in the law.

If the Committee of Ministers is satisfied with the measures taken by the offending State, it passes a resolution to this effect (for example, *X* v *UK* DH (83) 2). A resolution adopted under Article 54 states that the Committee of Ministers considers that it has exercised its supervisory functions, and the matter is closed.

Further reading
Sharpe, J., 'Awards of costs and expenses under Article 50 of the European Convention on Human Rights' (1984) 81 *Law Society Gazette* 905

CONCLUSION

Figure 1 indicates the frequency with which the UK has been summoned to answer alleged violations of the Convention, while from Figures 2 and 3 it is clear that applications against the UK exceed those against many of the other Contracting States, and certainly most of the other member States of the European Union. One reason for this may be that the lack of a Bill of Rights in the UK encourages individual applicants to proceed to Strasbourg. On the other hand, even if there were to be a Bill of Rights, the requirements for admissibility, particularly Articles 25 and 26, would still have to be satisfied. Contracting States which have human rights incorporated into their constitutions are still summoned to answer alleged violations of the Convention. The existence of a Bill of Rights by itself would not, therefore, provide a complete solution. One aspect which it could remedy, and which currently may be a reason why so many applications are brought against the UK, is the continuing reluctance of a number of judges to take into account the provisions of the Convention. Although the Convention is not part of domestic law, proactive judges can take it into account by adopting an approach to the facts before them 'as if' the Convention was part of UK domestic law. Many judges, however, when presented with arguments drawing the court's attention to possible violations of the Convention, still adopt the approach that as the Convention is not part of English law, the Court need not take its provisions into account. The difficulty facing victims of human rights violations at present is that there is a very limited domestic forum for litigating those rights in the UK. As a result it would almost seem that a tradition of taking a case to Strasbourg has developed.

Moreover, reflection on the case law suggests that there are certain areas of human rights where applications against the UK are most likely to be made. These include Article 8 and Articles 5 and 6. This may partly be attributed to the wide scope of the articles themselves, but must also indicate something about the shortcomings of UK law in the areas of privacy and judicial process. Indeed, these shortcomings have not escaped the concern or interest of a number of reform proposals within the UK.

Some of the circumstances giving rise to the cases brought before the Commission and the Court have themselves changed and may result in fewer cases in future – for example, changes in Northern Ireland. Also, it should be remembered that the delays involved in processing a case before Strasbourg means that in some cases domestic law has already changed before a final decision in the relevant case has been made. Where this has happened there is cause for optimism, provided, of course, that the legal reforms which have been made actually do change the law for the better protection of human rights and do not still leave deficiencies. As time passes, these reforms are themselves likely to be subject to the scrutiny of the European Court.

Also, it should be remembered that perceptions of human rights change over time. This is evident in cases involving corporal punishment, the treatment of prisoners, the response to transsexuals and unmarried parents. One of the challenges facing the European Court of Human Rights is to interpret and adapt the provisions of the Convention to meet changing social norms and legal expectations. In effect, each case that comes to Strasbourg is a 'test case', not just for the applicant, but for society at large.

Figure 1 Frequency with which the UK has been summoned to answer alleged violations

	Files opened				Application registered				Struck off/declared inadmissible				Declared admissible				Friendly settlement				Report on the merits				Referred to Government			
	91	92	93	94	91	92	93	94	91	92	93	94	91	92	93	94	91	92	93	94	91	92	93	94	91	92	93	94
France	1728	1648	1383	1637	400	353	399	439	247	444	335	338	25	27	38	63	3	3	5	5	—	—	25	43	70	113	90	118
Germany	620	601	672	836	139	137	148	188	154	103	112	140	5	5	1	4	—	—	—	2	16	15	7	1	10	5	11	3
Spain	159	194	228	254	75	78	90	138	80	84	94	125	1	2	5	1	—	—	—	—	1	2	6	1	8	11	4	7
Italy	463	474	3032	1858	133	196	142	507	74	54	87	107	64	64	90	298	—	—	—	—	51	99	71	237	79	122	122	356
Belgium	158	139	128	212	67	62	70	78	90	69	87	47	4	3	4	5	1	3	1	—	3	—	3	4	4	13	10	9
UK	843	908	648	946	202	222	205	236	178	206	226	141	38	12	10	16	1	3	2	1	32	8	12	11	22	45	42	46

Source: European Commission of Human Rights Survey of Activities and Statistics 1992, 1994

Figure 2   Referrals to and judgments of the Court 1993

State	Cases referred	At least one violation	Non-violation	Struck off
Belgium	32	19	6	4
France	44	23	8	6
Germany	27	10	15	–
Italy	114	79	9	18
Spain	10	4	—	—
UK	57	31	15	3

Source: Survey of Activities: European Court of Human Rights

Figure 3   Nationality of applicants

	1991	1992	1993	1994
France	231	263	315	358
Germany	141	122	135	156
Spain	71	73	84	122
Italy	116	195	143	520
Belgium	47	50	55	71
UK	174	186	187	225

Source: European Commission of Human Rights Survey of Activities and Statistics 1991, 1992, 1993 and 1994

Index

Abortions
  family life right   211–12
  foetus right to life   29, 30–1
Access to court   147–8
  Article 6   147–8
  individual and collective access   147
  limitations   147
  patient in mental hospital   157–9
  Prison Board of Visitors   159–66
  solicitor consultation
    delayed   173–5
    denied   149–53
  time limits on civil claims   180–1
Admissibility of applications   16
  decisions   8–12
  exhaustion of domestic remedies
    9–12
  immediate ruling   7
Adoptions
  uncles   215–17
  unmarried fathers   212–15
Advertising, General Medical Council
    and   278–9
Age of consent   200–2
Aircraft seizure, without criminal
    charge   178–80, 369–72
Allitt affair   37–9
Anti-terrorism measures
  derogation under Article 15   345–51
  Gibraltar killings   39–47
  inhuman or degrading treatment
    75–7
  joyriders   34–7
  plastic baton rounds   31–4

Anti-terrorism measures – *continued*
  pre-trial detention   87–111
  prohibition of rallies and
    demonstrations   292
  proportionality   28, 33–4, 35, 40, 43
  right of liberty   87–111
  right to life   28, 31–7, 39–47
  Sinn Fein broadcast prohibition
    279–80
  solicitor consultation delayed   173–5
  'special category' prisoners   75–7
Appeals
  Article 6   148
  custody pending   112–14
  legal aid refused   169–71, 181–4
  loss of remission following
    unsuccessful application   167–9
Applicants
  nationalities   392
  see also Victims
Applications
  admissibility   16
    decisions   8–12
    exhaustion of domestic remedies
      9–12
    immediate ruling   7
  Commission procedure rules   6–7
  examination of case   12–13
  inter-state   16
  limitation   11–12
  procedure   5–17
  relevant date   11–12
  six-month rule   11–12
  solutions

Applications – *continued*
    friendly settlement   13, 16, 384–5
    friendly settlements   13
    proceeding with case   13–17
    satisfaction to injured party   385–8
    victims *see* Victims
Armed services, minors joining and
    servitude   81–2
Article 1 *see* Jurisdiction
Article 2 *see* Life, right to
Article 3 *see* Inhuman or degrading
    treatment; Torture
Article 4 *see* Slavery
Article 5 *see* Detention: Liberty, right of
Article 6 *see* Court proceedings
Article 7 *see* Retrospective legislation
Article 8 *see* Private life, right to
Article 9 *see* Freedom of thought,
    conscience and religion: Religious
    freedom
Article 10 *see* Freedom of expression
Article 11 *see* Freedom of association
    and assembly
Article 12 *see* Marriage
Article 13 *see* Domestic remedies
Article 14 *see* Discrimination
Article 15-Article 18 *see* Restrictions
Assembly *see* Freedom of association
    and assembly
Association *see* Freedom of association
    and assembly
Asylum
    detention prior to deportation   140
    domestic remedy requirement
        318–20
    inhuman or degrading treatment
        51–4

Birth certificates, changes for
    transsexuals   208–10, 295–302
Blasphemous libel
    freedom of expression   260–1
    retrospective legislation   187–9

Capital punishment
    extradition where likelihood of
        domestic remedy requirement
        315–18
    inhuman or degrading treatment
        55–60
    jurisdiction   23–6

Capital punishment – *continued*
    right to life   30
Case law, relevance to domestic law
    4–5
Censorship
    blasphemous libel   260–1
    freedom of expression   255–64
    libel   264–5
    Little Red Schoolbook   255–60
    obscenity   255–60
    pacifist views   261–4
    protection of national security   262
Civil rights
    court proceedings   143–4
    to conduct insurance business
        153–7
Closed shop agreements   283–6
Commission
    membership   6–7
    procedure rules   6, 7–8
Committee of Ministers   15
Community charge, detention for failure
    to pay   139–40
Confiscation orders
    retrospective legislation   191–4
    without criminal charge   178–80,
        369–72
Conscience *see* Freedom of thought,
    conscience and religion
Contempt of court
    criminal   189–91
    freedom of expression   265–75
    pressing social need   265–70
    Spycatcher   189–91, 270–5
    Thalidomide   265–70
Corporal punishment
    education provision and   64–6, 373,
        374–9
    inhuman or degrading treatment
        birching   61–4
        refusal to accept school discipline
        64–6
Corporations   3
    as victims   8–9
Correspondence   199
    interception of mail   236–40
    prisoners   227–36, 306–8
        domestic remedy requirement
        306–8, 312, 313–14
        opening and reading   234–6

Correspondence – *continued*
    prior ventilation rule   162, 166,
        229
    stopping letters   227–34
Costs   387
Court *see* European Court of Human
    Rights
Court proceedings
    access to court   147–8
        individual and collective access
            147
        limitations   147
        patient in mental hospital   157–9
        Prison Board of Visitors   159–66
        solicitor consultation
            delayed   173–5
            denied   149–53
        time limits on civil claims   180–1
    anti-terrorism measures   173–5
    appeals   148
    Article 6   142
        cases   149–85
        scope   143–9
    care proceedings (Scotland)   175–7
    civil rights   143–4
        to conduct insurance business
            153–7
    court-martial hearing   184–5
    delay   50, 106–11, 145–6, 171–5
    equality of parties   148–9
        leave to appeal applications
            167–9
    fair hearing   144–6
        care proceedings   175–7
        comprehension   145
        delays   145–6
        disciplinary proceedings   171–2
        leave to appeal applications   167
        no access to documentation
            175–7
        press campaigns   145
        racial bias in jury   184, 342
        statement to DTI used in
            proceedings   184
    independent and impartial tribunal
        146
    Prison Board of Visitors   161–2
    jurors
        employed by prosecution witness
            185
        racial bias   184, 342

Court proceedings – *continued*
    leave to appeal applications   166–9
    legal aid   149
        discrimination because of poverty
            339–40
        to fund appeal   169–71, 181–4
    retrial   3, 147
    silence inferences   173–4
Criminal contempt, retrospective
    interpretation   189–91

Death penalty
    extradition where likelihood of
        domestic remedy
            requirement   315–18
        inhuman or degrading treatment
            55–60
        jurisdiction   23–6
        right to life   30
Defamation action, legal aid refusal
    339–4
Degrading treatment *see* Inhuman or
    degrading treatment
Delay
    between sentence and punishment
        50
    bringing before judge   106–8,
        109–11
    consultation with solicitor   173–5
    fair hearing right   145–6
    termination of employment
        proceedings   171–2
Deportation
    asylum seekers
        detention prior to   140
        domestic remedy requirement
            318–20
    detention with view to   85, 140
    inhuman or degrading treatment
        51–4
    national security grounds   79
    see also Immigration
Detention
    anti-terrorism measures   87–111
    convicted persons   112–14
        see also Prisoners
    delay in bringing before judge
        106–8, 109–11
    failure to pay community charge
        tax   139–40

Detention – *continued*
  informing of reasons   85, 93, 98,
      118–24
  judicial review   85–6
  lawfulness   84–6
  life sentences   124–39
    indeterminate   124–35
    periodic reviews   130–5, 137–9,
        141
    re-detention for minor offences
        124–30
    revocation of licence   124–37
  mental patients   85, 114–24, 157–9
    decisions on transfer   115–18
    inhuman or degrading treatment
        77–9
    recall   118–24
    right of liberty   85, 114–24
    solitary confinement   77–9
  pre-trial detention   86–111
    promptness of bringing before
        judge   106–8, 109–11
  review claimed   85–6
  right of liberty and   84–6
  with view to deportation   85, 140
Disciplinary proceedings
  fairness   171–2
  prisoners   159–66, 308–10
Discrimination
  Article 14   325
    cases   327–42
    scope   325–7
  comparison requirement   326
  differential treatment   325
  political, proportional
      representation   330–1
  racial   328–9, 342
  sex   331–4, 342
  sexual orientation   334–5
  status
    civilians and servicemen   335–6
    leaseholders   338–9
    licence to reside in Guernsey
        340–1
    poverty   339–40
    prisoners   339
    taxation and marriage   336–8
    unmarried fathers   341–2
Dismissal
  fairness of disciplinary proceedings
      171–2

Dismissal – *continued*
  refusal to join trade union   21–3
Domestic remedies
  Article 13   303
    cases   306–24
    scope   303–6
  asylum refusal   318–20
  burden of proof   10
  exhaustion requirement   9–12, 171
  extradition to face possible death
      sentence   315–18
  husbands unable to join wives
      310–12
  noise levels from Heathrow   320–4
  none   10
  not effective   9
  prisoners
    correspondence   306–8
    disciplinary loss of remission
        308–10
  requirement for   303–24

Education
  corporal punishment   373, 374–9
    inhuman or degrading treatment
        64–6
  failure to meet required standard
      379–80
  First Protocol, Article 2   372
    cases   374–81
    scope   372–4
  particular form   372
  philosophical convictions of parents
      373, 374–9
  in prison   380–1
Elections
  First Protocol, Article 3   381–3
  proportional representation   381–3
Enforcement machinery   6–8
European Convention on Human rights
  case law   4–5
  drafting   1
  rights protected   3
  role   1–2
  UK and   3–5
  see also individual Articles
European Court of Human Rights
  judges   16
  jurisdiction   14, 16
  majority judgments   14
  not permanent court   15

European Court of Human Rights –
  continued
  organisation 14
  permanent court 17
  purpose of court 14
  see also Court proceedings
European Union law 4
Examination of case 12–13
Exhaustion of domestic remedies
  9–12, 171
Expression *see* Freedom of expression
Extradition
  family life 217–21
    dependency 218
    husbands not permitted to remain
      218–21
    proof of marriage 218
  where likelihood of capital
    punishment
    domestic remedy requirement
      315–18
    inhuman or degrading treatment
      55–60
    jurisdiction 23–6
    right to life 30

Fair hearing right 144–6
  Article 6 144–6
  care proceedings 175–7
  comprehension 145
  delays 145–6
  disciplinary proceedings 171–2
  leave to appeal applications 167
  no access to documentation 175–7
  press campaigns 145
  racial bias in jury 184, 342
  statement to DTI used in proceedings
    184
Family life 197–9
  abortions 211–12
  adoptions 212–17
  Article 8 197–8
  care orders 215–17
  deportation 217–21
  extradition
    dependency 218
    husbands not permitted to remain
      218–21
    proof of marriage 218
  husbands unable to join wives

Family life – *continued*
  domestic remedy requirement
    310–12
  extradition 218–21
  inhuman or degrading treatment
    69–72
  racial discrimination 328–9
  sex discrimination 331–4
  immigration laws 218–21
  marriage for immigration reasons
    198, 293
  prisoners 312, 314–15
  unmarried fathers
    abortions 211–12
    adoptions 212–15
    discriminatory treatment 341–2
    parental rights 212–15
  welfare of child paramount 217
  see also Marriage
Fees, lawyers' 387
Filtering 13
First Protocol
  Article 1 352
    cases 354–72
    scope 352–4
    see also Peaceful enjoyment of
      possessions
First Protocol, Article 2 372
  cases 374–81
  scope 372–4
  see also Education
First Protocol, Article 3 381–3
  see also Elections
Foetus, right to life *see* Abortions
Forfeiture of property, peaceful
  enjoyment and 365–72
Freedom of association and assembly
  Article 11 282
    cases 283–92
    scope 282–3
  prisoners 283
  refusal of permission to hold rally
    291–3
  trade unions
    closed shop agreements 283–6
    compulsion to join 289–91
    GCHQ 286–9
    membership prohibited 286–9
Freedom of expression
  Article 10 253
    cases 255–80

Freedom of expression – *continued*
   scope   253–5
   censorship
      blasphemous libel   260–1
      freedom of expression   255–64
      libel   264–5
      Little Red Schoolbook   255–60
      obscenity   255–60
      pacifist views   261–4
      protection of national security
         262
   contempt of court
      freedom of expression   265–75
      pressing social need   265–70
      Spycatcher   270–5
      Thalidomide   265–70
   defamatory material   254
   exceptions   255
   receipt and dissemination of
      information   275–80
      advertising by doctors   278–9
      local authority refusal   275–7
      Sinn Fein broadcasts   279–80
Freedom of thought, conscience and
   religion
   Article 9   244
      cases   246–52
      scope   244–6
   pacifism   246–7
   religion
      cults   245
      Hindu Faith   250–2
      meaning   244–5
      Muslims and Friday working
         247–50
   thought and conscience   246–7
Friendly settlements   13, 16, 384–5

General Medical Council, advertising
   prohibition   278–9
Government Communication
   Headquarters (GCHQ), trade
   union membership   286–9
Grand Chamber   16
Guernsey, licence to live on   221–2,
   340–1, 362–5
Gypsy sites   225–7

Home   197
   gypsy sites   225–7

Home – *continued*
   leasehold property legislation reform
      338–9, 354–60
   licence to live on Guernsey   221–2
   discrimination because of status
      340–1
   peaceful enjoyment of possessions
      362–5
   right to private life   221–2
   lifestyle of own choosing   224–7
   noise nuisance from Heathrow
      223–4, 320–4
   planning controls   223
   protection from harassment in   221
Homosexual relationships
   age of consent   200–2
   conduct restriction in
      N.Ireland   203–8, 324–5
   sexual orientation discrimination
      334–5
Hospital safety inquiry   37–9
Husbands unable to join wives
   domestic remedy requirement
      310–12
   extradition   218–21
   inhuman or degrading treatment
      69–72
   racial discrimination   328–9
   sex discrimination   331–4

Immigration
   family life right and   218–21
   husbands unable to join wives
      domestic remedy requirement
         310–12
      family life right   218–21
      inhuman or degrading treatment
         69–72
      racial discrimination   328–9
      sex discrimination   331–4
   marriage for reasons of   198, 293
Impartial tribunal *see* Independent and
   impartial tribunal
Independent and impartial tribunal
   146
   Prison Board of Visitors   161–2
   see also Access to court: Fair hearing
      right
Individuals
   direct concern requirement   3
   right to petition   2–3

Inhuman or degrading treatment
  aggravating circumstances   50
  Article 3   48
    cases   51–79
    scope   48–51
  corporal punishment
    birching   61–4
    refusal to accept school
      discipline   64–6
  delay between sentence and
    punishment   50
  deportation   51–4
    national security grounds   79
  extradition where likelihood of death
    sentence   55–60
  husbands not permitted to join
    wives   69–72
  institutionalised violence   50–1
  mental patient detention   77–9
  political asylum refusal   51–4
  prisoners
    sex offender ill treatment and
      harassment   72–5
    'special category'   75–7
  punishment or treatment   50–1
  torture   48–9
Inter-State breach   20

Judges   16
Judgments
  finality of   16
  majority decisions   14
Jurisdiction   14, 16
  Article One   19–26
    cases   21–6
    scope   19–21
  dismissal for refusal to join
    union   21–3
  extradition to face death penalty
    23–6
  territorial limit   19
Jurors
  employed by prosecution witness
    185
  racial bias   184, 342

Krugerrands, smuggled   365–9

Leasehold legislation reform
  compulsory transfer   354–60

Leasehold legislation reform – *continued*
  peaceful enjoyment of possessions
    and   354–60
  status discrimination   338–9
Legal aid   149
  costs covered by   387
  discrimination because of poverty
    339–40
  to fund appeal   169–71, 181–4
Legal fees   387
Libel
  blasphemous
    freedom of expression   260–1
    retrospective legislation   187–9
  freedom of expression and   264–5
Liberty, right of
  Article 5   83–4
    cases   86–141
    scope of Article   84–6
  delay in bringing before judge
    106–8, 109–11
  detention *see* Detention
  political asylum   140
  procedural safeguards   84–6
Life, right to
  abortions   29, 30–1
  agents of State   27
  anti-terrorism measures   28, 31–7,
    39–47
    Gibraltar killings   39–47
    joyriders   34–7
    plastic baton rounds   31–4
    proportionality   28, 33–4, 35, 40,
      43
  Article 2   27
    cases   30–47
    scope   27–30
  death penalty   30
  exclusions   29
  exposure to nuclear tests   47, 185
  foetus   29
  hospital safety inquiry   37–9
  meaning   28
  prison officers   27
  victims   27
Life sentences   124–39
  indeterminate   124–35
  periodic reviews   130–5, 137–9, 141
  re-detention for minor offences
    124–30
  revocation of licence   124–37

Loss of time orders   112–14

Marriage
    Article 12   293
        cases   294–302
        scope   293–4
    discrimination in taxation   336–8
    in prison   294–5
    rape within   187, 194–5
    to obtain admission into UK   198,
        293
    transsexuals   208–10, 295–302
    see also Family life
Meetings see Freedom of association and
    assembly
Mental Health Review Tribunal   114,
    118
Mental patients
    denial of access to court   157–9
    detention   85, 114–24, 157–9
        decisions on transfer   115–18
        inhuman or degrading treatment
            77–9
        recall   118–24
        right of liberty   85, 114–24
        solitary confinement   77–9

Nationalisation   360–2
Nationalities of applicants   392
Next-of-kin, as victims   9
Noise nuisance, Heathrow   223–4,
    320–4, 354
Northern Ireland
    homosexual conduct restriction in
        203–8, 324–5
    see also Anti-terrorism measures
Nuclear testing exposure   47, 185
Nuisance
    noise from Heathrow   223–4,
        320–4, 354
    private life and home, right to   197

Pacifism
    censorship of views   261–4
    freedom of thought and conscience
        246–7
Pardons   3
Parole Board   135–9, 141
Peaceful enjoyment of possessions
    aircraft noise   223–4, 320–4, 354
    arbitrary confiscation   353

Peaceful enjoyment of possessions –
    continued
    compulsory transfer   354–60
    First Protocol, Article 1   352
        cases   354–72
        scope   352–4
    forfeiture   365–72
    leasehold property legislation reform
        354–60
    licence to live on Guernsey   362–5
    nationalisation   360–2
    prohibition on importation   367–9
    taxation   354
Petitions
    abuse   8
    procedure   6
    rights of individuals   2–3
Planning control, material change of use
    250–2
Plastic baton rounds, anti-terrorism
    measures   31–4
Political activity
    of aliens   343
    discrimination   330–1
    elections   381–3
    propaganda   8
    proportional representation   330–1,
        381–3
Political asylum
    detention prior to deportation   85,
        140
    domestic remedy requirement
        318–20
    inhuman or degrading treatment
        51–4
Possessions see Peaceful enjoyment of
    possessions
'Prior ventilation rule'   162, 166, 229
Prison Board of Visitors proceedings
    159–66
Prison officers, right to life and   27
Prisoners
    classification   3
    consultation with solicitor
        delayed   173–5
        denied   149–53
    correspondence
        domestic remedy requirement
            306–8, 312, 313–14
        opening and reading   234–6

Prisoners – *continued*
  prior ventilation rule   162, 166, 229
  stopping letters   227–34
  custody pending appeal   112–14
  disciplinary proceedings   159–66, 308–10
  discrimination by status   339
  domestic remedy requirement
    correspondence   306–8, 312, 313–14
    disciplinary loss of remission 308–10
  education provision   380–1
  family life right   312, 314–15
  freedom of association and assembly 283
  inhuman or degrading treatment
    mental patients   77–9
    sex offender ill treatment and harassment   72–5
    'special category' prisoners   75–7
  loss of time orders   112–14
  marriage   294–5
  'prior ventilation rule'   162, 166, 229
  Prison Board of Visitors disciplinary proceedings   159–66
  remission forfeiture   160, 166–9
Privacy   199–200
  interception of mail   236–40
  secret surveillance   199–200, 236–43
  telephone tapping   236–42
Private life, right to
  Article 8   196
  cases   200–43
  scope   197–200
  correspondence   199
    interception of mail   236–40
    opening and reading   234–6
    prisoners   227–36, 306–8
    stopping letters   227–34
  family life   197–9
    abortions   211–12
    adoptions   212–17
    care orders   215–17
    deportation   217–21
    extradition   217–21
      dependency   218
      husbands not permitted to remain   218–21

Private life, right to – *continued*
    proof of marriage   218
    husbands unable to join wives
      domestic remedy requirement 310–12
      extradition   218–21
      racial discrimination   328–9
      sex discrimination   331–4
    immigration laws   218–21
    prisoners   312, 314–15
    unmarried fathers
      abortions   211–12
      adoptions   212–15
      parental rights   212–15
    welfare of child paramount   217
    see also Marriage
  home   197
    gypsy sites   225–7
    licence to live on Guernsey   221–2
    lifestyle of own choosing   224–7
    noise nuisance from Heathrow 223–4, 320–4, 354
    planning controls   223
    protection from harassment in 221
  nuisance   197
  privacy   199–200
    interception of mail   236–40
    secret surveillance   199–200, 236–43
    telephone tapping   236–42
  sexual relationships
    homosexual
      age of consent   200–2
      conduct restriction in N.Ireland 203–8, 324–5
    transsexuals
      changing birth certificate 208–10, 295–302
      inability to marry   208–10, 295–302
Private prosecutions   3
Proportional representation   330–1, 381–3
Public emergency, Article 15 exceptions 343
Publicity   8

Racial discrimination
  husbands unable to join wives 328–9

Racial discrimination – *continued*
jury bias 184, 342
Rape within marriage 187, 194–5
Reforms, Eleventh Protocol 15–17
Religious freedom
cults 245
Hindu Faith 250–2
meaning of religion 244–5
Muslims and Friday working
247–50
see also Freedom of thought,
conscience and religion
Remedies
costs 387
domestic *see* Domestic remedies
friendly settlement 13, 16, 384–5
legal aid 387
legal fees 387
satisfaction to injured party 385–8
Residence 3
Restrictions
anti-terrorism measures 345–51
Articles 15 to 18 343–4
cases 345–61
scope 344–5
political activity of aliens 343
public emergencies 343
wars 343
Retrial 3, 147
Retrospective legislation
Article 7 187
cases 187–95
scope 187–8
blasphemous libel 187–9
confiscation order 191–4
criminal contempt 189–91
rape within marriage 187, 194–5
Right to life *see* Life, right to
Right to private life *see* Private life, right
to

School discipline, corporal punishment
64–6, 373, 374–9
Secret surveillance 199–200, 236–43
Security of person *see* Detention:
Liberty, right of
Seizure of aircraft, without criminal
charge 178–80, 369–72
Servitude
Article 4 81
cases 81–2

Servitude – *continued*
scope of article 80
minors joining armed services 81–2
Settlement
costs 387
friendly 13, 16, 384–5
satisfaction to injured party 385–8
Sex discrimination 331–4, 342
Sexual abuse 180–1
Sexual orientation discrimination
334–5
Sexual relationships
homosexual
age of consent 200–2
conduct restriction in N.Ireland
203–8, 324–5
discrimination 334–5
transsexuals
changing birth certificate 208–10,
295–302
inability to marry 208–10,
295–302
Silence, inferences from 173–4
Sinn Fein broadcast prohibition
279–80
Six-month rule 11–12
Slavery
Article 4 81
cases 81–2
scope of article 80
minors joining armed services 81–2
Solicitors
consultation delayed, anti-terrorism
measures 173–5
consultation denied 149–53
Solutions
friendly settlement 13, 16, 384–5
proceeding with case 13–17
satisfaction to injured party 385–8
Spycatcher contempt of court
freedom of expression and 270–5
retrospective interpretation 189–91
Status discrimination
civilians and servicemen 335–6
leaseholders 338–9
licence to reside in Guernsey 340–1
poverty 339–40
prisoners 339
taxation and marriage 336–8
unmarried fathers 341–2
Surveillance, secret 199–200, 236–43

Taxation
  detention for community charge
    non-payment 139–40
  discrimination by marital status
    336–8
  peaceful enjoyment of possessions
    and 354
Telephone tapping 236–42
Terrorism *see* Anti-terrorism measures
Thought, freedom of *see* Freedom of
  thought, conscience and religion
Torture
  Article 3 48–9
  see also Inhuman or degrading
    treatment
Trade unions
  closed shop agreements 283–6
  compulsion to join 289–91
  dismissal for refusal to join,
    jurisdiction 21–3
  GCHQ 286–9
  membership prohibited 286–9
Transsexuals
  changing birth certificates 208–10,
    295–302
  inability to marry 208–10, 295–302

Tribunal, independent and impartial
  Article 6 146
  Prison Board of Visitors 161–2
  see also Access to court: Fair hearing
    right

Unmarried fathers
  abortions 211–12
  adoptions 212–15
  discriminatory treatment 341–2
  parental rights 212–15

Victims
  consequences of own conduct 9
  corporations 8–9
  establishing if applicant is victim
    203
  next-of-kin 9
  parents acting for children 9
  potential father 30–1
  requirement 8–9
  right to life 27

Wars, Article 15 exceptions 343
Wednesbury principles 318